*Oracle Press*

ORACLE:
The Complete Reference,
Third Edition

ORACLE® Oracle Press

ORACLE:
The Complete Reference,
Third Edition

George Koch &
Kevin Loney

Osborne **McGraw-Hill**

Berkeley New York St. Louis San Francisco
Auckland Bogotá Hamburg London Madrid
Mexico City Milan Montreal New Delhi Panama City
Paris São Paulo Singapore Sydney Tokyo Toronto

Osborne **McGraw-Hill**
2600 Tenth Street
Berkeley, California 94710
U.S.A.

For information on translations or book distributors outside the U.S.A., or to
arrange bulk purchase discounts for sales promotions, premiums, or fundraisers,
please contact Osborne **McGraw-Hill** at the above address.

Oracle: The Complete Reference, Third Edition

234567890 DOC 998765

ISBN 0-07-882097-9

Publisher Lawrence Levitsky	**Computer Designer** Roberta Steele
Acquisitions Editor Claire Splan	**Illustrator** Rhys Elliott
Copy Editor Gary Morris	**Series Designer** Jani Beckwith
Proofreader Pat Mannion	**Quality Control Specialist** Joe Scuderi
Indexer Valerie Robbins	**Cover Designer** Ted Mader & Associates

About the Authors

George Koch is a leading authority on relational database applications. A popular speaker and widely published author, he is also the creator of THESIS, the securities trading, accounting, and portfolio management system that was the first major commercial applications product in the world to employ a relational database (ORACLE) and provide English language querying to its users. He is a former senior vice president of Oracle Corporation.

Kevin Loney, a veteran ORACLE developer and DBA, is the author of the *ORACLE DBA Handbook* and has written technical articles for *ORACLE Magazine* since 1990. He frequently makes presentations at international ORACLE conferences.

To Elwood Brant, Jr. (Woody), 1949-1990

Contents At A Glance

PART III
The Hitchhiker's Guide to the ORACLE7 Data Dictionary

PART IV
Designing for Productivity

PART V
Alphabetical Reference

PART VI
Appendixes

Contents

PART II
SQL: Going from Beginner to Expert

PART III
The Hitchhiker's Guide to the ORACLE7 Data Dictionary

PART IV
Designing for Productivity

PART V
Alphabetical Reference

PART VI
Appendixes

Acknowledgments

It's not until you undertake a book project like this one that you realize how massive an effort it really is, or how much you must rely upon the selfless efforts and goodwill of others. There were many who helped me with this project, and I very much want to thank them all.

The first help came from back in the early days at KOCH Systems Corporation, when we developed the world's first major relational application product, using a database named ORACLE from a small startup company in Menlo Park. My thanks go to Neill Brownstein, for his vision, Bill Younger, for his care, Howard Ervin, for his thoughtful counsel, and David Loar, for his faith, effort, and unflagging optimism. To all the folks at KOCH in those days, and in the years following: Thanks. We learned a lot from each other, about ORACLE and about life.

The first edition of this book was written before I joined Oracle as Senior Vice President of its Worldwide Applications Division. This is a business which has grown remarkably and is now one of the largest in the world. I finally left Oracle in 1994, and have many fond memories of my time there, and many friends and employees around the world whom I still hold in high regard. I hope this *Complete Reference* will continue to be of value to them in the years ahead.

Many fine folks at Oracle Corporation contributed repeatedly and well when the book was created. Tom Siebel always offered friendship, wisdom, insight, and a skilled hand when things needed to get done. MaryBeth Pierantoni helped me find references and manuals others didn't even know existed (and became an extraordinary Executive Assistant to me when I joined Oracle), and Nasreen Husain flawlessly got them to me in an instant, often with no notice.

I want to acknowledge Lynn Healy's brilliance and contributions (now wandering around Europe as an Oracle consultant), and Kevin Kraemer's creative genius on SQL*FORMS. Hal Steger, SQL*FORMS product manager, was able to uncover hidden truths that I wouldn't have otherwise found.

My thanks also go to Larry Ellison, for writing a foreword for the earlier editions in the midst of running a company with 10,000 employees and a personal schedule filled to the micro-second. His wit has sustained a company through unparalleled growth.

Lastly, my heartfelt thanks to Jenny Overstreet, who, as many people know, quietly runs Oracle and most of the Western world. She solves problems before anybody else has even realized there are problems.

Bob Muller was a helpful and responsive technical editor, often offering suggestions of alternative (and better) solutions to problems posed in the book, and he contributed to the second edition by adding material for the first release of ORACLE7.

Kevin Loney has taken on the great task of the third edition, by updating the book for ORACLE7.1 and 7.2, as well as eliminating unneeded references to earlier ORACLE versions. Chapters 20 to 24 are his original creation and are evidence of his understanding and experience of Oracle's products, and particularly of ORACLE7. I appreciate his thoroughness and care and the obvious good work he has done.

Linda Allen, my agent, found a company with the interest and wherewithal to publish this masssive a volume. And, at Osborne/McGraw-Hill, none of this would have happened at all without the persistence of Larry Levitsky, Jeff Pepper, Ann Wilson, Claire Splan, Gary Morris, Pat Mannion, Valerie Robbins, Jani Beckwith, Roberta Steele, and Peter Hancik.

Last, but not least, I must thank my family, not only for putting up with me during months of mania during the original writing of this book, but also for real work. My wife, Victoria, keyed in many definitions and the index of the first edition, as did our 13-year-old son, George (when he was just 9). Isaiah, our 10-year-old, contributed (at age 6) regular hugs and affection, and sustained us through many a long day. Thanks also are due to my brother, Bob, an Oracle and communications magician, who, during a particularly intense period, ably and without complaint assisted in the creation of some of the sections in the Alphabetical Reference.

What a delight all of you have been!

George Koch
Wheaton, Illinois
February 1995

Participating in an effort like this is a humbling experience; you become acutely aware of the degree to which other people support both the writer and the project. On the home front, that support came in oceans from my family, whose love and understanding made my contributions and edits for the third edition possible. They teach me every day without fail, and this completed work is as much their achievement as it is mine.

At work, the Information Integration Team at Astra Merck (Cheryl Bittner, Mary Blazak, Eric Erickson, John Hunt, Mike Janesch, Karen Rodgers, Steve Rodi, Mary Romano, and Pat Smith) again provided cover and support for me. Like the rest of the I/T staff at Astra Merck, the IIT's level of expertise and professionalism is awe-inspiring. Thanks also go to my users over the years who asked the questions that this book answers.

And over at the Oracle Press side of the house, Claire Splan, Ann Wilson (in a swan song), Jeff Pepper, Gary Morris, Janet Walden (in a cameo role), Jani Beckwith, and Julie Gibbs again provided the support necessary to generate the finished product. My long-held rule is that editors are always right (this cuts down on the creative differences); their efforts and abilities proved that rule once again. Thanks also to Rama Velpuri for his timely assistance.

Thanks to George Koch and Robert Muller for their efforts on the previous editions and to George for his edits of my work on the current edition. The earlier editions provided a very strong foundation for the current version. Thanks to Perry Trimble for introducing me to this book during its earlier incarnation, and to all of the folks (like Rob, Marie, Karen, Decky, Bill, and Jan) who have supported my writing efforts over the years.

Kevin Loney

Introduction

ORACLE is the most widely used database in the world. It runs on virtually every kind of computer, from PCs and Macintoshes, to minicomputers and giant mainframes. It functions virtually identically on all these machines, so when you learn it on one, you can use it on any other. This fact makes knowledgeable ORACLE users and developers very much in demand, and makes your ORACLE knowledge and skills very portable.

ORACLE documentation is thoroughgoing and voluminous, currently spanning more than 50 volumes. *ORACLE: The Complete Reference* is the first entity that has gathered all of the major ORACLE definitions, commands, functions, features, and products together in a single, massive core reference—one volume that every ORACLE user and developer can keep handy on his or her desk.

The audience for this book will usually fall into one of three categories:

■ *An ORACLE end user*   ORACLE can easily be used for simple operations such as entering data and running standard reports. But such an approach would ignore its great power; it would be like buying a high-performance racing car, and then pulling it around with a horse. With the introduction provided in the first two sections of this book, even an end user with little or no data processing background can become a proficient ORACLE user--generating ad hoc, English-language reports, guiding developers in the creation of new features and functions, and improving the speed and accuracy of the real work done in a business. The language of the book is simple, clear English without data processing jargon, and with few assumptions about previous knowledge of computers or databases. It will help beginners to become experts with an easy-to-follow format and numerous real examples.

■ *A developer who is new to ORACLE*   With as many volumes of documentation as ORACLE provides, finding a key command or concept can be a time-consuming effort. This book attempts to provide a more organized and efficient manner of learning the essentials of the product. The format coaches a developer new to ORACLE quickly through the basic concepts, covers areas of common difficulty, examines misunderstanding of the product and relational development, and sets clear guidelines for effective application building.

■ *An experienced ORACLE developer*   As with any product of great breadth and sophistication, there are important issues about which little, if anything, has been published. Knowledge comes through long experience, but is often not transferred to others. This book delves deeply into many such subject areas (such as precedence in UNION, INTERSECTION, and MINUS operators, using SQL*PLUS as a code-generator, inheritance and CONNECT BY, eliminating NOT IN with an outer join, and many others). The text also reveals many common misconceptions and suggests rigorous guidelines for naming conventions, application development techniques, and design and performance issues.

For every user and developer, nearly 400 pages of this book are devoted to a comprehensive Alphabetical Reference containing all major ORACLE concepts, commands, functions, features, and products, including proper syntax, cross-references, and examples. This is the largest single reference published on the subject.

How This Book Is Organized

There are six major parts to this book.

Part 1 is an introduction to "Critical Database Concepts." These chapters are essential reading for any ORACLE user, new or veteran, from key-entry clerk to Database Administrator. They establish the common vocabulary that both end users and developers can use to coherently and intelligently share concepts and assure the success of any development effort. This introductory section is intended for both developers and end users of ORACLE. It explores the basic ideas and vocabulary of relational databases and points out the dangers, classical errors, and profound opportunities in relational database applications.

Part 2, "SQL: Going from Beginner to Expert," teaches the theory and techniques of relational database systems and applications, including SQL (Structured Query Language) and SQL*PLUS. The section begins with relatively few assumptions about data processing knowledge on the part of the reader, and then advances step-by-step, through some very deep issues and complex techniques. The method very consciously uses clear, conversational English, with unique and interesting examples, and strictly avoids the use of undefined terms or jargon. This section is aimed primarily at developers and end users who are new to ORACLE, or need a quick review of certain ORACLE features. It moves step by step through the basic capabilities of SQL and ORACLE's interactive query facility, SQL*PLUS. When you've completed this section you should have a thorough understanding of all SQL key words, functions, and operators. You should be able to produce complex reports, create tables, and insert, update, and delete data from an ORACLE database.

The later sections of Part 2 provide some very advanced methods in SQL*PLUS, ORACLE's simple, command-line interface, and in-depth descriptions of the new and very powerful features of ORACLE7. This is intended for developers who are already familiar with ORACLE, and especially those familiar with previous versions of ORACLE, but who have discovered needs they couldn't readily fill. Some of these techniques are previously unpublished and, in some cases, have been thought impossible. The tips and advanced techniques covered here demonstrate how to use ORACLE7 in powerful and creative ways. These include code-generation, programmatic loading of variables, and nesting of start files and host processes in SQL*PLUS, as well as taking advantage of distributed database capabilities, triggers and stored procedures, and the other new features in ORACLE7.

Part 3, "The Hitchhiker's Guide to the ORACLE7 Data Dictionary," provides a user-oriented guide to the ORACLE7 data dictionary—the database equivalent of the Yellow Pages. Rather than list the available data dictionary views alphabetically, this section groups them by subject, thereby shortening the time it takes to discover which data dictionary view you need to use. Real-world examples are given to illustrate the proper usage of the available views.

Part 4, "Designing for Productivity," addresses vital issues in the design of useful and well-received applications. ORACLE tools provide a great opportunity to create applications that are effective and well-loved by their users, but many developers are unaware of some of the approaches and successes that are possible. This section of the book is aimed specifically at developers—those individuals whose responsibility it is to understand a business (or other) application, and design and program an ORACLE application to satisfy it. This section should not be completely incomprehensible to an end user, but the audience is assumed to have a technical data processing background, and experience in developing computer application programs. The purpose here is to discuss the techniques of developing with ORACLE that have proven effective and valuable to end users, as well as to propose some new approaches to design in areas that have been largely, and sadly, ignored. This section ends with "The Ten Commandments of Humane Design," a list of all of the vital rules of the development process.

Part 5, the "Alphabetical Reference," is the complete reference for ORACLE7. Reading the introductory pages to this reference will make its use much more effective and understandable. This section contains references for most major ORACLE commands, keywords, products, features and functions, with extensive cross-referencing of topics. Subtopics within a reference can be found in the index. The reference is intended for use by both developers and users of ORACLE but assumes some familiarity with the products. To make the most productive use of any of the entries, it would be worthwhile to read the first six pages of the reference. These explain in greater detail what is and is not included and how to read the entries.

Part 6, "Appendixes," contains the table creation statements and row insertions for all of the tables used in this book. For anyone learning ORACLE, having these tables available on your own ORACLE ID, or on a practice ID, will make trying or expanding on the examples very easy. There is also an appendix covering Oracle Glue.

A Brief Overview of the Chapters

Chapter 1, "Sharing Knowledge and Success," explains the basic ideas of the relational model, and the opportunity for successful application development by sharing design responsibilities with knowledgeable end users.

Chapter 2, "The Dangers in a Relational Database," exposes some of the risks that are inherent in developing within a fast-paced, relational environment, and discusses many of the classic errors that have been made in the past. This chapter also introduces methods of risk control.

Chapter 3, "The Basic Parts of Speech in SQL," is an introduction to the SQL language, the style used in this book, logic and value, subqueries, table joins, and view creation.

Chapter 4, "Basic SQLPLUS Reports and Commands," shows how to build a basic report in SQLPLUS, use an editor, use SQLPLUS commands, and understand the differences between SQLPLUS and SQL.

Chapter 5, "Getting Text Information and Changing It," introduces the idea of character strings, examines character functions, and distinguishes between characters, numbers, and dates in ORACLE.

Chapter 6, "Playing the Numbers," explores numbers and number functions, including single value, group value, and list functions.

Chapter 7, "Dates: Then, Now, and the Difference," shows how to use ORACLE's exceptional date-handling functions, calculate differences between dates, and format dates for display.

Chapter 8, "Conversion and Transformation Functions," looks at functions that convert one data type into another, or that "transform" data into some form other than that in which it normally appears.

Chapter 9, "Grouping Things Together," shows how information in ORACLE can be grouped and summarized, and how views of summarized data can be created.

Chapter 10, "When One Query Depends Upon Another," looks at advanced subqueries, "correlated subqueries," a technique called the "outer join," and the use of UNION, INTERSECT, and MINUS operators to combine ORACLE tables. This chapter also contains an advanced discussion of precedence, and the use of outer joins to replace the NOT IN operator.

Chapter 11, "Some Complex Possibilities," shows how to build very complex views, and contains an extensive discussion of inheritance and CONNECT BY.

Chapter 12, "Building a Report in SQLPLUS," explores advanced reporting and formatting techniques in SQLPLUS, weighted averages, variable use in titles, number formatting, and multi-statement SQL in reports.

Chapter 13, "Changing Data: insert, update, and delete," discusses how data in ORACLE tables is changed, and the importance and effect of commit and rollback processing.

Chapter 14, "Advanced Use of Functions and Variables," introduces methods for creating graphs and bar charts, inserting commas in numbers, doing complex cut-and-paste, and dynamically loading variables.

Chapter 15, "DECODE—Amazing Power in a Single Word," goes into considerable depth about the use of the powerful DECODE function in ORACLE, including how to flip a table onto its side, age invoices, control paper movement in printers, or regulate commit processing for large groups of records.

Chapter 16, "Creating, Dropping, and Altering Tables and Views," details the basics of table manipulation, including constraint specification, as well as the system views that contain information about tables.

Chapter 17, "By What Authority?," explores security provisions in ORACLE—the authority of the Database Administrators, and the access privileges that each user can be granted, or can grant to others, and how changes in authority affect users dependent on other users. It also covers the use of roles in application and database administration.

Chapter 18, "Changing the ORACLE Surroundings," looks at indexes, space usage, the structure of the database, the technique of clustering tables together, sequences, and basic ORACLE technical terms.

Chapter 19, "SQL*PLUS," is an advanced chapter for experienced ORACLE developers and users. It shows methods for using SQL*PLUS to generate code, load variables, create views with variable numbers of tables, and use host processes interactively.

Chapter 20, "Accessing Remote Data," describes the methods used to access data that is in a remote database and shows methods for creating and maintaining database links.

Chapter 21, "Triggers," describes the types of triggers available in ORACLE7 and shows examples of the most commonly used triggers.

Chapter 22, "Procedures," shows how to use procedures, packages, and functions in ORACLE7 and how to create, compile, debug, and manage those objects.

Chapter 23, "Snapshots," shows how to use ORACLE7's snapshot objects to manage the replication of remote data. It also shows how the snapshot actually works, the objects that are created in local and remote databases, and how to manage the replication schedule.

Chapter 24, "The Hitchhiker's Guide to the ORACLE7 Data Dictionary," shows the most-used data dictionary views in a user-oriented fashion; the views are organized by function to make it easy to find the proper view to use.

Chapter 25, "Good Design Has a Human Touch," provides firm guidance on how to build applications that will be meaningful to their users and will genuinely support the tasks they have to accomplish. This approach is fundamental to real success in application development.

Chapter 26, "Performance and Design," looks at some of the issues and fallacies surrounding normalization and design methods, and provides some explicit suggestions for improving both performance and design in ORACLE applications.

Chapter 27, "The Ten Commandments of Humane Design," introduces some new ideas to the relational community for the next steps in design methodology, including level-name integrity, object-name normalization, and singularity, as well as addressing related areas that have traditionally been fraught with difficulty. It concludes with ten basic rules for design.

Chapter 28, "Alphabetical Reference," is the complete list of major ORACLE commands, keywords, functions, and so on.

Appendix A, "Tables Used in This Book," includes complete listings of all tables used in the examples in this book.

Appendix B, "Oracle Glue," covers Glue, which lets you connect your desktop applications to ORACLE7 and other dBASE and mail servers.

Style Conventions Used in This Book

Except when testing for an equality (such as, City = 'CHICAGO'), ORACLE ignores upper- and lowercase. In the formal listing of commands, functions, and their format (syntax) in the Alphabetical Reference, this book will follow ORACLE's documentation style of putting all SQL in UPPERCASE, and all variables in lowercase italic.

Most users and developers of ORACLE, however, never key all their SQL in uppercase. It's too much trouble, and ORACLE doesn't care anyway. This book therefore will follow somewhat different style conventions in its examples (as opposed to its formal command and function formats, mentioned earlier), primarily for readability. They are as follows:

- Italic and boldface will not be used in example listings.

- **select**, **from**, **where**, **order by**, **having**, and **group by** will be in lowercase.

- SQLPLUS commands will be in lowercase: **column**, **set**, **save**, **ttitle**, and so on.

- SQL operators and functions will be in uppercase, such as **IN**, **BETWEEN**, **UPPER**, **SOUNDEX**, and so on.

- Columns will use upper- and lowercase, as in Feature, EastWest, Longitude, and so on.

- Tables will be in uppercase, such as in NEWSPAPER, WEATHER, LOCATION, and so on.

- Chapter 3 contains an introduction to the style for chapters of the book through 27. Chapter 28, the Alphabetical Reference, contains an important introductory section on style conventions that should be read carefully before the alphabetical listings are used.

Ordering a Disk of the Tables in This Book

To order a 3.5" disk (IBM format) with a complete copy of all the tables used in this book as listed below, send $40 to:

George Koch Disk Offer
0 North 512 Herrick Drive
Wheaton, IL 60187-3069

Payment must accompany order. No purchase orders. Non-U.S. price is $44 (U.S. dollars only). Shipping is included.

Please allow 3 to 6 weeks for shipment from receipt of order. Osborne/McGraw-Hill assumes NO responsibility for this offer. This is solely an offer of the author, and not of Osborne/McGraw-Hill.

PART 1

Critical Database Concepts

CHAPTER 1

Sharing Knowledge and Success

For an ORACLE application to be built and used rapidly and effectively, users and developers must share a common language and a deep and common understanding of both the business application and the ORACLE tools.

This is a new approach to development. Historically, the systems analyst studied the business requirements and built an application to meet those needs. The user was involved only in describing the business and perhaps in reviewing the functionality of the application after it was completed.

With the new tools and approaches available, and especially with ORACLE, applications can be built that more closely match the needs and work habits of the business—but only if a common understanding exists.

This book is aimed specifically at fostering this understanding, and at providing the means for both user and developer to exploit ORACLE's full potential. The end user will know details about the business that the developer will not comprehend. The developer will understand internal functions and features of ORACLE and the computer environment that will be too technically complex for the end user. But these areas of exclusive expertise will be minor compared with what both end users and developers can share in using ORACLE. There is a remarkable opportunity here.

It is no secret that "business" people and "systems" people have been in conflict for decades. Reasons for this include differences in knowledge, culture, professional interests, and goals, and the alienation that simple physical separation between groups can often produce. To be fair, this syndrome is not peculiar to data processing. The same thing occurs between people in accounting, personnel, or senior management, as members of each group gather apart from other groups in a separate floor or building or city. Relations between the individuals from one group to another become formalized, strained, and abnormal. Artificial barriers and procedures that stem from this isolationism become established, and these also contribute to the syndrome.

This is all very well, you say, and may be interesting to sociologists, but what does it have to do with ORACLE?

Because it isn't cloaked in arcane language that only systems professionals can comprehend, ORACLE fundamentally changes the nature of the relationship between business and systems people. Anybody can understand it. Anybody can use it. Information previously trapped in computer systems until someone in systems created a new report and released it now is accessible, instantly, to a business person, simply by typing an English query. This changes the rules of the game.

Where ORACLE is used, it has radically improved the understanding between the two camps, has increased their knowledge of one another, and has even begun to normalize relations between them. This has also produced superior applications and end results.

Since its first release, ORACLE has been based on the easily understood relational model (explained shortly), so non-programmers readily understood what ORACLE did and how it did it. This made it approachable and unimposing.

And it was created to run identically on virtually any kind of computer. It didn't matter which manufacturer sold you your equipment; ORACLE worked on it. These features all contributed directly to the profound success of the product and the company.

In a marketplace populated by computer companies with "proprietary" hardware, "proprietary" operating systems, "proprietary" databases, and "proprietary" applications, ORACLE gave business users and systems departments new control over their lives and futures. They were no longer bound to the database product of a single hardware vendor. ORACLE could run on nearly every kind of computer they could own. This is a basic revolution in the workplace and in application development, with consequences that will extend far into the future.

Some individuals haven't accepted or understood this yet, nor realized just how vital it is that the dated and artificial barriers between "users" and "systems" continue to fall. But the advent of cooperative development will profoundly affect applications and their usefulness.

However, many application developers have fallen into an easy trap with ORACLE: carrying forward unhelpful methods from previous generation system designs. There is a lot to unlearn. Many of the techniques (and limitations) that were indispensable to a previous generation of systems are not only unnecessary in designing with ORACLE, they are positively counterproductive. In the process of explaining ORACLE, the burden of these old habits and approaches must be lifted. There are refreshing new possibilities available.

Throughout this book, the intent will be to explain ORACLE in a way that is clear and simple, in terms that both users and developers can understand and share. Outdated or inappropriate design and management techniques will be exposed and replaced.

The Cooperative Approach

ORACLE is a *relational database*. This concept is an extremely simple way of thinking about and managing the data used in a business. It is nothing more than a collection of tables of data. We all encounter tables every day: weather reports, stock charts, sports scores. These are all tables, with column headings and rows of information simply presented. Even so, the relational approach can be sophisticated and powerful enough for even the most complex of businesses.

Unfortunately, the very people who can benefit most from a relational database, the business users, usually understand it the least. Application developers, who must build systems that these users need to do their jobs, often find relational concepts difficult to explain in simple terms. A common language is needed to make this cooperative approach work.

The first two sections of this book explain, in readily understandable terms, just what a relational database is, and how to use it effectively in business. It may seem that this discussion is for the benefit of "users" only. An experienced relational application designer may be inclined to skip these early chapters and simply use the book as a primary source ORACLE reference. Resist that temptation! Although much of this material may seem like elementary review, it is an opportunity for an application designer to acquire a clear, consistent, and workable terminology with which to talk to users about their needs and how these needs might be quickly met. If you are an application designer, this discussion may also help you unlearn some unnecessary and probably unconscious design habits. Many of these will be uncovered in the course of introducing the relational approach. It is important to realize that even ORACLE's power can be diminished considerably by design methods appropriate only to non-relational development.

If you are an end user, understanding the basic ideas behind relational databases will help you express your needs cogently to application developers and comprehend how those needs can be met. An average person working in a business role can be brought from beginner to expert in short order. With ORACLE you'll have the power to get and use information, have hands-on control over reports and data, and possess a clear-eyed understanding of what the application does and how it does it. ORACLE gives you, the user, the ability to control an application or query facility expertly and *know* if you are not getting all the flexibility and power that's available.

You also will be able to unburden programmers of their least favorite task: writing new reports. In large organizations as much as 95 percent of all programming backlog is composed of new report requests. Because you can do it yourself, in minutes instead of months, you will be delighted to have the responsibility.

Everyone Has "Data"

A library keeps lists of members, books, and fines. The owner of a baseball card collection keeps track of players' names, dates, averages, and card value. In any business, certain pieces of information about customers, products, prices, financial status, and so on must be saved. These pieces of information are called *data*.

Information philosophers like to say that data is just data until it is organized in a meaningful way, at which point it becomes "information." If this is true, then ORACLE is also a means of easily turning data into information. ORACLE will sort through and manipulate data to reveal pieces of knowledge hidden there—such as totals, buying trends, or other relationships—which are as yet undiscovered. You will learn how to make these discoveries. The main point here is that you have data, and you do three basic things with it: acquire it, store it, and retrieve it.

Once you've achieved the basics, you can make computations with data, move it from one place to another, or modify it. This is called processing, and, fundamentally, involves the same three steps that affect how information is organized.

You could do all of this with a cigar box, pencil, and paper, but as the volume of data increases, your tools tend to change. You may use a file cabinet, calculators, pencils, and paper. While at some point it makes sense to make the leap to computers, your tasks remain the same.

A *Relational Database Management System* (often called an RDBMS for short) such as ORACLE gives you a way of doing these tasks in an understandable and reasonably uncomplicated way. ORACLE basically does three things:

- ▪ Lets you put data into it.
- ▪ Keeps the data.
- ▪ Lets you get the data out and work with it.

Figure 1-1 shows how simple it is.

ORACLE supports this in-keep-out approach and provides clever tools that allow you considerable sophistication in how the data is captured, edited, modified, and put in; how you keep it securely; and how you get it out to manipulate and report on it.

The Familiar Language of ORACLE

The information stored in ORACLE is kept in tables—much like a weather table from the daily newspaper shown in Figure 1-2.

This table has four vertical columns: City, Temperature, Humidity, and Condition. It also has a horizontal row for each city from Athens to Sydney. Last, it has a table name: WEATHER.

These are the three major characteristics of most tables you'll see in print: *columns, rows,* and a *name.* The same is true in a relational database. Anyone can understand the words and the ideas they represent because the words used to

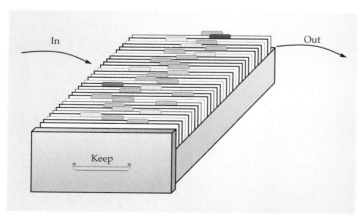

FIGURE 1-1. *What ORACLE does with data*

WEATHER

City	Temperature	Humidity	Condition
Athens.......	97	89	Sunny
Chicago......	66	88	Rain
Lima.........	45	79	Rain
Manchester...	66	98	Fog
Paris........	81	62	Cloudy
Sparta.......	74	63	Cloudy
Sydney.......	29	12	Snow

FIGURE 1-2. *A weather table from a newspaper*

describe the parts of a table in an ORACLE database are the same ones used in everyday conversation. The words have no special, unusual, or esoteric meanings. What you see is what you get.

Tables of Information

ORACLE stores information in tables, as Figure 1-3 shows. Each of these tables has one or more columns. The headings, such as City, Temperature, Humidity, and Condition, describe the kind of information kept in the column. The information

A column   **WEATHER** ← Table name

City	Temperature	Humidity	Condition
----------	-----------	--------	---------
ATHENS	97	89	SUNNY
CHICAGO	66	88	RAIN
LIMA	45	79	RAIN
MANCHESTER	66	98	FOG	← A row
PARIS	81	62	CLOUDY
SPARTA	74	63	CLOUDY
SYDNEY	29	12	SNOW

FIGURE 1-3. *A WEATHER table from ORACLE*

is stored row after row, city after city. Each unique set of data, such as the temperature, humidity, and condition for the city of Manchester, gets its own row.

ORACLE avoids specialized, academic terminology in order to make the product more approachable. In research papers on relational theory, a column name may be called an "attribute," a row may be called a "tuple" (rhymes with "couple"), and a table may be called an "entity." For an end user, however, these terms are confusing. More than anything, they are an unnecessary renaming of things for which there are already commonly understood names in our shared everyday language. ORACLE takes advantage of this shared language, and developers can too. It is imperative to recognize the wall of mistrust and misunderstanding that the use of unnecessary technical jargon produces. Like ORACLE, this book will stick with "tables," "columns," and "rows."

Structured Query Language

Oracle was the first company to release a product that used the English-based *Structured Query Language*, or SQL. This allowed end users to extract information themselves, without using a systems group for every little report.

ORACLE's query language is not without structure, any more than is English or any other language. It has rules of grammar and syntax, but they are basically the normal rules of careful English speech, and can be readily understood.

SQL, pronounced either "sequel" or "S.Q.L.," is an astonishingly capable tool, as you will see. Using it does not require any programming experience.

Here's an example of how you might use it. If someone asked you to select the city from the weather table where the humidity is 89, you would quickly respond "Athens." If you were asked to select cities from the weather table where the temperature is 66, you would respond "Chicago and Manchester."

ORACLE is able to answer these same questions, nearly as easily as you are, and with a simple query very much like the one you were just asked. The key words used in a query to ORACLE are **select**, **from**, **where**, and **order by**. They are clues to ORACLE to help it understand your request and respond with the correct answer.

A Simple ORACLE Query

If ORACLE had the WEATHER table in its database, your first query to it would be simply this:

```
select City from WEATHER where Humidity = 89
```

ORACLE would respond:

```
City
----------
ATHENS
```

Your second query would be this:

```
select City from WEATHER where Temperature = 66
```

For this query, ORACLE would respond:

```
City
-----------
MANCHESTER
CHICAGO
```

And how about **order by**? Suppose you wanted to see all the cities in order by their temperature. You'd simply type this:

```
select City, Temperature from WEATHER
  order by Temperature
```

and ORACLE would instantly respond with this:

```
City          Temperature
----------- -----------
SYDNEY                29
LIMA                  45
MANCHESTER            66
CHICAGO               66
SPARTA                74
PARIS                 81
ATHENS                97
```

ORACLE has quickly reordered your table by temperature. (This table lists lowest temperatures first; in a later chapter you'll learn to specify whether you want low numbers or high numbers first.)

There are many other questions you can ask with ORACLE's query facility, but these examples show how easy it is to obtain the information you need from an ORACLE database in the form that will be most useful to you. You can build complicated requests from simple pieces, but the method used to do this will always be understandable. For instance, you can combine the **where** and **order by**, both simple by themselves, and tell ORACLE to select those cities where the temperature is greater than 80, and show them in order by increasing temperature. You would type this:

```
select City, Temperature from WEATHER
  where Temperature > 80              (> means "greater than")
  order by Temperature
```

and ORACLE would instantly respond with this:

```
City          Temperature
----------    -----------
PARIS               81
ATHENS              97
```

Or, to be even more specific, request cities where the temperature is greater than 80 and the humidity is less than 70:

```
select City, Temperature, Humidity from WEATHER
  where Temperature > 80
        and Humidity < 70            (< means "less than")
  order by Temperature
```

and ORACLE would respond with this:

```
City          Temperature Humidity
----------    ----------- --------
PARIS               81       62
```

Why It Is Called Relational

Notice that the WEATHER table lists cities from several countries, and some countries have more than one city listed. Suppose you need to know in which country a particular city is located. You could create a separate LOCATION table of cities and their countries, as shown in Figure 1-4.

For any city in the WEATHER table, you can simply look at the LOCATION table, find the name in the City column, look over to the Country column in the same row, and see the country's name.

LOCATION

City	Country
ATHENS	GREECE
CHICAGO	UNITED STATES
CONAKRY	GUINEA
LIMA	PERU
MADRAS	INDIA
MADRID	SPAIN
MANCHESTER	ENGLAND
MOSCOW	RUSSIA
PARIS	FRANCE
ROME	ITALY
SHENYANG	CHINA
SPARTA	GREECE
SYDNEY	AUSTRALIA
TOKYO	JAPAN

WEATHER

City	Temperature	Humidity	Condition
ATHENS	97	89	SUNNY
CHICAGO	66	88	RAIN
LIMA	45	79	RAIN
MANCHESTER	66	98	FOG
PARIS	81	62	CLOUDY
SPARTA	74	63	CLOUDY
SYDNEY	29	12	SNOW

FIGURE 1-4. *WEATHER and LOCATION tables*

These are two completely separate and independent tables. Each contains its own information in columns and rows. They have one significant thing in common: the City column. For each city name in the WEATHER table, there is an identical city name in the LOCATION table.

For instance, what is the current temperature, humidity, and condition in an Australian city? Look at the two tables, figure it out, and then resume reading this.

How did you solve it? You found just one AUSTRALIA entry, under the Country column, in the LOCATION table. Next to it, in the City column of the same row, was the name of the city, SYDNEY. You took this name, SYDNEY, and then looked for it in the City column of the WEATHER table. When you found it, you moved across the row and found the Temperature, Humidity, and Condition: 29, 12, and SNOW.

Even though the tables are independent, you can easily see that they are related. The city name in one table is *related* to the city name in the other. This relationship is the basis for the name *relational* database. See Figure 1-5.

This is the basic idea of a relational database (sometimes called a relational model). Data is stored in tables. Tables have columns, rows, and names. Tables can be related to each other if they each have a column with a common type of information.

That's it. It's as simple as it seems.

LOCATION

City	Country
ATHENS	GREECE
CHICAGO	UNITED STATES
CONAKRY	GUINEA
LIMA	PERU
MADRAS	INDIA
MADRID	SPAIN
MANCHESTER	ENGLAND
MOSCOW	RUSSIA
PARIS	FRANCE
ROME	ITALY
SHENYANG	CHINA
SPARTA	GREECE
SYDNEY	AUSTRALIA
TOKYO	JAPAN

WEATHER

City	Temperature	Humidity	Condition
ATHENS	97	89	SUNNY
CHICAGO	66	88	RAIN
LIMA	45	79	RAIN
MANCHESTER	66	98	FOG
PARIS	81	62	CLOUDY
SPARTA	74	63	CLOUDY
SYDNEY	29	12	SNOW

Relationship

FIGURE 1-5.   *The relationship between the WEATHER and LOCATION tables*

Some Common, Everyday Examples

Once you understand the basic idea of relational databases, you'll begin to see tables, rows, and columns everywhere. Not that you didn't see them before, but you probably didn't think about them in quite the same way. Many of the tables that you are accustomed to seeing could be stored in ORACLE. They can be used to quickly answer questions that would take you quite some time to answer nearly any other way.

A typical stock market report in the paper might look like the one in Figure 1-6. This is a small portion of a dense, alphabetical listing that fills several narrow columns on several pages in a newspaper. Which stock traded the most shares? Which had the biggest percentage change in its price, either positively or negatively? The answers to these questions are simple English queries in ORACLE, which can find the answer much faster than you could by searching the columns on the newspaper page.

Figure 1-7 lists the standings of hockey teams. What's the relative standing of all the teams? Which have played the most games? The answers to these questions are simple English queries in ORACLE.

Company	Close Yesterday	Close Today	Shares Traded
Ad Specialty	31.75	31.75	18,333,876
Apple Cannery	33.75	36.50	25,787,229
AT Space	46.75	48.00	11,398,323
August Enterprises	15.00	15.00	12,221,711
Brandon Ellipsis	32.75	33.50	25,789,769
General Entropy	64.25	66.00	7,598,562
Geneva Rocketry	22.75	27.25	22,533,944
Hayward Antiseptic	104.25	106.00	3,358,561
IDK	95.00	95.25	9,443,523
India Cosmetics	30.75	30.75	8,134,878
Isaiah James Storage	13.25	13.75	22,112,171
KDK Airlines	80.00	85.25	7,481,566
Kentgen Biophysics	18.25	19.50	6,636,863
LaVay Cosmetics	21.50	22.00	3,341,542
Local Development	26.75	27.25	2,596,934
Maxtide	8.25	8.00	2,836,893
MBK Communications	43.25	41.00	10,022,980
Memory Graphics	15.50	14.25	4,557,992
Micro Token	77.00	76.50	25,205,667
Nancy Lee Features	13.50	14.25	14,222,692
Northern Boreal	26.75	28.00	1,348,323
Ockham Systems	21.50	22.00	7,052,990
Oscar Coal Drayage	87.00	88.50	25,798,992
Robert James Apparel	23.25	24.00	19,032,481
Soup Sensations	16.25	16.75	22,574,879
Wonder Labs	5.00	5.00	2,553,712

FIGURE 1-6. *A stock market table*

Figure 1-8 is an index to a newspaper. What's in section F? If you read the paper from front to back, in what order would you read the articles? The answers to these questions are simple English queries in ORACLE. You will learn how to do all of these queries, and even build the tables to store the information, in the course of using this reference.

OVERALL STANDINGS

Team	Won	Lost	Tied
Boston.................	17	13	3
Buffalo................	21	9	4
Calgary................	14	11	9
Chicago................	19	13	2
Detroit................	10	18	5
Edmonton...............	16	11	7
Hartford...............	16	17	1
Los Angeles............	16	14	3
Minnesota..............	17	15	2
Montreal...............	20	13	4
New Jersey.............	15	15	3
N.Y. Rangers...........	15	14	5
N.Y. Islanders.........	11	20	4
Philadelphia...........	16	14	4
Pittsburgh.............	13	16	3
Quebec.................	6	23	4
St Louis...............	14	12	6
Toronto................	16	18	0
Vancouver..............	11	16	6
Washington.............	13	15	4
Winnipeg...............	14	13	5

FIGURE 1-7. *A table of hockey results*

Feature	Sections	Page
Births	F	7
Bridge	B	2
Business	E	1
Classified	F	8
Comics	C	4
Doctor's In	F	6
Editorials	A	12
Modern Life	B	1
Movies	B	4
National News	A	1
Obituaries	F	6
Sports	D	1
Television	B	7
Weather	C	2

FIGURE 1-8. *A table based on the sections of a newspaper*

A 100-Year-Old Example

An old, decaying ledger book, first dated in 1896 and belonging to a "G. B. Talbot," contains the entries shown in Figure 1-9.

Entries like these go on for pages, day after day, through 1905. Dora Talbot paid her workers a dollar a day for their efforts, and George B. Talbot (perhaps her

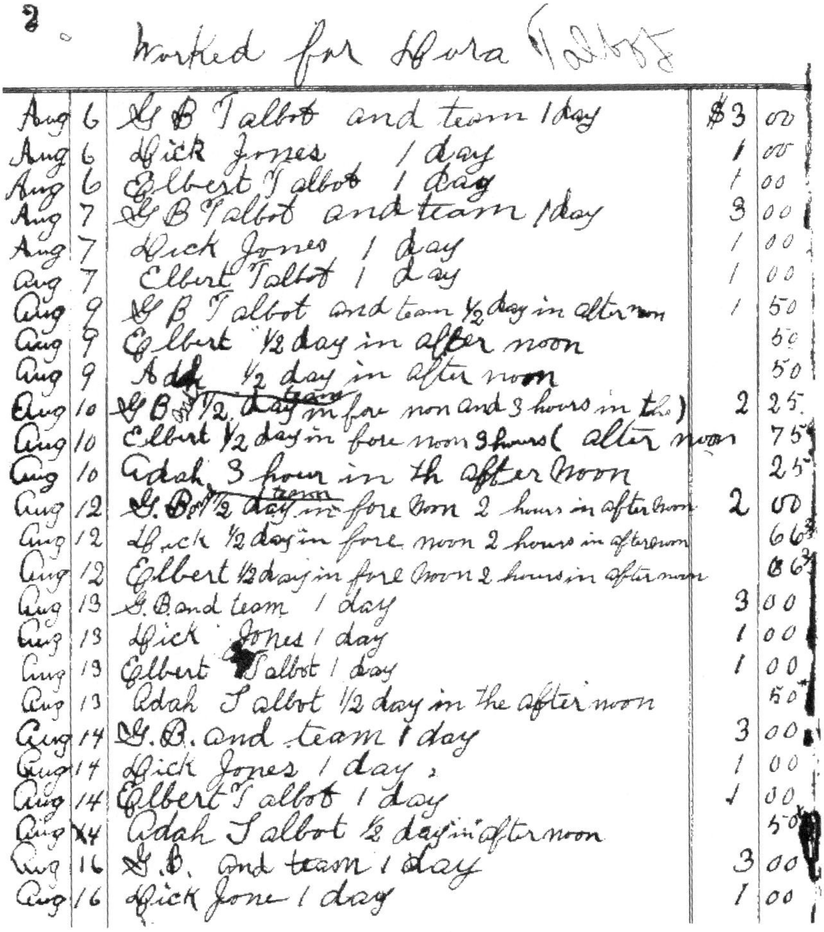
2. Worked for Dora Talbott

Aug	6	G B Talbot and team 1 day	$3	00
Aug	6	Dick Jones 1 day	1	00
Aug	6	Elbert Talbot 1 day	1	00
Aug	7	G B Talbot and team 1 day	3	00
Aug	7	Dick Jones 1 day	1	00
Aug	7	Elbert Talbot 1 day	1	00
Aug	9	G B Talbot and team 1/2 day in after noon	1	50
Aug	9	Elbert 1/2 day in after noon		50
Aug	9	Adah 1/2 day in after noon		50
Aug	10	G B and team 1/2 day in fore non and 3 hours in the)	2	25
Aug	10	Elbert 1/2 day in fore noon 3 hours (after noon		75
Aug	10	Adah 3 hour in th after noon		25
Aug	12	G. B. team 1/2 day in fore noon 2 hours in after noon	2	00
Aug	12	Dick 1/2 day in fore noon 2 hours in afternoon		66 2/3
Aug	12	Elbert 1/2 day in fore noon 2 hours in after noon		66 2/3
Aug	13	G. B. and team 1 day	3	00
Aug	13	Dick Jones 1 day	1	00
Aug	13	Elbert Talbot 1 day	1	00
Aug	13	Adah Talbot 1/2 day in the after noon		50
Aug	14	G. B. and team 1 day	3	00
Aug	14	Dick Jones 1 day	1	00
Aug	14	Elbert Talbot 1 day	1	00
Aug	14	Adah Talbot 1/2 day in afternoon		50
Aug	16	G. B. and team 1 day	3	00
Aug	16	Dick Jone 1 day	1	00

FIGURE 1-9. *G. B. Talbot's ledger book*

son) kept the books. A few of the workers appear in the book many times, others only once or twice.

George also had a few pages with the names and addresses of the workers, as shown in Figure 1-10. The relationship that links these two tables is the worker's name. If George wanted to send a boy around, with cash in pay envelopes, to each of the workers at the end of the month, what would he have to do? He'd first have

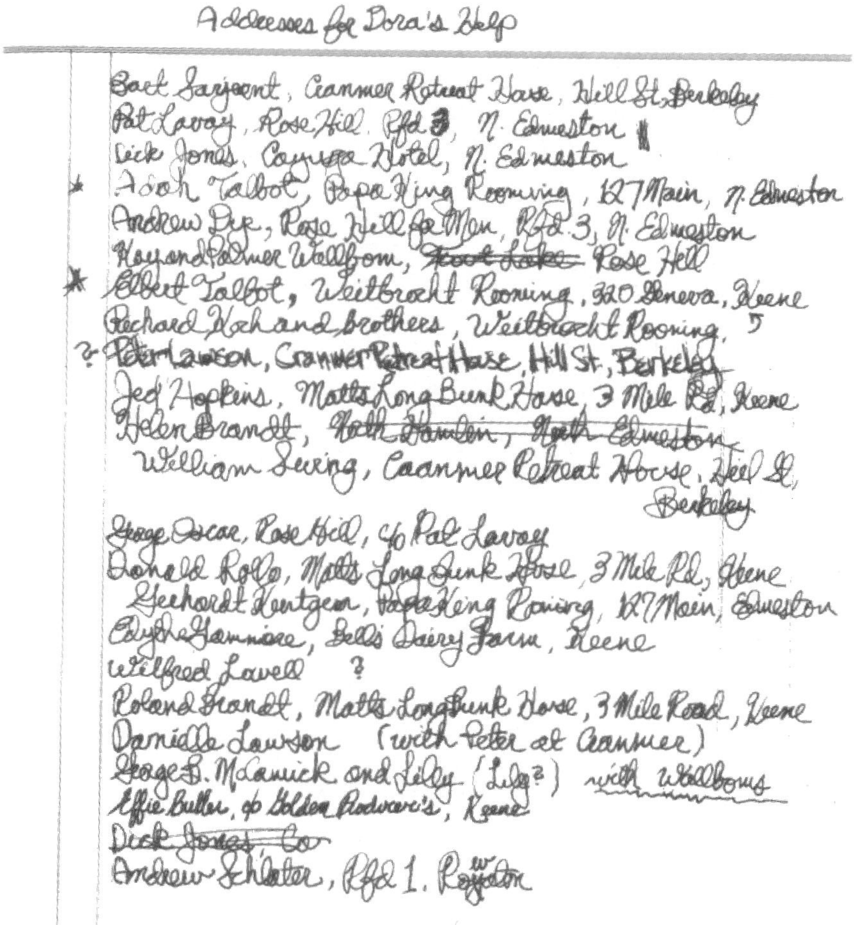

Addresses for Dora's Help

Bart Sarjeant, Cranmer Retreat House, Hill St, Berkeley
Pat Lavay, Rose Hill, Rfd 3, N. Edmeston
Dick Jones, Cayuga Hotel, N. Edmeston
Adah Talbot, Papa King Rooming, 127 Main, N. Edmeston
Andrew Dye, Rose Hill for Men, Rfd 3, N. Edmeston
Raymond Palmer Wellbom, ~~Fool Lake~~ Rose Hill
Elbert Talbot, Weitbrocht Rooming, 320 Geneva, Keene
Richard Koch and brothers, Weitbrocht Rooming
Peter Lawson, Cranmer Retreat House, Hill St, Berkeley
Jed Hopkins, Matts Long Bunk House, 3 Mile Rd, Keene
Helen Brandt, ~~North Hamlin, North Edmeston~~
William Swing, Cranmer Retreat House, Hill St, Berkeley
George Oscar, Rose Hill, c/o Pat Lavay
Donald Rollo, Matts Long Bunk House, 3 Mile Rd, Keene
Gerhardt Kentgen, Papa King Rooming, 127 Main, Edmeston
Blythe Gammon, Bells Dairy Farm, Keene
Wilfred Lowell ?
Roland Brandt, Matts Long Bunk House, 3 Mile Road, Keene
Danielle Lawson (with Peter at Cranmer)
George B. McCormick and Lily (Lily?) with Wellboms
Effie Buller, c/o Golden Hardware's, Keene
~~Dick Jones Co~~
Andrew Schlater, Rfd 1. Rogerston

FIGURE 1-10. *Addresses of workers in Talbot's ledger book*

to sum up the wages paid for each worker, put those total amounts in each envelope, and write each worker's name on the front. Then he'd look up each address in the second section of his ledger book, write it on the front of the envelope, and send the boy off.

G. B. Talbot has a genuine relational database. It uses paper and ink to store its information, rather than a computer disk drive. Even though the joining of the tables is done by his fingers, eyes, and mind rather than a CPU, it is a real, legitimate relational database. It is even fairly close to what a relational application designer would call *normalized*, a word that simply means the data is collected into natural groupings: daily pay and addresses are not mixed together in a single section (table) of the ledger.

The entries in this ledger, both for wages and addresses, could easily be ORACLE tables. The questions or tasks G. B. Talbot must have faced could be made much simpler. You will learn how to do this in the pages ahead, using both current examples and Talbot's old ledger entries to discover ORACLE's power.

CHAPTER 2

The Dangers in a
Relational Database

As with any new technology or new venture, it's sensible to think through not only the benefits and opportunities that are presented, but also the costs and risks. In a relatively new technology such as a relational database, enough time has not elapsed for most companies to have "old hands" around who know what to avoid and how to avoid it.

Combine a relational database with a series of powerful and easy-to-use tools, as ORACLE does, and the possibility of being seduced into disaster by its simplicity becomes real.

This chapter discusses some of the dangers that both developers and users need to consider. Part Four will cover these and additional issues in more depth, especially those of interest to developers in their task of building an accommodating and productive application.

Is It Really as Easy as They Say?

According to the relational vendors—the industry evangelists—developing an application using a relational database and the associated "fourth generation" tools will be as much as 20 times faster than traditional system development. And it will be very easy: ultimately, programmers and systems analysts will be used less, and end users will completely control their own destinies.

Critics of the relational approach warn that relational systems are inherently slower than others, that users given control of query and report writing will overwhelm computers, and that a company will lose face and fortune if a more traditional approach is not taken. The press cites stories of huge applications that simply failed to run when they were put into production.

So what's the truth? The truth is that the rules of the game have changed. Fourth generation relational development makes very different demands upon companies and management than does traditional development. There are issues and risks that are brand new, and not obvious. Once these are identified and understood, the risk is no greater, and probably much smaller, than in traditional development.

What Are the Risks?

The primary risk is that it *is* as easy as they say. Understanding tables, columns, and rows isn't difficult. The relationship between two tables is conceptually simple. Even *normalization,* the process of analyzing the inherent or "normal" relationships between the various elements of a company's data, is fairly easy to learn.

Unfortunately, this often produces instant "experts," full of confidence and naivete, but with little experience in building real, production-quality, relational applications. For a tiny marketing database, or a home inventory application, this doesn't matter very much. The mistakes made will reveal themselves in time, the lessons will be learned, and the errors will be avoided the next time around. In an important application, however, this is a sure formula for disaster. This lack of experience is usually behind the press's stories of major project failures.

Older development methods are generally slower. There are imposed project controls for review and quality assurance, but primarily the tasks of the older methods—coding, submitting a job for compilation, linking, and testing—result in a slower pace. The cycle, particularly on a mainframe, is often so tedious that programmers spend a good deal of time "desk-checking" in order to avoid going through the delay of another full cycle because of an error in the code.

Fourth generation tools seduce developers into rushing into production. Changes can be made and implemented so quickly that testing is given short shrift. The elimination of virtually all desk-checking compounds the problem. When the negative incentive (the long cycle) that encouraged desk-checking disappeared, desk-checking went with it. The attitude of many seems to be "If the application isn't quite right, we can fix it quickly. If the data gets corrupted, we can patch it with a quick update. If it's not fast enough, we can tune it on the fly. Let's get it in ahead of schedule and show the stuff we're made of."

This problem is made worse by an interesting sociological phenomenon: many of the developers of relational applications are recent college graduates. They've learned relational theory and design in school, and are ready to make their mark. More seasoned developers, as a class, haven't learned the new technology: they're busy supporting and enhancing the technologies they know, which support their companies' current information systems. The result is that inexperienced developers tend to end up on the relational projects, are sometimes less inclined to test, and are less sensitive to the consequences of failure than those who have already lived through several complete application developments.

The testing cycle in an important ORACLE project should be longer and more thorough than in a traditional project. This is true even if proper project controls are in place, and even if seasoned project managers are guiding the project, because there will be less desk-checking and an inherent overconfidence. This testing must check the correctness of data entry screens and reports, of data loads and updates, of data integrity and concurrence, and particularly of transaction and storage volumes during peak loads.

Because it really is as easy as they say, application development with ORACLE's tools can be breathtakingly rapid. But this automatically reduces the amount of testing done as a normal part of development, and the planned testing and quality assurance must be consciously lengthened to compensate. This is not usually foreseen by those new to either ORACLE or fourth generation tools, but you must budget for it in your project plan.

The Importance of the New Vision

Many of us look forward to the day when we can simply say, like Captain Kirk, "Computer. . .," make our query in English, and have our answer readily at hand. Perhaps, closer to home, we look to the day when we can type a "natural" language query in English, and have the answer back, on our screen, in seconds.

We are closer to these goals than most of us realize. The limiting factor is no longer technology, but rather the rigor of thought in our application designs. ORACLE can straightforwardly build English-based systems that are easily understood and exploited by unsophisticated users. The potential is there, already available in ORACLE's database and tools, but only a few have understood and used it.

Clarity and understandability should be the hallmarks of any ORACLE application. Applications can operate in English, be understood readily by end users who have no programming background, and provide information based on a simple English query.

How? First of all, a major goal of the design effort must be to make the application easy to understand and simple to use. If you err, it must always be in this direction, even if it means consuming more CPU or disk space. The limitation of this approach is that one could make an application exceptionally easy to use by creating overly complex programs that are nearly impossible to maintain or enhance. This would be an equally bad mistake. However, all things being equal, an end-user orientation should never be sacrificed for clever coding.

Changing Environments

Consider that in 1969 the cost to run a computer with a processing speed of 4 million instructions per second (MIPS) was about $1000 per hour. By 1989 that cost was about 45¢ per hour, and continues to plummet to this day. Labor costs, on the other hand, have risen steadily, not just because of the general trend, but also because salaries of individual employees increase the longer they stay with a company, and the better they become at their jobs. This means that any work that can be shifted from human laborers to machines is a good investment.

Have we factored this incredible shift into our application designs? The answer is "somewhat," but terribly unevenly. The real progress has been in *environments*, such as the visionary work first done at Xerox, and then on the Macintosh, and now in X-Windows, MS-Windows, Presentation Manager, New Wave, NeXT, and other graphical, icon-based systems. These environments are much easier to learn and understand than the older, character-based environments, and people who use them produce in minutes what previously took many days. The improvement in some cases has been so huge we've entirely lost sight of how hard some tasks used to be.

Unfortunately, this concept of an accommodating and friendly environment hasn't been grasped by many application developers. Even when they work in these environments, they continue old habits that are just no longer appropriate.

Codes, Abbreviations, and Naming Standards

This problem is most pronounced in codes, abbreviations, and naming standards, which are almost completely ignored when the needs of end users are considered. When these three issues are thought about at all, usually only the needs and conventions of the systems groups are considered. This may seem like a dry and uninteresting problem to be forced to think through, but it can make the difference between great success and grudging acceptance, between an order-of-magnitude leap in productivity and a marginal gain, between interested, effective users and bored, harried users who make continual demands on the developers.

Here's what happened. It used to be that business records were kept in ledgers and journals. Each event or transaction was written down, line by line, in English. Take a look at Talbot's ledger in Figure 2-1. Any codes? Nope. Any abbreviations? Yes, a few everyday ones that any English-speaking reader would understand immediately. When Talbot sold a cord of wood on January 28th, he wrote "Jan 28 (1 Crd) Wood Methest Church 2.00."

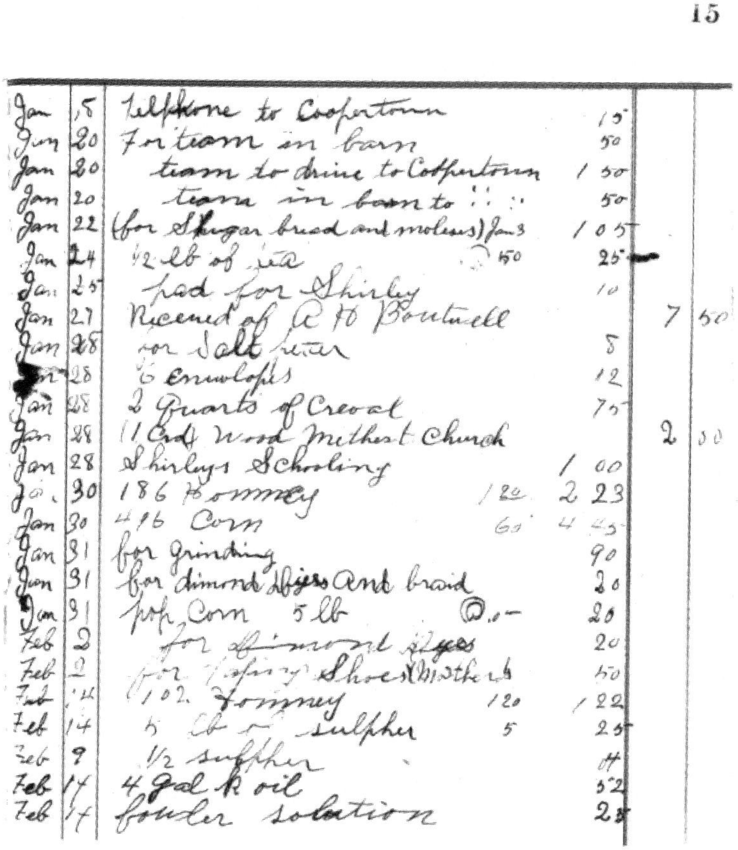

FIGURE 2-1. *A page from Talbot's ledger*

In many applications today, this same transaction would be represented in the computer files with something like "028 04 1 4 60227 3137"—that is, the Julian date for the 28th day of the year, transaction code 04 (a sell) of quantity 1 of quantity type 4 (cord) of item 60227 (60=wood, 22=unfinished, 7=cut) to customer 3137 (Methodist Church). Key entry clerks would actually have to know or look up most of these codes, and type them in at the appropriately labeled fields on their screens. This is an extreme example, but literally thousands of applications take exactly this approach and are every bit as difficult to learn or understand.

This problem has been most pronounced in large, conventional mainframe systems development. As relational databases are introduced into these groups, they are used simply as replacements for older input/output methods such as VSAM and IMS. The power and features of the relational database are virtually wasted when used in such a fashion.

Why Is Coding Used Instead of English?

Why use codes at all? There are two primary justifications usually offered:

- A category has so many items in it that all of them can't reasonably be represented or remembered in English.
- To save space in the computer.

The second point is an anachronism, an artifact of the days when 4 MIPS cost $1000 per hour (and more). Memory (at one time doughnut-shaped ferrite mounted on wire grids) and permanent storage (tapes or big magnetic drums) were once so expensive, and CPUs so slow (with less power than a hand-held calculator), that programmers had to cram every piece of information into the smallest possible space. Numbers, character for character, take half of the computer storage space of letters, and codes (such as 3137 for Kentgen, Gerhardt) reduce the demands on the machine even more.

Because machines were expensive, developers had to use codes for *everything* to make *anything* work at all. It was a technical solution to an economic problem. For users, who had to learn all sorts of meaningless codes, the demands were terrible. Machines were too slow and too expensive to accommodate the humans, so the humans were trained to accommodate the machines. It was a necessary evil.

This economic justification for codes vanished years ago. Computers are now fast enough and cheap enough to accommodate the humans, and work in human languages with words that humans understand. It's high time that they did so. Yet, without really thinking through the justifications, developers and designers continue to use codes willy-nilly, as if it were still 1969.

The first point—that of too many items per category—is more substantive, but much less so than it first appears. One idea is that it takes less effort (and is therefore less expensive) for someone to key in the numbers "3137" than "Kentgen, Gerhardt." This justification is untrue in ORACLE. Not only is it more costly to train people to know the correct customer, product, transaction, and other codes, and more expensive because of the cost of mistakes (which are high with code-based systems), but using codes means not using ORACLE fully; ORACLE is able to take the first few characters of "Kentgen, Gerhardt," and fill in the rest of the name itself. It can do the same thing with product names, transactions (a "b" will automatically fill in with "buy" and "s" with "sell"), and so on, throughout an application. It does this with very robust pattern-matching abilities that have gone virtually unexploited.

The Benefit of User Feedback

There is an immediate additional benefit: key entry errors drop almost to zero because the users get immediate feedback, in English, of the business information they're entering. Digits don't get transposed, codes don't get remembered incorrectly, and in financial applications, money rarely is lost in suspense accounts due to entry errors, with very significant savings.

Applications also become much more comprehensible. Screens and reports are transformed from arcane arrays of numbers and codes into a readable and understandable format. The change of application design from code-oriented to English-oriented has a profound and invigorating effect on a company and its employees. For users who have been burdened by code manuals, an English-based application produces a tremendous psychological release.

How to Reduce the Confusion

Another version of the "too many items per category" justification is that the number of products, customers, or transaction types is just too great to differentiate each by name, or there are too many items in a category that are identical or very similar (customers named "John Smith," for instance). A category can contain too many entries to make the options easy to remember or differentiate, but more often this is evidence of an incomplete job of categorizing information: too many dissimilar things are crammed into too broad a category. Developing an application with a strong English-based (or French, German, Spanish, and so on) orientation, as opposed to code-based, requires time spent with users and developers—taking apart the information of the business, understanding its natural relationships and categories, and then carefully constructing a database and naming scheme that simply and accurately reflects these discoveries.

There are three basic steps to doing this:

1. Normalize the data.

2. Choose English names for the tables and columns.

3. Choose English names for the data.

Each of these steps will be explained in order. The goal is to design an application where the data is sensibly organized, where the data is stored in tables and columns whose names are familiar to the user, and where the data itself is named in familiar terms, not codes.

Normalization

Relations between countries, or between departments in a company, or between users and developers, are usually the product of particular historical circumstances, which may define current relations even though the circumstances have long since passed. The result of this can be abnormal relations, or, in current parlance, dysfunctional relations. History and circumstance often have the same effect on data—on how it is collected, organized, and reported. And data, too, can become abnormal and dysfunctional.

Normalization is the process of putting things right, making them normal. The origin of the term is the Latin word *norma,* which was a carpenter's square that was used for assuring a right angle. In geometry, when a line is at a right angle to another line, it is said to be "normal" to it. In a relational database the term also has a specific mathematical meaning having to do with separating elements of data (such as names, addresses, or skills) into *affinity groups,* and defining the normal, or "right," relationships between them.

The basic concepts of normalization are being introduced here so that users can contribute to the design of an application they will be using, or better understand one that's already been built. It would be a mistake, however, to think that this process is really only applicable to designing a database or a computer application. Normalization results in deep insights into the information used in a business, and how the various elements of that information are related to each other. This will prove educational in areas apart from databases and computers.

The Logical Model
An early step in the analysis process is the building of a *logical model,* which is simply a normalized diagram of the data used by the business. Knowing why and how the data gets broken apart and segregated is essential to understanding the model, and the model is essential to building an application that will support the

business for a long time, without requiring extraordinary support. Part Four of this book covers this more completely, particularly as it applies to developers.

Normalization is usually discussed in terms of *form:* First, Second, and Third Normal Form are the most common, with Third representing the most highly normalized state. G. B. Talbot keeps track of the various people who work for him. Most of these people do pick-up work, and stay at one of the many lodging houses in town. He's developed a simple form to collect this information, which looks like Figure 2-2.

If Talbot were to follow older techniques, he may well design a database that matches the basic layout of this form. It seems like a straightforward enough approach, basically following the "pieces of paper in the cigar box" model. Many applications have been designed in this manner. The application designers took copies of existing forms—invoices, sales receipts, employment applications, statements, worker information sheets—and built systems based on their content and layout.

Thinking this through, however, reveals some lurking problems. Assume that Talbot's form became the table design in ORACLE. The table might be called WORKER, and the columns might be Name, Age, Lodging, Manager, Address, Skill1, Skill2, and Skill3. See Figure 2-3. The users of this table already have a

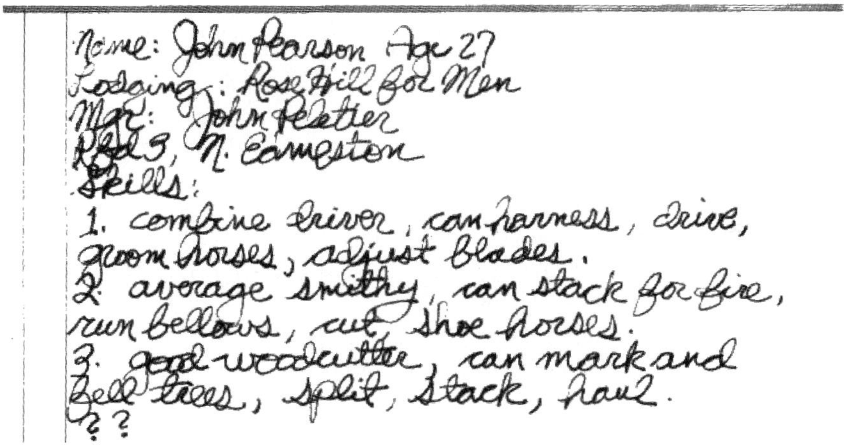
Name: John Pearson Age 27
Lodging: Rose Hill for Men
Mgr: John Peletier
Rfd 3, N. Edmeston
Skills:
1. combine driver, can harness, drive,
groom horses, adjust blades.
2. average smithy, can stack for fire,
run bellows, cut, shoe horses.
3. good woodcutter, can mark and
fell trees, split, stack, haul.
??

FIGURE 2-2. *Worker information*

```
WORKER Table
------------
Name
Age
Lodging
Manager
Address
Skill1
Skill2
Skill3
 .
 .
 .
 ?
```

FIGURE 2-3. *Talbot's WORKER table with lurking problems*

problem: on Talbot's piece of paper he can list as many skills as he likes, while in the WORKER table, users have been limited to just three.

Suppose that in addition to pieces of paper in the cigar box, Talbot enters the same elements of information in ORACLE to test his database WORKER table. Every piece of paper becomes a row of information. But what happens when Peletier (the manager on Talbot's form) moves to New Hampshire, and a new manager takes over? Someone has to go through every worker form in the cigar box (and row, in the WORKER table) and correct all those that say "Peletier." And when Rose Hill (where Pearson lives) is bought by Major Resorts International, the address changes to "One Major Resorts Way," and again all of the workers' records must be changed. What will Talbot do when John Pearson adds a fourth skill? And is "good" or "average" really a legitimate part of a skill, or is it a level of ability that perhaps should be a separate column?

These are not really computer or technical issues, even though they were apparent because you were designing a database. They are much more basic issues of how to sensibly and logically organize the information of a business. They are the issues that normalization addresses. This is done with a step-by-step reorganization of the elements of the data into affinity groups, by eliminating dysfunctional relationships and by assuring normal relationships.

First Normal Form Step one is to put the data into First Normal Form. This is done by moving data into separate tables where the data in each table is of a similar type, and giving each table a *primary key*—a unique label or identifier. This eliminates repeating groups of data, such as the skills in Talbot's paper form (which became just three skills in the first attempt at a WORKER table).

Instead of having only three skills allowed per worker, each worker's skills are placed in their own separate table, with a row per name, skill, and skill description. This eliminates the need for a variable number of skills in the WORKER table (impossible in ORACLE anyway), and is a better design than limiting the WORKER table to just three skills.

Next, you define the primary key to each table: what will uniquely identify and allow you to extract one row of information. For simplicity's sake, assume the workers' names are unique, so "name" is the primary key to the WORKER table. Since each worker may have several rows in the SKILL table, "name" plus "skill" is the whole primary key to the SKILL table (two parts are combined to make a whole). See Figure 2-4.

To find out what John Pearson's ability is as a woodcutter, as well as get a description of what skills a woodcutter has, you would simply type this query:

```
select Ability, Description
  from SKILL
 where Name = 'John Pearson' and Skill = 'Woodcutter';
```

ORACLE would respond with this:

```
Ability Description
------- ---------------------------------------
Good    Mark And Fell Trees, Split, Stack, Haul
```

What will lead you to a unique row in the SKILL table? It's both Name and Skill. But skill Description is only dependent on Skill, regardless of whose name is there. This leads to the next step.

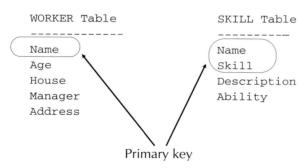

FIGURE 2-4.   *Talbot's workers in First Normal Form*

Second Normal Form   Step two, Second Normal Form, entails taking out data that's only dependent on a part of the key. To put things in Second Normal Form, you take Skill and Description off to a third table. The primary key to the third table is just Skill, and its long-winded description appears only once. If left in the First Normal Form SKILL table, the long descriptions would be repeated for every worker that had the skill. Further, if the last worker with smithy skills left town, when he was eliminated from the database, the description of smithy skills would vanish. With Second Normal Form, the skill and description can be in the database even if no one currently has the skill. Skills can even be added, like "job descriptions," before locating anyone who has them. See Figure 2-5.

Third Normal Form   Step three, Third Normal Form, means getting rid of anything in the tables that doesn't depend solely on the primary key. The lodging information for the worker is *dependent* on his living there (if he moves, you update his row with the name of the new lodging he lives in), but the lodging manager's name and the lodging address are *independent* of whether this worker lives there or not. Lodging information is therefore moved out to a separate table, and for the sake of convenience, a shorthand version of the lodging house name is used as the primary key, and the full name is kept as LongName. Figure 2-6 shows the tables in Third Normal Form, and Figure 2-7 graphically shows the relationships of the tables.

Anytime the data is in Third Normal Form, it is already automatically in Second and First Normal Form. The whole process can therefore actually be accomplished less tediously than by going from form to form. Simply arrange the data so that the columns in each table, other than the primary key, are dependent only on the *whole primary key*.

Third Normal Form is sometimes described as "the key, the whole key, and nothing but the key."

```
WORKER Table          WORKER SKILL Table        SKILL Table
-------------         ------------------        -----------
Name                  Name                      Skill
Age                   Skill                     Description
Lodging               Ability
Manager
Address
```

FIGURE 2-5.   *Talbot's workers in Second Normal Form*

```
WORKER Table       WORKER SKILL Table     SKILL Table       LODGING Table
------------       ------------------     -----------       -------------
Name               Name                   Skill             Lodging
Age                Skill                  Description        LongName
Lodging            Ability                                  Manager
                                                            Address
```

FIGURE 2-6.   *Talbot's workers in Third Normal Form*

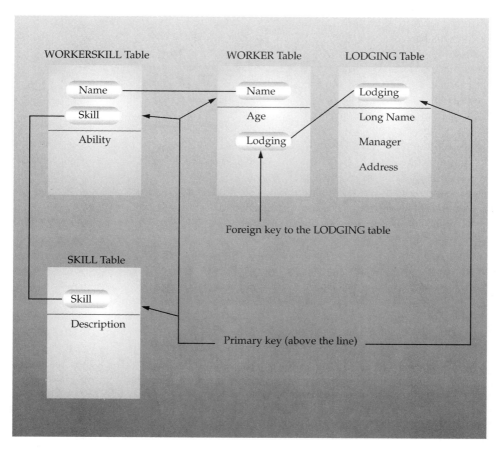

FIGURE 2-7.   *Relationships between the worker tables*

Navigating Through the Data

Talbot's database is now in Third Normal Form. Figure 2-8 shows a sample of what these tables might contain. It's easy to see how these four tables are related. You navigate from one to the other to pull out information on a particular worker, based on the keys to each table. The primary key in each table is able to uniquely identify a single row. Choose John Pearson, for instance, and you can readily discover his age in the WORKER table, because Name is the primary key.

Look up his name and the skill "Woodcutter" in the WORKER SKILL table, and you'll find his Ability, "Good." Name and Skill together are the primary key for this table, meaning that they will pick out only one row. Look up "Woodcutter" in the SKILL table and you will see a full description of what a woodcutter needs to be able to do.

When you looked up John Pearson in the WORKER table, you also saw that his Lodging was Rose Hill. This is the primary key to the LODGING table. When you look up Rose Hill there, you find its LongName, "Rose Hill For Men," the Manager, "John Peletier," and the Address, "Rfd 3, N. Edmeston." When the primary key of the LODGING table appears in another table, as it does in the WORKER table, it is called a *foreign key*—sort of like an embassy or consulate that is a local "key" to a foreign country.

These tables also show real-world characteristics: Talbot doesn't know where Brandt or Lowell live, doesn't have a skill listed for Sarjeant or Hopkins, and doesn't assess Pearson's ability as a combine driver. Because the data is organized logically, he's also able to keep a record of a grave digger's expected skills, even though none of the current workers has those skills.

This is a sensible and logical way to organize information, even if the "tables" are written in a ledger book, or on scraps of paper in cigar boxes. Of course, there is still some work to do to turn this into a real database. For instance, you probably ought to break Address up into component parts, such as Street, City, State, and so on. Name probably ought to be broken into first and last, and you might want to find a way to restrict the options for the Ability column in the WORKER SKILL table.

This whole process is called normalization. It really isn't any trickier than this. There are some other issues involved in a good design, but the basics of analyzing the "normal" relationships among the various elements of data are as they've just been explained—there's not that much to it. It makes sense whether or not a relational database or a computer is involved at all.

One caution needs to be raised, however. Normalization is a part of the process of analysis. It is not design. Design of a database application includes many other considerations, and it is a fundamental mistake to believe that the normalized tables of the logical model are the "design" for the actual database. This fundamental confusion of analysis and design contributes to the stories in the press

```
                         The WORKER Table
NAME                              AGE              LODGING
-------------------------         -----            ----------
Adah Talbot                       23               Papa King
Bart Sarjeant                     22               Cranmer
Dick Jones                        18               Rose Hill
Elbert Talbot                     43               Weitbrocht
Helen Brandt                      15
Jed Hopkins                       33               Matts
John Pearson                      27               Rose Hill
Victoria Lynn                     32               Mullers
Wilfred Lowell                    67


                       The WORKER SKILL Table
NAME                              SKILL            ABILITY
-------------------------         -------------    ---------
Adah Talbot                       Work             Good
Dick Jones                        Smithy           Excellent
Elbert Talbot                     Discus           Slow
Helen Brandt                      Combine Driver   Very Fast
John Pearson                      Combine Driver
John Pearson                      Woodcutter       Good
John Pearson                      Smithy           Average
Victoria Lynn                     Smithy           Precise
Wilfred Lowell                    Work             Average
Wilfred Lowell                    Discus           Average



                         The SKILL Table
SKILL              DESCRIPTION
-------------      --------------------------------------------
Combine Driver     Harness, Drive, Groom Horses, Adjust Blades
Discus             Harness, Drive, Groom Horses, Blade Depth
Grave Digger       Mark and Cut Sod, Dig, Shore, Fill, Resod
Smithy             Stack for Fire, Run Bellows, Cut, Shoe Horses
Woodcutter         Mark and Fell Trees, Split, Stack, Haul
Work               General Unskilled Labor

                         The LODGING Table
LODGING       LONGNAME                MANAGER          ADDRESS
-----------   ---------------------   --------------   ---------------
Cranmer       Cranmer Retreat House   Thom Cranmer     Hill St, Berkeley
Matts         Matts Long Bunk House   Roland Brandt    3 Mile Rd, Keene
Mullers       Mullers Coed Lodging    Ken Muller       120 Main, Edmeston
Papa King     Papa King Rooming       William King     127 Main, Edmeston
Rose Hill     Rose Hill For Men       John Peletier    Rfd 3, N. Edmeston
Weitbrocht    Weitbrocht Rooming      Eunice Benson    320 Geneva, Keene
```

FIGURE 2-8.   *Information in Talbot's tables*

about the failure of major relational applications. These issues are addressed for developers more fully in Part Four.

English Names for Tables and Columns

Once the relationships between the various elements of the data in an application are understood and segregated appropriately, considerable thought must be devoted to choosing names for the tables and columns into which the data will be placed. This is an area given too little attention, even by those who should know better. Table and column names are often developed without consulting end users, and without rigorous review during the design process. Both of these failings have serious consequences when it comes to actually using an application.

For example, consider Talbot's tables from the last section. They contain these columns:

WORKER Table	WORKER SKILL Table	SKILL Table	LODGING Table
Name	Name	Skill	Lodging
Age	Skill	Description	LongName
Lodging	Ability		Manager
			Address

These table and column names are virtually all self-evident. An end user, even one new to relational ideas and SQL, would have little difficulty understanding or even replicating a query such as this:

```
select Name, Age, Lodging
   from WORKER
 order by Age;
```

Users understand this because the words are all familiar. There are no obscure or ill-defined terms. When tables with many more columns in them must be defined, naming the columns can be more difficult, but a few consistently enforced rules will help immensely. Consider some of the difficulties commonly caused by lack of naming conventions. What if Talbot had chosen these names instead?

WORKERS Table	WS	SKILL	ACCOMMODATIONS
wkrname	wswkrname	skil	alocnam
wage	wskil	des	alngname
locnam	ablty		mgr
			addr

The naming techniques in this table, as bizarre as they look, are unfortunately very common. They represent tables and columns named by following the conventions (and lack of conventions) used by several well-known vendors and developers. Table 2-1 shows some real examples of column and table names from these same sources.

Here are a few of the more obvious difficulties in the list of names:

- *Abbreviation is used without good reason*   This makes remembering the "spelling" of a table or column name virtually impossible. The names may as well be codes, because the users will have to look them up.

- *Abbreviation is inconsistent*   In one instance it's "LOW," in another its "LO." Which is it, "NUMBER," "NUM," or "NO"? Is it "EMPNO" or "ENO"? Is it "EMPNAME" or "ENAME"?

- *The purpose or meaning of a column or table is unapparent from the name*   In addition to abbreviations making the spelling of names difficult to remember, they obscure the nature of the data the column or table contains. What is "PE"? "SLSTAXPCT"? "CDLEXP"?

- *Underlines are used inconsistently*   Sometimes they are used to separate words in a name, other times they are not. How will anyone remember which name did or didn't have an underline?

- *Use of plurals is inconsistent*   Is it "EMP" or "EMPS"? Is it "NOTE" or "NOTES"?

- *Rules apparently used have immediate limitations*   If the first letter of the table name is to be used for a name column, as in "DNAME," what happens when a "DIVISION" table becomes necessary? Does the name column in that table also get called "DNAME"? If so, why isn't the column in both simply called "NAME"?

These are only a few of the most obvious difficulties. Users subjected to poor naming of tables and columns will not be able to simply type English queries. The queries won't have the intuitive and familiar "feel" that the WORKER table query has, and this will harm the acceptance and usefulness of the application significantly.

Programmers used to be required to create field and file names that were a maximum of six to eight characters in length. As a result, names were unavoidably confused mixes of letters, numbers, and cryptic abbreviations. Like so many other restrictions forced on users by older technology, this one is just no longer applicable. ORACLE allows table and column names up to 30 characters long. This gives designers plenty of room to create a full, unambiguous, and descriptive name.

TABLES	COLUMNS		
DEPT	AD1	EMPNO	NOTES
EMP	AU_LNAME	ENAME	ORD_NUM
EMPS	AU_ORD	ENUMBER	PNAME
MYEMPS	BLOC	ESAL	PROJNO
PE	CDLEXP	HIGHQTY	PUBDATE
PERSONNEL	DEPTNO	HIRANGE	QTYOH
PROJ	DISCOUNTTYPE	LORANGE	SLSTAXPCT
TITLES	DNAME	LOWQTY	WORKHRS

TABLE 2-1. *Table and Column Names from Various Sources*

The difficulties outlined here imply solutions, such as avoiding abbreviations and plurals, and either eliminating underlines or using them consistently. These quick rules of thumb will go a long way in solving the naming confusion so prevalent today. At the same time, naming conventions need to be simple, easily understood, and easily remembered. Chapter 27 will develop naming conventions more completely. In a sense, what is called for is a normalization of names. In much the same way that data is analyzed logically, segregated by purpose, and thereby normalized, the same sort of logical attention needs to be given to naming standards. The job of building an application is improperly done without it.

English Names for the Data

Having raised the important issue of naming conventions for tables and columns, the next step is to look at the data itself. After all, when the data from the tables is printed on a report, how self-evident the data is will determine how understandable the report is. In Talbot's example, Skill might have been a two-number code, with 01 meaning "smithy," 02 meaning "combine driver," and so on, and 99 meaning "general unskilled labor." Ability could have been a rating scale from 1 to 10. Is this an improvement? If you asked another person about Dick Jones, would you want to hear that he was a 9 at 01? Why should a machine be permitted to be less clear, particularly when it is simple to design applications that can say "excellent smithy"?

Additionally, keeping the information in English makes writing and understanding queries much simpler. Which of these two SQL requests and answers is more obvious? This one:

```
select wswkrname, ablty, wskil
   from ws;
```

```
WSWKRNAME                AB WS
-----------------------  -- --
Adah Talbot              07 99
Dick Jones               10 01
Elbert Talbot            03 03
Helen Brandt             08 02
John Pearson                02
John Pearson             07 04
John Pearson             05 01
Victoria Lynn            09 01
Wilfred Lowell           05 99
Wilfred Lowell           05 03
```

or this one:

```
select Name, Ability, Skill
   from WORKERSKILL;
```

NAME	ABILITY	SKILL
Adah Talbot	Good	Work
Dick Jones	Excellent	Smithy
Elbert Talbot	Slow	Discus
Helen Brandt	Very Fast	Combine Driver
John Pearson		Combine Driver
John Pearson	Good	Woodcutter
John Pearson	Average	Smithy
Victoria Lynn	Precise	Smithy
Wilfred Lowell	Average	Work
Wilfred Lowell	Average	Discus

Case in Names and Data

ORACLE makes it slightly easier to remember table and column names by ignoring whether you type in uppercase or lowercase. It stores table and column names in its internal data dictionary in uppercase. When you type a query, it instantly converts the table and column names to uppercase, and then checks for them in the dictionary. Some other relational systems are case sensitive. If users type a column name as "Ability," but the database thinks it is "ability" or "ABILITY" (depending on what it was told when the table was created), it will not understand the query.

This is promoted as a benefit because it allows programmers to create many tables with, for instance, similar names. They can make a worker table, a Worker table, a wORker table, and so on, ad infinitum. These will all be separate tables. How is anyone, including the programmer, supposed to remember the differences? This is a drawback, not a benefit, and ORACLE was wise not to fall into this trap.

A similar case can be made for data stored in a database. There are ways, using certain commands, to find information from the database regardless of whether it is in uppercase or lowercase, but these methods impose an unnecessary burden. With few exceptions, such as legal text or form letter paragraphs, it is much easier to store data in the database in uppercase. It makes queries easier, and provides a more consistent appearance on reports. When and if some of this data needs to be put into lowercase, or mixed uppercase and lowercase (such as the name and address on a letter), then the ORACLE functions that make the conversion can be invoked. It will be less trouble overall, and less confusing, to store and report data in uppercase.

Looking back over this chapter, you'll see that this practice was not followed. Rather, it was delayed until the subject could be introduced and put in its proper context. From here on, with the exception of one or two tables, and a few isolated instances, data in the database will be in uppercase.

Normalizing Names

There are several "natural language" products that have come on the market whose purpose is to let you make queries using common English words instead of the odd conglomerations such as those found in Table 2-1. These products work by building a logical map between the common English words and the hard-to-remember, non-English column names, table names, and codes. The mapping takes careful thought, but once completed, makes the user's interaction with the application easy. Why not put the care in at the beginning? Why create a need for yet another layer, another product, and more work, when much of the confusion could have been solved by simply doing a good job the first time around?

For performance reasons it may be that some of an application's data must be stored in a coded fashion within the computer's database. These codes should *not* be exposed to users, either during data entry or retrieval, and ORACLE allows them to be easily hidden.

The instant that data entry requires codes, key entry errors increase. When reports contain codes, instead of English, errors of interpretation begin. And when users wish to create new or ad hoc reports, their ability to do so quickly and accurately is severely impaired both by codes and by not being able to remember strange column and table names.

Seizing the Opportunity

ORACLE gives users the power to see and work with English throughout the entire application. It is a waste of ORACLE's power to ignore this opportunity, and it will without question produce a less understandable and less productive application. Developers should seize the opportunity. Users should demand it. Both will benefit immeasurably.

PART 2

SQL: Going from Beginner to Expert

CHAPTER 3

The Basic Parts of Speech in SQL

With the Structured Query Language, or SQL, you tell ORACLE which information you want it to **select**, **insert**, **update**, or **delete**. In fact, these four verbs are the primary words you will use to give ORACLE instructions.

In Chapter 1 you saw what is meant by "relational," how tables are organized into columns and rows, and how to instruct ORACLE to select certain columns from a table and show you the information in them row by row.

In this and the following chapters you will learn to do this more completely. You also will learn how to interact with SQL*PLUS, a powerful ORACLE product that can take your instructions for ORACLE, check them for correctness, submit them to ORACLE, and then modify or reformat the response ORACLE gives, based on orders or directions that you've set in place. It *interacts* with you, which means you can "talk" to it, and it will "talk" back. You can give it directions, and it will follow them precisely. It will tell you if it doesn't understand something you've told it to do.

It may be a little confusing at first to understand the difference between what SQL*PLUS is doing and what ORACLE is doing, especially since the error messages that ORACLE produces are simply passed on to you by SQL*PLUS, but you will see as you work through this book where the differences lie.

As you get started, just think of SQL*PLUS as a coworker—an assistant who follows your instructions and helps you do your work more quickly. You interact with this coworker by typing on your keyboard.

You may follow the examples in this and subsequent chapters by typing the commands shown. Your ORACLE and SQL*PLUS programs should respond just as they do in these examples. You do need to make certain that the tables used in this book have been loaded into your copy of ORACLE.

You can understand what is described in this book without actually typing it in yourself; for example, you can use the commands shown with your own tables. It will probably be clearer and easier, though, if you have the same tables loaded into ORACLE that are used here, and practice using the same queries.

Appendix A contains instructions on loading the tables. Assuming that this has been done, connect to SQL*PLUS and begin working by typing this:

```
SQLPLUS
```

This starts SQL*PLUS. (Note that you don't type the * that is in the middle of the official product name. From here on SQLPLUS will be referred to without the asterisk.) Since ORACLE is careful to guard who can access the data it stores, it always requires an ID and PASSWORD in order for you to connect to it. ORACLE will display a copyright message, and then ask for your username and password. To gain access to the tables described in this book, enter the word **practice** for both username and password. SQLPLUS will announce that you're connected to ORACLE, and then display this prompt:

```
SQL>
```

You are now in SQLPLUS, and it awaits your instructions. If you are on a PC, and get this message:

```
Bad command or filename.
```

it means one of three things: you are not on the proper subdirectory to use ORACLE, ORACLE is not in your path, or ORACLE hasn't been installed properly

on your computer. On other computers, similar messages will let you know
ORACLE isn't ready to go. If you get this message:

```
ERROR: ORA-1017: invalid username/password; logon denied
```

it means either that you've entered the username or password incorrectly, or that
the practice username has not yet been set up on your copy of ORACLE. After three
unsuccessful attempts to enter a username and password that ORACLE recognizes,
SQLPLUS will terminate the attempt to log on with this message:

```
unable to CONNECT to ORACLE after 3 attempts, exiting SQL*Plus
```

If you get this message, either contact your company's database administrator
or follow the installation guidelines in Appendix A. Assuming everything is
in order, and the SQL> prompt has appeared, you may now begin working
with SQLPLUS.

When you want to quit working and leave SQLPLUS, type this:

```
quit
```

Style

First, some comments on style. SQLPLUS doesn't care if the SQL commands you
type are in uppercase or lowercase. This command:

```
SeLeCt feaTURE, section, PAGE FROM newsPaPeR;
```

will produce exactly the same result as this one:

```
select Feature, Section, Page from NEWSPAPER;
```

Case matters only when SQLPLUS or ORACLE is checking a value for equality
in the database. If you tell ORACLE to find a row where Section = 'f' and Section
is really equal to 'F', ORACLE won't find it (since f and F are not identical). Aside
from this use, case is completely irrelevant. (Incidentally, the letter 'F', as used
here, is called a literal, meaning that you want Section to be tested literally against
the letter 'F', not a column *named* F. The single quote marks on either side of the
letter tell ORACLE that this is a literal, and not a column name.)

As a matter of style, this book follows certain conventions about case to make
text and listings easier to read:

   - **select, from, where, order by**, **having**, and **group by** will always be
     lowercase and boldface.

- SQLPLUS commands also will be lowercase and boldface: **column**, **set**, **save**, **ttitle**, and so on.

- **IN, BETWEEN, UPPER, SOUNDEX**, and other SQL operators and functions will be uppercase and boldface.

- Column names will be uppercase and lowercase without boldface: Feature, EastWest, Longitude, and so on.

- Tables will be uppercase without boldface: NEWSPAPER, WEATHER, LOCATION, and so on.

You may wish to follow similar conventions in creating your own queries, or your company already may have standards it would like you to use, or you may choose to invent your own. The goal of any such standards should always be to make your work simple to read and understand.

Using SQL to select Data from Tables

Figure 3-1 shows a table of features from a local newspaper. If this were an ORACLE table, rather than just paper and ink on the front of the local paper, SQLPLUS would display it for you if you typed this:

```
select Feature, Section, Page from NEWSPAPER;

FEATURE          S      PAGE
--------------- - ----------
National News    A         1
Sports           D         1
Editorials       A        12
Business         E         1
Weather          C         2
Television       B         7
Births           F         7
Classified       F         8
Doctor Is In     F         6
Modern Life      B         1
Comics           C         4
Movies           B         4
Bridge           B         2
Obituaries       F         6

14 rows selected.
```

Feature	Section	Page
Births	F	7
Bridge	B	2
Business	E	1
Classified	F	8
Comics	C	4
Doctor Is In	F	6
Editorials	A	12
Modern Life	B	1
Movies	B	4
National News	A	1
Obituaries	F	6
Sports	D	1
Television	B	7
Weather	C	2

FIGURE 3-1.   *A table of newspaper sections*

What's different between the table in the listing and the one from the newspaper in Figure 3-1? Both tables have the same information but the format differs. For example, the column headings differ slightly. In fact, they even differ slightly from the columns you just asked for in the **select** statement.

The column named Section shows up as just the letter "S," and although you used uppercase and lowercase letters to type this:

```
select Feature, Section, Page from NEWSPAPER;
```

the columns came back with all of the letters in uppercase.

These changes are the result of the assumptions SQLPLUS makes about how information should be presented. You can change these, and you will, but until you give it different orders, this is how SQLPLUS changes what you input:

- It changes all the column headings to uppercase.

- It allows columns to be only as wide as the column is defined to be in ORACLE.

■ It squeezes out any spaces if the column heading is a function. (This will be demonstrated in Chapter 5.)

The first point is obvious. The column names you used were shifted to uppercase. The second point is not obvious. How *are* the columns defined? To find out, ask ORACLE. Simply tell SQLPLUS to describe the table, as shown here:

```
describe NEWSPAPER

Name                              Null?    Type
--------------------------------- -------- -------
FEATURE                           NOT NULL VARCHAR2(15)
SECTION                                    CHAR(1)
PAGE                                       NUMBER
```

This display is a descriptive table that lists the columns and their definitions for the NEWSPAPER table; **describe** works for any table.

The first column tells the names of the columns in the table being described.

The second column, Null?, is really a rule about the column named to its left. When this table was created by entering **NOT NULL**, its creator instructed ORACLE not to allow anyone to enter information into it unless he or she put in a real Feature title. No one is allowed to add a new row to this table with the Feature column empty (**NULL** means empty).

Of course, in a table such as NEWSPAPER, it probably would have been worthwhile to make the same rule about all three columns. What good is it to know the title of a Feature without also knowing what Section it's in and what Page it's on? But, for the sake of this example, only Feature was created with the specific rule that it could not be **NULL**.

Because Section and Page have nothing in the Null? column, it means they are allowed to be empty in any row of the NEWSPAPER table.

The third column, Type, tells the basic nature of the individual columns. Feature is a VARCHAR2 (variable-length character) column that can be up to 15 characters (letters, numbers, symbols, or spaces) long.

Section is a character column as well, but it is only one character long! The creator of the table knew that newspaper sections in the local paper are only a single letter, so the column was defined to be only as wide as it needed to be. It was defined using the CHAR datatype, which is used for fixed-length character strings. When SQLPLUS went to display the results of your query:

```
select Feature, Section, Page from NEWSPAPER;
```

it knew from ORACLE that Section was a maximum of only one character. It assumed that you did not want to use up more space than this, so it displayed a column just one character wide, and used as much of the column name as it could: "S".

The third column in the NEWSPAPER table is Page, and this is simply a number.

You'll notice that the Page column in the NEWSPAPER table shows up as ten spaces wide, even though there are no pages using more than two numbers. This is because numbers are not usually defined as having a specific maximum width, so SQLPLUS assumes one just to get started.

You also may have noticed that the heading for the only column composed solely of numbers, Page, was *right-justified*—that is, it sits over on the right side of the column, whereas the headings for columns that contain characters sit over on the left. This is standard alignment for column titles in SQLPLUS. Like other column features, you'll later be able to change these as needed.

Finally, SQLPLUS tells you how many rows it found in ORACLE's NEWSPAPER table. (Notice the "14 rows selected" notation at the bottom of the NEWSPAPER table.) This is called *feedback*. You can make SQLPLUS stop giving feedback by typing the **feedback** command, as shown here:

```
set feedback off
```

or you can set a minimum number of rows for **feedback** to work:

```
set feedback 25
```

This last use of the command tells ORACLE that you don't want to know how many rows have been displayed until there have been at least 25. Unless you tell SQLPLUS differently, **feedback** is set to 6.

The **set** command is a SQLPLUS command, which means that it is an instruction telling SQLPLUS how to act. There are many features of SQLPLUS, such as **feedback**, that you can set. Several of these will be shown and used in this chapter, and in the chapters to follow. For a complete list, look up **set** in the Alphabetical Reference section of this book.

The **set** command has a counterpart named **show** that will allow you to see what instructions you've given to SQLPLUS. For instance, you can check the setting of **feedback** by typing

```
show feedback
```

SQLPLUS will respond with

```
feedback ON for 25 or more rows
```

The width used to display numbers also is changed by the **set** command. You check it by typing

```
show numwidth
```

SQLPLUS will reply as shown here:

```
numwidth 10
```

Since 10 is a wide width for displaying page numbers that never contain more than two digits, shrink the display by typing

```
set numwidth 5
```

However, this means that all number columns will be five digits wide. If you anticipate having numbers with more than five digits, you must use a number higher than 5. Individual columns in the display also can be set independently. This will be covered in Chapter 4.

select, from, where, and order by

You will use four primary keywords in SQL when selecting information from an ORACLE table: **select**, **from**, **where**, and **order by**. You will use **select** and **from** in every ORACLE query you do.

The **select** keyword tells ORACLE which columns you want, and **from** tells ORACLE the names of the table or tables those columns are in. The NEWSPAPER table example showed how these are used. In the first line you entered, a comma follows each column name except the last. You'll notice that a correctly typed SQL query reads pretty much like an English sentence. A query in SQLPLUS usually ends with a semicolon (sometimes called the *SQL terminator*). The **where** keyword tells ORACLE what qualifiers you'd like to put on the information it is selecting for you. For example, if you input this:

```
select Feature, Section, Page from NEWSPAPER
 where Section = 'F';
```

```
FEATURE          S  PAGE
---------------  -  -----
Births           F     7
Classified       F     8
Obituaries       F     6
Doctor Is In     F     6
```

ORACLE checks each row it found in the NEWSPAPER table before sending them back to you. It skipped over those without the single letter "F" in their Section column. It returned those where the Section was "F", and SQLPLUS displayed them to you.

To tell ORACLE that you want the information it returns sorted in the order you specify, use **order by**. You can be as elaborate as you like about the order you request. Consider these examples:

```
select Feature, Section, Page from NEWSPAPER
  where Section = 'F'
  order by Feature;


FEATURE           S  PAGE
---------------   -  -----
Births            F    7
Classified        F    8
Doctor Is In      F    6
Obituaries        F    6
```

They are nearly reversed when ordered by page, as shown here:

```
select Feature, Section, Page from NEWSPAPER
  where Section = 'F'
  order by Page;


FEATURE           S  PAGE
---------------   -  -----
Obituaries        F    6
Doctor Is In      F    6
Births            F    7
Classified        F    8
```

In the next example, ORACLE first puts the Features in order by Page (see the previous listing to observe the order they are in when they are ordered only by Page). It then puts them in further order by Feature, listing "Doctor Is In" ahead of "Obituaries."

```
select Feature, Section, Page from NEWSPAPER
  where Section = 'F'
  order by Page, Feature;
```

```
FEATURE          S   PAGE
--------------   -   -----
Doctor Is In     F      6
Obituaries       F      6
Births           F      7
Classified       F      8
```

Using **order by** also can reverse the normal order, like this:

```
select Feature, Section, Page from NEWSPAPER
 where Section = 'F'
 order by Page desc, Feature;
```

```
FEATURE          S   PAGE
--------------   -   -----
Classified       F      8
Births           F      7
Doctor Is In     F      6
Obituaries       F      6
```

The **desc** keyword stands for descending. Because it followed the word "Page" in the **order by** line, it put the page numbers in descending order. It would have the same effect on the Feature column if it followed the word "Feature" in the **order by** line.

Notice that **select**, **from**, **where**, and **order by** each have their own way of structuring the words that follow them. In relational terms the groups of words including these keywords are often called *clauses*. See examples of each clause in Figure 3-2.

Logic and Value

Just as the **order by** clause can have several parts, so can the **where** clause, but with a significantly greater degree of sophistication. You control the extent to which you use **where** through the careful use of logical instructions to ORACLE on

Select Feature, Section, Page	<--**select clause**
from NEWSPAPER	<--**from clause**
where Section = 'F'	<--**where clause**

FIGURE 3-2.   *Relational clauses*

what you expect it to return to you. These instructions are expressed using mathematical symbols called *logical operators.* These are explained shortly, and also are listed in the Alphabetical Reference section, both individually by name, and grouped under the heading "Logical Operators."

```
select Feature, Section, Page
   from NEWSPAPER
 where Page = 6;


FEATURE          S  PAGE
--------------- - -----
Obituaries       F    6
Doctor Is In     F    6
```

This is a simple example of logic and value where the values in the Page column are tested to see if any equals 6. Every row where this is true is returned to you. Any rows where Page is not equal to 6 are skipped (in other words, those rows for which Page = 6 is false).

The equal sign is called a logical operator, because it operates by making a logical test by comparing the values on either side of it—in this case, the value of Page and the value 6—to see if they are equal.

In this example, there were no quotes placed around the value being checked. That's because the column the value is compared to (the Page column) is defined as a NUMBER datatype. Number values do not require quotes around them during comparisons.

Single Value Tests

You can use one of several logical operators to test against a single value, as shown in the special boxed section "Logical Tests Against a Single Value." Take a few examples from this list. They all work similarly, and can be combined at will, although they must follow certain rules about how they'll act together.

Equal, Greater Than, Less Than, Not Equal
Logical tests can compare values, both for equality and for relative value. Here a simple test is made for all sections equal to B:

```
select Feature, Section, Page
   from NEWSPAPER
 where Section = 'B';
```

```
FEATURE          S   PAGE
---------------  -   -----
Television       B     7
Modern Life      B     1
Movies           B     4
Bridge           B     2
```

The following is the test for all pages greater than 4:

```
select Feature, Section, Page
  from NEWSPAPER
 where Page > 4;
```

```
FEATURE          S   PAGE
---------------  -   -----
Editorials       A    12
Television       B     7
Births           F     7
Classified       F     8
Obituaries       F     6
Doctor Is In     F     6
```

The following is the test for sections greater than B (this means further into the alphabet than B is):

```
select Feature, Section, Page
  from NEWSPAPER
 where Section > 'B';
```

```
FEATURE          S   PAGE
---------------  -   -----
Sports           D     1
Business         E     1
Weather          C     2
Births           F     7
Classified       F     8
Comics           C     4
Obituaries       F     6
Doctor Is In     F     6
```

Logical Tests Against a Single Value

All of these operators work with letters or numbers, and with columns or literals.

EQUAL, GREATER THAN, LESS THAN, NOT EQUAL

Page=	6	Page *is equal to 6*
Page>	6	Page *is greater than 6*
Page>=	6	Page *is greater than or equal to 6*
Page<	6	Page *is less than 6*
Page<=	6	Page *is less than or equal to 6*
Page!=	6	Page *is not equal to 6*
Page^=	6	Page *is not equal to 6*
Page<>	6	Page *is not equal to 6*

Because some keyboards lack an exclamation mark (!) or a caret (^), ORACLE allows three ways of typing the not equal operator. The final alternative, <>, qualifies as a not equal operator because it permits only numbers less than 6 (in this example), or greater than 6, but not 6 itself.

LIKE

Feature LIKE 'Mo%'	Feature begins with the letters Mo
Feature LIKE '_ _ l%'	Feature has an l in the third position
Feature LIKE '%o%o%'	Feature has two o's in it

LIKE performs pattern matching. An underline (_) represents one space. A percent sign (%) represents any number of spaces or characters.

IS NULL, IS NOT NULL

Precipitation IS NULL	"Precipitation is unknown"
Precipitation IS NOT NULL	"Precipitation is known"

NULL tests to see if data exists in a column for a row. If the column is completely empty, it is said to be **NULL**. The word "IS" must be used with **NULL** and **NOT NULL**. Equal signs, greater than, or less than will not work.

Just as a test can be made for greater than, so can a test for less than, as shown here:

```
select Feature, Section, Page
   from NEWSPAPER
 where Page < 8;
```

```
FEATURE           S        PAGE
--------------- - ----------
National News     A           1
Sports            D           1
Business          E           1
Weather           C           2
Television        B           7
Births            F           7
Modern Life       B           1
Comics            C           4
Movies            B           4
Bridge            B           2
Obituaries        F           6
Doctor Is In      F           6
```

The opposite of the test for equality is *not equal*, as given here:

```
select Feature, Section, Page
   from NEWSPAPER
 where Page != 1;
```

```
FEATURE           S        PAGE
--------------- - ----------
Editorials        A          12
Weather           C           2
Television        B           7
Births            F           7
Classified        F           8
Comics            C           4
Movies            B           4
Bridge            B           2
Obituaries        F           6
Doctor Is In      F           6
```

Be careful when using the *greater than* and *less than* operators against numbers that are stored in character datatype columns. All values in VARCHAR2 and CHAR columns will be treated as characters during comparisons. Therefore, numbers that are stored in those types of columns will be compared as if they were character strings, not numbers. If the column's datatype is NUMBER, then 12 is greater than 9. If it is a character column, then 9 is greater than 12 because the character '9' is greater than the character '1'.

LIKE

One of the most powerful logical features of SQL is a marvelous pattern-matching operator called **LIKE**. **LIKE** is able to search through the rows of a database column for values that look like a pattern you describe. It uses two special characters to denote which kind of matching you wish to do: a percent sign called a *wild card*, and an underline called a *position marker*. To look for all of the Features that begin with the letters "Mo," use the following:

```
select Feature, Section, Page from NEWSPAPER
 where Feature LIKE 'Mo%';


FEATURE           S       PAGE
--------------- - ----------
Modern Life      B          1
Movies           B          4
```

The percent sign (%) means anything is acceptable here: one character, a hundred characters, or no characters. If the first letters are 'Mo', **LIKE** will find the Feature. If the query had used 'MO%' as its search condition instead, then no rows would have been returned due to Oracle's case-sensitivity in data values. If you wish to find those Features that have the letter "i" in the third position of their titles, and you don't care which two characters precede the "i" or what set of characters follows, two underlines specify that any character in those two positions is acceptable. Position three must have a lowercase "i"; the percent sign after that says anything is okay.

```
select Feature, Section, Page from NEWSPAPER
 where Feature LIKE '__i%';


FEATURE           S       PAGE
--------------- - ----------
Editorials       A         12
Bridge           B          2
Obituaries       F          6
```

Multiple percent signs also can be used. In order to find those words with two lowercase "o's" anywhere in the Feature title, three percent signs are used, as shown here:

```
select Feature, Section, Page from NEWSPAPER
  where Feature LIKE '%o%o%';


FEATURE           S       PAGE
--------------- - ----------
Doctor Is In      F          6
```

For the sake of comparison, the following is the same query, but it is looking for two "i's":

```
select Feature, Section, Page from NEWSPAPER
  where Feature LIKE '%i%i%';


FEATURE           S       PAGE
--------------- - ----------
Editorials        A         12
Television        B          7
Classified        F          8
Obituaries        F          6
```

This pattern-matching feature can play an important role in making an application friendlier by simplifying searches for names, products, addresses, and other partially remembered items.

NULL and NOT NULL

The NEWSPAPER table has no columns in it that are **NULL**, even though the **describe** you did on it showed that they were allowed. The COMFORT table following contains, among other data, the precipitation for San Francisco and Keene, New Hampshire, for four sample dates during 1993.

```
select City, SampleDate, Precipitation
  from COMFORT;
```

```
CITY            SAMPLEDAT PRECIPITATION
------------- --------- -------------
SAN FRANCISCO 21-MAR-93            .5
SAN FRANCISCO 22-JUN-93            .1
SAN FRANCISCO 23-SEP-93            .1
SAN FRANCISCO 22-DEC-93           2.3
KEENE         21-MAR-93           4.4
KEENE         22-JUN-93           1.3
KEENE         23-SEP-93
KEENE         22-DEC-93           3.9
```

You can find out the city and dates on which precipitation was not measured with this query:

```
select City, SampleDate, Precipitation
  from COMFORT;
 where Precipitation IS NULL;

CITY            SAMPLEDAT PRECIPITATION
------------- --------- -------------
KEENE         23-SEP-93
```

IS NULL essentially means where the data is missing. You don't know for that day whether the value should be 0, 1, or 5 inches. Because it is unknown, the value in the column is not set to 0; it stays empty. By using **NOT**, you also can find those cities and dates for which data exists, with this query:

```
select City, SampleDate, Precipitation
  from COMFORT;
 where Precipitation IS NOT NULL;

CITY            SAMPLEDAT PRECIPITATION
------------- --------- -------------
SAN FRANCISCO 21-MAR-93            .5
SAN FRANCISCO 22-JUN-93            .1
SAN FRANCISCO 23-SEP-93            .1
SAN FRANCISCO 22-DEC-93           2.3
KEENE         21-MAR-93           4.4
KEENE         22-JUN-93           1.3
KEENE         22-DEC-93           3.9
```

ORACLE lets you use the relational operators (=, !=, and so on) with **NULL**, but this kind of comparison will not return meaningful results. Use **IS** or **IS NOT NULL** for comparing values to **NULL**.

Simple Tests Against a List of Values

If there are logical operators that test against a single value, are there others that will test against many values, such as a list? The special boxed section entitled "Logical Tests Against a List of Values" shows just such a group of operators. Here are a few examples of how they are used:

Logical Tests Against a List of Values
With numbers:

Page IN (1,2,3)	Page is in the list (1,2,3)
Page NOT IN (1,2,3)	Page is not in the list (1,2,3)
Page BETWEEN 6 AND 10	Page is equal to 6,10, or anything in between
Page NOT BETWEEN 6 AND 10	Page is below 6 or above 10

With letters (or characters):

Section IN ('A','C','F')	Section is in the list ('A', 'C', 'F')
Section NOT IN ('A', 'C', 'F')	Section is not in the list ('A', 'C', 'F')
Section BETWEEN 'B' AND 'D'	Section is equal to 'B', 'D', or anything in between (alphabetically)
Section NOT BETWEEN 'B' AND 'D'	Section is below 'B' or above 'D' (alphabetically)

```
select Feature, Section, Page
  from NEWSPAPER
 where Section IN ('A','B','F');
```

```
FEATURE          S        PAGE
---------------  -  ----------
National News    A           1
Editorials       A          12
Television        B          7
Births           F           7
Classified       F           8
Modern Life      B           1
Movies           B           4
Bridge           B           2
Obituaries       F           6
Doctor Is In     F           6
```

```
select Feature, Section, Page
   from NEWSPAPER
 where Section NOT IN ('A','B','F');
```

```
FEATURE          S        PAGE
---------------  -  ----------
Sports           D           1
Business         E           1
Weather          C           2
Comics           C           4
```

```
select Feature, Section, Page
   from NEWSPAPER
 where Page BETWEEN 7 and 10;
```

```
FEATURE          S        PAGE
---------------  -  ----------
Television        B          7
Births           F           7
Classified       F           8
```

These logical tests also can be combined, as in this case:

```
select Feature, Section, Page
   from NEWSPAPER
 where Section = 'F'
  AND Page > 7;
```

```
FEATURE           S        PAGE
--------------- - ----------
Classified        F           8
```

The **AND** command has been used to combine two logical expressions, and requires any row ORACLE examines to pass *both* tests; both "Section = 'F'" and "Page > 7" must be true for a row to be returned to you. Alternatively, **OR** can be used, and will allow rows to be returned to you if *either* logical expression turns out to be true:

```
select Feature, Section, Page
  from NEWSPAPER
 where Section = 'F'
    OR Page > 7;
```

```
FEATURE           S  PAGE
--------------- - -----
Editorials        A    12
Births            F     7
Classified        F     8
Obituaries        F     6
Doctor Is In      F     6
```

There are some Sections here that qualify even though they are not equal to 'F' because their Page is greater than 7, and there are others whose Page is less than or equal to 7, but whose Section is equal to 'F'.

Finally, choose those features in section F between pages 7 and 10 with this query:

```
select Feature, Section, Page
  from NEWSPAPER
 where Section = 'F'
   and Page BETWEEN 7 AND 10;
```

```
FEATURE           S  PAGE
--------------- - -----
Births            F     7
Classified        F     8
```

There are a few additional *many-value operators* whose use is more complex; they will be covered in Chapter 6. They also can be found, along with those just discussed, in the Alphabetical Reference section under "Logical Operators."

Combining Logic

Both **AND** and **OR** follow the commonsense meaning of the words. They can be combined in a virtually unlimited number of ways, but care must be used because **AND**s and **OR**s get convoluted very easily.

Suppose you wanted to find the Features in the paper that the editors tended to bury, those that are placed somewhere past page 2 of section A or B. You might try this:

```
select Feature, Section, Page
  from NEWSPAPER
 where Section = 'A'
    or Section = 'B'
  and Page > 2;

FEATURE            S  PAGE
---------------    -  -----
National News      A     1
Editorials         A     12
Television          B     7
Movies             B     4
```

But the result you got back from ORACLE was not what you wanted. Somehow, page 1 of section A was included. Apparently, the "and Page > 2" only affected the rows for section B. If you now move the "and Page > 2" up to the middle of the **where** clause, the result is different, but still wrong:

```
select Feature, Section, Page
  from NEWSPAPER
 where Section = 'A'
   and Page > 2
    or Section = 'B';

FEATURE            S  PAGE
---------------    -  -----
Editorials         A     12
Television          B     7
Modern Life        B     1
Movies             B     4
Bridge             B     2
```

What happens if you put the "Page > 2" first? Still wrong:

```
select Feature, Section, Page
  from NEWSPAPER
 where Page > 2
   and Section = 'A'
    or Section = 'B';


FEATURE          S  PAGE
--------------   -  -----
Editorials       A    12
Television       B     7
Modern Life      B     1
Movies           B     4
Bridge           B     2
```

Why is this happening? Is there a way to get ORACLE to answer the question correctly? Although both **AND** and **OR** are logical connectors, **AND** is stronger. It binds the logical expressions on either side of it more strongly than the **OR** does (technically, it is said to have *higher precedence*). This means this **where** clause:

```
where Section = 'A'
    or Section = 'B'
  and Page > 2;
```

is interpreted to read, "where Section = 'A', or where Section = 'B' *and* Page > 2". If you look at each of the failed examples just given, you'll see how this interpretation affected the result. The **AND** is always acted on first.

You can break this bonding by using parentheses that enclose those expressions you want to be interpreted together. Parentheses override the normal precedence:

```
select Feature, Section, Page
  from NEWSPAPER
 where Page > 2   and ( Section = 'A'
        or Section = 'B' );


FEATURE          S PAGE
----------------  -  -----
Editorials       A    12
Television       B     7
Movies           B     4
```

The result is exactly what you wanted in the first place. Note that while you can type this with the sections listed first, the result is identical, because the parentheses tell ORACLE what to interpret together. Compare this to the different results caused by changing the order in the first three examples, where parentheses were not used:

```
select Feature, Section, Page
   from NEWSPAPER
 where ( Section = 'A'
         or Section = 'B' )
   and Page > 2;
```

```
FEATURE          S  PAGE
--------------   -  -----
Editorials       A    12
Television       B     7
Movies           B     4
```

Another Use for where–Subqueries

What if the logical operators in the special boxed sections "Logical Tests Against a Single Value" and "Logical Tests Against a List of Values" could be used not just with a single literal value (such as 'F') or a typed list of values (such as 4,2,7 or 'A','C','F'), but with values brought back by an ORACLE query? In fact, this is a powerful feature of SQL.

   Imagine that you are the author of the "Doctor Is In" feature, and each newspaper that publishes your column sends along a copy of the table of contents that includes your piece. Of course, each editor rates your importance a little differently, and places you in a section he or she deems suited to your feature. Without knowing ahead of time where your feature is, or with what other features you are placed, how could you write a query to find out where this local paper places you? You might do this:

```
select Section from NEWSPAPER
 where Feature = 'Doctor Is In';
```

```
S
-
F
```

   The result is 'F'. Knowing this, you could do this query:

```
select FEATURE from NEWSPAPER
 where Section = 'F';

FEATURE
---------------
Births
Classified
Obituaries
Doctor Is In
```

You're in there with births, deaths, and classified ads. Could the two separate queries have been combined into one? Yes, as shown here:

```
select FEATURE from NEWSPAPER
 where Section = (select Section from NEWSPAPER
                  where Feature = 'Doctor Is In');

FEATURE
---------------
Births
Classified
Obituaries
Doctor Is In
```

Single Values from a Subquery

In effect, the **select** in parentheses (called a *subquery*) brought back a single value, F. The main query then treated this F as if it were a literal 'F', as was used in the previous query. Remember that the equal sign is a single value test (refer back to Figure 3-2). It can't work with lists, so if your subquery brought back more than one row, you'd get an error message like this one:

```
select * from NEWSPAPER
 where Section = (select Section from NEWSPAPER
                  where Page = 1);

ERROR: ORA-1427:  single-row subquery returns more than one row
```

All of the logical operators that test single values can work with subqueries, as long as the subquery returns a single row. For instance, you can ask for all of the features in the paper where the section is *less than* (lower in the alphabet) the section that carries your column. The asterisk in this **select** shows a shorthand way to request all the columns in a table without listing them individually. They will be displayed in the order in which they were created in the table.

```
select * from NEWSPAPER
  where Section < (select Section from NEWSPAPER
                    where Feature = 'Doctor Is In');
```

```
FEATURE          S  PAGE
--------------- - -----
National News    A    1
Sports           D    1
Editorials       A   12
Business         E    1
Weather          C    2
Television       B    7
Modern Life      B    1
Comics           C    4
Movies           B    4
Bridge           B    2

10 rows selected.
```

Ten other features rank ahead of your medical advice in this local paper.

Lists of Values from a Subquery

Just as the single-value logical operators can be used on a subquery, so can the many-value operators. If a subquery brings back one or more rows, the value in the column for each row will be stacked up in a list. For example, suppose you wished to know the cities and countries where it is cloudy. You could have a table of complete weather information for all cities, and a location table for all cities and their countries, as shown here:

```
select City, Country from LOCATION;
```

```
CITY                          COUNTRY
----------------------------- ---------------------------
ATHENS                        GREECE
CHICAGO                       UNITED STATES
CONAKRY                       GUINEA
LIMA                          PERU
MADRAS                        INDIA
```

```
MANCHESTER          ENGLAND
MOSCOW              RUSSIA
PARIS               FRANCE
SHENYANG            CHINA
ROME                ITALY
TOKYO               JAPAN
SYDNEY              AUSTRALIA
SPARTA              GREECE
MADRID              SPAIN
```

```
select City, Condition from WEATHER;

CITY           CONDITION
-----------    -----------
LIMA           RAIN
PARIS          CLOUDY
MANCHESTER     FOG
ATHENS         SUNNY
CHICAGO        RAIN
SYDNEY         SNOW
SPARTA         CLOUDY
```

First, you'd discover which cities were cloudy:

```
select City from WEATHER
 where Condition = 'CLOUDY';

CITY
-----------
PARIS
SPARTA
```

Then you would build a list including those cities, and use it to query the LOCATION table:

```
select City, Country from LOCATION
  where City IN ('PARIS', 'SPARTA');

CITY                        COUNTRY
--------------------------  --------------------------
PARIS                       FRANCE
SPARTA                      GREECE
```

The same task can be accomplished by a subquery, where the **select** in parentheses builds a list of cities that are tested by the **IN** operator, as shown here:

```
select City, Country from LOCATION
  where City IN (select City from WEATHER
                   where Condition = 'CLOUDY');


CITY                             COUNTRY
------------------------------   --------------------------
PARIS                            FRANCE
SPARTA                           GREECE
```

The other many-value operators work similarly. The fundamental task is to build a subquery that produces a list that can be logically tested. The following are some relevant points:

- The subquery either must have only one column, or it must compare its selected columns to multiple columns in parentheses in the main query (covered in Chapter 10).

- The subquery must be enclosed in parentheses.

- Subqueries that produce only one row can be used with *either* single- or many-value operators.

- Subqueries that produce more than one row can be used *only* with many-value operators.

- BETWEEN *cannot* be used with a subquery; that is,

```
select * from WEATHER
  where Temperature BETWEEN 60
                   AND (select Temperature
                          from WEATHER
                          where City = 'PARIS');
```

will not work. All other many-value operators will work with subqueries.

Combining Tables

This is all very well when all the columns you need to display are in a single table, or when a simple test can be made with a subquery to another table. But if you've normalized your data, you'll probably need to combine two or more tables to get all the information you want.

Suppose you are the Oracle at Delphi. The Athenians come to ask about the forces of nature that might affect the expected attack by the Spartans, as well as the direction from which they are likely to appear:

```
select City, Condition, Temperature from WEATHER;

CITY          CONDITION    TEMPERATURE
-----------   -----------  -----------
LIMA          RAIN              45
PARIS         CLOUDY            81
MANCHESTER    FOG               66
ATHENS        SUNNY             97
CHICAGO       RAIN              66
SYDNEY        SNOW              29
SPARTA        CLOUDY            74
```

You realize your geography is rusty so you query the LOCATION table:

```
select City, Longitude, EastWest, Latitude, NorthSouth
  from LOCATION;

CITY                         LONGITUDE E LATITUDE N
--------------------------   --------- - -------- -
ATHENS                          23.43 E    37.58 N
CHICAGO                         87.38 W    41.53 N
CONAKRY                         13.43 W     9.31 N
LIMA                            77.03 W    12.03 S
MADRAS                          80.17 E    13.05 N
MANCHESTER                       2.15 W    53.3  N
MOSCOW                          37.35 E    55.45 N
PARIS                            2.2  E    48.52 N
SHENYANG                       123.3  E    41.48 N
ROME                            12.29 E    41.54 N
TOKYO                          139.5  E    35.42 N
SYDNEY                         151.1  E    33.52 S
SPARTA                          22.27 E    37.05 N
MADRID                           3.14 W    40.24 N
```

This is much more than you need, and it doesn't have any weather information. Yet these two tables, WEATHER and LOCATION, have a column in common: City. You can therefore put the information from the two tables together by joining them. You merely use the **where** clause to tell ORACLE what the two tables have in common (this is similar to the example given in Chapter 1):

```
select WEATHER.City, Condition, Temperature, Latitude,
       NorthSouth, Longitude, EastWest
  from WEATHER, LOCATION
 where WEATHER.City = LOCATION.City;


CITY          CONDITION    TEMPERATURE LATITUDE N LONGITUDE E
-----------   -----------  ----------- -------- - --------- -
ATHENS        SUNNY                 97    37.58 N     23.43 E
CHICAGO       RAIN                  66    41.53 N     87.38 W
LIMA          RAIN                  45    12.03 S     77.03 W
MANCHESTER    FOG                   66     53.3 N      2.15 W
PARIS         CLOUDY                81    48.52 N       2.2 E
SPARTA        CLOUDY                74    37.05 N     22.27 E
SYDNEY        SNOW                  29    33.52 S     151.1 E
```

Notice that the only rows in this combined table are those where the city is in *both* tables. The **where** clause is still executing your logic, as it did earlier in the case of the NEWSPAPER table. It is the logic you gave it that described the relationship between the two tables. It says, "select those rows in the WEATHER table and the LOCATION table where the cities are equal." If a city was only in one table, it would have nothing to be equal to in the other table. The notation used in the **select** statement is "TABLE.ColumnName"—in this case, WEATHER.City.

The **select** clause has chosen those columns from the two tables that you'd like to see displayed; any columns in either table that you did not ask for are simply ignored. If the first line had simply said this:

```
select City, Condition, Temperature, Latitude
```

then ORACLE would not have known to which City you were referring. ORACLE would tell you that the column name City was ambiguous. The correct wording in the **select** clause is "WEATHER.City" or "LOCATION.City". In this example, it won't make a bit of difference which of these alternatives is used, but you will encounter cases where the choice of identically named columns from two or more tables will contain very different data.

The **where** clause also requires the names of the tables to accompany the identical column name by which the tables are combined: "where weather dot city equals location dot city"—that is, where the City column in the WEATHER table equals the City column in the LOCATION table.

Consider that the combination of the two tables looks like a single table with seven columns and seven rows. Everything that you excluded is gone. There is no Humidity column here, even though it is a part of the WEATHER table. There is no Country column here, even though it is a part of the LOCATION table. And of the

14 cities in the LOCATION table, only those that are in the WEATHER table are here in this table. Your **where** clause didn't allow the others to be selected.

A table that is built from columns in one or more tables is sometimes called a *projection*, or a *result table*.

Creating a View

There is even more here than meets the eye. Not only does this look like a new table; you can give it a name and treat it like one. This is called creating a view. A *view* is a way of hiding the logic that created the joined table just displayed. It works this way:

```
create view INVASION AS
select WEATHER.City, Condition, Temperature, Latitude,
       NorthSouth, Longitude, EastWest
  from WEATHER, LOCATION
 where WEATHER.City = LOCATION.City;

View created.
```

Now you can act as if INVASION were a real table with its own rows and columns. You can even ask ORACLE to describe it to you:

```
describe INVASION

Name                             Null?     Type
-------------------------------- --------  ----
CITY                                       VARCHAR2(11)
CONDITION                                  VARCHAR2(9)
TEMPERATURE                                NUMBER
LATITUDE                                   NUMBER
NORTHSOUTH                                 CHAR(1)
LONGITUDE                                  NUMBER
EASTWEST                                   CHAR(1)
```

You can query it, too (note that you will not have to specify which table the City columns were from, because that logic is hidden inside the view):

```
select City, Condition, Temperature, Latitude, NorthSouth,
       Longitude, EastWest
  from INVASION;
```

```
CITY          CONDITION    TEMPERATURE LATITUDE N LONGITUDE E
----------    -----------  ----------- -------- - --------- -
ATHENS        SUNNY                 97    37.58 N     23.43 E
CHICAGO       RAIN                  66    41.53 N     87.38 W
LIMA          RAIN                  45    12.03 S     77.03 W
MANCHESTER    FOG                   66     53.3 N      2.15 W
PARIS         CLOUDY                81    48.52 N       2.2 E
SPARTA        CLOUDY                74    37.05 N     22.27 E
SYDNEY        SNOW                  29    33.52 S     151.1 E
```

There will be some ORACLE functions you won't be able to use on a view that you can use on a plain table, but they are few, and mostly involve modifying rows and indexing tables, which will be discussed in later chapters. For the most part, a view behaves and can be manipulated just like any other table.

Suppose now you realize that you don't really need information about Chicago or other cities outside of Greece, so you change the query. Will the following work?

```
select City, Condition, Temperature, Latitude, NorthSouth,
       Longitude, EastWest
  from INVASION
 where Country = 'GREECE';
```

SQLPLUS passes back this message from ORACLE:

```
where Country = 'GREECE'
      *
ERROR at line 4: ORA-0704:  invalid column name
```

Why? Because even though Country is a real column in one of the tables behind the view called "INVASION", it was not in the **select** clause when the view was created. It is as if it does not exist. So you must go back to the **create view** statement, and include only the country of Greece there.

```
create or replace view INVASION as
select WEATHER.City, Condition, Temperature, Latitude,
       NorthSouth, Longitude, EastWest
  from WEATHER, LOCATION
 where WEATHER.City = LOCATION.City
   and Country = 'GREECE';

View created.
```

Using the **create or replace view** command allows you to create a new version of a view without first dropping the old one. This command will make it easier to administer users' privileges to access the view, as will be described in Chapter 17.

The logic of the **where** clause has now been expanded to include both joining two tables and a single-value test on a column in one of those tables. Now, query ORACLE. You'll get this response:

```
select City, Condition, Temperature, Latitude, NorthSouth,
       Longitude, EastWest
  from INVASION;


CITY         CONDITION    TEMPERATURE LATITUDE N LONGITUDE E
-----------  -----------  ----------- -------- - --------- -
ATHENS       SUNNY                 97    37.58 N     23.43 E
SPARTA       CLOUDY                74    37.05 N     22.27 E
```

This allows you to warn the Athenians that the Spartans are likely to appear from the southwest, but will be overheated and tired from their march. With a little trigonometry you could even make ORACLE calculate how far they will have marched. The old Oracle at Delphi was always ambiguous in her predictions. She would have said, "the Spartans the Athenians will conquer." You can at least offer some facts.

Expanding the View of View

This power of views to hide or even modify data can be used for a variety of useful purposes. Very complex reports can be built up by the creation of a series of simple views, and specific individuals or groups can be restricted to seeing only certain pieces of the whole table.

In fact, any qualifications you put into a query can become part of a view. You could, for instance, let supervisors looking at a payroll table see only their own salaries and those of the people working for them, or restrict operating divisions in a company to seeing only their own financial results, even though the table actually contains results for all divisions. Most importantly, views are *not* snapshots of the data at a certain point in the past. They are dynamic, and always reflect the data in the underlying tables. The instant data in a table is changed, any views created with that table change as well.

For example, you may create a view that restricts values based on column values. As shown here, a query that restricts the LOCATION table on the Country column could be used to limit the rows that are visible via the view:

```
create or replace view PERU_LOCATIONS as
select * from LOCATION
where Country = 'PERU';
```

A user querying PERU_LOCATIONS would not be able to see any rows from any country other than Peru.

NOTE
Using * to define the columns in a view does not cause administrative problems in ORACLE7. In earlier versions of ORACLE, using * for this purpose required that the view be dropped and re-created if its base table's structure changed.

The queries used to define views may also reference *pseudo-columns.* A pseudo-column is a "column" that returns a value when it is selected, but is not an actual column in a table. The User pseudo-column, when selected, will always return the ORACLE username that executed the query. So if a column in the table contains usernames, then those values can be compared against the User pseudo-column to restrict its rows, as shown in the following listing. In this example, the NAME table is queried. If the value of its Name column is the same as the name of the user entering the query, then rows will be returned.

```
create or replace view RESTRICTED_NAMES
select * from NAME
where Name = User;
```

This type of view is very useful when users require access to selected rows in a table. It prevents them from seeing any rows that do not match their ORACLE username.

Views are powerful tools. There will be more to come on the subject in a later chapter.

The **where** clause can be used to join two tables based on a common column. The resulting set of data can be turned into a view (with its own name), which can be treated as if it were a regular table itself. The power of a view is in its ability to limit or change the way data if seen by a user, even though the underlying tables themselves are not affected.

CHAPTER 4

Basic SQLPLUS Reports and Commands

S QLPLUS is usually thought of as a kind of interactive report writer. It uses SQL
to get information from the ORACLE database, and lets you create polished,
well-formatted reports by giving you easy control over titles, column headings,
subtotals and totals, reformatting of numbers and text, and much more. It also can
be used to change the database by using **insert**, **update**, and **delete** commands in
SQL. SQLPLUS can even be used as a *code generator*, where a series of commands
in SQLPLUS can dynamically build a program and then execute it. This
little-known property is explored in detail in Chapter 19.

SQLPLUS is most commonly used for simple queries and printed reports. Getting SQLPLUS to format information in reports according to your taste and needs requires only a handful of *commands*, or key words that instruct SQLPLUS about how to behave. They are listed in Table 4-1. Detailed explanations, examples, and additional features of each of these are given in the Alphabetical Reference in Part Five.

In this chapter you will see a basic report that was written using SQLPLUS, along with an explanation of the features used to create it. If building a report at first seems a bit daunting, don't worry. Once you try the steps, you'll find them simple to understand, and they will soon become familiar.

You can write SQLPLUS reports while working interactively with SQLPLUS—that is, you can type commands about page headings, column titles, format, breaks, and totals, and so on, and then execute a SQL query, and SQLPLUS will immediately produce the report formatted to your specifications. For quick answers to simple questions that aren't likely to recur, this is a fine approach. More common, however, are complex reports that need to be produced periodically, and that you'll want to print rather than just view on the screen. Unfortunately, when you quit SQLPLUS, it promptly forgets every instruction you've given it. If you were restricted to using SQLPLUS only in this interactive way, then running the same report at a later time would require typing everything in all over again.

The alternative is very straightforward. You simply type the commands, line by line, into a file. SQLPLUS can then read this file as if it were a script, and execute your commands just as if you were typing them in. In effect, you've created a report program, but you've done it without a programmer, COBOL, or a compiler. You create this file using any of the popular editor programs available or even (given certain restrictions) a word processor.

The editor is not a part of ORACLE. Editors come in hundreds of varieties, and every company or person seems to have a favorite. Oracle realized this, and decided to let you choose which editor program to use rather than packaging a program with ORACLE and forcing you to use it. When ready to use your editor program, you suspend SQLPLUS, jump over to the editor program, create or change your SQLPLUS report program (also called a *start file*), then jump back to SQLPLUS right at the spot you left, and run that report. See Figure 4-1.

SQLPLUS also has a tiny, built-in editor of its own, sometimes called the *Command Line Editor*, which allows you to quickly modify a SQL query without leaving SQLPLUS. Its use will be covered later in this chapter.

COMMAND	DEFINITION
remark	Tells SQLPLUS that the words to follow are to be treated as comments, not instructions.
set headsep	The **head**ing **sep**arator identifies the single character that tells SQLPLUS to split a title onto two or more lines.
ttitle	Sets the **t**op **title** for each page of a report.
btitle	Sets the **b**ottom **title** for each page of a report.
column	Gives SQLPLUS a variety of instructions on the heading, format, and treatment of a column.
break on	Tells SQLPLUS where to put spaces between sections of a report, or where to break for subtotals and totals.
compute sum	Makes SQLPLUS calculate subtotals.
set linesize	Sets the maximum number of characters allowed on any line of the report.
set pagesize	Sets the maximum number of lines per page.
set newpage	Sets the number of blank lines between pages.
spool	Moves a report you would normally see displayed on the screen into a file, so you can print it.
/**/	Marks the beginning and end of a comment within a SQL query. Similar to **remark**.
- -	Marks the beginning of an inline comment within a SQL query. Treats everything from the mark to the end of the line as a comment. Similar to **remark**.
set pause	Makes screen display stop between pages of display.
save	Saves the SQL query you're creating into the file of your choice.
host	Sends any command to the host operating system.
start	Tells SQLPLUS to follow (execute) the instructions you've saved in a file.
edit	Pops you out of SQLPLUS and into an editor of your choice.
define _editor	Tells SQLPLUS the name of the editor of your choice.

TABLE 4-1.   *Basic SQLPLUS commands*

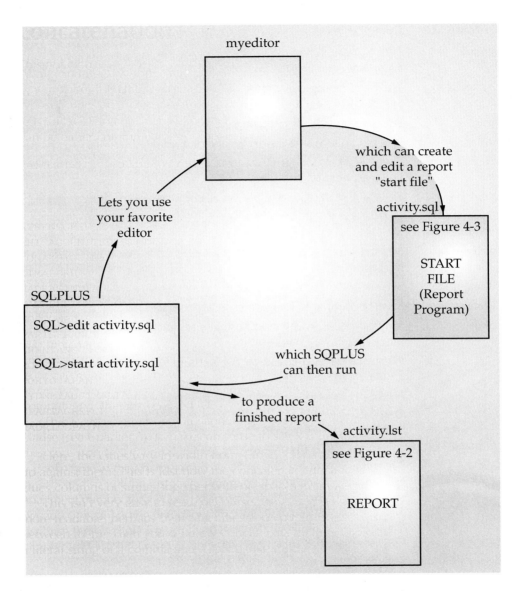

FIGURE 4-1. *SQLPLUS lets you use your favorite editor to create report programs*

Building a Simple Report

Figure 4-2 shows a quick and easy report produced for G. B. Talbot, detailing items he sold during the second half of 1901 and his income for that period.

Figure 4-3 shows the SQLPLUS start file that produced this report, in this case named ACTIVITY.SQL. To run this report program in SQLPLUS, type this:

```
start activity.sql
```

NOTE
How to Distinguish Between SQLPLUS and SQL. The **select** statement toward the bottom of Figure 4-3, beginning with the word "select" and ending with the semicolon (;), is Structured Query Language (SQL)—the language you use to talk to the ORACLE database. Every other command on the page is a SQLPLUS command, used to format the results of a SQL query into a report.

This causes SQLPLUS to read the file ACTIVITY.SQL and execute the instructions you've placed in it. Reviewing this start file will show the basic SQLPLUS instructions you can use to produce reports or change the way SQLPLUS interacts with you. Depending on your experience, this may look formidable or elementary. It is made up of a series of simple instructions to SQLPLUS.

① remark

The first five lines of Figure 4-3, at Circle 1, are documentation about the file itself. These lines begin with the letters:

```
rem
```

which stand for **remark**. SQLPLUS ignores anything on a line that begins with these letters, thus allowing you to add comments, documentation, and explanations to any start file you create. It is always a good idea to place remarks at the top of a start file, giving the file name, its creator and date of creation, the name of anyone who has modified it, the date of modification, what was modified, and an explanation of the purpose of the file. This will prove invaluable later on, as dozens of reports begin to accumulate.

```
Sat Feb 03                                                        page      1
                          Sales by Product During 1901
                          Second Six Months (Jul-Dec)


                         What Was
Date        To Whom Sold  Sold                Quan  Type    RATE      Ext
---------   ------------- -------------------  ----  ------ -----    -----
15-OCT-01   GENERAL STORE  BEEF                935   LB      0.03    28.05
15-NOV-01   FRED FULLER                         37   LB      0.04     1.48
21-NOV-01   ROLAND BRANDT                      116   LB      0.06     6.96
22-NOV-01   GERHARDT KENTGEN                   118   LB      0.06     7.08
                          ******************                        -----
                          sum                                       43.57


03-OCT-01   GARY KENTGEN   BOOT BETWEEN HORSE    1   EACH   12.50    12.50
11-NOV-01   PAT LAVEY                            1   EACH    6.00     6.00
                          ******************                        -----
                          sum                                       18.50


29-AUG-01   GERHARDT KENTGEN BUTTER              5   LB      0.23     1.15
11-NOV-01   PAT LAVEY                            1   LB      0.15     0.15
16-NOV-01   VICTORIA LYNN                        5   LB      0.16     0.80
18-NOV-01   JOHN PEARSON                         6   LB      0.16     0.96
                          ******************                        -----
                          sum                                        3.06

                         What Was
Date        To Whom Sold  Sold                Quan  Type    RATE      Ext
---------   ------------- -------------------  ----  ------ -----    -----
25-JUL-01   SAM DYE        CALF                  1   EACH    1.00     1.00
                          ******************                        -----
                          sum                                        1.00


03-JUL-01   SAM DYE        HEFER                 1   EACH   35.00    35.00
12-OCT-01   GEORGE B.                            1   EACH   35.00    35.00
            MCCORMICK
10-NOV-01   PAT LAVEY                            1   EACH   28.00    28.00
14-NOV-01   MORRIS ARNOLD                        1   EACH   35.00    35.00
20-NOV-01   PALMER WALBOM                        1   EACH   30.00    30.00
                          ******************                        ------
                          sum                                      163.00

                     from G. B. Talbot's Ledger
```

FIGURE 4-2.   *SQLPLUS report for G. B. Talbot*

```
rem         Name: activity.sql   Type: start file report
rem   Written by: G. Koch        Date: 4/1/95
rem
rem Description: Report of G. B. Talbot sales by product
rem              during second half of 1901.


set headsep !

ttitle 'Sales by Product During 1901!Second Six Months (Jul-Dec)'
btitle 'from G. B. Talbot''s Ledger'

column Item heading 'What Was!Sold'
column Item format a18
column Item truncated

column Person heading 'To Whom Sold' format a18 word_wrapped
column Rate format 90.99
column ActionDate heading 'Date'
column QuantityType heading 'Type' format a8 truncated
column Quantity heading 'Quan' format 9990
column Ext format 990.99
break on Item skip 2
compute sum of Ext on Item

set linesize 79
set pagesize 50
set newpage 0

spool activity.1st

select ActionDate, Person, Item, Quantity, QuantityType,
       Rate, Quantity * Rate "Ext"
  from Ledger
 where Action = 'SOLD'                /* last 6 months only */
       and ActionDate BETWEEN '01-JUL-01' AND '31-DEC-01'
 order by Item, ActionDate;

spool off
```

FIGURE 4-4.   *Start file ACTIVITY.SQL used to produce report*

② set headsep

The punctuation that follows **set headsep** (for **head**ing **sep**arator) at Circle 2 in Figure 4-3 tells SQLPLUS how you will indicate where you wish to break a page title or a column heading that runs longer than one line. When you first activate SQLPLUS, the default **headsep** character is the broken vertical bar (¦), but some keyboards do not have this character. If your keyboard doesn't, or if you prefer a different character (such as the exclamation character as shown in the example), you may choose any character on the keyboard.

```
set headsep !
```

CAUTION
Choosing a character that may otherwise appear in a title or column heading will cause unexpected splitting.

③ ttitle and btitle

The line at Circle 3 indicates immediately how **headsep** is used.

```
ttitle 'Sales by Product During 1901!Second Six Months (Jul-Dec)'
```

instructs SQLPLUS to put this **top title** at the top of each page of the report. The exclamation mark between "1901" and "Second" produces the split title you see in Figure 4-2. The title you choose must be enclosed in single quotation marks.

```
btitle 'from G. B. Talbot''s Ledger'
```

works similarly to **ttitle**, except that it goes on the **b**ottom of each page (as the **b** indicates), and also must be in single quotation marks. Note the pair of single quotation marks at the end of "Talbot," and look at the effect in Figure 4-2. Because single quotes are used to enclose the entire title, an apostrophe (the same character on your keyboard) would trick SQLPLUS into believing the title had ended. To avoid this, put two single quotation marks right next to each other when you want to print a single quotation mark. Because both SQL and SQLPLUS rely on single quotation marks to enclose strings of characters, this technique is used throughout SQL and SQLPLUS whenever an apostrophe needs to be printed or displayed. This can confuse even veteran SQL users, however, so whenever possible avoid possessives and contractions that call for an apostrophe.

When using **ttitle** this way, SQLPLUS will always center the title you choose based on the **linesize** you set (**linesize** will be discussed presently), and will always place the day, month, and date the report was run in the upper-left corner, and the page number in the upper-right corner.

There is another, more sophisticated method of using both **ttitle** and **btitle** that allows you to control placement of title information yourself, and even include variable information from your query in the title. These techniques will be covered in Chapter 12.

④ column

column allows you to change the heading and format of any column in a **select** statement. Look at the report in Figure 4-2. The third column is actually called Item in the database and in the first line of the **select** statement at the bottom of Figure 4-3. However, look at Circle 4:

```
column Item heading 'What Was!Sold'
```

relabels the column and gives it a new heading. This heading, like the report title, breaks onto two lines because it has the headsep character (!) embedded in it.

```
column Item format a18
```

sets the width for display at 18. The "a" in "a18" tells SQLPLUS that this is an alphabetic column, as opposed to a number column. The width can be set to virtually any value, quite irrespective of how the column is defined in the database. If you look at the LEDGER table from which this report is produced, you see this:

```
describe LEDGER
```

Name	Null?	Type
ACTIONDATE		DATE
ACTION		VARCHAR2(8)
ITEM		VARCHAR2(30)
QUANTITY		NUMBER
QUANTITYTYPE		VARCHAR2(10)
RATE		NUMBER
AMOUNT		NUMBER(9,2)
PERSON		VARCHAR2(25)

The Item column is defined as 30 characters wide, so it's possible that some items will have more than 18 characters. If you did nothing else in defining this column on the report, any item more than 18 characters long (such as "BOOT BETWEEN HORSES") would wrap onto the next line, as in the following:

```
What Was
Sold
-----------------
BOOT BETWEEN HORSE
S
```

The results look peculiar. To solve this, another column instruction is given:

```
column Item truncated
```

This instruction tells SQL to chop off any extra characters that go beyond the width specified in the line "column Item format a18". In Figure 4-2, look at "What Was Sold" for October 3rd, 1901, and you'll see that the "S" on "HORSES" was simply trimmed away. ("BOOT BETWEEN HORSES," incidentally, refers to plowing a field.)

Although the three column instructions given here for the Item column were placed on three separate lines, it is possible to combine them on a single line, as Circle 5 points out:

⑤ `column Person heading 'To Whom Sold' format a18 word_wrapped`

This instruction is very similar to that used for the Item column, except that here "word_wrapped" takes the place of "truncated". Notice "GEORGE B. MCCORMICK" in Figure 4-2 (on October 12). It was too long to fit in the 18 spaces allotted by this column command, so it was wrapped on to a second line, but the division was between the words or names. This is what **word_wrapped** does.

Circle 6 in Figure 4-3 shows an example of formatting a number:

⑥ `column Rate format 90.99`

This defines a column with room for four digits and a decimal point. If you'll count the spaces in the report for the Rate column, you'll see six spaces. Just looking at the **column** command might lead you to believe the column would be five spaces wide, but this would leave no room for a minus sign if the number were negative, so an extra space on the left is always provided for numbers. The "0" in "90.99" tells SQLPLUS that for a number below 1.00, such as .99, a zero rather than a blank will be put in the dollar position: "0.99". If you look at the report in Figure 4-2, you'll see it does just that.

Circle 7 in Figure 4-3 refers to a column that didn't appear in the table when we had SQLPLUS describe it:

⑦ `column Ext format 990.99`

What is Ext? Look at the **select** statement at the bottom of Figure 4-3. Ext appears in the line:

`Quantity * Rate Ext`

which tells SQL to multiply the Quantity column times the Rate column and treat the result as if it were a new column named Ext. In bookkeeping, a quantity times a rate is often called the *extension*. What you see here is SQL's ability to do a computation on the fly and rename the computation with a simpler column name (Ext as an abbreviation of extension). As a consequence, SQLPLUS sees a column named Ext, and all of its formatting and other commands will act as if it were a real column in the table. The column command for **Ext** is an example.

"Ext" is referred to as a *column alias*—another name to use when referring to a column. In ORACLE7.1, column aliases can be specified in a slightly different way. You can use the **as** clause to identify column aliases in queries. Doing this would change that part of the **select** command in the preceding example to

`Quantity * Rate AS Ext`

Using the **as** clause helps to visually separate the column aliases from the columns. In the remainder of this book, the **as** clause will not be shown because it is not supported in ORACLE7.0. Users of ORACLE7.1 and above should take advantage of this feature.

⑧ break on

Look at Circle 8 in Figure 4-3. Note on the report in Figure 4-2 how the transactions for each kind of Item are grouped together under "What Was Sold." This effect was produced by the line:

`break on Item skip 2`

as well as by the line:

`order by Item`

in the **select** statement near the end of the start file.

SQLPLUS looks at each row as it is brought back from ORACLE, and it keeps track of the value in Item. For the first four rows, this value is "BEEF", so SQLPLUS displays the rows it has gotten. On the fifth row, Item changes from "BEEF" to "BOOT BETWEEN HORSES". SQLPLUS remembers your break instructions, which tell it that when Item changes, it should break away from the normal display of row after row, and skip two lines. You'll notice two lines between the Item sections on the report. Unless the items were collected together because of the **order by**, it wouldn't make sense for **break on** to skip two lines every time the Item changed. This is why the **break on** command and the **order by** clause must be coordinated.

You also may notice that "BEEF" is only printed on the first line of its section, as are "BOOT BETWEEN HORSE," "BUTTER," "CALF," and "HEFER" (this is the spelling in the original ledger). This is in order to eliminate the duplicate printing of each of these items for every row in each section, which is visually unattractive. If you wish, you can force it to duplicate the item on each row of its section by altering the **break on** command to read:

```
break on Item duplicate skip 2
```

If you look at the report output in Figure 4-2, you'll notice that there is no grand total for the report. To be able to get a grand total for a report, add an additional break using the **break on report** command. Be careful when adding breaks, since they all need to be created by a single command; entering two consecutive **break on** commands will cause the first command's instructions to be overwritten by the second command.

To add a grand total for this report, modify the **break on** command to read:

```
break on Item duplicate skip 2 on report
```

⑨ compute sum

The totals calculated for each section on the report were produced by the **compute sum** command at Circle 9. This command always works in conjunction with the **break on** command, and the totals it computes will always be for the section specified by the **break on**. It is probably wise to consider these two related commands as a single unit:

```
break on Item skip 2
compute sum of Ext on Item
```

In other words, this tells ORACLE to compute the sum of the extensions for each item. ORACLE will do this first for BEEF, then BOOT BETWEEN HORSES, BUTTER, CALF, and HEFER. Every time SQLPLUS sees a new Item, it calculates and prints a total for the previous Item. **compute sum** also puts a row of asterisks below the column that **break on** is using, and prints the word "sum" underneath. For reports with many columns that need to be added, a separate **compute sum** statement is used for each total. It also is possible to have several different kinds of breaks on a large report (for Item, Person, and Date, for example) along with coordinated **compute sum** commands. See Chapter 12 for details.

You can use a **break on** command without a **compute sum** command, such as for organizing your report into sections where no totals are needed (addresses with a **break on** City would be an example), but the reverse is not true.

NOTE
Every **compute sum** command must have a **break on** to guide it, and the "**on**" portion of each must match (such as "**on** Item" in **compute sum** of Ext on Item).

The following are the basic rules:

- Every **break on** must have a related **order by**.
- Every **compute sum** must have a related **break on**.

This makes sense, of course, but it's easy to forget one of the pieces.

⑩ set linesize

The three commands at Circle 10 in Figure 4-3 control the gross dimensions of your report. The command **set linesize** governs the maximum number of characters that will appear on a single line. For letter-size paper, this number is usually around 70 or 80, unless your printer uses a very compressed (narrow) character font.

If you put more columns of information in your SQL query than will fit into the **linesize** you've allotted, SQLPLUS will wrap the additional columns down onto the next line, and stack columns under each other. You actually can use this to very good effect when a lot of data needs to be presented. Chapter 12 gives an example of this.

SQLPLUS also uses **linesize** to determine where to center the **ttitle**, and where to place the date and page number. Both date and page number appear on the top line, and the distance between the first letter of the date and the last number of the page number will always equal the **linesize** you set.

set pagesize

The **set pagesize** command sets the total number of lines SQLPLUS will place on each page, including the **ttitle**, **btitle**, **column** headings, and any blank lines it prints. On letter- and computer-size paper this is usually 66 (6 lines per inch times 11 inches). **set pagesize** is coordinated with **set newpage**.

set newpage

A better name for **set newpage** might have been "set blank lines" because what it really does is print blank lines before the top line (date, page number) of each page in your report. This is useful both in adjusting the position of reports coming out on single pages on a laser printer, and for skipping over the perforations between the pages of computer paper.

NOTE
set pagesize does not set the size of the body of the report (the number of printed lines from the date down to the **btitle**); it sets the total length of the page, measured in lines.

Thus, if you typed this:

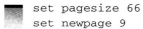

```
set pagesize 66
set newpage 9
```

SQLPLUS would produce a report starting with nine blank lines, followed by 57 lines of information (counting from the date down to the **btitle**). If you increase the size of **newpage**, SQLPLUS will put fewer rows of information on each page, but produce more pages altogether.

That's understandable, you say, but what is it that's been done at Circle 10 on Figure 4-3? It says

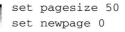

```
set pagesize 50
set newpage 0
```

This is a strange size for a report page—is SQLPLUS to put zero blank lines between pages? No. Instead, the zero after **newpage** switches on a special property it has: **set newpage 0** will produce a *top-of-form character* (usually a hex 13) just before the date on each page. Most modern printers will respond to this by moving immediately to the top of the next page, where the printing of the report will begin. The combination of **set pagesize 50** and **set newpage 0** produces a report whose body of information is exactly 50 lines long, and which has a top-of-form character at the beginning of each page. This is a cleaner and simpler way to control page printing than jockeying around with blank lines and lines per page.

⑪ spool

In the early days of computers most file storage was done on spools of either magnetic wire or tape. Writing information into a file and spooling a file were virtually synonymous. The term has survived, and spooling now generally refers to any process of moving information from one place to another. In SQLPLUS,

```
spool activity.lst
```

tells SQL to take all of the output from SQLPLUS and write it to the file named ACTIVITY.LST. Once you've told SQLPLUS to spool, it continues to do so until you tell it to stop, which you do by inputting

```
spool off
```

This means, for instance, that you could type

```
spool work.fil
```

and then type in a SQL query, such as

```
select Feature, Section, Page from NEWSPAPER
 where Section = 'F';
```

```
FEATURE           S   PAGE
---------------   -   ----
Births            F      7
Classified        F      8
Obituaries        F      6
Doctor Is In      F      6
```

or a series of SQLPLUS commands such as

```
set pagesize 60
column Section heading 'My Favorites'
```

or anything else. Whatever prompts SQLPLUS produced, whatever error messages you got, whatever appeared on the computer screen while spooling, would all end up in the file WORK.FIL. Spooling doesn't discriminate. It records everything that happens from the instant you use the **spool** command until you use **spool off**, which brings us back to G. B. Talbot's report at Circle 11 of Figure 4-3:

```
spool activity.lst
```

The above phrase is carefully placed as the command just before the **select** statement, and **spool off** immediately follows. Had **spool activity.lst** appeared any earlier, the SQLPLUS commands you were issuing would have ended up on the first page of your report file. Instead, it goes into the file ACTIVITY.LST, which is what you see in Figure 4-2: the results of the SQL query, formatted according to your instructions, and nothing more. You are now free to print the file, confident that a clean report will show up on your printer.

⑫ **/ * * /**

Circle 12 of Figure 4-3 shows how a comment can be embedded in a SQL statement. This is different in method and use from the **remark** statement discussed earlier. **remark** (or **rem**) must appear at the beginning of a line, and works only for the single line on which it appears. Furthermore, a multiple-line SQL statement is not permitted to have a **remark** within it. That is,

```
select Feature, Section, Page
rem this is just a comment
  from NEWSPAPER
 where Section = 'F';
```

is wrong. It will not work, and you'll get an error message. However, you can embed remarks in SQL following the method shown at Circle 12, or like this:

```
select Feature, Section, Page
 /* this is just a comment */
  from NEWSPAPER
 where Section = 'F';
```

The secret lies in knowing that /* tells SQLPLUS a comment has begun. Everything it sees from that point forward, even if it continues for many words and lines, is regarded as a comment until SQLPLUS sees */, which tells it that the comment has ended. In ORACLE7, you can use the characters "--" to begin a comment. The end of the line ends the comment. This kind of comment works just like **remark** except that you use -- (two dashes) instead of **rem**.

Some Clarification on Column Headings

It's possible that the difference between the renaming that occurs in this:

```
Quantity * Rate Ext
```

and the new heading given the column Item in this:

```
column Item heading 'What Was!Sold'
```

is not quite clear, particularly if you look at this command:

```
compute sum of Ext on Item
```

Why isn't it "compute sum of Ext on 'What Was!Sold'"? The reason is that SQLPLUS commands are aware only of columns that actually appear in the **select** statement. Every **column** command refers to a column in the **select** statement. Both **break on** and **compute** refer only to columns in the **select** statement. The only reason a **column** command or **compute** is aware of the column Ext is because it got its name in the **select** statement itself. The renaming of "Quantity * Rate" to "Ext" is something done by SQL, *not* by SQLPLUS.

Other Features

It's not terribly difficult to look at a start file and the report it produces and see how all of the formatting and computation was accomplished. It's possible to begin by creating the start file, typing into it each of the commands you expect to need, and then running it in SQLPLUS to see if it was correct. But when creating reports for the first time, it is often much simpler to experiment interactively with SQLPLUS, adjusting column formats, the SQL query, the titles, and the totals, until what you really want begins to take shape.

Command Line Editor

When you type in a SQL statement, SQLPLUS remembers each line as you enter it, storing it in what is called the SQL buffer (a fancy name for a computer scratchpad where your SQL statements are kept). Suppose you'd entered this query:

```
select Featuer, Section, Page
  from NEWSPAPER
 where Section = 'F';
```

ORACLE responds with the following:

```
select Featuer, Section, Page
       *
ERROR at line 1: ORA-0704:  invalid column name
```

You realize you've misspelled Feature. You do not have to retype the entire query. The Command Line Editor is already present and waiting for instructions. First, ask it to list your query:

```
list
```

SQLPLUS immediately responds with this:

```
1    select Featuer, Section, Page
2    from NEWSPAPER
3*   where Section = 'F'
```

Notice that SQLPLUS showed all three lines, and numbered them. It also placed an asterisk next to line 3, which means it is the line your editing commands are able to affect. But you want to change line 1, so you type, and SQLPLUS lists this:

```
list 1

  1* select Featuer, Section, Page
```

Line 1 is displayed and is now the current line. You can change it by typing this:

```
change /Featuer/Feature

  1* select Feature, Section, Page
```

You can check the whole query again with this:

```
list

  1   select Feature, Section, Page
  2     from NEWSPAPER
  3*   where Section = 'F'
```

If you believe this is correct, enter a single slash after the prompt. This slash has nothing to do with the **change** command or the editor. Instead, it tells SQLPLUS to execute the SQL in the buffer.

You can enter a block of PL/SQL statements into a buffer, too. But since these statements each end with a semicolon, the semicolon doesn't run the statement. In this case, when you finish the block, enter a slash to finish editing. See BLOCK STRUCTURE in the Alphabetical Reference in Part Five. You also can use a dot or period (.) to finish editing without running the statement.

```
/

FEATURE          S   PAGE
---------------  -   ----
Births           F    7
Classified       F    8
Obituaries       F    6
Doctor Is In     F    6
```

The **change** command requires that you mark the start and end of the text to be changed with a slash (/) or some other character.

```
change $Featuer$Feature
```

would have worked just as well. SQLPLUS looks at the first character after the word "change" and assumes that will be the one you've chosen to mark the start and end of the incorrect text (these markers are usually called *delimiters*). You can also delete the current line, as shown here:

```
list

  1   select Feature, Section, Page
  2      from NEWSPAPER
  3*   where Section = 'F'

del

list

  1   select Feature, Section, Page
  2      from NEWSPAPER
```

The letters "del" will delete just what is on the current line. The word "delete" (spelled out) will erase all of the lines and put the word "delete" as line 1. This will only cause problems, so avoid typing the whole word "delete." If your goal is to clear out the **select** statement completely, type this:

```
clear buffer
```

If you'd like to append something to the current line, you can use the **append** command:

```
list 1

  1* select Feature, Section, Page

append  "Where It Is"

  1* select Feature, Section, Page "Where It Is"
```

append places its text right up against the end of the current line, with no spaces between. To put a space in, as was done here, type *two* spaces between the word **append** and the text.

You may also **input** a whole new line after the current line, as shown here:

```
list

  1  select Feature, Section, Page "Where It Is"
  2*    from NEWSPAPER

input where Section = 'A'

list

  1  select Feature, Section, Page "Where It Is"
  2     from NEWSPAPER
  3* where Section = 'A'
```

and then set the column heading for the WhereItIs column:

```
column WhereItIs heading "WhereItIs"
```

and then run the Query:

```
/

FEATURE          S Where It Is
---------------- - -----------
National News    A           1
Editorials       A          12
```

To review, the Command Line Editor can **list** the SQL you've typed in, **change** or **del**ete the current line (marked by the asterisk), **append** something onto the end of the current line, or **input** an entire line after the current line. Once your corrections are made, the SQL will execute if you type in a **/** (slash) at the SQL> prompt. Each of these commands can be abbreviated to its own first letter except **del**, which must be exactly the three letters "del."

The Command Line Editor can edit only your SQL statement. It cannot edit SQLPLUS commands. If you've typed **column Item format a18**, for instance, and want to change it to "column Item format a20", you must retype the whole thing (this is in the SQLPLUS interactive mode—if you've got the commands in a file you obviously can change them with your own editor). You also can use the Command Line Editor to change SQLPLUS commands. This will be discussed in Chapter 12.

Also note that in interactive mode, once you've started to type a SQL statement, you must complete it before you can enter any additional SQLPLUS commands, such as **column** formats or **ttitle**. As soon as SQLPLUS sees the word "select" it assumes everything to follow is part of the **select** statement, until it sees *either* a semicolon (;) at the end of the last SQL statement line, *or* a slash (/) at the beginning of the line after the last SQL statement line.

This is correct:

```
select * from LEDGER;

select * from LEDGER
/
```

This is not:

```
select * from LEDGER/
```

set pause

During the development of a new report or when using SQLPLUS for quick queries of the database, it's usually helpful to set the **linesize** at 79 or 80, the **pagesize** at 24, and **newpage** at 1. You accompany this with two related commands, as shown here:

```
set pause 'More. . .'
set pause on
```

The effect of this combination is to produce exactly one full screen of information for each page of the report that is produced, and to pause at each page for viewing ("More. . ." will appear in the lower-left corner) until the ENTER key is hit. After the various column headings and titles are worked out, the **pagesize** can be readjusted for a page of paper, and the pause eliminated with this:

```
set pause off
```

save

If the changes you wish to make to your SQL statement are extensive, or you simply wish to work in your own editor, save the SQL you've created so far, in interactive mode, by writing the SQL to a file, like this:

```
save fred.sql
```

SQLPLUS responds with

```
Wrote file fred.sql
```

Your SQL (but not any **column**, **ttitle**, or other SQLPLUS commands) is now in a file named FRED.SQL (or a name of your choice), which you can edit using your own editor.

If the file already exists, then you must use the **replace** option (abbreviated **repl**) of the **save** command in order to save the new query in a file with that name. For this example, the syntax would be

```
save fred.sql repl
```

editing

Everyone has a favorite editor. Popular editors include KEDIT, BRIEF, vi, and many more. Word processing programs such as WordPerfect, Word, and others also can be used with SQLPLUS, but only if you save the files they create in ASCII format (see your word processor manual for details on how to do this). Editors are just programs themselves. They are normally invoked simply by typing their names at the operating system prompt. On a PC it usually looks something like this:

```
C> myedit activity.sql
```

In this example, **myedit** is your editor's name, and ACTIVITY.SQL represents the file you want to edit (the start file described previously was used here only as an example—you would enter the real name of whatever file you want to edit).

Other kinds of computers won't necessarily have the C> prompt, but there will be something equivalent. If you can invoke an editor this way on your computer, it is nearly certain you can do it from within SQLPLUS, *except* that you will not type in the name of your editor, but rather the word **edit**:

```
SQL> edit activity.sql
```

You cannot do this, however, until you first tell SQLPLUS your editor's name. You do this while in SQLPLUS by *defining* the editor, like this:

```
define _editor = "myedit"
```

(That's an underline before the "e" in editor.) SQLPLUS will then remember the name of your editor (until you **quit** SQLPLUS), and allow you to use it anytime you wish. See the special box "Using LOGIN.SQL to Define the Editor" for directions on making this happen automatically.

host

In the unlikely event that none of this works, but you do have an editor you'd like to use, you can invoke it by typing this:

```
host myedit activity.sql
```

The **host** tells SQLPLUS that this is a command to simply hand back to the operating system for execution (a **$** will work in place of the word "host"), and is the equivalent of typing **myedit activity.sql** at the **C>** prompt. Incidentally, this same **host** command can be used to execute almost any operating system command from within SQLPLUS, including **dir**, **copy**, **move**, **erase**, **cls**, and others.

Adding SQLPLUS Commands

Once you've saved a SQL statement into a file such as FRED.SQL, you can add to the file any SQLPLUS commands you wish. Essentially, you can build it in a similar fashion to ACTIVITY.SQL in Figure 4-3. When you've finished working on it, you can exit your editor and be returned to SQLPLUS.

Using LOGIN.SQL to Define the Editor

If you'd like SQLPLUS to define your editor automatically, put the **define _editor** command in a file named:

```
login.sql
```

This is a special file name that SQLPLUS always looks for whenever it starts up. If it finds LOGIN.SQL, it executes any commands in it as if you had entered them by hand. It looks first at the directory you are in when you type in **SQLPLUS**. If it doesn't find LOGIN.SQL there, it then looks in the home directory for ORACLE. If it doesn't find LOGIN.SQL there, it stops looking.

You can put virtually any command in LOGIN.SQL that you can use in SQLPLUS, including both SQLPLUS commands and SQL statements; all of them will be executed before SQLPLUS gives you the SQL> prompt. This can be a convenient way to set up your own individual SQLPLUS environment, with all the basic layouts the way you prefer them. Advanced use of LOGIN.SQL is covered in Chapter 12. Here's an example of a typical LOGIN.SQL file:

```
prompt Login.sql loaded.
set feedback off
set sqlprompt 'What now, boss? '
set sqlnumber off
set numwidth 5
set pagesize 24
set linesize 79
define _editor="kedit"
```

Another file, named GLOGIN.SQL, is used to establish default SQLPLUS settings for all users of a database. This file, usually stored in the administrative directory for SQLPLUS, is useful in enforcing column and environment settings for multiple users.

The meaning of each of these commands can be found in the Alphabetical Reference section.

start

Once back in SQLPLUS, test your editing work by executing the file you've just edited:

```
start fred.sql
```

   All of the SQLPLUS and SQL commands in that file will execute, line by line, just as if you'd entered each one of them by hand. If you've included a **spool** and a **spool off** command in the file, you can use your editor to view the results of your work. This is just what was shown in Figure 4-2—the product of starting **activity.sql** and spooling its results into **activity.lst**.

   To develop a report, use steps like these, in cycles:

1. Use SQLPLUS to build a SQL query interactively. When it appears close to being satisfactory, save it under a name such as **test.sql**. (The extension **.sql** is usually reserved for start files, scripts that will execute to produce a report.)

2. Edit the file **test.sql** using a favorite editor. Add **column** commands, **break**s, **compute**s, **set**s, and **spool** commands to the file. You usually spool to a file with the extension **.lst**, such as **test.lst**. Exit the editor.

3. Back in SQLPLUS, the file **test.sql** is **start**ed. Its results fly past on the screen, but also go into the file **test.lst**. The editor examines this file.

4. You incorporate any necessary changes into **test.sql**, and run it again.

5. You continue this process until the report is correct and polished.

Checking the SQLPLUS Environment

You saw earlier that the Command Line Editor couldn't change SQLPLUS commands, because the only things it could affect were SQL statements—those lines stored in the SQL buffer. You also saw that you could **save** SQL statements into a file, where they could be modified using your own editor. This is fine for SQL, but what about SQLPLUS commands? Is there any way to know which SQLPLUS commands you've entered or changed, and is there any way to save them? Checking is easy but saving is a bit more difficult, and will be covered in Chapter 12.

   If you'd like to check how a particular column was defined, type

```
column Item
```

without anything following the column name. SQLPLUS will then list all of the instructions you've given about that column, as shown here:

```
column   Item ON
heading  'What Was!Sold' headsep '!'
```

```
format     a18
truncate
```

If you type just the word **column**, without any column name following it, then
all of the columns will be listed:

```
column     Ext ON
format     990.99

column     Quantity ON
heading    'Quan'
format     9990

column     QuantityType ON
heading    'Type'
format     a8
truncate

column     ActionDate ON
heading    'Date'

column     Rate ON
format     90.99

column     Person ON
heading    'To Whom Sold'
format     a18
word_wrap

column     Item ON
heading    'What Was!Sold' headsep '!'
format     a18
truncate
```

ttitle, **btitle**, **break**, and **compute** are displayed simply by typing their names,
with nothing following. SQLPLUS answers back immediately with the current
definitions. The first line in each of the next examples is what you type; the
following lines show SQLPLUS' replies:

```
ttitle
ttitle ON and is the following 56 characters:
Sales by Product During 1901!Second Six Months (Jul-Dec)
```

```
btitle
btitle ON and is the following 26 characters:
from G. B. Talbot's Ledger
```

```
break
break on Item skip 2 nodup
```

```
compute
COMPUTE sum OF Ext ON Item
```

Looking at those settings (also called *parameters*) that follow the **set** command requires using the word **show**:

```
show headsep
headsep "!" (hex 21)
```

```
show linesize
linesize 79
```

```
show pagesize
pagesize 50
```

```
show newpage
newpage 0
```

See the Alphabetical Reference under **set** and **show** for a complete list of parameters.

The ttitle and btitle settings can be disabled by using the **btitle off** and **ttitle off** commands. The following listing shows these commands. SQLPLUS does not reply to the commands.

```
ttitle off
```

```
btitle off
```

The settings for columns, breaks, and computes can be disabled via the **clear columns**, **clear breaks**, and **clear computes** commands. The first line in each example in the following listings is what you type; the following lines show what SQLPLUS replies:

```
clear columns
columns cleared
```

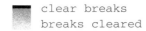

```
clear breaks
breaks cleared
```

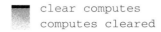

```
clear computes
computes cleared
```

Building Blocks

This has been a fairly dense chapter, particularly if SQLPLUS is new to you, yet on reflection you'll probably agree that what was introduced here is not really difficult. If Figure 4-3 looked daunting when you began the chapter, look at it again now. Is there any line on it that you don't understand, or don't have a sense of what is being done and why? You could, if you wished, simply copy this file (**activity.sql**) into another file with a different name, and begin to modify it to suit your own tastes, and to query against your own tables. The structure of any reports you produce will after all be very similar.

There is a lot going on in **activity.sql**, but it is made up of simple building blocks. This will be the approach used throughout the book. ORACLE provides building blocks, and lots of them, but each separate block is understandable and useful.

In the previous chapter you learned how to select data out of the database, choosing certain columns and ignoring others, choosing certain rows based on logical restrictions you set up, and combining two tables to give you information not available from either one on its own.

In this chapter you learned how to give orders that SQLPLUS can follow in formatting and producing the pages and headings of polished reports.

In the next several chapters (where the pace is a little more moderate), you'll change and format your data row by row. Your expertise and confidence should grow chapter by chapter; by the end of Part Two of this book, you should be able to produce very sophisticated reports in short order, to the considerable benefit of your company and to you.

CHAPTER 5

Getting Text
Information and
Changing It

This chapter introduces *string functions*, which are software tools that allow
you to manipulate a string of letters or other characters. To quickly reference
individual functions, look them up by name in the Alphabetical Reference section.
    Functions generally produce two different kinds of results: the creation of new
objects from old ones, and description of the objects.

In a restaurant, for instance, one of the prep cook's job "functions" is to turn oranges into orange juice, vegetables into salad, and roasts into slices of meat. This function takes an object (orange, vegetable, roast) and changes it (into juice, salad, slices). The "result" of the function is a modified version of the original object.

The buyer for the restaurant *counts* the oranges, the vegetables, and the roasts. This job function does not change the objects, but instead describes them. It still produces a "result" in the form of a number. It tells you "how many."

Functions in ORACLE also work in these two ways. Some functions produce a result that is a modification of the original information, such as turning lowercase characters into uppercase in a sentence. Other functions produce a result that tells you something about the information, such as how many characters there are in a word or sentence. The two types of functions are really no more conceptually difficult than this.

NOTE
If you are using PL/SQL, you can create your own functions for use within PL/SQL blocks with the **create function** statement. Look up "Function" in the Alphabetical Reference section for details.

Data Types

Just as people can be classified into different types, based on certain characteristics (shy, ornery, outgoing, smart, silly), different kinds of data can be classified into what are called data "types" based on certain characteristics.

Data types in ORACLE include NUMBER, CHAR (short for CHARACTER), DATE, VARCHAR2, LONG, RAW, and LONG RAW. The first three are probably obvious. The last four are special data types that you'll encounter later. A full explanation of each of these can be found by name or under "Data Types" in the Alphabetical Reference section. Each will be covered in detail in the chapters ahead. As with people, some of the "types" overlap and some are fairly rare.

If the information is the character (VARCHAR2 or CHAR) type of information—a mixture of letters, punctuation marks, numbers, and spaces (also called *alphanumeric*)—you'll need string functions to modify or inform you about it. ORACLE's SQL provides quite a few such tools.

What Is a String?

A *string* is a simple concept: a bunch of things in a line, like a string of houses, popcorn or pearls, numbers, or a string of characters in a sentence or a soap opera.

Strings are frequently encountered in managing information. Names are strings of characters, as in "Juan L'Heureaux." Phone numbers are strings of numbers, dashes, and sometimes parentheses, as in "(415) 555-2676." Even a pure number, such as "5443702," can be considered as either a number or a string of characters.

NOTE
Data types that are restricted to pure numbers (plus a decimal point and minus sign, if needed) are called "NUMBER," and are not usually referred to as strings. A number can be used in certain ways that a string cannot, and vice versa.

Strings that can include any mixture of letters, numbers, spaces, and other symbols (such as those above the numbers on your keyboard) are called *character strings,* or just *character* for short.

In ORACLE, character is abbreviated "CHAR". This is pronounced "care," like the first part of the word "character." It is not pronounced "CHAR" as in "CHARcoal," or "car." The latter two pronunciations are inappropriate because they take the user a step further away from the actual meaning (the abbreviation is bad enough) and can confuse nonprogrammers.

There are two string data types in ORACLE7. In older versions of ORACLE, the CHAR data type was a varying length string. In ORACLE7, CHAR strings are always a fixed length. If you set a value to a string with a length less than that of a CHAR column, ORACLE automatically pads the string with blanks. When you compare CHAR strings, ORACLE compares the strings by padding them out to equal lengths with blanks. This means that if you compare "character " with "character" in CHAR columns, ORACLE considers the strings to be the same. The VARCHAR2 data type is a varying-length string with the same behavior as CHAR in previous versions of ORACLE. The VARCHAR data type is synonymous with VARCHAR2, but this may change in future versions of ORACLE, so you should avoid using VARCHAR. Use CHAR for fixed-length character string fields and VARCHAR2 for all other character string fields.

The simple ORACLE string functions, explained in this chapter, are shown in Table 5-1. You will learn more advanced string functions and how to use them in Chapter 14.

FUNCTION NAME	USE
¦¦	Glues or *concatenates* two strings together. The ¦ symbol is called a *broken vertical bar*.
INITCAP	**INIT**ial **CAP**ital. Changes the first letter of a word or series of words into uppercase.
INSTR	Finds the location of a character **IN** a **STR**ing.
LENGTH	Tells the **LENGTH** of a string.
LOWER	Converts every letter in a string to **LOWER**case.
LPAD	**L**eft **PAD**. Makes a string a certain length by adding a certain set of characters to the left.
LTRIM	**L**eft **TRIM**. Trims all the occurrences of any one of a set of characters off of the left side of a string.
RPAD	**R**ight **PAD**. Makes a string a certain length by adding a certain set of characters to the right.
RTRIM	**R**ight **TRIM**. Trims all the occurrences of any one of a set of characters off of the right side of a string.
SOUNDEX	Finds words that **SOUND** like an **EX**ample.
SUBSTR	SUBSTRing. Clips out a piece of a string.
UPPER	Converts every letter in a string into **UPPER**case.

TABLE 5-1. *Simple ORACLE string functions*

Notation

Functions will be shown with this kind of notation:

```
FUNCTION(string [,option])
```

The function itself will be in uppercase. The thing it affects (usually a string) will be shown in lowercase italics. Anytime the word *string* appears, it represents either a literal string of characters, or the name of a character column in a table. When you actually use a string function, any literal must be in single quotes; any column name must appear without quotes.

Every function has only one pair of parentheses. Everything that function is to affect, as well as additional instructions you can give the function, go between its parentheses.

Some functions have *options,* parts that are not always required to make the function work as you wish. Options are always shown in square brackets: [ ]. See the discussion on **LPAD** and **RPAD** in the following section for an example of how this is used.

A simple example of how the **LOWER** function is printed follows.

```
LOWER(string)
```

The word "LOWER" with the two parentheses is the function itself, so it is shown here in uppercase. *string* stands for the actual string of characters to be converted to lowercase, and is shown in lowercase italics. Therefore,

```
LOWER('CAMP DOUGLAS')
```

would produce

```
camp douglas
```

The string 'CAMP DOUGLAS' is a literal, (which you learned about in Chapter 3), meaning that it is literally the string of characters that the function **LOWER** is to work on. ORACLE uses single quotation marks to denote the beginning and end of any literal string. The string in **LOWER** also could have been the name of a column from a table, in which case the function would have operated on the contents of the column for every row brought back by a **select** statement. For example,

```
select City, LOWER(City), LOWER('City') from WEATHER;
```

would produce this result:

```
CITY          LOWER(CITY) LOWER('CITY')
----------    ----------- -------------
LIMA          lima        city
PARIS         paris       city
MANCHESTER    manchester  city
ATHENS        athens      city
CHICAGO       chicago     city
SYDNEY        sydney      city
SPARTA        sparta      city
```

At the top of the second column, in the **LOWER** function, CITY is not inside quotation marks. This tells ORACLE that it is a column name, not a literal.

In the third column's **LOWER** function, CITY is inside single quotation marks. This means you literally want the function **LOWER** to work on the word 'City' (that is, the string of letters c-i-t-y), not the column by the same name.

Concatenation (¦¦)

This notation:

string ¦¦ string

tells ORACLE to concatenate, or stick together, two strings. The strings, of course, can be either column names or literals. For example:

```
select City¦¦Country from LOCATION;

CITY ¦¦ COUNTRY
---------------------------------------------------
ATHENSGREECE
CHICAGOUNITED STATES
CONAKRYGUINEA
LIMAPERU
MADRASINDIA
MANCHESTERENGLAND
MOSCOWRUSSIA
PARISFRANCE
SHENYANGCHINA
ROMEITALY
TOKYOJAPAN
SYDNEYAUSTRALIA
SPARTAGREECE
MADRIDSPAIN
```

Here, the cities vary in width from 4 to 12 characters. The countries push right up against them. This is just how the concatenate function is supposed to work: it glues columns or strings together with no spaces in between.

This isn't very easy to read, of course. What if you wanted to make this a little more readable, perhaps by listing cities and countries with a comma and a space between them? Then you'd simply concatenate the City and Country columns with a literal string of a comma and a space, like this:

```
select City¦¦', '¦¦Country from LOCATION;
```

```
CITY ||',' ||COUNTRY
-------------------------------------------------------
ATHENS, GREECE
CHICAGO, UNITED STATES
CONAKRY, GUINEA
LIMA, PERU
MADRAS, INDIA
MANCHESTER, ENGLAND
MOSCOW, RUSSIA
PARIS, FRANCE
SHENYANG, CHINA
ROME, ITALY
TOKYO, JAPAN
SYDNEY, AUSTRALIA
SPARTA, GREECE
MADRID, SPAIN
```

Notice the column title. See Chapter 4 for a review of column titles.

How to Cut and Paste Strings

In this section you learn about a series of functions that often confuse users: **LPAD**, **RPAD**, **LTRIM**, **RTRIM**, **LENGTH**, **SUBSTR**, and **INSTR**. These all serve a common purpose: they allow you to *cut* and *paste*.

Each of these functions does some part of cutting and pasting. For example, **LENGTH** tells you how many characters are in a string. **SUBSTR** lets you clip out and use a *substring,* a portion of a string, starting at one position in the string and ending at another. **INSTR** lets you find the location of a group of characters within another string. **LPAD** and **RPAD** allow you to easily concatenate spaces or other characters on the left or right side of a string. And, finally, **LTRIM** and **RTRIM** clip characters off of the ends of strings. Most interesting is that all of these functions can be used in combination with each other, as you'll soon see.

RPAD and LPAD

RPAD and **LPAD** are very similar functions. **RPAD** allows you to "pad" the right side of a column with any set of characters. The character set can be almost anything: spaces, periods, commas, letters or numbers, pound signs (#), or even exclamation marks (!). **LPAD** does the same thing as **RPAD**, but to the left side.

Here are the formats for **RPAD** and **LPAD**:

```
RPAD(string,length [,'set'])

LPAD(string,length [,'set'])
```

string is the name of a CHAR or VARCHAR2 column from the database (or a literal string), *length* is the total number of characters long that the result should be (in other words, its width), and *set* is the set of characters that do the padding. The set must be enclosed in single quotation marks. The square brackets mean that the set (and the comma that precedes it) are optional. If you leave this off, the function will automatically pad with spaces. This is sometimes called the *default*; that is, if you don't tell the function which set of characters to use, it will use spaces by default.

Many users produce tables with dots to help guide the eye from one side of the page to the other. Here's how **RPAD** does this:

```
select RPAD(City,35,'.'), Temperature from WEATHER;

RPAD(CITY,35,'.')                        TEMPERATURE
----------------------------------- -----------
LIMA...............................          45
PARIS..............................          81
MANCHESTER.........................          66
ATHENS.............................          97
CHICAGO............................          66
SYDNEY.............................          29
SPARTA.............................          74
```

Notice what happened here. **RPAD** took each city string, from Lima through Sparta, and concatenated dots on the right of it, adding just enough for each city so that the result (City plus dots) is exactly 35 characters long. The concatenate function (||) could not have done this. It would have added the same number of dots to every city, leaving a ragged edge on the right.

LPAD does the same sort of thing, only on the left. Let's say you want to reformat cities and temperatures so that the cities are right justified, that is, that they all align at the right:

```
select LPAD(City,11), Temperature from WEATHER;
```

```
LPAD(CITY,1 TEMPERATURE
----------- -----------
       LIMA          45
      PARIS          81
 MANCHESTER          66
     ATHENS          97
    CHICAGO          66
     SYDNEY          29
     SPARTA          74
```

LTRIM and RTRIM

LTRIM and **RTRIM** are like hedge trimmers. They trim off unwanted characters from the left and right ends of strings. For example, suppose you had a MAGAZINE table with a column in it that contained the titles of magazine articles, but the titles were entered by different people. Some always put the titles in quotes, while others simply entered the words; some used periods, others didn't; some started titles with "the," while others did not. How do you to trim these?

```
select Title from MAGAZINE;

TITLE
---------------------------------------
THE BARBERS WHO SHAVE THEMSELVES.
"HUNTING THOREAU IN NEW HAMPSHIRE"
THE ETHNIC NEIGHBORHOOD
RELATIONAL DESIGN AND ENTHALPY
"INTERCONTINENTAL RELATIONS."
```

Here are the formats for **RTRIM** and **LTRIM**:

```
RTRIM(string [,'set'])

LTRIM(string [,'set'])
```

string is the name of the column from the database (or a literal string) and *set* is the collection of characters you want to trim off. If no set of characters is specified, the functions trim off spaces.

You can trim off more than one character at a time; to do so simply make a list (a string) of the characters you want removed. First, let's get rid of the quotes and periods on the right, as shown here:

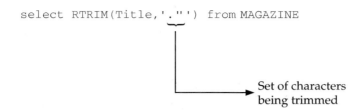

Set of characters
being trimmed

The preceding produces this:

```
RTRIM(TITLE,'."')
----------------------------------
THE BARBERS WHO SHAVE THEMSELVES
"HUNTING THOREAU IN NEW HAMPSHIRE
THE ETHNIC NEIGHBORHOOD
RELATIONAL DESIGN AND ENTHALPY
"INTERCONTINENTAL RELATIONS
```

RTRIM removed both the double quotation marks and the periods from the right side of each of these titles. The *set* of characters you want to remove can be as long as you wish. ORACLE will check and recheck the right side of each title until every character in your string has been removed—that is, until it runs into the first character in the string that is *not* in your *set*.

Combining Two Functions

Now what? How do you get rid of the quotes on the left? **Title** is buried there in the middle of the **RTRIM** function. Here you will learn how to combine functions.
  You know that when you ran the **select** statement:

```
select Title from MAGAZINE;
```

the result you got back was the content of the Title column:

```
THE BARBERS WHO SHAVE THEMSELVES.
"HUNTING THOREAU IN NEW HAMPSHIRE"
THE ETHNIC NEIGHBORHOOD
RELATIONAL DESIGN AND ENTHALPY
"INTERCONTINENTAL RELATIONS."
```

Remember that the purpose of this:

```
RTRIM(Title,'."')
```

is to take each of these strings and remove the quotes on the right side, effectively producing a result that is a *new* column whose contents are shown here:

```
THE BARBERS WHO SHAVE THEMSELVES
"HUNTING THOREAU IN NEW HAMPSHIRE
THE ETHNIC NEIGHBORHOOD
RELATIONAL DESIGN AND ENTHALPY
"INTERCONTINENTAL RELATIONS
```

Therefore, if you pretend **RTRIM(Title,'."')** is simply a column name itself, you can substitute it for the *string* in this:

```
LTRIM(string,'set')
```

So you simply type your select statement to look like this:

```
select LTRIM(RTRIM(Title,'."'),'"') from MAGAZINE;
```

Taking this apart for clarity, you see

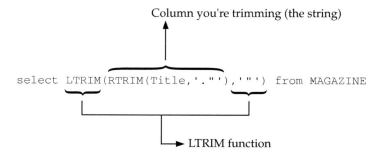

Is this how you want it? And what is the result of this combined function?

```
LTRIM(RTRIM(TITLE,'."'),'"')
------------------------------------
THE BARBERS WHO SHAVE THEMSELVES
HUNTING THOREAU IN NEW HAMPSHIRE
THE ETHNIC NEIGHBORHOOD
RELATIONAL DESIGN AND ENTHALPY
INTERCONTINENTAL RELATIONS
```

Voilà! Your titles are cleaned up.

It doesn't seem that simple to you? Well, take heart. Looking at a combination of functions the first (or the thousandth) time can be confusing, even for an experienced query user. It's difficult to assess which commas and parentheses go with which functions, particularly when a query you've written isn't working correctly; discovering where a comma is missing, or which parenthesis isn't properly matched with another, can be a real adventure.

One simple solution to this is to break functions onto separate lines, at least until they're all working the way you wish. SQLPLUS doesn't care at all where you break a SQL statement, as long as it's not in the middle of a word or a literal string. To better visualize how this **RTRIM** and **LTRIM** combination works, you could type it like this:

```
select LTRIM(
          RTRIM(Title,'."')
                              ,'"')
  from MAGAZINE;
```

This makes what you are trying to do obvious, and it will actually work even if it is typed on four separate lines with lots of spaces. SQLPLUS simply ignores extra spaces.

Suppose now you decide to trim off "THE" from the front of two of the titles, as well as the space that follows it (and of course the double quote you removed before). You might do this:

```
select LTRIM(RTRIM(Title,'."'),'"THE ')
  from MAGAZINE;
```

which produces the following:

```
LTRIM(RTRIM(TITLE,'."'),'"THE')
---------------------------------
BARBERS WHO SHAVE THEMSELVES
UNTING THOREAU IN NEW HAMPSHIRE
NIC NEIGHBORHOOD
RELATIONAL DESIGN AND ENTHALPY
INTERCONTINENTAL RELATIONS
```

Whoa! What happened? The second and third row got trimmed more than expected. Why? Because **LTRIM** was busy looking for and trimming off anything that was a **double quote**, a **T**, an **H**, an **E**, or a **space**. It was not looking for the word "THE". It was looking for the letters in it, and it didn't quit the first time it saw any of the letters it was looking for. It quit when it saw a character that wasn't in its *set*.

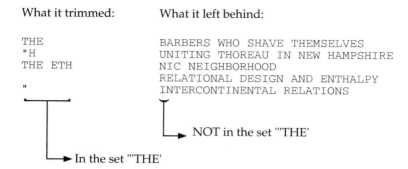

What it trimmed:

```
THE
"H
THE ETH

"
```

In the set '"THE'

What it left behind:

```
BARBERS WHO SHAVE THEMSELVES
UNITING THOREAU IN NEW HAMPSHIRE
NIC NEIGHBORHOOD
RELATIONAL DESIGN AND ENTHALPY
INTERCONTINENTAL RELATIONS
```

NOT in the set '"THE'

In other words, all these:

```
'"THE'
'HET"'
'E"TH'
'H"TE'
'ET"H'
```

and many other combinations of the letters will have the same effect when used as the *set* of an **LTRIM** or **RTRIM**. The order of the letters of the *set* has no effect on how the function works. Note, however, that the *case* of the letters is important. ORACLE will check the case of both the letters in the *set* and in the string. It will remove only those with an exact match.

LTRIM and **RTRIM** are designed to remove any characters in a *set* from the left or right of a string. They're not intended to remove words. To do that you'll need clever use of **INSTR**, **SUBSTR**, and even **DECODE**, which you will learn in later chapters.

The previous example makes one point clear: it's better to make certain that data gets cleaned up or edited before it is stored in the database. It would have been a lot less trouble if the individuals typing in these magazine article titles had simply avoided the use of quotes, periods, and the word "THE."

Adding One More Function

Suppose that you decide to **RPAD** your trimmed up **Title** with dashes and carets, perhaps also asking for a magazine Name and Page number. Your query would look like this:

```
select Name, RPAD(RTRIM(LTRIM(Title,'"'),'."'),47,'-^'), Page
  from MAGAZINE;

NAME               RPAD(RTRIM(LTRIM(TITLE,'"'),'."'),47,'-^')   PAGE
---------------    ------------------------------------------   -----
BERTRAND MONTHLY   THE BARBERS WHO SHAVE THEMSELVES-^-^-^-^-^      70
LIVE FREE OR DIE   HUNTING THOREAU IN NEW HAMPSHIRE-^-^-^-^-^     320
PSYCHOLOGICA       THE ETHNIC NEIGHBORHOOD-^-^-^-^-^-^-^-^-^-     246
FADED ISSUES       RELATIONAL DESIGN AND ENTHALPY-^-^-^-^-^-^     279
ENTROPY WIT        INTERCONTINENTAL RELATIONS-^-^-^-^-^-^-^-^      20
```

Each function has parentheses that enclose the column it is going to affect, so the real trick in understanding combined functions in **select** statements is to read from the outside to the inside on both left and right, watching (and even counting) the pairs of parentheses.

LOWER, UPPER, and INITCAP

These are three other related and very simple functions that often are used together. **LOWER** takes any string or column and converts any letters in it to lowercase. **UPPER** does the opposite, converting any letters to uppercase. **INITCAP** takes the initial letter of every word in a string or column, and converts just those letters to uppercase.

Here are the formats for these three functions:

```
LOWER(string)
UPPER(string)
INITCAP(string)
```

Returning to the WEATHER table, recall that each city is stored in uppercase letters, like this:

```
LIMA
PARIS
ATHENS
CHICAGO
MANCHESTER
SYDNEY
SPARTA
```

Therefore,

```
select City, UPPER(City), LOWER(City), INITCAP(LOWER(City))
  from WEATHER;
```

produces this:

```
City          UPPER(CITY) LOWER(CITY) INITCAP(LOW
-----------   ----------- ----------- -----------
LIMA          LIMA        lima        Lima
PARIS         PARIS       paris       Paris
MANCHESTER    MANCHESTER  manchester  Manchester
ATHENS        ATHENS      athens      Athens
CHICAGO       CHICAGO     chicago     Chicago
SYDNEY        SYDNEY      sydney      Sydney
SPARTA        SPARTA      sparta      Sparta
```

Look carefully at what is produced in each column, and at the functions that produced it in the SQL statement. The fourth column shows how you can apply **INITCAP** to **LOWER**(City) and have it appear with normal capitalization, even though it is stored as uppercase.

Another example is the Name column as stored in a MAGAZINE table:

```
NAME
----------------
BERTRAND MONTHLY
LIVE FREE OR DIE
PSYCHOLOGICA
FADED ISSUES
ENTROPY WIT
```

and then retrieved with the combined **INITCAP** and **LOWER** functions, as shown here:

```
select INITCAP(LOWER(Name)) from MAGAZINE;

INITCAP(LOWER(NA
----------------
Bertrand Monthly
Live Free Or Die
Psychologica
Faded Issues
Entropy Wit
```

and as applied to the Name, cleaned up Title, and Page (note that you'll also rename the columns):

```
select INITCAP(LOWER(Name)) Name,
       INITCAP(LOWER(RTRIM(LTRIM(Title,'"'),'."'))) Title,
       Page
  from Magazine;
```

```
NAME               TITLE                                 PAGE
---------------    -----------------------------------   -----
Bertrand Monthly   The Barbers Who Shave Themselves         70
Live Free Or Die   Hunting Thoreau In New Hampshire        320
Psychologica       The Ethnic Neighborhood                 246
Faded Issues       Relational Design And Enthalpy          279
Entropy Wit        Intercontinental Relations               20
```

LENGTH

This one is easy. **LENGTH** tells you how long a string is—how many characters it has in it, including letters, spaces, and anything else.

This is the format for **LENGTH**:

LENGTH(*string*)

For example:

```
select Name, LENGTH(Name) from MAGAZINE;
```

```
NAME               LENGTH(NAME)
---------------    ------------
BERTRAND MONTHLY         16
LIVE FREE OR DIE        16
PSYCHOLOGICA            12
FADED ISSUES            12
ENTROPY WIT             11
```

This isn't normally useful by itself, but it can be used as part of another function, for calculating how much space you'll need on a report, or as part of a **where** or an **order by** clause.

SUBSTR

You can use the SUBSTR function to clip out a piece of a string.

This is the format for **SUBSTR**:

SUBSTR(*string,start* [*,count*])

This tells SQL to clip out a subsection of the *string*, beginning at position *start* and continuing for *count* characters. If you don't specify the *count*, **SUBSTR** will clip beginning at *start* and continue to the end of the string. For example, this:

```
select SUBSTR(Name,6,4) from MAGAZINE;
```

gives you this:

```
SUBS
----
AND
FREE
OLOG
 ISS
PY W
```

You can see how the function works. It clipped out the piece of the magazine name starting in position 6 (counting from the left) and including a total of four characters.

A more practical use might be in separating out phone numbers from a personal address book. For example, assume that you have an ADDRESS table that contains, among other things, last names, first names, and phone numbers, as shown here:

```
select LastName, FirstName, Phone from ADDRESS;
```

LASTNAME	FIRSTNAME	PHONE
BAILEY	WILLIAM	213-293-0223
ADAMS	JACK	415-453-7530
SEP	FELICIA	214-522-8383
DE MEDICI	LEFTY	312-736-1166
DEMIURGE	FRANK	707-767-8900
CASEY	WILLIS	312-684-1414
ZACK	JACK	415-620-6842
YARROW	MARY	415-787-2178
WERSCHKY	ARNY	415-235-7387
BRANT	GLEN	415-526-7512
EDGAR	THEODORE	415-525-6252
HARDIN	HUGGY	617-566-0125
HILD	PHIL	603-934-2242
LOEBEL	FRANK	202-456-1414
MOORE	MARY	718-857-1638
SZEP	FELICIA	214-522-8383
ZIMMERMAN	FRED	503-234-7491

Suppose you want just those phone numbers in the 415 area code. One solution would be to have a separate column called AreaCode. Thoughtful planning about tables and columns will eliminate a good deal of fooling around later with reformatting. However, in this instance, area codes and phone numbers are combined in a single column, so a way must be found to separate out the numbers in the 415 area code.

```
select LastName, FirstName, Phone from ADDRESS
 where Phone like '415-%';
```

LASTNAME	FIRSTNAME	PHONE
ADAMS	JACK	415-453-7530
ZACK	JACK	415-620-6842
YARROW	MARY	415-787-2178
WERSCHKY	ARNY	415-235-7387
BRANT	GLEN	415-526-7512
EDGAR	THEODORE	415-525-6252

Next, since you do not want to dial your own area code when calling friends, you can eliminate this from the result by using another **SUBSTR**:

```
select LastName, FirstName, SUBSTR(Phone,5) from ADDRESS
 where Phone like '415-%';
```

LASTNAME	FIRSTNAME	SUBSTR(P
ADAMS	JACK	453-7530
ZACK	JACK	620-6842
YARROW	MARY	787-2178
WERSCHKY	ARNY	235-7387
BRANT	GLEN	526-7512
EDGAR	THEODORE	525-6252

Notice that the default version of **SUBSTR** was used here. **SUBSTR**(Phone,5) tells SQL to clip out the substring of the phone number, *start*ing at position 5 and going to the end of the string. Doing this eliminates the area code.

Of course, this:

```
SUBSTR(Phone,5)
```

has exactly the same effect as the following:

```
SUBSTR(Phone,5,8)
```

You can combine this with the concatenation and column renaming techniques discussed in Chapter 4 to produce a quick listing of local friends' phone numbers, as shown here:

```
select LastName ¦¦', ' ¦¦FirstName Name, SUBSTR(Phone,5) Phone
   from ADDRESS
 where Phone like '415-%';
```

```
NAME                                                              PHONE
----------------------------------------------------------    --------
ADAMS, JACK                                                    453-7530
ZACK, JACK                                                     620-6842
YARROW, MARY                                                   787-2178
WERSCHKY, ARNY                                                 235-7387
BRANT, GLEN                                                    526-7512
EDGAR, THEODORE                                                525-6252
```

To produce a dotted line in the **RPAD** add this:

```
select RPAD(LastName ¦¦', ' ¦¦FirstName,25,'.') Name,
   SUBSTR(Phone,5) Phone
   from ADDRESS
 where Phone like '415-%';
```

```
NAME                      PHONE
------------------------  --------
ADAMS, JACK.............. 453-7530
ZACK, JACK.............. 620-6842
YARROW, MARY............ 787-2178
WERSCHKY, ARNY.......... 235-7387
BRANT, GLEN............. 526-7512
EDGAR, THEODORE......... 525-6252
```

The use of negative numbers in the **SUBSTR** function is undocumented, but it works. Normally, the position value you specify for the starting position is relative to the start of the string. When using a negative number for the position value, it is relative to the *end* of the string. For example,

```
SUBSTR(Phone,-4)
```

would use the fourth column from the end of the Phone column's value as its starting point. Since no length parameter is specified in this example, the remainder of the string will be returned.

NOTE
Use this feature only for VARCHAR2 datatype columns. Do NOT use this feature with columns that use the CHAR datatype. CHAR columns are fixed-length columns, so their values are padded with spaces to extend them to the full length of the column. Using a negative number for the **SUBSTR** position value in a CHAR column will determine the starting position relative to the end of the column, not the end of the string.

The following example shows the result of this feature when it is used on a VARCHAR2 column.

```
select SUBSTR(Phone,-4)
from   ADDRESS
where  Phone like '415-5%';

SUBS
----
7512
6252
```

The *count* value of the **SUBSTR** function must always be positive or unspecified. Using a negative length will return a NULL result.

INSTR

The **INSTR** function allows for simple or sophisticated searching through a string for a set of characters, not unlike **LTRIM** and **RTRIM**, except that **INSTR** doesn't clip anything off. It simply tells you where in the string it found what you were searching for. This is similar to the **LIKE** logical operator described in Chapter 3, except that **LIKE** can only be used in a **where** or **having** clause, and **INSTR** can be used anywhere except in the **from** clause. Of course, **LIKE** can be used for complex pattern searches that would be quite difficult, if even possible, using **INSTR**.

This is the format for **INSTR**:

```
INSTR(string,set [,start [,occurrence ] ])
```

INSTR searches in the *string* for a certain *set* of characters. It has two options, one within the other. The first option is the default; it will look for the set *start*ing at position 1. If you specify the location to *start*, it will skip over all the characters up to that point and begin its search there.

The second option is *occurrence*. A *set* of characters may occur more than once in a string, and you may really be interested only in whether something occurs more than once. By default, **INSTR** will look for the first occurrence of the set. By adding the option *occurrence* and making it equal to 3, for example, you can force **INSTR** to skip over the first two occurrences of the set and give the location of the third.

Some examples will make all of this simpler to grasp. Recall the table of magazine articles. Here is a list of their authors:

```
select Author from MAGAZINE;

AUTHOR
------------------------
BONHOEFFER, DIETRICH
CHESTERTON, G. K.
RUTH, GEORGE HERMAN
WHITEHEAD, ALFRED
CROOKES, WILLIAM
```

To find the location of the first occurrence of the letter 'O', **INSTR** is used without its options, and with *set* as 'O' (note the single quotation marks, since this is a literal):

```
select Author, INSTR(Author,'O') from MAGAZINE;

AUTHOR                     INSTR(AUTHOR,'O')
------------------------ -----------------
BONHOEFFER, DIETRICH                     2
CHESTERTON, G. K.                        9
RUTH, GEORGE HERMAN                      9
WHITEHEAD, ALFRED                        0
CROOKES, WILLIAM                         3
```

This is, of course, the same as this:

```
select Author, INSTR(Author,'O',1,1) from MAGAZINE;
```

If it had looked for the second occurrence of the letter 'O' it would have found:

```
select Author, INSTR(Author,'O',1,2) from MAGAZINE;

AUTHOR                         INSTR(AUTHOR,'O',1,2)
------------------------       ---------------------
BONHOEFFER, DIETRICH                               5
CHESTERTON, G. K.                                  0
RUTH, GEORGE HERMAN                                0
WHITEHEAD, ALFRED                                  0
CROOKES, WILLIAM                                   4
```

INSTR found the second 'O' in Bonhoeffer's name, at position 5, and in Crookes' name, at position 4. Chesterton has only one 'O', so for him, Ruth, and Whitehead the result is zero, meaning no success—no second 'O' was found.

In order to tell **INSTR** to look for the second occurrence, you also must tell it where to start looking (in this case, position 1). The default value of *start* is 1, which means that's what it uses if you don't specify anything, but the *occurrence* option requires a *start*, so you have to specify both.

If *set* is not just one character but several, **INSTR** gives the location of the first letter of the set, as shown here:

```
select Author, INSTR(Author,'WILLIAM') from MAGAZINE;

AUTHOR                         INSTR(AUTHOR,'WILLIAM')
------------------------       -----------------------
BONHOEFFER, DIETRICH                                 0
CHESTERTON, G. K.                                    0
RUTH, GEORGE HERMAN                                  0
WHITEHEAD, ALFRED                                    0
CROOKES, WILLIAM                                    10
```

This has many useful applications. In the MAGAZINE table, for instance:

```
select Author, INSTR(Author,',') from MAGAZINE;

AUTHOR                         INSTR(AUTHOR,',')
------------------------       -----------------
BONHOEFFER, DIETRICH                          11
CHESTERTON, G. K.                             11
RUTH, GEORGE HERMAN                            5
WHITEHEAD, ALFRED                             10
CROOKES, WILLIAM                               8
```

Here, **INSTR** searched the strings of author names for a comma, and then reported back the position in the string where it found it.

Suppose you wish to reformat the names of the authors from the formal "last name/comma/first name" approach, and present them as they are normally spoken, as shown here:

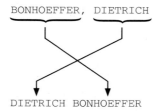

To do this using **INSTR** and **SUBSTR**, find the location of the comma, and use this to tell **SUBSTR** where to clip. Taking this step by step, first find the comma:

```
select Author, INSTR(Author,',')    from MAGAZINE;

AUTHOR                      INSTR(AUTHOR,',')
------------------------    -----------------
BONHOEFFER, DIETRICH                       11
CHESTERTON, G. K.                          11
RUTH, GEORGE HERMAN                         5
WHITEHEAD, ALFRED                          10
CROOKES, WILLIAM                            8
```

Two **SUBSTR**s will be needed, one that clips out the author's last name up to the position before the comma, and one that clips out the author's first name from two positions after the comma through to the end.

First, look at the one that clips from position 1 to just before the comma:

```
select Author, SUBSTR(Author,1,INSTR(Author,',')-1)
   from MAGAZINE;

AUTHOR                      SUBSTR(AUTHOR,1,INSTR(AUT
------------------------    -------------------------
BONHOEFFER, DIETRICH        BONHOEFFER
CHESTERTON, G. K.           CHESTERTON
RUTH, GEORGE HERMAN         RUTH
WHITEHEAD, ALFRED           WHITEHEAD
CROOKES, WILLIAM            CROOKES
```

Next, look at the one that clips from two positions past the comma to the end of the string:

```
select Author, SUBSTR(Author,INSTR(Author,',')+2) from MAGAZINE;

AUTHOR                    SUBSTR(AUTHOR,INSTR(AUTHO
------------------------  -------------------------
BONHOEFFER, DIETRICH      DIETRICH
CHESTERTON, G. K.         G. K.
RUTH, GEORGE HERMAN       GEORGE HERMAN
WHITEHEAD, ALFRED         ALFRED
CROOKES, WILLIAM          WILLIAM
```

Look at the combination of these two with the concatenation function putting a space between them, and a quick renaming of the column to "ByFirstName":

```
column ByFirstName heading "By First Name"

select Author, SUBSTR(Author,INSTR(Author,',')+2)
               ||' '||
               SUBSTR(Author,1,INSTR(Author,',')-1)
               ByFirstName
   from MAGAZINE;

AUTHOR                    By First Name
------------------------  -------------------------
BONHOEFFER, DIETRICH      DIETRICH BONHOEFFER
CHESTERTON, G. K.         G. K. CHESTERTON
RUTH, GEORGE HERMAN       GEORGE HERMAN RUTH
WHITEHEAD, ALFRED         ALFRED WHITEHEAD
CROOKES, WILLIAM          WILLIAM CROOKES
```

It is daunting to look at a SQL statement like this one, but it was built using simple logic, and it can be broken down the same way. Bonhoeffer can provide the example.

The first part looks like this:

```
SUBSTR(Author,INSTR(Author,',')+2)
```

This tells SQL to get the **SUBSTR** of Author starting two positions to the right of the comma and going to the end. This will clip out "DIETRICH"—the author's first name.

The beginning of the author's first name is found by locating the comma at the end of his last name (**INSTR** does this), and then sliding over two steps to the right (where his first name begins).

The following illustration shows how the **INSTR** function (plus 2) serves as the *start* for the **SUBSTR** function:

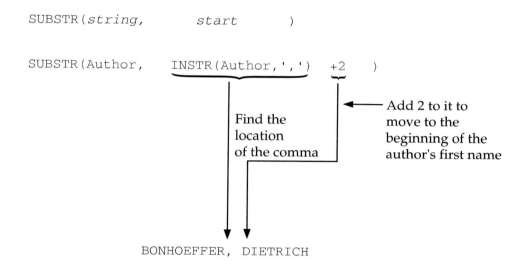

```
SUBSTR (string,        start        )
```

```
SUBSTR (Author,    INSTR (Author, ', ')   +2   )
```

Find the location of the comma

Add 2 to it to move to the beginning of the author's first name

```
BONHOEFFER,  DIETRICH
```

This is the second part of the combined statement:

```
||' '||
```

which, of course, simply tells SQL to concatenate a space in the middle.

This is the third part of the combined statement:

```
SUBSTR (Author, 1, INSTR (Author, ', ')-1)
```

This tells SQL to clip out the portion of the author's name starting at position 1 and ending one position before the comma, which results in the author's last name:

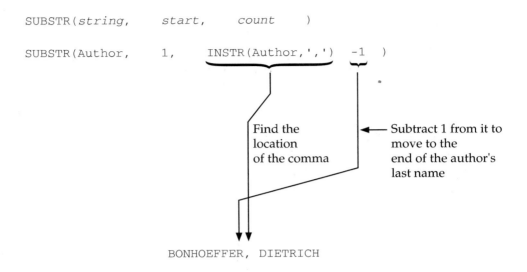

```
SUBSTR(string,      start,      count      )

SUBSTR(Author,      1,       INSTR(Author,',')   -1  )
```

Find the
location
of the comma

Subtract 1 from it to
move to the
end of the author's
last name

```
BONHOEFFER, DIETRICH
```

The fourth part simply renames the column:

```
"By First Name"
```

It was only possible to accomplish this transposition because each Author record in the MAGAZINE table followed the same formatting conventions. In each record, the last name was always the first word in the string and was immediately followed by a comma. This allowed you to use the **INSTR** function to search for the comma. Once the comma's position was known, you could determine which part of the string was the last name, and the rest of the string was treated as the first name.

This is not often the case. Names are difficult to force into standard formats. Last names may include prefixes (such as "von" in "von Hagel") or suffixes (such as "Jr.", "Sr.", and "III"). Using the previous example's SQL, the name "Richards, Jr., Bob" would have been transformed into "Jr., Bob Richards".

Because of the lack of a standard formatting for names, many applications store the first and last names separately. Titles (such as "MD") are usually stored in yet another column. A second option when storing such data is to force it into a single format, and use **SUBSTR** and **INSTR** to manipulate that data when needed.

order by and where with String Functions

String functions can be used in a **where** clause, as shown here:

```
select City
  from WEATHER
 where LENGTH(City) < 7;

CITY
----------
LIMA
PARIS
ATHENS
SPARTA
SYDNEY
```

They can also be used in an **order by** clause, as shown here:

```
select City
  from WEATHER
 order by LENGTH(City);

CITY
----------
LIMA
PARIS
ATHENS
SPARTA
SYDNEY
CHICAGO
MANCHESTER
```

These are simple examples; much more complex clauses could be used. For example, you could find all the authors with more than one 'O' in their names by using **INSTR** in the **where** clause:

```
select Author from MAGAZINE
 where INSTR(Author,'O',1,2) > 0;

AUTHOR
-------------------------
BONHOEFFER, DIETRICH
CROOKES, WILLIAM
```

This works by finding a second occurrence of the letter 'O' in the author names. The "> 0" is a logical technique: recall that functions generally produce two different kinds of results, one that creates new objects, and the other that tells you something about them.

The **INSTR** function tells something about a string, specifically the position of the set it has been asked to find. Here it is asked to locate the second 'O' in the Author string. Its result will be a number that will be greater than zero for those names with at least two O's, and zero for those with one or less (when **INSTR** doesn't find something, its result is a zero). So, a simple test for a result greater than zero checks for the success of the **INSTR** search for a second O.

The **where** clause using **INSTR** produces the same result as this:

```
where Author LIKE '%O%O%'
```

Remember that the percent sign (%) is a wild card, meaning it takes the place of anything, so the **like** clause here tells SQL to look for two O's with anything before, between, or after them. This is probably easier to understand than the previous example of **INSTR**.

This brings up the fact that there are often several ways to produce the same result in ORACLE. Some will be easier to understand, some will work more quickly, some will be more appropriate in certain situations, and some will be simply a matter of personal style.

SOUNDEX

There is one string function that is used almost exclusively in a **where** clause: **SOUNDEX**. It has the unusual ability to find words that sound like other words, virtually regardless of how either is spelled. This is especially useful when you're not certain how a word or name is really spelled.

This is the format for **SOUNDEX**:

```
SOUNDEX(string)
```

Here are a few of examples of its use:

```
select City, Temperature, Condition from WEATHER
 where SOUNDEX(City) = SOUNDEX('Sidney');

CITY          TEMPERATURE CONDITION
----------- ----------- ---------
SYDNEY                 29 SNOW

select City, Temperature, Condition from WEATHER
 where SOUNDEX(City) = SOUNDEX('menncestr');
```

```
CITY         TEMPERATURE CONDITION
-----------  ----------- ---------
MANCHESTER            66 SUNNY


select Author from MAGAZINE;
 where SOUNDEX(Author) = SOUNDEX('Banheffer');


AUTHOR
------------------------
BONHOEFFER, DIETRICH
```

SOUNDEX compares the sound of the entry in the selected column with the sound of the word in single quotation marks, and looks for a close match. **SOUNDEX** makes certain assumptions about how letters and combinations of letters are usually pronounced in English, and the two words being compared must begin with the same letter. It will not always find the word you're searching for or have misspelled, but it can help.

It is not necessary that one of the two **SOUNDEX**s in the **where** clause have a literal in it. **SOUNDEX** could be used to compare two columns to find those that sound alike.

One useful purpose for this function is cleaning up mailing lists. Many lists have duplicate entries with slight differences in spelling or format of the customers' names. By using **SOUNDEX** to list all the names that sound alike, many of these duplicates could be discovered and eliminated.

Let's apply this to the ADDRESS table:

```
select LastName, FirstName, Phone
  from ADDRESS;
```

```
LASTNAME                  FIRSTNAME                 PHONE
------------------------  ------------------------  ------------
BAILEY                    WILLIAM                   213-293-0223
ADAMS                     JACK                      415-453-7530
SEP                       FELICIA                   214-522-8383
DE MEDICI                 LEFTY                     312-736-1166
DEMIURGE                  FRANK                     707-767-8900
CASEY                     WILLIS                    312-684-1414
ZACK                      JACK                      415-620-6842
YARROW                    MARY                      415-787-2178
WERSCHKY                  ARNY                      415-235-7387
BRANT                     GLEN                      415-526-7512
EDGAR                     THEODORE                  415-525-6252
HARDIN                    HUGGY                     617-566-0125
```

```
HILD                    PHIL                    603-934-2242
LOEBEL                  FRANK                   202-456-1414
MOORE                   MARY                    718-857-1638
SZEP                    FELICIA                 214-522-8383
ZIMMERMAN               FRED                    503-234-7491
```

To accomplish this, you must force ORACLE to compare each LastName in the table to all the others in the same table.

Join the ADDRESS table to itself by creating an alias for the table, calling it first 'a' and then 'b'. Now it is as if there are two tables, a and b, with the common column LastName.

In the **where** clause, any column where the LastName in one table is identical to the LastName in the other table is eliminated. This prevents a LastName from matching to itself.

Those that sound alike are then selected.

```
select a.LastName, a.FirstName, a.Phone
  from ADDRESS a, ADDRESS b
 where a.LastName != b.LastName
   and SOUNDEX(a.LastName) = SOUNDEX(b.LastName);
```

```
LASTNAME                FIRSTNAME               PHONE
----------------------- ----------------------- ------------
SZEP                    FELICIA                 214-522-8383
SEP                     FELICIA                 214-522-8383
```

National Language Support

ORACLE7 doesn't have to use English characters; it can represent data in any language through its implementation of *National Language Support.* By using characters made up of longer pieces of information than ordinary characters, ORACLE can represent Japanese and other such strings. See NLSSORT, NLS_INITCAP, NLS_LOWER, and NLS_UPPER in the Alphabetical Reference.

Review

Data comes in several types, primarily DATE, NUMBER, and CHARACTER. Character data is basically a string of letters, numbers, and other symbols, and is often called a "character string," or just a "string." These strings can be changed or described by string functions. ORACLE7 features two types of character datatypes: variable length strings (the VARCHAR2 datatype) and fixed-length strings (the

CHAR datatype). Values in CHAR columns are padded with spaces to the full column length if they are shorter than the defined length of the column.

Functions such as **RPAD, LPAD, LTRIM, RTRIM, LOWER, UPPER, INITCAP,** and **SUBSTR** actually change the contents of a string or column before displaying them to you.

Functions such as **LENGTH, INSTR,** and **SOUNDEX** describe the characteristics of a string, such as how long it is, where in it a certain character is located, or what it sounds like.

All of these functions can be used alone or in combination to select and present information from an ORACLE database. This is a straightforward process, built up from simple logical steps that can be combined to accomplish very sophisticated tasks.

CHAPTER 6

Playing the Numbers

Virtually everything we do, particularly in business but also in other aspects of our lives, is measured, explained, and often guided by numbers. While ORACLE cannot correct our obsession with numbers and the illusion of control they often give us, it will facilitate capable and thorough analysis of the information in a database. Good mathematical analysis of familiar numbers will often show trends and facts that were initially not apparent.

The Three Classes of Number Functions

ORACLE functions deal with three classes of numbers: single values, groups of values, and lists of values. As with string functions (discussed in Chapter 5), some of these functions change the values they are applied to, while others merely report information about the values. The classes are distinguished in this way:

A *single value* is one number, such as these:

- A literal number, such as 544.3702

- A variable in SQLPLUS or SQL*FORMS

- One number from one column and one row of the database

ORACLE single-value functions usually change these values through a calculation.

A *group of values* is all the numbers in one column from a series of rows, such as the closing stock price for all the rows of stocks in the STOCK table. ORACLE group-value functions tell you about the whole group, such as average stock price, but not about the individual members of the group.

A *list of values* is a series of numbers that can include

- Literal numbers, such as 1, 7.3, 22, 86

- Variables in SQLPLUS or SQL*FORMS

- Columns, such as OpeningPrice, ClosingPrice, Bid, Ask

ORACLE list functions choose one member of a list of values.

Table 6-1 shows these functions by class. Some functions fit into more than one of these classes. Other functions fall somewhere between string and number functions, or are used to convert data from one to the other. These are covered in Chapter 8, and are organized by function type in Table 8-1.

Notation

Functions will be shown with this kind of notation:

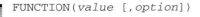

```
FUNCTION(value [,option])
```

The function itself will be uppercase. Values and options will be shown in lowercase italics. Anytime the word *value* appears this way, it represents one of the following: a literal number; the name of a number column in a table; the result of a calculation; or a variable. Because ORACLE does not allow numbers to be used as column names, a literal number should not be in single quotation marks (as a literal string would be in a string function). Column names also must not have quotation marks.

Every function has only one pair of parentheses. Everything that function is to affect, as well as additional instructions you can give the function, goes between its two parentheses.

SINGLE-VALUE FUNCTIONS

FUNCTION	DEFINITION
value1 + *value2*	Addition
value1 − *value2*	Subtraction
value1 * *value2*	Multiplication
value1 / *value2*	Division
ABS(*value*)	**ABS**olute value
CEIL(*value*)	Smallest integer larger than or equal to *value*
COS(*value*)	**COS**ine of *value*
COSH(*value*)	**H**yperbolic **COS**ine of *value*
EXP(*value*)	e raised to *value* **EXP**onent
FLOOR(*value*)	Largest integer smaller than or equal to *value*
LN(*value*)	Natural logarithm of *value*
LOG(*value*)	Base 10 **LOG**arithm of *value*
MOD(*value,divisor*)	**MOD**ulus
NVL(*value,substitute*)	Substitute for *value* if *value* is NULL
POWER(*value,exponent*)	*value* raised to an *exponent* **POWER**
ROUND(*value,precision*)	**ROUND**ing of *value* to *precision*
SIGN(*value*)	1 if *value* is positive, 1 if negative, 0 if zero
SIN(*value*)	**SIN**e of *value*
SINH(*value*)	**H**yperbolic **SIN**e of *value*
SQRT(*value*)	**SQ**uare **R**oo**T** of *value*
TAN(*value*)	**TAN**gent of *value*
TANH(*value*)	**H**yperbolic **TAN**gent of *value*
TRUNC(*value,precision*)	*Value* **TRUNC**ated to *precision*
VSIZE(*value*)	Storage size of *value* in ORACLE

GROUP-VALUE FUNCTIONS

FUNCTION	DEFINITION
AVG(*value*)	**AV**era**G**e of *value* for group of rows
COUNT(*value*)	**COUNT** of rows for column
MAX(*value*)	**MAX**imum of all *values* for group of rows

TABLE 6-1. *ORACLE number functions by class*

MIN(*value*)	**MIN**imum of all *values* for group of rows
STDDEV(*value*)	**ST**an**D**ard **DEV**iation of all *values* for group of rows
SUM(*value*)	**SUM** of all *values* for group of rows
VARIANCE(*value*)	**VARIANCE** of all *values* for group of rows

LIST FUNCTIONS

FUNCTION	**DEFINITION**
GREATEST(*value1,value2,...*)	**GREATEST** *value* of a list
LEAST(*value1,value2,...*)	**LEAST** *value* of a list

TABLE 6-1. *ORACLE number functions by class* (continued)

Some functions have options, or parts not required to make the function work but which can give you more control if you choose to use them. Options are always shown in square brackets: [ ]. The necessary parts of a function always come before the optional parts.

Single-Value Functions

Most single-value functions are pretty straightforward. This section gives short examples, and shows both the results of the functions and how they correspond to columns, rows, and lists. After the examples, you'll see how to combine these functions.

A table named MATH was created expressly to show the calculation effects of the many math functions. It has only four rows and four columns, as shown here:

```
select Name, Above, Below, Empty from MATH;

NAME            ABOVE    BELOW EMPTY
------------    -------  ------- -----
WHOLE NUMBER        11      -22
LOW DECIMAL      33.33   -44.44
MID DECIMAL       55.5    -55.5
HIGH DECIMAL    66.666  -77.777
```

This table is useful because it has values with a variety of characteristics, which are spelled out by the names of the rows. WHOLE NUMBER contains no decimal parts. LOW DECIMAL has decimals that are less than .5, MID DECIMAL decimals are equal to .5, and HIGH DECIMAL has decimals greater than .5. This range is particularly important when using **ROUND** and **TRUNC**ate functions and in understanding how they affect the value of a number.

To the right of the Name column are three other columns: Above, which contains only numbers above zero (positive numbers); Below, which contains only numbers below zero; and Empty, which is **NULL**.

NOTE
In ORACLE a number column may have no value in it at all: when it is **NULL** it is not zero, it is simply empty. This has important implications in making computations, as you will see.

Not all of the rows in this MATH table are needed to demonstrate how most math functions work, so the examples primarily use the last row, HIGH DECIMAL. Additionally, note that column formatting has been adjusted intentionally to show the precision of the calculation. Since SQLPLUS can affect the format of the numbers by a **column** command, it was important not to hide the effect of these SQL math functions with inappropriate SQLPLUS **column** commands, so care has been taken to display just what SQL calculates. If you'd like to look at the SQL and SQLPLUS commands that produced the results that follow, the file **math.sql** (in Appendix A) contains them. Chapter 12 discusses numeric formatting issues.

Addition, Subtraction, Multiplication, and Division (+ - * /)

This query shows each of the four basic arithmetic functions, using Above and Below:

```
select Name, Above, Below, Empty,
       Above + Below  Plus,
       Above - Below  Minus,
       Above * Below  Times,
       Above / Below  Divided
  from MATH where Name = 'HIGH DECIMAL';
```

NAME	ABOVE	BELOW	EMPTY	PLUS	MINUS	TIMES	DIVIDED
HIGH DECIMAL	66.666	-77.777		-11.111	144.443	-5185.081482	.857143

NULL

The same four arithmetic operations are now done again, except instead of using Above and Below, Above and Empty are used. Note that any arithmetic operation that includes a **NULL** value has **NULL** as a result. The calculated columns (columns whose values are the result of a calculation) Plus, Minus, Times, and Divided are all empty.

```
select Name, Above, Below, Empty,
       Above + Empty  Plus,
       Above - Empty  Minus,
       Above * Empty  Times,
       Above / Empty  Divided
  from MATH where Name = 'HIGH DECIMAL';
```

NAME	ABOVE	BELOW	EMPTY	PLUS	MINUS	TIMES	DIVIDED
HIGH DECIMAL	66.666	-77.777					

What you see here is evidence that a **NULL** value cannot be used in a calculation. **NULL** isn't the same as zero; think of **NULL** as a value that is unknown. For example, suppose you have a table with the names of your friends and their ages, but the Age column for PAT SMITH is empty, because you don't know it. What's the difference in your ages? It's clearly not your age minus zero. Your age minus an unknown age is also unknown, or **NULL**. You can't fill in an answer because you don't have an answer. Because you can't make the computation, the answer is **NULL**.

This is also the reason you cannot use **NULL** with an equal sign in a **where** clause (see Chapter 3). It makes no sense to say x is unknown and y is unknown, therefore x and y are equal. If Mrs. Wilkins's and Mr. Adams's ages are unknown, it doesn't mean they're the same age.

There also will be instances where **NULL** means irrelevant, such as an apartment number for a house. In some cases the apartment number might be **NULL** because it is unknown (even though it really exists), while in other cases it is **NULL** because there simply isn't one. **NULL**s will be explored in more detail later in this chapter under "NULLs in Group-Value Functions."

NVL—NULL-Value Substitution

The previous section states the general case about **NULL**s—that **NULL** represents an unknown or irrelevant value. In particular cases, however, although a value is unknown, you may be able to make a reasonable guess. If you're a package carrier, for instance, and 30 percent of the shippers that call you for pickups can't tell you the weight or volume of their packages, will you declare it completely impossible to estimate how many cargo planes you'll need tonight? Of course not. You know from experience the average weight and volume of your packages, so you'd plug in these numbers for those customers that didn't supply you with the information. Here's the information as supplied by your clients:

```
select Client, Weight from SHIPPING;

CLIENT          WEIGHT
------------    ------
JOHNSON TOOL        59
DAGG SOFTWARE       27
TULLY ANDOVER
```

This is what the **NULL**-value substitution (**NVL**) function does:

```
select Client, NVL(Weight,43) from SHIPPING;

CLIENT          NVL(WEIGHT,43)
------------    --------------
JOHNSON TOOL                59
DAGG SOFTWARE               27
TULLY ANDOVER               43
```

Here, you know that the average package weight is 43 pounds, so you use the **NVL** function to plug in 43 any time a client's package has an unknown weight—that is, where the value in the column is **NULL**. In this case, TULLY ANDOVER didn't know the weight of their package when they called it in, but you can still total these and have a fair estimate.

This is the format for **NVL**:

```
NVL(value,substitute)
```

If *value* is **NULL**, this function is equal to *substitute*. If *value* is not **NULL**, this function is equal to *value*. *substitute* can be a literal number, another column, or a computation. If you really were a package carrier with this problem, you could even have a table join in your **select** statement where *substitute* was from a view that actually averaged all non-**NULL** packages.

NVL is not restricted to numbers. It can be used with CHAR, VARCHAR2, DATE, and other data types as well, but the *value* and *substitute* must be the same data type, and it is really useful only in cases where the data is unknown, not where it's irrelevant.

ABS—Absolute Value

Absolute value is the measure of the magnitude of something. For instance, in a temperature change, or a stock index change, the magnitude of the change has meaning in itself, regardless of the direction of the change (which is important in its own right). Absolute value is always a positive number.

This is the format for **ABS**:

```
ABS(value)
```

Note these examples:

```
ABS(146) = 146
ABS(-30) =  30
```

CEIL

CEIL (for ceiling) simply produces the smallest *integer* (or whole number) that is greater than or equal to a specific value. Pay special attention to its effect on negative numbers.

The following is the format for **CEIL** and some examples:

```
CEIL(value)

CEIL(2)    =  2
CEIL(1.3)  =  2
CEIL(-2)   = -2
CEIL(-2.3) = -2
```

FLOOR

FLOOR is the intuitive opposite of **CEIL**. This is the format for **FLOOR**:

```
FLOOR(value)

FLOOR(2)    =  2
FLOOR(1.3)  =  1
FLOOR(-2)   = -2
FLOOR(-2.3) = -3
```

MOD

MODulus is an odd little function primarily used in data processing for esoteric tasks, such as "check digits," which helps assure the accurate transmission of a string of numbers. An example of this is given in the "Using MOD in DECODE" section of Chapter 15. What **MOD** does is divide a value by a divisor and tell you the remainder. **MOD**(23,6) = 5 means divide 23 by 6. The answer is 3 with 5 left over, so 5 is the result of the modulus.

This is the format for **MOD**:

```
MOD(value,divisor)
```

Both *value* and *divisor* can be any real number. The value of **MOD** is zero if *divisor* is zero or negative. Note the following examples:

```
MOD(100,10)      =   0
MOD(22,23)       =  22
MOD(10,3)        =   1
MOD(-30.23,7)    =  -2.23
MOD(4.1,.3)      =   .2
```

The second example shows what **MOD**ulus does whenever the divisor is larger than the dividend (the number being divided). It produces the dividend as a result. Also note this important case where *value* is an integer:

```
MOD(value,1)     = 0
```

The preceding is a good test to see if a number is an integer.

POWER

POWER is simply the ability to raise a value to a given positive exponent, as shown here:

```
POWER(value,exponent)
```

```
POWER(3,2)         =      9
POWER(3,3)         =     27
POWER(-77.777,2)   = 6049.261729
POWER(3,1.086)     =      3.297264
POWER(64,.5)       =      8
```

Before ORACLE7, the exponent had to be an integer; now it can be any real number.

SQRT—Square Root

ORACLE has a separate square root function that gives results equivalent to **POWER**(*value*,.5):

```
SQRT(value)
```

```
SQRT(64)      = 8
SQRT(66.666)  = 8.16492
SQRT(4)       = 2
SQRT(-9)      = NULL
```

The square root of a negative number is an imaginary number. ORACLE doesn't support imaginary numbers, so it returns a **NULL** if you attempt to find the square root of a negative number.

EXP, LN, and LOG

The **EXP, LN**, and **LOG** functions are rarely used in business calculations but are quite common in scientific and technical work. **EXP** is e (2.71828183...) raised to the specified power; **LN** is the "natural," or base e, logarithm of a value. The first two functions are reciprocals of one another; **LN**(**EXP**(*value*)) = *value*. The **LOG** function takes a base and a positive value. **LN**(*value*) is the same as **LOG**(2.71828183,*value*).

```
EXP(value)
```

```
EXP(3)        =  20.085537
EXP(5)        = 148.413159
```

```
LN(value)
```

```
LN(3)         = 1.098612
LN(20.085536) = 3
```

```
LOG(value)
```

```
LOG(EXP(1),3)  = 1.098612
LOG(10,100)    = 2
```

ROUND and TRUNC

ROUND and **TRUNC** are two related single-value functions. **TRUNC** truncates or chops off digits of precision from a number; **ROUND** rounds numbers to a given number of digits of precision.

Here are the formats for **ROUND** and **TRUNC**:

```
ROUND(value,precision)
TRUNC(value,precision)
```

There are some properties worth paying close attention to here. First, look at this simple example of a **select** from the MATH table. Two digits of precision are called for (counting toward the right from the decimal point).

```
select Name, Above, Below,
       ROUND(Above,2),
       ROUND(Below,2),
       TRUNC(Above,2),
       TRUNC(Below,2)
   from MATH;
```

NAME	ABOVE	BELOW	ROUND (ABOVE,2)	ROUND (BELOW,2)	TRUNC (ABOVE,2)	TRUNC (BELOW,2)
WHOLE NUMBER	11	-22	11	-22	11	-22
LOW DECIMAL	33.33	-44.44	33.33	-44.44	33.33	-44.44
MID DECIMAL	55.5	-55.5	55.5	-55.5	55.5	-55.5
HIGH DECIMAL	66.666	-77.777	66.67	-77.78	66.66	-77.77

Only the bottom row is affected, because only it has three digits beyond the decimal point. Both the positive and negative numbers in the bottom row were rounded or truncated: the 66.666 was rounded to a higher number, 66.67, but the -77.777 was rounded to a lower (more negative) number, -77.78. When rounding is done to zero digits, this is the result:

```
select Name, Above, Below,
       ROUND(Above,0),
       ROUND(Below,0),
       TRUNC(Above,0),
       TRUNC(Below,0)
   from MATH;
```

NAME	ABOVE	BELOW	ROUND (ABOVE,0)	ROUND (BELOW,0)	TRUNC (ABOVE,0)	TRUNC (BELOW,0)
WHOLE NUMBER	11	-22	11	-22	11	-22
LOW DECIMAL	33.33	-44.44	33	-44	33	-44
MID DECIMAL	55.5	-55.5	56	-56	55	-55
HIGH DECIMAL	66.666	-77.777	67	-78	66	-77

Note that the decimal value of .5 was rounded up when 55.5 went to 56. This follows the most common American rounding convention (some rounding conventions round up only if a number is larger than .5). Compare these results with **CEIL** and **FLOOR**. They have significant differences:

```
ROUND(55.5) = 56     ROUND(-55.5) = -56
TRUNC(55.5) = 55     TRUNC(-55.5) = -55
CEIL(55.5)  = 56     CEIL(-55.5)  = -55
FLOOR(55.5) = 55     FLOOR(-55.5) = -56
```

Finally, note that both **ROUND** and **TRUNC** can work with negative precision, moving to the left of the decimal point:

```
select Name, Above, Below,
       ROUND(Above,-1),
       ROUND(Below,-1),
       TRUNC(Above,-1),
       TRUNC(Below,-1)
  from MATH;
```

NAME	ABOVE	BELOW	ROUND (ABOVE,-1)	ROUND (BELOW,-1)	TRUNC (ABOVE,-1)	TRUNC (BELOW,-1)
WHOLE NUMBER	11	-22	10	-20	10	-20
LOW DECIMAL	33.33	-44.44	30	-40	30	-40
MID DECIMAL	55.5	-55.5	60	-60	50	-50
HIGH DECIMAL	66.666	-77.777	70	-80	60	-70

Rounding with a negative number can be useful when producing such things as economic reports, where populations or dollar sums need to be rounded up to the millions, billions, or trillions.

SIGN

SIGN is the flip side of absolute value. Whereas **ABS** tells you the magnitude of a value but not its sign, **SIGN** tells you the sign of a value but not its magnitude.

This is the format for **SIGN**:

```
SIGN(value)
```

```
Examples:  SIGN(146)  =   1   Compare to:  ABS(146)  =  146
           SIGN(-30)  =  -1                ABS(-30)  =   30
```

The **SIGN** of 0 is 0:

```
SIGN(0)=0
```

The **SIGN** function is often used in conjunction with the **DECODE** function. **DECODE** will be described in Chapter 15.

SIN, SINH, COS, COSH, TAN, and TANH

The trigonometric functions sine, cosine, and tangent are scientific and technical functions not used much in business. **SIN**, **COS**, and **TAN** give you the standard trigonometric function values for an angle expressed in radians (degrees multiplied by *pi* divided by 180). **SINH**, **COSH**, and **TANH** give you the hyperbolic functions for an angle.

```
SIN(value)
```

```
SIN(30*3.141593/180) = .5
```

```
COSH(value)
```

```
COSH(0)                = 1
```

Group-Value Functions

Group-value functions are those statistical functions such as **SUM**, **AVG**, **COUNT**, and the like, that tell you something about a group of values taken as a whole: the average age of all of the friends in the table mentioned earlier, for instance, or the oldest member of the group, or the youngest, or the number of members in the whole group, and more. Even when one of these functions is supplying information about a single row—such as the oldest person—it is still information that is defined by its relation to the group.

NULLs in Group-Value Functions

Group-value functions treat **NULL** values differently than single-value functions do. Group functions ignore **NULL** values and calculate a result in spite of them.

Take **AVG** as an example. Suppose you had a list of 100 friends and their ages. If you picked 20 of them at random, and averaged their ages, how different would the result be than if you picked a different list of 20, also at random, and averaged it, or if you averaged all 100? In fact, the averages of these three groups would be very close. What this means is that **AVG** is somewhat insensitive to missing records, even when the missing data represents a high percentage of the total number of records available.

NOTE
Average is not immune to missing data, and there can be cases where it will be significantly off (such as when missing data is not randomly distributed), but these will be less common.

The relative insensitivity to missing data of **AVG** needs to be contrasted with, for instance, **SUM**. How close to correct is the **SUM** of the ages of only 20 friends to the **SUM** of all 100 friends? Not close at all. So if you had a table of friends, but only 20 out of 100 supplied their ages, and 80 out of 100 had **NULL** for age, which would be a more reliable statistic about the whole group, and less sensitive to the absence of data, the **AVG** age of those 20 names, or the **SUM** of them? Note that this is an entirely different issue than whether it is possible to estimate the sum of all 100 based on only 20 (in fact, it is precisely the **AVG** of the 20, times 100). The point is, if you don't know how many rows are **NULL**, you can use the following to provide a fairly reasonable result:

```
select AVG(Age) from LIST;
```

You cannot get a reasonable result from this, however:

```
select SUM(Age) from LIST;
```

This same test of whether or not results are reasonable defines how the other group functions respond to **NULL**s. **STDDEV** and **VARIANCE** are measures of central tendency; they, too, are relatively insensitive to missing data. (These will be covered in the "STDDEV and VARIANCE" section later in this chapter.)

MAX and **MIN** measure the extremes of your data. They can fluctuate wildly while **AVG** stays relatively constant: add a 100-year-old man to a group of 99 people who are 50 years old, and the average age only goes up to 50.5—but the maximum age has doubled. Add a newborn baby, and the average goes back to 50 but the minimum age is now zero. It's clear that missing unknown **NULL** values can profoundly affect **MAX**, **MIN**, and **SUM**, so be cautious when using them, particularly if a significant percentage of the data is **NULL**.

Is it possible to create functions that also take into account how sparse the data is and how many values are **NULL** compared to how many have real values, and make good guesses about **MAX**, **MIN**, and **SUM**? Yes, but such functions would be statistical projections, which must make explicit their assumptions about a particular set of data. It is not an appropriate task for a general-purpose group function. Some statisticians would argue that these functions should return **NULL** if they encounter any **NULL**s, since returning any value can be misleading. ORACLE returns something rather than nothing, but leaves it up to you to decide if the result is reasonable.

COUNT is a special case. It can go either way with **NULL** values, but it always returns a number; it will never evaluate to **NULL**. Format and usage for **COUNT** will be shown shortly, but to simply contrast it with the other group functions, it will count all of the non-**NULL** rows of a column, or it will count all of the rows. In other words, if asked to count the ages of 100 friends, **COUNT** will return a value of 20 (since only 20 of the 100 gave their age). If asked to count the rows in a table of friends without specifying a column, it will return 100. An example of these differences is given in the section "DISTINCT in Group Functions" later in this chapter.

Examples of Single- and Group-Value Functions

Neither the group-value functions nor the single-value functions are particularly difficult to understand, but a practical overview of how each function works is helpful in fleshing out some of the options and consequences of their use.

The COMFORT table in these examples contains basic temperature data by city at noon and midnight on each of four sample days each year: the equinoxes (about March 21 and September 23) and the solstices (about June 22 and December 22). You ought to be able to characterize cities based on their temperatures on these days each year.

For the sake of these examples, this table has only eight rows: the data from the four dates in 1993 for San Francisco and Keene, New Hampshire. You can use ORACLE's number functions to analyze these cities, their average temperature, the volatility of the temperature, and so on, for 1993. With more years and data on more cities, an analysis of temperature patterns and variability throughout the century could be made.

The table looks like this:

```
describe COMFORT

Name                             Null?    Type
-------------------------------  ------   ----
CITY                                      VARCHAR2(13)
SAMPLEDATE                                DATE
NOON                                      NUMBER
MIDNIGHT                                  NUMBER
```

It contains this data:

```
select * from COMFORT;

CITY          SAMPLEDAT NOON MIDNIGHT
------------- --------- ---- --------
SAN FRANCISCO 21-MAR-93 62.5     42.3
SAN FRANCISCO 22-JUN-93 51.1     71.9
SAN FRANCISCO 23-SEP-93         61.5
SAN FRANCISCO 22-DEC-93 52.6     39.8
KEENE         21-MAR-93 39.9     -1.2
KEENE         22-JUN-93 85.1     66.7
KEENE         23-SEP-93 99.8     82.6
KEENE         22-DEC-93 -7.2     -1.2
```

AVG, COUNT, MAX, MIN, and SUM

Due to a power failure, the noon temperature in San Francisco on September 23 did not get recorded. The consequences of this can be seen in the following query:

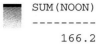

```
select AVG(Noon), COUNT(Noon), MAX(Noon), MIN(Noon), SUM(Noon)
  from COMFORT
 where City = 'SAN FRANCISCO';

AVG(NOON) COUNT (NOON)  MAX(NOON) MIN(NOON) SUM(NOON)
--------- -----------  --------- --------- ---------
     55.4           3      62.5      51.1     166.2
```

The **AVG**(Noon) is the average of the three temperatures that are known. **COUNT**(Noon) is of those that are not **NULL**. **MAX** and **MIN** are self-evident. **SUM**(Noon) is the sum of only three dates, because of the **NULL** for September 23. Note that:

```
SUM(NOON)
---------
    166.2
```

is by no coincidence exactly three times the **AVG**(Noon).

Combining Group-Value and Single-Value Functions

Suppose you would like to know how much the temperature changes in the course of a day. This is a measure of *volatility*. Your first attempt to answer the question might be to subtract the temperature at midnight from the temperature at noon:

```
select City, SampleDate, Noon-Midnight
  from COMFORT
 where City = 'KEENE';


CITY          SAMPLEDAT NOON-MIDNIGHT
------------- --------- -------------
KEENE         21-MAR-93          41.1
KEENE         22-JUN-93          18.4
KEENE         23-SEP-93          17.2
KEENE         22-DEC-93            -6
```

With only four rows to consider in this table, you can quickly convert (or ignore) the pesky minus sign. Volatility in temperature is really a magnitude—which means it asks by how much the temperature changed. It doesn't include a sign, so the -6 isn't really correct. If it goes uncorrected, and is included in a further calculation such as the average change in a year, the answer you get will be absolutely wrong, as shown here:

```
select AVG(Noon-Midnight)
  from COMFORT
 where City = 'KEENE';


AVG(NOON-MIDNIGHT)
------------------
             17.68
```

The correct answer requires an absolute value, as shown here:

```
select AVG(ABS(Noon-Midnight))
  from COMFORT
 where City = 'KEENE';


AVG(ABS(NOON-MIDNIGHT))
-----------------------
                  20.68
```

Combining functions this way follows the same technique given in Chapter 5 in the section on string functions. An entire function such as

```
ABS(Noon-Midnight)
```

is simply plugged into another function as its value like this:

```
AVG(value)
```

which produces

```
AVG(ABS(Noon-Midnight))
```

This shows both single-value and group-value functions at work. You see that you can place single-value functions inside group functions. The single-value functions will calculate a result for every row, and the group-value functions will view that result as if it were the actual value for the row. Single-value functions can be combined (*nested* inside each other) almost without limit. Group-value functions can contain single-value functions in place of their value. They can, in fact, contain many single-value functions in place of their value.

What about combining group functions? First of all, it doesn't make any sense to nest them this way:

```
select SUM(AVG(Noon)) from COMFORT;
```

The preceding will produce this error:

```
ERROR at line 1: ORA-0978:  nested set function without GROUP BY
```

Besides, if it actually worked, it would produce exactly the same result as this:

```
AVG(Noon)
```

because the result of **AVG**(Noon) is just a single value. The **SUM** of a single value is just the single value, so it is not meaningful to nest group functions. The exception to this rule is in the use of **group by** in the **select** statement, the absence of which is why ORACLE produced the error message here. This is covered in Chapter 9.

It *can* be meaningful to add, subtract, multiply, or divide the results of two or more group functions. For example,

```
select MAX(Noon) - MIN(Noon)
  from COMFORT
 where City = 'SAN FRANCISCO';


MAX(NOON)-MIN(NOON)
-------------------
              11.4
```

gives the range of the temperatures in a year. In fact, a quick comparison of San Francisco and Keene could be done with just a bit more effort:

```
select City, AVG(Noon), MAX(Noon), MIN(Noon),
       MAX(Noon) - MIN(Noon) Swing
  from COMFORT
 group by City;


CITY          AVG(NOON) MAX(NOON) MIN(NOON) SWING
------------- --------- --------- --------- -----
KEENE              54.4      99.8      -7.2   107
SAN FRANCISCO      55.4      62.5      51.1  11.4
```

This query is a good example of discovering information in your data: the average temperature in the two cities is nearly identical, but the huge temperature swing in Keene, compared to San Francisco, says a lot about the yearly temperature volatility of the two cities, and the relative effort required to dress (or heat and cool a home) in one city compared to the other. The **group by** clause will be explained in detail in Chapter 9. Briefly, in this example it forced the group functions to work not on the total table, but on the subgroups of temperatures by city.

STDDEV and VARIANCE

Standard deviation and *variance* have their common statistical meanings, and use the same format as all group functions.

```
select MAX(Noon), AVG(Noon), MIN(Noon), STDDEV(Noon),
       VARIANCE(Noon)
  from COMFORT
 where City = 'KEENE';


MAX(NOON) AVG(NOON) MIN(NOON) STDDEV(NOON) VARIANCE(NOON)
--------- --------- --------- ------------ --------------
     99.8      54.4      -7.2        48.33           2336
```

DISTINCT in Group Functions

All group-value functions have a **DISTINCT** versus **ALL** option. **COUNT** provides a good example of how this works.

This is the format for **COUNT** (¦ means "or"):

```
COUNT([DISTINCT ¦ ALL] value)
```

Here is an example:

```
select COUNT(DISTINCT City), COUNT(City), COUNT(*)
   from COMFORT;

COUNT(DISTINCTCITY) COUNT(CITY) COUNT(*)
------------------- ----------- --------
                  2           8        8
```

This query shows a couple of interesting results. First, **DISTINCT** forces **COUNT** to count only the number of unique city names. If asked to count the **DISTINCT** midnight temperatures, it would return 7, because two of the eight temperatures were the same. When **COUNT** is used on City but not forced to look at **DISTINCT** cities, it finds 8.

This also shows that **COUNT** can work on a character column. It's not making a computation on the values in the column, as **SUM** or **AVG** must; it is merely counting how many rows have a value in the City column.

COUNT has another unique property: *value* can be an asterisk, meaning that **COUNT** tells you how many rows there are in the table, regardless of whether any specific columns in it are **NULL**. It will count a row even if all of its fields are **NULL**.

The other group functions do not share **COUNT**'s ability to use an asterisk, nor its ability to use a character column for *value* (although **MAX** and **MIN** can). They do all share its use of **DISTINCT**, which forces each of them to operate only on unique values. A table with values such as this:

```
select FirstName, Age from BIRTHDAY;

FIRSTNAME            AGE
---------------      ----
GEORGE                40
ROBERT                50
NANCY                 40
VICTORIA              40
FRANK                 40
```

would produce this result:

```
select AVG(DISTINCT Age) Average, SUM(DISTINCT Age) Total
   from BIRTHDAY;

AVERAGE TOTAL
------- -----
     45    90
```

which, if you wanted to know the average age of your friends, is not the right answer. The use of **DISTINCT** other than in **COUNT** is likely to be extremely rare, except perhaps in some statistical calculations. **MAX** and **MIN** produce the same result with or without **DISTINCT**.

The alternative option to **DISTINCT** is **ALL**, which is the default. **ALL** tells SQL to check every row, even if the value is a duplicate of the value in another row. You do not need to type **ALL**; if you don't type in **DISTINCT**, **ALL** is used automatically.

List Functions

Unlike the group-value functions, which work on a group of rows, the list functions work on a group of columns, either actual or calculated values, within a single row. In other words, list functions compare the values of each of several columns and pick either the greatest or least of the list. Consider the COMFORT table, shown here:

```
select * from COMFORT;

CITY          SAMPLEDAT NOON  MIDNIGHT
------------- --------- ----  -------
SAN FRANCISCO 21-MAR-93 62.5      42.3
SAN FRANCISCO 22-JUN-93 51.1      71.9
SAN FRANCISCO 23-SEP-93           61.5
SAN FRANCISCO 22-DEC-93 52.6      39.8
KEENE         21-MAR-93 39.9      -1.2
KEENE         22-JUN-93 85.1      66.7
KEENE         23-SEP-93 99.8      82.6
KEENE         22-DEC-93 -7.2      -1.2
```

Now compare this query result with the following one. Note especially June and September in San Francisco, and December in Keene:

```
select City, SampleDate, GREATEST(Midnight,Noon) High,
       LEAST(Midnight,Noon) Low
  from COMFORT;


CITY           SAMPLEDAT  High   Low
-------------  ---------  ----   ----
SAN FRANCISCO  21-MAR-93  62.5   42.3
SAN FRANCISCO  22-JUN-93  71.9   51.1
SAN FRANCISCO  23-SEP-93
SAN FRANCISCO  22-DEC-93  52.6   39.8
KEENE          21-MAR-93  39.9   -1.2
KEENE          22-JUN-93  85.1   66.7
KEENE          23-SEP-93  99.8   82.6
KEENE          22-DEC-93  -1.2   -7.2
```

September in San Francisco has a **NULL** result, because **GREATEST** and **LEAST** couldn't legitimately compare an actual midnight temperature with an unknown noon temperature. In the other two instances, the midnight temperature was actually higher than the noon temperature.

These are the formats for **GREATEST** and **LEAST**:

```
GREATEST(value1,value2,value3. . .)
LEAST(value1,value2,value3. . .)
```

Both **GREATEST** and **LEAST** can be used with many values, and the values can be columns, literal numbers, calculations, or combinations of other columns. **GREATEST** and **LEAST** can also be used with character columns. For example, they can choose the names that fall last (**GREATEST**) or first (**LEAST**) in alphabetical order:

```
GREATEST('Bob','George','Andrew','Isaiah') = Isaiah
   LEAST('Bob','George','Andrew','Isaiah') = Andrew
```

Finding Rows with MAX or MIN

Which city had the highest temperature ever recorded, and on what date? The answer is easy with just eight rows to look at, but what if you have data from every city in the country and for every day of every year for the last 50 years? Assume for now that the highest temperature for the year occurred closer to noon than midnight. The following won't work:

```
select City, SampleDate, MAX(Noon)
  from COMFORT;
```

ORACLE flags the City column and gives this error message:

```
select City, SampleDate, MAX(Noon)
          *
ERROR at line 1: ORA-0937:   not a single group set function
```

This error message is a bit opaque. It means that ORACLE has detected a flaw in the logic of the question. Asking for columns means you want individual rows to appear; asking for **MAX**, a group function, means you want a group result for all rows. These are two different kinds of requests. The first asks for a set of rows, the second requests just one computed row, so there is a conflict. Here is how to construct the query:

```
select City, SampleDate, Noon
   from COMFORT
 where Noon = (select MAX(Noon) from COMFORT);


CITY          SAMPLEDAT  NOON
------------ ---------- -----
KEENE         23-SEP-93  99.8
```

This only produces one row. You might think, therefore, that the combination of a request for the City and SampleDate columns along with the **MAX** of noon is not so contradictory as was just implied. But what if you'd asked for minimum temperature instead?

```
select City, SampleDate, Midnight
   from COMFORT
 where Midnight = (select MIN(Midnight) from COMFORT);


CITY          SAMPLEDAT MIDNIGHT
------------ --------- --------
KEENE         21-MAR-93    -1.2
KEENE         22-DEC-93    -1.2
```

Two rows! More than one satisfied the **MIN** request, so there is a conflict in trying to combine a regular column request with a group function.

It is also possible to use two subqueries, each with a group-value function in it (or two subqueries where one does and the other doesn't have a group function). Suppose you want to know the highest and lowest noon temperatures for the year?

```
select City, SampleDate, Noon
   from COMFORT
 where Noon = (select MAX(Noon) from COMFORT)
    or Noon = (select MIN(Noon) from COMFORT);

CITY          SAMPLEDAT NOON
------------  --------- -----
KEENE         23-SEP-93  99.8
KEENE         22-DEC-93  -7.2
```

Precedence and Parentheses

When more than one arithmetic or logical operator is used in a single calculation, which one is executed first, and does it matter what order they are in? Consider the following:

```
select 2/2/4 from DUAL;

2/2/4
-----
  .25
```

When parentheses are introduced, although the numbers and the operation (division) stay the same, the answer changes considerably:

```
select 2/(2/4) from DUAL;

2/(2/4)
-------
      4
```

The reason for this is *precedence.* Precedence defines the order in which mathematical computations are made, not just in ORACLE but in mathematics in general. The rules are simple: parentheses have the highest precedence, then multiplication and division, then addition and subtraction. When an equation is computed, any calculations inside of parentheses are made first. Multiplication and division are next. Finally, any addition and subtraction are completed. When operations of equal precedence are to be performed, they are executed from left to right. Here are a few examples:

```
2*4/2*3 = 12              (the same as ( (2*4)/2 )*3)
(2*4)/(2*3) = 1.333
4-2*5 = -6                (the same as 4 - (2*5))
(4-2)*5 = 10
```

AND or **OR** also obey precedence rules, with **AND** having the higher precedence. Observe the effect of the **AND**, and also the left-to-right order, in these two queries:

```
select * from NEWSPAPER
 where Section = 'B' AND Page = 1 OR Page = 2;

FEATURE           S   PAGE
--------------    -   -----
Weather           C     2
Modern Life       B     1
Bridge            B     2

3 rows selected.

select * from NEWSPAPER
 where Page = 1 OR Page = 2 AND Section = 'B';

FEATURE           S   PAGE
--------------    -   -----
National News     A     1
Sports            D     1
Business          E     1
Modern Life       B     1
Bridge            B     2

5 rows selected.
```

If what you really desire is page 1 or 2 in Section B, then parentheses are needed to overcome the precedence of the **AND**. Parentheses override any other operations.

```
select * from NEWSPAPER
 where Section = 'B' AND (Page = 1 OR Page = 2);

FEATURE           S   PAGE
--------------    -   -----
Modern Life       B     1
Bridge            B     2

2 rows selected.
```

The truth is, even experienced programmers and mathematicians have trouble remembering what will execute first when they write a query or an equation. It is always wise to make explicit the order you want ORACLE to follow. Use parentheses whenever there could be the slightest risk of confusion.

Review

Single-value functions work on values in a row-by-row fashion. List functions compare columns and choose just one, again in a row-by-row fashion. Single-value functions almost always change the value of the column they are applied to. This doesn't mean, of course, that they have modified the database from which the value was drawn, but they do make a calculation with that value, and the result is different than the original value. For example:

```
ROUND(99.308,-1) = 90
```

The result of the **ROUND** function is to *change* the 99.308 value to 90. List functions don't change values in this way, but rather they simply choose (or report) the **GREATEST** or **LEAST** of a series of values in a row. Both single-value and list functions will not produce a result if they encounter a value that is **NULL**.

Both single-value and list functions can be used anywhere an expression can be used, such as in the **select** and **where** clauses.

The group-value functions tell something about a whole group of numbers—all of the rows in a set. The group-value functions tell you the average of those numbers, or the largest of them, or how many there are, or the standard deviation of the values, and so on. Group functions ignore **NULL** values, and this fact must be kept firmly in mind when reporting about groups of values; otherwise there is considerable risk of misunderstanding the data.

Group-value functions also can report information on subgroups within a table, or be used to create a summary view of information from one or more tables. Chapter 9 gives details on these additional features.

Finally, mathematical and logical precedence affect the order in which queries are evaluated, and this can have a dramatic effect on query results. Get into the habit of using parentheses to make the order you desire both explicit and easy to understand.

CHAPTER 7

Dates: Then, Now, and the Difference

One of ORACLE's more unusual strengths is its ability to store and calculate dates, and the number of seconds, minutes, hours, days, months, and years between dates. It also has the remarkable ability to format dates in virtually any manner you can conceive of, from a simple "01-APR-95" to "April 1st in the 769th Year of the Reign of Louis IX." You probably won't use many of these date formatting and computing functions, but the most basic ones will prove to be very important.

Date Arithmetic

DATE is an ORACLE data type, just as CHAR and NUMBER are, and it has its own unique properties. The DATE data type is stored in a special internal ORACLE format that includes not just the month, day, and year, but also the hour, minute, and second. The benefit of all this detail should be obvious. If you have, for instance, a customer help desk, for each call that is logged in, ORACLE can automatically store the date and time of the call in a single date column. You can format the date column on a report to show just the date, or the date and the hour, or the date, hour, and minute, or the date, hour, minute, and second.

SQLPLUS and SQL recognize columns that are of the DATE data type, and understand that instructions from you to do arithmetic with them call for *date arithmetic,* not regular math. Adding 1 to a date, for instance, will give you another *date:* the next day. Subtracting one date from another will give you a *number:* the count of days between the two dates.

However, since ORACLE dates can include hours, minutes, and seconds, doing date arithmetic can prove to be tricky, since ORACLE could tell you the difference between today and tomorrow is .516 days! (This will be explained later in this chapter.)

SysDate

ORACLE taps into the computer's operating system for the current date and time. It makes these available to you through a special column called SysDate. Think of SysDate as a function whose result is always the current date and time, and that can be used anywhere any other ORACLE function can be used. You also can regard it as a hidden column or pseudo-column that is in every table. Here, SysDate shows today's date:

```
select SysDate from DUAL;

SYSDATE
---------
01-APR-95
```

NOTE
DUAL is a small but useful ORACLE table created for testing functions or doing quick calculations. A special boxed section in this chapter entitled "The DUAL Table for Quick Tests and Calculations" describes DUAL.

The Difference Between Two Dates

HOLIDAY is a table of some of the important secular holidays in the United States during 1995.

```
select Holiday, ActualDate, CelebratedDate from HOLIDAY;

HOLIDAY                      ACTUALDAT CELEBRATE
------------------------     --------- ---------
NEW YEAR DAY                 01-JAN-95 01-JAN-95
MARTIN LUTHER KING, JR.      15-JAN-95 16-JAN-95
LINCOLNS BIRTHDAY            12-FEB-95 20-FEB-95
WASHINGTONS BIRTHDAY         22-FEB-95 20-FEB-95
FAST DAY, NEW HAMPSHIRE      22-FEB-95 22-FEB-95
MEMORIAL DAY                 30-MAY-95 29-MAY-95
INDEPENDENCE DAY             04-JUL-95 04-JUL-95
LABOR DAY                    04-SEP-95 04-SEP-95
COLUMBUS DAY                 08-OCT-95 09-OCT-95
THANKSGIVING                 23-NOV-95 23-NOV-95
```

The DUAL Table for Quick Tests and Calculations

DUAL is a tiny table ORACLE provides with only one row and one column in it.

```
describe DUAL

Name                             Null?       Type
------------------------------   ----------- ----
DUMMY                                        CHAR(1)
```

Since ORACLE's many functions work on both columns and literals, using DUAL lets you see some functioning using just literals. In these examples the **select** statement doesn't care which columns are in the table, and a single row is sufficient to demonstrate a point. For example, suppose you wanted to quickly calculate **POWER**(4,3)}—four "cubed."

(continued)

```
select POWER(4,3) from DUAL;

POWER(4,3)
----------
        64
```

The actual column in DUAL is irrelevant. This means that you can experiment with date formatting and arithmetic using the DUAL table and the date functions in order to understand how they work. Then those functions can be applied to actual dates in real tables.

Date Functions

- **ADD_MONTHS**(*date,count*) **adds** *count* **months** to *date*.

- **GREATEST**(*date1,date2,date3,...*) picks latest date from list of dates.

- **LEAST**(*date1,date2,date3,...*) picks earliest date from list of dates.

- **LAST_DAY**(*date*) gives date of **last day** of month that *date* is in.

- **MONTHS_BETWEEN**(*date2,date1*) gives *date2-date1* in **months** (can be fractional months).

- **NEXT_DAY**(*date,'day'*) gives date of **next day** after *date*, where 'day' is 'Monday', 'Tuesday', and so on.

- **NEW_TIME**(*date,'this','other'*) gives the *date* (and time) in *this* time zone. *this* will be replaced by a three-letter abbreviation for the current time zone. *other* will be replaced by a three-letter abbreviation for the other time zone for which you'd like to know the time and date.

(continued)

Time zones are as follows:

AST/ADT	Atlantic standard/daylight time
BST/BDT	Bering standard/daylight time
CST/CDT	Central standard/daylight time
EST/EDT	Eastern standard/daylight time
GMT	Greenwich mean time
HST/HDT	Alaska-Hawaii standard/daylight time
MST/MDT	Mountain standard/daylight time
NST	Newfoundland standard time
PST/PDT	Pacific standard/daylight time
YST/YDT	Yukon standard/daylight time

■ **ROUND**(*date,'format'*) without format specified, *round*s a *date* to 12 A.M. (midnight, the beginning of that day) if time of date is before noon, otherwise rounds up to next day. For use of *format* for rounding, see "ROUND" in the Alphabetical Reference.

■ **TRUNC**(*date,'format'*) without *format* specified, sets a *date* to 12 A.M. (midnight, the beginning of that day). For use of *format* for truncating, see "TRUNC" in the Alphabetical Reference Section.

■ **TO_CHAR**(*date,'format'*) reformats *date* according to *format*.*

■ **TO_DATE**(*string,'format'*) converts a *string* in a given *'format'* into an ORACLE date. Will also accept a *number* instead of a string, with certain limits. 'format' is restricted.*

*See the special boxed section "Date Formats" later in this chapter.

Which holidays are not celebrated on the actual date of their anniversary during 1995? This can be easily answered by subtracting the CelebratedDate from the ActualDate. If the answer is not zero, then there is a difference between the two dates:

```
select Holiday, ActualDate, CelebratedDate
   from Holiday
 where CelebratedDate - ActualDate != 0;


HOLIDAY                      ACTUALDAT CELEBRATE
------------------------     --------- ---------
MARTIN LUTHER KING, JR.      15-JAN-95 16-JAN-95
LINCOLNS BIRTHDAY            12-FEB-95 20-FEB-95
WASHINGTONS BIRTHDAY         22-FEB-95 20-FEB-95
MEMORIAL DAY                 30-MAY-95 29-MAY-95
COLUMBUS DAY                 08-OCT-95 09-OCT-95
```

Adding Months

If February 22 is "Fast Day" in New Hampshire, perhaps six months later could be celebrated as "Feast Day." If so, what would the date be? Simply use the **ADD_MONTHS** function, adding a **count** of six months as shown here:

```
column FeastDay heading "Feast Day"

select ADD_MONTHS(CelebratedDate,6) FeastDay
   from HOLIDAY
 where Holiday like 'FAST%';

Feast Day
---------
22-AUG-95
```

Subtracting Months

If picnic area reservations have to be made at least six months before Columbus Day, what's the last day you can make them? Take the CelebratedDate for Columbus Day, and use **ADD_MONTHS** adding a *negative* **count** of six months (this is the same as subtracting months). This will tell you the date six months before Columbus Day. Then subtract one day.

```
column LastDay heading "Last Day"

select ADD_MONTHS(CelebratedDate,-6) - 1 LastDay
   from HOLIDAY
 where Holiday = 'COLUMBUS DAY';


Last Day
---------
08-APR-95
```

GREATEST and LEAST

Which comes first for each of the holidays that were moved to fall on Mondays, the actual or the celebrated date? The **LEAST** function chooses the earliest date from a list of dates, whether columns or literals; **GREATEST** chooses the latest date. These **GREATEST** and **LEAST** functions are exactly the same ones that are used with numbers and character strings:

```
select Holiday, LEAST(ActualDate, CelebratedDate) First,
       ActualDate, CelebratedDate
   from HOLIDAY
 where ActualDate - CelebratedDate != 0;


HOLIDAY                   FIRST     ACTUALDAT CELEBRATE
------------------------- --------- --------- ---------
MARTIN LUTHER KING, JR.   15-JAN-95 15-JAN-95 16-JAN-95
LINCOLNS BIRTHDAY         12-FEB-95 12-FEB-95 20-FEB-95
WASHINGTONS BIRTHDAY      20-FEB-95 22-FEB-95 20-FEB-95
MEMORIAL DAY              29-MAY-95 30-MAY-95 29-MAY-95
COLUMBUS DAY              08-OCT-95 08-OCT-95 09-OCT-95
```

Here **LEAST** worked just fine, because it operated on DATE columns from a table. What about literals?

```
select LEAST('20-JAN-95','20-DEC-95') from DUAL;


LEAST('20
---------
20-DEC-95
```

This is quite wrong, almost as if you'd said **GREATEST** instead of **LEAST**. December 20, 1995, is not earlier than January 20, 1995. Why did this happen? Because **LEAST** treated these literals as *strings*.

It did not know to treat them as dates. The **TO_DATE** function converts these literals into an internal DATE format that ORACLE can use for its date-oriented functions:

```
select LEAST( TO_DATE('20-JAN-95'), TO_DATE('20-DEC-95') )
   from DUAL;

LEAST(TO_
---------
20-JAN-95
```

See the special boxed section entitled "A Warning about GREATEST and LEAST."

NEXT_DAY

NEXT_DAY figures the date of the next named day of the week (that is, Sunday, Monday, Tuesday, Wednesday, Thursday, Friday, or Saturday) after the given date. For example, suppose payday is always the first Friday after the 15th of the month. The table PAYDAY contains only the pay cycle dates, each one being the 15th of the month, with one row for each month of the year:

```
select CycleDate from PAYDAY;

CYCLEDATE
---------
15-JAN-95
15-FEB-95
15-MAR-95
15-APR-95
15-MAY-95
15-JUN-95
15-JUL-95
15-AUG-95
15-SEP-95
15-OCT-95
15-NOV-95
15-DEC-95
```

What will be the actual paydates?

A Warning about GREATEST and LEAST

Unlike many other ORACLE functions and logical operators, the GREATEST and LEAST functions will not evaluate literal strings that are in date format as dates. The dates are treated as strings:

```
select Holiday, CelebratedDate
  from HOLIDAY
 where CelebratedDate =  LEAST('16-JAN-95', '04-SEP-95');


HOLIDAY                      CELEBRATE
---------------------- ---------
LABOR DAY                    04-SEP-95
```

In order for LEAST and GREATEST to work properly, the function TO_DATE must be applied to the literal strings.

```
select Holiday, CelebratedDate
  from HOLIDAY
 where CelebratedDate = LEAST( TO_DATE('16-JAN-95'),
                               TO_DATE('04-SEP-95') );


HOLIDAY                        CELEBRATE
-------------------------- ---------
MARTIN LUTHER KING, JR.     16-JAN-95
```

```
column Payday heading "Pay Day!"

select NEXT_DAY(CycleDate,'FRIDAY') Payday
  from PAYDAY;

Pay Day!
---------
20-JAN-95
17-FEB-95
```

```
17-MAR-95
21-APR-95
19-MAY-95
16-JUN-95
21-JUL-95
18-AUG-95
22-SEP-95
20-OCT-95
17-NOV-95
22-DEC-95
```

This is nearly correct, except for September and December, because **NEXT_DAY** is the date of the *next* Friday after the cycle date. Since September 15 and December 15 are Fridays, this (wrongly) gives the following Friday instead. The correct version is as follows:

```
column Payday heading "Pay Day!"

select NEXT_DAY(CycleDate-1,'FRIDAY') PayDay
   from PAYDAY;


Pay Day!
---------
20-JAN-95
17-FEB-95
17-MAR-95
21-APR-95
19-MAY-95
16-JUN-95
21-JUL-95
18-AUG-95
15-SEP-95
20-OCT-95
17-NOV-95
15-DEC-95
```

NEXT_DAY is really a "greater than" kind of function. It asks for the next date *greater than* the given date, that falls on a 'FRIDAY'. To catch those cycle dates that are already on Friday, subtract one from the cycle date. This makes every cycle date appear one day earlier to **NEXT_DAY**. The paydays are then always the correct Friday. (If you like, consider what happens if one of the cycle dates is a Saturday, and you've set up this **select**. Will it be right?)

LAST_DAY

LAST_DAY produces the date of the last day of the month. Say that commissions and bonuses are always paid on the last day of the month. What are those dates in 1995?

```
column EndMonth heading "End Month"

select LAST_DAY(CycleDate) EndMonth
  from PAYDAY;


End Month
---------
31-JAN-95
28-FEB-95
31-MAR-95
30-APR-95
31-MAY-95
30-JUN-95
31-JUL-95
31-AUG-95
30-SEP-95
31-OCT-95
30-NOV-95
31-DEC-95
```

MONTHS_BETWEEN Two Dates

A group of friends have all given their ages, but recently you've come upon a file with their actual birthdates. You load the information into a table called BIRTHDAY and display it:

```
select * from BIRTHDAY;

FIRSTNAME        LASTNAME         BIRTHDATE   AGE
---------------- ---------------- --------- -----
GEORGE           SAND             12-MAY-46    42
ROBERT           JAMES            23-AUG-37    52
NANCY            LEE              02-FEB-47    42
VICTORIA         LYNN             20-MAY-49    45
FRANK            PILOT            11-NOV-42    42
```

Clearly, these are not their actual ages. Everyone except Victoria has fudged. To calculate real ages compute the months between today's date (in 1995) and their birthdates, and divide by 12 to get the years:

```
select FirstName, LastName, Birthdate, Age,
       MONTHS_BETWEEN(SysDate,Birthdate)/12 "Actual Age"
  from BIRTHDAY;
```

```
FIRSTNAME        LASTNAME         BIRTHDATE   AGE Actual Age
---------------  ---------------  ---------   --- ----------
GEORGE           SAND             12-MAY-46    42      48.89
ROBERT           JAMES            23-AUG-37    52      57.61
NANCY            LEE              02-FEB-47    42      48.16
VICTORIA         LYNN             20-MAY-49    45      45.87
FRANK            PILOT            11-NOV-42    42      52.39
```

Combining Date Functions

You are hired on April 1, 1995 at a great new job, with a starting salary that is lower than you had hoped, but with a promise of a review the first of the month after six months have passed. When is your review date?

```
select SysDate Today,
       LAST_DAY(ADD_MONTHS(SysDate,6)) + 1 Review
  from DUAL;
```

```
TODAY      REVIEW
---------  ---------
02-APR-95  01-NOV-95
```

ADD_MONTHS takes the SysDate and adds six months to it. **LAST_DAY** takes this result and figures the last day of that month. You then add 1 to the date to get the first day of the next month. How many days until that review? You simply subtract today's date from it. Note the use of parentheses to assure the proper order of the calculation.

```
select (LAST_DAY(ADD_MONTHS(SysDate,6))+ 1)-SysDate  Wait
  from DUAL;
```

```
WAIT
-----
  213
```

ROUND and TRUNC in Date Calculations

Here is today's SysDate:

```
SYSDATE
---------
01-APR-95
```

In the beginning of the chapter it was noted that ORACLE could subtract one date from another, such as tomorrow minus today, and come up with an answer other than a whole number. Let's look at it:

```
select TO_DATE('02-APR-95') - SysDate from DUAL;

TO_DATE('02-APR-95')-SYSDATE
----------------------------
                        .516
```

The reason for the fractional number of days between today and tomorrow is that ORACLE keeps hours, minutes, and seconds with its dates, and SysDate is always current, up to the second. It is obviously less than a full day until tomorrow.

In order to simplify some of the difficulties you might encounter using fractions of days, ORACLE makes a couple of assumptions about dates:

- A date entered as a literal, such as '01-APR-95', is given a default time of 12 A.M. (midnight) at the beginning of that day.

- A date entered through SQLFORMS, unless a time is specifically assigned to it, is set to 12 A.M. (midnight) at the beginning of that day.

- SysDate always includes both the date and the time, unless you intentionally round it off. The **ROUND** function on any date sets it to 12 A.M. of that day, if the time is before exactly noon, and to 12 A.M., the next day, if it is after noon. The **TRUNC** function acts similarly, except that it sets the time to 12 A.M. for any time up to and including one second before midnight.

To get the rounded number of days between today and tomorrow, use this:

```
select TO_DATE('02-APR-95') - ROUND(SysDate) from DUAL;

TO_DATE('02-APR-95')-ROUND(SYSDATE)
-----------------------------------
                                  1
```

ROUND, without a 'format' (see the boxed section "Date Functions") always rounds a date to 12 A.M. of the closest day. If dates that you will be working with contain times other than noon, either use **ROUND** or accept possible fractional results in your calculations. The **TRUNC** works similarly, but sets the time to 12 A.M. of the current day.

TO_DATE and TO_CHAR Formatting

TO_DATE and **TO_CHAR** are alike in that they both have powerful formatting capabilities. They are opposite in that **TO_DATE** converts a character string or a number into an ORACLE date, and **TO_CHAR** converts an ORACLE date into a character string. The formats for these two functions are as follows:

```
TO_CHAR(date[,'format'[,'NLSparameters']]))

TO_DATE(string[,'format'[,'NLSparameters]]))
```

date must be a column defined as a DATE data type in ORACLE. It cannot be a string even if it is in the default date format of DD-MON-YY. The only way to use a string where *date* appears in the **TO_CHAR** function is to enclose it within a **TO_DATE** function.

string is a literal string, a literal number, or a database column containing a string or a number. In every case but one, their format must correspond to that which is described by the *format*. Only if a string is in the default format can the *format* be left out. The default starts out as 'DD-MON-YY', but you can change this with

```
alter session set NLS_DATE_FORMAT
```

for a given SQL session or with the NLS_DATE_FORMAT INIT.ORA parameter.

format is a dizzying collection of more than 40 options, which can be combined in virtually an infinite number of ways. The special boxed section entitled "Date Formats" lists these options with explanations. Once you understand the basic method of using the options, putting them into practice is simple.

NLSparameters is a string that sets the NLS_DATE_LANGUAGE option to a specific language, as opposed to using the language for the current SQL session. You shouldn't need to use this option often. ORACLE will return day and month names in the language set for the session with **alter session.**

TO_CHAR will be used as an example of how the options work. The first thing to do is define a column format for the **TO_CHAR** function results. This is done because, without it, **TO_CHAR** will produce a column in SQLPLUS nearly 100 characters wide. By renaming the column for readability, and setting its format to 30 characters, a practical display is produced:

```
column Formatted format a30 word_wrapped
select BirthDate, TO_CHAR(BirthDate,'MM/DD/YY') Formatted
  from BIRTHDAY
 where FirstName = 'VICTORIA';


BIRTHDATE FORMATTED
--------- ------------------------------
20-MAY-49 05/20/49
```

Date Formats

These date formats are used with both TO_CHAR and TO_DATE.

MM	Number of month: 12
RM	Roman numeral month: XII
MON	Three-letter abbreviation of Month: AUG
MONTH	Month fully spelled out: AUGUST
DDD	Number of days in year, since Jan 1: 354
DD	Number of days in month: 23
D	Number of days in week: 6
DY	Three-letter abbreviation of day: FRI
DAY	Day fully spelled out: FRIDAY
YYYY	Full four-digit year: 1946
SYYYY	Signed year, 1000 B.C.=-1000
YYY	Last three digits of year: 946
YY	Last two digits of year: 46
Y	Last one digit of year: 6
IYYY	Four-digit year from ISO standard*
IYY	Three-digit year from ISO standard
IY	Two-digit year from ISO standard
I	One-digit year from ISO standard

* ISO is the International Standard Organization, which has a different set
  of standards for dates than the US formats.

(continued)

RR	Last two digits of year relative to current date
YEAR	Year spelled out: NINETEEN-FORTY-SIX
Q	Number of quarter: 3
WW	Number of weeks in year: 46
IW	Weeks in year from ISO standard
W	Number of weeks in month: 3
J	"Julian"—days since December 31, 4713 B.C.: 2422220
HH	Hours of day, always 1-12:11
HH12	Same as HH
HH24	Hours of day, 24-hour clock: 17
MI	Minutes of hour: 58
SS	Seconds of minute: 43
SSSSS	Seconds since midnight, always 0-86399: 43000
/,-:.	Punctuation to be incorporated in display for **TO_CHAR** or ignored in format for **TO_DATE**
A.M.	Displays A.M. or P.M., depending upon time of day
P.M.	Same effect as A.M.
AM or PM	Same as A.M. but without periods
B.C.	Displays B.C. or A.D., depending upon date
A.D.	Same as B.C.
BC or AD	Same as B.C. but without periods

These date formats work only with **TO_CHAR**. They do not work with **TO_DATE**:

"string"	string is incorporated in display for **TO_CHAR**.
fm	Prefix to Month or Day: fmMONTH or fmday. Suppresses padding of Month or Day (defined earlier) in format. Without fm, all months are displayed at same width. Similarly true for days. With fm, padding is eliminated. Months and days are only as long as their count of characters.

(continued)

TH	Suffix to a number: ddTH or DDTH produces 24th or 24TH. Capitalization comes from the case of the number—DD—not from the case of the TH. Works with any number in a date: YYYY, DD, MM, HH, MI, SS, and so on.
SP	Suffix to a number that forces number to be spelled out: DDSP, DdSP, or ddSP produces THREE, Three, or three. Capitalization comes from case of number—DD—not from the case of SP. Works with any number in a date: YYYY, DD, MM, HH, MI, SS, and so on.
SPTH	Suffix combination of TH and SP that forces number to be both spelled out and given an ordinal suffix: Ddspth produces Third. Capitalization comes from case of number—DD—not from the case of SP. Works with any number in a date: YYYY, DD, MM, HH, MI, SS, and so on.
THSP	Same as SPTH.

BirthDate shows the default ORACLE date format: DD-MON-YY, or day of month, dash, three-letter abbreviation for month, dash, last two digits of year. The **TO_CHAR** function in the **select** is nearly self-evident. The MM, DD, and YY in the TO_CHAR statement are key symbols to ORACLE in formatting the date. The slashes (/) are just punctuation, and ORACLE will accept a wide variety of punctuation. It doesn't even need to be sensible. For example, here you see > used as punctuation:

```
select BirthDate, TO_CHAR(BirthDate,'YYMM>DD') Formatted
  from BIRTHDAY
 where FirstName = 'VICTORIA';


BIRTHDATE FORMATTED
--------- ------------------------------
20-MAY-49 4905>20
```

In addition to standard punctuation, ORACLE also allows you to insert text into the **format**. This is done by enclosing the desired text in *double* quotation marks:

```
select BirthDate, TO_CHAR(BirthDate,"Month, DDth    "in, um,"
YyyY')        Formatted
  from BIRTHDAY ;

BIRTHDATE FORMATTED
--------- -----------------------------
12-MAY-46 May       , 12TH   in, um, 1946
23-AUG-37 August    , 23RD   in, um, 1937
02-FEB-47 February  , 02ND   in, um, 1947
20-MAY-49 May       , 20TH   in, um, 1949
11-NOV-42 November  , 11TH   in, um, 1942
```

Several consequences of the **format** are worth observing here. The full word **Month** told ORACLE to use the full name of the month in the display. Because it was typed with the first letter in uppercase and the remainder in lowercase, each month in the result was formatted exactly the same way. The options for month are as follows:

- Month produces August
- month produces august
- Mon produces Aug
- mon produces aug

The day of the month is produced by the DD in the **format**. A suffix of **th** on the DD tells ORACLE to use *ordinal* suffixes such as "TH", "RD", and "ND" with the number. In this instance, the suffixes are also case sensitive, but their case is set by the DD, not the th:

- DDth or DDTH produces 11TH
- Ddth or DdTH produces 11Th
- ddth or ddTH produces 11th

This same approach holds true for all numbers in the **format**, including century, year, quarter, month, week, day of the month (DD), Julian day, hours, minutes, and seconds.

The words between double quotation marks are simply inserted where they are found. Spaces between any of these format requests are reproduced in the result (look at the three spaces before the word "in"). YyyY is included simply to show that case is irrelevant unless a suffix such as Th is being used (ORACLE would regard yyyy, Yyyy, yyyY, yYYy, and yYYY as equivalent).

For simplicity's sake, consider this format request:

```
select BirthDate, TO_CHAR(BirthDate,'Month, ddth, YyyY')
          Formatted
   from BIRTHDAY;


BIRTHDATE FORMATTED
--------- ------------------------------
12-MAY-46 May       , 12th, 1946
23-AUG-37 August    , 23rd, 1937
02-FEB-47 February  , 02nd, 1947
20-MAY-49 May       , 20th, 1949
11-NOV-42 November  , 11th, 1942
```

This is a reasonably normal format. The days are all aligned, which makes comparing the rows easy. This is the default alignment, and ORACLE accomplishes it by padding the month names on the right with spaces up to a width of nine spaces. There will be circumstances when it is more important for a date to be formatted normally, at the top of a letter for instance. The spaces between the month and the comma would look odd. To eliminate the spaces, fm is used as a prefix for the words "month" or "day":

- Month, ddth produces August   , 20th
- fmMonth, ddth produces August, 20th
- Day, ddth produces Monday   , 20th
- fmDay, ddth produces Monday, 20th

This is illustrated in the following:

```
select BirthDate, TO_CHAR(BirthDate,'fmMonth, ddth, YyyY')
Formatted
   from BIRTHDAY;


BIRTHDATE FORMATTED
--------- ------------------------------
12-MAY-46 May, 12th, 1946
23-AUG-37 August, 23rd, 1937
02-FEB-47 February, 2nd, 1947
```

```
20-MAY-49 May, 20th, 1949
11-NOV-42 November, 11th, 1942
```

By combining all of these format controls and adding hours and minutes, you can produce a birth announcement:

```
select FirstName, Birthdate, TO_CHAR(BirthDate,
'"Baby Girl on" fmMonth ddth, YYYY, "at" HH:MI "in the Morning"')
     Formatted
  from BIRTHDAY
 where FirstName = 'VICTORIA';

FIRSTNAME       BIRTHDATE FORMATTED
--------------- --------- -----------------------------
VICTORIA        20-MAY-49 Baby Girl on May 20th, 1949,
                          at 3:27 in the Morning
```

Suppose after looking at this, you decide you'd rather spell out the date. Do this with the **sp** control:

```
select FirstName, Birthdate, TO_CHAR(BirthDate,
'"Baby Girl on the" Ddsp "of" fmMonth, YYYY, "at" HH:MI')
     Formatted
  from BIRTHDAY
 where FirstName = 'VICTORIA';

FIRSTNAME       BIRTHDATE FORMATTED
--------------- --------- -----------------------------
VICTORIA        20-MAY-49 Baby Girl on the Twenty of
                          May, 1949, at 3:27
```

Well, 20 was spelled out, but it still doesn't look right. Add the **th** suffix to the **sp**:

```
select FirstName, Birthdate, TO_CHAR(BirthDate,
'"Baby Girl on the" Ddspth "of" fmMonth, YYYY, "at" HH:MI')
     Formatted
  from BIRTHDAY
 where FirstName = 'VICTORIA';

FIRSTNAME       BIRTHDATE FORMATTED
--------------- --------- -----------------------------
VICTORIA        20-MAY-49 Baby Girl on the Twentieth of
                          May, 1949, at 3:27
```

But was it 3:27 A.M. or 3:27 P.M.? These could be added inside of double quotation marks, but then the result would always say "A.M." or "P.M.", regardless of the actual time of the day (since double quotation marks enclose a literal). Instead, ORACLE lets you add *either* "A.M." or "P.M." after the time, but not in double quotation marks. ORACLE then interprets this as a request to display whether it is A.M. or P.M. Note how the **select** has this formatting control entered as P.M., but the result shows A.M., because the birth occurred in the morning:

```
select FirstName, Birthdate, TO_CHAR(BirthDate,
'"Baby Girl on the" Ddspth "of" fmMonth, YYYY, "at" HH:MI P.M.')
       Formatted    from BIRTHDAY
 where FirstName = 'VICTORIA';


FIRSTNAME         BIRTHDATE FORMATTED
---------------   --------- ------------------------------
VICTORIA          20-MAY-49 Baby Girl on the Twentieth of
                            May, 1949, at 3:27 A.M.
```

The RR format lets you use the last two digits of the year in the usual way, where "95" means 1995 and "06" means "2006". Although this sounds useful, in fact you may be referring to "1906"—and who's to know which is which? Avoid this format and use four-digit dates whenever possible.

Consult the boxed section "Date Formats" earlier in the chapter for a list of all of the possible date options. How would you construct a date format for the 769th Year of the Reign of Louis IX? Use date arithmetic to alter the year from A.D. to A.L. (Louis' reign began in 1226, so subtract 1226 years from the current year) and then simply format the result, using **TO_CHAR**.

The Most Common TO_CHAR Error

Always check the date formats when using the **TO_CHAR** function. The most common error is to interchange the 'MM' (Month) format with the 'MI' (Minutes) format when formatting the time portion of a date.

For example, to view the current time, use the **TO_CHAR** function to query the time portion of SysDate:

```
select TO_CHAR(SysDate,'HH:MI:SS') Now
from DUAL;


Now
--------
10:01:30
```

This example is correct, since it uses 'MI' to show the minutes. However, users often select 'MM' instead—partly because they are also selecting two other pairs of double letters, 'HH' and 'SS'. Selecting 'MM' will return the Month, not the Minutes:

```
select TO_CHAR(SysDate,'HH:MM:SS') NowWrong
from DUAL;

NowWrong
--------
10:04:30
```

This time is incorrect, since the Month was selected in the Minutes place. Since Oracle is so flexible and has so many different supported date formats, it does not prevent you from making this error.

NEW_TIME—Switching Time Zones

The **NEW_TIME** function tells you the time and date of a date column or literal date in other time zones. Currently, this function works only for the zones between Greenwich, England, and Hawaii.

This is the format for **NEW_TIME**:

```
NEW_TIME(date,'this','other')
```

date is the date (and time) in *this* time zone. *this* will be replaced by a three-letter abbreviation for the current time zone. *other* will be replaced by a three-letter abbreviation of the other time zone for which you'd like to know the time and date. The time zone options are given in the boxed section "Date Functions" earlier in this chapter. To compare just the date, without showing the time, of Victoria's birth between Eastern standard time and Hawaiian standard time, use this:

```
select Birthdate, NEW_TIME(Birthdate,'EST','HST')
  from BIRTHDAY
 where FirstName = 'VICTORIA';

BIRTHDATE NEW_TIME(
--------- ---------
20-MAY-49 19-MAY-49
```

But how could Victoria have been born on two different days? Since every date stored in ORACLE also contains a time, it is simple enough using **TO_CHAR** and

NEW_TIME to discover both the date and the time differences between the two zones. This will answer the question:

```
select TO_CHAR(Birthdate,'fmMonth Ddth, YYYY "at" HH:MI AM') Birth,
       TO_CHAR(NEW_TIME(Birthdate,'EST','HST'),
       'fmMonth ddth, YYYY "at" HH:MI AM') Birth
  from BIRTHDAY
 where FirstName = 'VICTORIA';


BIRTH                               BIRTH
-----------------------------       -----------------------------
May 20th, 1949 at 3:27 AM           May 19th, 1949 at 10:27 PM
```

TO_DATE Calculations

TO_DATE follows the same formatting conventions as **TO_CHAR**, with some restrictions. The purpose of **TO_DATE** is to turn a literal string, such as MAY 20, 1949, into an ORACLE date format. This then allows the date to be used in date calculations.

This is the format for **TO_DATE**:

```
TO_DATE(string[,'format'])
```

To put the string 22-FEB-95 into ORACLE date format, use this:

```
select TO_DATE('22-FEB-95','DD-MON-YY') from DUAL;

TO_DATE('
---------
22-FEB-95
```

Note, however, that the 22-FEB-95 format is already in the default format in which ORACLE displays and accepts dates. When a literal *string* has a date in this format, the *format* in the **TO_DATE** can be left out, with exactly the same result:

```
select TO_DATE('22-FEB-95') from DUAL;

TO_DATE('
---------
22-FEB-95
```

If the string is in a familiar format, but not the default ORACLE format of DD-MON-YY, **TO_DATE** fails:

```
select TO_DATE('02/22/95') from DUAL;

ERROR: ORA-1843:  not a valid month
```

When the format matches the literal string, the string is successfully converted to a date and is then displayed in default date format:

```
select TO_DATE('02/22/95','MM/DD/YY') from DUAL;

TO_DATE('
---------
22-FEB-95
```

Suppose you needed to know the day of the week of February 22. The **TO_CHAR** function will not work, even with the literal string in the proper format, because **TO_CHAR** requires a date (see its format at the very beginning of the "TO_DATE and TO_CHAR Formatting" section):

```
select TO_CHAR('22-FEB-95','Day') from DUAL
                   *
ERROR at line 1: ORA-1481:  invalid TO_CHAR format string
```

The message is somewhat misleading, but the point is that the query fails. It will work if you first convert the string to a date. Do this by combining the two functions **TO_CHAR** and **TO_DATE**:

```
select TO_CHAR( TO_DATE('22-FEB-95'), 'Day') from DUAL;

TO_CHAR(TO_DATE('22-FEB-95'),'DAY')
-----------------------------------
Wednesday
```

TO_DATE can also accept numbers, without single quotation marks, instead of strings, as long as they are formatted consistently. Here is an example:

```
select TO_DATE(11051946,'MM DD YYYY') from DUAL;

TO_DATE(1
---------
05-NOV-46
```

The punctuation in the **format** is ignored, but the number must follow the order of the format controls. The number itself must not have punctuation.

How complex can the format control be in **TO_DATE**? Suppose you simply reversed the **TO_CHAR select** statement shown earlier, put its result into the **string** portion of **TO_DATE**, and kept its format the same as **TO_CHAR**.

```
select TO_DATE('Baby Girl on the Twentieth of May, 1949, at 3:27 A.M.',
'"Baby Girl on the" Ddspth "of" fmMonth, YYYY, "at" HH:MI P.M.')
      Formatted
  from BIRTHDAY
 where FirstName = 'VICTORIA';

ERROR: ORA-1858:  a letter was found in a date where a number was expected
```

This clearly failed. As it turns out, only a limited number of the **format** controls can be used.

These are the restrictions on **format** that govern **TO_DATE**:

- No literal strings are allowed, such as "Baby Girl on the".
- Days cannot be spelled out. They must be numbers.
- Punctuation is permitted.
- fm is not necessary. If used, it is ignored.
- If Month is used, the month in the string must be spelled out. If Mon is used, the month must be a three-letter abbreviation. Upper- and lowercase are ignored.

This **select** does work:

```
select TO_DATE('August, 20, 1949, 3:27 A.M. ', 'fmMonth, Dd,
YYYY, HH:MI P.M. ')
      Formatted
  from BIRTHDAY
where FirstName = 'VICTORIA';

FORMATTED
---------
20-AUG-49
```

Dates in where Clauses

Early in this chapter you saw an example of date arithmetic used in a **where** clause:

```
select Holiday, ActualDate, CelebratedDate
  from Holiday
 where CelebratedDate - ActualDate != 0;


HOLIDAY                     ACTUALDAT CELEBRATE
------------------------    --------- ---------
MARTIN LUTHER KING, JR.     15-JAN-95 16-JAN-95
LINCOLNS BIRTHDAY           12-FEB-95 20-FEB-95
WASHINGTONS BIRTHDAY        22-FEB-95 20-FEB-95
MEMORIAL DAY                30-MAY-95 29-MAY-95
COLUMBUS DAY                08-OCT-95 09-OCT-95
```

Dates can be used with other ORACLE logical operators as well, with some warnings and restrictions. The **BETWEEN** operator will do date arithmetic if the column preceding it is a date, even if the test dates are literal strings:

```
select Holiday, CelebratedDate
  from HOLIDAY
 where CelebratedDate BETWEEN '01-JAN-95' and '22-FEB-95';


HOLIDAY                     CELEBRATE
------------------------    ---------
NEW YEAR DAY                01-JAN-95
MARTIN LUTHER KING, JR.     16-JAN-95
LINCOLNS BIRTHDAY           20-FEB-95
WASHINGTONS BIRTHDAY        20-FEB-95
FAST DAY, NEW HAMPSHIRE     22-FEB-95
```

The logical operator **IN** works as well with literal strings:

```
select Holiday, CelebratedDate
  from HOLIDAY
 where CelebratedDate IN ('01-JAN-95', '22-FEB-95');


HOLIDAY                     CELEBRATE
------------------------    ---------
NEW YEAR DAY                01-JAN-95
FAST DAY, NEW HAMPSHIRE     22-FEB-95
```

LEAST and **GREATEST** do not work, because they assume the literal strings are *strings,* not *dates.*

```
select Holiday, CelebratedDate
  from HOLIDAY
 where CelebratedDate = LEAST('16-JAN-95', '04-SEP-95');


HOLIDAY                   CELEBRATE
------------------------  ---------
LABOR DAY                 04-SEP-95
```

In order for **LEAST** and **GREATEST** to work properly, the **TO_DATE** function must be applied to the literal strings. All other logical operators will work properly with dates given as literal strings in the default ORACLE date format 'DD-MON-YY'.

CHAPTER 8

Conversion and Transformation Functions

This chapter looks at functions that convert, or transform, one data type into another.

Four data types and their associated functions have been covered thus far: CHAR (fixed length character strings), VARCHAR2 (variable length character strings), NUMBERs, and DATEs.

■ CHAR and VARCHAR2 include any letter of the alphabet, any number, and any of the symbols on the keyboard. Character literals must be enclosed in single quotation marks: 'Sault Ste. Marie!'

■ NUMBER includes just the digits 0 through 9, a decimal point, and a minus sign, if necessary. NUMBER literals are not enclosed in quotation marks: –246.320

■ DATE is a special type that includes information about the date, time, and time zone. It has a default format of DD-MON-YY, but can be displayed in many ways using the **TO_CHAR** function as you saw in Chapter 7. DATE literals must be enclosed in single quotation marks: '26-AUG-81'

Each of these data types has a group of functions designed especially to manipulate data of its own type, as shown in Table 8-1. String functions are used with character columns or literals, arithmetic functions are used with NUMBER columns or literals, and date functions are used with DATE columns or literals. Most group and miscellaneous functions work with any of these types. Some of these functions change the object they affect (whether CHAR, VARCHAR2, NUMBER, or DATE), while others report information about the object.

STRING FUNCTIONS FOR CHAR & VARCHAR2 DATA TYPES	ARITHMETIC FUNCTIONS FOR NUMBER DATA TYPE	DATA FUNCTIONS FOR DATE DATA TYPE
¦¦ (concatenation)	+ (addition)	ADD_MONTHS
ASCII	–(subtraction)	LAST_DAY
CHR	* (multiplication)	MONTHS_BETWEEN
CONCAT	/(division)	NEW_TIME
CONVERT	ABS	NEXT_DAY
INITCAP	CEIL	ROUND
INSTR	COS	s
INSTRB	COSH	
LENGTH	EXP	
LENGTHB	FLOOR	
LOWER	LN	
LPAD	LOG	
LTRIM		

TABLE 8-1. *Functions by data type*

STRING FUNCTIONS FOR CHAR & VARCHAR2 DATA TYPES	ARITHMETIC FUNCTIONS FOR NUMBER DATA TYPE	DATA FUNCTIONS FOR DATE DATA TYPE
NLS_INITCAP	MOD	
NLS_LOWER	POWER	
NLS_UPPER	ROUND	
NLSSORT	SIGN	
REPLACE	SIN	
RPAD	SINH	
RTRIM	SQRT	
SOUNDEX	TAN	
SUBSTR	TANH	
SUBSTRB	TRUNC	
TRANSLATE		
UID		
UPPER		
USER		
USERENV		

GROUP FUNCTIONS	CONVERSION FUNCTIONS	MISCELLANEOUS FUNCTIONS
AVG	CHARTOROWID	DECODE
COUNT	CONVERT	DUMP
GLB	HEXTORAW	GREATEST
LUB	RAWTOHEX	GREATEST_LB
MAX	ROWIDTOCHAR	LEAST
MIN	TO_CHAR	LEAST_UB
STDDEV	TO_DATE	NVL
SUM	TO_MULTI_BYTE	VSIZE
VARIANCE	TO_NUMBER	
	TO_SINGLE_BYTE	

TABLE 8-1. *Functions by data type* (continued)

In one sense, most of the functions studied so far have been *transformation functions*, meaning they changed their objects. However, the functions covered in this chapter change their objects in an unusual way: they transform them from one data type into another, or they make a profound transformation of the data in them. Table 8-2 describes these functions.

FUNCTION NAME	DEFINITION
CHARTOROWID	**CHAR**acter **TO ROW ID**entifier. Changes a character string to act like an internal ORACLE row identifier, or RowID.
CONVERT	**CONVERT**s a character string from one national language character set to another.
DECODE	**DECODE**s a CHAR, VARCHAR2, or a NUMBER into any of several different character strings or NUMBERs, based on value. This is a very powerful IF, THEN, ELSE function. Chapter 15 is devoted to **DECODE**.
HEXTORAW	**HEX**adecimal **TO RAW**. Changes a character string of hex numbers into binary.
RAWTOHEX	**RAW TO HEX**adecimal. Changes a string of binary numbers to a character string of hex numbers.
ROWIDTOCHAR	**ROW ID**entifier **TO CHAR**acter. Changes an internal ORACLE row identifier, or RowID, to act like a character string.
TO_CHAR	**TO CHAR**acter. Converts a NUMBER or DATE so that it acts like a character string.
TO_DATE	**TO DATE**. Converts a NUMBER, CHAR, or VARCHAR2 to act like a DATE (a special ORACLE data type).
TO_MULTI_BYTE	**TO MULTI_BYTE**. Converts the single-byte characters in a character string to multi-byte.
TO_NUMBER	**TO NUMBER**. Converts a CHAR or VARCHAR2 to act like a number.
TO_SINGLE_BYTE	**TO SINGLE BYTE**. Converts the multi-byte characters in a CHAR or VARCHAR2 to single bytes.
TRANSLATE	**TRANSLATE**s characters in a string into different characters.

TABLE 8-2. *Conversion and transformation functions*

The use of two of these functions, **TO_CHAR** and **TO_DATE**, has already been demonstrated in Chapter 7. **TO_CHAR** transforms a date into a character string (in the format you request). **TO_CHAR** can convert not just DATEs but also NUMBERs into character strings. **TO_DATE** is also a transformation function. It takes either a character string or a number, and converts it into the DATE data type. It then can be used in date arithmetic in order to calculate **MONTHS_BETWEEN**, **NEXT_DAY**, and other date functions.

Elementary Conversion Functions

There are three elementary ORACLE functions whose purpose is to convert one data type into another:

- **TO_CHAR** transforms a DATE or NUMBER into a character string
- **TO_DATE** transforms a NUMBER, CHAR, or VARCHAR2 into a DATE
- **TO_NUMBER** transforms a CHAR or VARCHAR2 into a NUMBER

Why are these transformations important? **TO_DATE** is obviously necessary to accomplish date arithmetic. **TO_CHAR** allows you to manipulate a number as if it were a string, using string functions. **TO_NUMBER** allows you to use a string that happened to contain only numbers as if it were a number: using it, you can add, subtract, multiply, divide, and so on.

This means that if you stored a nine-digit zip code as a number, you could transform it into a string, and then use **SUBSTR** and concatenation to add a dash (such as when printing addresses on envelopes):

```
select SUBSTR(TO_CHAR(948033515),1,5)||'-'||
       SUBSTR(TO_CHAR(948033515),6)  Zip
  from DUAL;


ZIP
----------------------------------------
94803-3515
```

Here, the **TO_CHAR** function transforms the pure number 948033515 (notice that it has no single quotation marks around it, as a CHAR or VARCHAR2 string must) into a character string. **SUBSTR** then clips out positions 1 to 5 of this "string," producing 94803. A dash is concatenated on the right end of this string, and then another **TO_CHAR** creates another "string," which another **SUBSTR** clips out from position 6 to the end. The second string, 3515, is concatenated after the dash. The whole rebuilt string is relabeled "Zip," and ORACLE displays it: 94803-3515. This

TO_CHAR function lets you use string manipulation functions on numbers (and dates), as if they were actually strings. Handy? Yes. But watch this:

```
select SUBSTR(948033515,1,5)||'-'||
       SUBSTR(948033515,6) Zip
  from DUAL;

ZIP
----------------------------------------
94803-3515
```

But this shouldn't work! 948033515 is a NUMBER, not a character string. Yet the string function **SUBSTR** clearly worked anyway. Would it work with an actual NUMBER database column? Here's a table with Zip as a NUMBER:

```
describe ADDRESS

Name                             Null?    Type
-------------------------------- -------- ----
LASTNAME                                  VARCHAR2(25)
FIRSTNAME                                 VARCHAR2(25)
STREET                                    VARCHAR2(50)
CITY                                      VARCHAR2(25)
STATE                                     CHAR(2)
ZIP                                       NUMBER
PHONE                                     VARCHAR2(12)
EXT                                       VARCHAR2(5)
```

Select just the zip code for all the Marys in the table:

```
select SUBSTR(Zip,1,5)||'-'||
       SUBSTR(Zip,6)  Zip
  from ADDRESS
 where FirstName = 'MARY';

ZIP
----------------------------------------
94941-4302
60126-2460
```

SUBSTR works here just as well as it does with strings, even though Zip is a NUMBER column from the ADDRESS table. Will other string functions also work?

```
select Zip, RTRIM(Zip,20)
  from ADDRESS
 where FirstName = 'MARY';

       ZIP RTRIM(ZIP,20)
---------- --------------------------------------
 949414302 9494143
 601262460 60126246
```

The column on the left demonstrates that Zip is a NUMBER; it is even right-justified, as numbers are by default. But the **RTRIM** column is left-justified, just as strings are, and it has removed zeros and twos from the right side of the zip codes. There is something else peculiar here. Recall from Chapter 5 the format for **RTRIM**, shown here:

RTRIM(*string* [,'*set*'])

The *set* to be removed from the string is enclosed within single quotation marks, yet in this example:

RTRIM(Zip,20)

there are no quotation marks. So what is going on?

Automatic Conversion of Data Types

ORACLE is automatically converting these numbers, both the Zip and the 20, into strings, almost as if they both had **TO_CHAR** functions in front of them. In fact, with a few clear exceptions, ORACLE will automatically transform any data type into any other data type, based on the function that is going to affect it. If it's a string function, ORACLE will convert a NUMBER or a DATE instantly into a string, and the string function will work. If it's a DATE function, and the column or literal is a string in the format DD-MON-YY, ORACLE will convert it into a DATE. If the function is arithmetic, and the column or literal is a character string, ORACLE will convert it into a NUMBER, and do the calculation.

Will this always work? No. To have ORACLE automatically convert one data type into another, the first data type must already "look" like the data type it is being converted to. The basic guidelines are given in the special boxed section, "Guidelines for Automatic Conversion of Data Types." These may well be confusing, so a few examples should help to clarify this. The following are the effects of several randomly chosen string functions on NUMBERs and DATEs:

```
select INITCAP(LOWER(SysDate)) from DUAL;

INITCAP(LOWER(SYSDATE))
-----------------------
01-Apr-95
```

Note that the **INITCAP** function put the first letter of "apr" into uppercase even though "apr" was buried in the middle of the string "01-apr-95." This is a feature of **INITCAP** that is not confined to dates, although it is illustrated here for the first time. It works because the following works:

```
select INITCAP('this-is_a.test,of:punctuation;for+initcap')
   from DUAL;

INITCAP('THIS-IS_A.TEST,OF:PUNCTUATION;FO
-----------------------------------------
This-Is_A.Test,Of:Punctuation;For+Initcap
```

INITCAP puts the first letter of every word into uppercase. It determines the beginning of a word based on its being preceded by any character other than a letter. You can also cut and paste dates using string functions, just as if they were strings:

```
select SUBSTR(SysDate,4,3) from DUAL;

SUB
---
APR
```

Here a DATE is left padded with nines for a total length of 20:

```
select LPAD(SysDate,20,'9') from DUAL;

LPAD(SYSDATE,20,'9')
--------------------
9999999999901-APR-95
```

Note that you would get the same results if the character to be used for padding, 9, were not in single quotation marks. This is because 9 is a literal NUMBER. If you wished to pad with a character, single quotation marks would be required:

```
select LPAD(SysDate,20,'-') from DUAL;
```

```
LPAD(SYSDATE,20,'-')
--------------------
----------01-APR-95
```

LPAD, or any other string function, also can be used on NUMBERs, whether literal (as shown here) or columns:

```
select LPAD(9,20,0) from DUAL;

LPAD(9,20,0)
--------------------
00000000000000000009
```

These examples show how string functions treat both NUMBERs and DATEs as if they are character strings. The result of the function (what you see displayed) is

Guidelines for Automatic Conversion of Data Types

These guidelines describe the automatic conversion of data from one type to another, based on the function that will use the data.

- Any NUMBER or DATE can be converted into a character string. As a consequence, *any* string function can be used on a NUMBER or DATE column. Literal NUMBERs do not have to be enclosed in single quotation marks when used in a string function; literal DATEs do.

- A CHAR or VARCHAR2 will be converted to a NUMBER if it contains only numbers, a decimal point, or a minus sign on the left. There must be no embedded spaces or other characters.

- A CHAR or VARCHAR2 will be converted to a DATE only if it is in the format DD-MON-YY, such as 07-AUG-95. This is true for all functions except **GREATEST** and **LEAST**, which will treat it as a string, and true for **BETWEEN** only if the column to the left after the word **BETWEEN** is a DATE. Otherwise **TO_DATE** must be used, with a proper format.

- A DATE will not be converted to a NUMBER.

- A NUMBER will not be converted to a DATE.

itself a character string. In this next example, a string (note the single quotation marks) is treated as a NUMBER by the number function **FLOOR**:

```
select FLOOR('-323.78') from DUAL;

FLOOR('-323.78')
----------------
            -324
```

Here, two literal character strings are converted to DATEs for the DATE function **MONTHS_BETWEEN**. This works only because the literal strings are in the default date format DD-MON-YY:

```
select MONTHS_BETWEEN('16-MAY-95','01-APR-95') from DUAL;

MONTHS_BETWEEN('16-MAY-95','01-APR-95')
---------------------------------------
                             1.48387097
```

One of the guidelines in this chapter's special boxed section says that a DATE will not be converted to a NUMBER. Yet, here is an example of addition and subtraction with a DATE. Does this violate the guideline?

```
select SysDate, SysDate + 1, SysDate - 1 from DUAL;

SYSDATE    SYSDATE+1 SYSDATE-1
--------- --------- ---------
01-APR-95 02-APR-95 31-MAR-95
```

It does not, because the addition and subtraction were date arithmetic, not regular arithmetic. Date arithmetic (covered in Chapter 7) works only with addition and subtraction, and only with DATEs. Most functions will automatically convert a character string in default date format into a DATE. An exception is this attempt at date addition with a literal:

```
select '01-APR-95' + 1 from DUAL;

ERROR: ORA-1722:  invalid number
```

Date arithmetic, even with actual DATE data types, works only with addition and subtraction. Any other arithmetic function attempted with a date will fail. Dates are not converted to numbers, as this attempt to divide a date by two illustrates:

```
select SysDate / 2 from DUAL;
      *
ERROR at line 1: ORA-0932:   inconsistent data types
```

Finally, a NUMBER will never be automatically converted to a DATE, because a pure number cannot be in the default format for a DATE, which is DD-MON-YY:

```
select NEXT_DAY(040195,'FRIDAY') from DUAL;
               *
ERROR at line 1: ORA-0932:   inconsistent data types
```

To use a NUMBER in a date function, **TO_DATE** is required.

A Warning About Automatic Conversion

There are arguments on either side of the issue on whether it is a good practice to allow SQL to do automatic conversion of data types. On the one hand, it considerably simplifies and reduces the functions necessary to make a **select** statement work. On the other hand, if your assumption about what will be in the column is wrong (for example, you assume a particular character column will always have a number in it, so you can use it in a calculation), then at some point a report will stop working, ORACLE will produce an error, and time will have to be spent trying to find the problem. Further, another person reading your **select** statement may be confused by what appear to be inappropriate functions at work on characters or numbers.

A simple rule of thumb might be that it is best to use functions where the risk is low, such as string manipulation functions on numbers, rather than arithmetic functions on strings. For your benefit and that of others using your work always put a note near the **select** statement signaling the use of automatic type conversion.

Specialized Conversion Functions

There are several specialized conversion functions in ORACLE. Their names and formats are as follows:

CHARTOROWID(*string*)	Converts character string to a row id
ROWIDTOCHAR(*rowid*)	Converts a row id to a character string
HEXTORAW(*hexnumber*)	Converts a hexadecimal number to a binary
RAWTOHEX(*raw*)	Converts a binary number to hexadecimal
TO_MULTI_BYTE	Converts single-byte characters to multi-byte characters
TO_SINGLE_BYTE	Converts multi-byte characters to single-byte characters

If you expect to use SQLPLUS and ORACLE simply to produce reports, you probably won't ever need any of these functions. If, on the other hand, you will use SQLPLUS to **update** the database, or if you expect to build ORACLE applications, or if you are using National Language Support, this information will eventually prove valuable. Chapter 13 shows the use of RowID. The other functions can be found, by name, in the Alphabetical Reference in Part Five.

■ Transformation Functions

Although in one sense any function that changes its object could be called a transformation function, there are two unusual functions that you can use in many interesting ways to control your output based on your input instead of simply transforming it. These are **TRANSLATE** and **DECODE**.

TRANSLATE

TRANSLATE is a simple function that does an orderly character-by-character substitution in a string.

This is the format for **TRANSLATE**:

```
TRANSLATE(string,if,then)
```

TRANSLATE looks at each character in *string*, and then checks *if* to see if that character is there. If it is, it notes the position in *if* where it found the character, and then looks at the same position in *then*. **TRANSLATE** substitutes whichever character it finds there for the character in *string*. Normally the function is written on a single line, like this:

```
select TRANSLATE(7671234,234567890,'BCDEFGHIJ')
   from DUAL;

TRANSLATE(7671234,234567890,'BCDEFGHIJ
------------------------------------
GFG1BCD
```

But it might be easier to understand if simply broken onto two lines (SQLPLUS doesn't care, of course):

```
select TRANSLATE(7671234,234567890,
                        'BCDEFGHIJ')
   from DUAL;
```

```
TRANSLATE(7671234,234567890,'BCDEFGHIJ
---------------------------------------
GFG1BCD
```

When **TRANSLATE** sees a 7 in the *string*, it looks for a 7 in the *if*, and translates it to the character in the same position in the *then* (an uppercase "G"). If the character is not in the *if*, it is not translated (observe what it did with the "1").

TRANSLATE is technically a string function but, as you can see, it will do automatic data conversion and work with a mix of strings and numbers. Following is an example of a very simple code cipher, where every letter in the alphabet is shifted one position. Many years ago spies used such character-substitution methods to encode messages before sending them. The recipient simply reversed the process. Do you remember the smooth-talking computer, HAL, in the movie *2001: A Space Odyssey?* If you **TRANSLATE** HAL's name with a one-character shift in the alphabet you get this:

```
select TRANSLATE('HAL', 'ABCDEFGHIJKLMNOPQRSTUVWXYZ',
                        'BCDEFGHIJKLMNOPQRSTUVWXYZA')    Who
  from DUAL;


WHO
----
IBM
```

DECODE

If **TRANSLATE** is a character-by-character substitution, **DECODE** can be considered a value-by-value substitution. For every value it sees in a field, **DECODE** checks for a match in a series of *if/then* tests. **DECODE** is an incredibly powerful function, with a broad range of areas where it can be useful. Chapter 15 is devoted entirely to advanced use of **DECODE**.

This is the format for **DECODE**:

```
DECODE(value,if1,then1,if2,then2,if3,then3,. . . ,else)
```

Only three *if/then* combinations are illustrated here, but there is no practical limit. To see how this function works, recall the NEWSPAPER table you saw earlier:

```
select * from NEWSPAPER;
```

```
FEATURE          S . PAGE
---------------  -  -----
National News    A     1
Sports           D     1
Editorials       A    12
Business         E     1
Weather          C     2
Television       B     7
Births           F     7
Classified       F     8
Modern Life      B     1
Comics           C     4
Movies           B     4
Bridge           B     2
Obituaries       F     6
Doctor Is In     F     6
```

Suppose you wished to change the name of a couple of the regular features.
DECODE will check each Feature *value*, row by row. *if* the *value* it finds is 'Sports',
then it will substitute 'Games People Play'; *if* it finds 'Movies', *then* it will substitute
'Entertainment'; if it finds anything *else* in the value, then it will use the value of **Feature**.

```
select DECODE(Feature, 'Sports','Games People Play',
                       'Movies','Entertainment',Feature),
       Section, Page
  from NEWSPAPER;
```

```
DECODE(FEATURE,'S S  PAGE
---------------- - -----
National News    A    1
Games People Play D   1    ◄─────────────── Changed from 'Sports'
Editorials       A   12
Business         E    1
Weather          C    2
Television       B    7
Births           F    7
Classified       F    8
Modern Life      B    1
Comics           C    4
Entertainment    B    4    ◄─────────────── Changed from 'Movies'
Bridge           B    2
Obituaries       F    6
Doctor Is In     F    6
```

In the next example, the page number is decoded. *if* the page number is one, *then* the words 'Front Page' are substituted. If the page number is anything *else*, the words 'Turn to' are concatenated with the page number. This illustrates that *else* can be a function, a literal, or another column.

```
select Feature, Section,
       DECODE(Page,'1','Front Page','Turn to '||Page)
  from NEWSPAPER;


FEATURE          S DECODE(PAGE,'1','FRONTPAGE','TURNTO'PAGE
---------------- - -------------------------------------------
National News    A Front Page
Sports           D Front Page
Editorials       A Turn to 12
Business         E Front Page
Weather          C Turn to 2
Television       B Turn to 7
Births           F Turn to 7
Classified       F Turn to 8
Modern Life      B Front Page
Comics           C Turn to 4
Movies           B Turn to 4
Bridge           B Turn to 2
Obituaries       F Turn to 6
Doctor Is In     F Turn to 6
```

There are some restrictions on data types in the list of *if*s and *then*s, which will be covered in Chapter 15.

Review

Most functions in ORACLE, although they are intended for a specific data type, such as CHAR, VARCHAR2, NUMBER, and DATE, will actually work with other data types as well. They do this by performing an automatic type conversion. With a few logical exceptions, and the hope of future compatibility, they will do this as long as the data to be converted "looks" like the data type required by the function.

Character functions will convert any NUMBER or DATE. NUMBER functions will convert a CHAR or VARCHAR2 if it contains only the digits 0 through 9, a decimal point, or a minus sign on the left. NUMBER functions will not convert DATEs. DATE functions will convert character strings if they are in the format DD-MON-YY. They will not convert NUMBERs.

Two functions, **TRANSLATE** and **DECODE**, will fundamentally change the data they affect. **TRANSLATE** will do a character substitution according to any pattern you specify, and **DECODE** will do a value substitution, again for any pattern you specify.

CHAPTER 9

Grouping Things Together

U p to this point you've seen how SQL can **select** rows of information from database tables, how the **where** clause can limit the number of rows being returned to only those that meet certain rules that you define, and how the rows returned can be sorted in ascending or descending sequence using **order by**. You've also seen how the values in columns can be modified by character, NUMBER, and DATE data types, and how group functions can tell you something about the whole set of rows.

Beyond the group functions you've seen, there are also two group clauses: **having** and **group by**. These are parallel to the **where** and **order by** clauses, except that they act on groups, not on individual rows. These clauses can provide very powerful insights into your data.

In order to make the display of information consistent and readable in this chapter, the following column definitions have been given to SQLPLUS:

```
column Amount format 999.90
column Average format 999.90
column Item format a16
column Month format a9
column Percent format 99.90
column Person format a25
column Total format 999.90
column YearTotal format 999.90
```

Figure 9-1 is a listing of the ActionDate, Item, Person, and Amount paid to each worker by G. B. Talbot during 1901. The SQL statement that created Figure 9-1 is as follows:

```
select ActionDate, Item, Person, Amount
  from LEDGER
 where Action = 'PAID'
 order by ActionDate;
```

```
ACTIONDAT    ITEM               PERSON                      AMOUNT
---------    ----------------   -------------------------   ------
04-JAN-01    WORK               GERHARDT KENTGEN              1.00
12-JAN-01    WORK               GEORGE OSCAR                 1.00
19-JAN-01    WORK               GERHARDT KENTGEN             1.00
30-JAN-01    WORK               ELBERT TALBOT                 .50
04-FEB-01    WORK               ELBERT TALBOT                 .50
28-FEB-01    WORK               ELBERT TALBOT                1.00
05-MAR-01    WORK               DICK JONES                   1.00
14-MAR-01    DIGGING OF GRAVE   JED HOPKINS                  3.00
20-MAR-01    WORK               DICK JONES                   1.00
21-MAR-01    WORK               VICTORIA LYNN                1.00
01-APR-01    PLOWING            RICHARD KOCH AND BROTHERS    3.00
16-APR-01    PLOWING            RICHARD KOCH AND BROTHERS    3.00
27-APR-01    PLOWING            RICHARD KOCH AND BROTHERS    3.00
02-MAY-01    WORK               DICK JONES                   1.00
11-MAY-01    WORK               WILFRED LOWELL               1.20
24-MAY-01    WORK               WILFRED LOWELL               1.20
```

FIGURE 9-1.   *Dates and amounts paid by G.B. Talbot during 1901*

```
ACTIONDAT    ITEM              PERSON                         AMOUNT
---------    ----------------  -----------------------------  ------
03-JUN-01    WORK              ELBERT TALBOT                    1.00
13-JUN-01    WORK              PETER LAWSON                     1.00
18-JUN-01    THRESHING         WILLIAM SWING                     .50
26-JUN-01    PAINTING          KAY AND PALMER WALBOM              .25
14-JUL-01    WORK              WILFRED LOWELL                   1.20
15-JUL-01    WORK              KAY AND PALMER WALBOM            2.25
28-JUL-01    SAWING            DICK JONES                        .75
06-AUG-01    PLOWING           VICTORIA LYNN                    1.80
06-AUG-01    PLOWING           ANDREW DYE                       4.00
10-AUG-01    WORK              HELEN BRANDT                     1.00
11-AUG-01    WORK              HELEN BRANDT                     2.00
18-AUG-01    WEEDING           ELBERT TALBOT                     .90
22-AUG-01    SAWING            PETER LAWSON                     1.00
23-AUG-01    SAWING            PETER LAWSON                     1.00
09-SEP-01    WORK              ADAH TALBOT                      1.00
11-SEP-01    WORK              ROLAND BRANDT                     .75
23-SEP-01    DISCUS            RICHARD KOCH AND BROTHERS        1.50
29-SEP-01    WORK              GERHARDT KENTGEN                 1.00
07-OCT-01    PLOWING           RICHARD KOCH AND BROTHERS        1.50
07-OCT-01    WORK              JED HOPKINS                      1.00
09-OCT-01    WORK              DONALD ROLLO                      .63
22-0CT-01    PLOWING           DICK JONES                       1.80
07-NOV-01    SAWED WOOD        ANDREW DYE                        .50
10-NOV-01    WORK              JOHN PEARSON                      .63
12-NOV-01    WORK              PAT LAVAY                        1.50
13-NOV-01    CUT LOGS          PAT LAVAY                         .25
13-NOV-01    DRAWED LOGS       PAT LAVAY                         .75
12-DEC-01    WORK              BART SARJEANT                    1.00
13-DEC-01    SAWED WOOD        PAT LAVAY                         .50
17-DEC-01    SAWING            DICK JONES                        .75

46 rows selected
```

FIGURE 9-1. *Dates and amounts paid by G.B. Talbot during 1901* (continued)

A careful inspection of this table will reveal that many of the items are repeated.

The Use of group by and having

If Talbot wanted to get a total of the amount he had paid out, grouped by item, he'd write a query like this one:

```
select Item, SUM(Amount) Total, COUNT(Item)
  from LEDGER  where Action = 'PAID'
 group by Item;

ITEM                 TOTAL COUNT(ITEM)
---------------- ------- -----------
CUT LOGS               .25           1
DIGGING OF GRAVE      3.00           1
DISCUS               1.50           1
DRAWED LOGS           .75           1
PAINTING             1.75           1
PLOWING             18.10           7
SAWED WOOD           1.00           2
SAWING               3.50           4
THRESHING             .50           1
WEEDING               .90           1
WORK                27.36          26

11 rows selected.
```

Notice the mix of a column name, Item, and two group functions, **SUM** and **COUNT**, in the **select** clause. This mix is possible only because Item is referenced in the **group by** clause. Were it not there, the opaque message first encountered in Chapter 6 would have resulted in this:

```
select Item, SUM(Amount) Total, COUNT(Item)
       *
ERROR at line 1: ORA-0937:  not a single group set function
```

This is because the group functions, such as **SUM** and **COUNT**, are designed to tell you something about a group of rows, not the individual rows of the table. The error is avoided by the use of Item in the **group by** clause, which forces the **SUM** to sum up all of the rows grouped within each Item. **COUNT** tells how many rows each of the Items actually has within its group.

The **having** clause works very much like a **where** clause, except that its logic is only related to the results of group functions, as opposed to columns or expressions for individual rows, which can still be selected by a **where** clause. Here the rows in the previous example are further restricted to just those where the **SUM** of the Amount, by Item group, is greater than 3 dollars.

```
select Item, SUM(Amount) Total    from LEDGER
 where Action = 'PAID'  group by Item
having SUM(Amount) > 3;


ITEM                   TOTAL
----------------   -------
PLOWING                18.10
SAWING                  3.50
WORK                   27.36
```

You also could find the items where the average Amount spent per item in the course of the year was greater than the average of all the items. First, let's check to see what the **AVG** of all the items was for the year:

```
select AVG(Amount) Average
   from LEDGER
 where ACTION = 'PAID';


AVERAGE
-------
   1.27
```

Next, incorporate this average as a subquery (similar to those you did with a **where** clause in Chapter 3), to test each group of items against the average:

```
select Item, SUM(Amount) Total, AVG(Amount) Average
   from LEDGER
 where Action = 'PAID'
 group by Item
having AVG(Amount) > (select AVG(Amount)
                        from LEDGER
                       where ACTION = 'PAID');


ITEM                   TOTAL AVERAGE
----------------   ------- -------
DIGGING OF GRAVE        3.00    3.00
DISCUS                  1.50    1.50
PAINTING                1.75    1.75
PLOWING                18.10    2.59
```

Note that the **having** clause tests the average amount by Item (because the items are **group**ed **by** Item) against the average amount for all the Items paid during the year. Also note the differences and similarities between the Total column and the Average column. Grouping the data from the LEDGER table by Item tells you how much money was paid out, by Item, as well as the average amount paid, by Item. Talbot's LEDGER table can also yield similar information by Person:

```
select Person, SUM(Amount) Total
   from LEDGER
 where Action = 'PAID'
 group by Person;


PERSON                          TOTAL
-------------------------       -------
ADAH TALBOT                      1.00
ANDREW DYE                       4.50
BART SARJEANT                    1.00
DICK JONES                       6.30
DONALD ROLLO                      .63
ELBERT TALBOT                    3.90
GEORGE OSCAR                     1.00
GERHARDT KENTGEN                 3.00
HELEN BRANDT                     3.00
JED HOPKINS                      4.00
JOHN PEARSON                      .63
KAY AND PALMER WALBOM            4.00
PAT LAVAY                        3.00
PETER LAWSON                     3.00
RICHARD KOCH AND BROTHERS       12.00
ROLAND BRANDT                     .75
VICTORIA LYNN                    2.80
WILFRED LOWELL                   3.60
WILLIAM SWING                     .50

19 rows selected.
```

This is a useful summary alphabetized by Person, but what about an alternative order for display? You can't use this:

```
group by SUM(Amount)
```

because then the rows for each person would no longer be collected (grouped) together. Besides, the purpose of **group by** is not to produce a desired sequence, but to collect "like" things together. The order they appear in after **group by** is done is a by-product of how it functions; **group by** is not meant to be used to change the sorting order.

Adding an order by

The solution is the addition of an **order by** clause following the **having** clause. You could add this:

```
order by Person desc
```

which would reverse the order of the list, or you could add this:

```
order by SUM(Amount) desc
```

For example, 19 people worked for Talbot in 1901, doing some 46 tasks over the course of the year (see Figure 9-1). Of those that Talbot paid more than a dollar during 1901, who did Talbot pay the most, and what is the relative rank of the workers by income?

```
select Person, SUM(Amount) Total
  from LEDGER
 where Action = 'PAID'
 group by Person
having SUM(Amount) > 1.00
  order by SUM(Amount) desc;
```

```
PERSON                      TOTAL
------------------------- -------
RICHARD KOCH AND BROTHERS   12.00
DICK JONES                   6.30
ANDREW DYE                   4.50
JED HOPKINS                  4.00
KAY AND PALMER WALBOM        4.00
ELBERT TALBOT                3.90
WILFRED LOWELL               3.60
GERHARDT KENTGEN             3.00
PETER LAWSON                 3.00
PAT LAVAY                    3.00
HELEN BRANDT                 3.00
VICTORIA LYNN                2.80

12 rows selected.
```

An alternative method of telling SQL which column to use for the **order by** is the sequence number of the column. The **order by** clause in the previous query could also have been written like this:

```
order by 2 desc
```

If SQL sees a number in an **order by**, it looks back at the **select**, and counts the columns listed, from left to right. The second column over in the **select** was **SUM**(Amount), so SQL will use it as the column in which to order the results.

NOTE
Starting with ORACLE7.1, the ability to use ordinal column positions in **order by** clauses is being phased out. This change is due to a change in the ANSI SQL standard. ORACLE7.1 and above support the use of column aliases in the **order by** clause, which is more reliable than ordinal positions as a method of specifying order. See **order by** in the Alphabetical Reference.

Order of Execution

The previous query has quite a collection of competing clauses! Here are the rules ORACLE uses to execute each of them, and the order in which execution takes place:

1. It chooses rows based on the **where** clause.

2. It groups those rows together based on the **group by**.

3. It calculates the results of the group functions for each group.

4. It chooses and eliminates groups based on the **having** clause.

5. It orders the groups based on the results of the group functions in the **order by**. The **order by** must use either a group function or a column in the **group by** clause.

Why is the order of execution important? Because it has a direct impact on the perfomance of your queries. In general, the more records that can be eliminated via **where** clauses, the faster the query will execute. This performance benefit is due to the reduction in the number of rows that must be processed during the **group by** operation.

If a query is written to use a **having** clause to eliminate groups, then you should check to see if the **having** condition can be re-written as a **where** clause. In many cases, this re-write won't be possible. It is usually only available when the **having** clause is used to eliminate groups based on the grouping columns.

For example, if you had this query:

```
select Person, SUM(Amount) Total
  from LEDGER
 where Action = 'PAID'
 group by Person
having Person like 'P%'
 order by SUM(Amount) desc;
```

then the order of execution would, in order:

1. Eliminate rows based on

```
where Action = 'PAID'
```

2. Group the remaining rows based on

```
group by Person
```

3. For each Person, calculate the

```
SUM(Amount)
```

4. Eliminate groups based on

```
having Person like 'P%'
```

5. Order the remaining groups.

This query will run faster if the *groups* eliminated in Step 4 can be eliminated as *rows* in Step 1. If they are eliminated at Step 1, then fewer rows will be grouped (Step 2), fewer calculations will be performed (Step 3), and no groups will be eliminated (Step 4). Each of these steps in the execution will run faster if this can be done.

Since the **having** condition in this example is not based on a calculated column, it is easily changed into a **where** condition:

```
select Person, SUM(Amount) Total
  from LEDGER
 where Action = 'PAID'
   and Person like 'P%'
 group by Person
 order by SUM(Amount) desc;
```

Views of Groups

In Chapter 3, just as SQL and SQLPLUS were beginning to be explored, a view called INVASION was created for the Oracle at Delphi, which joined together the WEATHER and LOCATION tables. This view appeared to be a table in its own right, with columns and rows, but it contained columns in each of its rows that actually came from two separate tables.

The same process of creating a view can be used with groups. The difference is that each row will contain information about a group of rows—a kind of subtotal table. For example, consider this group query:

```
select LAST_DAY(ActionDate) MONTH,
       SUM(Amount) Total
  from LEDGER
 where Action = 'PAID'
 group by LAST_DAY(ActionDate);
```

```
MONTH        TOTAL
---------    -------
31-JAN-01     3.50
28-FEB-01     1.50
31-MAR-01     6.00
30-APR-01     9.00
31-MAY-01     3.40
30-JUN-01     4.25
31-JUL-01     4.20
31-AUG-01    11.70
30-SEP-01     4.25
31-OCT-01     4.93
30-NOV-01     3.63
31-DEC-01     2.25

12 rows selected.
```

What's being done here is really rather simple. This is a table (technically, a view) of the monthly amounts Talbot paid out for all items combined. This expression:

```
LAST_DAY(ActionDate)
```

forces every real ActionDate encountered to be the last day of the month. If ActionDate were the column in the **select**, you'd get subtotals by day, instead of by month. The same sort of thing could have been accomplished with this:

```
TO_CHAR(ActionDate,'MON')
```

except that the result would have ended up in alphabetical order by month, instead of in normal month order. You now can give this result a name, and create a view:

```
create or replace view MONTHTOTAL as
select LAST_DAY(ActionDate) MONTH,
       SUM(Amount) Total
  from LEDGER
 where Action = 'PAID'
 group by LAST_DAY(ActionDate);

View created.
```

Renaming Columns with Aliases

Notice the names MONTH and Total in the **select** clause. These *rename* the columns they follow. These new names are called *aliases,* because they are used to disguise the real names of the underlying columns (which are complicated because they have functions). This is similar to what you saw in the SQLPLUS report in Chapter 4 in Figure 4-3, when Quantity times Rate was renamed Ext:

```
Quantity * Rate Ext
```

In fact, now that this view is created, you can describe it, like this:

```
describe MONTHTOTAL

Name                                Null?    Type
---------------------------------  -------- ----
MONTH                                        DATE
TOTAL                                        NUMBER
```

When you query the table, you can (and must) now use the new column names:

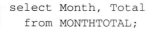

```
select Month, Total
   from MONTHTOTAL;


MONTH        TOTAL
---------   -------
31-JAN-01    3.50
28-FEB-01    1.50
31-MAR-01    6.00
30-APR-01    9.00
31-MAY-01    3.40
30-JUN-01    4.25
31-JUL-01    4.20
31-AUG-01   11.70
30-SEP-01    4.25
31-OCT-01    4.93
30-NOV-01    3.63
31-DEC-01    2.25


12 rows selected.
```

"Total" is referred to as a *column alias*—another name to use when referring to a column. In ORACLE7.1, column aliases can be specified in a slightly different way. You can use the **as** clause to identify column aliases in queries. Doing this would change that part of the select command in the preceding example to

```
SUM(Amount) AS Total
```

Using the **as** clause helps to visually separate the column aliases from the columns. In this book, the **as** clause will not be shown because it is not supported in ORACLE7.0. Users of ORACLE7.1 and above should take advantage of this feature.

In the description of the view, and in the query, there is no evidence of the **LAST_DAY**(ActionDate) or **SUM**(Amount)—just their new names, MONTH and TOTAL. It is as if the view MONTHTOTAL was a real table with rows of monthly sums. Why?

ORACLE automatically takes a single word, without quotes, and uses it to rename the column it follows. When it does this, ORACLE forces the word—the alias—into uppercase, regardless of how it was typed. You can see evidence of this by comparing the column names in the **create view** and the **describe** commands. Even though MONTH was typed in uppercase and Total in mixed uppercase and lowercase in the **create view**, they are both in uppercase in the table description that ORACLE keeps internally. When creating a view, *never put double quotes around your column aliases.* Always leave aliases in **create view** statements without quotes. This will cause them to be stored in uppercase, which is required for ORACLE to find them. See the boxed section entitled "Aliases in View Creation" for a warning on aliases.

Aliases in View Creation

Internally, ORACLE works with all column and table names in uppercase. This is how they are stored in its data dictionary, and this is how it always expects them to be. When aliases are typed to create a view, they should always be naked, without quotation marks around them. Putting double quotation marks around an alias can force the column name stored internally by ORACLE to be in mixed case. If you do this, ORACLE will never be able to find the column when you execute a **select**.

Never use double quotation marks in creating aliases for a view.

You now have monthly totals collected together in a view. A total for the entire year could also be created, using YEARTOTAL as both the view name and the column alias for **SUM**(Amount):

```
create or replace view YEARTOTAL as
select SUM(Amount) YEARTOTAL
  from LEDGER
 where Action = 'PAID';

View created.
```

If you query the view, you'll discover it has only one record:

```
select YEARTOTAL
  from YEARTOTAL;

YEARTOTAL
---------
    58.61
```

The Power of Views of Groups

Now you'll see the real power of a relational database. You've created views of Talbot's underlying ledger that contain totals by groups: by Item, by Person, by Month, and by Year. These views can now be *joined* together, just like the tables were in Chapter 3, to reveal information never before apparent. For instance, what percentage of the year's payments were made each month?

```
select Month, Total, (Total/YearTotal)*100 Percent
  from MONTHTOTAL, YEARTOTAL
 order by Month;
```

```
MONTH       TOTAL PERCENT
--------- ------- -------
31-JAN-01    3.50    5.97
28-FEB-01    1.50    2.56
31-MAR-01    6.00   10.24
30-APR-01    9.00   15.36
31-MAY-01    3.40    5.80
30-JUN-01    4.25    7.25
31-JUL-01    4.20    7.17
31-AUG-01   11.70   19.96
30-SEP-01    4.25    7.25
31-OCT-01    4.93    8.41
30-NOV-01    3.63    6.19
31-DEC-01    2.25    3.84

12 rows selected.
```

In this query, two views are listed in the **from** clause, but they are not joined in a **where** clause. Why not?

In this particular case, no **where** clause is necessary because one of the views, YEARTOTAL, will only return one row (as was shown in the previous listing). Both the MONTHTOTAL and the YEARTOTAL views were created with the assumption that only one year's data would be stored in the LEDGER table. If data for multiple years is to be stored in the LEDGER table, then both of these views will need to be re-created to **group by** a Year column as well. That column would then be used to join them (since the YEARTOTAL view might then return more than one row).

The same results could have been obtained by directly joining the LEDGER *table* with the YEARTOTAL *view,* but as you can see, the query is immensely more complicated and difficult to understand:

```
select LAST_DAY(ActionDate) MONTH,
       SUM(Amount) Total,
       (SUM(Amount)/YearTotal)*100  Percent
  from LEDGER, YEARTOTAL
 where Action = 'PAID'
 group by LAST_DAY(ActionDate), YearTotal;


MONTH        TOTAL PERCENT
--------- ------- -------
31-JAN-01    3.50    5.97
28-FEB-01    1.50    2.56
31-MAR-01    6.00   10.24
30-APR-01    9.00   15.36
31-MAY-01    3.40    5.80
30-JUN-01    4.25    7.25
31-JUL-01    4.20    7.17
31-AUG-01   11.70   19.96
30-SEP-01    4.25    7.25
31-OCT-01    4.93    8.41
30-NOV-01    3.63    6.19
31-DEC-01    2.25    3.84

12 rows selected.
```

Would it be possible to go one step further, and simply join the LEDGER table to itself, once for monthly totals and once for the yearly total, without creating any views at all? The answer is no, because the **group by** for monthly totals is in conflict with the **group by** for a yearly total. In order to create queries that compare one grouping of rows (such as by month) with another grouping of rows (such as by year), at least one of the groupings must be a view. Beyond this technical restriction, however, it is just simpler and easier to understand doing the queries with views. Compare the last two examples, and the difference in clarity is apparent. Views hide complexity.

The views also give you more power to use the many character, NUMBER, and DATE data types at will, without worrying about things like months appearing in alphabetical order. Now that the MONTHTOTAL view exists, you can modify the display of the month with a simple **SUBSTR** (TO_CHAR could also be used):

```
select SUBSTR(Month,4,3), Total,
       (Total/YearTotal)*100 Percent
  from MONTHTOTAL, YEARTOTAL
 order by Month;

SUB    TOTAL  PERCENT
---    -----  -------
JAN     3.50     5.97
FEB     1.50     2.56
MAR     6.00    10.24
APR     9.00    15.36
MAY     3.40     5.80
JUN     4.25     7.25
JUL     4.20     7.17
AUG    11.70    19.96
SEP     4.25     7.25
OCT     4.93     8.41
NOV     3.63     6.19
DEC     2.25     3.84

12 rows selected.
```

Logic in the having Clause

In the **having** clause, the choice of the group function, and the column on which it operates, might bear no relation to the columns or group functions in the **select** clause.

```
select Person, SUM(Amount) Total
  from LEDGER
 where Action = 'PAID'
 group by Person
having COUNT(Item) > 1
 order by SUM(Amount) desc;
```

```
PERSON                    TOTAL
------------------------  -------
RICHARD KOCH AND BROTHERS  12.00
DICK JONES                  6.30
ANDREW DYE                  4.50
JED HOPKINS                 4.00
KAY AND PALMER WALBOM       4.00
ELBERT TALBOT               3.90
WILFRED LOWELL              3.60
GERHARDT KENTGEN            3.00
PETER LAWSON                3.00
PAT LAVAY                   3.00
HELEN BRANDT                3.00
VICTORIA LYNN               2.80

12 rows selected.
```

Here the **having** clause selected only those persons (the **group by** collected all the rows into groups by Person) that had more than one Item. Anyone who only did a task once for Talbot is eliminated. Those who did any task more than once are included.

The sort of query shown in the last listing is very effective for determining which rows in a table have duplicate values in specific columns. For example, if you are trying to establish a new unique index on a column (or set of columns) in a table, and the index creation fails due to uniqueness problems with the data, then you can easily determine which rows caused the problem.

First, select the columns that you want to be unique, followed by a **COUNT**(*) column. **Group by** the columns you want to be unique, and use the **having** clause to return only those groups having **COUNT**(*)>1. The only records returned will be duplicates. The following query shows this check being performed for the Person column of the LEDGER table.

```
select Person, COUNT(*)
  from LEDGER
 group by Person
having COUNT(*)>1
 order by Person;
```

order by with Columns and Group Functions

The **order by** clause is executed after the **where**, **group by**, and **having** clauses. It can employ group functions, or columns from the **group by**, or a combination. If it uses a group function, that function operates on the groups, then the **order by** sorts the *results* of the function in order. If the **order by** uses a column from the **group by**, it sorts the rows that are returned based on that column. Group functions and single columns (so long as the column is in the **group by**) can be combined in the **order by**.

In the **order by** clause you can specify a group function and the column it affects even though they have nothing at all to do with the group functions or columns in the **select**, **group by**, or **having** clause. On the other hand, if you specify a column in the **order by** that is not part of a group function, it must be in the **group by** clause. This query shows the count of Items and the total amount paid per Person, but it puts them in order by the average Amount they were paid per item:

```
select Person, COUNT(Item), SUM(Amount) Total
   from LEDGER
 where Action = 'PAID'
 group by Person
having COUNT(Item) > 1
 order by AVG(Amount);
```

```
PERSON                       COUNT(ITEM)   TOTAL
------------------------     -----------   -------
PAT LAVAY                              4    3.00
ELBERT TALBOT                          5    3.90
GERHARDT KENTGEN                       3    3.00
PETER LAWSON                           3    3.00
DICK JONES                             6    6.30
WILFRED LOWELL                         3    3.60
VICTORIA LYNN                          2    2.80
HELEN BRANDT                           2    3.00
JED HOPKINS                            2    4.00
KAY AND PALMER WALBOM                  2    4.00
ANDREW DYE                             2    4.50
RICHARD KOCH AND BROTHERS              5   12.00

12 rows selected.
```

If this is a little hard to believe, look at the same query with the **AVG**(Amount) added to the **select** clause:

```
select Person, COUNT(Item), SUM(Amount) Total, AVG(Amount)
   from LEDGER
 where Action = 'PAID'
 group by Person
having COUNT(Item) > 1
 order by AVG(Amount);
```

```
PERSON                        COUNT(ITEM)   TOTAL AVG(AMOUNT)
----------------------------- ----------- ------- -----------
PAT LAVAY                               4    3.00         .75
ELBERT TALBOT                           5    3.90         .78
GERHARDT KENTGEN                        3    3.00           1
PETER LAWSON                            3    3.00           1
DICK JONES                              6    6.30        1.05
WILFRED LOWELL                          3    3.60         1.2
VICTORIA LYNN                           2    2.80         1.4
HELEN BRANDT                            2    3.00         1.5
JED HOPKINS                             2    4.00           2
KAY AND PALMER WALBOM                   2    4.00           2
ANDREW DYE                              2    4.50        2.25
RICHARD KOCH AND BROTHERS               5   12.00         2.4

12 rows selected.
```

You can check any of these results by hand with the full ledger listings given in Figure 9-1.

Join Columns

As explained in Chapters 1 and 3, joining two tables together requires that they have a relationship defined by a common column. This is also true in joining views, or tables and views. The only exception is when one of the tables or views has just a single row, as the YEARTOTAL table does. In this case, SQL joins the single row to every row in the other table or view, and no reference to the joining columns needs to be made in the **where** clause of the query.

Any attempt to join two tables that each have more than one row, without specifying the joined columns in the **where** clause, will produce what's known as a *Cartesian product,* usually a giant result where every row in one table is joined with every row in the other table. A small 80-row table joined to a small 100-row table in this way would produce 8000 rows in your display, and few of them would be at all meaningful.

where, having, group by, and order by

Tables in ORACLE can be grouped into collections of related rows, such as by Item, or Date, or Person. This is done using the **group by** clause. The **group by** collects only those rows in the table that pass the logical test of the **where** clause:

```
where Action = 'PAID'
group by person
```

The **having** clause looks at these groups, and eliminates any based on whether they pass the logical test of the group function used in the **having** clause, such as:

```
having SUM(Amount) > 5
```

Those groups whose **SUM**(Amount) is greater than 5 are returned to you. Each group has just one row in the resulting table that is displayed. The **having** clause need not (and often will not) correspond to the group functions in the **select** clause. After these rows have been chosen by the **having** clause, they can be placed in the desired sequence by an **order by**:

```
order by AVG(Amount)
```

The **order by** must use either a column named in the **group by**, or any appropriate group function that can reference any column without regard to the **select** or the **having** clause. Its group function will make its computation row by row for each group created by the **group by** clause.

All of these powerful grouping features can be combined to create complex summary views of the underlying table, which appear very simple. Once created, their columns can be manipulated, and their rows selected, just as with any other table. These views also can be joined to each other, and to tables, to produce deep insights into the data.

CHAPTER 10

When One Query Depends upon Another

This chapter and Chapter 11 introduce more difficult concepts than we've previously seen. While many of these are rarely used in the normal course of running queries or producing reports, there will be occasions that call for the techniques taught in these chapters. If they seem too challenging as you study them, read on anyway. The odds are that by the time you need these methods, you'll be able to use them.

Advanced Subqueries

You've encountered subqueries—those **select** statements that are part of a **where** clause in a preceding **select** statement—in Chapters 3, 6, and 9. Subqueries also can be used in **insert**, **update**, and **delete** statements. This use will be covered in Chapter 13.

Often a subquery will provide an alternative approach to a query. For example, suppose George Talbot needs a combine driver quickly (a combine is a machine that moves through a field to harvest, head, thresh, and clean grains such as wheat and oats). He can't afford to send someone off to another town to search for a driver, so he has to find someone in Edmeston or North Edmeston. One way to locate such a person is with a three-way table join, using the tables that were normalized back in Chapter 2. These are shown in Figure 10-1.

```
select WORKER.Name, WORKER.Lodging
  from WORKER, WORKERSKILL, LODGING
 where WORKER.Name = WORKERSKILL.Name
   and WORKER.Lodging = LODGING.Lodging
   and Skill = 'COMBINE DRIVER'
   and Address LIKE '%EDMESTON%';

NAME                          LODGING
-------------------------     ---------------
JOHN PEARSON                  ROSE HILL
```

Three tables are joined in the same way that two tables are. The common columns are set equal to each other in the **where** clause, as shown in Figure 10-2. To join three tables together, two of them must each be joined to a third.

NOTE
Not every table is joined to every other table. In fact, the number of links between the tables (such as WORKER.Name = WORKERSKILL.Name) is usually one less than the number of tables being joined.

Once the tables are joined, as shown in the first two lines of the **where** clause, then Skill and Address can be used to find a nearby combine driver.

The WORKER Table

NAME	AGE	LODGING
ADAH TALBOT	23	PAPA KING
ANDREW DYE	29	ROSE HILL
BART SARJEANT	22	CRANMER
DICK JONES	18	ROSE HILL
DONALD ROLLO	16	MATTS
ELBERT TALBOT	43	WEITBROCHT
GEORGE OSCAR	41	ROSE HILL
GERHARDT KENTGEN	55	PAPA KING
HELEN BRANDT	15	
JED HOPKINS	33	MATTS
JOHN PEARSON	27	ROSE HILL
KAY AND PALMER WALLBOM		ROSE HILL
PAT LAVAY	21	ROSE HILL
PETER LAWSON	25	CRANMER
RICHARD KOCH AND BROTHERS		WEITBROCHT
ROLAND BRANDT	35	MATTS
VICTORIA LYNN	32	MULLERS
WILFRED LOWELL	67	
WILLIAM SWING	15	CRANMER

The WORKERSKILL Table

NAME	SKILL	ABILITY
ADAH TALBOT	WORK	GOOD
DICK JONES	SMITHY	EXCELLENT
ELBERT TALBOT	DISCUS	SLOW
HELEN BRANDT	COMBINE DRIVER	VERY FAST
JOHN PEARSON	COMBINE DRIVER	
JOHN PEARSON	WOODCUTTER	GOOD
JOHN PEARSON	SMITHY	AVERAGE
VICTORIA LYNN	SMITHY	PRECISE
WILFRED LOWELL	WORK	AVERAGE
WILFRED LOWELL	DISCUS	AVERAGE

FIGURE 10-1. *Information in Talbot's tables*

```
              The SKILL Table

SKILL              DESCRIPTION
---------------    ----------------------------------------------
COMBINE DRIVER     HARNESS, DRIVE, GROOM HORSES, ADJUST BLADES
DISCUS             HARNESS, DRIVE, GROOM HORSES, BLADE DEPTH
GRAVE DIGGER       MARK AND CUT SOD, DIG, SHORE, FILL, RESOD
SMITHY             STACK FOR HIRE, RUN BELLOWS, CUT, SHOE HORSES
WOODCUTTER         MARK AND FELL TREES, SPLIT, STACK, HAUL
WORK               GENERAL UNSKILLED LABOR

              The LODGING Table

LODGING     LONGNAME              MANAGER          ADDRESS
----------  --------------------  --------------   ------------------
CRANMER     CRANMER RETREAT HOUSE THOM CRANMER     HILL ST, BERKELEY
MATTS       MATTS LONG BUNK HOUSE ROLAND BRANDT    3 MILE RD, KEENE
MULLERS     MULLERS COED LODGING  KEN MULLER       120 MAIN, EDMESTON
PAPA KING   PAPA KING ROOMING     WILLIAM KING     127 MAIN, EDMESTON
ROSE HILL   ROSE HILL FOR MEN     JOHN PELETIER    RFD 3, N. EDMESTON
WEITBROCHT  WEITBROCHT ROOMING    EUNICE BENSON    320 GENEVA, KEENE
```

FIGURE 10-1. *Information in Talbot's tables* (continued)

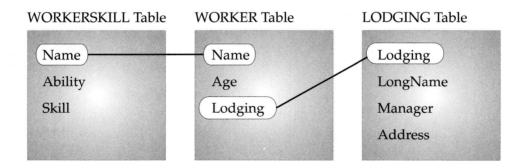

FIGURE 10-2. *A three-way table join*

Correlated Subqueries

Is there another way to accomplish this same result? Recall that a **where** clause can contain a subquery **select**. Subquery **selects** can be nested—that is, a **where** clause in a subquery also can contain a **where** clause with a subquery, which can contain a **where** clause with a subquery—on down for more levels than you are ever likely to need. It's common wisdom, widely published, that you can do this down to 16 levels. The number is actually higher, but you'll never even need 16, and performance can become very poor with more than a few levels. The following shows three **selects**, each connected to another through a **where** clause:

```
select Name, Lodging
  from WORKER
 where Name IN
       (select Name
          from WORKERSKILL
         where Skill = 'COMBINE DRIVER'
           and Lodging IN
               (select Lodging
                  from LODGING
                 where Address LIKE '%EDMESTON%'));


NAME                       LODGING
------------------------   ---------------
JOHN PEARSON               ROSE HILL
```

This query selects any workers who drive a combine and live in lodging located in Edmeston. It does this by simply requesting a worker whose Name is in the WORKERSKILL table with a Skill of 'COMBINE DRIVER' and whose Lodging is in the LODGING table with an Address LIKE '%EDMESTON%'. This is an example of a subquery that contains subqueries, but it has an additional feature. Look at the **where** clause of the second **select** statement:

```
(select Name
   from WORKERSKILL
  where Skill = 'COMBINE DRIVER'
    and Lodging IN
```

At first glance this looks reasonable, but it contains the Lodging column. Is the Lodging column in the WORKERSKILL table? It is not. So why does this query work? The reason is that because this is a subquery, ORACLE assumes the column Lodging to be from the first **select** statement, the one that contains the subquery in its **where** clause. This is called a *correlated* subquery, because for every Name in the outer query that has a Skill of 'COMBINE DRIVER', the Lodging is correlated in the second **where** clause.

Said differently, a subquery may refer to a column in a table used in its main query (the query that has the subquery in its **where** clause).

```
select Name, Lodging
  from WORKER
 where Name IN
       (select Name
          from WORKERSKILL
         where skill = 'COMBINE DRIVER'
           and Lodging IN
               (select Lodging
                  from LODGING
                 where Address LIKE ('%EDMESTON%')));
```

Correlated, same column

This correlated subquery in effect joins information from three tables to answer the question of whether there are any combine drivers that live nearby.

You've also seen how this same query can be accomplished with a three-way table join. Can any correlated subquery be replaced by a table join? No. Suppose Talbot wanted to know which of his workers were the oldest in each lodging house. Here are the maximum ages by house:

```
select Lodging, MAX(Age)
  from WORKER
 group by Lodging;
```

```
LODGING      MAX(AGE)
---------- --------
                 67
CRANMER          25
MATTS            35
MULLERS          32
PAPA KING        55
ROSE HILL        41
WEITBROCHT       43
```

How would you incorporate this into a query? The Lodging column in the upper **select** is correlated with the Lodging column in the subquery **select**:

```
select Name, Age, Lodging
  from WORKER W
 where Age =
```

```
(select MAX(Age) from WORKER
   where W.Lodging = Lodging);
```

```
NAME                            AGE LODGING
------------------------        ----- ----------
ELBERT TALBOT                   43 WEITBROCHT
GEORGE OSCAR                    41 ROSE HILL
GERHARDT KENTGEN                55 PAPA KING
PETER LAWSON                    25 CRANMER
ROLAND BRANDT                   35 MATTS
VICTORIA LYNN                   32 MULLERS
```

You'll observe some new notation here. WORKER has been given an alias of W, and one of the Lodging columns in the lower **where** clause has been designated W.Lodging. This is done because both the top **select** and the subquery use the same table, and each has a column named Lodging. Without this ability to rename (give an alias to) one of the tables, there would be no way for the lower **where** clause to distinguish one Lodging from the other. Would it work to give the second WORKER table the alias instead?

```
select Name, Age, Lodging
   from WORKER
 where Age =
       (select MAX(Age)
           from WORKER W
        where W.Lodging = Lodging);
```

```
NAME                            AGE LODGING
------------------------        ----- ----------
GERHARDT KENTGEN                55 PAPA KING
```

Clearly, it does not. The second **where** clause does not detect that Lodging should belong to the main query's WORKER table, and therefore believes that W.Lodging and Lodging are each their own Lodging column. Since these are always equal (except for **NULL**s), the subquery does not produce the maximum age for each lodging; instead, it produces the maximum age from all the lodgings.

This brings up one of the effects of equality tests with **NULL**s, as discussed in Chapter 3: The oldest person overall is Wilfred Lowell, but this last query produced Gerhardt Kentgen, and the query just before produced only those workers who had real values in their Lodging column (the column was not **NULL**). Both of these effects are due to this **where** clause:

```
where W.Lodging = Lodging);
```

The mere existence of this test, with the equal sign, excludes any Lodging whose value is **NULL**. To include those workers for whom you do not have a Lodging value, use the **NVL** function:

```
select Name, Age, Lodging
  from WORKER W
 where Age =
       (select MAX(Age)
          from WORKER
         where NVL(W.Lodging,'X') = NVL(Lodging,'X'));
```

```
NAME                             AGE LODGING
------------------------------ ----- ----------
ELBERT TALBOT                     43 WEITBROCHT
GEORGE OSCAR                      41 ROSE HILL
GERHARDT KENTGEN                  55 PAPA KING
PETER LAWSON                      25 CRANMER
ROLAND BRANDT                     35 MATTS
VICTORIA LYNN                     32 MULLERS
WILFRED LOWELL                    67
```

The substitute of X could have been anything, as long as the same substitute was used in both **NVL** functions. If the **NVL** function were to be added to the query that produced only GERHARDT KENTGEN, the result would have been WILFRED LOWELL instead. Another way to write the same query (oldest person per lodging house) is shown here:

```
select Name, Age, Lodging
  from WORKER
 where (Lodging, Age) IN
       (select Lodging, MAX(Age)
          from WORKER
         group by Lodging);
```

```
NAME                             AGE LODGING
------------------------------ ----- ----------
PETER LAWSON                      25 CRANMER
ROLAND BRANDT                     35 MATTS
VICTORIA LYNN                     32 MULLERS
GERHARDT KENTGEN                  55 PAPA KING
GEORGE OSCAR                      41 ROSE HILL
ELBERT TALBOT                     43 WEITBROCHT
```

These two columns are being tested simultaneously against a subquery. The **IN** is necessary because the subquery produces more than one row; otherwise, an equal sign could have been used. When two or more columns are tested at the same time against the results of a subquery, they must be enclosed in parentheses, as shown with (Lodging, Age). Note that this query did not find WILFRED LOWELL, because the **IN** ignores **NULL** values.

Coordinating Logical Tests

John Pearson falls ill. He's been a stalwart of the Talbot crew for many months. Who else has his skills, and where do they live? A list of the workers that have skills Talbot knows about is easily retrieved from the WORKER and WORKERSKILL tables:

```
select WORKER.Name, Lodging, Skill
  from WORKER, WORKERSKILL
 where WORKER.Name = WORKERSKILL.Name;
```

NAME	LODGING	SKILL
ADAH TALBOT	PAPA KING	WORK
DICK JONES	ROSE HILL	SMITHY
ELBERT TALBOT	WEITBROCHT	DISCUS
HELEN BRANDT		COMBINE DRIVER
JOHN PEARSON	ROSE HILL	COMBINE DRIVER
JOHN PEARSON	ROSE HILL	WOODCUTTER
JOHN PEARSON	ROSE HILL	SMITHY
VICTORIA LYNN	MULLERS	SMITHY
WILFRED LOWELL		WORK
WILFRED LOWELL		DISCUS

Rather than search by hand through this list (or the much longer list a business is likely to have of its workers' skills), let ORACLE do it for you. This query simply asks which workers have Pearson's skills, and where each lives:

```
select WORKER.Name, Lodging, Skill
  from WORKER, WORKERSKILL
 where WORKER.Name = WORKERSKILL.Name
   and Skill IN
       (select Skill
         from WORKERSKILL
```

```
        where Name = 'JOHN PEARSON')
  order by WORKER.Name;


NAME                         LODGING    SKILL
--------------------------   ---------- --------------
DICK JONES                   ROSE HILL  SMITHY
HELEN BRANDT                            COMBINE DRIVER
JOHN PEARSON                 ROSE HILL  COMBINE DRIVER
JOHN PEARSON                 ROSE HILL  WOODCUTTER
JOHN PEARSON                 ROSE HILL  SMITHY
VICTORIA LYNN                MULLERS    SMITHY
```

Not surprisingly, it turns out that Pearson has Pearson's skills. To exclude him from the query, another **and** is added to the **where** clause:

```
select WORKER.Name, Lodging, Skill
  from WORKER, WORKERSKILL
 where WORKER.Name = WORKERSKILL.Name
   and Skill IN
        (select Skill
           from WORKERSKILL
          where Name = 'JOHN PEARSON')
   and WORKER.Name != 'JOHN PEARSON'
  order by WORKER.Name;


NAME                         LODGING    SKILL
--------------------------   ---------- --------------
DICK JONES                   ROSE HILL  SMITHY
HELEN BRANDT                            COMBINE DRIVER
VICTORIA LYNN                MULLERS    SMITHY
```

This **and** is a part of the main query, even though it follows the subquery.

EXISTS and Its Correlated Subquery

EXISTS is a test for existence. It is placed the way **IN** might be with a subquery, but differs in two ways:

1. It does not match a column or columns.

2. It is typically used only with a correlated subquery.

Suppose Talbot wanted the names and skills of workers possessing more than one skill. Finding just the *names* of those with more than one skill is simple:

```
select Name
   from WORKERSKILL
 group by Name
having COUNT(Skill) > 1;


NAME
------------------------
JOHN PEARSON
WILFRED LOWELL
```

Attempting to find both Name and Skill fails, however, because the **group by** made necessary by the **COUNT**(Skill) is on the primary key of the WORKERSKILL table (Name, Skill). Since each primary key, by definition, uniquely identifies only one row, the count of skills for that one row can never be greater than one, so the **having** clause always tests false—it doesn't find any rows:

```
select Name, Skill
   from WORKERSKILL
 group by Name, Skill
having COUNT(Skill) > 1;


no rows selected.
```

EXISTS provides a solution. The following subquery asks if for each Name selected in the main (outer) query, there exists a Name in the WORKERSKILL table with a count of skills greater than one. If the answer for a given name is yes, the **EXISTS** test is true, and the outer query **select**s a Name and Skill. The worker names are correlated by the WS alias given to the first WORKERSKILL table.

```
select Name, Skill
   from WORKERSKILL WS
 where EXISTS
       (select *
          from WORKERSKILL
         where WS.Name = Name
         group by Name
        having COUNT(Skill) > 1);
```

```
NAME                     SKILL
------------------------ --------------
JOHN PEARSON             COMBINE DRIVER
JOHN PEARSON             SMITHY
JOHN PEARSON             WOODCUTTER
WILFRED LOWELL           WORK
WILFRED LOWELL           DISCUS
```

This same query could have been built using **IN** and a test on the column Name. No correlated subquery is necessary here:

```
select Name, Skill
  from WORKERSKILL WS
 where Name IN
       (select Name
          from WORKERSKILL
        group by Name)
       having COUNT(Skill) > 1;
```

```
NAME                     SKILL
------------------------ --------------
JOHN PEARSON             COMBINE DRIVER
JOHN PEARSON             WOODCUTTER
JOHN PEARSON             SMITHY
WILFRED LOWELL           WORK
WILFRED LOWELL           DISCUS
```

There are some logical anomalies using **EXISTS** and its "almost" opposite, **NOT EXISTS**, as well as **ANY** and **ALL**, particularly as they relate to **NULL**s. These are discussed under **EXISTS** in the Alphabetical Reference section of this book. **NOT EXISTS** is also discussed in the "Replacing **NOT IN** with **NOT EXISTS**" section later in this chapter.

Outer Joins

The WORKER table contains all of Talbot's employees and ages, but doesn't list skills. The WORKERSKILL table contains only those employees that have skills. How would you go about producing a report of all employees, with their ages and skills, regardless of whether they have skills or not? Your first attempt might be to join the two tables. Notice the extensive use of aliases in this query. For convenience each table is renamed, one A and the other B, and A and B appear anywhere the table names normally would appear.

```
select A.Name, Age, Skill
  from WORKER A, WORKERSKILL B
 where A.Name = B.Name
 order by A.Name;
```

```
NAME                      AGE SKILL
------------------------- ----- --------------
ADAH TALBOT                23 WORK
DICK JONES                 18 SMITHY
ELBERT TALBOT              43 DISCUS
HELEN BRANDT               15 COMBINE DRIVER
JOHN PEARSON               27 COMBINE DRIVER
JOHN PEARSON               27 SMITHY
JOHN PEARSON               27 WOODCUTTER
VICTORIA LYNN              32 SMITHY
WILFRED LOWELL             67 WORK
WILFRED LOWELL             67 DISCUS
```

Unfortunately, this result only includes those employees that have skills. The solution to producing a complete list is an *outer join.* This is a technique in which ORACLE adds extra matching rows with nothing in them to one table (in this case the WORKERSKILL table), so that the result is as long as the other table (the WORKER table). Basically, every row in the WORKER table that couldn't find a match in WORKERSKILL gets listed anyway:

```
select A.Name, Age, Skill
  from WORKER A, WORKERSKILL B
 where A.Name = B.Name(+)
 order by A.Name;
```

```
NAME                      AGE SKILL
------------------------- ----- --------------
ADAH TALBOT                23 WORK
ANDREW DYE                 29
BART SARJEANT              22
DICK JONES                 18 SMITHY
DONALD ROLLO               16
ELBERT TALBOT              43 DISCUS
GEORGE OSCAR               41
GERHARDT KENTGEN           55
HELEN BRANDT               15 COMBINE DRIVER
JED HOPKINS                33
JOHN PEARSON               27 COMBINE DRIVER
```

```
JOHN PEARSON                    27 WOODCUTTER
JOHN PEARSON                    27 SMITHY
KAY AND PALMER WALLBOM
PAT LAVAY                       21
PETER LAWSON                    25
RICHARD KOCH AND BROTHERS
ROLAND BRANDT                   35
VICTORIA LYNN                   32 SMITHY
WILFRED LOWELL                  67 WORK
WILFRED LOWELL                  67 DISCUS
WILLIAM SWING                   15
```

Think of the (+), which must immediately follow the join column of the shorter table, as saying add an extra (null) row of B.Name anytime there's no match for A.Name. As you can see, all workers are listed, along with age and skill. Those for whom there was no match simply got an empty Skill column.

Replacing NOT IN with an Outer Join

The various logical tests that can be done in a **where** clause all have their separate performance measures. The all-time slowest test is probably **NOT IN**, because it forces a full read of the table in the subquery **select**. Suppose Talbot needed workers for a particular project, but wanted to be sure not to call anyone who had smithy skills, as he knew he'd need them for another project. To select workers without smithy skills, and their lodging, he could construct a query like this one:

```
select A.Name, Lodging
  from WORKER A
 where A.Name NOT IN
        (select Name
           from WORKERSKILL
          where Skill = 'SMITHY')
order by A.Name;


NAME                            LODGING
------------------------------- ----------
ADAH TALBOT                     PAPA KING
ANDREW DYE                      ROSE HILL
BART SARJEANT                   CRANMER
DONALD ROLLO                    MATTS
ELBERT TALBOT                   WEITBROCHT
```

```
GEORGE OSCAR                    ROSE HILL
GERHARDT KENTGEN                PAPA KING
HELEN BRANDT
JED HOPKINS                     MATTS
KAY AND PALMER WALLBOM          ROSE HILL
PAT LAVAY                       ROSE HILL
PETER LAWSON                    CRANMER
RICHARD KOCH AND BROTHERS WEITBROCHT
ROLAND BRANDT                   MATTS
WILFRED LOWELL
WILLIAM SWING                   CRANMER
```

This is typically the way such a query would be written, even though experienced ORACLE users know it will be slow. The following query uses an outer join, and produces the same result. The difference is that this one is *much* faster:

```
select A.Name, Lodging
  from WORKER A, WORKERSKILL B
 where A.Name = B.Name(+)
   and B.Name is NULL
   and B.Skill(+) = 'SMITHY' order by A.Name;
```

```
NAME                        LODGING
--------------------------- ----------
ADAH TALBOT                 PAPA KING
ANDREW DYE                  ROSE HILL
BART SARJEANT               CRANMER
DONALD ROLLO                MATTS
ELBERT TALBOT               WEITBROCHT
GEORGE OSCAR                ROSE HILL
GERHARDT KENTGEN            PAPA KING
HELEN BRANDT
JED HOPKINS                 MATTS
KAY AND PALMER WALLBOM      ROSE HILL
PAT LAVAY                   ROSE HILL
PETER LAWSON                CRANMER
RICHARD KOCH AND BROTHERS WEITBROCHT
ROLAND BRANDT               MATTS
WILFRED LOWELL
WILLIAM SWING               CRANMER
```

Why does it work and give the same results as the **NOT IN**? The outer join between the two tables assures that all rows are available for the test, including those workers for whom no skills are listed in the WORKERSKILL table. The

```
B.Name is NULL
```

produces only those workers that don't appear in the WORKERSKILL table (no skills listed), and the

```
B.Skill(+) = 'SMITHY'
```

adds those who are in the WORKERSKILL table but who don't have a skill of 'SMITHY' (therefore, the B.Skill(+) invented one).

The logic here is extremely obscure, but it works. The best way to use this technique is simply to follow the model. Save this method for use where a **NOT IN** will be searching a big table, and put plenty of explanatory comments nearby.

Replacing NOT IN with NOT EXISTS

A faster and more straightforward way of performing this type of query requires using the **NOT EXISTS** clause. **NOT EXISTS** is typically used to determine which values in one table do not have matching values in another table. In usage, it is identical to the **EXISTS** clause; in the following examples you'll see the difference in the query logic and the records returned.

Retrieving data from two tables such as these typically requires that they be joined. However, joining two tables—such as SKILL and WORKERSKILL—will by definition exclude the records that exist only in one of those tables. But what if *those* are the records you care about?

For example, what if you want to know which Skills in the SKILL table are not covered by the skills of the current staff of workers? The workers' skills are listed in the WORKERSKILL table, so a query that joins SKILL and WORKERSKILL on the Skill column will exclude the Skills that are not covered:

```
select SKILL.Skill
  from SKILL, WORKERSKILL
 where SKILL.Skill = WORKERSKILL.Skill;
```

NOT EXISTS allows you to use a correlated subquery to eliminate from a table all records that may successfully be joined to another table. For this example, that means that you can eliminate from the SKILL table all Skills that are present in the Skill column of the WORKERSKILL table. The following query shows how this is done.

```
select SKILL.Skill
  from SKILL
 where NOT EXISTS
      (select 'x' from WORKERSKILL
        where WORKERSKILL.Skill = SKILL.Skill);

SKILL
-------------
GRAVE DIGGER
```

As this query shows, there are no workers in the WORKERSKILL table that have `'GRAVE DIGGER'` as a Skill. How does this query work?

For each record in the outer query (from the SKILL table), the **NOT EXISTS** subquery is checked. If the join of that record to the WORKERSKILL table returns a row, then the subquery succeeds. **NOT EXISTS** tells the query to reverse that return code; therefore, any row in SKILL that can be successfully joined to WORKERSKILL will not be returned by the outer query. The only row left is the one skill that does not have a record in WORKERSKILL.

NOT EXISTS is a very efficient way to perform this type of query, especially when multiple columns are used for the join. Because it uses a join, **NOT EXISTS** is frequently able to use available indexes, whereas **NOT IN** is not able to use those indexes. The ability to use indexes for this type of query can have a dramatic impact on the query's performance.

UNION, INTERSECT, and MINUS

Sometimes you need to combine information of a similar type from more than one table. A classic example of this would be two or more mailing lists that were being merged prior to a mailing campaign. Depending upon the purpose of a particular mailing, you might want to send letters to any of these combinations of people:

- Everyone in both lists (while avoiding sending two letters to someone who happens to be in both lists)

- Only those people who are in both lists

- Those in only one of the lists

These three combinations of lists are known in ORACLE as **UNION**, **INTERSECT**, and **MINUS**. Suppose Talbot has two lists, one of his longtime employees and the other of prospective workers that he has acquired from another employer. The longtime employee list includes these eight names:

```
select Name from LONGTIME;

NAME
--------------
ADAH TALBOT
DICK JONES
DONALD ROLLO
ELBERT TALBOT
GEORGE OSCAR
PAT LAVAY
PETER LAWSON
WILFRED LOWELL
```

The prospective worker list includes these eight employees:

```
select Name from PROSPECT;

NAME
--------------
ADAH TALBOT
DORY KENSON
ELBERT TALBOT
GEORGE PHEPPS
JED HOPKINS
PAT LAVAY
TED BUTCHER
WILFRED LOWELL
```

The most straightforward use of **UNION** is this combination of the two tables. Note that it contains 12, not 16, names. Those in both lists appear only once:

```
select Name from LONGTIME
 UNION
select Name from PROSPECT;

NAME
--------------
ADAH TALBOT
DICK JONES
DONALD ROLLO
DORY KENSON
ELBERT TALBOT
GEORGE OSCAR
```

```
GEORGE PHEPPS
JED HOPKINS
PAT LAVAY
PETER LAWSON
TED BUTCHER
WILFRED LOWELL
```

In ORACLE7, you can use the **UNION ALL** operator as well. When you use **UNION ALL**, any duplicates from the two lists are given twice in the result. For example, the preceding query would have 16 names rather than 12 if you used **UNION ALL**.

In the following, the two lists of eight are intersected. This list contains only those names that are in *both* underlying tables:

```
select Name from LONGTIME
  INTERSECT
select Name from PROSPECT;


NAME
--------------
ADAH TALBOT
ELBERT TALBOT
PAT LAVAY
WILFRED LOWELL
```

Next, the names in the second table are subtracted from those in the first table. Here PROSPECT is subtracted from LONGTIME. The only names remaining are those that are in the LONGTIME table and not in the PROSPECT table:

```
select Name from LONGTIME
  MINUS
select Name from PROSPECT;


NAME
--------------
DICK JONES
DONALD ROLLO
GEORGE OSCAR
PETER LAWSON
```

This is not the same, of course, as subtracting LONGTIME from PROSPECT. Here the only names remaining are those listed in PROSPECT but not in LONGTIME:

```
select Name from PROSPECT
 MINUS
select Name from LONGTIME;

NAME
--------------
DORY KENSON
GEORGE PHEPPS
JED HOPKINS
TED BUTCHER
```

You've just learned the basics of **UNION**, **INTERSECT**, and **MINUS**. Now let's go into details. In combining two tables, ORACLE does not concern itself with column names on either side of the combination operator—that is, ORACLE will require that each **select** statement be valid and have valid columns for its own table(s), but the column names in the first **select** statement do not have to be the same as those in the second. ORACLE does have these stipulations:

- The **select**s must have the same number of columns.

- The matching top and bottom columns must be the same data type (they needn't be the same length).

The following query is nonsensical, getting lodging from one table and names from the other, but because both Lodging and Name are the same data type, the query will run.

```
select Lodging from LONGTIME
 UNION
select Name from PROSPECT;

LODGING
-------------------------
ADAH TALBOT
CRANMER
DORY KENSON
ELBERT TALBOT
GEORGE PHEPPS
JED HOPKINS
MATTS
```

```
PAPA KING
PAT LAVAY
ROSE HILL
TED BUTCHER
WEITBROCHT
WILFRED LOWELL
```

Next, three columns are selected. Since the LONGTIME table is similar in structure to the WORKER table, it has Name, Lodging, and Age columns. The PROSPECT table, however, has only a Name and Address column. The following **select** matches Lodging and Address (since they contain similar information), and adds a literal 0 to the PROSPECT table **select** statement to match the numeric Age column in the LONGTIME **select** statement:

```
select Name, Lodging, Age from LONGTIME
  UNION
select Name, Address, 0 from PROSPECT;
```

NAME	LODGING	AGE
ADAH TALBOT	23 ZWING, EDMESTON	0
ADAH TALBOT	PAPA KING	23
DICK JONES	ROSE HILL	18
DONALD ROLLO	MATTS	16
DORY KENSON	GEN. DEL., BAYBAC	0
ELBERT TALBOT	3 MILE ROAD, WALPOLE	0
ELBERT TALBOT	WEITBROCHT	43
GEORGE OSCAR	ROSE HILL	41
GEORGE PHEPPS	206 POLE, KINGSLEY	0
JED HOPKINS	GEN. DEL., TURBOW	0
PAT LAVAY	1 EASY ST, JACKSON	0
PAT LAVAY	ROSE HILL	21
PETER LAWSON	CRANMER	25
TED BUTCHER	RFD 1, BRIGHTON	0
WILFRED LOWELL		0
WILFRED LOWELL		67

You'll quickly see that many names appear twice. This is because the checking for duplicates that **UNION** always does operates over *all* of the columns being selected.

NOTE
The duplicate checking that **UNION** does ignores **NULL** columns. If this previous query had not included Age, WILFRED LOWELL would only have appeared once. This may not seem entirely logical, since a **NULL** in one table isn't equal to a **NULL** in the other one, but that's how **UNION** works.

The **INTERSECT** of these same columns produces no records, because no rows in both tables (that include these columns) are identical. If this next query had excluded Age, only WILFRED LOWELL would have shown up. **INTERSECT** also *ignores* **NULL** columns.

```
select Name, Lodging, Age from LONGTIME
  INTERSECT
select Name, Address, 0 from PROSPECT;

no rows selected
```

How about **order by**? If these operators normally sort the results according to the columns that appear, how can that sorting be changed? Because ORACLE ignores the column names in combining the two **select** statements, column names cannot be used in the **order by**:

```
select Name, Lodging, Age from LONGTIME
  UNION
select Name, Address, 0 from PROSPECT
 order by Age;
            *
ERROR at line 4: ORA-1785:  order-by item must be the number of a
select-list expression
```

order by must be the *number* of the column in the **select** clause. This means the positional number of the column. The following lets you **order by** Age, which is the third column from the left:

```
select Name, Lodging, Age from LONGTIME
  UNION
select Name, Address, 0 from PROSPECT
 order by 3;
```

```
NAME            LODGING                          AGE
--------------  ------------------------------  -----
ADAH TALBOT     23 ZWING, EDMESTON                  0
DORY KENSON     GEN. DEL., BAYBAC                   0
ELBERT TALBOT   3 MILE ROAD, WALPOLE                0
GEORGE PHEPPS   206 POLE, KINGSLEY                  0
JED HOPKINS     GEN. DEL., TURBOW                   0
PAT LAVAY       1 EASY ST, JACKSON                  0
TED BUTCHER     RFD 1, BRIGHTON                     0
WILFRED LOWELL                                      0
DONALD ROLLO    MATTS                              16
DICK JONES      ROSE HILL                          18
PAT LAVAY       ROSE HILL                          21
ADAH TALBOT     PAPA KING                          23
PETER LAWSON    CRANMER                            25
GEORGE OSCAR    ROSE HILL                          41
ELBERT TALBOT   WEITBROCHT                         43
WILFRED LOWELL                                     67
```

NOTE

This is the only case in which you should use the positional number of columns in the **order by** clause in ORACLE7.1 and above. When you are *not* using **UNION, INTERSECT,** and **MINUS,** you should use column aliases in the **order by** clause instead. See **order by** in the Alphabetical Reference.

You can use combination operators with two or more tables, but when you do, precedence becomes an issue, especially if **INTERSECT** and **MINUS** appear. Use parentheses to force the order you desire.

IN Subqueries

Combination operators can be used in subqueries, but, with one exception, they have equivalent constructions using the operators **IN, AND,** and **OR**.

UNION

Here the WORKER list is checked for those names that are in either the PROSPECT or the LONGTIME table. Of course, the names also must be in the WORKER table. Unlike the combinations of two tables *not* in a subquery, this **select** is restricted to the names in only one of the three tables, those already in the WORKER table:

```
select Name
   from WORKER
  where Name IN
        (select Name from PROSPECT)
           UNION
        (select Name from LONGTIME);
```

```
NAME
--------------
ADAH TALBOT
DICK JONES
DONALD ROLLO
ELBERT TALBOT
GEORGE OSCAR
JED HOPKINS
PAT LAVAY
PETER LAWSON
WILFRED LOWELL
```

The preceding seems to be the logical equivalent to this:

```
select Name
   from WORKER
  where Name IN
        (select Name from PROSPECT)
     OR Name IN
        (select Name from LONGTIME);
```

```
NAME
--------------
ADAH TALBOT
DICK JONES
DONALD ROLLO
ELBERT TALBOT
GEORGE OSCAR
JED HOPKINS
```

```
PAT LAVAY
PETER LAWSON
WILFRED LOWELL
```

It appears that an **OR** construction can be built that is equivalent to the **UNION**.

A Warning About UNION

Reverse the order of the tables that are **UNION**ed and watch what happens. (The asterisks were added after the fact to highlight the differences.)

```
select Name from WORKER
 where Name IN
        (select Name from LONGTIME)
          UNION
        (select Name from PROSPECT);

NAME
--------------------------
ADAH TALBOT
DICK JONES
DONALD ROLLO
DORY KENSON         *
ELBERT TALBOT
GEORGE OSCAR
GEORGE PHEPPS       *
JED HOPKINS
PAT LAVAY
PETER LAWSON
TED BUTCHER         *
WILFRED LOWELL
```

Three names appear in the result that are not in the previous two versions of the query, and they are not even in the WORKER table! Why? Because the **IN** has higher precedence than the **UNION**. This means the test of this:

```
Name IN
(select Name from LONGTIME)
```

is first evaluated, and its result is then **UNION**ed with this:

```
(select Name from PROSPECT)
```

This result is not at all intuitive. If this is the kind of effect you want a query to produce, put plenty of comments near your SQL statement, because no one will ever guess this is what you intended. Otherwise, always enclose a **UNION**ed set of **select**s in parentheses, to force precedence:

```
select Name from WORKER
 where Name IN (
        (select Name from LONGTIME)
          UNION
        (select Name from PROSPECT) );


NAME
-------------------------

ADAH TALBOT
DICK JONES
DONALD ROLLO
ELBERT TALBOT
GEORGE OSCAR
JED HOPKINS
PAT LAVAY
PETER LAWSON
WILFRED LOWELL
```

INTERSECT

Here the WORKER table is checked for those names that are in both the PROSPECT table and the LONGTIME table. Reversing the order of the **INTERSECT**ed tables will not affect the result.

```
select Name
  from WORKER
 where Name IN
        (select Name from PROSPECT)
         INTERSECT
        (select Name from LONGTIME);


NAME
--------------

ADAH TALBOT
ELBERT TALBOT
PAT LAVAY
WILFRED LOWELL
```

The following gives you the same result:

```
select Name
   from WORKER
 where Name IN
       (select Name from PROSPECT)
   AND Name IN
       (select Name from LONGTIME);

NAME
--------------
ADAH TALBOT
ELBERT TALBOT
PAT LAVAY
WILFRED LOWELL
```

MINUS

The PROSPECT table **MINUS** the LONGTIME table produces only one name that is in the WORKER table. Reversing the order of the **MINUS**ed tables *will* change the results of this query, as will be shown shortly:

```
select Name
   from WORKER
 where Name IN
       (select Name from PROSPECT)
          MINUS
       (select Name from LONGTIME);

NAME
--------------
JED HOPKINS
```

Here is the equivalent query without **MINUS**:

```
select Name
   from WORKER
 where Name IN
       (select Name from PROSPECT)
   and Name NOT IN
       (select Name from LONGTIME);

NAME
--------------
JED HOPKINS
```

Reversing the order of the tables produces these results:

```
select Name from WORKER
 where Name IN
       (select Name from LONGTIME)
         MINUS
       (select Name from PROSPECT);


NAME
------------------------
DICK JONES
DONALD ROLLO
GEORGE OSCAR
PETER LAWSON
```

This is a much more intuitive result than the reversal of tables in **UNION**, because here which table is subtracted from the other has obvious consequences (see the earlier section, "UNION, INTERSECT, and MINUS," for details of **MINUS**ed tables), and the precedence of the **IN** will not change the result.

A Warning About MINUS

It is not uncommon to use **MINUS** when one of the tables in the subquery is the same as the outer query table. The danger here is that if that is the table after the **MINUS**, it is subtracted *from itself*. Without other qualifiers (such as in the **where** clause of the **select** following the **MINUS**), no records will be selected.

```
select Name
   from PROSPECT
 where Name IN
       (select Name from LONGTIME)
         MINUS
       (select Name from PROSPECT);

no rows selected
```

Restrictions on UNION, INTERSECT, and MINUS

Queries that use a **UNION**, **INTERSECT**, or **MINUS** in their **where** clause must have the same number and type of columns in their **select** list:

```
select Name from WORKER
 where (Name, Lodging) IN
       (select Name, Lodging from LONGTIME)
         MINUS
       (select Name, Address from PROSPECT);
```

```
ERROR at line 1: ORA-1789:  query block has incorrect number of
result columns
```

But an equivalent **IN** construction does not have this limitation:

```
select Name from WORKER
 where (Name, Lodging) IN
       (select Name, Lodging from LONGTIME)
   AND (Name, Lodging) NOT IN
       (select Name, Address from PROSPECT);
```

```
NAME
-------------------------
ADAH TALBOT
DICK JONES
DONALD ROLLO
ELBERT TALBOT
GEORGE OSCAR
PAT LAVAY
PETER LAWSON
```

To make the **MINUS** version work, all of the columns in the **where** clause must be in the **select** clause. They must also, of course, be in the **select** clause of the **MINUS**ed **select** statements:

```
select Name, Lodging from WORKER
 where (Name, Lodging) IN
       (select Name, Lodging from LONGTIME)
         MINUS
       (select Name, Address from PROSPECT);
```

```
NAME                      LODGING
------------------------- -----------------------------------
ADAH TALBOT               PAPA KING
DICK JONES                ROSE HILL
DONALD ROLLO              MATTS
ELBERT TALBOT             WEITBROCHT
```

```
GEORGE OSCAR            ROSE HILL
PAT LAVAY               ROSE HILL
PETER LAWSON            CRANMER
```

Some books and other published materials suggest that combination operators cannot be used in subqueries. This is untrue. Here is an example of how to use them:

```
select Name from WORKER
 where (Name, Lodging) IN
        (select Name, Lodging from WORKER
         where (Name, Lodging) IN
                (select Name, Address from PROSPECT)
                  UNION
                (select Name, Lodging from LONGTIME) );
```

```
NAME
-------------------------
ADAH TALBOT
DICK JONES
DONALD ROLLO
ELBERT TALBOT
GEORGE OSCAR
PAT LAVAY
PETER LAWSON
```

The use of combination operators in place of **IN**, **AND**, and **OR** is a matter of personal style. Most SQL users regard **IN**, **AND**, and **OR** as being clearer and easier to understand.

CHAPTER 11

Some Complex Possibilities

This chapter continues the study of the more complex ORACLE functions and features. Of particular interest here is the creation of simple and group queries that can be turned into views, the use of totals in calculations, and the creation of reports showing tree structure. Like those in Chapter 10, these techniques are not essential for most reporting needs, and if they look overly difficult, don't be frightened off. If you are new to ORACLE and the use of its query facilities, it is enough to know that these exist and can be turned to if needed.

Creating a Complex View

Views can build upon each other. In Chapter 9, you saw the concept of creating a view of a grouping of rows from a table. Here the concept is extended to show how views can be joined to other views and tables to produce yet another view. This technique, although it sounds a bit complicated, actually simplifies the task of querying and reporting. Here is a list of expenses G. B. Talbot incurred during March of 1901. It was a difficult month. These items, spellings, and prices are directly from the ledger.

```
column Amount format 999.90
column Item format a23
column Person format a16 column

select ActionDate, Item, Person, Amount
  from LEDGER
 where ActionDate BETWEEN '01-MAR-01' AND '31-MAR-01'
   and Action IN ('BOUGHT','PAID')
 order by ActionDate;


ACTIONDAT ITEM                     PERSON              AMOUNT
--------- ----------------------- ----------------- ------
05-MAR-01 TELEPHONE CALL           PHONE COMPANY         .20
06-MAR-01 MEDISON FOR INDIGESTION DR. CARLSTROM         .40
06-MAR-01 PANTS                    GENERAL STORE         .75
07-MAR-01 SHOEING                  BLACKSMITH            .35
07-MAR-01 MAIL BOX                 POST OFFICE          1.00
08-MAR-01 TOBACCO FOR LICE         MILL                  .25
10-MAR-01 STOVE PIPE THIMBLES      VERNA HARDWARE       1.00
13-MAR-01 THERMOMETER              GENERAL STORE         .15
14-MAR-01 LOT IN CEMETERY NO. 80   METHODIST CHURCH    25.00
14-MAR-01 DIGGING OF GRAVE         JED HOPKINS          3.00
16-MAR-01 GRINDING                 MILL                  .16
20-MAR-01 WORK                     DICK JONES           1.00
22-MAR-01 MILK CANS                VERNA HARDWARE       5.00
23-MAR-01 CLOTH FOR DRESS LINING   GENERAL STORE         .54
25-MAR-01 BOOTS FOR SHIRLEY        GENERAL STORE        2.50
27-MAR-01 HOMINY                   MILL                  .77
30-MAR-01 FIXING SHIRLEYS WATCH    MANNER JEWELERS       .25
```

When reordered by Person, you can see how Talbot's expenditures were concentrated:

```
select ActionDate, Item, Person, Amount
   from LEDGER
 where ActionDate BETWEEN '01-MAR-01' AND'31-MAR-01'
   and Action IN ('BOUGHT','PAID')
 order by Person, ActionDate;
```

```
ACTIONDAT ITEM                         PERSON              AMOUNT
--------- ----------------------       ------------------  ------
07-MAR-01 SHOEING                      BLACKSMITH             .35
20-MAR-01 WORK                         DICK JONES            1.00
06-MAR-01 MEDISON FOR INDIGESTION DR. CARLSTROM              .40
06-MAR-01 PANTS                        GENERAL STORE          .75
13-MAR-01 THERMOMETER                  GENERAL STORE          .15
23-MAR-01 CLOTH FOR DRESS LINING       GENERAL STORE          .54
25-MAR-01 BOOTS FOR SHIRLEY            GENERAL STORE         2.50
14-MAR-01 DIGGING OF GRAVE             JED HOPKINS           3.00
30-MAR-01 FIXING SHIRLEYS WATCH        MANNER JEWELERS        .25
14-MAR-01 LOT IN CEMETERY NO. 80       METHODIST CHURCH     25.00
08-MAR-01 TOBACCO FOR LICE             MILL                   .25
16-MAR-01 GRINDING                     MILL                   .16
27-MAR-01 HOMINY                       MILL                   .77
05-MAR-01 TELEPHONE CALL               PHONE COMPANY          .20
07-MAR-01 MAIL BOX                     POST OFFICE           1.00
10-MAR-01 STOVE PIPE THIMBLES          VERNA HARDWARE        1.00
22-MAR-01 MILK CANS                    VERNA HARDWARE        5.00
```

A View of a Group

A view is created of this table, **group**ed **by** Person, so you can see how much Talbot spent with each supplier. Note the use of aliases for the computed column:

```
create or replace view ITEMTOTAL as
select Person, SUM(Amount) ItemTotal
   from LEDGER
 where ActionDate BETWEEN '01-MAR-01' AND '31-MAR-01'
   and Action IN ('BOUGHT','PAID')
 group by Person;

View created.
```

Here is what the view contains:

```
column ItemTotal format 99,999.90

select * from ITEMTOTAL;

PERSON             ITEMTOTAL
----------------   ---------
BLACKSMITH               .35
DICK JONES             1.00
DR. CARLSTROM           .40
GENERAL STORE          3.94
JED HOPKINS            3.00
MANNER JEWELERS         .25
METHODIST CHURCH      25.00
MILL                   1.18
PHONE COMPANY           .20
POST OFFICE            1.00
VERNA HARDWARE         6.00
```

A View of the Total

Next, another view is created of exactly the same information, but without a **group by** clause. This creates a complete total for all of the records:

```
create or replace view TOTAL as
select SUM(Amount) TOTAL
   from LEDGER
 where ActionDate BETWEEN '01-MAR-01' AND '31-MAR-01'
   and Action IN ('BOUGHT','PAID');

View created.
```

This view contains just one record:

```
select * from TOTAL;

   TOTAL
-------
   42.32
```

The Combined View

Finally, yet another view is created. This one contains the base table, LEDGER; the view of totals by item, ITEMTOTAL; and the view of the total expense for all items, TOTAL. Note again the use of aliases both for computed columns and for the underlying table and view names. This view is in effect a three-way join of a table to itself, using views that summarize the table in two different ways:

```
create or replace view ByItem as
select L.Person Person, Item, Amount,
       100*Amount/ItemTotal ByPerson, 100*Amount/Total ByTotal
  from LEDGER L, ITEMTOTAL I, TOTAL
 where L.PERSON = I.PERSON
   and ActionDate BETWEEN '01-MAR-01' AND '31-MAR-01'
   and Action IN ('BOUGHT','PAID');

View created.
```

Now three **compute sum**s are put into place, along with a **break on** to force the summing (addition) to occur. Look at how simple the **select** statement is here:

```
column ByPerson format 9,999.99
column ByTotal format 9,999.99

break on Person skip 1
compute sum of ByPerson on Person
compute sum of ByTotal  on Person
compute sum of Amount   on Person

select Person, Item, Amount, ByPerson, ByTotal
  from ByItem
 order by Person;
```

Yet look at the tremendous wealth of information it produces! Not only are each item and its price shown, but also its percentage of all the expenses to that person, and its percentage of all expenses, are shown on the same line:

```
PERSON            ITEM                        AMOUNT BYPERSON BYTOTAL
----------------  ------------------------    ------ -------- -------
BLACKSMITH        SHOEING                        .35   100.00     .83
* * * * * * * * * * * * * * * *                 ------ -------- -------
sum                                              .35   100.00     .83


DICK JONES        WORK                         1.00   100.00    2.36
* * * * * * * * * * * * * * * *                 ------ -------- -------
sum                                            1.00   100.00    2.36


DR. CARLSTROM     MEDISON FOR INDIGESTION       .40   100.00     .95
* * * * * * * * * * * * * * * *                 ------ -------- -------
sum                                              .40   100.00     .95


GENERAL STORE     PANTS                          .75    19.04    1.77
                  CLOTH FOR DRESS LINING         .54    13.71    1.28
                  THERMOMETER                    .15     3.81     .35
                  BOOTS FOR SHIRLEY             2.50    63.45    5.91
* * * * * * * * * * * * * * * *                 ------ -------- -------
sum                                            3.94   100.00    9.31


JED HOPKINS       DIGGING OF GRAVE             3.00   100.00    7.09
* * * * * * * * * * * * * * * *                 ------ -------- -------
sum                                            3.00   100.00    7.09


MANNER JEWELERS   FIXING SHIRLEYS WATCH         .25   100.00     .59
* * * * * * * * * * * * * * * *                 ------ -------- -------
sum                                              .25   100.00     .59


METHODIST CHURCH  LOT IN CEMETERY NO. 80      25.00   100.00   59.07
* * * * * * * * * * * * * * * *                 ------ -------- -------
sum                                           25.00   100.00   59.07


MILL              TOBACCO FOR LICE              .25    21.19     .59
                  HOMINY                        .77    65.25    1.82
                  GRINDING                      .16    13.56     .38
* * * * * * * * * * * * * * * *                 ------ -------- -------
sum                                            1.18   100.00    2.79
```

```
PHONE COMPANY      TELEPHONE CALL              .20    100.00      .47
* * * * * * * * * * * * * * * *                ------  --------  -------
sum                                            .20    100.00      .47


POST OFFICE        MAIL BOX                   1.00    100.00     2.36
* * * * * * * * * * * * * * * *                ------  --------  -------
sum                                          1.00    100.00     2.36


VERNA HARDWARE     STOVE PIPE THIMBLES        1.00     16.67     2.36
                   MILK CANS                  5.00     83.33    11.81
* * * * * * * * * * * * * * * *                ------  --------  -------
sum                                          6.00    100.00    14.18
```

With this technique of using both summary views of a table joined to itself, and views of several tables joined together, you can create views and reports that include weighted averages, effective yield, percentage of total, percentage of subtotal, and many similar calculations. There is no effective limit to how many views can be built on top of each other, although even the most complex calculations seldom require more than three or four levels of views built upon views. The **break on report** command, which is used for grand totals, is discussed in Chapter 12.

Family Trees and connect by

One of ORACLE's more interesting but little used or understood facilities is its **connect by** clause. Put simply, it is a method to report in order the branches of a *family tree*. Such trees are encountered often: the genealogy of human families, livestock, horses, corporate management, company divisions, manufacturing, literature, ideas, evolution, scientific research, and theory—even views built upon views.

The **connect by** clause provides a means to report on all of the family members in any of these many trees. It lets you exclude branches or individual members of a family tree, and allows you to travel through the tree either up or down, reporting on the family members encountered during the trip.

The earliest ancestor in the tree is technically called the *root node*. In everyday English this would be called the trunk. Extending from the trunk are branches, which have other branches, which have still other branches. The forks where one or more branches split away from a larger branch are called *nodes*, and the very end of a branch is called a *leaf*, or a *leaf node*. Figure 11-1 shows a picture of such a tree.

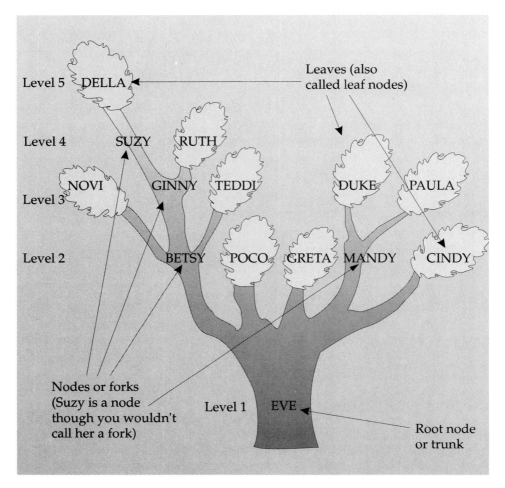

FIGURE 11-1. *Talbot's cows and bulls, born starting with EVE*

The following is a table of cows and bulls born between January 1900 and October 1908. Each offspring, as born, is entered as a row in the table, along with its sex, parents (the cow and bull), and its birthdate. If you compare the Cows and Offspring in this table with Figure 11-1, you'll find they correspond. EVE has no cow or bull parent, as she was the first generation, and ADAM and BANDIT are bulls brought in for breeding, again with no parents in the table.

```
column Cow format a6
column Bull format a6
column Offspring format a10
column Sex format a3

select * from BREEDING
 order by Birthdate;

OFFSPRING  SEX COW    BULL   BIRTHDATE
---------- --- ------ ------ ---------
EVE        F
ADAM       M
BANDIT     M
BETSY      F   EVE    ADAM   02-JAN-00
POCO       M   EVE    ADAM   15-JUL-00
GRETA      F   EVE    BANDIT 12-MAR-01
MANDY      F   EVE    POCO   22-AUG-02
CINDY      F   EVE    POCO   09-FEB-03
NOVI       F   BETSY  ADAM   30-MAR-03
GINNY      F   BETSY  BANDIT 04-DEC-03
DUKE       M   MANDY  BANDIT 24-JUL-04
TEDDI      F   BETSY  BANDIT 12-AUG-05
SUZY       F   GINNY  DUKE   03-APR-06
PAULA      F   MANDY  POCO   21-DEC-06
RUTH       F   GINNY  DUKE   25-DEC-06
DELLA      F   SUZY   BANDIT 11-OCT-08
```

Next, a query is written to illustrate the family relationships visually. This is done using **LPAD** and a special column, Level, that comes along with **connect by**. Level is a number, from 1 for EVE to 5 for DELLA, that is really the *generation.* If EVE is the first generation of cattle Talbot keeps, then DELLA is the fifth generation. Whenever the **connect by** clause is used, the Level column can be added to the **select** statement to discover the generation of each row. Level is a *pseudo-column,* like SysDate and User. It's not really a part of the table, but it is available under specific circumstances. The next listing shows an example using Level.

The results of this query are apparent in the following table, but why did the **select** statement produce this? How does it work?

```
select Cow, Bull, LPAD(' ',6*(Level-1))||Offspring Offspring,
       Sex, Birthdate
  from BREEDING
 start with Offspring = 'EVE'
 connect by Cow = PRIOR Offspring;
```

COW	BULL	OFFSPRING					SEX	BIRTHDATE
		EVE					F	
EVE	ADAM		BETSY				F	02-JAN-00
BETSY	ADAM			NOVI			F	30-MAR-03
BETSY	BANDIT			GINNY			F	04-DEC-03
GINNY	DUKE				SUZY		F	03-APR-06
SUZY	BANDIT					DELLA	F	11-OCT-08
GINNY	DUKE				RUTH		F	25-DEC-06
BETSY	BANDIT			TEDDI			F	12-AUG-05
EVE	ADAM	POCO					M	15-JUL-00
EVE	BANDIT	GRETA					F	12-MAR-01
EVE	POCO	MANDY					F	22-AUG-02
MANDY	BANDIT			DUKE			M	24-JUL-04
MANDY	POCO			PAULA			F	21-DEC-06
EVE	POCO	CINDY					F	09-FEB-03

Note that this is really Figure 11-1 turned clockwise onto its side. EVE isn't centered, but she is the root node (trunk) of this tree. Her children are BETSY, POCO, GRETA, MANDY, and CINDY. BETSY's children are NOVI, GINNY, and TEDDI. GINNY's children are SUZY and RUTH. And SUZY's child is DELLA. MANDY also has two children, DUKE and PAULA.

This tree started with EVE as the first "offspring." If the SQL statement had said **start with** MANDY, only MANDY, DUKE, and PAULA would have been selected. **start with** defines the beginning of that portion of the tree that will be displayed, and it includes only branches stretching out from the individual that **start with** specifies. **start with** acts just as its name implies.

The **LPAD** in the **select** statement is probably very confusing in its construction. Recall from Chapter 5 the format for **LPAD**:

```
LPAD(string,length [,'set'])
```

Compare this to the **LPAD** in the **select** statement shown earlier:

```
LPAD(' ',6*(Level-1))
```

The two single quotation marks separated by a space do *not* define the character to be used in padding. It is a literal column, a *string* one character long. The 6*(Level-1) is the *length*, and because the **set** is not defined, the default, also a space, is used. In other words, this tells SQL to take this string of one space and left-pad it to the number of spaces determined by 6*(Level-1). What is that number?

```
6*(Level-1)
```

is a calculation made by first subtracting 1 from the Level. For EVE the Level is 1, so 1-1 is zero. For BETSY, the Level (her generation) is 2, so 2-1 is one. This result is then multiplied by 6, and that number is how many spaces will be concatenated to the left of the Offspring column. Note that **LPAD** is not padding Offspring directly, but is concatenated to Offspring. The effect is obvious in the result just shown. Each generation, or level, is left padded with spaces corresponding to its Level.

Why is this padding and concatenation done, instead of simply using **LPAD** directly on Offspring? For two reasons. First, a direct **LPAD** on Offspring would cause the names to be right justified. The names at each level would end up having their last letters lined up vertically. Second, if **Level-1** is equal to 0, as it is for EVE, the resulting **LPAD** of EVE will be 0 characters wide. EVE will vanish:

```
select Cow, Bull, LPAD(Offspring,6*(Level-1),' ') Offspring,
       Sex, Birthdate   from BREEDING
  start with Offspring = 'EVE'
connect by Cow = PRIOR Offspring;


COW     BULL    OFFSPRING                        SEX BIRTHDATE
------  ------  ------------------------------   --- ---------
                                                 F
EVE     ADAM    BETSY                            F   02-JAN-00
BETSY   ADAM          NOVI                       F   30-MAR-03
BETSY   BANDIT        GINNY                      F   04-DEC-03
GINNY   DUKE               SUZY                  F   03-APR-06
SUZY    BANDIT                DELLA              F   11-OCT-08
GINNY   DUKE               RUTH                  F   25-DEC-06
BETSY   BANDIT        TEDDI                      F   12-AUG-05
EVE     ADAM     POCO                            M   15-JUL-00
EVE     BANDIT  GRETA                            F   12-MAR-01
EVE     POCO    MANDY                            F   22-AUG-02
MANDY   BANDIT        DUKE                       M   24-JUL-04
MANDY   POCO          PAULA                      F   21-DEC-06
EVE     POCO    CINDY                            F   09-FEB-03
```

Thus, to get the proper spacing for each level, to assure that EVE appears, and to make the names line up vertically on the left, the **LPAD** should be used with the concatenate function, and not directly on the Offspring column.

Now, how does **connect by** work? Look again at Figure 11-1. Starting with NOVI and traveling downward, which cows are the offspring prior to NOVI? The first is BETSY. And the offspring just prior to BETSY is EVE. Even though it is not instantly readable, this clause:

```
connect by Cow = PRIOR Offspring
```

tells SQL to find the next row in which the value in the Cow column is equal to the value in the Offspring column in the prior row. Look at the table and you'll see this is true.

Excluding Individuals and Branches

There are two methods of excluding cows from a report. One uses the normal **where** clause technique, and the other uses the **connect by** clause itself. The difference is that the exclusion using the **connect by** clause will exclude not just the cow mentioned, but all of its children as well. If you use **connect by** to exclude BETSY, then NOVI, GINNY, TEDDI, SUZY, RUTH, and DELLA all vanish as well. The **connect by** really tracks the tree structure. If BETSY had never been born, none of her offspring would have been either. In this example, the **and** clause modifies the **connect by** clause.

```
select Cow, Bull, LPAD(' ',6*(Level-1))||Offspring Offspring,
       Sex, Birthdate
  from BREEDING
 start with Offspring = 'EVE'
connect by Cow = PRIOR Offspring
    AND Offspring != 'BETSY';
```

COW	BULL	OFFSPRING		SEX	BIRTHDATE
		EVE		F	
EVE	ADAM	POCO		M	15-JUL-00
EVE	BANDIT	GRETA		F	12-MAR-01
EVE	POCO	MANDY		F	22-AUG-02
MANDY	BANDIT		DUKE	M	24-JUL-04
MANDY	POCO		PAULA	F	21-DEC-06
EVE	POCO	CINDY		F	09-FEB-03

The **where** clause removes only the cow or cows it mentions. If BETSY dies, she is removed from the chart, but her offspring are not. In fact, notice that BETSY is still there under the Cow column as mother of her children, NOVI, GINNY, and TEDDI:

```
select Cow, Bull, LPAD(' ',6*(Level-1))||Offspring Offspring,
       Sex, Birthdate
  from BREEDING
 where Offspring != 'BETSY'
 start with Offspring = 'EVE'
connect by Cow = PRIOR Offspring;
```

```
COW     BULL    OFFSPRING                               SEX BIRTHDATE
------  ------  ------------------------------------    --- ---------
                EVE                                     F
BETSY   ADAM              NOVI                          F   30-MAR-03
BETSY   BANDIT            GINNY                         F   04-DEC-03
GINNY   DUKE                    SUZY                    F   03-APR-06
SUZY    BANDIT                        DELLA             F   11-OCT-08
GINNY   DUKE                  RUTH                      F   25-DEC-06
BETSY   BANDIT          TEDDI                           F   12-AUG-05
EVE     ADAM      POCO                                  M   15-JUL-00
EVE     BANDIT    GRETA                                 F   12-MAR-01
EVE     POCO      MANDY                                 F   22-AUG-02
MANDY   BANDIT            DUKE                          M   24-JUL-04
MANDY   POCO            PAULA                           F   21-DEC-06
EVE     POCO      CINDY                                 F   09-FEB-03
```

The order in which the family tree is displayed when using **connect by** is basically level by level, left to right, as shown in Figure 11-1, starting with the lowest level, Level 1. For example, you may wish to alter this to collect the cows and their offspring by birthdate.

```
select Cow, Bull, LPAD(' ',6*(Level-1))||Offspring Offspring,
       Sex, Birthdate   from BREEDING
 start with Offspring = 'EVE'
connect by Cow = PRIOR Offspring
 order by Cow, Birthdate;
```

```
COW     BULL    OFFSPRING                               SEX BIRTHDATE
------  ------  ------------------------------------    --- ---------
                EVE                                     F
BETSY   ADAM              NOVI                          F   30-MAR-03
BETSY   BANDIT            GINNY                         F   04-DEC-03
BETSY   BANDIT            TEDDI                         F   12-AUG-05
EVE     ADAM      BETSY                                 F   02-JAN-00
EVE     ADAM      POCO                                  M   15-JUL-00
EVE     BANDIT    GRETA                                 F   12-MAR-01
```

```
EVE      POCO      MANDY                            F    22-AUG-02
EVE      POCO      CINDY                            F    09-FEB-03
GINNY    DUKE                         SUZY          F    03-APR-06
GINNY    DUKE                         RUTH          F    25-DEC-06
MANDY    BANDIT         DUKE                         M    24-JUL-04
MANDY    POCO           PAULA                        F    21-DEC-06
SUZY     BANDIT                              DELLA   F    11-OCT-08
```

The generations are still obvious in the display, but Offspring are more closely grouped with their mother. Another way to look at the same family tree is by Birthdate, as follows:

```
select Cow, Bull, LPAD(' ',6*(Level-1))||Offspring Offspring,
       Sex, Birthdate
  from BREEDING
 start with Offspring = 'EVE'
connect by Cow = PRIOR Offspring
 order by Birthdate;
```

```
COW      BULL    OFFSPRING                            SEX BIRTHDATE
------   ------  ------------------------------       --- ---------
                 EVE                                   F
EVE      ADAM      BETSY                               F    02-JAN-00
EVE      ADAM      POCO                                M    15-JUL-00
EVE      BANDIT    GRETA                               F    12-MAR-01
EVE      POCO      MANDY                               F    22-AUG-02
EVE      POCO      CINDY                               F    09-FEB-03
BETSY    ADAM           NOVI                           F    30-MAR-03
BETSY    BANDIT         GINNY                          F    04-DEC-03
MANDY    BANDIT         DUKE                           M    24-JUL-04
BETSY    BANDIT         TEDDI                          F    12-AUG-05
GINNY    DUKE                SUZY                      F    03-APR-06
MANDY    POCO           PAULA                          F    21-DEC-06
GINNY    DUKE                RUTH                      F    25-DEC-06
SUZY     BANDIT                     DELLA              F    11-OCT-08
```

Now the order of the rows no longer shows generations, as in a tree, but the indenting still preserves this information. You can't tell what offspring belong to which parents without looking at the Cow and Bull columns, though.

Traveling Toward the Roots

Thus far, the direction of travel in reporting on the family tree has been from parents toward children. Is it possible to start with a child, and move backward to parent, grandparent, great-grandparent, and so on? To do so, the word PRIOR is simply moved to the other side of the equal sign. The following traces DELLA's ancestry:

```
select Cow, Bull, LPAD(' ',6*(Level-1))||Offspring Offspring,
       Sex, Birthdate
  from BREEDING
 start with Offspring = 'DELLA'
connect by Offspring = PRIOR Cow;
```

COW	BULL	OFFSPRING				SEX	BIRTHDATE
SUZY	BANDIT	DELLA				F	11-OCT-08
GINNY	DUKE		SUZY			F	03-APR-06
BETSY	BANDIT			GINNY		F	04-DEC-03
EVE	ADAM				BETSY	F	02-JAN-00
						EVE	F

This shows DELLA's own roots, but is a bit confusing if compared to the previous displays. It looks like DELLA is the ancestor, and EVE the great-great-granddaughter. Adding an **order by** for Birthdate helps, but EVE is still further to the right:

```
select Cow, Bull, LPAD(' ',6*(Level-1))||Offspring Offspring,
       Sex, Birthdate
  from BREEDING
 start with Offspring = 'DELLA'
connect by Offspring = PRIOR Cow
 order by Birthdate;
```

COW	BULL	OFFSPRING				SEX	BIRTHDATE
					EVE	F	
EVE	ADAM				BETSY	F	02-JAN-00
BETSY	BANDIT			GINNY		F	04-DEC-03
GINNY	DUKE		SUZY			F	03-APR-06
SUZY	BANDIT	DELLA				F	11-OCT-08

The solution is simply to change the calculation in the **LPAD**:

```
select Cow, Bull, LPAD(' ',6*(5-Level))||Offspring Offspring,
       Sex, Birthdate
  from BREEDING
 start with Offspring = 'DELLA'
connect by Offspring = PRIOR Cow
 order by Birthdate;
```

```
COW     BULL    OFFSPRING                               SEX BIRTHDATE
------  ------  --------------------------------------  --- ---------
                EVE                                     F
EVE     ADAM          BETSY                             F   02-JAN-00
BETSY   BANDIT               GINNY                      F   04-DEC-03
GINNY   DUKE                        SUZY                F   03-APR-06
SUZY    BANDIT                             DELLA        F   11-OCT-08
```

Finally, look how different this report is when the **connect by** tracks the parentage of the Bull. Here are Adam's offspring:

```
select Cow, Bull, LPAD(' ',6*(Level-1))||Offspring Offspring,
       Sex, Birthdate
  from BREEDING
 start with Offspring = 'ADAM'
connect by PRIOR Offspring = Bull;
```

```
COW     BULL    OFFSPRING                               SEX BIRTHDATE
------  ------  --------------------------------------  --- ---------
                ADAM                                    M
EVE     ADAM          BETSY                             F   02-JAN-00
EVE     ADAM          POCO                              M   15-JUL-00
EVE     POCO                MANDY                       F   22-AUG-02
EVE     POCO                CINDY                       F   09-FEB-03
MANDY   POCO                PAULA                       F   21-DEC-06
BETSY   ADAM          NOVI                              F   30-MAR-03
```

ADAM and BANDIT were the original bulls at the initiation of the herd. In order to create a single tree that reported both ADAM's and BANDIT's offspring, you would have to invent a "father" for the two of them, which would be the root of the tree. One of the advantages that these alternative trees have over the type of tree shown earlier is that many inheritance groups, from families to projects to divisions within companies, can be accurately portrayed in more than one way.

```
select Cow, Bull, LPAD(' ',6*(Level-1))||Offspring Offspring,
       Sex, Birthdate
   from BREEDING
  start with Offspring = 'BANDIT'
 connect by PRIOR Offspring = Bull;
```

```
COW     BULL    OFFSPRING                       SEX BIRTHDATE
------  ------  ------------------------------- --- ---------
                BANDIT                          M
EVE     BANDIT      GRETA                       F   12-MAR-01
BETSY   BANDIT      GINNY                       F   04-DEC-03
MANDY   BANDIT      DUKE                        M   24-JUL-04
GINNY   DUKE            SUZY                    F   03-APR-06
GINNY   DUKE            RUTH                    F   25-DEC-06
BETSY   BANDIT      TEDDI                       F   12-AUG-05
SUZY    BANDIT      DELLA                       F   11-OCT-08
```

The Basic Rules

Using **connect by** and **start with** to create treelike reports is not difficult, but certain basic rules must be followed:

■ The order of the clauses when using **connect by** is

   select
   from
   where
   start with
   connect by
   order by

■ **prior** forces reporting to be from the root out toward the leaves (if the **prior** column is the parent) or from a leaf toward the root (if the **prior** column is the child).

■ A **where** clause eliminates individuals from the tree, but not their descendants (or ancestors, if **prior** is on the right side of the equal sign).

■ A qualification in the **connect by** (particularly a not equal) eliminates both an individual and all of its descendants (or ancestors, depending on how you trace the tree).

■ **connect by** cannot be used with a table join in the **where** clause.

This particular set of commands is one that few people are likely to remember correctly. However, with a basic understanding of the tree and inheritance, constructing a proper **select** statement to report on a tree should just be a matter of referring to this chapter for correct syntax.

C H A P T E R 12

Building a Report in SQLPLUS

Chapter 4 showed basic formatting of reports and Chapters 3 and 9 gave methods for using groups and views. This chapter will look at more advanced formatting methods as well as more complex computations of weighted averages. A number of interrelationships among various SQLPLUS commands are not documented in any of the manuals or books on ORACLE. This chapter will review these interrelationships as well.

Advanced Formatting

Chapter 1 showed an example of a stock table from the newspaper. Here you will actually manipulate that table to draw nonobvious information from it. For the sake of brevity, the stocks examined will be limited to a small number in three industries: electronics, space, and the medical field. These are the column commands in effect:

```
column Net format 99.90
column Industry format a11
column Company format a18
column CloseToday heading 'Close|Today' format 999.90
column CloseYesterday heading 'Close|Yest.' format 999.90
column Volume format 999,999,999
```

The first **select** simply pulls out the stocks in the three industries, does a simple calculation of the difference in closing prices between today and yesterday, and then sorts them in order by Industry and Company, as shown in Figure 12-1.

This is a good beginning, but in order to make it more meaningful, some additional features are added. A new column is calculated to show the percentage of change between one day's trading and the next:

```
(CloseToday/CloseYesterday)*100 - 100 Percent,
```

The calculation is given the alias Percent, and column formatting is put in place for it. Additionally, both Company and Industry columns are cut back considerably to make room for additional columns, which will be added shortly. Of course, on a wide report, such as one with 132 columns, this may not be necessary. It is done here for space considerations.

```
column Percent heading 'Percent|Change' format 9999.90
column Company format a8 trunc
column Industry heading 'Ind' format a5 trunc
```

Formatting Problems with Numbers

Note that problems occasionally occur with numbers whose column headings are wider than their formatting definitions. For example, a column named Interest with a format of 99.90 has eight characters in the name but only four digits in the allotted space.

SQLPLUS picks up its formatting information for internal calculations from the number format, and not from the column heading. Therefore, a column being

```
select  Industry, Company,
        CloseYesterday, CloseToday,
        (CloseToday - CloseYesterday) Net,
        Volume    from STOCK
 where Industry in ('ELECTRONICS', 'SPACE', 'MEDICAL')
 order by Industry, Company
/
```

INDUSTRY	COMPANY	Close Yest.	Close Today	NET	VOLUME
ELECTRONICS	IDK	95.00	95.25	.25	9,443,523
ELECTRONICS	MEMORY GRAPHICS	15.50	14.25	-1.25	4,557,992
ELECTRONICS	MICRO TOKEN	77.00	76.50	-.50	25,205,667
MEDICAL	AT SPACE	46.75	48.00	1.25	11,398,323
MEDICAL	AUGUST ENTERPRISES	15.00	15.00	.00	12,221,711
MEDICAL	HAYWARD ANTISEPTIC	104.25	106.00	1.75	3,358,561
MEDICAL	KENTGEN BIOPHYSICS	18.25	19.50	1.25	6,636,863
SPACE	BRANDON ELLIPSIS	32.75	33.50	.75	25,789,769
SPACE	GENERAL ENTROPY	64.25	66.00	1.75	7,598,562
SPACE	GENEVA ROCKETRY	22.75	28.00	1.25	22,533,944
SPACE	NORTHERN BOREAL	26.75	28.00	1.25	1,348,323
SPACE	OCKHAM SYSTEMS	21.50	22.00	.50	7,052,990
SPACE	WONDER LABS	5.00	5.00	.00	2,553,712

FIGURE 12-1. *Closing stock prices and volume*

displayed or printed in SQLPLUS, whose name exceeds the total number of digits, will sometimes have spurious characters appear in the report and cause incorrect printing or a peculiar look. The solution to this is to be certain that the digits in the format statement are always at least as wide as the column title, less one (for the minus sign):

```
Interest
 9999.99
```

break on

Next, a **break on** is set up to put a blank line between the end of an Industry group and the beginning of the next Industry; the sum of the daily Volume, by Industry, is then computed. Note the coordination between **break on** and **compute sum** in Figure 12-2.

```
break on Industry skip 1

compute sum of Volume on Industry

select Industry,
       Company,
       CloseYesterday, CloseToday,
       (CloseToday - CloseYesterday) Net,
       (CloseToday/CloseYesterday)*100 - 100 Percent,
       Volume
  from STOCK
 where Industry in ('ELECTRONICS', 'SPACE', 'MEDICAL')
 order by Industry, Company
/
```

```
              Close   Close           Percent
Ind   COMPANY  Yest.   Today    NET    Change         VOLUME
----- -------- ------- ------- ------ ------- ------------
ELECT IDK       95.00   95.25    .25     .26     9,443,523
      MEMORY G  15.50   14.25  -1.25   -8.06     4,557,992
      MICRO TO  77.00   76.50   -.50    -.65    25,205,667
*****                                          ------------
sum                                             39,207,182


MEDIC AT SPACE  46.75   48.00   1.25    2.67    11,398,323
      AUGUST E  15.00   15.00    .00     .00    12,221,711
      HAYWARD  104.25  106.00   1.75    1.68     3,358,561
      KENTGEN   18.25   19.50   1.25    6.85     6,636,863
*****                                          ------------
sum                                             33,615,458


SPACE BRANDON   32.75   33.50    .75    2.29    25,789,769
      GENERAL   64.25   66.00   1.75    2.72     7,598,562
      GENEVA R  22.75   27.25   4.50   19.78    22,533,944
      NORTHERN  26.75   28.00   1.25    4.67     1,348,323
      OCKHAM S  21.50   22.00    .50    2.33     7,052,990
      WONDER L   5.00    5.00    .00     .00     2,553,712
*****                                          ------------
sum                                             66,877,300
```

FIGURE 12-2. *Stock report with a **break on** Industry and **compute sum** of Volume*

The **break on** and **compute sum** are now expanded. The order of the columns in the **break on** is critical, as will be explained shortly. The **compute sum** has been instructed to calculate the Volume on both the Industry and Report. See Figure 12-3.

```
break on Report on Industry skip 1

compute sum of Volume on Industry Report

select Industry,
       Company,
       CloseYesterday,
       CloseToday,
       (CloseToday - CloseYesterday) Net,
       (CloseToday/CloseYesterday)*100 - 100 Percent,
       Volume
  from STOCK
 where Industry in ('ELECTRONICS', 'SPACE', 'MEDICAL')
 order by Industry, Company
/
```

```
Current Portfolio                                   April 1st,1995
                          Industry Listings
                  Close   Close          Percent
Ind   COMPANY     Yest.   Today   NET    Change       VOLUME
----- --------    ------- ------- ------ -------   ------------
ELECT IDK          95.00   95.25    .25      .26     9,443,523
      MEMORY G     15.50   14.25  -1.25    -8.06     4,557,992
      MICRO TO     77.00   76.50   -.50     -.65    25,205,667
*****                                             ------------
sum                                                39,207,182

MEDIC AT SPACE     46.75   48.00   1.25     2.67    11,398,323
      AUGUST E     15.00   15.00    .00      .00    12,221,711
      HAYWARD     104.25  106.00   1.75     1.68     3,358,561
      KENTGEN      18.25   19.50   1.25     6.85     6,636,863
*****                                             ------------
sum                                                33,615,458

SPACE BRANDON      32.75   33.50    .75     2.29    25,789,769
      GENERAL      64.25   66.00   1.75     2.72     7,598,562
      GENEVA R     22.75   27.25   4.50    19.78    22,533,944
      NORTHERN     26.75   28.00   1.25     4.67     1,348,323
      OCKHAM S     21.50   22.00    .50     2.33     7,052,990
      WONDER L      5.00    5.00    .00      .00     2,553,712
*****                                             ------------
sum                                                66,877,300

                                                  ------------
                                                  139,699,940
portfoli.sql
```

FIGURE 12-3. **break on** *and* **compute sum** *on Report for grand totals*

The Volume is shown for each Industry as before, but now a total volume for all industries has been added as well. The **compute** command has been expanded to allow you to compute **on Report**. This must be coordinated with the **break on**:

```
break on Report on Industry skip 1
compute sum of Volume on Industry Report
```

This will produce a sum of Volume for the entire report. This is the **break on** and **compute** in Figure 12-3. The placement of **on Report** in the **break on** command is unimportant: **on Report** will always be the final break.

Next, the report is given a top title and a bottom title, using the newer method for **ttitle** and **btitle** that permits extensive formatting. See the special boxed section "ttitle and btitle Formatting Commands" for an explanation of this.

```
ttitle left 'Current Portfolio' -
       right 'April 1st, 1995'      skip 1 -
       center 'Industry Listings   '  skip 4;

btitle left 'portfoli.sql';
```

Order of Columns in break on

You can get into trouble if the order of the columns in **break on** is incorrect. Suppose that you wish to report on a company's revenues by company, division, department, and project (where a division has departments, and departments have projects). If you input this:

```
break on Project on Department on Division on Company
```

then the totals for each of these would be calculated every time the project changed, and they wouldn't be accumulated totals, only those for the project. This would be worthless. Instead, the **break on** must be in order from the largest grouping to the smallest, like this:

```
break on Company on Division on Department on Project
```

ttitle and btitle Formatting Commands

The results of these **ttitle** and **btitle** commands can be seen later in this chapter in Figure 12-5.

```
ttitle left 'Current Portfolio' -
       right xINDUSTRY                    skip 1 -
       center 'Industry Listings     '   skip 4;
```

left, **right**, and **center** define where the string that follows is to be placed on the page. A dash at the end of a line means another line of title commands follows. **skip** tells how many blank lines to print after printing this line. Text in single quotation marks is printed as is. Words not inside of single quotation marks are usually variables. If they've been defined by **accept**, **NEW_VALUE**, or **define**, their values will print in the title. If they have not been defined, the name of the variable will print instead.

```
btitle left 'portfoli.sql on ' xTODAY -
       right 'Page ' format 999 sql.pno;
```

sql.pno is a variable that contains the current page number. Formatting commands can be placed anywhere in a title, and they will control formatting for any variables from there forward in the **ttitle** or **btitle** unless another format is encountered.

For additional options for these commands, look in the Alphabetical Reference at the end of this book under **ttitle**.

break on Row

SQLPLUS also allows **compute**s and **break**s to be made **on Row**. Like **on Report,** the **break on** and **compute** must be coordinated.

Adding Views

In order for the full report to be useful, computations of each stock in relation to its industry segment, and to the whole, are important. Two views are therefore created. The first summarizes stock Volume, grouped by Industry. The second summarizes total stock volume.

```
create or replace view INDUSTRY as
select Industry, sum(Volume) Volume
  from STOCK
 where Industry in ('ELECTRONICS', 'SPACE', 'MEDICAL')
 group by Industry
/

create or replace view MARKET as
select sum(Volume) Volume
  from STOCK
 where Industry in ('ELECTRONICS', 'SPACE', 'MEDICAL')
/
```

Note that this practice of creating views in a SQLPLUS report is intended only for temporary views that have no particular use outside of the report. More widely used views that are shared by others and used as if they were regular tables in the database would be neither dropped nor created in a SQLPLUS start file that was used just for a report. They would simply be a part of the **from** clause in the **select** statement.

Columns Used with ttitle and btitle

Some additional column definitions are now added, along with a new column, PartOfInd (explained presently). See Circle A in Figure 12-4.

Now two columns that will appear in **ttitle** and **btitle** are put in with the **NEW_VALUE** command. Look at Circle B in Figure 12-4, and its effect in Circle 1 in Figure 12-5. The column Today was used to produce today's date in the **btitle**. How did this work? First of all, Today is an alias for a formatted SysDate in the **select** statement:

```
TO_CHAR(SysDate,'fmMonth ddth, yyyy') Today
```

```
column User noprint

column PartOfInd heading 'Part of Ind' format 999.90          (A)

column Today    NEW-VALUE xTODAY noprint format a1 trunc
column Industry NEW_VALUE xINDUSTRY                            (B)

ttitle left 'Current Portfolio' -
       right xINDUSTRY                    skip 1 -
       center 'Industry Listings  '  skip 4
btitle left 'portfoli.sql on ' xTODAY -
       right 'Page ' format 999 sql.pno

clear breaks                             (C)
clear computes

break on Report page on Industry page                         (D)

compute sum of Volume on Report Industry
compute sum of PartOfInd on Industry                          (E)
compute avg of Net Percent on Industry
compute avg of Net Percent PartOfInd on Report

select S.Industry,
       Company,
       CloseYesterday, CloseToday,
       (CloseToday - CloseYesterday) Net,
       (CloseToday - CloseYesterday)*(S. Volume/I.Volume) PartOfInd,
       (CloseToday/CloseYesterday)*100 - 100 Percent,
       S.Volume,
       TO_CHAR(SysDate,'fmMonth ddth, yyyy') Today
  from STOCK S, INDUSTRY I
 where S.Industry = I.Industry
   AND I.Industry in ('ELECTRONICS', 'SPACE', 'MEDICAL')
 order by I.Industry, Company
/
```

FIGURE 12-4. *SQLPLUS commands for report by industry*

```
Current Portfolio                                    ②———→   ELECTRONICS
                              Industry Listings

                    Close    Close              Part Percent
Ind     COMPANY     Yest.    Today      NET   of Ind  Change         VOLUME
----    --------    -------  -------   ------  ------- -------    ------------
ELECT  IDK          95.00    95.25      .25      .06      .26     9,443,523
       MEMORY G     15.50    14.25    -1.25     -.15    -8.06     4,557,992
       MICRO TO     77.00    76.50     -.50     -.32     -.65    25,205,667
*****                                 ------  ------- -------    ------------
avg                                    -.50             -2.82
sum                                            -.41             39,207,182

portfoli.sql on April 1st, 1995←———   ①                      Page       1
```

```
Current Portfolio                                    ③———→      MEDICAL
                              Industry Listings

                    Close    Close              Part Percent
Ind     COMPANY     Yest.    Today      NET   of Ind  Change         VOLUME
-----   --------    -------  -------   ------  ------- -------    ------------
MEDIC  AT SPACE     46.75    48.00     1.25      .42     2.67    11,398,323
       AUGUST E     15.00    15.00      .00      .00      .00    12,221,711
       HAYWARD     104.25   106.00     1.75      .17     1.68     3,358,561
       KENTGEN      18.25    19.50     1.25      .25     6.85     6,636,863
*****                                 ------  ------- -------    ------------
avg                                    1.06             2.80
sum                                             .85             33,615,458

portfoli.sql on April 1st, 1995                              Page       2
```

FIGURE 12-5.   *Report by industry, one industry per page*

NEW_VALUE placed the contents of the Today column (April 1st, 1995) into a variable named xToday, which is then used in **btitle**:

```
btitle left 'portfoli.sql on ' xToday -
       right 'Page ' format 999 sql.pno;
```

```
Current Portfolio                              4 ──────▶ SPACE

                        Industry Listings

            Close   Close           Part Percent
Ind   COMPANY Yest.   Today    NET  of Ind Change      VOLUME
----- -------- ------- ------- ------ ------- ------- ------------
SPACE BRANDON  32.75   33.50    .75    .29    2.29   25,789,769
      GENERAL  64.25   66.00   1.75    .20    2.72    7,598,562
      GENEVA R 22.75   27.25   4.50   1.52   19.78   22,533,944
      NORTHERN 26.75   28.00   1.25    .03    4.67    1,348,323
      OCKHAM S 21.50   22.00    .50    .05    2.33    7,052,990
      WONDER L  5.00    5.00    .00    .00     .00    2,553,712
*****                          ------ ------- ------- ------------
avg                5 ──▶ 1.46                 5.30
sum                                    2.08          66,877,300

portfoli.sql on April 1st, 1995                   Page      3
```

```
Current Portfolio                                       SPACE

                        Industry Listings

            Close   Close           Part Percent
Ind   COMPANY Yest.   Today    NET  of Ind Change      VOLUME
----- -------- ------- ------- ------ ------- ------- ------------
                               ------ ------- ------- ------------
                 6 ──▶ .88     .19    2.66
                                             139,699,940

portfoli.sql on April 1st, 1995                   Page      4
```

FIGURE 12-5. *Report by industry, one industry per page* (continued)

The variable could have had any name. xToday was chosen to make it easy to spot in the listing, but it could even have the same name as the column Today, or something else like DateVar or XYZ. **portfoli.sql** is simply the name of the start file used to produce this report. It's a useful practice to print the name of the start file used to create a report somewhere on the report, so that if it needs to be rerun, it can be found quickly.

You'll also notice **format 999 sql.pno**. The last part of this, **sql.pno,** is a variable that always contains the current page number. You can use it anywhere in either **ttitle** or **btitle**. By placing it in the **btitle** after the word "right", it shows up on the bottom-right corner of each page.

The format 999 that precedes it designates the format for the page number. Anytime a formatting command like this appears in **ttitle** or **btitle**, it defines the format of any number or characters in the variables that follow it, all the way to the end of the **ttitle** or **btitle** command, unless another format command is encountered.

A Warning about Variables

There are two other items of importance in the column command:

```
column Today NEW_VALUE xToday noprint format a1 trunc
```

noprint tells SQLPLUS not to display this column when it prints the results of the SQL statement. Without it, the date would appear on every row of the report. The **format a1 trunc** is a bit more esoteric. Dates that have been reformatted by **TO_CHAR** get a default width of about 100 characters (this was discussed in Chapter 7). Even though the **noprint** option is in effect, SQLPLUS gets confused and counts the width of the Today column in deciding whether **linesize** has been exceeded. The effect is to completely foul up the formatting of the rows as they are displayed or printed. By changing the format to a1 trunc, this effect is minimized.

The other column with **NEW_VALUE** is Industry. This column already has some column definitions in effect:

```
column Industry heading 'Ind' format a5 trunc
```

and now a new one is added (remember that different instructions for a column may be given on several lines):

```
column Industry NEW_VALUE xIndustry
```

Like Today, this column command inserts the contents of the column from the **select** statement into a variable called xIndustry. The value in this variable is coordinated with the **break on**. It gets the value of Industry when the *first* row is read, and keeps it until a new value is encountered and the **break on** forces a new page, as shown at Circles 2, 3, and 4 in Figure 12-5. Here's what SQLPLUS does.

■ It delays printing anything on a page until the **break on** detects a change in the value of Industry or enough rows are retrieved to fill the page.

■ It prints the ttitle with the value xIndustry had before the value changed (or the page got full).

■ It moves the value of xIndustry into an OLD_VALUE variable and saves it.

■ It prints the rows on the page.

■ It loads the new value into xIndustry.

■ It prints the btitle.

■ It begins collecting rows for the next page, and goes back to the first step.

What this means is that if xIndustry had been placed in the **btitle** instead of the **ttitle**, it would contain the Industry for the following page, instead of the one being printed. MEDICAL (Circle 3) would be at the bottom of page 1, SPACE (Circle 4) at the bottom of page 2, and so on. To use the **btitle** properly for column values retrieved in the query, you would use this:

```
column Industry OLD_VALUE xIndustry;
```

More on break and compute

Circle C in Figure 12-4 just precedes the **break on** and **compute** commands. Once a **compute** command is in place it continues to be active until you either clear it or leave SQLPLUS. This means you can have **compute** commands from previous reports that will execute on a current report, producing all sorts of unwanted effects.

The **break on** command also persists, although any new **break on** command will completely replace it. It is good practice to **clear breaks** and **clear computes** just before setting up new ones.

Here are the options available for **break on**:

■ **break on** *column*

■ **break on row**

■ **break on page**

■ **break on report**

column can be a column name, an alias, or an expression such as **SUBSTR**(Industry,1,4). Each of these can be followed by one of these actions:

■ **skip** *n*

■ **skip page**

or by nothing. **break on** *column* will produce the action anytime the value in the selected column changes. **break on row** will force a break with every row. **break on page** will force a break every time a page is filled up (in the current example, xIndustry will always contain the value in the Industry column for the first row of the page with this option). **break on report** will take the specified action every time a report ends.

The **skip** actions are to skip one or more lines (that is, print them blank), or go to the top of a new page. Recall from Chapter 3 that **break on** is used only once, with all of the columns and actions you wish. See Circle D in Figure 12-4.

The command **compute**, on the other hand, can be reused for each type of computation and for one or more columns at once. Circle E shows a variety of ways in which it can be used. Note how columns appear on either side of the **on** in the **compute** commands. No commas are used anywhere in either **break on** or **compute** commands.

Here are possible computations:

- **compute avg**
- **compute count**
- **compute max**
- **compute min**
- **compute std**
- **compute sum**
- **compute var**
- **compute num**

These have the same meanings for a column in a SQLPLUS report that **AVG(20)**, **COUNT( )**, **MAX( )**, **MIN( )**, **STDDEV( )**, **SUM( )**, and **VARIANCE( )** have in SQL. All of them except **num** ignore **NULL**s, and none of them is able to use the **DISTINCT** keyword. **compute num** is similar to **compute count**, except that **compute count** produces the count of non-**NULL** rows, and **compute num** produces the count of *all* rows.

Displaying Current breaks and computes

Entering just the word **break** or **compute** in SQLPLUS will cause it to display the breaks and computes it has in effect at the moment.

Running Several computes at Once

Figure 12-4 contains the following **compute** statements:

```
compute sum of Volume on Report Industry
compute sum of PartOfInd on Industry
compute avg of Net Percent on Industry
compute avg of Net Percent PartOfInd on Report
```

Look at Circles 5 and 6 in Figure 12-5, and you'll see the effects of all of these. Observe that the **avg** calculation for each column appears on one line, and the **sum** (where there is one) appears on the following line. Further, the words **sum** and **avg** appear *under the column* that follows the word **on** in the **compute** statement. They're missing at Circle 6 for the grand totals, because these are made on Report, and Report is not a column, so **sum** and **avg** can't appear under a column.

The Volume **sum** at Circle 5 is just for the Space industry stocks. The Volume **sum** at Circle 6 is for all industries (page 4 of this report contains only the grand totals and averages). Note that the first **compute** here is for the **sum** of one column, Volume, on both Report and Industry. (Incidentally, the order of the columns in a **compute** is irrelevant, unlike in a **break on**.)

The next **compute**, for PartOfInd on Industry, requires some explanation. (Part of Industry refers to its part of the industry point shift or a change in stock price over all the stocks in the industry.) PartOfInd comes from a portion of the **select** statement:

```
(CloseToday - CloseYesterday)*(S.Volume/I.Volume) PartOfInd,
```

This is a calculation that weights the net change in a stock versus the other stocks in its Industry, based on the volume traded. Compare the actual Net change between BRANDON and NORTHERN in the SPACE industry. BRANDON changed only .75 but traded over 25 million shares. NORTHERN changed 1.25 but traded only about a million shares. The contribution of BRANDON to the upward shift in the SPACE industry is thus considerably greater than that of NORTHERN; this is reflected in the relative values for the two under the PartOfInd column.

Now compare the **sum** of the PartOfInd column, 2.08, with the **avg** of the Net column, 1.46 (from the very next **compute**). Which is more representative of the change in stock price in this industry? It is the **sum** of PartOfInd, because its values are weighted by stock volume. This example is given to show the difference between a simple average in a column and a weighted average, and also to show how summary information is calculated. In one case it is done by averaging, in another by summing.

This is not the place to launch a detailed discussion of weighted averages, percentages, or statistical calculations, but it is appropriate to point out that significant differences will result from various methods of calculation. This will often affect decisions that are being made, so care and caution are in order.

The final **compute** calls for the average of Net, Percent, and PartOfInd on Report. These values are shown at Circle 6 as .88, .19, and 2.66, respectively. Look now at Circle 7 at the bottom of Figure 12-6. This is the same report as that in Figure 12-5, with a few exceptions. It is on one page instead of four; its upper-right

```
Current Portfolio                                        April 1st, 1995
                              Industry Listings

                  Close    Close            Part  Percent
Ind    COMPANY    Yest.    Today     NET   of Ind  Change         VOLUME
-----  --------   ------   ------   -----  ------- -------   ------------
ELECT  IDK         95.00    95.25     .25     .06     .26      9,443,523
       MEMORY G    15.50    14.25   -1.25    -.15   -8.06      4,557,992
       MICRO TO    77.00    76.50    -.50    -.32    -.65     25,205,667
*****                              ------  ------- -------   ------------
avg                                  -.50           -2.82
sum                                          -.41            39,207,182


MEDIC  AT SPACE    46.75    48.00    1.25     .42    2.67     11,398,323
       AUGUST E    15.00    15.00     .00     .00     .00     12,221,711
       HAYWARD    104.25   106.00    1.75     .17    1.68      3,358,561
       KENTGEN     18.25    19.50    1.25     .25    6.85      6,636,863
*****                              ------  ------- -------   ------------
avg                                  1.06            2.80
sum                                           .85            33,615,458


SPACE  BRANDON     32.75    33.50     .75     .29    2.29     25,789,769
       GENERAL     64.25    66.00    1.75     .20    2.72      7,598,562
       GENEVA R    22.75    27.25    4.50    1.52   19.78     22,533,944
       NORTHERN    26.75    28.00    1.25     .03    4.67      1,348,323
       OCKHAM S    21.50    22.00     .50     .05    2.33      7,052,990
       WONDER L     5.00     5.00     .00     .00     .00      2,553,712
*****                              ------  ------- -------   ------------
avg                                  1.46            5.30
sum                                          2.08            66,877,300


                                   ------  ------- -------   ------------
                                     .88     .19    2.66
                                                            139,699,940


Market Averages and Totals          1.09            2.66   139,699,940   (7)
```

FIGURE 12-6.   *Revised report with correct market averages and totals*

title is the date, not the industry segment; and its bottom line has an additional and different result for averages and totals:

```
Market Averages and Totals        1.09        2.66   139,699,940
```

These are the correct results, and they differ from those that are or can be calculated from the columns displayed using *any* **compute** statement. This is because the **compute** statements lack the weighting of the total industry volume. So how was this result produced? The answer is in Figure 12-7. At Circle F the **btitle**

```
ttitle left 'Current Portfolio'   right xTODAY skip 1 -
       center 'Industry Listings'    skip 4;

btitle off ←——————( F )

clear breaks
clear computes


break on Report on Industry skip 1


compute sum of Volume on Report Industry
compute sum of PartOfInd on Industry
compute avg of Net Percent on Industry
compute avg of Net Percent PartOfInd on Report

select S.Industry,
       Company,
       CloseYesterday, CloseToday,
       (CloseToday - CloseYesterday) Net,
       (CloseToday - CloseYesterday)*(S.Volume/I.Volume) PartOfInd,
       (CloseToday/CloseYesterday)*100 - 100 Percent,
       S.Volume, User,
       To_CHAR(SysDate,'fmMonth ddth, yyyy')Today
  from STOCK S, INDUSTRY I
 where S.Industry = I.Industry
   AND I.Industry in ('ELECTRONICS', 'SPACE', 'MEDICAL')
 order by I.Industry, Company
/
set heading off
ttitle off
select 'Market Averages and Totals    ',                          ( G )
       SUM(((CloseToday-CloseYesterday)*S.Volume)/M.Volume) Net,
       '         ',
       AVG((CloseToday/CloseYesterday))*100 - 100 Percent,
       SUM(S.Volume) Volume
  from STOCK S, MARKET M
 where Industry in ('ELECTRONICS', 'SPACE', 'MEDICAL')
/
```

FIGURE 12-7. *How the correct market averages and totals were produced*

was turned off, and at Circle G, just following the **select** that produced the main body of the report, is an additional **select** that includes the label Market Averages and Totals, and a proper calculation of them.

This **select** statement is preceded by **set heading off** and **ttitle off**. These are necessary because a new **select** will normally force a new top title to print. The **set heading off** command is used to turn off the *column* titles that normally would appear above this line. The **btitle** at Circle F had to be turned off before the first **select** executed, because the completion of the first **select** would cause the **btitle** to print before the second **select** could even execute.

set termout off and set termout on

Another useful pair of commands is **set termout off** and **set termout on**. The former is often used in a start file just before the **spool** command, and the latter just after it. The effect is to suppress the display of the report to the screen. For reports to be printed, this saves time (they'll run faster) and avoids the annoying rolling of data across the screen. The spooling to a file continues to work properly.

Variables in SQLPLUS

If you're using SQLPLUS interactively, you can check on the current **ttitle** and **btitle** at any time by typing their names alone on a line. SQLPLUS immediately shows you their contents:

```
ttitle
ttitle ON and is the following 113 characters:
left 'Current Portfolio'          right xTODAY
skip 1          center 'Industry Listings  ' skip 4
```

Note the presence of xTODAY, which is a variable, rather than its current contents, such as April 1st, 1995. SQLPLUS is capable of storing and using many variables—those used in **ttitle** and **btitle** are only some of them. The current variables and their values can be discovered by typing **define**:

```
define

DEFINE _EDITOR       = "vi" (CHAR)
DEFINE _O_VERSION    = "Oracle7 Server Release 7.1.4.1.0 - Production Release
With the distributed and parallel query options
PL/SQL Release 2.1.4.0.0 - Production" (CHAR)
DEFINE _O_RELEASE    = "701040100" (CHAR)
DEFINE XINDUSTRY   = "SPACE" (CHAR)
DEFINE XTODAY      = "April 1st, 1995" (CHAR)
```

The first is the editor you use when you type the word **edit**. You saw how to set this up in your **login.sql** file back in Chapter 4. The second and third of these identify which version and release of ORACLE you are using.

The next two are the variables defined in the stock market queries, and their contents are just those displayed in the reports. SQLPLUS stores variables for **ttitle** and **btitle** by defining them as equal to some value, and then allows you to use them whenever a query is being executed. In fact, variables can be used many places in a report other than in titles.

Suppose your stock database were updated automatically by a pricing service, and you wished to check regularly the closing prices and volumes on a stock-by-stock basis. This could be easily accomplished with variables in the **where** clause. Normally you would type this query:

```
select Company, CloseYesterday, CloseToday, Volume
   from STOCK   where Company = 'IDK';
```

```
                      Close   Close
COMPANY               Yest.   Today       VOLUME
------------------    -------  -------  ------------
IDK                    95.00   95.25    9,443,523
```

Alternatively, you could type this into a start file named, for example, **closing.sql**:

```
column CloseToday heading 'Close!Today' format 999.90
column CloseYesterday heading 'Close!Yest.' format 999.90
column Volume format 999,999,999

accept xCompany prompt 'Enter Company name: '

select Company, CloseYesterday, CloseToday, Volume
   from STOCK
 where Company = '&xCompany';
```

In this file, xCompany is a variable you have invented, such as xIndustry or xToday. **accept** tells SQLPLUS to accept input from the keyboard, and **prompt** tells it to display a message. Note that the variable name must be preceded by the ampersand (&) when it appears in the SQL **select** statement, but not when it appears in the **accept** or in a title. Then, when you type this:

```
start closing.sql
```

the screen displays this:

```
Enter Company name:
```

You then type in **MEMORY GRAPHICS**. SQLPLUS will display the following:

```
select Company, CloseYesterday, CloseToday, Volume
  from STOCK
 where Company = '&xCompany';

old   3:  where Company = '&xCompany'
new   3:  where Company = 'MEMORY GRAPHICS'


                        Close   Close
COMPANY                 Yest.   Today        VOLUME
------------------     ------- ------- ------------
MEMORY GRAPHICS          15.50   14.25     4,557,992
```

First, it shows you the query you have set up. Next, it shows you the **where** clause first with the variable in it, then with the value you typed in. Finally, it shows you the results of the query. If you then typed **start closing.sql** again, but typed **IDK** for Company name, the **old** and **new** would show this:

```
old   3:  where Company = 'MEMORY GRAPHICS'
new   3:  where Company = 'IDK'
```

and the result would be for IDK. It is unnecessary for the **select** and the **old** and **new** to be displayed each time. Both of these can be controlled, the first by the **set echo** command and the second by **set verify**. To see what these are set at currently, type the **show** command followed by the keyword **verify** or **echo**.

```
show verify
verify ON

show echo
echo ON
```

The revised version of the start file looks like this:

```
column CloseToday heading 'Close|Today' format 999.90
column CloseYesterday heading 'Close|Yest.' format 999.90
column Volume format 999,999,999
```

```
set echo off
set verify off
set sqlcase upper
accept xCompany prompt 'Enter company name: '

select Company, CloseYesterday, CloseToday, Volume
  from STOCK
 where Company = '&xCompany';
```

The **set sqlcase upper** tells SQLPLUS to convert anything keyed into the variable (using the **accept**) to uppercase before executing the query. This can be helpful if you've stored your data in uppercase (which is a good practice) but don't want to force people to type in uppercase anytime they want to run a query. Now when the start file is executed this is what happens:

```
start closing.sql

Enter company name: memory graphics


                     Close   Close
COMPANY              Yest.   Today       VOLUME
------------------- ------- ------- ------------
MEMORY GRAPHICS      15.50   14.25    4,557,992
```

The use of variables in start files can be very helpful, particularly for reports run on an ad hoc basis where the basic format of the report stays the same but certain parameters change, such as date, company division, stock name, project, client, and so on. When the report starts, it asks the person using it for these details and then it runs. As just shown, typing only the word **define** will result in a list of all the variables currently defined. Typing **define** with just one name will show only that variable's contents:

```
define xCompany

DEFINE XCOMPANY      = "memory graphics" (CHAR)
```

After a start file has completed, any variables are held by SQLPLUS until you exit or intentionally **undefine** them:

```
undefine xCompany
```

An attempt now to see the variable's value produces the following:

```
define xCompany

symbol xcompany is UNDEFINED
```

You also can define a variable within the start file, without using the **accept** command. Simply assign a value directly, as shown here:

```
define xCompany = 'idk'
```

Any place that &xCompany appears in the start file will have 'idk' substituted instead.

Other Places to Use Variables

Any variable that you define using either **accept** or **define** can be used directly in a **btitle** or **ttitle** command, without using the **NEW_VALUE** column command. All that **NEW_VALUE** does is take the contents of a column and issue its own **define** command for the variable name following **NEW_VALUE**. The single difference in using the variable in titles, as opposed to the SQL statement, is that in titles the variable is not preceded by an ampersand.

Variables also can be used in a setup start file, explained later in this chapter under the heading "Using mask.sql."

Numeric Formatting

The default method SQLPLUS uses for formatting numbers is simply to right-justify them in a column, without commas, using decimal points only if the number is not an integer. The table NUMBERTEST contains columns named Value1 and Value2, which have identical numbers in each column. These will be used to show how numeric formatting works. The first query shows the default formatting:

```
select Value1, Value2 from NUMBERTEST;

    VALUE1       VALUE2
------------ ------------
           0            0
       .0001        .0001
        1234         1234
      1234.5       1234.5
```

```
    1234.56        1234.56
    1234.567       1234.567
98761234.567 98761234.567
```

Row five is **NULL**. Notice how the decimal point moves from row to row. Just as columns can be formatted individually in queries, the default format can be changed:

```
set numformat 9,999,999

select Value1, Value2 from NUMBERTEST;

    VALUE1        VALUE2
---------- ----------

     1,234         1,234
     1,235         1,235

     1,235         1,235
     1,235         1,235
  #,###,###     #,###,###
```

But rows one and two have vanished, and row eight is filled with pound signs. The difficulty with row eight is that the format defined is too narrow. You can prevent this by adding another digit on the left, as shown here:

```
set numformat 99,999,999

select Value1, Value2 from NUMBERTEST;

    VALUE1        VALUE2
---------- ----------

     1,234         1,234
     1,235         1,235
     1,235         1,235
     1,235         1,235
98,761,235    98,761,235
```

With this default format left in place, the formatting for Value1 will now be altered. The zero at the end will assure that at least a zero is produced for each row with a value. Because no decimal places have been specified in either of the formats, both .0001 and 0 display as zero.

```
column value1 format 99,999,990

select Value1, Value2 from NUMBERTEST;

    VALUE1      VALUE2
----------- -----------
          0
          0
      1,234       1,234
      1,235       1,235

      1,235       1,235
      1,235       1,235
 98,761,235  98,761,235
```

Additional options for formatting are described in the boxed section entitled "Numeric Formatting Options."

Using mask.sql

Columns used in one report may also need to be used regularly in several reports. Rather than retype the formatting commands for these columns in every start file, it can be useful to keep all of the basic column commands in a single file. This file might be called **mask.sql**, because it contains formatting (also called *masking*) information for columns. For example, the file might look like the following:

```
REM    File mask.sql
set numwidth 12
set numformat 999,999,999.90

column Net format 99.90
column Industry format a11
column Company format a18
column CloseToday heading 'Close|Today' format 999.90
column CloseYesterday heading 'Close|Yest.' format 999.90
column Volume format 999,999,999

define xDepartment = 'Systems Planning Dept. 3404'
```

This is then effectively embedded in a start file (usually near the top) simply by including this line:

```
start mask.sql
```

Numeric Formatting Options

These options work with both **set numformat** and the **column format** command.

9999990	Count of 9s and 0s determines maximum digits that can be displayed.
999,999,999.99	Commas and decimals will be placed in the pattern shown. Display will be blank if the value is zero.
999990	Displays a zero if the value is zero.
099999	Displays numbers with leading zeros.
$99999	Dollar sign placed in front of every number.
B99999	Display will be blank if value is zero. This is the default.
99999MI	If number is negative, minus sign follows the number. Default is negative sign on left.
99999PR	Negative numbers displayed with < and >.
9.999EEEE	Display will be in scientific notation.
999V99	Multiplies number by 10^n where n is number of digits to right of V. 999V99 turns 1234 into 123400.

Alternatively, this line could be inserted in the **login.sql** file described in Chapter 4. It will then load automatically every time SQLPLUS is begun. Observe the final line in the **mask.sql** file. Variables also can be defined here, and could be used to set up site-specific information that can be used in **ttitle**, **btitle**, or **where** clauses for reports.

Using Buffers to Save SQLPLUS Commands

Normally, using the command line editor in SQLPLUS (see Chapter 4 under "Command Line Editor") allows you to affect only the SQL statement. It is for this reason that a separate editor is normally used for editing start files. There is another alternative intended only for initial efforts in developing a start file. It is cumbersome and confusing to use with larger files.

When the Command Line Editor is being used, the SQL commands (but *no* SQLPLUS commands) are stored in a scratchpad area of the computer's memory called the *SQL buffer*. When you edit lines, using **change**, **append**, **del**, and so on, the lines stored in this SQL buffer are what actually change. Because in initial work on a query you may want to change SQLPLUS commands such as **column**, **ttitle**, and the like, as well as SQL commands, ORACLE provides the means to use a buffer to save SQL commands and SQLPLUS commands.

The default buffer is named **sql**. If you change the name of the buffer from **sql** to anything else (up to seven characters) using the **set buffer** command, from that moment on SQLPLUS commands also will be stored in the buffer. For example, to create a buffer named **A**, begin putting **input** into it, and include a **column** definition and a **select** statement. Here is what you would type:

```
set buffer A
input
column Volume format 999,999,999
select Company, Volume from STOCK;
```

set buffer A sets aside the scratch area for what is to follow. **input** tells SQLPLUS you are about to begin keying information into this scratchpad. Two lines are typed in, followed by a blank line (just an ENTER) that tells SQLPLUS you have finished keying in information. The buffer is now "full" and closed. This means, of course, that you cannot use this method to put blank lines in a file. You can use **show** to check to see if this buffer is still active (that is, that it is the buffer currently in use), as shown in the following:

```
show buffer

buffer A
```

It is, and you can use the Command Line Editor **list**, **del**, **append**, and **change** commands on any of the lines in it. (Refer to Chapter 4.)

```
list

  1   column Volume format 999,999,999
  2*  select Company, Volume from STOCK;
```

You also can **save** the buffer's contents to a file, and **get** them back from the file into the buffer for more editing. Here the preceding lines are saved in a file named **check**:

```
save check

Wrote file check
```

The opposite of **save** is **get**. If you have a start file you'd like to edit with the Command Line Editor, you can move it into a buffer named **test**, for instance, by typing:

```
set buffer test

get check
```

This will move everything in **check** into the buffer **test**, where the Command Line Editor can affect it. Unfortunately, you cannot execute either the SQLPLUS or the SQL commands in the buffer **test**. You can save the changes you make using the **save check** command again (using the **repl** parameter to replace the current **check.sql** file), and execute them with **start check**, but there is no way to execute the buffer itself. You can, however, execute the SQL buffer. There are some restrictions on how this works:

- If the buffer is set to **sql**, any SQL typed directly on the line in SQLPLUS goes into the SQL buffer. A semicolon (;) at the end of a word will cause the SQL in the buffer to execute immediately.

- After it executes, only the SQL, without the semicolon, remains in the sql buffer. To reexecute, type a slash (**/**), or the word **run** on a line by itself. This tells SQLPLUS to execute whatever is in the sql buffer.

- If the current buffer is set to **sql**, the **get** will pull the contents of a file into it. If that file contains any SQLPLUS commands, or a semicolon, you will not be able to execute it.

- Whenever you run a start file, the SQL in it will be automatically loaded into the **sql** buffer, and will reexecute if you type the word **run** or the **/**.

- Anytime a SQL command is executed, whether from the command line or from a start file, the buffer is automatically changed back to **sql**. The contents of buffer A do not disappear, but **set buffer A** must be typed in again in order to edit its contents.

To edit a buffer other than the SQL buffer, here are the basic rules:

- **set buffer** must be followed by one word from one to seven characters in length.

- The word **input** must be typed by itself on a line.

- Any SQLPLUS commands must be typed in, including titles, columns, spool, and the like.

- The SQL statement must be typed in.

- A blank line must be entered.

- The buffer must be saved to a file.

You can edit using the Command Line Editor before the buffer's contents are saved to the file. If the file is retrieved using the **get** command, its contents will go into the current buffer (whatever buffer was last **set**). You may have several buffers, each with different contents, in a single SQLPLUS session. All of the buffers are erased when you leave SQLPLUS. If you want to save the work you've done with a buffer, be certain to **save** it to a file before leaving SQLPLUS.

This may sound like a lot of trouble, and it can be. The rules are difficult to remember. Knowing which buffer you are in, and whether you can execute it, or (if it is the **sql** buffer) if its contents are executable, confuses even veteran ORACLE users. The buffers and the Command Line Editor are meant only for simple, spur-of-the-moment editing, and not as a comprehensive editing environment. It is generally much easier to simply use your own editor, include your SQLPLUS commands and SQL in it, and then **start** it in SQLPLUS.

spooling Current Definitions

There is one other method for saving SQLPLUS commands. Most commands can be displayed using the **show** command, or the single words **column**, **define**, **ttitle**, or **btitle**. If you wish to accumulate all of these into a file, simply use the **spool** command, as shown here:

```
spool saveit.sql
```

The **spool** command will **save** everything that subsequently appears on the screen into a file, for example, the file named **saveit.sql**. Once spooling is on, type this:

```
column
ttitle
btitle

spool off
```

This will load all of the current **column**, **ttitle**, and **btitle** definitions into the file **saveit.sql**, which you can then edit. The column commands will not be in precisely the order they need to be, but they'll be close enough to permit quick editing to get them into proper form. The same is true of the titles.

show all and spooling

You've seen several commands that use the **set** command, and whose current status can be determined using the **show** command, such as **feedback**, **echo**,

verify, **heading**, and so on. There are actually about 50 such commands that can be **set**. These can all be displayed at once using this:

```
show all
```

Unfortunately, these fly by so quickly on the screen that it's impossible to read most of them. You can solve this problem by spooling. Simply **spool** to a file, as in the previous example, execute **show all**, and then **spool off**. You can now look at the current status of all of the **set** commands using your editor on the file. You can look up these commands in the Alphabetical Reference at the end of this book under **set**.

Folding onto New Lines

Information retrieved from a database is often just fine with only one line of column titles and columns of data stacked below them. There are occasions, however, when a different kind of layout is preferable. Sometimes this can be accomplished using literal columns of nothing but blank spaces in order to properly position real data on more than one line, and have it line up properly. These literal columns are given an alias in the SQL, and then a blank heading in the **column** command. The technique parallels what was done for the total line in Figure 12-6. For example, look at this:

```
column Industry format a14 trunc
column B format a21 heading ' '
column Company format a20
column Volume format 999,999,999 justify left

select Industry, ' ' B,
       Company,
       CloseYesterday, CloseToday,
       (CloseToday - CloseYesterday) Net,
       Volume
  from STOCK
 where Industry in ('ADVERTISING','GARMENT')
 order by Industry, Company;
```

```
INDUSTRY                                COMPANY
-------------- -------------------- --------------------
CLOSEYESTERDAY CLOSETODAY      NET VOLUME
-------------- ---------- ---------- ------------
ADVERTISING                             AD SPECIALTY
        31.75       31.75         0    18,333,876
ADVERTISING                             MBK COMMUNICATIONS
        43.25          41     -2.25    10,022,980
ADVERTISING                             NANCY LEE FEATURES
         13.5       14.25       .75    14,222,692
GARMENT                                 ROBERT JAMES APPAREL
        23.25          24       .75    19,032,481
```

A literal column of one space, given an alias of B, is defined by the **column** command as 21 characters wide with a blank heading. This is used specifically to move the company names over so that the columns line up as desired, with stock Volume directly below the Company name, and column B for CloseToday and Net lining up with the blank.

fold_after and fold_before

Next, look at how the column command **fold_after** affects every column in the **select**:

```
clear columns
column Net format 99.90
column A format a15 fold_after 1
column Company format a20 fold_after 1
column CloseToday heading 'Close│Today' format 999.90 -
   fold_after
column CloseYesterday heading 'Close│Yest.' format 999.90 -
   fold_after 1
column Net fold_after 1
column Volume format 999,999,999 fold_after 1
set heading off

select Industry││',' A,
       Company,
       CloseYesterday,
       CloseToday, (CloseToday - CloseYesterday) Net,
       Volume
  from STOCK
 where Industry in ('ADVERTISING','GARMENT')
 order by Industry, Company;
```

The previous query produces this effect:

```
ADVERTISING,
AD SPECIALTY
   31.75
   31.75     .00
   18,333,876


ADVERTISING, MBK COMMUNICATIONS
   43.25
   41.00   -2.25
   10,022,980


ADVERTISING,
NANCY LEE FEATURES
   13.50
   14.25     .75
   14,222,692


GARMENT,
ROBERT JAMES APPAREL
   23.25
   24.00     .75
   19,032,481
```

The **fold_after** is effective after every column except CloseToday because CloseToday lacks the number required following its **fold_after** command. This number can be any integer, although 1 is recommended. The number currently has no effect on anything (it must simply be present), but may be used in a future ORACLE release to denote the number of lines to advance. **fold_before** accomplishes a similar end, but causes a line feed before a column is printed, rather than after. One obvious use for the **fold_after** and **fold_before** commands is in preparing mailing labels, client lists, and the like.

Additional Reporting Controls

Many of the commands illustrated here, as well as in other chapters, have options considerably beyond those used in these examples. All of the options for each of these commands can be found in the Alphabetical Reference, under the individual command names.

CHAPTER 13

Changing Data: insert, update, and delete

U ntil now, virtually everything you've learned about ORACLE, SQL, and SQLPLUS has been about selecting data from tables in the database. This chapter shows how to *change* the data in a table: how to **insert** new rows, how to **update** the values of columns in rows, and how to **delete** rows entirely. Although these topics have not been covered explicitly, nearly everything you already know about SQL, including data types, calculations, string formatting, **where** clauses, and the like, can be used here, so there really isn't much new to learn.

Previous versions of ORACLE did not permit users to **insert**, **update**, and **delete** data in tables in remote databases. ORACLE7 gives you a transparent, distributed database capability that lets you do what you want wherever you want to do it (see Chapter 20).

321

insert

The SQL command **insert** lets you place a row of information directly into a table (or indirectly, through a view. See the section in Chapter 16 entitled "Creating a View"). The COMFORT table tracks temperatures at noon and midnight and daily precipitation, city by city, for a series of four sample dates through the year:

```
describe COMFORT

Name                               Null?     Type
--------------------------------   --------  ----
CITY                                         VARCHAR2(13)
SAMPLEDATE                                   DATE
NOON                                         NUMBER
MIDNIGHT                                     NUMBER
PRECIPITATION                                NUMBER
```

To add a new row to this table, use this:

```
insert into COMFORT
values ('WALPOLE', '21-MAR-93', 56.7, 43.8, 0);

1 row created.
```

The word **values** must precede the list of data to be inserted. Note that a character string must be in single quotation marks. A date must be in single quotation marks and in the default ORACLE date format. Numbers can stand by themselves. Each field is separated by commas, and the fields must be in the same order as the columns are when the table is described.

To insert a date not in default format, use the **TO_DATE** function, with a formatting mask as shown in the following:

```
insert into COMFORT
values ('WALPOLE', TO_DATE('06/22/93','MM/DD/YY'),
        56.7, 43.8, 0);

1 row created.
```

inserting a Time

Both of these methods for inserting dates will produce a default time of midnight, the very beginning of the day. If you wish to insert a date with a time other than midnight, simply use the **TO_DATE** function and include a time:

```
insert into COMFORT
values ('WALPOLE', TO_DATE('06/22/93 1:35','MM/DD/YY HH24:MI'),
        56.7, 43.8, 0);

1 row created.
```

Columns also can be inserted out of the order they appear when described, if you first (before the word **values**) list the order the data is in. This doesn't change the fundamental order of the columns in the table. It simply allows you to list the data fields in a different order.

NOTE
You also can "insert" a **NULL**. This simply means the column will be left empty for this row, as shown in the following:

```
insert into COMFORT
        (SampleDate,  Precipitation, City, Noon, Midnight)
values ('23-SEP-93', NULL,'WALPOLE', 86.3, 72.1);

1 row created.
```

insert with select

You also can **insert** information that has been selected from a table. Here a mix of columns selected from the COMFORT table, together with literal values for SampleDate (22-DEC-93) and City (WALPOLE), are inserted. Note the **where** clause in the **select**, which will retrieve only one row. Had the **select** retrieved five rows, five new ones would have been inserted, if ten, then ten, and so on:

```
insert into COMFORT
      (SampleDate, Precipitation, City, Noon, Midnight)
select '22-DEC-93', Precipitation, 'WALPOLE', Noon, Midnight
  from COMFORT
 where City = 'KEENE' and SampleDate = '22-DEC-93';

1 row created.
```

NOTE
You cannot use the **insert into...select from** syntax with LONG datatypes.

Of course, you don't need to simply insert the value in a selected column. You can modify the column using any of the appropriate string, date, or number functions within the **select** statement. The results of those functions are what will be inserted. You can attempt to **insert** a value in a column that exceeds its width (for character data types) or its precision (for number data types). You have to fit within the constraints you defined on your columns. These attempts will produce a "value too large for column" or "mismatched data type" error message. If you now query the COMFORT table for the city of Walpole, the results will be the records you inserted:

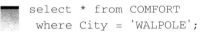

```
select * from COMFORT
 where City = 'WALPOLE';
```

CITY	SAMPLEDAT	NOON	MIDNIGHT	PRECIPITATION
WALPOLE	21-MAR-93	56.7	43.8	0
WALPOLE	22-JUN-93	56.7	43.8	0
WALPOLE	23-SEP-93	86.3	72.1	
WALPOLE	22-DEC-93	-7.2	-1.2	3.9

```
4 rows selected.
```

rollback, commit, and autocommit

When you **insert**, **update**, or **delete** data from the database you can reverse or *rollback* the work you've done. This can be very important when an error is discovered. The process of committing or rolling back work is controlled by two SQLPLUS commands, **commit** and **rollback**. Additionally, SQLPLUS has the facility to automatically commit your work without your explicitly telling it to do so. This is controlled by the **autocommit** feature of **set**. Like other **set** features, you can **show** it, like this:

```
show autocommit

autocommit OFF
```

OFF is the default. This means **insert**s, **update**s, and **delete**s are not made final until you **commit** them:

```
commit;

commit complete
```

Until you **commit**, only you can see how your work affects the tables. Anyone else with access to these tables will continue to get the old information. You will see *new* information whenever you **select** from the table. Your work is, in effect, in a "staging" area, which you interact with until you **commit**. You can do quite a large number of **insert**s, **update**s, and **delete**s, and still undo the work (return the tables to the way they used to be) by issuing this command:

```
rollback;

rollback complete
```

However, the message "rollback complete" can be misleading. It means only that it has rolled back any work that hasn't been committed. If you commit a series of transactions, either explicitly with the word **commit**, or implicitly by another action (an example of which is shown next), the "rollback complete" message won't really mean anything. The two special boxed sections "How commit and rollback Work" and "How commit and rollback Work in SQL" give a picture of how **commit** and **rollback** affect a table of dogs' names.

Implicit commit

The actions that will force a **commit** to occur, even without your instructing it to, are **quit**, **exit** (equivalent of **quit**), **create table** or **create view**, **drop table** or **drop view**, **grant** or **revoke**, **connect** or **disconnect**, **alter**, **audit**, and **noaudit**. Using any of these commands is just like using **commit**.

Auto rollback

If you've completed a series of **insert**s, **update**s, or **delete**s, but have not yet explicitly or implicitly committed them, and you experience serious difficulties, such as a computer failure, ORACLE will automatically **rollback** any uncommitted work. If the machine or database goes down, it does this as cleanup work the next time the database is brought back up.

How commit and rollback Work

A database table has only one column and row in it. The table is CANINE and the column is Name. It already has one dog in it, TROUBLE, which is incorrectly spelled as "TRAUBLE," and the diagrams show the attempts of TROUBLE's keeper to add other dogs to the table and correct the spelling of his name. This assumes the **autocommit** feature of SQLPLUS is off. See the next boxed section to view the SQL equivalent of the actions in this diagram:

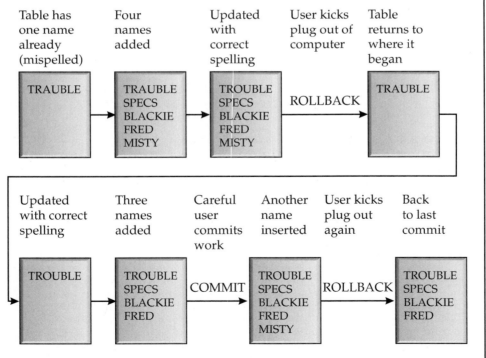

Misty will have to be added again later, after the user plugs the machine back in.

How commit and rollback Work in SQL

In SQL, this same sequence would look like this:

```
select * from CANINE:

NAME
-------
TRAUBLE

insert into CANINE values ('SPECS');
insert into CANINE values ('BLACKIE');
insert into CANINE values ('FRED');
insert into CANINE values ('MISTY');

update CANINE set Name = 'TROUBLE' where Name = 'TRAUBLE';

rollback;

select * from CANINE:

NAME
--------
TRAUBLE

update CANINE set Name = 'TROUBLE' where Name = 'TRAUBLE';

insert into CANINE values ('SPECS');
insert into CANINE values ('BLACKIE');
insert into CANINE values ('FRED');

commit;

insert into CANINE values ('MISTY');

rollback;

select * from CANINE:

NAME
-------
TROUBLE
SPECS
BLACKIE
FRED
```

delete

Removing a row or rows from a table requires the **delete** command. The **where** clause is essential to removing only the rows you intend. **delete** without a **where** clause will empty the table completely.

```
delete from COMFORT where City = 'WALPOLE';

4 rows deleted.
```

Of course, a **where** clause in a **delete**, just as in an **update** or a **select** that is part of an **insert**, can contain as much logic as any **select** statement you've seen thus far, and may include subqueries, unions, intersects, and so on. You can always roll back a bad **insert**, **update**, or **delete**, but you really should experiment with the **select** before actually making the change to the database to make sure you are doing the right thing.

Now that you've just deleted the rows where City = 'WALPOLE', you can test the effect of that **delete** with a simple query:

```
select * from COMFORT
 where City = 'WALPOLE';

no rows selected
```

Now roll back the **delete** and run the same query:

```
rollback;
rollback complete

select * from COMFORT
 where City = 'WALPOLE';

CITY          SAMPLEDAT      NOON   MIDNIGHT PRECIPITATION
------------- ---------  ---------- ---------- -------------
WALPOLE       21-MAR-93      56.7       43.8             0
WALPOLE       22-JUN-93      56.7       43.8             0
WALPOLE       23-SEP-93      86.3       72.1
WALPOLE       22-DEC-93      -7.2       -1.2           3.9

4 rows selected.
```

This illustrates that recovery is possible, so long as a **commit** hasn't occurred.

An additional command for deleting records, **truncate**, does not behave the same as **delete**. Whereas **delete** allows you to **commit** or **rollback** the deletion, **truncate** automatically deletes all records from the table. The **truncate** transaction cannot be rolled back or committed; the truncated records are irrecoverable. See the **truncate** command in the Alphabetical Reference for further details.

update

update requires setting specific values for each column you wish to change, and specifying which row or rows you wish to affect by using a carefully constructed **where** clause:

```
update COMFORT set Precipitation = .5, Midnight = 73.1
  where City = 'WALPOLE' and SampleDate = '22-DEC-93';

1 row updated.
```

Here is the effect:

```
select * from COMFORT
  where City = 'WALPOLE';

CITY          SAMPLEDAT     NOON    MIDNIGHT PRECIPITATION
------------- ---------   ---------- ---------- -------------
WALPOLE       21-MAR-93     56.7      43.8            0
WALPOLE       22-JUN-93     56.7      43.8            0
WALPOLE       23-SEP-93     86.3      72.1
WALPOLE       22-DEC-93     -7.2      73.1           .5

4 rows selected.
```

What if you later discover that the thermometer used in Walpole consistently reports its temperatures low by one degree? You also can do calculations, string functions, and almost any other legitimate function in setting a value for the **update** (just as you can for an **insert**, or in the **where** clause of a **delete**). Here each temperature in WALPOLE is increased by one degree:

```
update COMFORT set Midnight = Midnight + 1, Noon = Noon + 1
  where City = 'WALPOLE';

4 rows updated.
```

Here is the effect of the **update**:

```
select * from COMFORT
 where City = 'WALPOLE';

CITY          SAMPLEDAT      NOON    MIDNIGHT PRECIPITATION
------------- ---------  ---------- ---------- -------------
WALPOLE       21-MAR-93      57.7      44.8              0
WALPOLE       22-JUN-93      57.7      44.8              0
WALPOLE       23-SEP-93      87.3      73.1
WALPOLE       22-DEC-93      -6.2      74.1             .5

4 rows selected.
```

As with **delete**, the **where** clause is critical. Without one, every row in the database will be updated. With an improperly constructed **where** clause, the wrong rows will be updated, often in ways that are hard to discover or fix, especially if your work has been committed. Always **set feedback on** when doing **update**s, and look at the result to be sure the number is what you expected it to be. Query the rows after you **update** to see if the expected change took place.

update with Embedded select

It is possible to set values in an **update** by embedding a **select** statement right in the middle of it. Note that this **select** has its own **where** clause, picking out the temperature from the City of MANCHESTER from the WEATHER table, and the **update** has its own **where** clause to affect just the City of WALPOLE on a certain day:

```
update COMFORT set Midnight =
        (select Temperature
           from WEATHER
          where City = 'MANCHESTER')
 where City = 'WALPOLE'
   AND SampleDate = '22-DEC-93';

1 row updated.
```

Here is the effect of the **update**:

```
select * from COMFORT
 where City = 'WALPOLE';

CITY           SAMPLEDAT     NOON    MIDNIGHT PRECIPITATION
------------   ---------   ----------  ---------- -------------
WALPOLE        21-MAR-93     57.7        44.8            0
WALPOLE        22-JUN-93     57.7        44.8            0
WALPOLE        23-SEP-93     87.3        73.1
WALPOLE        22-DEC-93     -6.2          66           .5

4 rows selected.
```

When using subqueries with updates, you must be certain that the subquery
will return no more than one record for each of the updated records; otherwise, the
update will fail. See Chapter 10 for details on correlated queries.

You also can use an embedded **select** to **update** multiple columns at once. The
columns must be in parentheses and separated by a comma, as shown here:

```
update COMFORT set (Noon, Midnight) =
        (select Humidity, Temperature
           from WEATHER
          where City = 'MANCHESTER')
 where City = 'WALPOLE'
    AND SampleDate = '22-DEC-93';

1 row updated.
```

Here is the effect:

```
select * from COMFORT
 where City = 'WALPOLE';

CITY           SAMPLEDAT     NOON    MIDNIGHT PRECIPITATION
------------   ---------   ----------  ---------- -------------
WALPOLE        21-MAR-93     57.7        44.8            0
WALPOLE        22-JUN-93     57.7        44.8            0
WALPOLE        23-SEP-93     87.3        73.1
WALPOLE        22-DEC-93       98          66           .5

4 rows selected.
```

You also can generate a series of updates by using SQLPLUS as a code generator. This will be covered in Chapter 19.

update with NULL

You also can update a table and set a column equal to **NULL**. This is the sole instance of using the equal sign with **NULL**, instead of the word "is." For example, this:

```
update COMFORT set Noon = NULL
 where City = 'WALPOLE'
   AND SampleDate = '22-DEC-93';

1 row updated.
```

will set the noon temperature to **NULL** for Walpole on December 22, 1993.

NOTE
The primary issues with **insert**, **update**, and **delete** are careful construction of **where** clauses to affect (or **insert**) only the rows you really wish, and the normal use of SQL functions within these **insert**s, **update**s, and **delete**s. It is extremely important that you exercise caution about committing work before you are certain it is correct. These three commands extend the power of ORACLE well beyond simple query, and allow direct manipulation of data.

CHAPTER 14

Advanced Use of Functions and Variables

In previous chapters you've seen definitions and examples for character, number, and date functions, as well as for the use of variables. The examples ranged from simple to fairly complex, and enough explanation was provided so that you could construct rather sophisticated combined functions on your own.

This chapter expands upon some of the earlier uses, and shows examples of how functions can be combined to solve more difficult problems. ORACLE7 has made solving some of these problems easier using SQL itself, but the examples in this chapter can expand your thinking about how to apply functions to solve real problems.

Functions in order by

Functions can be used in an **order by** to change the sorting sequence. Here these **SUBSTR** functions cause the list of authors to be put in alphabetical order by first name:

```
select Author
  from MAGAZINE
 order by SUBSTR(Author,INSTR(Author,',')+2);


AUTHOR
-------------------------
WHITEHEAD, ALFRED
BONHOEFFER, DIETRICH
CHESTERTON, G.K.
RUTH, GEORGE HERMAN
CROOKES, WILLIAM
```

Bar Charts and Graphs

You also can produce simple bar charts and graphs in SQLPLUS, using a mix of **LPAD** and a numeric calculation. First, look at the column formatting commands that will be used:

```
column Name format a16
column Age Format 999
column Graph Heading 'Age!    1    2    3    4    5    6    7-
!....0....0....0....0....0....0....0' justify c
column Graph format a35
```

The first two of these are straightforward. The third requires some explanation. The dash at the end of the third line tells SQLPLUS the column command is wrapped down onto the next line. If the dash appears at the end of a line, SQLPLUS assumes that it means another line of this command follows.

CAUTION
SQLPLUS will insert a space in a heading where it sees this dash. It is important to put the ! at the beginning of the second line, rather than at the end of the first line.

Had the command looked like this:

```
column Graph Heading 'Age¦    1    2    3    4    5    6    7-
¦....0....0....0....0....0....0....0' justify c
```

this heading would have been produced:

```
Age
     1    2    3    4    5    6    7
 ....0....0....0....0....0....0....0
```

instead of what you see in Figure 14-1. Here is the SQL statement that produced the horizontal bar chart. Workers for whom age is unknown are not included:

```
select Name, Age, LPAD('o',ROUND(Age/2,0),'o') Graph
  from WORKER
 where Age is NOT NULL
 order by Age;
```

```
                                     Age
                         1    2    3    4    5    6    7
NAME              AGE  ....0....0....0....0....0....0....0
--------------- ---- ----------------------------------
HELEN BRANDT      15 oooooooo
WILLIAM SWING     15 oooooooo
DONALD ROLLO      16 oooooooo
DICK JONES        18 ooooooooo
PAT LAVAY         21 oooooooooo
BART SARJEANT     22 oooooooooo
ADAH TALBOT       23 ooooooooooo
PETER LAWSON      25 oooooooooooo
JOHN PEARSON      27 oooooooooooo
ANDREW DYE        29 ooooooooooooo
VICTORIA LYNN     32 oooooooooooooo
JED HOPKINS       33 oooooooooooooo
ROLAND BRANDT     35 ooooooooooooooo
GEORGE OSCAR      41 oooooooooooooooooooo
ELBERT TALBOT     43 ooooooooooooooooooooo
GERHARDT KENTGEN  55 ooooooooooooooooooooooooooo
WILFRED LOWELL    67 ooooooooooooooooooooooooooooooooo
```

FIGURE 14-1.   *Horizontal bar chart of age by person*

This use of **LPAD** is similar to what was done in Chapter 11, where Talbot's cows and bulls were shown in their family tree. Basically, a lowercase o is the column here, and it is padded on the left with a number of additional lowercase o's, to the maximum width determined by **ROUND**(Age/2,0).

Notice that the scale of the column heading is in increments of two. A simple change to the SQL will produce a classic graph, rather than a bar chart. The literal column is changed from a space to a lowercase x, and the padding on the left is done by spaces. The results of this SQL statement are shown in Figure 14-2.

```
select Name, Age, LPAD('x',ROUND(Age/2,0),' ') Graph
  from WORKER
 where Age is NOT NULL
 order by Age;
```

Another way to graph Age is by its distribution, rather than by person. First a view is created that puts each Age into its decade. Thus 15, 16, and 18 become 10; 20 through 29 become 20, 30 through 39 become 30, and so on:

```
                                      Age
                          1    2    3    4    5    6    7
NAME               AGE  ....0....0....0....0....0....0....0
---------------    ----  ----------------------------------
HELEN BRANDT        15        x
WILLIAM SWING       15        x
DONALD ROLLO        16        x
DICK JONES          18         x
PAT LAVAY           21          x
BART SARJEANT       22          x
ADAH TALBOT         23           x
PETER LAWSON        25            x
JOHN PEARSON        27             x
ANDREW DYE          29              x
VICTORIA LYNN       32               x
JED HOPKINS         33                x
ROLAND BRANDT       35                 x
GEORGE OSCAR        41                    x
ELBERT TALBOT       43                     x
GERHARDT KENTGEN    55                          x
WILFRED LOWELL      67                               x
```

FIGURE 14-2. *Graph of age by person*

```
create view AGERANGE as
select TRUNC(Age,-1) Decade
   from WORKER;
```

View created.

Next a column heading is set up, similar to the previous heading, although shorter and in increments of one:

```
column Graph Heading 'Count¦           1     1¦....5....0....5'-
justify c
column Graph format a15
column People Heading 'Head¦Count' format 9999
```

This SQL determines the count of workers that is represented in each decade. Since those with an unknown age were not excluded either here or in the view, a blank line appears at the top of the bar chart for those with a **NULL** age. See Figure 14-3.

```
select Decade, COUNT(Decade) People,
       LPAD('o',COUNT(Decade),'o') Graph
   from AGERANGE
 group by Decade;
```

Because **COUNT** ignores **NULL**s, it could not include the number of workers for whom the age is unknown in Figure 14-3. If, instead of **COUNT**ing the non-**NULL** rows in the Decade column, you use **COUNT**(*), every row will be

```
                         Count
               Head        1     1
    DECADE     Count   ....5....0....5
-------------- -----   ---------------

       10        4     oooo
       20        6     oooooo
       30        3     ooo
       40        2     oo
       50        1     o
       60        1     o
```

FIGURE 14-3.   *Distribution of age by decade; workers whose age is unknown don't get counted, but produce a blank line*

counted, and the bar chart will appear as shown in Figure 14-4. The SQL that produced it is this:

```
select Decade, COUNT(*) People,
       LPAD('o',COUNT(*),'o') Graph
  from AGERANGE
 group by Decade;
```

Using TRANSLATE

Recall that **TRANSLATE** converts characters in a string into different characters, based on a substitution plan you give it, from **if** to **then**.

```
TRANSLATE(string,if,then)
```

In the following SQL, the letters in a sentence are replaced. Anytime an uppercase **T** is detected, it is replaced by an uppercase **T**. In effect, nothing changes. Anytime an uppercase vowel is detected, however, it is replaced by a lowercase version of the same vowel.

Any letter not in the TAEIOU string is left alone; no change is made to it. When a letter is found in TAEIOU, its position is checked in the TAEIOU string, and the letter there is substituted. Thus the letter E, at position 3 in TAEIOU, is replaced by e, in position 3 of Taeiou:

```
                         Count
                Head         1     1
       DECADE Count  ....5....0....5
       ------------- ----- ---------------
                  2 oo
           10     4 oooo
           20     6 oooooo
           30     3 ooo
           40     2 oo
           50     1 o
           60     1 o
```

FIGURE 14-4. *Distribution of age, counting all workers*

```
select TRANSLATE('NOW VOWELS ARE UNDER ATTACK','TAEIOU','Taeiou')
   from DUAL;
```

```
TRANSLATE('NOWVOWELSAREUNDE
---------------------------
NoW VoWeLS aRe uNDeR aTTaCK
```

Eliminating Characters

Extending this logic, what happens if the *if* string is TAEIOU and the *then* string is only T? Checking for the letter E (as in the word VOWELS) finds it in position 3 of TAEIOU. Position 3 in the *then* string (which is just the letter T) has nothing. There is no position 3, so the value in position 3 is nothing. So E is replaced by nothing. This same process is applied to all of the vowels. They appear in the *if* string, but not in the *then* string. As a result, they disappear, as shown here:

```
select TRANSLATE('NOW VOWELS ARE UNDER ATTACK','TAEIOU','T')
   from DUAL;
```

```
TRANSLATE('NOWVOWELSAREUNDE
---------------------------
NW VWLS R NDR TTCK
```

This feature of **TRANSLATE**, the ability to eliminate characters from a string, can prove very useful in cleaning up data. Recall the magazine titles in Chapter 5:

```
select Title from MAGAZINE;
```

```
TITLE
--------------------------------------
THE BARBERS WHO SHAVE THEMSELVES.
"HUNTING THOREAU IN NEW HAMPSHIRE"
THE ETHNIC NEIGHBORHOOD
RELATIONAL DESIGN AND ENTHALPY
"INTERCONTINENTAL RELATIONS."
```

The method used in Chapter 5 to clean out the periods and double quotes was a nested combination of **LTRIM** and **RTRIM**.

```
select LTRIM( RTRIM(Title,'."') ,'"') from MAGAZINE;
```

The same purpose can be accomplished with a single use of **TRANSLATE**:

```
select TRANSLATE(Title,'T".','T') TITLE
   from MAGAZINE;

TITLE
---------------------------------------
THE BARBERS WHO SHAVE THEMSELVES
HUNTING THOREAU IN NEW HAMPSHIRE
THE ETHNIC NEIGHBORHOOD
RELATIONAL DESIGN AND ENTHALPY
INTERCONTINENTAL RELATIONS
```

Cleaning Up Dollar Signs and Commas

Suppose you have a file of data from an old accounting system, and you've stored it in the format in which you received it, including commas, decimal points, and even dollar signs. How would you clean up the data in the column, in order to move it into a *pure number column* that doesn't allow commas or dollar signs?

ORACLE version 6 introduced number formats into the **TO_CHAR** and **TO_NUMBER** functions, so in versions 6 and 7 you can convert the number directly using **TO_NUMBER**. But what if these formats didn't exist, as they didn't in version 5?

The COMMA table simply lists 11 rows of comma-formatted numbers. Here it is along with the translation that erases the commas:

```
select AmountChar, TRANSLATE(AmountChar,'1,$','1')
   from COMMA;

AMOUNTCHAR                TRANSLATE(AMOUNTCHAR
-------------------       --------------------
$0                        0
$0.25                     0.25
$1.25                     1.25
$12.25                    12.25
$123.25                   123.25
$1,234.25                 1234.25
$12,345.25                12345.25
$123,456.25               123456.25
$1,234,567.25             1234567.25
$12,345,678.25            12345678.25
$123,456,789.25           123456789.25
```

The SQL says, "Look for either a 1, a comma, or a dollar sign. If you find a 1, replace it with a 1. If you find a comma or a dollar sign, replace it with nothing." Why is there always at least one letter or number translated, a 1 here, and a T in the previous example? Because without at least one real character in the *then*, **TRANSLATE** produces nothing:

```
select AmountChar, TRANSLATE(AmountChar,',$','') from COMMA;

AMOUNTCHAR              TRANSLATE(AMOUNTCHAR
-------------------     --------------------
$0
$0.25
$1.25
$12.25
$123.25
$1,234.25
$12,345.25
$123,456.25
$1,234,567.25
$12,345,678.25
$123,456,789.25
```

The *then* string was blank, with no characters in it, and the *if* string held only those characters to be eliminated. But this approach does not work. There must be at least one character in both the *if* and *then* strings. If this approach can be used to get commas and other characters out of a string, is there a way to get them in, such as comma-editing a number to display it?

The way to put commas into a number is to use the **TO_CHAR** function. As its name implies, this function changes the number string to a character string, which allows the introduction of dollar signs and commas, among other symbols. See the "Number Formats" entry in the Alphabetical Reference for a complete listing of the format options for numbers. The following example shows how to format a number with commas. A format mask tells ORACLE7 how to format the character string that will be created by this command.

```
select TO_CHAR(123456789,"999,999,999") CommaTest
  from DUAL;

COMMATEST
-----------
123,456,789
```

Complex Cut and Paste

The NAME table contains a list of names as you might receive them from a mailing list company or another application. First name, last name, and initials are all in one column:

```
select Name from NAME;

NAME
-------------------------
HORATIO NELSON
VALDO
MARIE DE MEDICIS
FLAVIUS JOSEPHUS
EDYTHE P. M. GAMMIERE
```

Suppose you wanted to cut and paste these names, and put them into a table with FirstName and LastName columns. How would you go about it? The technique learned in Chapter 5 involved using **INSTR** to locate a space, and using the number it returns in a **SUBSTR** to clip out the portion up to that space. Here's an attempt to do just that for the first name:

```
select SUBSTR(Name,1,INSTR(Name,' '))
   from NAME;

SUBSTR(NAME,1,INSTR(NAME,
-------------------------
HORATIO

MARIE
FLAVIUS
EDYTHE
```

VALDO has vanished! The problem is that these names are not as consistent as the authors' names were in Chapter 5. One of these names (probably a magician) is only one name long, so there is no space for the **INSTR** to find. When **INSTR** has an unsuccessful search, it returns a zero. The **SUBSTR** of the name VALDO, starting at position 1 and going for 0 positions, is nothing, so he disappears. This is solved with **DECODE**. In place of this:

```
INSTR(Name,' ')
```

you put the entire expression like this:

```
DECODE(INSTR(Name,' '),0,99,INSTR(Name,' '))
```

Remember that **DECODE**'s format is this:

```
DECODE(value,if1,then1[,if2,then2,if3,then3]...,else)
```

In the example here, **DECODE** tests the value of **INSTR**(Name,' '). If it is equal to 0, it substitutes 99; otherwise, it returns the default value, which is also **INSTR**(Name,' '). The choice of 99 as a substitute is relatively arbitrary. It will create an effective **SUBSTR** function for VALDO that looks like this:

```
SUBSTR('VALDO',1,99)
```

This works because **SUBSTR** will clip out text from the starting number, 1, to the ending number or the end of the string, whichever comes first. With the **DECODE** function in place, the first names are retrieved correctly:

```
select SUBSTR(Name,1,
       DECODE(INSTR(Name,' '),0,99,INSTR(Name,' ')))
  from NAME;
SUBSTR(NAME,1,DECODE(INST
-------------------------
HORATIO
VALDO
MARIE
FLAVIUS
EDYTHE
```

How about the last names? You could use **INSTR** again to search for a space, and use this (plus 1) as the starting point for **SUBSTR**. No ending point is required for **SUBSTR** because you want it to go to the end of the name. This is what happens:

```
select SUBSTR(Name,INSTR(Name,' ')+1)
  from NAME;

SUBSTR(NAME,INSTR(NAME,''
-------------------------
NELSON
VALDO
DE MEDICIS
JOSEPHUS
P. M. GAMMIERE
```

This didn't quite work. One solution is to use three **INSTR** functions, looking successively for the first, second, or third occurrence of a space in the name. Each of these **INSTR**s will return either the location where it found a space, or a zero if it didn't find any. In a name with only one space, the second and third **INSTR**s will both return zero. The **GREATEST** function therefore will pick the number returned by the **INSTR** that found the space furthest into the name:

```
select SUBSTR(Name,
GREATEST(INSTR(Name,' '),INSTR(Name,' ',1,2),INSTR(Name,' ',1
,3)) +1)
   from NAME;


SUBSTR(NAME,GREATEST(INST
-------------------------
NELSON
VALDO
MEDICIS

JOSEPHUS
GAMMIERE
```

Except for the fact that you also got VALDO again, this worked. (**GREATEST** also could have been used similarly in place of **DECODE** in the previous example.) There is a second and simpler method:

```
select SUBSTR(Name,INSTR(Name,' ',-1)+1)
   from NAME;

SUBSTR(NAME,INSTR(NAME,''
-------------------------
NELSON
VALDO
MEDICIS
JOSEPHUS
GAMMIERE
```

The –1 in the **INSTR** tells it to start its search in the final position and go *backward*, or right to left, in the Name. When it finds the space, **INSTR** returns its position, counting from the left as usual. All the –1 does is make **INSTR** start searching from the end, rather than the beginning. A –2 would make it start searching from the second position from the end, and so on.

The +1 in the **SUBSTR** command has the same purpose as in the previous example: once the space is found, **SUBSTR** has to move one position to the right to begin clipping out the Name. If no space is found, the **INSTR** returns 0, and **SUBSTR** therefore starts with position 1. That's why VALDO made the list.

How do you get rid of VALDO? Add an ending position to the **SUBSTR**, instead of its default (which goes automatically all the way to the end). The ending position is found by using this:

```
DECODE(INSTR(Name,' '),0,0,LENGTH(Name))
```

This says, "Find the position of a space in the Name. If the position is zero, return zero, otherwise return the **LENGTH** of the Name." For VALDO, the **DECODE** produces zero as the ending position for **SUBSTR**, so nothing is displayed. For any other name, because there is a space somewhere, the **LENGTH** of the Name becomes the ending position for the **SUBSTR**, so the whole last name is displayed.

This is similar to the **DECODE** used to extract the first name, except that the value 99 used there has been replaced by **LENGTH**(Name), which will always work, whereas 99 would fail for a name longer than 99 characters. This won't matter a whit here, but in other uses of **DECODE** and **SUBSTR** it could be important.

```
select SUBSTR(Name,
       INSTR(Name,' ',-1)+1,
       DECODE(INSTR(Name,' '), 0, 0, LENGTH(Name)))
   from NAME;

SUBSTR(NAME,INSTR(NAME,''
------------------------
NELSON

MEDICIS
JOSEPHUS
GAMMIERE
```

This **DECODE** also could have been replaced by a **GREATEST**:

```
select SUBSTR(Name,
       INSTR(Name,' ',-1)+1,
       GREATEST(INSTR(Name,' '),0))
   from NAME;
```

A third method to accomplish the same end uses **RTRIM**. Remember that **RTRIM** eliminates everything specified in its *set* from the right side of a string, until it encounters any character not in its *set*. The **RTRIM** here effectively erases all the letters on the right, until it hits the first space (just before the last name), or reaches the beginning of the string.

```
select
SUBSTR(Name,LENGTH(RTRIM(NAME,'ABCDEFGHIJKLMNOPQRSTUVWXYZ'))
    +1)
  from NAME;

SUBSTR(NAME,LENGTH(RTRIM(
-------------------------
NELSON
MEDICIS
JOSEPHUS
GAMMIERE
```

LENGTH then measures the resulting string (with the last name erased). This tells you the position of the space before the last name. Add 1 to this number, do a **SUBSTR** starting there, and you'll get just the last name. Let's create a table with first name and last name columns (you'll see complete details on creating tables in Chapter 16):

```
create table TWONAME(
FirstName      VARCHAR2(25),
LastName       VARCHAR2(25)
);

Table created.
```

Now use an insert with a subquery to load it with the first and last names from the NAME table:

```
insert into TWONAME (FirstName, LastName)
select
  SUBSTR(Name,1,DECODE(INSTR(Name,' '),0,99,INSTR(Name,' '))),
  SUBSTR(Name,LENGTH(RTRIM(NAME,'ABCDEFGHIJKLMNOPQRSTUVWXYZ'))+1)
  from NAME;
```

Check the contents of the TWONAME table:

```
select * from TWONAME;

FIRSTNAME                LASTNAME
------------------------  ------------------------
HORATIO                  NELSON
VALDO
MARIE                    MEDICIS
FLAVIUS                  JOSEPHUS
EDYTHE                   GAMMIERE
```

You can use similar techniques to extract the middle initial or initials, and apply these methods elsewhere as well, such as to addresses, product descriptions, company names, and so on.

When moving data from an old system to a new one, reformatting is frequently necessary and often difficult. The facilities exist in SQL but require some knowledge of how the functions work, and some thoughtfulness to avoid the kinds of difficulties shown here.

Variables and Spooled Substitution

Suppose you are preparing a report to be used by bank officers to determine when CDs they've issued are going to mature. The difficulty is the approach of the year 2000, and the fact that some securities will mature after 1999. First create a report of all CDs and their maturity dates:

```
ttitle 'CD Maturities'

select Account, Amount, MaturityDate
  from CD;

Sat Apr 1                        page    1
            CD Maturities


        ACCOUNT          AMOUNT MATURITYD
--------------  --------------  ---------
        573334           10000  15-JAN-09
        677654           25000  15-JAN-01
        976032           10000  15-JAN-95
        275031           10000  15-JAN-97
        274598           20000  15-JAN-99
        538365           45000  15-JAN-01
        267432           16500  15-JAN-04
```

There are several accounts, amounts, and years represented here. Your particular concern is about those maturing on January 15, 2001, so you modify the query:

```
select Account, Amount
  from CD
 where MaturityDate = '15-JAN-01';
```

```
no rows selected
```

Unfortunately, ORACLE assumes any two-digit year entered is in the current century. It thought you meant 1901. One way around this is to change the query so it has a **TO_DATE** that will take a four-digit year:

```
select Account, Amount
  from CD
 where MaturityDate = TO_DATE('15-JAN-2001','DD-MON-YYYY');
```

```
Sat Apr 1                          page    1
             CD Maturities

        ACCOUNT            AMOUNT
  --------------  --------------
         677654            25000
         538365            45000
```

However, this report is to be run by a bank officer who may know nothing about SQL or writing queries. You can make the officer's job easier by using a variable and the **accept** command:

```
set verify off
set echo off
accept Test prompt 'Enter Date as MM/DD/YYYY: '

spool maturity.lst
select Account, Amount
  from CD
 where MaturityDate = TO_DATE('&Test','MM/DD/YYYY');

spool off
```

When this code is put into a start file and started, it will prompt the officer with this:

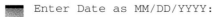
```
Enter Date as MM/DD/YYYY:
```

There is an alternative approach that will allow even a two-digit year to be entered, and that will automatically expand it into four digits with the correct century. You could, of course, use the "RR" date format for the year; this format interprets all two-digit years before 50 as being in the 21st century. But say you really wanted only the first 10 years treated this way. You can use **DECODE** to get this effect, or use an additional feature of SQLPLUS and start files. Look at the start file in Figure 14-5.

An even better approach is to set the default date format to a four-digit year in the **init.ora** file or for a session with the **alter session** statement.

At Circle 1, all of the controls that might produce extraneous messages on the display are turned off.

At Circle 2, the user is requested to enter a date with a two-digit year, in the format MM/DD/YY. Assume the user enters **01/15/01**.

At Circle 3, this start file begins spooling its results into another file named **t.sql**. These results are shown in Figure 14-6.

At Circle 4, a **select** statement is executed that compares the last two digits of the date, 01, with the test year, 90, using the dummy table DUAL, which has only one row. Because 01 is not greater than or equal to 90, this **select** statement will produce no records. Since **feedback** is **off**, not even the "no rows selected" message will appear.

At Circle 5, a nearly identical **select** statement is executed, but because 01 is less than 90, this succeeds, and it adds 2000 to 01. The results of this **select** are at Circle A in Figure 14-6. Notice how the literal 'define YYYY=' is now combined with the result of the calculation, 2001.

At Circle 6, the first portion of the date is clipped out of the variable Test, and defined as equal to the variable MonthDay. The effect is shown at Circle B in Figure 14-6.

A series of **prompt**s at Circle 7 now displays these messages:

```
set feedback on
set heading on
ttitle on
```

Because the main start file is still spooling to **t.sql**, the word **prompt** has the effect of writing any text that follows it directly into the spool file, and this is just what appears in **t.sql** at Circle C. The **prompt** not followed by any text wrote a blank line.

At Circle 8, spooling to **t.sql** is turned off. This, in effect, closes the file with the information shown in Figure 14-6 inside of it.

At Circle 9, the file **t.sql** is started! All of the commands in Figure 14-6 now execute. YYYY is defined to be 2001. MonthDay is defined to be 01/15/. **feedback**, **heading**, and **ttitle** are restored to their former states.

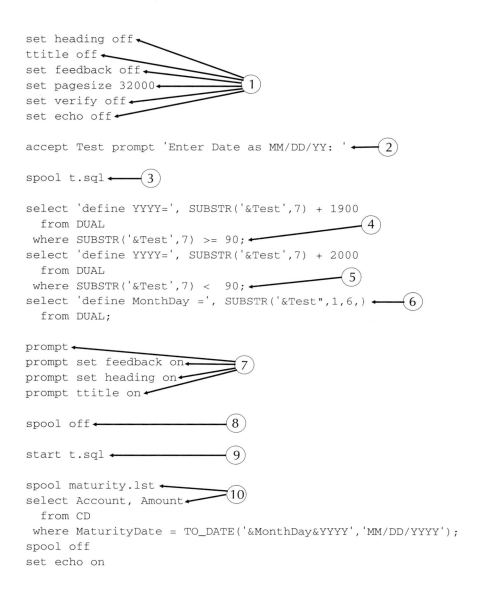

```
set heading off
ttitle off
set feedback off
set pagesize 32000
set verify off
set echo off

accept Test prompt 'Enter Date as MM/DD/YY: '

spool t.sql

select 'define YYYY=', SUBSTR('&Test',7) + 1900
  from DUAL
 where SUBSTR('&Test',7) >= 90;
select 'define YYYY=', SUBSTR('&Test',7) + 2000
  from DUAL
 where SUBSTR('&Test',7) <  90;
select 'define MonthDay =', SUBSTR('&Test",1,6,)
  from DUAL;

prompt
prompt set feedback on
prompt set heading on
prompt ttitle on

spool off

start t.sql

spool maturity.lst
select Account, Amount
  from CD
 where MaturityDate = TO_DATE('&MonthDay&YYYY','MM/DD/YYYY');
spool off
set echo on
```

FIGURE 14-5. *Start file for complex variable use*

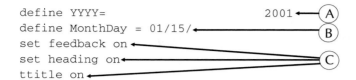

```
define YYYY=                              2001 ←(A)
define MonthDay = 01/15/ ←              (B)
set feedback on ←
set heading on ←                      (C)
ttitle on ←
```

FIGURE 14-6. *The spooled start file T.SQL*

At Circle 10, all of this work comes together. Spooling begins to the output file **maturity.lst**, and this **select** statement:

```
select Account, Amount
  from CD
 where MaturityDate = TO_DATE('&MonthDay&YYYY','MM/DD/YYYY');
```

is executed. Because &MonthDay and &YYYY are pushed right up against each other, they produce the net effect 01/15/2001, and the query executes, producing this report in the file **maturity.lst**:

```
Sat Apr 1                        page    1
              CD Maturities

        ACCOUNT          AMOUNT
    -------------- --------------
          677654           25000
          538365           45000

2 rows selected.
```

Some Additional Facts about Variables

The command **accept** forces SQLPLUS to **define** the variable as equal to the entered value, and it can do this with a text message, with control over the data type entered, and even with the response blanked out from viewing (such as for passwords; see **accept** in the Alphabetical Reference at the back of this book).

It is also possible to pass arguments to a start file when it is started by embedding numbered variables in the **select** statements (rather than variables with names).

To select all of Talbot's transactions between one date and another, the **select** statement might look like this:

```
select * from LEDGER
 where ActionDate BETWEEN '&1' AND '&2';
```

The query would then be started like this:

```
start ledger.sql 01-JAN-01 31-DEC-01
```

The start file **ledger.sql** would begin, with 01-JAN-01 substituted for &1 and 31-DEC-01 substituted for &2. As with other variables, character and DATE data types must be enclosed in single quotation marks in the SQL statement. One limitation of this is that each argument following the word **start** must be a single word without spaces.

Variable substitutions are not restricted to the SQL statement. The start file also may use variables for such things as SQLPLUS commands.

You saw earlier that variables can be concatenated simply by pushing them together. You can concatenate a variable with a constant using the period (.).

```
select sum(Amount)
   from LEDGER
 where ActionDate BETWEEN '01-&Month.-01'
                     AND LAST_DAY(TO_DATE('01-&Month.-01'));
```

This **select** will query once for a month, and then build the two dates using the period as a concatenation operator.

NOTE
No period is necessary before the variable, only after it. The ampersand tells SQLPLUS that a variable is beginning.

Related set Commands

Normally the ampersand (&) denotes a variable. This can be changed with **set define** followed by the single symbol you'd prefer to denote a variable.

set escape defines a character you can place just in front of the ampersand (or other defined symbol) so that SQLPLUS will treat the symbol as a literal, not as denoting a variable.

set concat can change the default concatenation operator for variables, which is the period (.), to another single symbol. This variable concatenation is used in addition to, and separately from, the SQL concatenation operator, which is usually two broken vertical bars (¦ ¦).

set scan turns variable substitution **off** or **on** for the SQL statement. If **scan** is **off**, any variable in a **select** statement is treated as a literal—for example, **&Test** is treated as the literal word **&Test**, not as the value it is defined as. Variables used in SQLPLUS commands, however, are still substituted as before.

CHAPTER 15

DECODE–Amazing Power in a Single Word

The **DECODE** function is without doubt one of the most powerful in ORACLE's SQL. It is one of several extensions ORACLE added to the standard SQL language, and is not yet available in the SQL supplied by other vendors. Until these vendors add it to their own SQL, they might claim that this makes ORACLE's SQL nonstandard. Although this is true, it is a poor criticism, somewhat like a buggy manufacturer complaining that Henry Ford's buggy is nonstandard because it has an engine in it. **DECODE** provides opportunities for manipulating data that are simply impossible to accomplish using any other SQL commands. Implementations of SQL that lack **DECODE** are impoverished by its absence. This chapter will explore a number of ways that **DECODE** can be used.

This is an advanced and often difficult chapter. Most of what is illustrated here is unnecessary for the vast majority of reporting; don't be concerned if it seems beyond your needs. Its real value is more for sophisticated reporting and programming.

if, then, else

In programming and logic, a common construction of a problem is in the pattern *if, then, else.* For example, *if* this day is a Saturday, *then* Adah will play at home; *if* this day is a Sunday, *then* Adah will go to her grandparent's home; *if* this day is a holiday, *then* Adah will go over to Aunt Dora's, *else* Adah will go to school. In each case "this day" was tested, and if it was one of a list of certain days, then a certain result followed, or else (if it was none of those days) another result followed. **DECODE** follows this kind of logic. Chapter 8 provided an introduction that demonstrated the basic structure and usage of **DECODE**.

This is **DECODE**'s format:

```
DECODE(value,if1,then1,if2,then2,if3,then3,. . . ,else)
```

value represents any column in a table (regardless of data type) or any result of a computation, such as one date minus another, a **SUBSTR** of a character column, one number times another, and so on. *value* is tested for each row. If *value* equals *if1*, then the result of the **DECODE** is *then1*, if *value* equals *if2*, then the result of the **DECODE** is *then2*, and so on, for virtually as many if/then pairs as you can construct. If *value* equals none of the *if*s, then the result of the **DECODE** is *else*. Each of the *if*s, *then*s, and the *else* also can be a column or the result of a function or computation.

Example: Aging Invoices

Suppose George Talbot had a table or a view called INVOICE that contained outstanding invoices, their dates, and the related client names. If he were to look at this on December 15, 1901, it might contain the results shown in Figure 15-1.

```
column ClientName format a14
column InvoiceDate heading 'Date of¦Invoice'

select ClientName, InvoiceDate, Amount
  from INVOICE;


                    Date of
CLIENTNAME          Invoice   AMOUNT
---------------     --------- ------
ELBERT TALBOT       23-OCT-01   5.03
JOHN PEARSON        09-NOV-01   2.02
DICK JONES          12-SEP-01  11.12
GENERAL STORE       09-NOV-01  22.10
ADAH TALBOT         17-NOV-01   8.29
GENERAL STORE       01-SEP-01  21.32
ADAH TALBOT         15-NOV-01   7.33
GENERAL STORE       04-OCT-01   8.42
KAY WALLBOM         04-OCT-01   1.43
JOHN PEARSON        13-OCT-01  12.41
DICK JONES          23-OCT-01   4.49
GENERAL STORE       23-NOV-01  40.36
GENERAL STORE       30-OCT-01   7.47
MORRIS ARNOLD       03-OCT-01   3.55
ROLAND BRANDT       22-OCT-01  13.65
MORRIS ARNOLD       21-SEP-01   9.87
```

FIGURE 15-1. *Clients and invoice amounts due*

As he looks through this list he realizes some of these invoices have been outstanding for some time. He asks you to try to analyze how serious a problem he has. Your first attempt is to put the clients in order by date, as shown in Figure 15-2.

This is more useful, but it still doesn't produce any real insights into the magnitude of Talbot's problem. Therefore, you create a **DECODE** expression to show how these invoices and amounts are spread through time. This is shown in

```
select ClientName, InvoiceDate, Amount
  from INVOICE
 order by InvoiceDate;
```

```
                     Date of
CLIENTNAME           Invoice     AMOUNT
----------------     ---------   ------
GENERAL STORE        01-SEP-01    21.32
DICK JONES           12-SEP-01    11.12
MORRIS ARNOLD        21-SEP-01     9.87
MORRIS ARNOLD        03-OCT-01     3.55
GENERAL STORE        04-OCT-01     8.42
KAY WALLBOM          04-OCT-01     1.43
VICTORIA LYNN        09-OCT-01     8.98
JOHN PEARSON         13-OCT-01    12.41
ROLAND BRANDT        22-OCT-01    13.65
GENERAL STORE        22-OCT-01    17.58
ELBERT TALBOT        23-OCT-01     5.03
DICK JONES           23-OCT-01     4.49
GENERAL STORE        30-OCT-01     7.47
JOHN PEARSON         09-NOV-01     2.02
GENERAL STORE        09-NOV-01    22.10
ADAH TALBOT          15-NOV-01     7.33
ADAH TALBOT          17-NOV-01     8.29
GENERAL STORE        23-NOV-01    40.36
```

FIGURE 15-2.   *Clients in order by invoice date*

Figure 15-3. Consider just the **DECODE** expression for NINETY days. This will show the logic used in each of the **DECODE** expressions.

```
DECODE(TRUNC((AsOf-InvoiceDate)/30),3,Amount,NULL) NINETY
```

AsOf is a date: December 15, 1901. The date here is from a small table, ASOF, created just for "as of" reporting and with only one date in it. SysDate also might be used if a query like this were always current, but AsOf is more useful when the report will be "as of" a certain day, rather than today. (A variable also could be used in a start file, with the **TO_DATE** function.)

```
select ClientName,
       TRUNC((AsOf-InvoiceDate)/30) DAYS
       DECODE(TRUNC((AsOf-InvoiceDate)/30),0,Amount, NULL) THIS,
       DECODE(TRUNC((AsOf-InvoiceDate)/30),1,Amount, NULL) THIRTY,
       DECODE(TRUNC((AsOf-InvoiceDate)/30),2,Amount, NULL) SIXTY,
       DECODE(TRUNC((AsOf-InvoiceDate)/30),3,Amount, NULL) NINETY,
  from INVOICE, ASOF
 order by InvoiceDate;
```

CLIENTNAME	DAYS	THIS	THIRTY	SIXTY	NINETY
GENERAL STORE	3				21.32
DICK JONES	3				11.12
MORRIS ARNOLD	2			9.87	
MORRIS ARNOLD	2			3.55	
GENERAL STORE	2			8.42	
KAY WALLBOM	2			1.43	
VICTORIA LYNN	2			8.98	
JOHN PEARSON	2			2.41	
ROLAND BRANDT	1		13.65		
GENERAL STORE	1		17.58		
ELBERT TALBOT	1		5.03		
DICK JONES	1		4.49		
GENERAL STORE	1		7.47		
JOHN PEARSON	1		2.02		
GENERAL STORE	1		22.10		
ADAH TALBOT	1		7.33		
ADAH TALBOT	0	8.29			
GENERAL STORE	0	40.36			

FIGURE 15-3.   **DECODE** *used to spread amounts due over time*

The value that is being decoded is a computation. It extends from the "T" after the opening parenthesis to the first comma. In this **DECODE**, the InvoiceDate of each row is subtracted from the AsOf date. The result is the number of days that have elapsed since the invoice date. This interval is now divided by 30, giving the number of 30-day periods since the invoice date.

For intervals other than exact multiples of 30, this will not be a whole number, so it's truncated, thereby assuring a whole number as a result. Any date less than 30 days before December 15 will produce a 0. A date 30 to 59 days before will produce a 1. A date 60 to 89 days before will produce a 2. A date 90 to 119 days before will produce a 3. The number 0, 1, 2, or 3 is the *value* in the **DECODE** statement.

Look again at the last **DECODE**. Following the first comma is a 3. This is the *if* test. If the *value* is 3, *then* the whole **DECODE** statement will be the Amount in this row. If the *value* is anything other than 3 (meaning less than 90 days or more than 119), the **DECODE** will be equal to **NULL**. Compare the invoice dates in Figure 15-2 with the amounts in the NINETY column of Figure 15-3, and you'll see how this logic works.

Collecting Clients Together

As the next step in your analysis, you may want to collect all the clients together, along with the amounts they owe by period. A simple **order by** added to the last SQL statement accomplishes this, as shown in Figure 15-4.

Unfortunately, each invoice produces its own row in this display. It would be more useful to total up the amounts owed if each client took up a single row, with the amount owed spread out by period. This is done with a view:

```
create or replace view AGING as
select ClientName,
       SUM(DECODE(TRUNC((AsOf-InvoiceDate)/30),0,Amount,NULL) THIS,
       SUM(DECODE(TRUNC((AsOf-InvoiceDate)/30),1,Amount,NULL)) THIRTY,
       SUM(DECODE(TRUNC((AsOf-InvoiceDate)/30),2,Amount,NULL)) SIXTY,
       SUM(DECODE(TRUNC((AsOf-InvoiceDate)/30),3,Amount,NULL)) NINETY,
       SUM(Amount) TOTAL
  from INVOICE, ASOF
 group by ClientName;
```

The view is followed by a simple query, with column headings, and **compute** and **break on** used to show totals by column. To get grand totals, the pseudo-column (a column that isn't really in the table, such as SysDate) User was employed here, rather than the **Report** option of **break on** explained in Chapter 12 (merely to show an alternative technique). The query is shown in Figure 15-5.

Each client is consolidated to a single row, showing the Amount owed per period, as well as in total. You may have noticed an interesting shorthand in the **select** statement. An asterisk (*) after a **select** will get all of the regular columns in

```
select ClientName,
       TRUNC((AsOf-InvoiceDate)/30) DAYS
       DECODE(TRUNC((AsOf-InvoiceDate)/30),0,Amount, NULL) THIS,
       DECODE(TRUNC((AsOf-InvoiceDate)/30),1,Amount, NULL) THIRTY,
       DECODE(TRUNC((AsOf-InvoiceDate)/30),2,Amount, NULL) SIXTY,
       DECODE(TRUNC((AsOf-InvoiceDate)/30),3,Amount, NULL) NINETY,
   from INVOICE, ASOF
 order by ClientName, InvoiceDate;
```

CLIENTNAME	DAYS	THIS	THIRTY	SIXTY	NINETY
ADAH TALBOT	1		7.33		
ADAH TALBOT	0	8.29			
DICK JONES	3				11.12
DICK JONES	1		4.49		
ELBERT TALBOT	1		5.03		
GENERAL STORE	3				21.32
GENERAL STORE	2			8.42	
GENERAL STORE	1		17.58		
GENERAL STORE	1		7.47		
GENERAL STORE	1		22.10		
GENERAL STORE	0	40.36			
JOHN PEARSON	2			12.41	
JOHN PEARSON	1		2.02		
KAY WALLBOM	2			1.43	
MORRIS ARNOLD	2			9.87	
MORRIS ARNOLD	2			3.55	
ROLAND BRANDT	1		13.65		
VICTORIA LYNN	2			8.98	

FIGURE 15-4. *Client invoices collected together*

the table or view. However, in addition to the real columns, the pseudo-column User was desired as well. To use the shorthand method and get additional columns, the table name and a period must precede the asterisk. The asterisk cannot stand alone if it will be followed by another column name (whether a pseudo-column or a real column). In other words, this:

```
select AGING.*, User
```

```
column User noprint
column This heading 'CURRENT'
compute sum of This Thirty Sixty Ninety Total on User
break on User skip 1

select AGING.*, User
  from AGING;
```

CLIENTNAME	CURRENT	THIRTY	SIXTY	NINETY	TOTAL
ADAH TALBOT	8.29	7.33			15.62
DICK JONES		4.49		11.12	15.61
ELBERT TALBOT		5.03			5.03
GENERAL STORE	40.36	47.15	8.42	21.32	117.25
JOHN PEARSON		2.02	12.41		14.43
KAY WALLBOM			1.43		1.43
MORRIS ARNOLD			13.42		13.42
ROLAND BRANDT		13.65			13.65
VICTORIA LYNN			8.98		8.98
	48.65	79.67	44.66	32.44	205.42

FIGURE 15-5. *Clients consolidated to a single row each*

is identical to this:

```
select ClientName, This, Thirty, Sixty, Ninety, Total, User
```

The User may be needed in a query in order to include it in a **ttitle** or **btitle** to show who ran the report. In the example in Figure 15-5 it is used in a more unusual way: it produces the same effect as **break on Report**. In other words, this:

```
column User noprint
column This heading 'CURRENT'
compute sum of This Thirty Sixty Ninety Total on User
break on User skip 1

select AGING.*, User
  from AGING;
```

will produce exactly the same result as this:

```
column This heading 'CURRENT'
compute sum of This Thirty Sixty Ninety Total on Report
break on Report skip 1

select *
  from AGING;
```

Compare the presence of Report in the second of these two SQL statements with the User in the first. The second is the normal technique for creating a report with totals. The first method produces the same result. It works because the User pseudo-column, which always contains your username, doesn't change from row to row. The **break on** doesn't detect a change in User until the last row has passed and the query is over. By also making the column User **noprint**, it doesn't show up on the report. This is the method that was used before the Report option for **break on** and **compute** became available in ORACLE, and it may have other applications for you. It is shown here not as a recommended alternative to Report (it is not), but just to let you know another technique is available.

Flipping a Table onto Its Side

A table, as we have seen again and again, is made up of columns and rows. The columns are *predefined:* they each have a specific name and data type, and there are a limited number of them per table. Rows are different: in any table they will vary in number from zero to millions, and the value in a column can change from row to row, and is not predefined. It can be virtually anything, so long as it fits the data type.

This states the general case—that is, it is true of tables in general. However, tables are often much more restricted, stable, and defined than this. A table of holiday names, for instance, won't require new rows of holidays very often. It isn't likely that a thirteenth month will ever be added to a table of month names.

Other tables are somewhat more volatile, but may remain stable for an extended period of time, or the values in certain columns, such as the names of major clients, may remain unchanged. Circumstances like these provide the opportunity to use **DECODE** in a most unusual way: to flip a table on its side, to turn some of the values in rows into columns. Here the INVOICE table is turned sideways in a view called ClientByDate. For each InvoiceDate, each ClientName becomes a number column containing the amount of the invoice on that date:

```
create or replace view ClientByDate as
select  InvoiceDate,
        SUM(DECODE(ClientName,'ADAH TALBOT',  Amount, 0)) AdahTalbot,
        SUM(DECODE(ClientName,'ELBERT TALBOT',Amount, 0)) ElbertTalbot,
        SUM(DECODE(ClientName,'VICTORIA LYNN',Amount, 0)) VictoriaLynn,
        SUM(DECODE(ClientName,'JOHN PEARSON', Amount, 0)) JohnPearson,
        SUM(DECODE(ClientName,'DICK JONES',   Amount, 0)) DickJones,
        SUM(DECODE(ClientName,'GENERAL STORE',Amount, 0)) GeneralStore,
        SUM(DECODE(ClientName,'KAY WALLBOM',  Amount, 0)) KayWallbom,
        SUM(DECODE(ClientName,'MORRIS ARNOLD',Amount, 0)) MorrisArnold,
        SUM(DECODE(ClientName,'ROLAND BRANDT',Amount, 0)) RolandBrandt
   from INVOICE
 group by InvoiceDate;
```

When this view is described, it reveals this:

```
describe CLIENTBYDATE

Name                              Null?    Type
-------------------------------   -------  ----
INVOICEDATE                                DATE
ADAHTALBOT                                 NUMBER
ELBERTTALBOT                               NUMBER
VICTORIALYNN                               NUMBER
JOHNPEARSON                                NUMBER
DICKJONES                                  NUMBER
GENERALSTORE                               NUMBER
KAYWALLBOM                                 NUMBER
MORRISARNOLD                               NUMBER
ROLANDBRANDT                               NUMBER
```

Querying this view reveals a row for every date, with either 0 or an amount owed under each column. Note that only five of the clients were included in this query, simply to make it easier to read. See Figure 15-6.

This view could have a further view built upon it, perhaps summing the totals by client for all dates, and consolidating horizontally all amounts for all clients. This method turns vertical calculations into horizontal ones, and horizontal calculations into vertical ones. It is especially powerful in complex array and matrix-like computations. In effect, this flipping is also what was done in the invoice aging example, where the InvoiceDate, broken into 30-day periods, was converted into four columns.

An even more sophisticated approach to this can be taken, in which a view is dynamically built from a query of the values of client names, creating new columns as new clients are added. This requires dropping and re-creating the view as new clients are added, but the **create view** and **select** can be automatic, using the code-generating techniques described in Chapter 19.

```
select InvoiceDate, ElbertTalbot, GeneralStore, DickJones, KayWallbom,
       RolandBrandt
  from CLIENTBYDATE;
```

Date of Invoice	ELBERTTALBOT	GENERALSTORE	DICKJONES	KAYWALLBOM	ROLANDBRANDT
01-SEP-01	0	21.32	0	0	0
12-SEP-01	0	0	11.12	0	0
21-SEP-01	0	0	0	0	0
03-OCT-01	0	0	0	0	0
04-OCT-01	0	8.42	0	1.43	0
09-OCT-01	0	0	0	0	0
13-OCT-01	0	0	0	0	0
22-OCT-01	0	17.58	0	0	13.65
23-OCT-01	5.03	0	4.49	0	0
30-OCT-01	0	7.47	0	0	0
09-NOV-01	0	22.10	0	0	0
15-NOV-01	0	0	0	0	0
17-NOV-01	0	0	0	0	0
23-NOV-01	0	40.36	0	0	0

FIGURE 15-6. *A table flipped onto its side*

Using MOD in DECODE

The modulus function, **MOD**, can be used in conjunction with **DECODE** and RowNum to produce some startling printing, paper-handling, and other effects. RowNum is another of the pseudo-columns, and is the number of each row counted as it is retrieved from the database; that is, when you execute a **select**, the first row returned is given the RowNum of 1, the second is 2, and so on. RowNum is not a part of the row's location in the table or database, and has nothing to do with RowID. It is a number tacked onto the row as it is being pulled from the database.

In Figure 15-7, a **select** statement retrieves the InvoiceDate and Amount from the INVOICE table. The RowNum also is displayed in the far-left column. The second column, however, is a combination of **DECODE** and **MOD**. Each RowNum is divided by 5 in the modulus function. The result is the value in the **DECODE**. If RowNum is evenly divided by 5, the result of **MOD** is 0, and then the result of the **DECODE** is RowNum. If RowNum is not a multiple of 5, the result of **MOD** will not be 0, so **DECODE** will produce a **NULL** result.

```
column Line Format 9999
select RowNum,DECODE(MOD(RowNum,5),0,RowNum, NULL) Line,
       InvoiceDate,Amount
  from INVOICE;
```

```
                 Date of
ROWNUM  LINE   Invoice      AMOUNT
--------  ----   ---------    -------
     1           23-OCT-01     5.03
     2           09-NOV-01     2.02
     3           12-SEP-01    11.12
     4           09-NOV-01    22.10
     5     5     17-NOV-01     8.29
     6           01-SEP-01    21.32
     7           15-NOV-01     7.33
     8           04-OCT-01     8.42
     9           04-OCT-01     1.43
    10    10     13-OCT-01    12.41
    11           23-OCT-01     4.49
    12           23-NOV-01    40.36
    13           30-OCT-01     7.47
    14           03-OCT-01     3.55
    15    15     22-OCT-01    13.65
    16           21-SEP-01     9.87
    17           22-OCT-01    17.58
    18           09-OCT-01     8.98
```

FIGURE 15-7. *Numbering lines using* **DECODE** *and* **MOD**

In Figure 15-8, the same basic approach is used, but RowNum is eliminated as a printed column, and the **DECODE** becomes a separate column following the Amount. Additionally, instead of every fifth row displaying the RowNum, a top-of-page character is put into the *then* in the **DECODE**. The **DECODE** column is renamed A, and a **column** command makes it just one character long, with no heading.

When this prints, the result will be a new page of data each time the printer receives the top-of-form character, as shown in Figure 15-9. The columns will line up correctly during printing. If your computer system will not permit you to key a *hexadecimal* (base 16) directly into a line of text, use the SQL expression CHR(12) instead of the literal.

```
column A format al heading ' '
select InvoiceDate, Amount,
       DECODE(MOD(RowNum,5),0,'♀',null) A
from INVOICE;

Date of
Invoice     AMOUNT
---------  --------
23-OCT-01      5.03
09-NOV-01      2.02
12-SEP-01     11.12
09-NOV-01     22.10
17-NOV-01      8.29 ♀
01-SEP-01     21.32
15-NOV-01      7.33
04-OCT-01      8.42
04-OCT-01      1.43
13-OCT-01     12.41 ♀
23-OCT-01      4.49
23-NOV-01     40.36
30-OCT-01      7.47
03-OCT-01      3.55
22-OCT-01     13.65 ♀
21-SEP-01      9.87
22-OCT-01     17.58
09-OCT-01      8.98
```

FIGURE 15-8.   *Listing with embedded top-of-form characters*

A hex character is not your only option. You also can use two line-feed characters, or a word surrounded by hex characters, and so on. The effect of this technique is to give you row-by-row procedural logic. Once you fully comprehend this, great possibilities open up, such as committing large blocks of **insert**s, **update**s, or **delete**s in small groups by substituting the word **commit** for the hex character in the last example.

order by and RowNum

Because RowNum can be used to such great benefit in **DECODE**, it's important to understand that this number is attached to a row just as it is first pulled from the

```
Date of
Invoice        AMOUNT
---------      --------
23-OCT-01        5.03
09-NOV-01        2.02
12-SEP-01       11.12
09-NOV-01       22.10
17-NOV-01        8.29
```

```
01-SEP-01       21.32
15-NOV-01        7.33
04-OCT-01        8.42
04-OCT-01        1.43
13-OCT-01       12.41
```

```
23-OCT-01        4.49
23-NOV-01       40.36
30-OCT-01        7.47
03-OCT-01        3.55
22-OCT-01       13.65
```

```
21-SEP-01        9.87
22-OCT-01       17.58
09-OCT-01        8.98
```

FIGURE 15-9.   *The effect of printing the table shown in Figure 15-8—four separate pages*

database, *before* ORACLE executes any **order by** you've given it. As a result, if you attempted to add an **order by** to the first query that used **DECODE** and **MOD**, you'd get the results shown in Figure 15-10.

```
select RowNum,DECODE(MOD(RowNum,5),0,RowNum,NULL) Line,
       InvoiceDate,Amount
  from INVOICE;
 order by InvoiceDate;
```

| | | Date of | |
ROWNUM	LINE	Invoice	AMOUNT
6		01-SEP-01	21.32
3		12-SEP-01	11.12
16		21-SEP-01	9.87
14		03-OCT-01	3.55
8		04-OCT-01	8.42
9		04-OCT-01	1.43
18		09-OCT-01	8.98
10	10	13-OCT-01	12.41
15	15	22-OCT-01	13.65
17		22-OCT-01	17.58
1		23-OCT-01	5.03
11		23-OCT-01	4.49
13		30-OCT-01	7.47
2		09-NOV-01	2.02
4		09-NOV-01	22.10
7		15-NOV-01	7.33
5	5	17-NOV-01	8.29
12		23-NOV-01	40.36

FIGURE 15-10. *The effect of* **order by** *on RowNum*

You can see that the **order by** has rearranged the order of the row numbers, which destroys the usefulness of the **DECODE**.

NOTE
If it is important to put the rows in a certain order, such as by InvoiceDate, and also to use the features of the **DECODE, MOD,** and RowNum combination, this can be accomplished by creating a view where a **group by** does the ordering. See the **"order by** in Views" section in Chapter 16 for warnings about this practice.

```
create or replace view DATEANDAMOUNT as
select InvoiceDate, Amount
  from INVOICE
 group by InvoiceDate, Amount;
```

The **select** statement then attaches row numbers to each row as it is retrieved from this view, and the goal of date order, and the use of **DECODE**, **MOD**, and RowNum, is accomplished, as shown in Figure 15-11.

Columns and Computations in then and else

Thus far the *value* portion of **DECODE** has been the only real location of column names or computations. These can easily occur in the *then* and *else* portions of

```
select RowNum,DECODE(MOD(RowNum,5),0,RowNum,NULL) Line,
       InvoiceDate,Amount
  from DATEANDAMOUNT;
```

		Date of	
ROWNUM	LINE	Invoice	AMOUNT
-------	----	---------	------
1		01-SEP-01	21.32
2		12-SEP-01	11.12
3		21-SEP-01	9.87
4		03-OCT-01	3.55
5	5	04-OCT-01	1.43
6		04-OCT-01	8.42
7		09-OCT-01	8.98
8		13-OCT-01	12.41
9		22-OCT-01	13.65
10	10	22-OCT-01	17.58
11		23-OCT-01	4.49
12		23-OCT-01	5.03
13		30-OCT-01	7.47
14		09-NOV-01	2.02
15	15	09-NOV-01	22.10
16		15-NOV-01	7.33
17		17-NOV-01	8.29
18		23-NOV-01	40.36

FIGURE 15-11. *Using* **group by** *in place of* **order by** *for RowNum*

```
column DailyRate format 9999999.9
select Name, DailyRate from PAY;

NAME                          DAILYRATE
------------------------      ----------
ADAH TALBOT                         1.00
ANDREW DYE                           .75
BART SARJEANT                        .75
DICK JONES                          1.00
GEORGE OSCAR                        1.25
PAT LAVAY                           1.25
```

FIGURE 15-12.   *Talbot's workers and daily rates of pay*

DECODE as well. Suppose Talbot has a PAY table that lists workers and their daily rates of pay, as shown in Figure 15-12.

He also constructs an AVERAGEPAY view, which calculates the average pay of all his workers:

```
create or replace view AVERAGEPAY as
select AVG(DailyRate) AveragePay
  from PAY;
```

Talbot then decides to give his workers a raise. Those workers earning just exactly the average wage continue to earn the (existing) average wage. The rest will get a 15 percent pay hike. In this **select** statement, the *value* in the DECODE is DailyRate. The *if* is AveragePay. The *then* is DailyRate. The *else* is DailyRate times 1.15. What this illustrates is the use of columns and computations in the *if, then,* and *else* portions of DECODE, as demonstrated in Figure 15-13.

Greater Than, Less Than, and Equal To in DECODE

The format of the **DECODE** statement would seem to imply that it really can only do a series of equality tests, since the *value* is successively tested for equality against a list of *if*s. However, clever use of functions and computations in the place of *value* can allow **DECODE** to have the effective ability to act based on a value being greater than, less than, or equal to another value.

```
column NewRate    format 9999999.9

select Name, DailyRate,
       DECODE( DailyRate, AveragePay, DailyRate,
       DailyRate*1.15) NewRate
  from PAY, AVERAGEPAY;


NAME                        DAILYRATE    NEWRATE
------------------------    ---------    -------
ADAH TALBOT                         1       1.00
ANDREW DYE                        .75        .86
BART SARJEANT                     .75        .86
DICK JONES                          1       1.00
GEORGE OSCAR                     1.25       1.44
PAT LAVAY                        1.25       1.44
```

FIGURE 15-13. *A 15 percent pay hike for workers not earning the average wage*

In Figure 15-14, for example, DailyRate is compared to AveragePay for each worker. Those who make more than the AveragePay are given 5 percent raises. Those who make less than average are given 15 percent raises. Those who make exactly average wages get no raise at all. How is this accomplished?

The DailyRate is divided by the AveragePay. For someone earning more than average, this ratio will be a number greater than one. For someone earning exactly the average wage, this ratio will be exactly the number one. And for those earning less than average wages, this ratio will be a number less than one but greater than zero.

Now subtract 1 from each of these numbers. Big earners will get a number above 0. Average earners will get a 0. Small earners will get a number below 0.

The **SIGN** of each of these is 1, 0, and –1 (see Chapter 6 for a review of **SIGN**). Thus the *value* in the **DECODE** is 1, 0, or –1, depending upon wages. If it is 1, DailyRate is multiplied by 1.05. If it is –1, DailyRate is multiplied by 1.15. If it is 0 (the *else*), the worker continues to get DailyRate.

This approach can be used to accomplish complex, single-pass updates, whereas the alternative would be a series of **update** statements with differing **set** statements and **where** clauses.

This same approach can be used with other functions as well. **GREATEST**, with a list of columns, could be the *value* in **DECODE**, or the *if, then,* or *else*. Extremely complex procedural logic can be accomplished when it is needed.

```
select Name, DailyRate,
       DECODE( SIGN( (DailyRate/AveragePay)-1 ),
       1, DailyRate*1.05, -1, DailyRate*1.15, DailyRate) NewRate
  from PAY, AVERAGEPAY;

NAME                          DAILYRATE    NEWRATE
------------------------      ---------    ---------
ADAH TALBOT                        1.00        1.00
ANDREW DYE                          .75         .86
BART SARJEANT                       .75         .86
DICK JONES                         1.00        1.00
GEORGE OSCAR                       1.25        1.31
PAT LAVAY                          1.25        1.31
```

FIGURE 15-14. *Pay hikes based on ratio of worker's rate to average*

To summarize this chapter, **DECODE** is a powerful function that uses *if, then, else* logic, and that can be combined with other ORACLE functions to produce spreads of values (such as aging of invoices), to effectively flip tables onto their sides, to control display and page movement, to make calculations, and to force row-by-row changes based on the *value* in a column (or computation) being tested.

CHAPTER 16

Creating, Dropping, and Altering Tables and Views

Until now, the emphasis has been on using tables; this chapter looks at creating, dropping, and changing tables, creating views, and creating a table from a table.

Creating a Table

Consider the TROUBLE table. This is similar to the COMFORT table, but is used to track cities with unusual weather patterns:

```
describe TROUBLE

Name                                Null?     Type
----------------------------------- --------- ----
CITY                                NOT NULL  VARCHAR2(13)
SAMPLEDATE                          NOT NULL  DATE
NOON                                          NUMBER(3,1)
MIDNIGHT                                      NUMBER(3,1)
PRECIPITATION                                 NUMBER
```

The five rows in the TROUBLE table represent the three major data types in ORACLE: VARCHAR2, DATE, and NUMBER, and each column was assigned one of these types when the table was created. Here is the SQL that created this ORACLE table:

```
create table TROUBLE (City VARCHAR2(13) NOT NULL, SampleDate DATE NOT NULL,
Noon NUMBER(3,1), Midnight NUMBER(3,1), Precipitation NUMBER);
```

Another style of entering the same command, one less prone to misplacing or miscounting parentheses, is this:

```
create table TROUBLE (
City          VARCHAR2(13) NOT NULL,
SampleDate    DATE NOT NULL,
Noon          NUMBER(3,1),
Midnight      NUMBER(3,1),
Precipitation NUMBER
);
```

These are the basic elements of this command:

- The words **create table**
- The name of the table
- An opening parenthesis

- Column definitions
- A closing parenthesis
- A SQL terminator

The individual column definitions are separated by commas. There is no comma after the last column definition. The table and column names must start with a letter of the alphabet but may include letters, numbers, and underscores. Names may be 1 to 30 characters in length, must be unique within the table, and cannot be an ORACLE reserved word (see "Object Names" in the Alphabetical Reference).

Case does not matter in creating a table. There are no options for DATE data types. Character data types must have their maximum length specified. NUMBERs may be either high precision (up to 38 digits) or specified precision, based on the maximum number of digits, and on the number of places allowed to the right of the decimal (an amount field for American currency, for instance, would have only two decimal places).

Character Width and NUMBER Precision

Specifying maximum length for character (CHAR and VARCHAR2) columns and precision for NUMBER columns has consequences that must be considered during the design of the table. Improper decisions can be corrected later using the **alter table** command, but the process can be difficult.

Deciding on a Proper Width

A character column that is not wide enough for the data you want to put in will cause an **insert** to fail and result in this error message:

```
ERROR at line 1: ORA-1401:  inserted value too large for column
```

Maximum width for CHAR (fixed-length) columns is 255 characters. VARCHAR2 columns can have up to 2000 characters. In assigning width to a column, allot enough space to allow for all real future possibilities. A CHAR(15) for a city name, for instance, is just going to get you in trouble later on. Either you'll have to alter the table, or truncate or distort the names of some cities.

NOTE
There is no penalty in ORACLE for defining a wide VARCHAR2 column. ORACLE is clever enough not to store blank spaces at the end of VARCHAR2 columns. The city name "SAN FRANCISCO," for example, will be stored in 13 spaces even if you've defined the column as VARCHAR2(50). There will not be 37 blank spaces stored with the name. The stored column will have just the actual characters. And if a column has nothing in it (NULL), ORACLE will store nothing in the column, not even a blank space (it does store a couple of bytes of internal database control information, but this is unaffected by the size you specify for the column). The only effect that choosing a higher number will have is in the default SQLPLUS column formatting. SQLPLUS will create a default heading the same width as the VARCHAR2 definition.

Choosing NUMBER Precision

A NUMBER column with incorrect precision will have one of two consequences. Either ORACLE will reject the attempt to **insert** the row of data, or it will drop some of the data's precision. Here are four rows of data about to be entered into ORACLE:

```
insert into TROUBLE values
      ('PLEASANT LAKE', '21-MAR-93', 39.99,   -1.31, 3.6);

insert into TROUBLE values
      ('PLEASANT LAKE', '22-JUN-93', 101.44,   86.2, 1.63);

insert into TROUBLE values
      ('PLEASANT LAKE', '23-SEP-93', 92.85,   79.6, 1.00003);

insert into TROUBLE values
      ('PLEASANT LAKE', '22-DEC-93', -17.445, -10.4, 2.4);
```

These are the results of this attempt:

```
1 row created.

insert into TROUBLE values ('PLEASANT LAKE', '22-JUN-93', 101.44, 86.2, 1.63)

ERROR at line 1: ORA-1438:  value larger than specified precision allows for
this column
```

```
1 row created.

1 row created.
```

The first, third, and fourth rows were inserted, but the second **insert** failed because 101.44 exceeded the precision set in the **create table** statement, where Noon was defined as NUMBER(3,1). The 3 here indicates the maximum number of digits ORACLE will store. The 1 means that one of those three digits is reserved for a position to the right of the decimal point. Thus, 12.3 would be a legitimate number, but 123.4 would not be.

Note carefully that the error here is caused by the 101, not the .44, because NUMBER(3,1) leaves only two positions available to the left of the decimal point. The .44 will not cause the "value larger than specified precision" error. It would simply be rounded to one decimal place. This will be demonstrated shortly, but first, look at the results of a query of the four rows we've attempted to **insert**:

```
select * from TROUBLE;

CITY          SAMPLEDAT   NOON MIDNIGHT PRECIPITATION
------------- --------- -------- -------- -------------
PLEASANT LAKE 21-MAR-93     39.9    -1.31           3.6
PLEASANT LAKE 23-SEP-93     92.9    79.6        1.00003
PLEASANT LAKE 22-DEC-93    -17.4    -10.4           2.4
```

The three rows were successfully inserted; only the problematic row is missing. ORACLE automatically backed out the single **insert** statement that failed.

Rounding During Insertion

If you correct the **create table** statement and increase the number of digits available for noon and midnight, as shown here:

```
create table TROUBLE (
City          VARCHAR2(13) NOT NULL,
SampleDate    DATE NOT NULL,
Noon          NUMBER(4,1),
Midnight      NUMBER(4,1),
Precipitation NUMBER
);
```

then the four **insert** statements will all be successful. A query now will reveal this:

```
select * from TROUBLE;

CITY          SAMPLEDAT    NOON MIDNIGHT PRECIPITATION
------------- --------- ------- -------- -------------
PLEASANT LAKE 21-MAR-93      40     -1.3           3.6
PLEASANT LAKE 22-JUN-93   101.4     86.2          1.63
PLEASANT LAKE 23-SEP-93    92.9     79.6       1.00003
PLEASANT LAKE 22-DEC-93   -17.4    -10.4           2.4
```

Look at the first **insert** statement. The value for noon is 39.99. In the query it is rounded to 40. Midnight in the **insert** is –1.31. In the query it is –1.3. ORACLE rounds the number based on the digit just to the right of the allowed precision. Table 16-1 shows the effects of precision in several examples.

Constraints in create table

The **create table** statement lets you enforce several different kinds of constraints on a table: candidate keys, primary keys, foreign keys, and check conditions. A **constraint** clause can constrain a single column or group of columns in a table. The point of these constraints is to get ORACLE to do most of the work in maintaining the integrity of your database. The more constraints you add to a table definition, the less work you have to do in applications to maintain the data. On the other hand, the more constraints there are in a table, the longer it takes to update the data.

There are two ways to specify constraints: as part of the column definition (a *column* constraint) or at the end of the **create table** statement (a *table* constraint). Clauses that constrain several columns must be table constraints.

The Candidate Key

A *candidate key* is a combination of one or more columns, the values of which uniquely identify each row of a table.

```
create table TROUBLE (
City            VARCHAR2(13) NOT NULL,
SampleDate      DATE NOT NULL,
Noon            NUMBER(4,1),
Midnight        NUMBER(4,1),
Precipitation   NUMBER,
UNIQUE (City, SampleDate)
);
```

IN INSERT STATEMENT	ACTUAL VALUE IN TABLE
For precision of NUMBER(4,1)	
123.4	123.4
123.44	123.4
123.45	123.5
123.445	123.4
1234.5	**insert** fails
For precision of NUMBER(4)	
123.4	123
123.44	123
123.45	123
123.445	123
1234.5	1235
12345	**insert** fails
For precision of NUMBER(4,-1)	
123.4	120
123.44	120
123.45	120
123.445	120
125	130
1234.5	1230
12345	**insert** fails
For precision of NUMBER	
123.4	123.4
123.44	123.44
123.45	123.45
123.445	123.445
125	125
1234.5	1234.5
12345.6789012345678	12345.6789012345678

TABLE 16-1. *Examples of the effect of precision on inserted value*

The key of this table is the combination of City and SampleDate. Notice that both columns are also declared to be **NOT NULL**. This feature allows you to prevent data from being entered into the table without certain columns having data in them. Clearly temperature and precipitation information is not useful without knowing where or when it was collected. This technique is common for columns that are the primary key of a table, but is also useful if certain columns are critical for the row of data to be meaningful. If **NOT NULL** isn't specified, the column can have **NULL** values.

The Primary Key

The *primary key* of a table is one of the candidate keys that you give some special characteristics. You can have only one primary key, and a primary key column cannot contain nulls:

```
create table TROUBLE (
City            VARCHAR2(13),
SampleDate      DATE,
Noon            NUMBER(4,1),
Midnight        NUMBER(4,1),
Precipitation NUMBER,
PRIMARY KEY (City, SampleDate)
);
```

This **create table** statement has the same effect as the previous one except that you can have several UNIQUE constraints but only one PRIMARY KEY constraint.

For single-column primary or candidate keys, you can define the key on the column with a column constraint instead of a table constraint:

```
create table WORKER (
Name            VARCHAR2(25) PRIMARY KEY,
Age             NUMBER,
Lodging         VARCHAR2(15)
);
```

In this case, the Name column is the primary key.

The Foreign Key

A *foreign key* is a combination of columns with values based on the primary key values from another table. A foreign key constraint, also known as a *referential integrity constraint,* specifies that the values of the foreign key correspond to actual values of the primary key in the other table. In the WORKER table, for example, the Lodging column refers to values for the Lodging column in the Lodging table.

```
create table WORKER (
Name            VARCHAR2(25) PRIMARY KEY,
Age             NUMBER,
Lodging         VARCHAR2(15) REFERENCES LODGING(Lodging)
);
```

You can refer to a primary or unique key, even in the same table. However, you can't refer to a table in a remote database in the **references** clause. You can use the table form (which was used in the prior example to create a PRIMARY KEY on the TROUBLE table) instead of the column form to specify foreign keys with multiple columns.

Sometimes you want to delete these dependent rows when you delete the row they depend on. In the case of WORKER and LODGING, if you delete LODGING, you want to make the Lodging column **NULL**. In another case, you might want to delete the whole row. The clause **on delete cascade** added to the **references** clause tells ORACLE to delete the dependent row when you delete the corresponding row in the parent table. This action automatically maintains referential integrity. For more information on the clauses **on delete cascade** and **references**, consult "Integrity Constraint" in the Alphabetical Reference.

The Check Constraint

Many columns must have values that are within a certain range or that satisfy certain conditions. With a *check constraint*, you can give an expression that must always be true for every row in the table. For example, if Talbot employs only workers between the ages of 18 and 65, the constraint would look like this:

```
create table WORKER (
Name            CHAR(25) PRIMARY KEY,
Age             NUMBER CHECK (Age BETWEEN 18 AND 65),
Lodging         CHAR(15) REFERENCES LODGING(Lodging)
);
```

You can't refer to values in other rows; you can't call the pseudo-columns SysDate, UID, User, Userenv, Currval, Nextval, Level, or RowNum. You can use the table constraint form (as opposed to the column constraint form) to refer to multiple columns in a check constraint.

Dropping Tables

Dropping tables is very simple. You use the words **drop table** and the table name, as shown here:

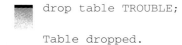

```
drop table TROUBLE;

Table dropped.
```

You drop a table only when you no longer need it. In ORACLE7, the **truncate** command lets you remove all the rows in the table and reclaim the space for other uses without removing the table definition from the database. In prior versions, you needed to drop and re-create the table to reclaim its space.

Truncating is also very simple.

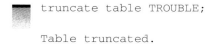

```
truncate table TROUBLE;

Table truncated.
```

Truncating can't be rolled back. If there are triggers that delete rows that depend on rows in the table, truncating does not execute those triggers. You should be *sure* you really want to **truncate** before doing it.

Altering Tables

Tables can be altered in one of two ways: by changing a column's definition, or by adding a column to an existing table. Adding a column is straightforward, and similar to creating a table. Suppose you decide to add two new columns to the TROUBLE table: Condition, which you believe should be **NOT NULL**, and Wind, for the wind speed. The first attempt looks like this:

```
alter table TROUBLE add (
Condition     VARCHAR2(9) NOT NULL,
Wind          NUMBER(3)
);

alter table TROUBLE add (
              *
ERROR at line 1: ORA-1758:  table must be empty to add mandatory (NOT NULL)
column
```

You get an error message because you cannot (logically) add a column defined as **NOT NULL**—when you try to add it, the column won't yet have anything in it. Each row in the table would have a new empty column defined as **NOT NULL**.

There are two alternatives. The **alter table** command's **add** clause will work with a **NOT NULL** column if the table is empty. But usually it is impractical to empty a table of all its rows just to add a **NOT NULL** column. And you can't

use EXPORT and IMPORT if you add a column after **EXPORT**ing but
before **IMPORT**ing.

The alternative is to first alter the table by adding the column without the
NOT NULL restriction:

```
alter table TROUBLE add (
Condition     VARCHAR2(9),
Wind          NUMBER(3)
);

Table altered.
```

Then fill the column with data for every row (either with legitimate data, or a
placeholder until legitimate data can be obtained):

```
update TROUBLE set Condition = 'SUNNY';
```

Then, finally, alter the table again with a **modify**, and change the column
definition to **NOT NULL**:

```
alter table TROUBLE modify (
Condition     VARCHAR2(9) NOT NULL,
City          VARCHAR2(17)
);

Table altered.
```

Note that the City column was also modified to enlarge it to 17 characters (just
to show how this is done). When the table is described, it shows this:

```
describe TROUBLE

Name                                  Null?     Type
------------------------------------- --------- ----
CITY                                  NOT NULL  VARCHAR2(17)
SAMPLEDATE                            NOT NULL  DATE
NOON                                            NUMBER(4,1)
MIDNIGHT                                        NUMBER(4,1)
PRECIPITATION                                   NUMBER
CONDITION                             NOT NULL  VARCHAR2(9)
WIND                                            NUMBER(3)
```

It contains the following:

```
select * from TROUBLE;

CITY            SAMPLEDAT   NOON MIDNIGHT PRECIPITATION CONDITION WIND
--------------- --------- ------ -------- ------------- --------- ----
PLEASANT LAKE   21-MAR-93     40     -1.3           3.6 SUNNY
PLEASANT LAKE   22-JUN-93  101.4     86.2          1.63 SUNNY
PLEASANT LAKE   23-SEP-93   92.9     79.6       1.00003 SUNNY
PLEASANT LAKE   22-DEC-93  -17.4    -10.4           2.4 SUNNY
```

Here you see the effect of the changes. City is now 17 characters wide, instead of 13. Condition has been added to the table as **NOT NULL** and is SUNNY (temporarily). WIND has been added, and is **NULL**.

To make a **NOT NULL** column nullable, use the **alter table** command with the **null** clause, as shown in the following listing.

```
alter table TROUBLE modify
(Condition NULL);
```

The Rules for Adding or Modifying a Column

These are the rules for adding a column to a table:

■ You may add a column at any time if **NOT NULL** isn't specified.

■ You may add a **NOT NULL** column in three steps:

1. Add the column without **NOT NULL** specified.

2. Fill every row in that column with data.

3. Modify the column to be **NOT NULL**.

These are the rules for modifying a column:

■ You can increase a character column's width at any time.

■ You can increase the number of digits in a NUMBER column at any time.

■ You can increase or decrease the number of decimal places in a NUMBER column at any time.

In addition, if a column is **NULL** for every row of the table, you can make any of these changes:

■ You can change its data type.

■ You can decrease a character column's width.

■ You can decrease the number of digits in a NUMBER column.

There are additional options available in different ORACLE versions, which are described under **alter table** in the Alphabetical Reference.

Creating a View

Since you've already seen the techniques for creating a view (in Chapters 3, 9, 11, 12, and 15), they will not be reviewed here. However, this section gives several additional points about views that will prove useful.

If a view is based on a single underlying table, you can **insert**, **update**, or **delete** rows in the view. This will actually **insert**, **update**, or **delete** rows in the underlying table. There are restrictions on your ability to do this, though they are quite sensible:

■ You cannot **insert** if the underlying table has any **NOT NULL** columns that don't appear in the view.

■ You cannot **insert** or **update** if any one of the view's columns referenced in the **insert** or **update** contains functions or calculations.

■ You cannot **insert**, **update**, or **delete** if the view contains **group by**, **distinct**, or a reference to the pseudo-column RowNum.

Stability of a View

Remember that the results of querying a view are built instantly from a table (or tables) when you execute the query. Until that moment, the view has no data of its own, as a table does. It is merely a description (a SQL statement) of what information to pull out of other tables, and how to organize it. As a consequence, if a table is dropped, the validity of a view is destroyed. Attempting to query a view where the underlying table has been dropped will produce an error message about the view. In the following sequence a view is created on an existing table, the table is dropped, and the view then is queried.

First the view is created:

```
create view RAIN as
select City, Precipitation
   from TROUBLE;

View created.
```

The underlying table is dropped:

```
drop table TROUBLE;

Table dropped.
```

The view is queried:

```
select * from RAIN
             *
ERROR at line 1: ORA-0942:  table or view does not exist
    .
```

Similarly, a view is created using the asterisk in the view creation:

```
create view RAIN as
select * from TROUBLE;

View created.
```

But then the underlying table is altered:

```
alter table TROUBLE add (
Warning       VARCHAR2(20)
);

Table altered.
```

Despite the change to the view's base table, the view is still valid and it will access the new columns in the TROUBLE table.

To re-create a view while keeping in place all of the privileges that have been granted for it, use the **create or replace view** command, as shown in the following listing. This command will replace the view text of an existing view with the new view text, while the old grants on the view will not be affected.

```
create or replace view RAIN as select * from TROUBLE;
```

order by in Views

You cannot use an **order by** in a **create view** statement. Occasionally, a **group by**, which can be used, may accomplish the purpose for which an **order by** might be used, as was demonstrated in Chapter 15, in the "**order by** and RowNum" section. However, even if there are no group functions in the **select** clause, the **group by**

can still consolidate rows. Consider this query from the COMFORT table, with an
order by:

```
select City, Precipitation
  from COMFORT
 order by Precipitation;
```

```
CITY            PRECIPITATION
------------- -------------
KEENE
SAN FRANCISCO            .1
SAN FRANCISCO            .1
SAN FRANCISCO            .5
KEENE                  1.3
SAN FRANCISCO          2.3
KEENE                  3.9
KEENE                  4.4

8 rows selected.
```

The same query, in a view, using a **group by** instead of an **order by**, causes the
two identical SAN FRANCISCO rows (with Precipitation of .1) to be compressed
into one:

```
create view DISCOMFORT as
select City, Precipitation
  from COMFORT
 group by Precipitation, City;

View created.
```

When queried, only seven rows remain:

```
select * from DISCOMFORT;

CITY            PRECIPITATION
------------- -------------
KEENE
SAN FRANCISCO            .1
SAN FRANCISCO            .5
KEENE                  1.3
FRANCISCO              2.3
```

```
KEENE                    3.9
KEENE                    4.4

7 rows selected.
```

This is probably not what you intended to occur. Although a **group by** will put a view in order, using it for this purpose can cause problems. It is generally better to simply use an **order by** in the **select** statement that queries the view.

Creating a Table from a Table

The view RAIN that was previously created from the TROUBLE table could alternatively have been a table. ORACLE lets you create a new table on the fly, based on a **select** statement on an existing table:

```
create table RAIN as
select City, Precipitation
   from TROUBLE;

Table created.
```

> **NOTE**
> The **create table ... as select ...** command will not work if one of the selected columns uses the LONG datatype.

When the new table is described, it reveals that it has "inherited" its column characteristics from the TROUBLE table. A table created in this fashion can include all columns, using an asterisk if you like, or a subset of columns from another table. It also can include "invented" columns, which are the product of functions or the combination of other columns, just as in a view. The character column definitions will adjust to the size necessary to contain the data in the invented columns. NUMBER columns that had specified precision in the source table, but which undergo computation in inventing a new column, will simply be NUMBER columns, with no specified precision, in the new table. When the table RAIN is described, it shows its column definitions:

```
describe RAIN

Name                                    Null?     Type
------------------------------------    --------  ----
CITY                                    NOT NULL  VARCHAR2(13)
PRECIPITATION                                     NUMBER
```

When RAIN is queried, it contains just the columns and data selected from the TROUBLE column as follows:

```
select * from RAIN;

CITY            PRECIPITATION
-------------   -------------
PLEASANT LAKE            3.6
PLEASANT LAKE           1.63
PLEASANT LAKE        1.00003
PLEASANT LAKE            2.4
```

You also can use this technique to create a table with column definitions like that of the source table, but with no rows in it, by building a **where** clause that will select no rows from the old table:

```
create table RAIN as
select City, Precipitation
  from TROUBLE
 where 1=2;

Table created.
```

Querying this table will show there is nothing in it:

```
select * from RAIN;

no rows selected.
```

In ORACLE7.2 you can create a table based on a query without generating redo log entries (chronological records of database actions used during database recoveries). Avoiding the generation of these entries is accomplished by using the **unrecoverable** keyword in the **create table** command. When the redo log entries are circumvented in this way, the performance of the **create table** command will improve, since less work is being done; the larger the table, the greater the impact. However, since the new table's creation is not being written to the *redo log files* (which record the redo log entries), the table will not be re-created if, following a database failure, those redo log files are used to recover the database. Therefore, you should consider performing a backup of the database soon after using the **unrecoverable** option if you want to be able to recover the new table. See the *ORACLE7 Server Administrator's Guide* for ORACLE7.2.

The following example shows how to use the **unrecoverable** keyword during table creations based on queries. By default, table creations based on queries generate redo log entries.

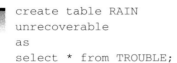

```
create table RAIN
unrecoverable
as
select * from TROUBLE;

Table created.
```

CHAPTER 17

By What Authority?

Information is vital to success, but when damaged or in the wrong hands, it can threaten success. ORACLE provides extensive security features in order to safeguard your information, from both unauthorized viewing and intentional or inadvertent damage. This security is provided by granting or revoking privileges on a person-by-person and privilege-by-privilege basis, and is in addition to (and independent of) any security your computer system already has. ORACLE7 uses the **create user**, **create role**, and **grant** commands to control data access.

Users, Roles, and Privileges

Every ORACLE user has a name and password and owns any tables, views, and other resources that he or she creates. An ORACLE *role* is a set of *privileges* (or the type of access that each user needs depending on his or her status and responsibilities). You can grant or bestow specific privileges to roles and then assign roles to the appropriate users. A user can also grant privileges directly to other users.

Database system privileges let you execute specific sets of commands. The CREATE TABLE privilege, for example, lets you create tables. The GRANT ANY PRIVILEGE privilege allows you to grant any system privilege. See "Privilege" in the Alphabetical Reference at the back of this book for a complete list.

Database object privileges give you the ability to perform some operation on various objects. The DELETE privilege, for example, lets you delete rows from tables and views. The SELECT privilege allows you to query with a **select** from tables, views, sequences, and snapshots. See "Privilege" in the Alphabetical Reference at the back of this book for a complete list.

Creating a User

The ORACLE system comes with two users already created, SYSTEM and SYS. You log onto the SYSTEM user to create other users, since SYSTEM has that privilege.

When installing ORACLE, you (or a system administrator) first create a user for yourself.

This is the format for the **create user** command:

```
create user user identified {by password ¦ externally};
```

There are other privileges that can be set via this command; see the **create user** command in the Alphabetical Reference for details.

To connect your computer system's userid and password into ORACLE's security so that only one logon is required, use "externally" instead of giving a password. A system administrator (who has a great many privileges) may want the extra security of having a separate password. Let's call the system administrator George in the following examples:

```
create user George identified by avocado;
```

Voilà! George's account now exists and is secured by a password.

You also can set up the user with specific *tablespaces* (space on disk for the user's tables—discussed in the following chapter) and *quotas* (limits) for space and resource usage. See **create user** in the Alphabetical Reference and Chapter 18 for a discussion of tablespaces and resources.

To change a password, use the **alter user** command.

```
alter user George identified by psyche;
```

Now George has the password "psyche" instead of "avocado".

Three Standard Roles

But what can George do in ORACLE? At this point, nothing—George has no system privileges.

ORACLE7 provides three standard roles for compatibility with previous versions: CONNECT, RESOURCE, and DBA.

The CONNECT Role

Occasional users, particularly those who do not need to create tables, will usually be given only the CONNECT role. CONNECT is simply the privilege to use ORACLE at all. This right becomes meaningful with the addition of access to specific tables belonging to other users, and the privilege to **select**, **insert**, **update**, and **delete** rows in these tables, as each of these rights is granted. Users who have the CONNECT role may also **create table**s, **view**s, **sequence**s, **cluster**s, **synonym**s (discussed presently), **session**s (see the Alphabetical Reference), and **link**s to other databases (see Chapter 20).

The RESOURCE Role

More sophisticated and regular users of the database may be granted the RESOURCE role. RESOURCE gives users the additional rights to **create** their own **table**s, **sequence**s, **procedure**s, **trigger**s, **index**es, and **cluster**s (the latter two are discussed in Chapter 18; see Chapter 21 for a discussion of triggers and Chapter 22 for a discussion of procedures).

The DBA Role

The DBA (*database administrator*) role has all system privileges—including unlimited space quotas—and the ability to grant all privileges to other users. In this chapter, dba refers to the person who is a database administrator and has the DBA role, while DBA will refer just to those privileges encompassed by the DBA role. SYSTEM is for use by a DBA user. Some of the rights that are reserved for the dba are never given to, nor needed by, normal users. Little time will be spent here on those rights. Other rights typically used by dbas are also regularly used by and important to users. This subset of DBA privileges will be explained shortly. In ORACLE7 the DBA is granted the EXP_FULL_DATABASE and

IMP_FULL_DATABASE roles, which in turn have privileges necessary for exporting and importing the full ORACLE database.

Format for the grant Command

Here is the format for the **grant** command for system privileges:

```
grant {system privilege | role}
      [, {system privilege | role},. . .]
      to {user | role} [, {user | role}]. . .
      [with admin option]
```

By using the **grant** command, you can **grant** any system privilege or role to another user or to another role. The **with admin option** clause permits the grantee to bestow the privilege or role on other users or roles. The grantor can **revoke** a role from a user as well.

Revoking Privileges

Privileges granted can be taken away. The **revoke** command is similar to the **grant** command:

```
revoke {system privilege | role}
       [, {system privilege | role},. . .]
       from {user | role} [, {user | role}]. . .
```

An individual with DBA role can **revoke** CONNECT, RESOURCE, and DBA or any other privilege or role from anyone, including another dba. This, of course, is dangerous, and is why DBA privileges should be given neither lightly nor to more than a tiny minority who really need them.

NOTE
Revoking everything from a given user does not eliminate that user from ORACLE, nor does it destroy any tables that user had created; it simply prohibits that user's access to them. Other users with access to the tables will still have exactly the same access they've always had.

To remove a user and all the resources owned by that user, use the **drop user** command like this:

```
drop user user [cascade];
```

The **cascade** option drops the user along with all the objects owned by the user including referential integrity constraints. The **cascade** option invalidates views, synonyms, stored procedures, functions, or packages that refer to objects in the dropped user's schema. If you don't use the **cascade** option and there are still objects owned by the user, ORACLE does not drop the user.

What Users Can Grant

A user can grant privileges on any object he or she owns. The dba can grant any system privilege (because the DBA role has **grant any privilege** and **grant any role** privileges).

Let's say that user George owns the COMFORT table and is a dba. He creates two new users, Bob and Judy, with these privileges:

```
create user Judy identified by sarah;

User created.

grant CONNECT to Judy;

Role granted.

create user Bob identified by carolyn;

User created.

grant CONNECT, RESOURCE to bob;

Role granted.
```

This sequence of commands gives both Judy and Bob the ability to connect to ORACLE, and gives Bob some extra capabilities. But can either do anything with George's tables? Not without explicit access.

To give others access to your tables, use a second form of the **grant** command:

```
grant object privilege [(column [, column])]
   on object to {user ¦ role}
   [with grant option];
```

The privileges a user can **grant** include these:

Tables and views (user's own only):

- **insert**
- **update**   (all or specific columns)
- **delete**

On tables only:

- **alter**   (table—all or specific columns—or sequence)
- **references**
- **index**   (columns in a table)
- **all**   (of the above)

On procedures, functions, and packages:

- **execute**

On tables, views, sequences, and snapshots:

- **select**

The object privilege granted must be one of the nine object privileges (ALL, ALTER, DELETE, EXECUTE, INDEX, INSERT, REFERENCES, SELECT, or UPDATE). These privileges give the grantee the ability to take some action on the object. The object can be a table, view, sequence, procedure, function, package, snapshot, or a synonym for any of these objects.

When you execute another user's procedure or function, you temporarily have the privileges of that user. This means that you don't need explicit access to the data the procedure or function uses; you see only the result of the execution, not the underlying data.

George gives Bob SELECT access to the COMFORT table:

```
grant select on COMFORT to Bob;

Grant succeeded.
```

The **with grant option** clause of the **grant** command allows the recipient of that grant to pass along the privileges he has received to other users. If the user George grants privileges on his tables to the user Bob **with grant option**, then Bob can make grants on George's tables to other users (Bob can only pass along those privileges—such as SELECT—that he has been granted). If you intend to create views based on another user's tables and to grant access to those views to other users, then you will need to have been granted access **with grant option** to the base tables.

Moving to Another User with connect

To test the success of his **grant**, George connects to Bob's username with the **connect** command. This may be used, as with other ORACLE products, by one of the following methods: entering both username and password on the same line as the command; entering the command alone and then responding to prompts; or entering the command and username and responding to the prompt for the password. The latter two methods will suppress display of the password, and are therefore inherently more secure.

```
connect Bob/carolyn

Connected.
```

Once **connect**ed, George selects from the table to which Bob's been given SELECT access.

NOTE
The table name must be preceded by the username of the table's owner. Without this, ORACLE will say the table does not exist.

```
select * from George.COMFORT;

CITY          SAMPLEDAT  NOON MIDNIGHT PRECIPITATION
------------- ---------- ---- -------- -------------
SAN FRANCISCO 21-MAR-93  62.5     42.3           .5
SAN FRANCISCO 22-JUN-93  51.1     71.9           .1
SAN FRANCISCO 23-SEP-93           61.5           .1
SAN FRANCISCO 22-DEC-93  52.6     39.8          2.3
KEENE         21-MAR-93  39.9     -1.2          4.4
KEENE         22-JUN-93  85.1     66.7          1.3
KEENE         23-SEP-93  99.8     82.6
KEENE         22-DEC-93  -7.2     -1.2          3.9
```

For convenience, a view named COMFORT is created which is simply a straight **select** from the table George.COMFORT.

```
create view COMFORT as select * from George.COMFORT;

View created.
```

Selecting from this view will produce exactly the same results as selecting from George.COMFORT:

```
select * from COMFORT;

CITY          SAMPLEDAT  NOON MIDNIGHT PRECIPITATION
------------- ---------- ---- -------- -------------
SAN FRANCISCO 21-MAR-93  62.5     42.3           .5
SAN FRANCISCO 22-JUN-93  51.1     71.9           .1
SAN FRANCISCO 23-SEP-93           61.5           .1
SAN FRANCISCO 22-DEC-93  52.6     39.8          2.3
KEENE         21-MAR-93  39.9     -1.2          4.4
KEENE         22-JUN-93  85.1     66.7          1.3
KEENE         23-SEP-93  99.8     82.6
KEENE         22-DEC-93  -7.2     -1.2          3.9
```

Now George returns to his own username and creates a view that selects only a part of the COMFORT table:

```
connect George/psyche
Connected.

create view SOMECOMFORT as
select * from COMFORT
```

```
where City = 'KEENE';

View created.
```

He then grants both SELECT and UPDATE privileges to Bob *on this view,* and revokes all privileges from Bob for the whole COMFORT table:

```
grant select, update on SOMECOMFORT to Bob;

Grant succeeded.

revoke all on COMFORT from Bob;

Revoke succeeded.
```

George then reconnects to Bob's username to test the effects of this change:

```
connect Bob/carolyn
Connected.

select * from COMFORT;
                  *
ERROR at line 1: ORA-0942:  table or view does not exist
```

Attempting to select from his COMFORT view fails, because the underlying table named in Bob's view was the George.COMFORT table. Not surprisingly, attempting to select from George.COMFORT would produce exactly the same message. Next, an attempt to select from George.SOMECOMFORT is made:

```
select * from George.SOMECOMFORT;

CITY           SAMPLEDAT  NOON MIDNIGHT PRECIPITATION
-------------- ---------- ----- -------- -------------
KEENE          21-MAR-93  39.9     -1.2           4.4
KEENE          22-JUN-93  85.1     66.7           1.3
KEENE          23-SEP-93  99.8     82.6
KEENE          22-DEC-93  -7.2     -1.2           3.9
```

This works perfectly well, even though direct access to the COMFORT table had been revoked, because George gave Bob access to a portion of COMFORT through the SOMECOMFORT view. It is just that portion of the table related to KEENE.

This shows a powerful security feature of ORACLE: you can create a view, using virtually any restrictions you like or any computations in the columns, and then give access to the view, rather than to the underlying tables, to other users. They will see only the information the view presents. This can even be extended to be user-specific. The "Security by User" section at the end of this chapter gives complete details on this feature.

Now the view LITTLECOMFORT is created under Bob's username, on top of the view SOMECOMFORT:

```
create view LITTLECOMFORT as select * from George.SOMECOMFORT,

View created.
```

and the row for September 23, 1993, is updated:

```
update LITTLECOMFORT set Noon = 88 where SampleDate = '23-SEP-93';

1 row updated.
```

When the view LITTLECOMFORT is queried, it shows the effect of the update:

```
select * from LITTLECOMFORT;

CITY          SAMPLEDAT  NOON MIDNIGHT PRECIPITATION
------------- ---------  ---- -------- -------------
KEENE         21-MAR-93  39.9     -1.2           4.4
KEENE         22-JUN-93  85.1     66.7           1.3
KEENE         23-SEP-93    88     82.6
KEENE         22-DEC-93  -7.2     -1.2           3.9
```

A query of George.SOMECOMFORT would show the same results, as would a query of COMFORT itself, if George made it on his own username. The update was successful against the underlying table, even though it went through two views (LITTLECOMFORT and SOMECOMFORT) to reach it.

NOTE
Starting with ORACLE7.1, you need to grant users SELECT access to any table in which they can **update** or **delete** records. This is in keeping with the evolving ANSI standard, and reflects the fact that a user who only had UPDATE or DELETE privilege on a table could use the database's feedback comments to discover information about the underlying data.

create synonym

An alternative method to creating a view that includes an entire table or view from another user is to create a synonym:

```
create synonym LITTLECOMFORT for George.SOMECOMFORT;
```

This synonym can be treated exactly like a view. See the **create synonym** command in the Alphabetical Reference.

Using Ungranted Privileges

Let's say an attempt is made to delete the row you just updated:

```
delete from LITTLECOMFORT where SampleDate = '23-SEP-92';
                    *
ERROR at line 1: ORA-1031:  insufficient privileges
```

Bob has not been given DELETE privileges by George, so the attempt fails.

Passing on Privileges

Bob can **grant** authority for other users to access his tables, but cannot bestow on other users access to tables that don't belong to him. Here, he attempts to give INSERT authority to Judy:

```
grant insert on George.SOMECOMFORT to Judy;
      *
ERROR at line 1: ORA-1712:  you cannot grant a privilege which
you do not have
```

Because Bob does not have this authority, he fails to give it to Judy. Next, Bob tries to pass on the privilege he does have, SELECT:

```
grant select on George.SOMECOMFORT to Judy;
      *
ERROR at line 1: ORA-1713:  GRANT OPTION does not exist for
that privilege
```

He cannot grant this privilege either because the view SOMECOMFORT does not belong to him. If he had been granted access to SOMECOMFORT **with grant option**, then the preceding grant command would have succeeded. The view LITTLECOMFORT does belong to him, though, so he can pass authority to that on to Judy:

```
grant select on LITTLECOMFORT to Judy;

Grant succeeded.
```

In addition, a new table, owned by Bob, is created and loaded with the current information from his view LITTLECOMFORT:

```
create table NOCOMFORT as
select * from LITTLECOMFORT;

Table created.
```

SELECT privileges on it are granted to Judy as well. Seemingly, these two tables ought to supply Judy with the same information.

```
grant select on NOCOMFORT to Judy;

Grant succeeded.
```

To test this, Judy's username is connected, like this:

```
connect Judy/sarah
Connected.
```

Queries are made against the view and table for which Bob granted SELECT privilege to Judy:

```
select * from Bob.LITTLECOMFORT;
                 *
ERROR at line 1: ORA-0942:  table or view does not exist

select * from Bob.NOCOMFORT;
```

```
CITY           SAMPLEDAT  NOON MIDNIGHT PRECIPITATION
-------------  ---------  ----- -------- -------------
KEENE          21-MAR-93  39.9     -1.2           4.4
KEENE          22-JUN-93  85.1     66.7           1.3
KEENE          23-SEP-93  99.8     82.6
KEENE          22-DEC-93  -7.2     -1.2           3.9
```

Only the second grant was successful, even though both gave the message "Grant succeeded." Why? The latter is more obvious. A NOCOMFORT table was created, and owned, by Bob's username. He was able to successfully give access to this table. But the LITTLECOMFORT view actually relied on one of George's views, and Bob cannot **grant** access to those. The "Grant succeeded" message occurred because Bob successfully gave Judy access to his *view*, but when Judy tried to use it, it failed as soon as it attempted to execute, because she did not have privileges to George's view. If LITTLECOMFORT had been created with the **create synonym** instead of **create view**, Bob's original attempt to **grant** Judy SELECT privileges would have failed when he attempted it.

If George wishes Bob to be able to pass on his privileges to others, he can add another clause to the **grant** statement:

```
grant select, update on SOMECOMFORT to Bob with grant option;

Grant succeeded.
```

The **with grant option** clause enables Bob to pass on access to SOMECOMFORT to Judy through his LITTLECOMFORT view. Note that attempts to access a table to which a user does not have **select** privilege always result in this message:

```
ERROR at line 1: ORA-0942:  table or view does not exist
```

This message appears rather than a message about not having access privilege so that a person without permission to query a table doesn't know that it even exists.

Creating a Role

In addition to the three system roles shown earlier in this chapter—CONNECT, RESOURCE, and DBA—you can create you own roles within ORACLE7. The roles you create can be comprised of table or system privileges, or a combination of both. In the following sections you will see how to create and administer roles.

In order to create a role, you need to have CREATE ROLE system privilege. The syntax for role creation is shown in the following listing.

```
create role role_name
[not identified|identified [by password|externally]];
```

When a role is first created, it has no privileges associated with it. Password options for roles are discussed in the "Adding a Password to a Role" section of this chapter.

Two sample **create role** commands are shown in the following example.

```
create role CLERK;
create role MANAGER;
```

The first command creates a role called CLERK that will be used in the examples in the following sections of this chapter. The second command creates a role called MANAGER, which will also be featured in those examples.

Granting Privileges to a Role

Once a role has been created, you may **grant** privileges to it. The syntax for the **grant** command is the same for roles as it was for users. When granting privileges to roles, you use the role name in the **to** clause of the **grant** command, as shown in the following listing.

```
grant select on COMFORT to CLERK;
```

As shown in this example, the role name takes the place of the user name in the **grant** command. The privilege to **select** from the COMFORT table will now be available to any user of the CLERK role.

If you are a dba, or have been granted the GRANT ANY PRIVILEGE system role, then you may grant system privileges—such as CREATE SESSION, CREATE SYNONYM, and CREATE VIEW—to roles. These privileges will then be available to any user of your role.

The ability to log into the database is given via the CREATE SESSION system privilege. In the following example, this privilege is granted to the CLERK role. This privilege is also granted to the MANAGER role, along with the CREATE DATABASE LINK system privilege.

```
grant CREATE SESSION to CLERK;
grant CREATE SESSION, CREATE DATABASE LINK to MANAGER;
```

Granting a Role to Another Role

Roles can be granted to other roles. You can do this via the **grant** command, as shown in the following example.

```
grant CLERK to MANAGER;
```

In this example, the CLERK role is granted to the MANAGER role. Even though you have not directly granted any table privileges to the MANAGER role, it will now inherit any privileges that have been granted to the CLERK role. Organizing roles in this way is a common design for hierarchical organizations.

When granting a role to another role (or to a user, as in the following section), you may grant the role using the **with admin option** clause, as shown in the following listing.

```
grant CLERK to MANAGER with admin option;
```

If the **with admin option** clause is used, then the grantee has the authority to grant the role to other users or roles. The grantee can also alter or drop the role.

Granting a Role to Users

Roles can be granted to users. When granted to users, roles can be thought of as named sets of privileges. Instead of granting each privilege to each user, you grant the privileges to the role and then grant the role to each user. This greatly simplifies the administrative tasks involved in the management of privileges.

NOTE
Privileges that are granted to users via roles should not be used as the basis for views, procedures, functions, packages, or foreign keys. When creating these types of database objects, you must rely on direct grants of the necessary privileges.

You can grant a role to a user via the **grant** command, as shown in the following example.

```
grant CLERK to Bob;
```

The user "Bob" in this example will have all of the privileges that were granted to the CLERK role (CREATE SESSION and SELECT privilege on COMFORT).

When granting a role to a user, you may grant the role using the **with admin option** clause, as shown in the following listing.

```
grant MANAGER to George with admin option;
```

George now has the authority to grant the MANAGER role to other users or roles, or to alter or drop the role.

Adding a Password to a Role

You can use the **alter role** command for only one purpose: to change the authority needed to enable it. By default, roles do not have passwords associated with them. To enable security for a role, use the **identified** keyword in the **alter role** command. There are two ways to implement this security.

First, you can use the **identified by** clause of the **alter role** command to specify a password, as shown in the following listing.

```
alter role MANAGER identified by cygnusxi;
```

Any time a user tries to activate that role, the password will be required. If, however, that role is set up as a default role for the user, then no password will be required for that role when the user logs in. See the "Enabling and Disabling Roles" section of this chapter for more details on these topics.

Roles can be tied to operating system privileges as well. If this capability is available on your operating system, then you use the **identified externally** clause of the **alter role** command. When the role is enabled, ORACLE7 will check the operating system to verify your access. Altering a role to use this security feature is shown in the following example.

```
alter role MANAGER identified externally;
```

In VMS, the verification process uses operating system rights identifiers. In most UNIX systems, the verification process uses the /etc/group file. In order to use this for any operating system, the OS_ROLES database startup parameter in the **init.ora** file must be set to TRUE.

The following example of this verification process is for a database instance called "Local" on a UNIX system. The server's /etc/group file may contain the following entry:

```
ora_local_manager_d:NONE:1:george
```

This entry grants the MANAGER role to the account named George. The "_d" suffix indicates that this role is to be granted by default when George logs in. An "_a" suffix would indicate that this role is to be enabled **with admin option**. If this role were also the user's default role, then the suffix would be "_ad". If more than one user were granted this role, then the additional usernames would be appended to the /etc/group entry, as shown in the following listing.

```
ora_local_manager_d:NONE:1:george,judy
```

If you use this option, then all roles in the database will be enabled via the operating system. For further details on implementing this, see the *ORACLE7 Server Administrator's Reference Guide* for your operating system.

Removing a Password from a Role

To remove a password from a role, use the **not identified** clause of the **alter role** command, as shown in the following listing. By default, roles do not have passwords.

```
alter role MANAGER not identified;
```

Enabling and Disabling Roles

When a user's account is altered, a list of default roles for that user can be created. This is done via the **default role** clause of the **alter user** command. The default action of this command sets all of a user's roles as default roles, enabling all of them every time the user logs in.

The syntax for this portion of the **alter user** command is

```
alter user username
default role {[role1, role2]
[all|all except role1, role2][NONE]};
```

As shown by this syntax, a user can be altered to have specific roles enabled, all roles enabled, all except specific roles enabled, and no roles enabled by default. For example, the following **alter user** command will enable the CLERK role whenever BOB logs in.

```
alter user Bob
default role CLERK;
```

To enable a non-default role, use the **set role** command, as shown in this example:

```
set role CLERK;
```

You may also use the **all** and **all except** clauses that were available in the **alter user** command:

```
set role all;
set role all except CLERK;
```

If a role has a password associated with it, then that password must be specified via an **identified by** clause:

```
set role MANAGER identified by cygnusxi;
```

To disable a role in your session, use the **set role none** command, as shown in the following listing. This will disable all roles in your current session. Once all of the roles have been disabled, re-enable the ones you want.

```
set role none;
```

Since you may find it necessary to execute a **set role none** command from time to time, you may wish to grant CREATE SESSION privilege to users directly rather than via roles.

Revoking Privileges from a Role

To revoke a privilege from a role, use the **revoke** command described earlier in this chapter. Specify the privilege, object name (if it is an object privilege), and role name, as shown in the following example.

```
revoke select on COMFORT from CLERK;
```

Users of the CLERK role will then be unable to query the COMFORT table.

Dropping a Role

To drop a role, use the **drop role** command, as shown in the following example.

```
drop role MANAGER;
drop role CLERK;
```

The roles you specify, and their associated privileges, will be removed from the database entirely.

Granting update to Specific Columns

You may wish to grant users SELECT privilege to more columns than you wish to grant them UPDATE privilege. Since SELECT columns can be restricted through a view, to further restrict the columns that can be updated requires a special form of the user's **grant** command. Here is an example for two COMFORT columns:

```
grant update (Noon, Midnight) on COMFORT to Judy;
```

Revoking Privileges

If object privileges can be granted, they can also be taken away. This is similar to the **grant** command:

```
revoke object privilege [, object privilege . . .]
on object
from {user ¦ role} [,{user ¦ role}]
[cascade constraints];
```

    revoke all removes any of the privileges listed previously, from SELECT through INDEX; revoking individual privileges will leave others that had also been granted intact. The **with grant option** is revoked along with the privilege to which it was attached.

    If a user defines referential integrity constraints on the object, ORACLE drops these constraints if you revoke privileges on the object using the **cascade constraints** option.

Security by User

Access to tables can be granted specifically, table by table and view by view, to each user. There is, however, an additional technique that will simplify this process in some cases. Recall Talbot's WORKER table:

```
select * from WORKER;
```

NAME	AGE	LODGING
ADAH TALBOT	23	PAPA KING
ANDREW DYE	29	ROSE HILL
BART SARJEANT	22	CRANMER
DICK JONES	18	ROSE HILL
DONALD ROLLO	16	MATTS
ELBERT TALBOT	43	WEITBROCHT

```
GEORGE OSCAR                 41 ROSE HILL
GERHARDT KENTGEN             55 PAPA KING
HELEN BRANDT                 15
JED HOPKINS                  33 MATTS
JOHN PEARSON                 27 ROSE HILL
KAY AND PALMER WALLBOM          ROSE HILL
PAT LAVAY                    21 ROSE HILL
PETER LAWSON                 25 CRANMER
RICHARD KOCH AND BROTHERS       WEITBROCHT
ROLAND BRANDT                35 MATTS
VICTORIA LYNN                32 MULLERS
WILFRED LOWELL               67
WILLIAM SWING                15 CRANMER
```

To enable each worker to access this table but restrict the access given to a view of only each worker's own single row, you could create 19 separate views, each with a different name in the **where** clause, and you could make separate **grant**s to each of these views for each worker. Alternatively, you could create a view whose **where** clause contained User, the pseudo-column, like this:

```
create view YOURAGE as
select * from WORKER
  where SUBSTR(Name,1,INSTR(Name,' ')-1) = User;

View created.
```

When George, the owner of this table, queries it through the view, the **where** clause finds his username, GEORGE, in the Name column (see the **where** clause), and produces this:

```
select * from YOURAGE;

NAME                      AGE LODGING
------------------------- ----- ---------------
GEORGE OSCAR                 41 ROSE HILL
```

Now George **grant**s **select** on this view to Bart Sarjeant:

```
grant select on YOURAGE to Bart;
```

He then **connect**s to Bart to check the effect:

```
connect Bart/stjohn
Connected.
```

```
select * from George.YOURAGE;

NAME                         AGE LODGING
------------------------- ----- ---------------
BART SARJEANT                 22 CRANMER
```

Amazingly, the result for Bart is his own row, not George's, because the pseudo-column User, in George's view, is always equal to the user of SQLPLUS at the moment the view is queried.

Granting Access to the Public

Rather than **grant** access to every worker, the **grant** command can be generalized to the **public**:

```
grant select on YOURAGE to public;
```

This gives everyone access, including users created after this grant was made. However, each still will have to access the table using George's username as a prefix. To avoid this, a dba may create a *public synonym* (which creates a name accessible to all users that stands for George.YOURAGE).

```
create public synonym YOURAGE for George.YOURAGE;
```

From this point forward, anyone can access YOURAGE without prefixing it with **George**. This approach gives tremendous flexibility for security. Workers could see only their own salaries, for instance, in a table that contained salaries for everyone. If, however, a user creates a table or view with the same name as a public synonym, any future SQL statements by this user will act on this new table or view, and not on the one by the same name to which the public has access.

Granting Limited Resources

When granting resource quotas in an ORACLE7 database, the **quota** parameter of the **create user** or **alter user** command is used, as shown in the following listing. In this example, Bob is granted a quota of 100M (100 megabytes) in the USERS tablespace.

```
alter user Bob
quota 100M on USERS;
```

A user's space quota may be set when the user is created, via the **create user** command. If there is no limit on the user's space quota, then you can grant that user the UNLIMITED TABLESPACE system privilege. See the **create user** and **alter user** commands in the Alphabetical Reference for further details on these commands.

CHAPTER 18

Changing the ORACLE Surroundings

L ike Chapter 17, this chapter looks at that subset of database administrator (DBA) functions used by most ORACLE users—functions not restricted to DBAs. These include indexes on tables, clusters, sequence generators, and allocations of space for tables and indexes. This chapter shows how ORACLE's databases are structured internally, which helps in understanding how its many features actually work and how they interrelate. Only limited options of the **create index**, **create tablespace**, and **create cluster** commands will be shown in this chapter. Full options are shown in the Alphabetical Reference later in this book.

Indexes

An *index* is a simple concept. It is typically a listing of *keywords* accompanied by the *location* of information on a subject. To find information on indexes, for instance, you look up the word "index" in the index at the back of this book. It will give the number of the page you are reading now. The word "index" is the key, and the page numbers given point you to the location of discussions about indexes in this book. This is related to the idea of primary keys in ORACLE, which was described in Chapter 2.

While indexes are not strictly necessary to running ORACLE, they do speed the process. For example, while you could find the information on indexes simply by reading through this book until you encountered the page with the information on it, this would be slow and time-consuming. Because the index at the back of the book is in alphabetical order, you can quickly go to the appropriate spot in the index (without reading every entry) where "index" will be found. This is quicker than reading through the book from front to back, obviously. These same principles apply to ORACLE indexes. Consider the HOCKEY table:

```
select * from HOCKEY;

TEAM            WON   LOST  TIED
------------    ----- ----- -----
Quebec             6    23     4
Detroit           10    18     5
Vancouver         11    16     6
NY Islanders      11    20     4
Washington        13    15     4
Pittsburgh        13    16     3
Calgary           14    11     9
St. Louis         14    12     6
Winnipeg          14    13     5
NY Rangers        15    14     5
New Jersey        15    15     3
Edmonton          16    11     7
Philadelphia      16    14     4
Los Angeles       16    14     3
Hartford          16    17     1
Toronto           16    18     0
Boston            17    13     3
Minnesota         17    15     2
Chicago           19    13     2
Montreal          20    13     4
Buffalo           21     9     4
```

Few tables that you will use in actual practice are as short as the HOCKEY table, and they will seldom be in alphabetical order. The following query asks ORACLE to find a specific team based on its win record:

```
select Team, Won, Lost, Tied
  from HOCKEY
 where Won = 20;
```

If the HOCKEY table does not have an index on the Won column, it means that ORACLE has to read every row in the table until it finds all Teams that match the **where** clause of your query.

To speed this process, you can create an index on the Won column. Then, when you execute the same query, ORACLE first looks in the index, which is in numerical order, thus finding the Team with 20 wins very quickly (ORACLE doesn't read every entry, but jumps directly to the close vicinity of the Team, much as you would in looking through the index of a book). The index entry then gives ORACLE the exact location in the table (and on disk) of the Montreal row.

Knowing this, it is clear how indexing an important column (one that's likely to appear in a **where** clause) will speed up ORACLE's response to a query. It will likewise speed up queries where two tables are joined together, if the columns that are related (by the **where** clause) are indexed. These are the basics of indexing; the rest of this chapter shows a number of additional features and issues related to indexing that will affect how quickly it works.

Creating an Index

This command is the most basic method of indexing:

```
create index index on table(column [,column]. . .);
```

index must be a unique name and follow the naming conventions of ORACLE columns. *table* is simply the name of the table on which the index will be established, and *column* is the name of the column. You can establish a single index on multiple columns by listing the columns one after the other, separated by commas. Recall the WORKERSKILL table. The primary key to this table is the combination of the worker Name and Skill. The following query produces the table shown at the top of Figure 18-1:

```
select RowID, Name, Skill, Ability
  from WORKERSKILL;
```

```
The WORKERSKILL Table with the RowID for Each Row:

ROWID               NAME            SKILL           ABILITY
------------------- --------------- --------------- ---------
0000204C.0001.0001  DICK JONES      SMITHY          EXCELLENT
0000204C.0002.0001  JOHN PEARSON    COMBINE DRIVER
0000204C.0003.0001  JOHN PEARSON    SMITHY          AVERAGE
0000204C.0004.0001  HELEN BRANDT    COMBINE DRIVER VERY FAST
0000204C.0005.0001  JOHN PEARSON    WOODCUTTER      GOOD
0000204C.0006.0001  VICTORIA LYNN   SMITHY          PRECISE
0000204C.0007.0001  ADAH TALBOT     WORK            GOOD
0000204C.0008.0001  WILFRED LOWELL  WORK            AVERAGE
0000204C.0009.0001  ELBERT TALBOT   DISCUS          SLOW
0000204C.000A.0001  WILFRED LOWELL  DISCUS          AVERAGE

The Index to the WORKERSKILL Table with the RowID of the Table:

ADAH TALBOT     WORK            0000204C.0007.0001
DICK JONES      SMITHY          0000204C.0001.0001
ELBERT TALBOT   DISCUS          0000204C.0009.0001
HELEN BRANDT    COMBINE DRIVER 0000204C.0004.0001
JOHN PEARSON    COMBINE DRIVER 0000204C.0002.0001
JOHN PEARSON    SMITHY          0000204C.0003.0001
JOHN PEARSON    WOODCUTTER      0000204C.0005.0001
VICTORIA LYNN   SMITHY          0000204C.0006.0001
WILFRED LOWELL DISCUS          0000204C.000A.0001
WILFRED LOWELL WORK            0000204C.0008.0001
```

FIGURE 18-1. *The WORKERSKILL table and its index*

For the sake of this example, the RowID was also selected. This is the internal location of the row (like a page number in a book) that ORACLE uses when it stores rows of data in a table. Now an index is created on the primary key:

```
create index WORKERSKILL_NAME_SKILL on WORKER(Name,Skill);
```

This is a practical and helpful technique to name the index by combining the table and column names, up to 30 characters. You will never need to know the name of the index for a query or other SQL command; ORACLE will use it automatically whenever it can. But when listing (or dropping) the indexes that you've created (their names are stored in the data dictionary view USER_INDEXES, which you can query), their names will tell you immediately what they do. The index in ORACLE looks like the second table in Figure 18-1.

When you execute a query such as this:

```
select Name, Skill, Ability
  from WORKERSKILL
 where Name = 'JOHN PEARSON'
   and Skill = 'WOODCUTTER';
```

ORACLE finds the Name and Skill in the index, takes the RowID (0000204C.0005.0001), and then reads the information at that RowID in the WORKERSKILL table. The index is in a format described as a *self-balancing B-Tree*, which means that it is organized in a structure like a tree, with nodes and leaves (similar to the cows in Chapter 11), and it *restructures* or balances itself automatically whenever a new row is inserted in the table. A discussion of the mechanisms of self-balancing B-Trees is beyond the scope of this book, but can be found in many good computer science texts.

The next few sections cover a number of issues related to the use of indexes.

Enforcing Uniqueness

Recall from Chapter 2 that a set of tables is said to be in Third Normal Form if all of the columns in a table's row are dependent only on the primary key. In the WORKERSKILL table, the primary key is the combination of the Name and Skill. In other tables, a primary key might be an employee ID, a client ID, an account number, or, in a bank, a combination of branch number and account number.

In each of these cases, the uniqueness of the primary key is critical. A bank with duplicate account numbers, or a billing system with duplicate client IDs, would wreak havoc as transactions were posted to accounts belonging to different people but having the same primary key (this is why names are not usually used as primary keys—there are too many duplicates). To avoid this danger, have your database help prevent the creation of duplicate primary keys. ORACLE offers two facilities that help: you can guarantee the uniqueness of a key through either indexing or constraints, or you can use the sequence generators. Sequence generators are discussed later in this chapter.

Creating a Unique Index

To create an index that will guarantee the uniqueness of the primary key (whether a single- or multiple-column primary key), such as on the WORKERSKILL table, use the primary key constraint on the key columns in the **create table** statement. You also can use a **create unique index** statement (and you must in versions of ORACLE prior to ORACLE7), but this statement will fail if any duplicates already exist. If you use the primary key constraint, you would never have duplicates. If the **create unique index** statement succeeds, then any future attempt to **insert** (or **update**) a row that would create a duplicate key will fail and result in this error message:

```
ERROR at line 1: ORA-0001:   duplicate value in index
```

There could be circumstances when you would want to enforce uniqueness on something other than a primary key, and the unique constraint lets you do this. For example, if you included a Social Security number for each person but the primary key was a sequence, you would want to ensure the uniqueness of the Social Security column as well with a unique constraint.

Consider the STOCK table, for example. Its primary key is the Company column. However, the Symbol column should be unique as well, even though Symbol is not the primary key. To enforce the uniqueness of both of these columns, create two separate constraints when creating the table, as shown in the following listing.

```
create table STOCK (
Company           VARCHAR2(20) primary key,
Symbol            VARCHAR2(6) unique,
Industry          VARCHAR2(15),
CloseYesterday    NUMBER(6,2),
CloseToday        NUMBER(6,2),
Volume            NUMBER);
```

When creating the primary key and unique constraints specified for the STOCK table, ORACLE7 will automatically create unique indexes to enforce those constraints. See "Placing an Index in the Database" later in this chapter for details concerning the location of the created indexes.

When to Create an Index

Indexes are most useful on larger tables, on columns that are likely to appear in **where** clauses either as a simple equality, such as this:

```
where Name = 'JOHN PEARSON'
   and Skill = 'WOODCUTTER'
```

or in joins, such as this:

```
where WORKER.Lodging = LODGING.Lodging
```

They also produce quicker retrievals for indexed columns in **where** clauses except those **where** clauses using **IS NOT NULL** and **IS NULL** on the indexed column. If there is no **where** clause, no index is used. Neither **distinct** nor **group by** currently uses indexes, although **order by** can. (This is described in detail later in this chapter.)

When Indexes Are Ignored

However, ORACLE needs to know that it is working with a simple column for which it can detect an index. If an indexed column is modified by a function, such as **SUBSTR** or ||, ORACLE will not use the index. Both **MIN** and **MAX**, if used alone with a column, will take advantage of the index.

Variety in Indexed Columns

Indexes are most useful on columns with a significant amount of variety in their data. For instance, a column that indicates whether a company is a current client with a Y or N would be a poor choice for an index, and could actually slow down a query. A telephone number column would be a good candidate. An area code column would be quite marginal.

When a primary key involves more than one column, it is better to put the column with the most variety first in the primary key constraint. If the columns have relatively equal variety, put the column likely to be accessed most often first.

Small tables are better left unindexed, except to enforce uniqueness in the primary key. A small table is one with fewer than 30 rows; in a given application a table with up to 100 or more rows may still be considered small. Beyond that, indexing will nearly always be productive.

How Many Indexes to Use on a Table

You can index up to 16 columns in one table in a single index (or a maximum of about 1000 to 2000 bytes per index, depending on your operating system). The trade-off for indexing too many columns is the speed of inserting new rows: every index also must have a new entry made in it when an **insert** is done. If your table will be used primarily for queries, the only cost of indexing as many columns as you can (that have variety, and will be used in **where** clauses, of course) is using some extra disk space. The indexing is usually more than worth the effort and space cost.

Except in cluster indexes (discussed later in this chapter), columns that are **NULL** will not appear in an index. If, for instance, you indexed the Noon column in the COMFORT table, as shown here:

```
select * from COMFORT;

CITY          SAMPLEDAT  NOON MIDNIGHT PRECIPITATION
------------- ---------- ----- -------- -------------
SAN FRANCISCO 21-MAR-93  62.5     42.3            .5
SAN FRANCISCO 22-JUN-93  51.1     71.9            .1
SAN FRANCISCO 23-SEP-93           61.5            .1
SAN FRANCISCO 22-DEC-93  52.6     39.8           2.3
KEENE         21-MAR-93  39.9     -1.2           4.4
KEENE         22-JUN-93  85.1     66.7           1.3
KEENE         23-SEP-93  99.8     82.6
KEENE         22-DEC-93  -7.2     -1.2           3.9
```

there would be an entry in the index for every row except 23-SEP-93, because the value for Noon on that date is **NULL**.

Indexes based on more than one column will have an entry if any of the columns are not **NULL**. If all columns are **NULL** for a given row, no entry will appear for it in the index.

Since indexes are typically used by **where** clauses that contain an equality, the row with a **NULL** column will not be returned to you by the **select** statement (remember that nothing is equal to **NULL**). This may be the desired effect. You might, for instance, keep a column of commissions for salespeople, but leave the column **NULL**, rather than 0, if a salesperson has no commission. A query that says this:

```
select Name, Commission
  from COMMISSION
 where Commission > 0;
```

will run faster because salespeople who have no commission will not even appear in the index on the Commission column.

Placing an Index in the Database

You can specify where the index to a table is placed by assigning it to a specific tablespace. As was briefly mentioned in Chapter 17, a tablespace is a section of disk where tables and indexes are stored, and one database may have several, each with its own name. An index for a table should be placed in a tablespace that is on a physically separate disk drive than the data tablespace. This will reduce the potential for disk contention between the tablespaces' files.

To specify the tablespace in which to locate an index, the normal **create index** statement is simply followed by the word **tablespace** and the tablespace name, as shown here:

```
create index workerskill_name_skill on WORKER(Name,Skill)
        tablespace GBTALBOT;
```

GBTALBOT is the name given to a tablespace previously created by the database administrator. The use of the **tablespace** option in a **create index** statement is usually necessary only with large databases where optimization or space usage is critical. Consult with your database administrator if you believe its use may be needed.

When you create a primary key or unique constraint, ORACLE7 will automatically create an index to enforce uniqueness. Unless you specify otherwise, that index will be created in the same tablespace as the table the constraint modifies, and will use the default storage parameters for that tablespace. Since that storage location is typically undesirable, you should take advantage of the **using index** clause when creating primary key and unique constraints.

The **using index** clause allows you to specify the storage parameters and tablespace location for an index created by a constraint. In the following example, a primary key is created on the Company column of the STOCK table. The primary key constraint is given the name PK_STOCK. The index associated with that primary key is directed to the INDEXES tablespace, with certain storage parameters. A unique constraint is created on the Symbol column, and its index is also placed in the INDEXES tablespace. Both constraints are specified at the table level (rather than at the column level) to better illustrate the **using index** syntax.

```
create table STOCK (
Company          VARCHAR2(20),
Symbol           VARCHAR2(6),
Industry         VARCHAR2(15),
CloseYesterday   NUMBER(6,2),
CloseToday       NUMBER(6,2),
Volume           NUMBER),
   constraint PK_STOCK  primary key (Company)
        using index tablespace INDEXES
      storage (initial 20K next 20K),
   constraint UQ_STOCK  unique (Symbol)
        using index tablespace INDEXES
      storage (initial 20K next 20K))
;
```

See "Integrity Constraint" in the Alphabetical Reference for further options for the **using index** clause, and see **create index** in the Alphabetical Reference for performance-related index creation options introduced in ORACLE7.1 and ORACLE7.2.

Tablespace and the Structure of the Database

People who have worked with computers for any period of time are familiar with the concept of a file; it's a place on disk where information is stored, and it has a name. Its size is usually not fixed: if you add information to the file, it can grow larger and take up more disk space, up to the maximum available. This process is managed by the operating system, and often will involve distributing the information in the file over several smaller sections of the disk that are not physically near each other. The operating system handles the logical connection of these smaller sections without your being aware of it at all. To you, the file looks like a single whole.

ORACLE uses files as a part of its organizational scheme, but its logical structure goes beyond the concept of a file. A tablespace is an area of disk, comprised of one or more disk files. A tablespace can contain many tables, indexes, or clusters. Because a tablespace has a fixed size, it can get full as rows are added to its tables. When this happens, the tablespace can be expanded by someone who has **dba** authority. The expansion is accomplished by creating a new disk file and adding it to the tablespace or, in ORACLE 7.2, by extending the existing datafiles. New rows can then be added to existing tables, and those tables will therefore have rows in both files. One or more tablespaces, together, make up a database.

Each table has a single area of disk space called a *segment* set aside for it in the tablespace. Each segment, in turn, has an initial area of disk space set aside for it in the tablespace called the *initial extent*. Once it has used up this space, the *next extent,* another single area of disk space, is set aside for it. When it has used this up as well, yet another next extent is set aside. This process continues with every table until the whole tablespace is full. At that point, someone has to add a new file to the tablespace or (if you're using ORACLE 7.2) extend the tablespace's files before any more growth in the tables can take place.

If this is confusing, an old parallel (see Figure 18-2) might help clarify it. Think of a database as a town block, and each tablespace as a fenced-in lot. At first, the block is fairly sparse: there are only a few fenced-in lots and plenty of open, unclaimed space. Lot one (tablespace one) is owned by G. B. Talbot, and he calls it "Homestead One." He plants several garden plots: rows of corn, rows of beans, rows of carrots. Each of these corresponds to a table with its rows, and each is planted in its own area, or "initial extent." After the carrots, he decides to plant more corn, but he's used up that section of the lot, so he plants more corn over on the other side of the yard. His corn is now in its next extent (its second extent). He continues similarly with additional rows of beans and carrots, until the yard is a patchwork of sections of each.

Eventually, he fills the lot entirely. His tablespace is full. He then purchases some empty land down at the other end of the block, fences in the lot, and dubs it

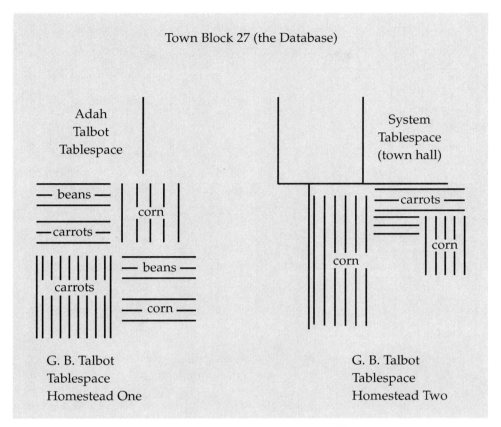

FIGURE 18-2. *ORACLE database structure as a town block*

"Homestead Two." His tablespace is now larger. Even though the lots (files) are not physically connected, Talbot still owns both of them. The tablespace is still "G. B. Talbot," and contains two lots, "Homestead One" and "Homestead Two." He can now plant more rows of corn, beans, and carrots in his second lot. They continue to consume additional "extents."

Every database also contains a *system* tablespace. This is the town hall for the block, where the ownership records and addresses are kept. It contains the data dictionary, and the names and locations of all of the tablespaces, tables, indexes, and clusters for this database.

Figure 18-3 shows how a database looks with a typical collection of tablespaces, tables, indexes, clusters, and extents. The database is created and named by the system database administrator, who usually also sets up tablespaces and grants use

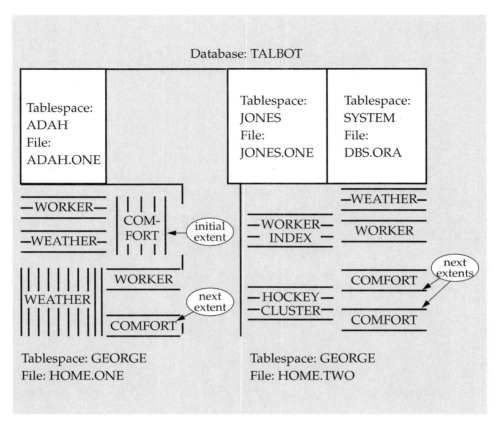

FIGURE 18-3. *ORACLE database structure as normally described*

of them to individual users. In this database, named TALBOT, tablespaces have been set up named ADAH, JONES, SYSTEM, and GEORGE.

Within a tablespace are tables, indexes, and clusters. Each table starts out with an initial extent allocated to it, and a next extent size that governs the amount of space allocated each time it grows beyond its current extent. In this figure, the COMFORT, WEATHER, and WORKER tables have all grown beyond their initial extent, and completely consumed the initial file, HOME.ONE, of the tablespace. COMFORT has grown into two additional extents in the second file, HOME.TWO. Both WEATHER and WORKER also have an additional extent in the second file. An index on the WORKER table was created after the second file became necessary, as was a cluster for the HOCKEY tables (you'll learn about clusters in the "Clusters" section near the end of this chapter).

create tablespace

The **create tablespace** command allows one or more files to be assigned immediately to the tablespace. It also specifies a default space for any tables created without an explicit storage clause mentioned in the **create table** statement.

This is the basic format for the **create tablespace** command:

```
create tablespace TALBOT datafile 'HOME.ONE' size 1000K
              default storage (initial 25K next 10K
              minextents 1 maxextents 100
              pctincrease 0);
```

> **NOTE**
> In ORACLE 7.1 and above, tablespaces can be designated READ ONLY. In ORACLE 7.2, datafiles associated with tablespaces can be extended. See **create tablespace** in the Alphabetical Reference for descriptions of these advanced options.

By default, an index's tablespace and storage are the same as the table's, but you can override these defaults with the **create index** statement. The initial file assigned to this tablespace is included in the command, as well as its size in *bytes,* not blocks. The number of bytes is an integer and can be followed by a K (to multiply by 1024—about a thousand) or an M (to be multiplied by 1048576—about a million). **default storage** sets up the storage a table will get if storage is not specified in the **create table** statement. Here the initial default extent is **25K** bytes (not blocks) and the next (incremental) extent is **10K** bytes.

minextents allows you to set aside additional extents beyond the first at the time a table is created. These will not necessarily be contiguous (physically adjacent) with the initial extent, or with each other, but the space will at least be reserved.

maxextents is the limit of additional extents allowed.

pctincrease is a growth factor for extents. When set to a non-zero value, each incremental extent will be the specified percentage larger than the one before it. This has the effect of reducing the number of extents, and noncontiguous space, used by a table that grows large.

The default values for storage are operating-system specific. The minimum and maximum values for each of these options are available in the Alphabetical Reference later in this book under **create table** and "Storage." These options may be changed with the **alter tablespace** command. The **create table** command for the LEDGER table looks like this:

```
create table LEDGER (
ActionDate      DATE,
Action          VARCHAR2(8),
Item            VARCHAR2(30),
Quantity        NUMBER,
QuantityType    VARCHAR2(10),
Rate            NUMBER,
Amount          NUMBER(9,2),
Person          VARCHAR2(25)
)
tablespace TALBOT
;
```

In this form, it will inherit the default storage definitions of the TALBOT tablespace. To override these, the **storage** clause is used in the **create table** command:

```
create table LEDGER (
ActionDate      DATE,
Action          VARCHAR2(8),
Item            VARCHAR2(30),
Quantity        NUMBER,
QuantityType    VARCHAR2(10),
Rate            NUMBER,
Amount          NUMBER(9,2),
Person          VARCHAR2(25)
)
tablespace TALBOT
storage (initial 5K next 5K
                 minextents 2 maxextents 50
                 pctincrease 0)
;
```

Clusters

Clustering is a method of storing tables that are intimately related and often joined together into the same area on disk. For example, instead of the WORKER table being in one section of the disk and the WORKERSKILL table being somewhere else, their rows could instead be interleaved together in a single area, called a *cluster*. The *cluster key* is the column or columns by which the tables are usually joined in a query (for example, Name for the WORKER and WORKERSKILL tables). To cluster tables, you must own the tables you are going to cluster together.

The following is the basic format of the **create cluster** command:

```
create cluster cluster (column datatype [,column
    datatype]. . .) [other options];
```

The *cluster* name follows the table-naming conventions, and *column datatype* is the name and datatype you will use as the cluster key. The *column* name may be the same as one of the columns of a table you will put in this cluster, or it may be any other valid name. It doesn't matter. Here's an example:

```
create cluster WORKERandSKILL ( Judy CHAR(25));

Cluster created.
```

This creates a cluster (a space is set aside, as it would be for a table) with nothing in it. The use of Judy for the cluster key is irrelevant; you'll never use it again. Next, tables are created to be included in this cluster:

```
create table WORKER (
Name            VARCHAR2(25) not null,
Age             NUMBER,
Lodging         VARCHAR2(15)
)
cluster WORKERandSKILL (Name)
;
```

Recall that the presence of a **cluster** clause here precludes the use of a **tablespace** or **storage** clause. Note how this structure differs from a standard **create table** statement:

```
create table WORKER (
Name            VARCHAR2(25) not null,
Age             number,
Lodging         VARCHAR2(15)
);
```

In the first **create table** statement, the cluster **WORKERandSKILL (Name)** clause *follows* the closing parentheses of the list of columns being created in the table. **WORKERandSKILL** is the name of the cluster previously created. Name is the column in this table that will be stored in the cluster key Judy. It is possible to have multiple cluster keys in the **create cluster** statement, and to have multiple columns stored in those keys in the **create table** statement. Notice that nowhere does either statement say explicitly that the Name column goes into the Judy cluster key. The matchup is done by position only: Name and Judy were both the first objects mentioned in their respective cluster statements. Multiple columns and cluster keys are matched first to first, second to second, third to third, and so on. Now a second table is added to the cluster:

```
create table WORKERSKILL (
Name            VARCHAR2(25) not null,
Skill           VARCHAR2(25) not null,
Ability         VARCHAR2(15)
)
cluster WORKERandSKILL (Name)
;
```

How the Tables Are Stored

Figure 18-4 illustrates how the data is stored in a cluster. Recall that the WORKER table has three columns: Name, Age, and Lodging. The WORKERSKILL table also has three columns: Name, Skill, and Ability. When these two tables are clustered, each unique Name is actually stored only once, in the cluster key. To each Name are attached the columns from both of these tables.

The data from both of these tables is actually stored in a single location, almost as if the cluster were a big table containing data drawn from both of the tables that make it up.

Sequences

ORACLE has solved the long-standing problem of assigning unique numbers, such as customer IDs, without having to create a special table and handle update and concurrence for it. This is done by using the **create sequence** command, as shown here:

```
create sequence CustomerID increment by 1 start with 1000;
```

This will create a sequence that can be accessed by **insert** and **update** statements (also **select**, although this is rare). Typically, the sequence is created with a statement like the following:

```
insert into CUSTOMER
            (Name, Contact, ID)
values
            ('COLE CONSTRUCTION', 'VERONICA',CustomerID.NextVal);
```

The NextVal attached to CustomerID tells ORACLE you want the next available sequence number from the CustomerID sequence. This is guaranteed to be unique; ORACLE will not give it to anyone else. To use the same number more than once (such as in a series of **insert**s into related tables), CurrVal is used instead of NextVal,

```
AGE LODGING      NAME                        SKILL           ABILITY
---- ----------  -------------------------   --------------  ---------
  23 PAPA KING   ADAH TALBOT                 WORK            GOOD
  29 ROSE HILL   ANDREW DYE
  22 CRANMER     BART SARJEANT
  18 ROSE HILL   DICK JONES                  SMITHY          EXCELLENT
  16 MATTS       DONALD ROLLO
  43 WEITBROCHT  ELBERT TALBOT               DISCUS          SLOW
  41 ROSE HILL   GEORGE OSCAR
  55 PAPA KING   GERHARDT KENTGEN
  15             HELEN BRANDT                COMBINE DRIVER  VERY FAST
  33 MATTS       JED HOPKINS
  27 ROSE HILL   JOHN PEARSON                COMBINE DRIVER
                                             WOODCUTTER      GOOD
                                             SMITHY          AVERAGE

     ROSE HILL   KAY AND PALMER WALLBOM
  21 ROSE HILL   PAT LAVAY
  25 CRANMER     PETER LAWSON
     WEITBROCHT  RICHARD KOCH AND BROTHERS
  35 MATTS       ROLAND BRANDT
  32 MULLERS     VICTORIA LYNN               SMITHY          PRECISE
  67             WILFRED LOWELL              WORK            AVERAGE
                                             DISCUS          AVERAGE
  15 CRANMER     WILLIAM SWING
```

from the WORKER table

from the WORKERSKILL table

cluster key

FIGURE 18-4. *How data is stored in clusters*

after the first use. That is, using NextVal assures that the sequence table gets incremented, and you get a unique number, so you've got to use NextVal first. Once you've used NextVal, that number is stored in CurrVal for your use anywhere, until you use NextVal again, at which point both NextVal and CurrVal change to the new sequence number.

If you use both NextVal and CurrVal in a single SQL statement, both will contain the value retrieved by NextVal. Neither of these can be used in subqueries, as columns in the **select** clause of a view, with **DISTINCT**, **UNION**, **INTERSECT**, or **MINUS**, or in the **order by**, **group by**, or **having** clause of a **select** statement.

You can also cache sequence values in memory for faster access, and you can make the sequence cycle back to its starting value once a maximum value is reached. See **create sequence** in the Alphabetical Reference.

CHAPTER 19

SQL*PLUS

SQLPLUS has a number of features that take it far beyond the realm of a report writer and interactive SQL environment, and allow it to be an actual code generator. It can dynamically create SQL and SQLPLUS code and execute it. This chapter explores some of the techniques for maximizing the use of SQLPLUS.

One of the real powers of SQL is its ability to foster thinking more and more deeply about your data. Because queries can be formulated, executed, and reformulated very quickly, naïve questions will regularly lead to further, more penetrating questions.

Generating Code for a Query

For example, suppose you wondered what tables existed currently in your userid.
You might use this query:

```
select Table_Name from USER_TABLES;
```

USER_TABLES contains information about all of your tables, and Table_Name
is the column that contains the table names. The following is the result of the query:

```
TABLE_NAME
------------------------------
BREEDING
LEDGER
LODGING
SKILL
WORKER
WORKERSKILL

6 rows selected.
```

Now you know the names of your tables, but how big are they? How many
rows does each contain? You could, for each of these table names, type a query
like this:

```
select COUNT(*) from BREEDING;
```

This would produce the answers you need, and you could set up a start file that
contained six such queries, and then run it on a regular basis to track the growth of
the various tables in the database. And if another table is added? Of course, you'd
need to go back and add the new table to the start file. You also could build a start
file named **master.sql** that looked like this:

```
rem master.sql - creates and executes slave.sql

set feedback off
set heading off
spool slave.sql
select 'select COUNT(*) from '||Table_Name||';' from
 USER_TABLES;
spool off
```

When this executes it will produce a file named **slave.sql**, which will contain the following:

```
select COUNT(*) from BREEDING;
select COUNT(*) from LEDGER;
select COUNT(*) from LODGING;
select COUNT(*) from SKILL;
select COUNT(*) from WORKER;
select COUNT(*) from WORKERSKILL;
```

Executing **slave.sql** produces row counts for each of these tables. The benefit of this approach is that it will always create as many **select** statements as there are tables listed in USER_TABLES. The trick is to make a **select** statement contain a literal column that is itself a **select** statement. Because the results are being spooled into a file, the result is executable code—in this case a whole series of **select** statements to count the rows in each table. **set feedback off** prevents a message like '**6 rows selected.**' from appearing in **slave.sql**, and **set heading off** does the same thing for column headings. Neither the "rows selected" messages nor the column headings would be executable SQL or SQLPLUS statements, so you don't want them in **slave.sql**.

You can expand this basic technique in a number of ways. For instance, make the execution of **slave.sql** automatic by including it in the original **master.sql** start file, and spooling its output to another file, **table.lst**:

```
rem master.sql - creates and executes slave.sql

set feedback off
set heading off

spool slave.sql
select 'select COUNT(*) from '||Table_Name||';' from
       USER_TABLES;
spool off

spool table.lst
start slave.sql
spool off
```

Of course, the **table.lst** file is only going to contain a column of numbers—the row counts from each of these tables. A slightly more complicated query is necessary to include the table names as well:

```
set feedback off
set heading off

spool slave.sql
select 'select '||''''||Table_Name||''''||', COUNT(*) from '||
       Table_Name||';' from USER_TABLES;
spool off

spool table.lst
start slave.sql
spool off
```

This produces a **slave.sql** file that looks like this:

```
select 'BREEDING', COUNT(*) from BREEDING;
select 'LEDGER', COUNT(*) from LEDGER;
select 'LODGING', COUNT(*) from LODGING;
select 'SKILL', COUNT(*) from SKILL;
select 'WORKER', COUNT(*) from WORKER;
select 'WORKERSKILL', COUNT(*) from WORKERSKILL;
```

The only new trick here is in including the table name as a literal, in quotation marks, to the left of the **COUNT(*)**. This is done using the following:

```
||''''||
```

The four single quotation marks produce a single quotation mark in the result because the center two are interpreted by ORACLE as meaning a literal single quotation mark, rather than a SQL delimiter. The outer two are no different than the single quotes that surround '**select** '. The net effect is to concatenate a single quotation mark between the '**select** ' and the Table_Name. The same thing is done on the right of the Table_Name.

Knowing that ORACLE will interpret two adjacent single quotation marks as a solitary single quotation mark, the following also could have been written:

```
select 'select '''||Table_Name||''', COUNT(*) from '||
       Table_Name||';' from USER_TABLES;
```

However, as the creation of code-generating start files becomes more complex, the management of literal single quotation marks also becomes more complicated. You may have instances of **select**s embedded in **select**s embedded in **select**s, where a long string of single quotation marks may be necessary to produce the desired result. Before long it becomes next to impossible to figure out how many consecutive single quotation marks you need. Always using ¦¦''''¦¦ whenever one literal single quotation mark is required makes managing this much easier.

When **slave.sql** executes now, it will produce a file named **table.lst** that looks like this:

```
BREEDING        16

LEDGER          225

LODGING         6

SKILL           6

WORKER          19

WORKERSKILL     10
```

In many cases, either **master.sql** or **slave.sql** also could contain SQLPLUS commands to format **report.lst** with formatted columns, such as **ttitle** and **btitle**, simply by placing these commands *after* **slave.sql** is created, but *before* it is executed, like this:

```
set feedback off
set heading off

spool slave.sql
select 'select '¦¦''''¦¦Table_Name¦¦''''¦¦', COUNT(*) from '¦¦
       Table_Name¦¦';' from USER_TABLES;
spool off

ttitle 'List of Tables and Sizes'
set heading on
set feedback 1
spool table.lst
start slave.sql
spool off
```

This would not work in this instance, however, because **ttitle** places a top title for every **select** statement that executes, and **slave.sql** has six of them. There would be a **ttitle** and column headings above every row in **table.lst**. Feedback would report '**1 row selected.**' for each row. It would not be a pretty sight.

How about creating a view? Could a report on rows per table be produced with a carefully constructed view from the USER_TABLES table, perhaps using a **union**

of the tables? No. SQL doesn't have the means currently to have a view that has a
dynamic number of **union**ed **select** statements. It can be approximated, however.
The first attempt is shown in Figure 19-1, and its result is shown in Figure 19-2.

Step by step, here is what is being done: At Circle 1, the **pagesize** and **linesize**
are set large enough to preclude formatting problems. If **linesize** is too small, some
long generated SQL statements may fold in the middle of a word. If the **pagesize** is
too short, a blank line will be inserted every time the page length is exceeded by
the generated statements. That is, if **slave.sql** had a 200-line SQL statement (not
uncommon), and **pagesize** were set to 50, there would be three blank lines in the
SQL statement, one after each 50 lines. This would cause the statement to fail to
execute. Therefore, **pagesize** is set very high.

At Circle 2, every SQLPLUS command that could produce messages, titles,
headings, feedback, or any other nonexecutable text is turned off, in order to assure
that the code generated into **slave.sql** is clean. An alternative to putting this laundry

```
rem master.sql - creates and executes slave.sql

set pagesize 30000
set linesize 200

set timing off
set time off
set feedback off
set heading off
set echo off
ttitle off
btitle off
spool slave.sql

prompt create or replace view USER_TABLE_SIZE as
select DECODE(RowNum,1,null,'union ')||
'select '||''''||Table_Name||''''||' Name'||
', COUNT(*) Row_Count from '||Table_Name
  from USER_TABLES;
prompt /
spool off
```

FIGURE 19-1. *The first attempt to create a view of table sizes*

```
create or replace view USER_TABLE_SIZE as (A)

select 'BREEDING' Name, COUNT(*) Row_Count from BREEDING      (B)
union select 'LEDGER' Name, COUNT(*) Row_Count from LEDGER    (C)
union select 'LODGING' Name, COUNT(*) Row_Count from LODGING
union select 'SKILL' Name, COUNT(*) Row_Count from SKILL
union select 'WORKER' Name, COUNT(*) Row_Count from WORKER
union select 'WORKERSKILL' Name, COUNT(*) Row_Count from WORKERSKILL
/
```

FIGURE 19-2.   *The result of the first attempt (contents of **slave.sql**)*

list into every such start file is to place all seven lines of it into a little start file of its own, called perhaps **off.sql**. Then, a single line like this:

```
start off
```

can replace these lines (a start file with the extension **.sql** can be abbreviated to just the file name when using the start command). You may use a similar technique at the very end of the **master.sql** file to turn on those SQLPLUS features you usually prefer to have functioning, such as **set feedback on** and **set heading on**.

At Circle 3, the **prompt** command is used to "write" the **create or replace view** statement to the spool file. Its effect is at Circle A in Figure 19-2.

Now things start to get complicated, at least at first viewing. Circle 4 contains a **DECODE** statement:

```
select DECODE(RowNum,1,null,'union ')||
```

When this **select** executes, the first row it retrieves returns a RowNum of 1, so the **DECODE** produces a result of **NULL**, which is to say, nothing. The effect can be seen at Circle B. For every row after that, RowNum is not 1, so the **DECODE** produces the word **union**. The effect is shown at Circle C in Figure 19-2. Every line except the first gets the word **union** at its beginning.

Circle 5 is similar to the method shown earlier, except that the Table_Name column (which will contain the actual table names for each table) has been given the alias of **Name**:

```
'select '||''''||Table_Name||''''||' Name'||
```

It is **Name** that will be the column name in the USER_TABLE_SIZE view. You also can see this effect in all of the lines containing **select** from Circle B onward. At Circle 6, **COUNT**(*) is similarly renamed, to be **Row_Count**.

At Circle 7, the **prompt** command is again used to produce a SQL terminator.

This attempt nearly works. The **create or replace view** is ignored because of the blank line that follows it. To correct this problem, the **prompt** command for the **create or replace view** is replaced by an addition to the **DECODE**:

```
select DECODE(RowNum,1,'create or replace view
  USER_TABLE_SIZE as
  ','union ')||
  'select '||''''||Table_Name||''''||' Name'||
', count(*) Row_Count from '||Table_Name
  from USER_TABLES;
prompt /
```

Now **slave.sql** contains the following:

```
create or replace view USER_TABLE_SIZE as
select 'BREEDING' Name, count(*) Row_Count from BREEDING
union select 'LEDGER' Name, count(*) Row_Count from LEDGER
union select 'LODGING' Name, count(*) Row_Count from LODGING
union select 'SKILL' Name, count(*) Row_Count from SKILL
union select 'WORKER' Name, count(*) Row_Count from WORKER
union select 'WORKERSKILL' Name, count(*) Row_Count from WORKERSKILL
/
```

After **slave.sql** is executed, the new view exists and can be queried:

```
select * from USER_TABLE_SIZE;

NAME        Row_Count
----------- ---------
BREEDING           16
LEDGER            225
LODGING             6
SKILL               6
WORKER             19
WORKERSKILL        10

6 rows selected.
```

Voilà! Of course, this **select**, and perhaps some title and other formatting commands, could all be included in the **master.sql** start file, simply following the creation and execution of **slave.sql**. Thereafter the running of **master.sql** will always easily produce a current list of tables and their sizes.

Loading Variables

This method of spooling to a file and creating executable code from SQL statements and **prompt** commands also can be used to load variables in SQLPLUS for use in subsequent SQL statements, **ttitle** or **btitle**, **prompt**s, and the like. For instance, suppose you have a series of reports to run, all of which will make calculations using the **SUM** and **AVG** of the Amount column in the LEDGER table. The previous method for doing this, as illustrated in Chapters 9 and 15, was to create a view that contained these calculations, and then join the view to other tables in a **select** statement. In most cases this approach is appropriate.

Suppose, however, that the table on which the **SUM** and **AVG** are being calculated is very large. With each subsequent SQL statement that is executed, the view recalculates **SUM** and **AVG** for the whole table. If these could be calculated just once, and then kept in a variable, the variable could be used in subsequent SQL statements without incurring the additional processing of the view. This is usually not a sensible approach if the table is very volatile while the reports are being produced, but if the reports are run at night, or the data is stable, it works well (you can also use a **lock table** in **row share** or **share update mode**). Here's an example of loading two variables with data from a query:

```
set pagesize 32000
set linesize 200

start off

column FoldIt newline

spool slave.sql
select 'define Average =', AVG(Amount),
       'define Total   =' FoldIt, SUM(Amount)
  from LEDGER;
spool off

start slave
```

This produces the start file **slave.sql**, which looks like this:

```
define Average =   4.57075556
define Total   =     1028.42
```

When **slave.sql** is started, these variables are defined to SQLPLUS, and can be used in subsequent SQL statements. The file **off.sql** assures clean output to **slave.sql**. While using this technique with a single variable is straightforward, defining two variables at once requires a little more work. SQLPLUS will not accept this:

```
define Average =   4.57075556   define Total    =      1028.42
```

because two **define**s appear on one line. Therefore, the literal column '**define Total =**' is given an alias of FoldIt, and a column command **column FoldIt newline** is placed up above. This causes a **newline** to be started for this column. If you have multiple columns, you could use the same alias, FoldIt, for each column where a new line needed to be started. The single column command would then control all of them. Incidentally, **newline** has the same effect as **fold_before 1**, which is discussed in Chapter 12.

Changing Variable Values

A variable, once defined, can undergo change. Here, just as an example, Average is added to itself (having already been defined once):

```
column B format 999999999.9999
spool slave.sql
select 'define Average =', (AVG(Amount) + &Average)   B,
       'define Total   =', SUM(Amount)
  from LEDGER;
spool off
start slave
```

The preceding produces this:

```
define Average =            9.1415
define Total   =     1028.42
```

Note how the use of **column B format 999999999.9999** affects the way the value for Average now appears, and compare it to that done previously, when only **set numwidth 10** was in effect.

Using Variables with ttitle

Since any variable also can be used in a **ttitle** or **btitle** (see Chapter 12 for details), you could create a SQL statement that would load a variable with a value, and use it in a **ttitle** command. This would prove particularly valuable when the value you wanted in the **ttitle** could not be obtained from the main **select** statement of the report for which **ttitle** is the heading.

Character Strings and Dates

When loading variables in this fashion, character strings and dates must be concatenated inside of single quotation marks, as shown here:

```
select 'define City = '||''''||City||''''
  from COMFORT
 where Noon is NULL;
```

This produces the following:

```
define City = 'San Francisco'
```

When the variable is then used inside a subsequent SQL statement, it is not surrounded by single quotation marks:

```
select Midnight
  from COMFORT
 where City = &City;
```

Failing to concatenate the string when the first **select** is run will cause the **define** to lose all but the first word of a multiword text string (like San Francisco). By concatenating dates and text strings, and leaving numbers bare during the creation of the variable, all variables will look the same—that is, they won't have quotes in subsequent **select** statements.

Creating and Nesting Start Files and Commands

Figure 19-3 shows a start file, **master.sql**, used for simple reporting on all of the tables in your database. Its purpose is to illustrate some additional techniques that can be employed in generating code into start files.

Circle 1 shows how a host or other command can be written into a slave start file. Recall that the **$** is equivalent to the word **host**, and is used here to execute a

```
rem master.sql - creates and executes slave.sql

set pagesize 32000
set linesize 200

start off

column FoldIt newline

spool slave.sql

prompt $cls
prompt spool table.lst                                    ─┐─①
prompt prompt Beginning Table Reports ─┐─②
prompt prompt

select 'define Table   = '||''''||Table_Name||'''',
       'prompt Working on '||''''||Table_Name||'''',
       'prompt                                ',          ─┐─③
       'start sizing.sql'
  from USER_TABLES;

prompt prompt Table Reports Completed ─┐
prompt spool off                                          ─┤─④
prompt $print table.lst ─┘

spool off

start slave
```

FIGURE 19-3. *Nested start files and commands*

```
$cls                                    ┐
spool table.lst                         ├─(A)
prompt Beginning Table Reports          ┐
prompt                                  ├─(B)

define Table    = 'BREEDING'            ┐
prompt Working on 'BREEDING'            ├─(C)
prompt                                  │
start sizing.sql                        ┘

define Table    = 'LEDGER'
prompt Working on 'LEDGER'
prompt
start sizing.sql

define Table    = 'LODGING'
prompt Working on 'LODGING'
prompt
start sizing.sql

define Table    = 'SKILL'
prompt Working on 'SKILL'
prompt
start sizing.sql

define Table    = 'WORKER'
prompt Working on 'WORKER'
prompt
start sizing.sql

define Table    = 'WORKERSKILL'
prompt Working on 'WORKERSKILL'
prompt
start sizing.sql

prompt Table Reports Completed          ┐
spool off                               ├─(D)
$print table.lst                        ┘
```

FIGURE 19-4.   *The effects of the **master.sql** file*

module named **cls** on the host operating system (in this case, a screen clear). Because this is a **prompt**, the **$cls** is simply written into the **slave.sql** file, as are the words **spool table.lst**. The effects can be seen in Figure 19-4 at Circle A.

Circle 2 of Figure 19-3 is a bit different. Here a **prompt** writes another **prompt** into the slave file. This means the message shown at Circle B in Figure 19-4 will appear on the screen later, when **slave.sql** is executed.

Circle 3 produces the effects shown at Circle C and in the lines following: a group of four commands for each table. When **slave.sql** runs, the **prompt**s will display on your screen, **sizing.sql** will be executed for each table, and the results will be spooled to **table.lst**.

When **slave.sql** is complete, the final line sends the **table.lst** file that's been created to the printer. See Circles 4 and D.

The start file **sizing.sql** (Circles 3 and C) contains the following code:

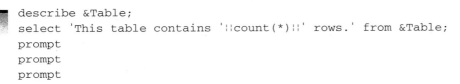

```
describe &Table;
select 'This table contains '||count(*)||' rows.' from &Table;
prompt
prompt
prompt
```

Note that **sizing.sql** relies on the **&Table** variable that is changed just before **sizing.sql** is executed each time. The result of all of this—**master.sql**, **slave.sql**, and **sizing.sql**—is the report shown in Figure 19-5.

Using Host Processes

Two host processes were used in producing this report. One cleared the screen and the other printed the report when it was completed. Substantially more complex host manipulation can also be used, for instance, to reformat the results of a query, or to erase work files that have been created. It is even possible to use SQLPLUS to create macros that a given editor will use, then call the editor, execute the macro, and return to SQLPLUS. A robust interactive English Query facility was built using SQLPLUS and an interpretive host language, where each repeatedly wrote code for and called the other, in order to support interaction with the user.

```
Beginning Table Reports

Working on 'BREEDING'

Name                             Null?      Type
------------------------------   --------   ----
OFFSPRING                                   VARCHAR2(10)
SEX                                         CHAR(1)
COW                                         VARCHAR2(10)
BULL                                        VARCHAR2(10)
BIRTHDATE                                   DATE

This table contains 16 rows.


Working on 'LEDGER'

Name                             Null?      Type
------------------------------   --------   ----
ACTIONDATE                                  DATE
ACTION                                      VARCHAR2(8)
ITEM                                        VARCHAR2(30)
QUANTITY                                    NUMBER
QUANTITYTYPE                                VARCHAR2(10)
RATE                                        NUMBER
AMOUNT                                      NUMBER(9,2)
PERSON                                      VARCHAR2(25)

This table contains 225 rows.
       .
       .
       .
```
(And so on, for each table. Additional tables not shown)
```
       .
       .
       .
Table Reports Completed
```

FIGURE 19-5.   *Report produced by **slave.sql** repeatedly calling **sizing.sql***

Review

The techniques shown in this chapter have been used for many complex reporting and data manipulation purposes, from creating a table report that calculated the average row size for each table (by dynamically constructing a **select** with a **VSIZE** for each column of each table), to a report showing which tables are affected by each SQLFORMS application, block by block, and whether tables have rows **select**ed, **insert**ed, **update**d, or **delete**d in each block. Other possibilities are numerous: for validating all indexes; for creating, copying, or dropping tables; even for creating dynamic batch files that can exit SQLPLUS (if necessary), then export, import, or load data, run programs, reports, or other ORACLE products, and then reenter SQLPLUS when finished.

Even very experienced SQLPLUS users sometimes must experiment to assure that **linesize**, **pagesize**, the **sqlprompt**, and other features and commands do not adversely affect the code being generated.

Generally, the cleanest approach is to divide the tasks into common start files, such as **off.sql**, and clearly defined processing start files, whether of SQL, SQLPLUS, or host programs. These start files are then all directed from a single master start file.

CHAPTER 20

Accessing Remote Data

As your databases grow in size and number, you will very likely need to share data among them. Sharing data requires a method of locating and accessing the data. In ORACLE7, remote data accesses such as queries and updates are enabled through the use of database links. As described in this chapter, database links allow users to treat a group of distributed databases as if they were a single, integrated database (advanced uses of database links to maintain remote copies of data are described in Chapter 23). In this chapter you will also find information about direct connections to remote databases, such as those used in client-server applications.

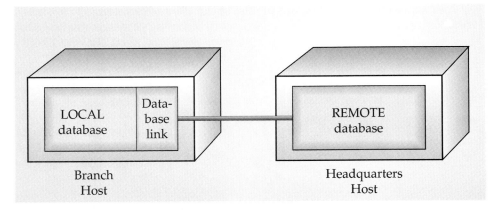

FIGURE 20-1. *Sample architecture for a database link*

Database Links

Database links tell ORACLE7 how to get from one database to another. You may also specify the access path in an ad hoc fashion (see the section "Dynamic Links: Using the SQLPLUS **copy** Command," later in this chapter). If you will frequently use the same connection to a remote database, then a database link is appropriate.

How a Database Link Works

A database link requires that SQL*Net be running on each of the machines ("*hosts*") involved in the remote database access. SQL*Net is usually started by the database administrator (DBA) or the system manager. A sample architecture for a remote access using a database link is shown in Figure 20-1. This figure shows two hosts, each running SQL*Net. There is a database on each of the hosts. A database link will be used to establish a connection from the first database (named "Local", on the "Branch" host) to the second database (named "Remote", on the "Headquarters" host).

The database link shown in Figure 20-1 is software that is located in the "Local" database.

Database links specify the following connection information:

- The communications protocol (such as TCP/IP) to use during the connection.

- The host on which the remote database resides.

- The name of the database on the remote host.
- The name of a valid account in the remote database.
- The password for that account.

When used, a database link will actually log in as a user in the remote database, then log out when the remote data access is complete. A database link can be *private*—owned by a single user—or *public*—in which case all users in the "local" database can use the link.

The syntax for creating a database link is shown in "Syntax for Database Links" later in this chapter.

Using a Database Link for Remote Queries

If you are a user in the "Local" database shown in Figure 20-1, you can access objects in the "Remote" database via the REMOTE_CONNECT database link. To do this, simply append the database link name to the name of any table or view that is accessible to the remote account. When appending the database link name to a table or view name, you must precede the database link name with an "@" sign (pronounced "at"), as shown in the following listing.

For local tables:

```
select *
from WORKER;
```

For remote tables, use the REMOTE_CONNECT database link:

```
select *
from WORKER@REMOTE_CONNECT;
```

When the database link in the last query above is used, Oracle will log into the database specified by the database link, using the username and password provided by the link. It will then query the WORKER table in that account and return the data to the user who initiated the query. This is shown graphically in Figure 20-2.

The REMOTE_CONNECT database link shown in Figure 20-2 is located in the "Local" database.

As shown in Figure 20-2, logging into the "Local" database and using the REMOTE_CONNECT database link in your **from** clause will return the same results as logging directly into the remote database and executing the query without the database link. It makes the remote database seem local.

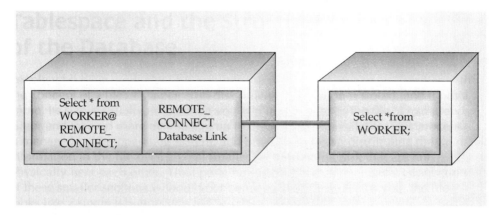

FIGURE 20-2. *Using a database link for a remote query*

The maximum number of database links that can be used in a single query is set via the OPEN_LINKS parameter in the database's INIT.ORA initialization file. It usually defaults to four.

There are restrictions to the queries that are executed using database links. You should avoid using database links in queries that use the **connect by**, **start with**, and **prior** keywords. Some queries using these keywords will work (for example, if **prior** is not used outside of the **connect by** clause, and **start with** does not use a subquery), but most uses of tree-structured queries will fail when using database links.

Using a Database Link for Synonyms and Views

You may create local synonyms and views that reference remote objects. To do this, reference the database link name, preceded by an "@" sign, wherever you refer to a remote table. The following example shows how to do this for synonyms. The **create synonym** command in this example is executed from an account in the "Local" database.

```
create synonym WORKER_SYN
for WORKER@REMOTE_CONNECT;
```

In this example, a synonym called WORKER_SYN is created for the WORKER table accessed via the REMOTE_CONNECT database link. Every time this synonym is used in a **from** clause of a query, the remote database will be queried. This is very similar to the remote queries shown earlier; the only real change is that the database link is now defined as part of a local object (in this case, a synonym).

What if the remote account that is accessed by the database link does not own the table being referenced? In that event, any synonyms that are available to the remote account (either private or public) can be used. If there are no such synonyms for a table that the remote account has been granted access to, then you must specify the table owner's name in the query, as shown in the following example.

```
create synonym WORKERSKILL_SYN
for TALBOT.WORKERSKILL@REMOTE_CONNECT;
```

In this example, the remote account used by the database link does not own the WORKERSKILL table, nor does the remote account have a synonym called WORKERSKILL. It does, however, have privileges on the WORKERSKILL table owned by the remote user TALBOT. Therefore, the owner and table name are specified; both are interpreted in the remote database. The syntax for these queries and synonyms is almost the same as if everything was in the local database; the only addition is the database link name.

To use a database link in a view, simply add it as a suffix to table names in the **create view** command. The following example creates a view in the local database of a remote table, using the REMOTE_CONNECT database link.

```
create view LOCAL_EMPLOYEE_VIEW
as
select * from WORKER@REMOTE_CONNECT
where Lodging = 'ROSE HILL';
```

The **from** clause in this example refers to WORKER@REMOTE_CONNECT. Therefore, the base table for this view is not in the same database as the view. Also note that a **where** clause is placed on the query to limit the number of records returned by it for the view.

This view may now be treated like any other view in the local database. Access to this view can be granted to other users, provided those users also have access to the REMOTE_CONNECT database link.

Using a Database Link for Remote Updates

The types of remote updates you can perform depend on which version of the ORACLE7 database you are using. If you are using ORACLE7 with the distributed option, then you can update tables in all remote ORACLE7 databases that are running the distributed option. If you are not using ORACLE7 with the distributed option, then you are limited to updating only remote databases that are on the same host as the local database.

The database link syntax for remote updates is the same as that for remote queries. Append the name of the database link to the name of the table being updated. For example, to change the Lodging values for workers in a remote WORKER table, you would execute the **update** command shown in the following listing.

```
update WORKER@REMOTE_CONNECT
set Lodging = 'CRANMER'
where Lodging = 'ROSE HILL';
```

This **update** command will use the REMOTE_CONNECT database link to log into the remote database. It will then update the WORKER table in that database, based on the **set** and **where** conditions specified.

It is also possible to use subqueries in the **set** portion of the **update** command (see Chapter 13). The **from** clause of such subqueries can reference either the local database or the remote database. To refer to the remote database in a subquery, append the database link name to the table names in the **from** clause of the subquery. An example of this is shown in the following listing.

```
update WORKER@REMOTE_CONNECT          /*in remote database*/
set Lodging =
    (select Lodging
     from LODGING@REMOTE_CONNECT  /*in remote database*/
     where Manager = 'KEN MULLER')
where Lodging = 'ROSE HILL';
```

NOTE
If you do not append the database link name to the table names in the **from** clause of **update** subqueries, then tables in the local database will be used. This will be true even if the table being updated is in a remote database.

In this example, the remote WORKER table is updated based on value on the remote LODGING table. If the database link is not used in the subquery, as in the following example, then the LODGING table in the local database will be used instead. If this was unintended, it will produce a nasty mixing of local data into the remote database table. If you're doing it on purpose, be *very* careful.

```
update WORKER@REMOTE_CONNECT          /*in remote database*/
set Lodging =
    (select Lodging
     from LODGING                 /*in local database*/
     where Manager = 'KEN MULLER')
where Lodging = 'ROSE HILL';
```

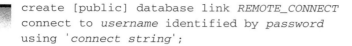

Syntax for Database Links

You can create a database link with the following command:

```
create [public] database link REMOTE_CONNECT
connect to username identified by password
using 'connect string';
```

The specific syntax to use when creating a database link depends upon three criteria:

- The "public" or "private" status of the database link.
- The use of default or explicit logins for the remote database.
- The version of SQL*Net in use.

Each of these criteria, and their associated syntax, will be described in the following sections.

NOTE

In order to create a database link, you must have CREATE DATABASE LINK system privilege. The account to which you will be connecting in the remote database must have CREATE SESSION privilege. Both of these system privileges are included as part of the CONNECT role in ORACLE7.

Public vs. Private Database Links

A *public* database link is available to all users in a database. By contrast, a *private* database link is only available to the user who created it. It is not possible for one user to grant access on a private database link to another user. The database link must either be public (available to all users) or private.

To specify a database link as a public database link, use the **public** keyword in the **create database link** command, as shown in the following example.

```
create public database link REMOTE_CONNECT
connect to username identified by password
using 'connect string';
```

NOTE

In order to create a public database link, you must have CREATE PUBLIC DATABASE LINK system privilege. This privilege is included in the DBA role in ORACLE7.

Default vs. Explicit Logins

In SQL*Net V2, you do not have to specify a "**connect to ... identified by ...**" clause when creating a database link. If you do not, then when that link is used, it will attempt to open a session in the remote database that has the same username and password as the local database account. This is called a *default login*, since the username/password combination will default to the combination in use in the local database.

The following listing shows an example of a public database link, created with a default login. The use of default logins will be described further in the "Using the User Pseudo-column in Views" section of this chapter.

```
create public database link REMOTE_CONNECT
using 'connect string';
```

When this database link is used, it will attempt to log into the remote database using the current user's username and password. If the current username is not valid in the remote database, or if the password is different, then the login attempt will fail. This failure will cause the SQL statement using the link to fail.

An *explicit* login specifies a username and password that the database link will use while connecting to the remote database. No matter which local account uses the link, the same remote account will be used. The following listing shows the creation of a database link with an explicit login.

```
create public database link REMOTE_CONNECT
connect to WAREHOUSE identified by ACCESS339
using 'connect string';
```

This example shows a common usage of explicit logins in database links. In the remote database, a user named WAREHOUSE was created, and was given the password ACCESS339. This account can then be granted SELECT access to specific tables, solely for use by database links. This **create public database link** then provides access to it for all local users.

SQL*Net V1 vs. SQL*Net V2

The "connect string" portion of the create database link command is dependent upon the version of SQL*Net you will be using. SQL*Net V1 uses *connect strings* in the following format:

> *T:hostname:dbname*
> where
> *T* is the abbreviation for the protocol to be used (in this example, TCP/IP).
> *hostname* is the name of the host on which the remote database resides.
> *dbname* is the name of the remote database (its instance name).

Because this information is specified when creating the database link, you must know these connection details before creating the link. If the database later moves to a different host, you must drop and re-create the link. The following listing shows an example of a public database link using an explicit login and a SQL*Net V1 connect string.

```
create public database link REMOTE_CONNECT
connect to WAREHOUSE identified by ACCESS339
using 'T:host1:remote';
```

In this example, the SQL*Net V1 connect string specifies that the remote database is called "remote", and that it resides on the host called "host1". The TCP/IP network protocol is specified for use during the connection.

SQL*Net V2 uses *service names* to identify remote connections. The connection details for these service names are contained in files that are distributed to each host in the network. When a service name is encountered, ORACLE7 checks the local SQL*Net V2 file (called TNSNAMES.ORA) to determine which protocol, host name, and database name to use during the connection. Thus, all of the connection information is removed from the data dictionary and placed in external files.

When using SQL*Net V2, you must know the name of the service that points to the remote database. For example, if the service name 'HQ' specifies the connection parameters for the database you need, then 'HQ' should be used as the connect string in the create database link command. The following example shows a private database link, using a default login and a SQL*Net V2 service name.

```
create database link REMOTE_CONNECT
using 'HQ';
```

When this link is used, ORACLE7 will check the TNSNAMES.ORA file on the local host to determine which database to connect to. When it attempts to log into that database, it will use the current user's username and password.

The TNSNAMES.ORA files for a network of databases should be coordinated by the DBAs for those databases. A typical entry in the TNSNAMES.ORA file (for a network using the TCP/IP protocol) is shown in the following listing.

```
HQ =(DESCRIPTION=
      (ADDRESS=
            (PROTOCOL=TCP)
            (HOST=HOST1)
            (PORT=1521))
      (CONNECT DATA=
            (SID=remote)))
```

In this listing, the `'HQ'` service name is mapped to a connect descriptor. This descriptor tells the database which protocol to use (TCP/IP), and which host (HOST1) and database (remote) to connect to. The "port" information refers to the port on the host that will be used for the connection; that data is environment-specific. Different protocols will have different keywords, but they all must convey the same content.

Using Synonyms for Location Transparency

Over the life span of an application, its data will very likely move from one database to another, or from one host to another. Therefore, it will simplify maintenance of an application if the exact physical location of a database object is shielded from the user (and the application).

The best way to implement such location transparency is through the use of synonyms. Instead of writing applications (or SQLPLUS reports) that contain queries that specify a table's owner, such as

```
select *
from TALBOT.WORKER;
```

you should instead create a synonym for that table, and then reference the synonym in the query:

```
create synonym WORKER
for TALBOT.WORKER;

select *
from WORKER;
```

The logic required to find the data has thus been moved out of your application and into the database. Moving the table location logic to the database will be a benefit any time you move the table (for example, when moving from a development database to a test database).

In addition to hiding the ownership of tables from an application, you can also hide the data's physical location through the use of database links and synonyms. By using local synonyms for remote tables, you move another layer of logic out of the application and into the database. For example, the local synonym WORKERSKILL, as defined in the following listing, refers to a table that is located in a different database, on a different host. If that table ever moves, only the link has to be changed; the application code, which uses the synonym, will not change.

```
create synonym WORKERSKILL
for WORKERSKILL@REMOTE_CONNECT;
```

If the remote account used by the database link is not the owner of the object being referenced, then you have two options. First, you can reference an available synonym in the remote database:

```
create synonym WORKERSKILL
for WORKERSKILL@REMOTE_CONNECT;
```

where WORKERSKILL, in the remote account used by the database link, is a synonym for another user's WORKERSKILL table.

The second option is to include the remote owner's name in creating the local synonym, as shown in the following listing.

```
create synonym WORKERSKILL
for TALBOT.WORKERSKILL@REMOTE_CONNECT;
```

These two examples will result in the same functionality for your queries, but there are differences. The second example, which includes the owner name, is potentially more difficult to maintain because you are not using a synonym in the remote database. The two examples also have slightly different functionality when the **describe** command is used. If the remote account accesses a synonym (instead of a table), then you will not be able to **describe** that table, even though you can **select** from it. For **describe** to work correctly, you will need to use the format shown in the last example and specify the owner.

Using the User Pseudo-column in Views

The User pseudo-column becomes very useful when you are using remote data access methods. For example, you may not wish for all remote users to see all records in a table. To solve this problem, you must think of remote users as special users within your database. To enforce the data restriction, you will need to create a view that the remote accounts will access.

But what can you use in the **where** clause to properly restrict the records? The User pseudo-column, combined with properly selected usernames, will allow you to enforce this restriction.

As you may recall from Chapter 3, queries used to define views may also reference *pseudo-columns*. A pseudo-column is a "column" that returns a value when it is selected, but is not an actual column in a table. The User pseudo-column, when selected, will always return the Oracle username that executed the query. So if a column in the table contains usernames, then those values can be compared against the User pseudo-column to restrict its records, as shown in the following example. In this example, the NAME table is queried. If the value of its Name column is the same as the name of the user entering the query, then records will be returned.

```
create or replace view RESTRICTED_NAMES
as select * from NAME
where Name = User;
```

NOTE
We need to shift our point of view for a moment. Since this discussion concerns operations on the database that owns the table being queried, that database will be referred to as the "local" database, and the users from other databases will be referred to as "remote" users.

When restricting remote access to the rows of your table, you should first consider which columns would be the best to use for the restriction. There are usually logical divisions to the data within a table, such as Department or State. For each distinct division, create a separate user account in your local database. For this example, let's add a Department column to the WORKER table.

```
alter table WORKER
add
(Department varchar2(10));
```

Suppose you had four major departments represented in your WORKER table, and you created an account for each department. You could then set up each remote user's database link to use his or her specific user account in your local database. For this example, let us assume the departments are called NORTH, EAST, SOUTH, and WEST. For each of the departments, there would be a specific database link created. For example, the members of the SOUTH department would use the database link shown in the following listing.

```
create database link SOUTH_LINK
connect to SOUTH identified by PAW
using 'T:host1:remote';
```

The database link shown in this example is a private database link with an explicit login to the SOUTH account in the remote database, using a SQL*Net V1 connect string.

When remote users query via their database links (such as SOUTH_LINK from the previous example), they will then be logged into the local database, with their Department name (such as SOUTH) as their username. Thus, the value of the User column for any table that user queries will be 'SOUTH'.

Now create a view of your base table, comparing the User pseudo-column to the value of the Department column in the view's **where** clause:

```
create or replace view RESTRICTED_WORKER
as select *
from WORKER
where Department = User;
```

A user who connects via the SOUTH_LINK database link—and thus is logged in as the SOUTH user—would only be able to see the WORKER records that had a Department value equal to 'SOUTH'. If users are accessing your table from a remote database, then their logins are occurring via database links—and you know the local accounts they are using because you set them up.

This type of restriction can also be performed in the remote database instead of in the database where the table resides. Users in the remote database may create views within their databases of the form

```
create or replace view SOUTH_WORKERS
as select *
from WORKER@REMOTE_CONNECT
where Department = 'SOUTH';
```

In this case, the Department restriction is still in force, but it is administered locally, and the Department restriction is coded into the view's query. Choosing between the two restriction options (locally or remotely) is based on the number of accounts required for the desired restriction to be enforced.

Dynamic Links: Using the SQLPLUS copy Command

The SQLPLUS **copy** command is an underutilized, underappreciated command. It allows data to be copied between databases (or within the same database) via SQLPLUS. Although it allows the user to select which columns to copy, it works best when all of the columns of a table are being chosen. The greatest benefit from using this command is its ability to commit after each array of data has been processed (explained shortly). This in turn generates transactions that are of a manageable size.

Consider the case of a large table (let's use WORKER). What if the WORKER table has 100,000 rows that use a total of 100M of space, and you need to make a copy of that table into a different database? The easiest option involves creating a database link and then using that link in a **create table ... as select** command. This option is shown in the following listing.

```
create database link REMOTE_CONNECT
connect to TALBOT identified by LEDGER
using 'T:host1:remote';

create table WORKER
as
select * from WORKER@REMOTE_CONNECT;
```

The first command creates the database link, and the second creates a new table based on all of the data in the remote table.

Unfortunately, this option creates a very large transaction (all 100,000 rows would be inserted into the new table as a single transaction). This will place a large burden on internal ORACLE7 structures called *rollback segments*. Rollback segments store the prior image of data until that data is committed to the database. Since this table is being populated by a single **insert,** a single, large transaction is generated, which will very likely exceed the space in the currently available rollback segments. This failure will, in turn, cause the table creation to fail.

To break the transaction into smaller entries, use the SQLPLUS **copy** command, The syntax for this command is

```
copy from
[remote username/remote password@connect string]
[to username/password@connect string]
{append|create|insert|replace}
table name
using subquery;
```

If the current account is to be the destination of the copied data, then the word **to** plus the local username, password, and connect string are not necessary. If the current account is to be the source of the copied data, then the remote connection information for the data source is not necessary.

To set the transaction entry size, use the SQLPLUS **set** command to set a value for the **arraysize** parameter. This determines the number of records that will be retrieved in each "batch." The **copycommit** parameter tells SQLPLUS how many batches should be committed at one time. The following SQLPLUS script accomplishes the same data-copying goal that the **create table as** command met; however, it breaks up the single transaction into multiple transactions. In this

OPTION	DESCRIPTION
APPEND	Inserts the rows into the destination table. Automatically creates the table if it does not exist.
CREATE	Creates the table, then inserts the rows.
INSERT	Inserts the rows into the destination table if it exists; otherwise returns an error. When using INSERT, all columns must be specified in the USING subquery.
REPLACE	Drops the existing destination table and replaces it with a new table containing the copied data.

TABLE 20-1. *Data options for the* ***copy*** *command*

example, the data is committed after every 1,000 records. This reduces the transaction's rollback segment entry size needed from 100M to 1M.

```
set copycommit 1
set arraysize 1000

copy from TALBOT/LEDGER@T:host1:remote -
create WORKER -
using -
select * from WORKER
```

NOTE
Except for the last line, each line in the **copy** command must be terminated with a dash (-), since this is a SQLPLUS command.

The different data options within the **copy** command are described in Table 20-1. The feedback provided by this command may be confusing at first. After the final commit is complete, the database reports to the user the number of records that were committed in the *last* batch. It does not report the total number of records committed (unless they are all committed in a single batch).

Connecting to a Remote Database

In addition to the inter-database connections described earlier in this chapter, you may also connect directly to a remote database via an Oracle tool. Thus, instead of typing

```
sqlplus username/password
```

and accessing your local database, you can go directly to a remote database. To do this, enter your username and password along with the SQL*Net connect string for the remote database. The following example uses the SQL*Net V1 connect string shown earlier in this chapter.

```
sqlplus username/password@T:host1:remote
```

This command will log you directly into the "remote" database. The host configuration for this type of login is shown in Figure 20-3. As shown there, the "Branch" host has the Oracle tools (such as SQLPLUS) on it, and is running SQL*Net. The "Remote" host is running SQL*Net and has an Oracle database. There may or may not be a database on the "Branch" host; specifying the SQL*Net connect string to the remote database forces Oracle to ignore any local databases.

For SQL*Net V2, you would use the service name as the connect string, as shown in the following example. This example uses the 'HQ' service name shown earlier in this chapter.

```
sqlplus username/password@HQ
```

As you can see from Figure 20-3, there are very few hardware requirements for the "Branch" host. All it has to support is the front-end tool and SQL*Net. This is a typical configuration for client-server applications. The client machine, such as the

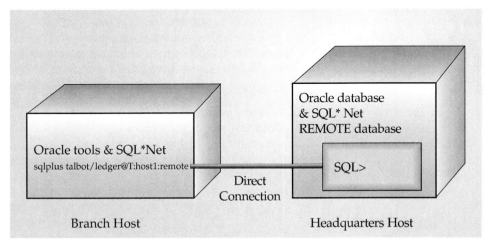

FIGURE 20-3. *Sample Architecture for a Remote Connection*

"Branch" host, is used primarily for presentation of the data via the database access tools. The server side, such as the "Headquarters" host, is used to maintain the data and process the data access requests from users.

Management Tools: Oracle*Names

There are a number of management tasks involved in the maintenance of remote data access. In this chapter you have seen synonyms, database links, views, and data-driven usernames. Within database links, there are SQL*Net V1 connect strings, SQL*Net V2 service names, and TNSNAMES.ORA files. Oracle*Names, which was released with SQL*Net 2.1, can be used to manage many of these.

With Oracle*Names, all of the tasks of managing distributed databases are handled via a global naming service, available to all hosts in a network. It is used to store information about

- connect strings
- connect descriptors
- database links
- object aliases

This changes the way in which database links are resolved. Previously, when a database link was specified, the database first looked at the user's private database links. If none with the matching name was found, then the available public database links were checked.

Oracle*Names adds an additional level to this. Now, if the first two checks do not return a match for the database link name, then the Oracle*Names server's list of global database link names is searched for the database link. If the link name is found there, Oracle*Names will return the link's specifications and resolve the query.

This greatly simplifies the administration of *location transparency*—the ability to mask the physical location of data—in a distributed environment. The information related to remote data access is now stored in a central location. The impact of this is felt every time a part of an object's location is changed. For example, if there were multiple links using explicit connections to a single remote database, then a pre-Oracle*Names modification to the user's password would require dropping and re-creating multiple database links. With Oracle*Names, this change is made once.

Oracle*Names also supports the *Domain Name Service* (DNS) structure that Oracle introduced with SQL*Net V2. DNS allows hosts within a network to be hierarchically organized. Each node within the organization is called a *domain*, and each domain is labeled by its function. These functions may include "COM" for companies and "EDU" for schools. Each domain may have many subdomains. Each server will be given a unique name within the network; its name contains information about how it fits into the network hierarchy. Oracle's DNS allows network hierarchies to be specified; thus, a server may be identified as HR.HQ.ACME.COM, which would be interpreted as the HR server in the HQ network of the ACME Company.

If connect descriptors are also stored in Oracle*Names, then the need for manually maintaining multiple copies of the TNSNAMES.ORA file rapidly diminishes. The centralized Oracle*Names server defines the relationships among the network objects. The database network may be divided into administrative regions, and the management tasks may be likewise divided. A change to one region will be transparently propagated to the other regions.

When implementing an application that uses SQL*Net V2.1, Oracle*Names will greatly simplify administration.

CHAPTER 21

Triggers

A *trigger* defines an action the database should take when some database-related event occurs. Triggers may be used to supplement declarative referential integrity, to enforce complex business rules, or to audit changes to data. The code within a trigger, called the *trigger body*, is made up of PL/SQL blocks.

The execution of triggers is transparent to the user. Triggers are executed by the database when specific types of data manipulation commands are performed on specific tables. Such commands may include **inserts**, **updates**, and **deletes**. Updates of specific columns may also be used as triggering events.

Because of their flexibility, triggers may supplement referential integrity; they should not be used to replace it. When enforcing the business rules in an application, you should first rely on the declarative referential integrity available with ORACLE7; use triggers to enforce rules that cannot be coded through referential integrity.

Triggers are available in any ORACLE7 database that has installed the Procedural option. This option is part of ORACLE7.1, but is not part of the default installation for ORACLE7.0. If you are using a version of ORACLE7 that precedes ORACLE7.1, you can install the Procedural option during database installation.

Required System Privileges

In order to create a trigger on a table, you must be able to alter that table. Therefore, you must either own the table, have ALTER privilege for the table, or have ALTER ANY TABLE system privilege. In addition, you must have the CREATE TRIGGER system privilege; to create triggers in another user's account (also called a *schema*), you must have CREATE ANY TRIGGER system privilege. The CREATE TRIGGER system privilege is part of the RESOURCE role provided with ORACLE7.

In order to alter a trigger, you must either own the trigger or have the ALTER ANY TRIGGER system privilege. You may also alter triggers by altering the tables they are based on, which requires that you either have the ALTER privilege for that table or the ALTER ANY TABLE system privilege. For information on altering triggers, see the "Enabling and Disabling Triggers" section of this chapter.

Required Table Privileges

Triggers may reference tables other than the one that initiated the triggering event. For example, if you use triggers to audit changes to data in the LEDGER table, then you may insert a record into a different table (say, LEDGER_AUDIT) every time a record is changed in LEDGER. In order to do this, you will need to have privileges to insert into LEDGER_AUDIT (to perform the triggered transaction).

NOTE
The privileges needed for triggered transactions cannot come from roles; they must be granted directly to the creator of the trigger.

Types of Triggers

There are twelve basic types of triggers. A trigger's type is defined by the type of triggering transaction, and by the level at which the trigger is executed. In the following sections you will see descriptions of these classifications, along with relevant restrictions.

Row-Level Triggers

Row-level triggers execute once for each row in a transaction. For the LEDGER table auditing example described above, each row that is changed in the LEDGER table may be processed by the trigger. Row-level triggers are the most common type of triggers; they are often used in data auditing applications. Row-level triggers are also useful for keeping distributed data in sync. Snapshots, which use row-level triggers for this purpose, are described in Chapter 23.

Row-level triggers are created using the **for each row** clause in the **create trigger** command. The syntax for triggers is shown in the "Trigger Syntax" section of this chapter.

Statement-Level Triggers

Statement-level triggers execute once for each transaction. For example, if a single transaction inserted 500 rows into the LEDGER table, then a statement-level trigger on that table would only be executed once. Statement-level triggers therefore are not often used for data-related activities; they are normally used to enforce additional security measures on the types of transactions that may be performed on a table.

Statement-level triggers are the default type of triggers created via the **create trigger** command. The syntax for triggers is shown in the "Trigger Syntax" section of this chapter.

BEFORE and AFTER Triggers

Since triggers occur because of events, they may be set to occur immediately before or after those events. Since the events that execute triggers are database transactions, triggers can be executed immediately before or after **inserts**, **updates**, and **deletes**.

Within the trigger, you will be able to reference the old and new values involved in the transaction. The access required for the old and new data may determine which type of trigger you need. "Old" refers to the data as it existed prior to the transaction. Updates and deletes usually reference old values. "New" values are the data values that the transaction creates (such as the columns in an inserted record).

If you need to set a column value in an inserted row via your trigger, then you will need to use a BEFORE INSERT trigger in order to access the "new" values. Using an AFTER INSERT trigger would not allow you to set the inserted value, since the row will already have been inserted into the table (and thus be "old").

AFTER row-level triggers are frequently used in auditing applications, since they do not fire until the row has been modified. Since the row has been successfully modified, this implies that it has successfully passed the referential integrity constraints defined for that table.

Valid Trigger Types

When combining the different types of triggering actions, there are twelve possible configurations:

BEFORE INSERT row
BEFORE INSERT statement
AFTER INSERT row
AFTER INSERT statement
BEFORE UPDATE row
BEFORE UPDATE statement
AFTER UPDATE row
AFTER UPDATE statement
BEFORE DELETE row
BEFORE DELETE statement
AFTER DELETE row
AFTER DELETE statement

UPDATE triggers may be dependent upon the columns being updated. See the "Trigger Syntax" section of this chapter for further details.

Restrictions for ORACLE7.0

In ORACLE7.0, you may have only one trigger of each type per table. Therefore, you are limited to twelve triggers per table. If a table is used as part of a snapshot, and has a snapshot log associated with it (see Chapter 23), then ORACLE7 will automatically create a series of **AFTER [*command*] row** triggers on the table (where [*command*] can be **insert**, **update**, or **delete**). These triggers will preclude the user from creating any additional **AFTER [*command*] row** triggers on the table. This restriction is not enforced in ORACLE7.1.

Trigger Syntax

The syntax for the **create trigger** command is shown in the following listing.

```
create [or replace] trigger trigger_name
[before|after]
  [delete|insert|update [of column]]
on [User.]TABLE
[for each row][when condition]
[PL/SQL block];
```

Clearly, there is a great deal of flexibility in the design of a trigger. The **before** and **after** keywords indicate whether the trigger should be executed before or after the triggering transaction. The **delete**, **insert**, and **update** keywords (the last of which may include a column list) indicate the type of data manipulation that will constitute a triggering event.

When the **for each row** clause is used, the trigger will be a row-level trigger; otherwise, it will be a statement-level trigger. The **when** clause is used to further restrict when the trigger is executed. The restrictions enforced in the **when** clause may include checks of old and new data values.

For example, suppose we want to monitor any adjustments to an Amount that are greater than 10 percent. The following row-level BEFORE UPDATE trigger will be executed only if the new value of the Amount column is more than 10 percent greater than its old value. This example also illustrates the use of the **new** keyword, which refers to the new value of the column, and the **old** keyword, which refers to the old value of the column.

```
create trigger ledger_bef_upd_row
before update on LEDGER
for each row
when (new.Amount/old.Amount>1.1)
begin
insert into LEDGER_AUDIT
 values (:old.Action_Date, :old.Action, :old.Item,
 :old.Quantity, :old.QuantityType, :old.Rate,
 :old.Amount, :old.Person)
end;
```

Breaking this **create trigger** command into its components makes it easier to understand. First, the trigger is named:

```
create trigger ledger_bef_upd_row
```

The name of the trigger contains the name of the table it acts upon and the type of trigger it is. See the "Naming Triggers" section later in this chapter for information on naming conventions.

```
before update on LEDGER
```

This trigger applies to the LEDGER table. It will be executed **before update** transactions have been committed to the database.

```
for each row
```

Because the **for each row** clause is used, the trigger will apply to each row in the transaction. If this clause is not used, then the trigger will execute only at the statement level.

```
when (new.Amount/old.Amount>1.1)
```

The **when** clause adds further criteria to the triggering condition. The triggering event must not only be an update of the LEDGER table, but also must reflect an increase of over 10 percent in the value of the Amount column.

```
begin
insert into LEDGER_AUDIT
 values (:old.Action_Date, :old.Action, :old.Item,
 :old.Quantity, :old.QuantityType, :old.Rate,
 :old.Amount, :old.Person);
end;
```

The PL/SQL code shown in the previous listing is the trigger body. The commands shown here are to be executed for every **update** of the LEDGER table that passes the **when** condition. In order for this to succeed, the LEDGER_AUDIT table must exist, and the owner of the trigger must have been granted privileges (directly, not via roles) on that table. This particular example inserts the old values from the LEDGER record into the LEDGER_AUDIT table before the LEDGER record is updated.

NOTE
When referencing the **new** and **old** keywords in the PL/SQL block, they are preceded by colons (:).

This example is typical of auditing triggers. The auditing activity is completely transparent to the user who performs the **update** of the LEDGER table.

Combining Trigger Types

Triggers for multiple **insert**, **update**, and **delete** commands on a table can be combined into a single trigger, provided they are all at the same level (row-level or statement-level). The following example shows a trigger that is executed whenever an **insert** or an **update** occurs. Two points (shown in bold) should stand out in this example: the **update** portion of the trigger only occurs when the Amount column is updated, and an **if** clause is used within the PL/SQL block to determine which of the two commands executed the trigger.

```
create trigger ledger_bef_upd_ins_row
before insert or update of Amount on LEDGER
for each row
begin
  IF INSERTING THEN
    insert into LEDGER_AUDIT
    values (:new.Action_Date, :new.Action, :new.Item,
    :new.Quantity, :new.QuantityType, :new.Rate,
    :new.Amount, :new.Person);
  ELSE  -- if not inserting, then we are updating Amount
    insert into LEDGER_AUDIT
    values (:old.Action_Date, :old.Action, :old.Item,
    :old.Quantity, :old.QuantityType, :old.Rate,
    :old.Amount, :old.Person);
end;
```

Again, look at the trigger in its component parts. First, it is named and identified as a **before insert** and **before update** (of Amount) trigger, executing **for each row**.

```
create trigger ledger_bef_upd_ins_row
before insert or update of Amount on LEDGER
for each row
```

The trigger body then follows. In the first part of the trigger body, shown in the following listing, the type of transaction is checked via an **if** clause. The valid transaction types are INSERTING, DELETING, and UPDATING. In this case, the trigger checks to see if the record is being inserted into the LEDGER table. If it is, then the first part of the trigger body is executed. The INSERTING portion of the trigger body inserts the new values of the record into the LEDGER_AUDIT table.

```
begin
  IF INSERTING THEN
    insert into LEDGER_AUDIT
    values (:new.Action_Date, :new.Action, :new.Item,
    :new.Quantity, :new.QuantityType, :new.Rate,
    :new.Amount, :new.Person);
```

Other transaction types can then be checked. In this example, since the trigger executed, the transaction must either be an **insert** or an **update** of the Amount column. Since the **if** clause in the first half of the trigger body checks for inserts, and the trigger is only executed for inserts and updates, the only conditions that should execute the second half of the trigger body are updates of Amount. Therefore, no additional **if** clauses are necessary to determine the transaction type.

This portion of the trigger body is the same as in the previous example: prior to being updated, the old values in the row are written to the LEDGER_AUDIT table.

```
ELSE  -- if not inserting, then we are updating Amount
   insert into LEDGER_AUDIT
     values (:old.Action_Date, :old.Action, :old.Item,
     :old.Quantity, :old.QuantityType, :old.Rate,
     :old.Amount, :old.Person);
end;
```

Combining trigger types in this manner may help you to coordinate trigger development among multiple developers, since it helps to consolidate all of the database events that depend on a single table.

Setting Inserted Values

You may use triggers to set column values during inserts and updates. For example, you may have partially denormalized your LEDGER table to include derived data, such as UPPER(Person). Storing this data in an uppercase format in a column of your table (for this example, UpperPerson) allows you to display data to the users in its natural format while using the uppercase column during queries.

Since UpperPerson is derived data, it may be out of sync with the Person column. That is, there may be times immediately after transactions during which UpperPerson does not equal UPPER(Person). Consider an insert into the LEDGER table; unless your application supplies a value for UpperPerson during inserts, that column's value will be NULL.

To avoid this synchronization problem, you can use a database trigger. Put a BEFORE INSERT and BEFORE UPDATE trigger on the table. They will act at the row level. As shown in the following listing, they will set a new value for UpperPerson every time Person is changed.

```
create trigger ledger_bef_upd_ins_row
before insert or update of Person on LEDGER
for each row
begin
   :new.UpperPerson := UPPER(:new.Person)
end;
```

In this example, the trigger body determines the value for UpperPerson by using the UPPER function on the Person column. This trigger will be executed every time a row is inserted into LEDGER and every time the Person column is updated. The two columns will thus be kept in sync.

In ORACLE7.0, this trigger will conflict with the auditing trigger shown in the previous section. The conflict arises because of the restriction on the number of triggers per table in ORACLE7.0 (see "Restrictions for ORACLE7.0" above). To resolve this conflict, you must either drop one of the triggers or combine the two into a single, larger trigger.

Maintaining Duplicated Data

The method of setting values via triggers, shown in the previous section, can be combined with the remote data access methods described in Chapter 20. Using triggers to duplicate data is redundant in databases that have the distributed option; snapshots serve that purpose (see Chapter 23 for details). However, if you do not have the distributed option, you may use triggers to maintain remote copies (on the same host) of your tables. As with snapshots, you may replicate all or part of the rows in a table.

For example, you may wish to create and maintain a second copy of your application's audit log. By doing so, you will safeguard against a single application wiping out the audit log records created by multiple applications. Duplicate audit logs are frequently used in security monitoring.

Consider the LEDGER_AUDIT table used in the prior examples in this chapter. A second table, LEDGER_AUDIT_DUP, could be created, possibly in a remote database. For this example, assume that a database link called AUDIT_LINK can be used to connect the user to the database in which LEDGER_AUDIT_DUP resides (see Chapter 20 for details on database links).

To automate the populating of the LEDGER_AUDIT_DUP table, the following trigger could be placed on the LEDGER_AUDIT table.

```
create trigger ledger_after_ins_row
before insert on LEDGER_AUDIT
for each row
begin
  insert into LEDGER_AUDIT_DUP@AUDIT_LINK
    values (:new.Action_Date, :new.Action, :new.Item,
    :new.Quantity, :new.QuantityType, :new.Rate,
    :new.Amount, :new.Person);
end;
```

As seen in its header, this trigger executes for each row that is inserted into the LEDGER_AUDIT table. It inserts a single record into the LEDGER_AUDIT_DUP table, in the database defined by the AUDIT_LINK database link. If you are using ORACLE7 with the distributed option, then AUDIT_LINK may point to a database located on a remote server, although you'd be better off using a snapshot in that case (see Chapter 23).

Customizing Error Conditions

Within a single trigger, you may establish different error conditions. For each of the error conditions you define, you may select an error message that appears when the error occurs. The error numbers and messages that are displayed to the user are set via the RAISE_APPLICATION_ERROR procedure. This procedure may be called from within any trigger.

The following example shows a statement-level BEFORE DELETE trigger on the LEDGER table. When a user attempts to **delete** a record from the LEDGER table, this trigger is executed and checks two system conditions: that the day of the week is neither Saturday nor Sunday, and that the Oracle username of the account performing the delete begins with the letters 'FIN'. The trigger's components will be described following the listing.

```
create trigger ledger_bef_del
before delete on LEDGER
declare
  weekend_error EXCEPTION;
  not_finance_user EXCEPTION;
begin
  IF TO_CHAR(SysDate,'DY') = 'SAT' or
     TO_CHAR(SysDate,'DY') = 'SUN' THEN
   RAISE weekend_error;
  END IF;
  IF SUBSTR(User,1,3) <> 'FIN' THEN
   RAISE not_finance_user;
EXCEPTION
  WHEN weekend_error THEN
    RAISE_APPLICATION_ERROR (-20001,
     'Deletions not allowed on weekends');
  WHEN not_finance_user THEN
    RAISE_APPLICATION_ERROR (-20002,
     'Deletions only allowed by Finance users');
end;
```

The header of the trigger defines it as a statement-level BEFORE DELETE trigger.

```
create trigger ledger_bef_del
before delete on LEDGER
```

There are no **when** clauses in this trigger, so the trigger body is executed for all deletes.

The next portion of the trigger declares the names of the two exceptions that are defined within this trigger:

```
declare
  weekend_error EXCEPTION;
  not_finance_user EXCEPTION;
```

The first part of the trigger body contains an **if** clause that uses the TO_CHAR function on the SysDate pseudo-column. If the current day is either Saturday or Sunday, then the WEEKEND_ERROR error condition is executed. This error condition, called an *exception*, must be defined within the trigger body.

```
begin
  IF TO_CHAR(SysDate,'DY') = 'SAT' or
     TO_CHAR(SysDate,'DY') = 'SUN' THEN
   RAISE weekend_error;
  END IF;
```

A second **if** clause checks the User pseudo-column to see if its first three letters are 'FIN'. If the username does not begin with 'FIN', then the NOT_FINANCE_USER exception is executed. In this example, the operator <> is used; this is equivalent to != (meaning "not equals").

```
IF SUBSTR(User,1,3) <> 'FIN' THEN
    RAISE not_finance_user;
```

The final portion of the trigger body tells the trigger how to handle the exceptions. It begins with the keyword EXCEPTIONS, followed by a WHEN clause for each of the exceptions. Each of the exceptions in this trigger calls the RAISE_APPLICATION_ERROR procedure.

The RAISE_APPLICATION_ERROR procedure takes two input parameters: the error number (which must be between -20001 and -20999), and the error message to be displayed. In this example, two different error messages are defined, one for each of the defined exceptions.

```
EXCEPTION
  WHEN weekend_error THEN
    RAISE_APPLICATION_ERROR (-20001,
     'Deletions not allowed on weekends');
  WHEN not_finance_user THEN
    RAISE_APPLICATION_ERROR (-20002,
     'Deletions only allowed by Finance users');
end;
```

The use of the RAISE_APPLICATION_ERROR procedure gives you great flexibility in managing the error conditions that may be encountered within your trigger. For a further description of procedures, see Chapter 22.

Naming Triggers

The name of a trigger should clearly indicate the table it applies to, the DML commands that trigger it, its before/after status, and whether it is a row-level or statement-level trigger. A standard naming convention is particularly important in ORACLE7.0 database, in which you may only have one trigger of each type.

Enabling and Disabling Triggers

Unlike declarative integrity constraints (such as NOT NULL and PRIMARY KEY), triggers do not affect all rows in a table. They only affect transactions of the specified type, and then only while the trigger is enabled. Any transactions created prior to a trigger's creation will not be affected by the trigger.

By default, a trigger is enabled when it is created. However, there are situations in which you may wish to disable a trigger. The two most common reasons involve data loads. During large data loads, you may wish to disable triggers that would execute during the load. Disabling the triggers during data loads may dramatically improve the performance of the data load. Once the data has been loaded, you will need to manually perform the data manipulation that the trigger would have performed had it been enabled during the data load.

The second data load-related reason for disabling a trigger occurs when a data load fails and has to be performed a second time. In such a case, it is likely that the data load partially succeeded—and thus the trigger was executed for a portion of the data load records. During a subsequent data load, the same records would be inserted. Thus, it is possible that the same trigger will be executed twice for the same transaction (when that transaction occurs during both loads). Depending on the nature of the transactions and the triggers, this may not be desirable. If the trigger was enabled during the failed load, then it may need to be disabled prior to the start of a second data load process. Once the data has been loaded, you will need to manually perform the data manipulation that the trigger would have performed had it been enabled during the data load.

To enable a trigger, use the **alter trigger** command with the **enable** keyword. In order to use this command, you must either own the table or have ALTER ANY TRIGGER system privilege. A sample **alter trigger** command is shown in the following listing.

```
alter trigger ledger_bef_upd_row enable;
```

A second method of enabling triggers uses the **alter table** command, with the **enable all triggers** clause. You may not enable specific triggers with this command; you must use the **alter trigger** command to achieve that. The following example shows the usage of the **alter table** command.

```
alter table LEDGER enable all triggers;
```

To use the **alter table** command , you must either own the table or have ALTER ANY TABLE system privilege.

You can disable triggers using the same basic commands (requiring the same privileges) with modifications to their clauses. For the **alter trigger** command, use the **disable** clause:

```
alter trigger ledger_bef_upd_row disable;
```

For the **alter table** command, use the **disable all triggers** clause, as shown in the following listing.

```
alter table LEDGER disable all triggers;
```

Replacing Triggers

The body of a trigger cannot be altered. As shown in the previous sections, the status of a trigger is the only portion that can be altered; to alter its body, a trigger must be re-created or replaced.

When replacing a trigger, use the **create or replace trigger** command (see "Trigger Syntax," above). Using the **or replace** option will maintain any grants made for the original version of the trigger. The alternative solution, dropping and re-creating the trigger, drops all grants made for the trigger.

Dropping Triggers

Triggers may be dropped via the **drop trigger** command. In order to drop a trigger, you must either own the trigger or have the DROP ANY TRIGGER system privilege. An example of this command is shown in the following listing.

```
drop trigger ledger_bef_upd_row;
```

CHAPTER 22

Procedures

Sophisticated business rules and application logic can be stored as *procedures* within ORACLE7. Stored procedures—groups of SQL and PL/SQL statements—allow you to move code that enforces business rules from your application to your database. As a result, the code will be stored once for use by multiple applications. Because ORACLE7 supports stored procedures, the code within your applications should become more consistent and easier to maintain.

You may group procedures and other PL/SQL commands into *packages.* In the following sections, you will see implementation details and recommendations for packages, procedures, and *functions* (procedures which can return values to the user). Depending on the version of the ORACLE7 RDBMS you are using, additional function extensions are available.

You may experience performance gains when using procedures, for two reasons. First, the processing of complex business rules may be performed within the database—and therefore by the server. In client-server applications, shifting complex processing from the application (on the client) to the database (on the server) may dramatically improve your performance. Second, since the procedural code is stored within the database and is fairly static, you may also benefit from the reuse of the same queries within the database. The Shared SQL Area in the System Global Area will store the parsed versions of the executed commands. Thus, the second time a procedure is executed, it may be able to take advantage of the parsing that was previously performed, improving the performance of the procedure's execution.

In addition to these advantages, your application development efforts may also benefit. By consolidating business rules within the database, they no longer need to be written into each application, saving time during application creation and simplifying the maintenance process.

Procedural objects (procedures, packages, and functions) can only be created in ORACLE7 databases that have installed the procedural option. The procedural option is part of ORACLE7.1; if you are using ORACLE7.0, then you will need to install the procedural option during the database installation and creation process.

Required System Privileges

In order to create a procedural object, you must have the CREATE PROCEDURE system privilege (which is part of the RESOURCE role). If the procedural object will be in another user's schema, then you must have CREATE ANY PROCEDURE system privilege.

Executing Procedures

Once a procedural object has been created, it may be executed. When a procedural object is executed, it relies on the table privileges of its owner, *not* those of the user who is executing it. A user executing a procedure does not need to have been granted access to the tables that the procedure accesses.

To allow other users to execute your procedural object, **grant** them EXECUTE privilege on that object, as shown in the following example.

```
grant execute on MY_PROCEDURE to Talbot;
```

The user Talbot will now be able to execute the procedure named MY_PROCEDURE—even if he does not have privileges on any of the tables that MY_PROCEDURE uses. If you do not **grant** EXECUTE privilege to users, then they must have the EXECUTE ANY PROCEDURE system privilege in order to execute the procedure.

When executed, procedures usually have variables passed to them. For example, a procedure that interacts with the LEDGER table may accept a value for the Person column as its input. In this example, we will assume that the procedure creates a new record in the WORKER table when a new employee is first paid (causing a LEDGER entry). This procedure can be called from any application within the database (provided the user calling the procedure has been granted EXECUTE privilege for it).

The syntax used to execute a procedure depends on the environment from which the procedure is being called. From within SQLPLUS, a procedure can be executed by using the **execute** command, followed by the procedure name. Any arguments to be passed to the procedure must be enclosed in parentheses following the procedure name, as shown in the following example (which uses a procedure called NEW_WORKER).

```
execute NEW_WORKER('ADAH TALBOT');
```

The command shown in the preceding example will execute the NEW_WORKER procedure, passing to it the value 'ADAH TALBOT'.

From within another procedure, function, package, or trigger, the procedure can be called without the **execute** command. If the NEW_WORKER procedure was called from a trigger on the LEDGER table, then the body of that trigger may include the command

```
NEW_WORKER(:new.Person);
```

In this example, the NEW_WORKER procedure will be executed using the new value of the Person column as its input. See Chapter 21 for further information on the use of old and new values within triggers.

To execute a procedure owned by another user, you must either create a synonym for that procedure or reference the owner's name during the execution, as shown in the following listing.

```
execute George.NEW_WORKER('ADAH TALBOT');
```

The command shown in the preceding example will execute the NEW_WORKER procedure owned by George. Alternatively, a synonym for the procedure could be created using the command

```
create synonym NEW_WORKER for George.NEW_WORKER;
```

The owner of that synonym would then no longer need to refer to the procedure's owner in order to execute the procedure. You could simply enter the command

```
execute NEW_WORKER('ADAH TALBOT');
```

and the synonym would point to the proper procedure.

When executing remote procedures, the name of a database link must be specified (see Chapter 20 for information on database links). The name of the database link must be specified after the procedure's name but before the variables, as shown in the following example.

```
execute NEW_WORKER@REMOTE_CONNECT('ADAH TALBOT');
```

The command shown in the preceding example uses the REMOTE_CONNECT database link to access a procedure called NEW_WORKER in a remote database. To make the location of the procedure transparent to the user, a synonym may be created for the remote procedure, as shown in the following example.

```
create synonym NEW_WORKER
    for NEW_WORKER@REMOTE_CONNECT;
```

Once this synonym has been created, the user may refer to the remote procedure by using the name of the synonym. ORACLE7 assumes that all remote procedure calls involve updates in the remote database; therefore, you must have installed the distributed option in order to call remote procedures.

Required Table Privileges

Procedural objects may reference tables. In order for the objects to execute properly, the owner of the procedure, package, or function being executed must have privileges on the tables it uses. The user who is executing the procedural object does not need privileges on its underlying tables; such a user only needs to have EXECUTE privilege on the procedural object.

NOTE
The privileges needed for procedures, packages, and functions cannot come from roles; they must be granted directly to the owner of the procedure, package, or function.

Procedures vs. Functions

Unlike procedures, functions can return a value to the caller (procedures cannot return values). This value is returned through the use of the RETURN keyword within the function. Examples of functions are shown in the "**create function** Syntax" section later in this chapter.

Functions may not use the IN OUT or OUT arguments, which *are* available for procedures. These arguments are described in the "**create procedure** Syntax" section later in this chapter.

Procedures vs. Packages

Packages are groups of procedures, functions, variables, and SQL statements grouped together into a single unit. To execute a procedure within a package, you must first list the package name, then the procedure name, as shown in the following example.

```
execute LEDGER_PACKAGE.NEW_WORKER('ADAH TALBOT');
```

In the preceding example, the NEW_WORKER procedure within the LEDGER_PACKAGE package was executed.

Packages allow multiple procedures to use the same variables and cursors. Procedures within packages may be available to the public (as the NEW_WORKER procedure is in the prior example) or they may be private, in which case they are only accessible via commands from within the package (such as calls from other procedures). Examples of packages will be shown in the "**create package** Syntax" section later in this chapter.

Procedures may also include commands that are to be executed each time the package is called, regardless of the procedure or function called within the package. Thus, they not only group procedures, but also give you the ability to execute commands that are not procedure-specific. See the "Initializing Packages" section later in this chapter for an example of code that is executed each time a package is called.

create procedure Syntax

The syntax for the **create procedure** command is

```
create [or replace] procedure [user.] procedure
[(argument [IN¦OUT¦IN OUT] datatype]
[,argument [IN¦OUT¦IN OUT] datatype]...)]
{IS¦AS} block;
```

Both the header and the body of the procedure are created by this command. The NEW_WORKER procedure is created by the command shown in the following listing.

```
create procedure NEW_WORKER (Person_Name IN varchar2)
AS
  BEGIN
    insert into WORKER
      (Name, Age, Lodging)
    values
      (Person_Name, null, null);
  END;
/
```

The NEW_WORKER procedure shown in this example will accept a person's name as its input. It can be called from any application. It inserts a record into the WORKER table, with null values for the Age and Lodging columns.

If a procedure already exists, you may replace it via the **create or replace procedure** command. The benefit of using this command (instead of dropping and re-creating the old procedure) is that the **execute** grants previously made on the procedure will remain in place.

The IN qualifier is used for arguments for which values must be specified when calling the procedure. In the NEW_WORKER examples earlier in this chapter, the Person argument would be declared as IN.

The OUT qualifier signifies that the procedure passes a value back to the caller through this argument.

The IN OUT qualifier signifies that the argument is both an IN and an OUT: a value must be specified for this argument when the procedure is called, and the procedure will return a value to the caller via this argument.

If no qualifier type is specified, then the default value is IN.

block refers to the PL/SQL block that the procedure will execute when called. In the NEW_WORKER example, the block is

```
  BEGIN
    insert into WORKER
      (Name, Age, Lodging)
    values
      (Person_Name, null, null);
  END;
```

The PL/SQL block shown in the preceding example is fairly simple, consisting of a single SQL statement. PL/SQL blocks within procedures can include any DML statement; they cannot be used for DDL statements (such as **create view**).

create function Syntax

The syntax for the **create function** command is very similar to the syntax for the **create procedure** command. It is

```
create [or replace] function [user.] function
[(argument IN datatype
[,argument IN datatype]...)]
RETURN datatype
{IS|AS} block;
```

Both the header and the body of the function are created by this command.

The only valid argument qualifier for functions is IN. Since IN is the default type of qualifier, it may be left out of the **create function** command.

The RETURN keyword specifies the datatype of the function's return value. This can be any valid PL/SQL data type. Every function must have a RETURN clause, since the function must, by definition, return a value to the calling environment.

The following example shows a function named BALANCE_CHECK. This function returns the status of the 'BOUGHT' and 'SOLD' transactions for a Person in the LEDGER table. The input is the Person's name, while the output is the balance for that Person.

```
create function BALANCE_CHECK (Person_Name IN varchar2)
  RETURN NUMBER
  IS
    balance NUMBER(10,2);
  BEGIN
    select sum(decode(Action,'BOUGHT',Amount,0))
      - sum(decode(Action,'SOLD',Amount,0))
      INTO balance
      from LEDGER
    where Person = Person_Name;
  RETURN(balance);
  END;
/
```

To show the differences between procedures and functions, we'll look at this function piece by piece. First, the function is named and the input is specified:

```
create function BALANCE_CHECK (Person_Name IN varchar2)
```

Next, we define the characteristics of the value to be returned. There are three parts to the definition of the variable whose value will be returned: its datatype, its name, and its length. The datatype in this example is set via the RETURN NUMBER clause. The variable is then named **balance**, and is defined here as a NUMBER(10,2). Thus all three parts of the variable—its datatype, its name, and its length—have been defined.

```
RETURN NUMBER
  IS
    balance NUMBER(10,2);
```

The PL/SQL block follows. In the SQL statement, the sum of all 'SOLD' amounts is subtracted from the sum of all 'BOUGHT' amounts for that Person. The difference between those sums is selected **into** a variable called *balance* (which we defined above). The RETURN(balance) command line then returns the value in the *balance* variable to the calling program.

```
BEGIN
    select sum(decode(Action,'BOUGHT',Amount,0))
      - sum(decode(Action,'SOLD',Amount,0))
      INTO balance
      from LEDGER
     where Person = Person_Name;
   RETURN(balance);
   END;
/
```

If a function already exists, you may replace it via the **create or replace function** command. If you use the **or replace** clause, then any EXECUTE grants previously made on the function will remain in place.

If the function is to be created in a different account (also known as a *schema*), then you must have the CREATE ANY PROCEDURE system privilege. If no schema is specified, then the function will be created in your schema. In order to create a function in your schema, you must have been granted the CREATE PROCEDURE system privilege (which is part of the RESOURCE role). Having the privilege to create procedures gives you the privilege to create functions and packages as well.

Referencing Remote Tables in Procedures

Remote tables can be accessed by the SQL statements in procedures. A remote table can be queried via a database link in the procedure, as shown in the following example. In this example, the NEW_WORKER procedure inserts a record into the WORKER table in the database defined by the REMOTE_CONNECT database link.

```
create or replace procedure NEW_WORKER
  (Person_Name IN varchar2)
AS
  BEGIN
      insert into WORKER@REMOTE_CONNECT
         (Name, Age, Lodging)
      values
         (Person_Name, null, null);
  END;
/
```

Data manipulation in remote databases—such as the **insert** shown in the preceding example—will usually require that the distributed option be installed in your database.

Procedures may also make use of local synonyms. For example, you may create a local synonym for a remote table, as shown in the following listing.

```
create synonym WORKER for WORKER@REMOTE_CONNECT;
```

You can then rewrite your procedure to remove the database link specifications:

```
create or replace procedure NEW_WORKER
  (Person_Name IN varchar2)
AS
  BEGIN
      insert into WORKER
         (Name, Age, Lodging)
      values
         (Person_Name, null, null);
  END;
/
```

Removing database link names from procedures allows you to remove the details of the table's physical location from the procedure. If the table changes location, only the synonym will change while the procedure will still be valid.

Debugging Procedures

The SQLDBA and SQLPLUS **show errors** command will display all of the errors associated with the most recently created procedural object. This command will check the USER_ERRORS data dictionary view for the errors associated with the most recent compilation attempt for that procedural object. **show errors** will display the line and column number for each error, as well as the text of the error message.

To view errors associated with previously created procedural objects, you may query USER_ERRORS directly, as shown in the following listing. Queries against USER_ERRORS are not common, since such a query would imply that you have errors with two or more procedures. The following example queries USER_ERRORS for error messages encountered during the creation of the BALANCE_CHECK function shown earlier in this chapter.

```
select Line,      /*Line number of the error./*
       Position,  /*Column number of the error.*/
       Text       /*Text of the error message.*/
  from USER_ERRORS
 where Name = 'BALANCE_CHECK'
   and Type = 'FUNCTION'
 order by Sequence;
```

Valid values for the Type column are PROCEDURE, PACKAGE, FUNCTION, PACKAGE, and PACKAGE BODY.

Two other data dictionary views—ALL_ERRORS and DBA_ERRORS—may also be used to retrieve information about errors involving procedural objects. For information on these views, see Chapter 24.

Using the DBMS_OUTPUT Package

In addition to the debugging information provided by the **show errors** command, you may also use the DBMS_OUTPUT package. DBMS_OUTPUT is created when the procedural option is installed in the database.

To use DBMS_OUTPUT, you must be using either SQLDBA or SQLPLUS. You must issue the

```
set server output on
```

command before executing the procedural object you will be debugging.

DBMS_OUTPUT allows you to use three debugging functions within your package:

PUT	Puts multiple outputs on the same line.
PUT_LINE	Puts each output on a separate line.
NEW_LINE	Used with PUT; signals the end of the current output line.

PUT and PUT_LINE are used to generate the debugging information you wish to display. For example, if you are debugging a procedure that includes a loop (see

"Loop" in the Alphabetical Reference), then you may wish to track the changes in a variable with each pass through the loop. To track the variable's value, you may use a command similar to the one shown in the following listing. In this example, the value of the Amount column is printed, prefixed by the literal string 'Amount:'.

```
PUT_LINE('Amount: '||Amount);
```

You may also use PUT and PUT_LINE outside of loops, but such uses may be better accomplished via the use of the RETURN command in functions (see the **create function** Syntax" section earlier in this chapter).

Extensions for ORACLE7.1 and Above

As of ORACLE7.1, you may use the custom functions you create within your SQL expressions (rather than just calling them via **execute** commands). This allows you to extend the available functionality of SQL, customizing it to your needs. Your functions can be used in the same manner as such ORACLE-provided functions as SUBSTR and TO_CHAR. The only restriction on their application is that your custom functions cannot be used in CHECK or DEFAULT constraints.

The functions you can call either must be stand-alone functions (created via the **create function** command shown in the previous sections) or must be declared in package specifications (to be covered in the "**create package** Syntax" section later in this chapter). Procedures are not directly callable from SQL, but may be called by the functions you create.

For example, consider the BALANCE_CHECK function shown earlier in this chapter. BALANCE_CHECK calculated the difference between the 'BOUGHT' and 'SOLD' balances for people. It had a single input variable—the person's name. However, to see the BALANCE_CHECK results for all of the workers, you would normally need to execute this procedure once for each record in the WORKER table.

Beginning with ORACLE7.1, you can extend SQL and improve the BALANCE_CHECK calculation process. Consider the following query:

```
select Name,
       BALANCE_CHECK(Name)
  from WORKER;
```

This single query will use your custom BALANCE_CHECK function to calculate the difference between the 'BOUGHT' and 'SOLD' balances for all workers.

In order to take advantage of this feature, your functions must follow the same guidelines as ORACLE's functions. Most notably, they must not update the database, and they must contain only IN parameters.

Customizing Error Conditions

As with triggers, you may establish different error conditions within procedural objects (see Chapter 21 for examples of customized error conditions within triggers). For each of the error conditions you define, you may select an error message that will appear when the error occurs. The error numbers and messages that are displayed to the user are set by you via the RAISE_APPLICATION_ERROR procedure, which may be called from within any procedural object.

You can call RAISE_APPLICATION_ERROR from within procedures, packages, and functions. It requires two inputs: the message number and the message text. You get to assign both the message number and the text that will be displayed to the user. This is a very powerful addition to the standard exceptions that are available in PL/SQL (see "Exception" in the Alphabetical Reference).

The following example shows the BALANCE_CHECK function shown earlier in this chapter. Now, however, it has an additional section (shown in **bold**). Titled EXCEPTIONS, the additional section tells ORACLE7 how to handle nonstandard processing. In this example, the NO_DATA_FOUND exception's standard message is overridden via the RAISE_APPLICATION_ERROR procedure.

```
create function BALANCE_CHECK (Person_Name IN varchar2)
  RETURN NUMBER
  IS
    balance NUMBER(10,2);
  BEGIN
    select sum(decode(Action,'BOUGHT',Amount,0))
      - sum(decode(Action,'SOLD',Amount,0))
      INTO balance
      from LEDGER
     where Person = Person_Name;
   RETURN(balance);
  EXCEPTIONS
    WHEN NO_DATA_FOUND THEN
      RAISE_APPLICATION_ERROR (-20100,
        'No BOUGHT or SOLD entries for that Person.');
  END;
/
```

In the preceding example, the NO_DATA_FOUND exception was used. If you wish to define custom exceptions, you need to name the exception in a DECLARE section of the procedure. The DECLARE section of the procedure immediately precedes the BEGIN command. As shown in the following listing, this section should include entries for each of the custom exceptions you have defined, listed as type "EXCEPTION".

```
declare
some_custom_error EXCEPTION;
```

NOTE
If you are using the exceptions already defined within PL/SQL, then you do not need to list them in the declare section of the procedural object. See "Exception" in the Alphabetical Reference for a list of the predefined exceptions.

In the EXCEPTIONS portion of the procedural object's code, you tell the database how to handle the exceptions. It begins with the keyword EXCEPTIONS, followed by a **WHEN** cause for each of the exceptions. Each exception may call the RAISE_APPLICATION_ERROR procedure.

The RAISE_APPLICATION_ERROR procedure takes two input parameters: the error number (which must be between -20001 and -20999) and the error message to be displayed. In the example shown above, only one exception was defined. Multiple exceptions can be defined as shown in the following listing; you may use the **when others** clause to handle all nonspecified exceptions.

```
EXCEPTIONS
    WHEN NO_DATA_FOUND THEN
        RAISE_APPLICATION_ERROR (-20100,
            'No BOUGHT or SOLD entries for that Person.');
    WHEN some_custom_error THEN
        RAISE_APPLICATION_ERROR (-20101,
            'Some custom error message.');
```

The use of the RAISE_APPLICATION_ERROR procedure gives you great flexibility in managing the error conditions that may be encountered within your procedural objects.

Naming Procedures

Procedures and functions should be named according to the business function they perform or business rule they enforce. There should be no ambiguity about their purpose.

The NEW_WORKER procedure shown earlier should be renamed. NEW_WORKER performs a business function—inserting records into WORKER —so its name should reflect that function. A better choice for the name would be ADD_NEW_WORKER. Since it performs a function, a verb (in this case, "add") must describe what it does. The name of the procedure should also include the name of the major table(s) it impacts. If the tables are properly named, then the name of the table should be the direct object upon which the verb acts (in this case, WORKER). See Chapter 27 for further information on object names.

For the sake of consistency, we will continue to refer to the procedure as NEW_WORKER for the remainder of this chapter.

create package Syntax

When creating packages, the package specification and the package body are created separately. Thus there are two commands to use: **create package** for the package specification, and **create package body** for the package body. Both of these commands require that you have the CREATE PROCEDURE system privilege. If the package is to be created in a schema other than your own, then you must have the CREATE ANY PROCEDURE system privilege.

The syntax for creating package specifications is

```
create [or replace] package [user.] package
{IS ¦ AS}
PL/SQL package specification;
```

A *package specification* consists of the list of functions, procedures, variables, constants, cursors, and exceptions that will be available to users of the package.

A sample **create package** command is shown in the following listing. In this example, the LEDGER_PACKAGE package is created. The BALANCE_CHECK function and NEW_WORKER procedure seen earlier in this chapter are shown.

```
create package LEDGER_PACKAGE
AS
   function BALANCE_CHECK(Person_Name VARCHAR2);
   procedure NEW_WORKER(Person_Name IN VARCHAR2);
end
```

NOTE
You may append the name of the procedural object to the **end** clause, as shown in the preceding example. This addition may make it easier to coordinate the logic within your code.

A *package body* contains the PL/SQL blocks and specifications for all of the public objects listed in the package specification. The package body may include objects that are not listed in the package specification; such objects are said to be *private* and are not available to users of the package. Private objects may only be called by other objects within the same package body. A package body may also include code that is run every time the package is invoked, regardless of the part of the package that is executed—see "Initializing Packages" later in this chapter for an example.

The syntax for creating package bodies is

```
create [or replace] package body [user.] package body
{IS ¦ AS}
PL/SQL package body;
```

The name of the package body should be the same as the name of the package specification. Continuing the LEDGER_PACKAGE example, its package body can be created via the **create package body** command shown in the following example.

```
create package body LEDGER_PACKAGE
AS
function BALANCE_CHECK (Person_Name IN varchar2)
  RETURN NUMBER
  IS
    balance NUMBER(10,2);
  BEGIN
     select sum(decode(Action,'BOUGHT',Amount,0))
       - select sum(decode(Action,'SOLD',Amount,0))
       INTO balance
       from LEDGER
       where Person = Person_Name;
   RETURN(balance);
  EXCEPTIONS
     WHEN NO_DATA_FOUND THEN
        RAISE_APPLICATION_ERROR (-20100,
           'No BOUGHT or SOLD entries for that Person.');
  END BALANCE_CHECK;
procedure NEW_WORKER
 (Person_Name IN varchar2)
AS
  BEGIN
     insert into WORKER
       (Name, Age, Lodging)
     values
       (Person_Name, null, null);
  END NEW_WORKER;
END LEDGER_PACKAGE;
/
```

The **create package body** command shown in the preceding example combines the **create function** command for the BALANCE_CHECK function with the **create procedure** command for the NEW_WORKER procedure. The **end** clauses all have the names of their associated objects appended to them (shown in **bold** in the prior listing). Modifying the **end** clauses in this manner helps to clarify the ending points of the object code.

Additional functions, procedures, exceptions, variables, cursors, and constants may be defined within the package body, but they will not be available to the public unless they have been declared within the package specification (via the **create package** command). If a user has been granted EXECUTE privilege on a package, then that user can access any of the public objects that are declared in the package specification.

Initializing Packages

Package specifications may include code that is to be run the first time a user executes the package. In the following example, the LEDGER_PACKAGE package body is modified to include a SQL statement that records the current user's username and the timestamp for the start of the package execution. Two new variables must also be declared in the package body in order to record these values.

Since the two new variables are declared within the package body, they are not available to the public. Within the package body, they are separated from the procedures and functions. The package initialization code is shown in bold in the following listing.

```
create or replace package body LEDGER_PACKAGE
AS
User_Name VARCHAR2;
Entry_Date DATE;
function BALANCE_CHECK (Person_Name IN varchar2)
  RETURN NUMBER
  IS
    balance NUMBER(10,2);
  BEGIN
      select sum(decode(Action,'BOUGHT',Amount,0))
        - select sum(decode(Action,'SOLD',Amount,0))
        INTO balance
        from LEDGER
```

```
      where Person = Person_Name;
   RETURN(balance);
  EXCEPTIONS
     WHEN NO_DATA_FOUND THEN
        RAISE_APPLICATION_ERROR (-20100,
           'No BOUGHT or SOLD entries for that Person.');
  END BALANCE_CHECK;
procedure NEW_WORKER
 (Person_Name IN varchar2)
AS
  BEGIN
     insert into WORKER
        (Name, Age, Lodging)
     values
        (Person_Name, null, null);
  END NEW_WORKER;
BEGIN
  select User, SysDate
     into User_Name, Entry_Date
     from DUAL;
END LEDGER_PACKAGE;
/
```

NOTE
The code that is to be run every time the package is executed is
stored in its own PL/SQL block, at the bottom of the package body.
It does not have its own **end** clause; it uses the package body's
end clause.

Every time the LEDGER_PACKAGE package is executed, the User_Name and
Entry_Date variables will be populated by the query shown in the previous listing.
These two variables can then be used by the functions and procedures within the
package.

To **execute** a procedure or function that is within a package, specify both the
package name and the name of the procedure or function in the **execute**
command, as shown in the following listing.

```
execute LEDGER_PACKAGE.BALANCE_CHECK('ADAH TALBOT');
```

Viewing Source Code for Existing Procedural Objects

The source code for existing procedures, functions, packages, and package bodies can be queried from the following data dictionary views:

USER_SOURCE   For procedural objects owned by the user.

ALL_SOURCE   For procedural objects owned by the user or to which the user has been granted access.

DBA_SOURCE   For all procedural objects in the database.

Select information from the USER_SOURCE view via a query similar to the one shown in the following listing. In this example, the Text column is selected, ordered by the Line number. The Name of the object and the object Type are used to define which object's source code is to be displayed. The following example uses the NEW_WORKER procedure shown earlier in this chapter.

```
select Text
  from USER_SOURCE
 where Name = 'NEW_WORKER'
   and Type = 'PROCEDURE'
 order by Line;

TEXT
---------------------------------------------------
procedure NEW_WORKER
 (Person_Name IN varchar2)
AS
  BEGIN
     insert into WORKER
       (Name, Age, Lodging)
     values
       (Person_Name, null, null);
  END;
```

As shown in the preceding example, the USER_SOURCE view contains one record for each line of the NEW_WORKER procedure. The sequence of the lines is maintained by the Line column; therefore, the Line column should be used in the **order by** clause, as shown.

Valid values for the Type column are PROCEDURE, FUNCTION, PACKAGE, and PACKAGE BODY.

Compiling Procedures, Functions, and Packages

ORACLE7 compiles procedural objects when they are created. However, these may become invalid if the database objects they reference change. The next time the procedural objects are executed, they will be recompiled by the database.

You can avoid this run-time compiling—and the performance degradation it may cause—by explicitly recompiling the procedures, functions, and packages. To recompile a procedure, use the **alter procedure** command, as shown in the following listing. The **compile** clause is the only valid option for this command.

```
alter procedure NEW_WORKER compile;
```

In order to use this command, you must either own the procedure or have ALTER ANY PROCEDURE system privilege.

To recompile a function, use the **alter function** command, with the **compile** clause:

```
alter function NEW_WORKER compile;
```

In order to use this command, you must either own the function or have ALTER ANY PROCEDURE system privilege.

When recompiling packages, you may either recompile both the package specification and body, or just the package body. By default, both the package specification and the package body will be recompiled. You cannot use the **alter function** or **alter procedure** command to recompile functions and procedures stored within a package.

If the source code for the procedures or functions within the package body has changed but the package specification has not, then you may wish to recompile only the package body. In most cases, it is appropriate to recompile both the specification and the package body.

The syntax for the **alter package** command is

```
alter package [user.] package_name
compile [PACKAGE | BODY];
```

To recompile a package, use the **alter package** command shown above, with the **compile** clause, as shown in the following example.

```
alter package LEDGER_PACKAGE compile;
```

In order to use this command, you must either own the package or have ALTER ANY PROCEDURE system privilege. Since neither 'PACKAGE' nor 'BODY' was specified in the preceding example, the default of 'PACKAGE' was used, resulting in the recompilation of both the package specification and the package body.

Replacing Procedures, Functions, and Packages

Procedures, functions, and packages may be replaced via their respective **create or replace** commands. Using the **or replace** clause keeps in place any existing grants that have been made for those objects. If you choose to drop and re-create procedural objects, then you will have to regrant any EXECUTE privileges that had previously been granted.

Dropping Procedures, Functions, and Packages

To drop a procedure, use the **drop procedure** command, as shown in the following listing. In order to drop a procedure, you must either own the procedure or have DROP ANY PROCEDURE system privilege.

```
drop procedure NEW_WORKER;
```

To drop a function, use the **drop function** command. In order to drop a function, you must either own the function or have DROP ANY PROCEDURE system privilege.

```
drop function BALANCE_CHECK;
```

To drop a package, use the **drop package** command, as shown in the following listing. In order to drop a package, you must either own the package or have DROP ANY PROCEDURE system privilege.

```
drop package LEDGER_PACKAGE;
```

To drop a package body, use the **drop package** command with the **body** clause, as shown in the following listing. In order to drop a package body, you must either own the package or have DROP ANY PROCEDURE system privilege.

```
drop package body LEDGER_PACKAGE;
```

CHAPTER 23

Snapshots

In order to improve the performance of an application that uses distributed data, you can make local copies of remote tables. ORACLE7 provides *snapshots* as a means of managing local copies of remote tables. Snapshots can be used to replicate all or part of a single table, or to replicate the result of a query against multiple tables; the refreshes of the replicated data can be done automatically by the database, at time intervals you specify. In this chapter, you'll see the commands and privileges needed to create and manage snapshots, along with relevant examples.

Depending on the version of ORACLE7 you are using, your snapshots may be updateable. In ORACLE7.0, snapshots cannot be updated. In ORACLE7.1, the ability to update snapshots was in Alpha release state when the ORACLE7.1 distributed option was released. If you are not sure of the support status for this feature for your platform for the version you are using, contact your Oracle support representative.

In order to use snapshots, you have to have installed the distributed option within your ORACLE7 database. This option can be installed via the ORACLE7 installation program, or it can be installed after the database has been created.

Using snapshots also requires the use of the procedural option within ORACLE7. The procedural option is part of ORACLE7.1; if you are using ORACLE7.0, then you will need to install the procedural option during the database installation and creation process.

Snapshots Functionality

Snapshots are copies (also known as *replicas*) of remote data, based upon queries. In their simplest form, they can be thought of as a table created by a command such as

```
create table LOCAL_LEDGER
as
select * from LEDGER@REMOTE_CONNECT;
```

In the preceding example, a table named LOCAL_LEDGER is created in the local database and is populated with data from a remote database (defined by the database link named REMOTE_CONNECT). Once the LOCAL_LEDGER table is created, though, its data may immediately become out of sync with the master table (LEDGER@REMOTE_CONNECT). Also, since it is a local table, LOCAL_LEDGER may be updated by local users, further complicating its synchronization with the master table.

Despite these synchronization problems, there are benefits to replicating data in this way. Creating local copies of remote data may be useful to improve the performance of distributed queries, particularly if the tables' data does not change frequently. Snapshots are also useful for decision support environments, during which complex queries are used to periodically "roll up" data into summary tables for use during analysis.

ORACLE7 lets you manage the synchronization of the master table with its snapshots. When snapshots are used, a *refresh interval* is established to schedule refreshes of replicated data. Local updates can be prevented, and transaction-based refreshes can be used. Transaction-based refreshes, available for some types of snapshots, send from the master database only those rows that have changed for the snapshot. This capability, described in the "Simple vs. Complex Snapshots" and "**create snapshot log** Syntax" sections later in this chapter, may significantly improve the performance of your snapshot refreshes.

Extensions for ORACLE7.1 and Above

Since snapshots were first introduced in ORACLE7.0, several new features have been added. Beginning with ORACLE7.1, you can create *refresh groups*—sets of snapshots that are refreshed as a group. If related snapshots are not refreshed as a group, then you may encounter referential integrity inconsistencies between related snapshots. The use and management of refresh groups is covered in the "Using Snapshot Refresh Groups" section later in this chapter.

Another feature that is available with ORACLE7.1 and above is the ability to update snapshots. This feature was in Alpha release when ORACLE7.1 was released. If you are not sure of the support status for this feature for your platform for the version you are using, contact your Oracle support representative.

Required System Privileges

In order to create a snapshot, you must have the privileges needed to create the underlying objects that the snapshot will use. You must have the CREATE SNAPSHOT, CREATE TABLE, CREATE VIEW, and CREATE INDEX (only for simple snapshots) system privileges. In addition, you must have either the UNLIMITED TABLESPACE system privilege or a sufficient specified space quota in a local tablespace.

The underlying objects that the snapshot will use are stored in your user account (also called a *schema*). If the snapshot is to be created in a schema other than your own, then you must have the CREATE ANY SNAPSHOT system privilege, as well as the CREATE ANY TABLE, CREATE ANY VIEW, and CREATE ANY INDEX (only for simple snapshots) system privileges. In addition, you must have either the UNLIMITED TABLESPACE system privilege or a sufficient specified space quota in a local tablespace.

Snapshots of remote tables require queries of remote tables; therefore, you must have privileges to use a database link that accesses the remote database. The link you use can either be a public or a private one. If the database link is private, then you will need to have the CREATE DATABASE LINK system privilege. See Chapter 20 for further information on database links.

Required Table Privileges

When creating a snapshot, you will reference tables in a remote database via a database link. The account that the database link uses in the remote database must have access to the tables and views used by the database link. You cannot create a snapshot based on objects owned by the user SYS.

Within the local database, you can grant SELECT privilege on your snapshot to other local users. Since most snapshots are read-only (updateable snapshots are only available in later versions of ORACLE7), no additional grants are necessary. If, however, you will be using a later version of ORACLE7.1 and wish to create an updateable snapshot, then you must grant your users UPDATE privilege on both the snapshot and the underlying local table it accesses. For information on the local objects created by snapshots, see the "Local and Remote Objects Created" section under the "**create snapshot** Syntax" section later in this chapter.

Simple vs. Complex Snapshots

The queries that form the basis of snapshots are grouped into two categories: *simple* and *complex*. If a snapshot uses a simple query (described below), then it is a simple snapshot. If the snapshot uses a complex query (that is, a query that does not qualify as a simple query), then it is a complex snapshot. The distinction between simple and complex snapshots affects the options that are available to you during snapshot refreshes. Those options will be described in the "Refreshing Snapshots" section later in this chapter, but it is important to keep these distinctions in mind while you are first considering how you will use snapshots.

A simple query

- selects rows from only one table (not a view).

- does not perform any set operations, joins, subqueries, **group by**s, or **connect by**s.

The result set of a simple query will contain records that each map to a single record in the master table. A simple snapshot does not need to contain all of the records from the master table; a **where** clause can be used to restrict the rows returned. If a snapshot uses a simple query, then it is a simple snapshot.

A complex snapshot is one whose query violates either of the rules specified for a simple snapshot. Therefore, any snapshot whose query contains a subquery or a **group by** clause is, by definition, a complex snapshot.

You do not specify the type (simple or complex) of snapshot to use when you create a snapshot. ORACLE7 will examine the snapshot's query and determine the snapshot type and the default refresh options available for your snapshot. You may override these options, as shown in the next section.

create snapshot Syntax

The syntax for creating a snapshot is shown in the following listing. Examples will be shown following the command description.

```
create snapshot [user.] snapshot
{ [ PCTFREE integer ¦
     PCTUSED integer ¦
     INITRANS integer ¦
     MAXTRANS integer ¦
     TABLESPACE tablespace ¦
     STORAGE storage] ¦
  [CLUSTER cluster (column[,column]...]}
 [REFRESH [FAST ¦ COMPLETE ¦ FORCE]
     [START WITH date] [NEXT date]]
AS query;
```

There are four distinct sections of the **create snapshot** command. First, there is the header, in which the snapshot is named (the first line in the listing). The snapshot will be created in your user account (schema) unless a different username is specified in the header. In the second section, the storage parameters for the snapshot are set. The storage parameters will be applied to a table that will be created in the local database to store the replicated data. For information about the available storage parameters, see the "Storage" entry in the Alphabetical Reference.

In the third section, the REFRESH options are set. The REFRESH option specifies the mechanism ORACLE7 should use when refreshing the snapshot. The three options available are FAST, COMPLETE, and FORCE. Fast refreshes are only available for simple snapshots; they use tables called *snapshot logs* to send specific rows from the master table to the snapshot. Complete refreshes completely re-create the snapshot. The FORCE option for refreshes tells ORACLE to use a fast refresh if it is available; otherwise, a complete refresh will be used. If you have created a simple snapshot, but want to use complete refreshes, specify REFRESH COMPLETE in your **create snapshot** command. The refresh options will be further described in the "Refreshing Snapshots" section later in this chapter.

The fourth section of the **create snapshot** command is the query that the snapshot will use. You can create snapshots of tables that are within your local database (to automate a refresh schedule, for example), but snapshots are usually created based on queries of remote tables.

The following example creates a snapshot called LOCAL_LEDGER in a local database, based on a remote table named LEDGER that is accessible via the REMOTE_CONNECT database link.

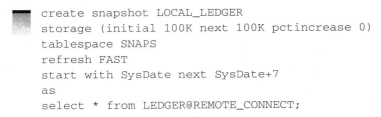

```
create snapshot LOCAL_LEDGER
storage (initial 100K next 100K pctincrease 0)
tablespace SNAPS
refresh FAST
start with SysDate next SysDate+7
as
select * from LEDGER@REMOTE_CONNECT;
```

The command shown in the preceding example will create a simple snapshot called LOCAL_LEDGER. Its underlying table will be created with the specified storage parameters, in a tablespace named SNAPS. Since the data in the snapshot's local base table will be changing over time, it is usually worthwhile to store snapshots in their own tablespace (SNAPS, in this example). Since the example creates a simple snapshot, the FAST refresh option is specified. The snapshot's query specifies that the entire LEDGER table, with no modifications, is to be copied to the local database. As soon as the LOCAL_LEDGER snapshot is created, its underlying table will be populated with the LEDGER data. Thereafter, the snapshot will be refreshed every seven days. The storage parameters that are not specified will use the default values for those parameters for the SNAPS tablespace.

The following example creates a complex snapshot named LOCAL_LEDGER_TOTALS in a local database, based on a remote table named LEDGER in a database accessed via the REMOTE_CONNECT database link. The major differences between this snapshot and the LOCAL_LEDGER snapshot are shown in bold in the following listing.

```
create snapshot LOCAL_LEDGER_TOTALS
storage (initial 50K next 50K pctincrease 0)
tablespace SNAPS
refresh COMPLETE
start with SysDate next SysDate+7
as
select Person, Action, SUM(Amount) Sum_Amount
  from LEDGER@REMOTE_CONNECT
group by Person, Action;
```

The query in the LOCAL_LEDGER_TOTALS example groups the Amount values by Person and Action (in the LEDGER table, the Action values are 'BOUGHT', 'SOLD', 'PAID', and 'RECEIVED').

There are several important points to note about the two examples shown in this section.

1. The **group by** query used in the LOCAL_LEDGER_TOTALS snapshot could be performed in SQLPLUS against the LOCAL_LEDGER snapshot. That is, the **group by** operation can be performed outside of the snapshot.

2. Since LOCAL_LEDGER_TOTALS uses a **group by** clause, it is a complex snapshot. Therefore, only complete refreshes may be used. LOCAL_LEDGER, as a simple snapshot, can use fast refreshes.

The two snapshots shown in the preceding examples reference the same table. Since one of the snapshots is a simple snapshot that replicates all columns and all rows of the master table, the second snapshot may at first appear to be redundant. However, there are times when the second, complex snapshot is the more useful of the two.

How can this be? First, remember that the snapshots are being used to service the query needs of local users. If those users always perform **group by** operations in their queries, and their grouping columns are fixed, then LOCAL_LEDGER_TOTALS may be more useful to them. Second, if the transaction volume on the master LEDGER table is very high, or the master LEDGER table is very small, then there may not be a significant difference in the refresh times of the fast and complete refreshes. The most appropriate snapshot is the one that is most productive for your users.

Local and Remote Objects Created

When you create a snapshot, a number of objects are created in the local and remote databases. The supporting objects created within a database are the same for both simple and complex snapshots. With simple snapshots, you have the ability to create additional objects called *snapshot logs*, which will be discussed in the **"create snapshot log** Syntax" section later in this chapter.

Consider the simple snapshot shown in the last section:

```
create snapshot LOCAL_LEDGER
storage (initial 100K next 100K pctincrease 0)
tablespace SNAPS
refresh FAST
start with SysDate next SysDate+7
as
select * from LEDGER@REMOTE_CONNECT;
```

Within the local database, this command will create the following objects in the snapshot owner's schema:

- A table named SNAP$_LOCAL_LEDGER that is the *local base table* for the snapshot of the remote table. This table contains the replicated data plus an extra column for the master ROWIDs.

- A view named LOCAL_LEDGER that is accessed by users of the local snapshot.

- A view named MVIEW$_LOCAL_LEDGER that is used by the database during refreshes. This view is only used by the RDBMS, never by the users.

- If the snapshot is a simple snapshot, then ORACLE7 will create an index, named PK$_LOCAL_LEDGER, on the snapshot's local base table (SNAP$_LOCAL_LEDGER).

NOTE
Because ORACLE7 uses the snapshot name in the name of its supporting objects, the snapshot's name should be kept to less than 23 characters.

There is only one permissible change that should be made to these underlying objects: the SNAP$_LOCAL_LEDGER table should be indexed to reflect the query paths that are normally used by your local users. If you do index the snapshot's local base table, then you need to factor in your indexes' storage requirements when you estimate the snapshot's space needs. See the "Indexing Snapshot Tables" section later in this chapter for further details.

When you, as a user in the local database, query the LOCAL_LEDGER snapshot, you are actually querying the LOCAL_LEDGER view of the SNAP$_LOCAL_LEDGER table. This layer was put in place to prevent direct access to the underlying table. If you are using your snapshots in read-only mode, then ORACLE effectively prevents updates of the snapshot's local base table. And since LOCAL_LEDGER is a view, you cannot create an additional simple snapshot based on it.

There are no supporting objects created in the remote database unless you use snapshot logs to record changes to rows in the master table. Snapshot logs are described in the "**create snapshot log** Syntax" section of this chapter.

Snapshot Naming Considerations
Since ORACLE7 uses the snapshot's name as the basis for the names of the snapshot's supporting objects, a snapshot's name cannot exceed 23 characters in length. Otherwise, its supporting objects' names will exceed the ORACLE7 maximum of 30 characters in length.

The name given to a snapshot used by an application should make it obvious to the application administrator that a snapshot is being used. In the example shown in the previous section, the snapshot was named LOCAL_LEDGER—implying that there is a remote copy of the LEDGER table somewhere. Since it uses the generic prefix "LOCAL", nothing is implied about its content. If the snapshot performs some restriction on the rows or columns returned, then those actions should be reflected in the snapshot's name. For example, a simple snapshot of the LEDGER table that only replicates the current year's data may be called LOCAL_CURR_YEAR_LEDGER.

In order to use the same application on multiple databases, the database object names should be the same. Therefore, in your local database, you may wish to create a synonym that points to your snapshot. That synonym may be named after the master table of the snapshot. The following example creates a private synonym for the LOCAL_CURR_YEAR_LEDGER snapshot owned by a user named Talbot.

```
create synonym LEDGER for Talbot.LOCAL_CURR_YEAR_LEDGER;
```

A local user of this synonym would reference the LOCAL_CURR_YEAR_LEDGER snapshot whenever LEDGER was referenced.

Indexing Snapshot Tables

As noted earlier, the SNAP$_*snapshotname* table, called the *local base table*, contains the data that has been replicated from a remote site (for the LOCAL_LEDGER snapshot, the local base table is SNAP$_LOCAL_LEDGER). Since that data has been replicated with a goal in mind (usually to improve performance in the database or the network), it is important to follow through to that goal after the snapshot has been created. Performance improvements are usually gained through the use of indexes. Columns that are frequently used in the **where** clauses of queries should be indexed; if a set of columns is frequently accessed in queries, then a concatenated index on that set of columns can be created. See Chapter 18 for more information on indexing.

If a simple snapshot is created, then ORACLE7 will automatically create an index on the primary key of the snapshot's local base table (this presumes that the master table has a defined primary key). Since the snapshot's master table has a primary key, the local base table's primary key's enforcement of uniqueness is redundant. The primary key index on the local base table will improve performance of queries that reference its columns in their **where** clauses. The name of the primary key constraint on the local base table will be PK$_*snapshotname*—such as PK$_LOCAL_LEDGER.

ORACLE7 does not automatically create indexes for complex snapshots. You will need to create these manually. To create indexes on your local base table, use the **create index** command (see the Alphabetical Reference section of this book). Do *not* create any constraints on the snapshot's local base table.

Refreshing Snapshots

The data in your snapshots may be replicated either once (at creation) or at intervals. The **create snapshot** command allows you to set the refresh interval, delegating the responsibility for performing the refreshes to the database. In the following sections you will see how to perform both manual and automatic refreshes.

Automatic Refreshes

Within the **create snapshot** command, you can specify the refresh schedule for the snapshot. Consider the LOCAL_LEDGER snapshot described earlier. Its refresh schedule settings, defined by its **create snapshot** command, are shown in bold in the following listing.

```
create snapshot LOCAL_LEDGER
storage (initial 100K next 100K pctincrease 0)
tablespace SNAPS
refresh FAST
start with SysDate next SysDate+7
as
select * from LEDGER@REMOTE_CONNECT;
```

There are three components to the refresh schedule. First, the type of refresh (FAST, COMPLETE, or FORCE) is specified. Fast refreshes use tables called *snapshot logs* (described later in this chapter) to send changed rows from the master table to the snapshot. They are only available for simple snapshots. Complete refreshes completely re-create the snapshot. The FORCE option for refreshes tells ORACLE to use a fast refresh if it is available; otherwise, a complete refresh will be used.

The **start with** clause tells the database when to perform the first replication from the master table to the local base table. It must evaluate to a future point in time. If you do not specify a **start with** time but specify a **next** value, then ORACLE7 will use the **next** clause to determine the start time. To maintain control over your replication schedule, you should specify a value for the **start with** clause.

The **next** clause tells ORACLE7 how long to wait between refreshes. Since it will be applied to a different base time each time the snapshot is refreshed, the **next** clause specifies a date expression instead of a fixed date. In the example shown above, the expression is

```
next SysDate+7
```

Every time the snapshot is refreshed, the next refresh will be scheduled for seven days thereafter. Although the refresh schedule in this example is fairly simple, you can use many of ORACLE7's date functions to customize your refresh schedule. For example, if you wished to refresh every Monday at noon, regardless of the current date, then you could set the **next** clause to

```
NEXT_DAY(TRUNC(SysDate,'MONDAY'))+12/24
```

This example will find the next Monday after the current system date; the time portion of that date will be truncated, and 12 hours will be added to the date. For information on date functions in ORACLE7, see Chapter 7.

In order for automatic snapshot refreshes to occur, you must have at least one background snapshot refresh process running in your database. The refresh process, called *SNPn* (where *n* is a number from 0 to 9) periodically "wakes up" and checks to see if any snapshots in the database need to be refreshed. The number of SNPn processes running in your database is determined by an initialization parameter called SNAPSHOT_REFRESH_PROCESSES. That parameter must be set (in your **init.ora** file) to a value greater than 0; for most cases, a value of 1 should be sufficient.

The interval, in seconds, between "wake up calls" to the SNPn processes is set by the SNAPSHOT_REFRESH_INTERVAL parameter in the **init.ora** parameter file. The default interval is 60 seconds. If you want ORACLE7 to maintain the connections it makes to remote databases during these checks, then set the SNAPSHOT_REFRESH_KEEP_CONNECTIONS parameter in the **init.ora** file to TRUE.

If you are not running the SNPn processes, then you will need to use manual refresh methods, described in the next section.

Manual Refreshes

In addition to the database's automatic refreshes, you can perform manual refreshes of your snapshots. These override the normally scheduled refreshes; the new **start with** value will be based on the time of your manual refresh.

The LOCAL_LEDGER_TOTALS snapshot defined earlier contained the following specifications about its refresh interval:

```
refresh COMPLETE
start with SysDate next SysDate+7
```

As noted in the previous section, the **start with** and **next** clauses provide input to ORACLE7's scheduling for refreshes of snapshots. However, you may wish to override these settings due to significant changes in the master table. For example, after a major data load in the master table, the snapshot should be refreshed in order to limit the amount of inconsistency between the snapshot and the master table.

You can manually refresh the snapshot via the DBMS_SNAPSHOT package provided in ORACLE7. This is a public package owned by the user SYS (for more information on packages and procedures, see Chapter 22). There is a procedure named REFRESH within this package that can be used to refresh a snapshot. An example of the command's usage is shown in the following listing. In this example, the user **execute**s the procedure, passing it two parameters. The parameters passed to the procedure are described following the example.

```
execute DBMS_SNAPSHOT.REFRESH('LOCAL_LEDGER_TOTALS','?');
```

The REFRESH procedure of the DBMS_SNAPSHOT package, as shown in this listing, takes two parameters. The first is the name of the snapshot, which should be prefixed by the name of the snapshot's owner (if other than the user executing this procedure). The second parameter is the manual refresh option. The available values for the manual refresh option are listed in Table 23-1.

MANUAL REFRESH OPTION	DESCRIPTION
F	Fast refresh.
f	Fast refresh.
C	Complete refresh.
c	Complete refresh.
?	Indicates that the default refresh option for the snapshot should be used.

TABLE 23-1. *Manual Refresh Option Values for the DBMS_SNAPSHOT.REFRESH Procedure*

Another procedure in the DBMS_SNAPSHOT package can be used to refresh all of the snapshots that are scheduled to be automatically refreshed. This procedure, named REFRESH_ALL, will refresh each snapshot separately. It does not accept any parameters. The following listing shows an example of its execution.

```
execute DBMS_SNAPSHOT.REFRESH_ALL;
```

When this command is run, every snapshot that is due to be automatically refreshed is refreshed, one by one. Since the snapshots are not all refreshed at the same time, a database or server failure during the execution of this procedure may cause the local snapshots to be out of synch with each other. If that happens, simply rerun this procedure after the database has been recovered.

NOTE
On many platforms, a utility named REFSNAP is available that executes the REFRESH_ALL procedure. Check your *Installation and User's Guide* for details.

Using Snapshot Refresh Groups

Related snapshots can be collected into *refresh groups* in ORACLE7.1 and above. The purpose of a refresh group is to coordinate the refresh schedules of its members. Snapshots whose master tables have relationships with other snapshot master tables are good candidates for membership in refresh groups. Coordinating the refresh schedules of the snapshots will maintain the master tables' referential integrity in the snapshots as well. If refresh groups are not used, then the data in the snapshots may be inconsistent with regard to the master tables' referential integrity.

All manipulation of refresh groups is achieved via the DBMS_REFRESH package. The procedures within that package are MAKE, ADD, SUBTRACT, CHANGE, DESTROY, and REFRESH. In the following sections you will see how to use these procedures to manage your refresh groups. Information about existing refresh groups can be queried from the USER_REFRESH and USER_REFRESH_CHILDREN data dictionary views.

NOTE
Snapshots that belong to a refresh group do not have to belong to the same schema, but they all have to be stored within the same database.

Creating a Refresh Group

Create a refresh group by executing the MAKE procedure in the DBMS_REFRESH package, using the following syntax:

```
execute DBMS_REFRESH.MAKE
(refresh_group_name,
snapshot [,snapshot...],
next_refresh_date,
interval_date_function,
implicit_destroy,   (DEFAULT FALSE)
lax,                (DEFAULT FALSE)
job,                (DEFAULT 0)
rollback_seg);      (DEFAULT NULL)
```

> **NOTE**
> The DEFAULT notes shown in these listings are not part of the command. They are purely informational.

The last four of the parameters for this procedure have default values that are usually acceptable. You can use the following command to create a refresh group for the LEDGER snapshots created earlier in this chapter.

```
execute DBMS_REFRESH.MAKE
('ledger_group','local_ledger, local_ledger_totals',
SysDate,SysDate+7)
```

> **NOTE**
> The snapshot list parameter, which is the second parameter in the listing, has a single quote at its beginning and at its end, with none between. In this example, two snapshots, LOCAL_LEDGER and LOCAL_LEDGER_TOTALS, are passed to the procedure via a single parameter. If you had enclosed each of them within its own set of quotes, then the first one would have been passed to the procedure as the snapshot list, while the second snapshot, since it was separately enclosed, would have been passed to the procedure as the "next_refresh_date" parameter.

The preceding command will create a refresh group named LEDGER_GROUP, with the two LEDGER-based snapshots as its members. Note that the refresh group name is enclosed in single quotes, as is the *list* of snapshot members—but not each member.

If the refresh group is going to contain a snapshot that is already a member of another refresh group (for example, during a move of a snapshot from an old refresh group to a newly created refresh group), then you must set the *lax* parameter to TRUE. A snapshot can only belong to one refresh group at a time.

Adding Members to a Refresh Group

To add snapshots to an existing refresh group, use the ADD procedure of the DBMS_REFRESH package, using the following syntax:

```
execute DBMS_REFRESH.ADD
(refresh_group_name,
snapshot [,snapshot...],
lax);            (DEFAULT FALSE)
```

As with the MAKE procedure, the ADD procedure's *lax* parameter does not have to be specified unless a snapshot is being moved between two refresh groups. When this procedure is executed with the *lax* parameter set to TRUE, the snapshot is moved to the new refresh group and is automatically deleted from the old refresh group.

Removing Members from a Refresh Group

To remove snapshots from an existing refresh group, use the SUBTRACT procedure of the DBMS_REFRESH package, using the following syntax:

```
execute DBMS_REFRESH.SUBTRACT
(refresh_group_name,
snapshot [,snapshot...]);
```

As with the MAKE and ADD procedures, a single snapshot or a list of snapshots (separated by commas) may serve as input to this procedure.

Changing a Refresh Group's Refresh Schedule

The refresh schedule for a refresh group may be altered via the CHANGE procedure of the DBMS_REFRESH package, using the following syntax:

```
execute DBMS_REFRESH.CHANGE
(refresh_group_name,
next_refresh_date,
interval_date_function,
implicit_destroy,  (DEFAULT FALSE)
rollback_seg);     (DEFAULT NULL)
```

The *next_refresh_date* parameter is analogous to the **start with** clause in the **create snapshot** command. The *interval_date_function* parameter is analogous to the **next** clause in the **create snapshot** command.

For example, to change the LEDGER_GROUP's schedule so that it will be replicated every three days, you can execute the following command (which specifies a null value for the *next_refresh_date* parameter, leaving that value unchanged).

```
execute DBMS_REFRESH.CHANGE('ledger_group',null,SysDate+3);
```

After this command is executed, the refresh cycle for the LEDGER_GROUP refresh group will be changed to every three days.

Deleting a Refresh Group

To delete a refresh group, use the DESTROY procedure of the DBMS_REFRESH package, as shown in the following example. Its only parameter is the name of the refresh group.

```
execute DBMS_REFRESH.DESTROY('ledger_group');
```

You may also implicitly destroy the refresh group. If you set the *implicit_destroy* parameter to TRUE when you created the group with the MAKE procedure, then the refresh group will be deleted (destroyed) when its last member is removed from the group (usually via the SUBTRACT procedure).

Manually Refreshing a Refresh Group

A refresh group may be manually refreshed via the REFRESH procedure of the DBMS_REFRESH package. The REFRESH procedure accepts the name of the refresh group as its only parameter. The command shown in the following listing will refresh the refresh group named LEDGER_GROUP.

```
execute DBMS_REFRESH.REFRESH('ledger_group');
```

Snapshots vs. Triggers

Instead of using snapshots to replicate data, you can also use triggers to replicate data on a transaction-by-transaction basis to remote copies of a table (see Chapter 21). When choosing between triggers and snapshots for your replication needs, consider the following points in favor of snapshots:

1. Replication-type triggers (such as those used for auditing applications) are executed each time a row changes in the master table. If your table is transaction-intensive, this may place a large burden on your application and network. Snapshots bundle all of the changes into a single (and potentially large) transaction.

2. Trigger transactions cannot be scheduled; they occur when the transaction on the master table occurs. Snapshot replications can be scheduled or executed manually; either method should allow you to avoid large replication transaction loads during peak usage times for the application.

3. As the complexity of the transactions on the master table changes, triggers must change as well. The snapshots, with declared relationships to the base tables, will not change.

4. If multiple related tables are being replicated, then the synchronization of the replications can be done via snapshot refresh groups (in ORACLE7.1 and above). Maintaining replicas of related tables via triggers is very code-intensive.

5. If the basis for the replication is a complex query (such as a join, a **group by**, or a **connect by**), then you will usually not want to reevaluate the query for every transaction in the master table. Snapshots can help you schedule the replication of complex queries.

There are two areas in which triggers are superior to snapshots for purposes of replication:

1. If the data in the replica has to be constantly synchronized with the master table, then you have to use triggers or very short refresh intervals. If the master table has a trigger on it, and the transaction on its remote copy fails, then the transaction on the master table will fail, thus maintaining the consistency of the two tables.

2. If you are using ORACLE7 versions prior to ORACLE7.1, and you need to maintain referential integrity between your snapshots, and you have to refresh frequently, then you may need to use triggers. Triggers will allow you to overcome the lack of snapshot refresh groups in early versions of ORACLE7.

In replication, as in referential integrity, you should use a declarative method (snapshots) instead of a procedural method (triggers) unless the declarative method is inappropriate for your needs.

create snapshot log Syntax

In simple snapshots, each record in the snapshot is based on a single row in a single master table. When simple snapshots are used, a *snapshot log* can be created on the master table. The snapshot log is a table that records the date on which every row within the master table last changed. The record of changed rows can then be used during refreshes to send out to the snapshots only those rows that have changed in the master table. Multiple simple snapshots based on the same table can use the same snapshot log.

The syntax for the **create snapshot log** command is shown in the following listing. As you may note from its syntax, it has all of the parameters normally associated with tables.

```
create snapshot log on [user.] table
[PCTFREE  integer |
 PCTUSED integer |
 INITRANS integer |
 MAXTRANS integer |
 TABLESPACE tablespace |
 STORAGE storage];
```

The **create snapshot log** command is executed in the master table's database, usually by the owner of the master table. Snapshot logs should not be created for tables that are only involved in complex snapshots (since they wouldn't be used). No name is specified for the snapshot log.

A snapshot log for the LEDGER table can be created via the following command, executed from within the account that owns the table:

```
create snapshot log on LEDGER
tablespace SNAP_LOGS
storage (initial 40K next 40K pctincrease 0);
```

The command shown in the preceding example creates a snapshot log in a tablespace named SNAP_LOGS. Since snapshot logs may grow unpredictably over time, you may wish to store their associated objects in tablespaces that are dedicated to snapshot logs.

Required System Privileges

In order to create the snapshot log, you must have CREATE TABLE and CREATE TRIGGER system privileges. If you are creating the snapshot log from a user account that does not own the master table, then you need to have CREATE ANY TABLE and CREATE ANY TRIGGER system privileges.

Local and Remote Objects Created

When a snapshot log is created, two objects are created in the master table's schema. From the perspective of the snapshot owner, the **create snapshot log** command occurs in the remote database, and the objects it creates are all in the remote database. The snapshot log creates a table and a trigger:

- A table is created to store the ROWIDs of the rows that change in the master table, along with a separate timestamp column to record the time the rows changed. This table is named MLOG$_*master_table_name*. If a snapshot log is created on the LEDGER table, the snapshot log's table will be named MLOG$_LEDGER.

- An AFTER ROW trigger is created to insert the ROWIDs and timestamps of updated, inserted, or deleted rows into the snapshot log table. This trigger is named TLOG$_*master_table_name*. If a snapshot log is created on the LEDGER table, the snapshot log's trigger will be named TLOG$_LEDGER.

> **NOTE**
> If you are using a version of ORACLE7 below ORACLE7.1, then you may not have any other AFTER ROW trigger on your master table when you create the snapshot log. ORACLE7.0 prevents you from having multiple triggers of the same type on the same table; this restriction is no longer in effect as of ORACLE7.1. See Chapter 21 for more details.

Because of the names used for the objects that are created for the snapshot logs, the name of the table on which the snapshot log is based may not exceed 24 characters in length.

Viewing Information about Existing Snapshots

To view data about snapshots, query the USER_SNAPSHOTS data dictionary view. For information on snapshots that are accessible to, but not owned by, the user, query ALL_SNAPSHOTS. A sample query against USER_SNAPSHOTS is shown in the following listing.

```
select
 Name,         /*Name of the view used for the snapshot*/
 Last_Refresh, /*Timestamp for the last refresh*/
 Type,         /*Type of refresh used for automatic refreshes*/
 Query         /*Query used to create the snapshot*/
  from USER_SNAPSHOTS;
```

This query will return the most used information for the snapshot. A full listing of the available columns is shown in Table 23-2.

COLUMN NAME	DESCRIPTION
Owner	Owner of the snapshot.
Name	Name of the snapshot.
Table_Name	The name of the local base table for the snapshot (SNAP$_*snapshotname*).
Master_View	The name of the local view used for refreshes (MVIEW$_*snapshotname*).
Master_Owner	The owner of the master table.
Master	The name of the master table.
Master_Link	The name of the database link to the master database used by the snapshot's query.
Can_Use_Log	A flag to indicate if the snapshot can use a snapshot log (values are YES and NO).
Last_Refresh	The date and time at the master site the last time the snapshot was refreshed.
Error	Any error that was returned during the last refresh attempt.
Type	The type of refresh to use during automatic refreshes (FAST, COMPLETE, or FORCE).
Next	The date function used to calculate the next refresh date and time.
Start_With	The date function used to calculate the first refresh date and time.
Query	The query that forms the basis of the snapshot.

TABLE 23-2. *Columns for USER_SNAPSHOTS*

COLUMN NAME	DESCRIPTION
Log_Owner	The owner of the snapshot log.
Master	The name of the master table the snapshot log applies to.
Log_Table	The name of the snapshot log table (MLOG$_*master_table_name*).
Log_Trigger	The name of the trigger on the master table that populates the snapshot log table (TLOG$_*master_table_name*).
Current_Snapshots	The date the snapshot of the master table was last refreshed.

TABLE 23-3. *Columns for USER_SNAPSHOT_LOGS*

You can query information about snapshot logs from the USER_SNAPSHOT_LOGS data dictionary view, whose columns are listed in Table 23-3.

You should query these data dictionary views periodically to determine if any snapshots have gone without refreshes for long periods of time. Long delays between refreshes may cause synchronization problems and can cause the snapshot logs to grow unacceptably large.

Altering Snapshots and Snapshot Logs

You may alter the storage parameters, refresh option, and refresh schedule for existing snapshots. If you are unsure of the current settings for a snapshot, check the USER_SNAPSHOTS data dictionary view as shown in the previous section.

The syntax for the **alter snapshot** command is

```
alter snapshot [user.] snapshot
[PCTFREE  integer ¦
 PCTUSED integer ¦
 INITRANS integer ¦
 MAXTRANS integer ¦
 STORAGE storage]
[refresh FAST ¦ COMPLETE ¦ FORCE]
[start with date next date];
```

For example, to alter the refresh option used by the LOCAL_LEDGER snapshot, execute the command

```
alter snapshot LOCAL_LEDGER
refresh COMPLETE;
```

All future refreshes of the LOCAL_LEDGER snapshot will refresh the entire local base table of the snapshot.

In order to alter a snapshot, you must either own the snapshot or have ALTER ANY SNAPSHOT system privilege.

The storage parameters for snapshot logs may be modified via the **alter snapshot log** command. The syntax is

```
alter snapshot log on [user.] table
[PCTFREE  integer |
 PCTUSED integer |
 INITRANS integer |
 MAXTRANS integer |
 STORAGE storage];
```

Changing these parameters will change the **storage** parameters on the snapshot log's table. For example, the following command will change the NEXT parameter within the **storage** clause for the snapshot log.

```
alter snapshot log on LEDGER
storage (next 100K);
```

In order to alter a snapshot log, you must either own the table, have ALTER privilege for the table, or have ALTER ANY TABLE system privilege.

Dropping Snapshots and Snapshot Logs

To drop a snapshot, you must have the system privileges required to drop both the snapshot and all of its related objects. Therefore, you must have the DROP SNAPSHOT, DROP TABLE, DROP VIEW, and the DROP INDEX (for simple snapshots) system privileges. If the snapshot is not in your schema, then you must have the DROP ANY SNAPSHOT, DROP ANY TABLE, DROP ANY VIEW, and DROP ANY INDEX system privileges. As of ORACLE7.1, these privileges have been simplified so that you only need to have DROP SNAPSHOT or DROP ANY SNAPSHOT system privilege to drop a snapshot.

The command shown in the following listing drops the LOCAL_LEDGER_TOTALS snapshot created earlier in this chapter.

```
drop snapshot LOCAL_LEDGER_TOTALS;
```

Snapshot logs can be dropped via the **drop snapshot log** command. Once the snapshot log is dropped from a master table, no fast refreshes can be performed for simple snapshots based on that table. A snapshot log should be dropped when there are no simple snapshots based on the master table. The command shown in the following example drops the snapshot log that was created on the LEDGER table earlier in this chapter.

```
drop snapshot log on LEDGER;
```

In order to drop a snapshot log, you must have the ability to drop both the snapshot log and its related objects. If you own the snapshot log, you must have the DROP TABLE and DROP TRIGGER system privileges. If you do not own the snapshot log, then you will need the DROP ANY TABLE and DROP ANY TRIGGER system privileges to execute this command.

Part 3

The Hitchhiker's Guide to the ORACLE7 Data Dictionary

CHAPTER 24

The Hitchhiker's Guide to the ORACLE7 Data Dictionary

ORACLE7's data dictionary stores all of the information that is used to manage the objects in the database. Although it is usually the domain of database administrators (DBAs), the data dictionary is a source of valuable information for developers and end users as well.

In this chapter, you will see the data dictionary—ORACLE's "Yellow Pages"—from the perspective of an end user; thus, the data dictionary tables and views are not listed alphabetically, but rather are grouped by function (tables, security, and so on). This organization is designed to let you quickly find your way to the information you need. The most-used data dictionary views are all shown here, along with examples of their usage.

Depending on which ORACLE7 configuration options you are using, some of the groups will not apply to your database. The most commonly used views are listed first. The groupings used in this chapter are, in order:

1. The Road Maps: DICTIONARY and DICT_COLUMNS

2. Things You Select From: Tables (and Columns), Views, Synonyms, and Sequences

3. Constraints and Comments

4. Indexes and Clusters

5. Database Links and Snapshots

6. Triggers, Procedures, Functions, and Packages

7. Space Allocation and Usage

8. Users and Privileges

9. Roles

10. Auditing

11. Monitoring: The V$ Dynamic Performance tables

12. Miscellaneous (ORACLE V6 and V5 views, CHAINED_ROWS, PLAN_TABLE, Interdependencies, DBA-only Views, Trusted Oracle Views, SQL*Loader Direct Load Option Views, and National Language Support [NLS] Views)

A Note About Nomenclature

With some exceptions, the names of the objects in the ORACLE7 data dictionary begin with one of three prefixes: "USER", "ALL", or "DBA". Records in the "USER" views usually record information about objects owned by the account performing the query. Records in the "ALL" views include the "USER" records plus information about objects on which privileges have been granted to PUBLIC or to the user. "DBA" views encompass all of the database objects, regardless of owner. For most database objects, "USER", "ALL," and "DBA" views are available.

In keeping with the user focus of this guide, the emphasis will be on the "USER" views or those which are accessible to all users. The "ALL" and "DBA" views will be described when they are applicable to the category.

The Road Maps: DICTIONARY (DICT) and DICT_COLUMNS

Descriptions for the objects that make up the ORACLE7 data dictionary are accessible via a view named DICTIONARY. This view, also accessible via the public synonym DICT, queries the database to determine which data dictionary views you can see. It also searches for public synonyms for those views.

The following example queries DICT for the names of all data dictionary views whose name includes the string 'TABLES'.

Selecting from DICT, as shown in the following listing, returns the object name and comments for each data dictionary object that matches your search criteria. There are only two columns in this view: Table_Name and the table's associated Comments.

```
column Comments format a50

select Table_Name, Comments
  from DICT
 where Table_Name like '%TABLES%';


TABLE_NAME               COMMENTS
-------------------      ----------------------------------------------
ALL_TABLES               Description of tables accessible to the user
DBA_TABLES               Description of all tables in the database
DBA_TABLESPACES          Description of all tablespaces
USER_TABLES              Description of the user's own tables
USER_TABLESPACES         Description of accessible tablespaces
```

The columns of the dictionary views can be queried via the DICT_COLUMNS view. Like the DICTIONARY view, DICT_COLUMNS displays the comments that have been entered into the database for the data dictionary views. DICT_COLUMNS has three columns: Table_Name, Column_Name, and Comments. Querying DICT_COLUMNS lets you determine which data dictionary views would be most useful for your current needs.

For example, if you want to view space allocation and usage information for your database objects, but are not sure which data dictionary views store that information, you can query DICT_COLUMNS as shown in this example. The query shown here looks for all the dictionary tables that have a column named Blocks.

```
select Table_Name
   from DICT_COLUMNS
 where Column_Name = 'BLOCKS'
   and Table_Name like 'USER%';


TABLE_NAME
--------------------
USER_EXTENTS
USER_FREE_SPACE
USER_SEGMENTS
USER_TABLES
USER_TS_QUOTAS
```

To list all of the available column names that you could have used in the last example, query DICT_COLUMNS:

```
select distinct Column_Name
   from DICT_COLUMNS
 order by Column_Name;
```

Whenever you're unsure where to find the data you want, just check DICTIONARY and DICT_COLUMNS. If it appears there are a large number of views that could be useful, query DICTIONARY (as in the first example) to see the Comments on each view.

Things You Select From: Tables (and Columns), Views, Synonyms, and Sequences

The set of objects owned by a user is referred to as the user's *catalog*. There is one catalog per user. The catalog lists all of those objects that the user can **select** records from—that is, an object that can be listed in the **from** clause of a query. Although sequences are not referenced directly in **from** clauses, ORACLE7 includes them in the catalog. In this section, you will see how to retrieve information about tables, columns, views, synonyms, sequences, and the user catalog.

Catalog: USER_CATALOG (CAT)

Querying USER_CATALOG will display all tables, views, synonyms, and sequences for which the user is the owner. The Table_Name column shows the name of the object (even if it is not a table), and the Table_Type column shows the type of object.

```
select Table_Name, Table_Type
  from USER_CATALOG
 where Table_Name like 'R%' or Table_Name like 'T%';

TABLE_NAME           TABLE_TYPE
-------------------- ----------
RAIN                 VIEW
ROSE                 TABLE
TROUBLE              TABLE
TWONAME              TABLE
```

USER_CATALOG may also be referred to by the public synonym CAT.

There are two additional catalogs that are available. ALL_CATALOG lists everything in your USER_CATALOG view, plus any objects that you have been granted access to. Any objects that have been granted to PUBLIC will also be displayed in ALL_CATALOG. DBA_CATALOG is a DBA-level version of the catalog, showing all tables, views, sequences, and synonyms in the database. In addition to the Table_Name and Table_Type columns shown in the USER_CATALOG query, ALL_CATALOG and DBA_CATALOG include an Owner column.

Objects: USER_OBJECTS (OBJ)

USER_CATALOG only displays information for specific types of objects. To retrieve information on *all* types of objects, query USER_OBJECTS. You can use this view to find out about the following types of objects: clusters, database links, functions, indexes, packages, package bodies, procedures, sequences, synonyms, tables, triggers, and views. USER_OBJECTS' columns are listed in Table 24-1.

USER_OBJECTS (also known by its public synonym OBJ) contains several vital pieces of information that are not found in other data dictionary views. It records the creation date of objects (the Created column) and the last time an object was altered (the Last_DDL_Time column). These columns are very useful when trying to reconcile different sets of tables in the same application.

The following example selects the creation date and last alteration date for several objects.

COLUMN NAME	DESCRIPTION
Object_Name	The name of the object.
Object_ID	A unique, Oracle-assigned ID for the object.
Object_Type	The object type ('TABLE', 'INDEX', and so on).
Created	The timestamp for the object's creation (a DATE column).
Last_DDL_Time	The timestamp for the last DDL command used on the object, including **alter**, **grant**, and **revoke**.
Timestamp	The timestamp for the object's creation (same as Created, but stored as a character column).
Status	The status of the object ('VALID' or 'INVALID').

TABLE 24-1. *Columns in USER_OBJECTS*

```
column Last_DDL_Time format a13

select Object_Name, Created, Last_DDL_Time
  from USER_OBJECTS
 where Object_Name like 'R%' or Object_Name like 'T%';

OBJECT_NAME          CREATED    LAST_DDL_TIME
-------------------- ---------- -------------
RAIN                 07-AUG-01  07-AUG-01
ROSE                 07-AUG-01  07-AUG-01
TROUBLE              07-AUG-01  14-AUG-01
TWONAME              07-AUG-01  07-AUG-01
```

This example shows the date on which these objects were last created, and the dates on which they were last altered. The data in this listing shows that the four objects were all created on the same day, but that the TROUBLE table was later altered.

NOTE
If you re-create objects in any way, such as via Import, their Created values will change to the last time they were created.

There are two additional object listings available. ALL_OBJECTS lists everything in your USER_OBJECTS view, plus any objects that you have been granted access to. Any objects that have been granted to PUBLIC will also be displayed in ALL_OBJECTS. DBA_OBJECTS is a DBA-level version of the object listing, showing all of the objects in the database. In addition to the Table_Name and Table_Type columns shown in the USER_OBJECTS view, ALL_OBJECTS and DBA_OBJECTS include an Owner column.

Tables: USER_TABLES (TABS)

Although all of a user's objects are shown in USER_OBJECTS, few attributes of those objects are shown there. To get more information about an object, you need to look at the view that is specific to that type of object. For tables, that view is USER_TABLES. It can also be referenced via the public synonym TABS.

NOTE
In earlier versions of ORACLE, there was a view called TAB. That view, which is similar in function to TABS, is still supported because of Oracle products that reference it. However, TAB does not contain the ORACLE7-related columns that TABS contains. Use TABS in your data dictionary queries.

The columns in USER_TABLES can be divided into three major categories ("Identification", "Space-Related", and "Statistics-Related"), as shown in Table 24-2.

IDENTIFICATION	SPACE-RELATED	STATISTICS-RELATED
Table_Name	Tablespace_Name	Num_Rows
Backed_Up	Cluster_Name	Blocks
	Pct_Free	Empty_Blocks
	Pct_Used	Avg_Space
	Ini_Trans	Chain_Cnt
	Max_Trans	Avg_Row_Len
	Initial_Extent	
	Next_Extent	
	Min_Extents	
	Max_Extents	

TABLE 24-2. *Columns in USER_TABLES*

The table's name is shown in the Table_Name column. The Backed_Up column shows whether or not the table has been backed up since its last modification. The "Space-Related" columns are described in the "Storage" entry of the Alphabetical Reference section of this book. The "Statistics-Related" columns are populated when the table is analyzed (see the **analyze** command in the Alphabetical Reference).

Querying the Table_Name column from USER_TABLES will display the names of all of the tables in the current account. The following example lists all of the tables whose names begin with the letter 'L'.

```
select Table_Name from USER_TABLES
 where Table_Name like 'L%';

TABLE_NAME
------------------------------
LEDGER
LOCATION
LODGING
LONGTIME
```

The ALL_TABLES view shows all of the tables owned by the user as well as any to which the user has been granted access. Most third-party reporting tools that list available tables for queries obtain that list by querying ALL_TABLES. Since ALL_TABLES can contain entries for multiple users, it contains an Owner column in addition to the columns shown in Table 24-2. DBA_TABLES, which lists all tables in the database, has the same column definitions as ALL_TABLES.

Columns: USER_TAB_COLUMNS (COLS)

Although users do not query from columns, the data dictionary view that shows columns is closely tied to the data dictionary view of tables. This view, called USER_TAB_COLUMNS, lists information specific to columns. USER_TAB_COLUMNS can also be queried via the public synonym COLS.

The columns you can query from USER_TAB_COLUMNS can be separated into three major categories, as shown in Table 24-3.

The Table_Name and Column_Name columns contain the names of your tables and columns. The usage of the "Definition-Related" columns is described in the "Data Types" entry in the Alphabetical Reference. The "Statistics-Related" columns are populated when the table is analyzed (see the **analyze** command in the Alphabetical Reference).

IDENTIFICATION	DEFINITION-RELATED	STATISTICS-RELATED
Table_Name	Data_Type	Num_Distinct
Column_Name	Data_Length	Low_Value
Column_ID	Data_Precision	High_Value
	Data_Scale	Density
	Nullable	
	Default_Length	
	Data_Default	

TABLE 24-3. *Columns in USER_TAB_COLUMNS*

To see the column definitions for a table, query USER_TAB_COLUMNS, specifying the Table_Name in the **where** clause.

```
select Column_Name, Data_Type
  from USER_TAB_COLUMNS
 where Table_Name = 'NEWSPAPER';


COLUMN_NAME    DATA_TYPE
------------   ---------
FEATURE        VARCHAR2
SECTION        CHAR
PAGE           NUMBER
```

The information in this example is also obtainable via the SQLPLUS **describe** command; however, **describe** does not give you the option of seeing the column defaults and statistics.

The ALL_TAB_COLUMNS view shows the columns for all of the tables and views owned by the user as well as any to which the user has been granted access. Since ALL_TAB_COLUMNS can contain entries for multiple users, it contains an Owner column in addition to the columns shown in Table 24-3. DBA_TAB_COLUMNS, which lists the column definitions for all tables and views in the database, has the same column definitions as ALL_TAB_COLUMNS.

Views: USER_VIEWS

The base query of a view is accessible via the USER_VIEWS data dictionary view, which contains three columns:

View_Name	The name of the view.
Text_Length	The length of the view's base query, in characters.
Text	The query that the view uses.

The Text column is a LONG datatype. This may cause a problem when querying USER_VIEWS via SQLPLUS, because LONGs are truncated in SQLPLUS. The point at which truncation occurs, however, can be changed by the user. USER_VIEWS provides a mechanism for determining the proper setting for the LONG truncation point, as you'll see in the following example.

The Text_Length column shows the length of the view's query. Therefore, the SQLPLUS LONG truncation point must be set to a value equal to or greater than the view's Text_Length value. For example, the following listing shows a view whose View_Name is AGING and whose Text_Length is 500.

```
select View_Name, Text_Length
  from USER_VIEWS
 where View_Name = 'AGING';

View_Name            Text_Length
-----------------    -------------
AGING                500
```

Since the length of the view's text is 500 characters, you must use the **set long** command shown in the following listing to increase the LONG truncation point to at least 500 (the default is 80). Otherwise, you will not see the full text of the view's query.

```
set long 500
```

Once the LONG truncation point value is set correctly, you can then query USER_VIEWS for the view's Text, using the query shown in the following listing.

```
select Text
  from USER_VIEWS
 where View_Name = 'AGING';
```

If you had not used the **set long** command, then the output would have been truncated at 80 characters, with no message telling you why the truncation occurred. Before querying other views, you will need to recheck their Text_Length values.

The column definitions for views can be seen by querying USER_TAB_COLUMNS, the same view you query for tables.

If you use column aliases in your views, and your column aliases are part of the view's query, then your data dictionary queries for information about views will be simplified. Since the entire text of the view's query is displayed in USER_VIEWS, the column aliases will be displayed as well.

It is also possible to create views using the format

```
create view NEWSPAPER_VIEW (SomeFeature, SomeSection)
    as select Feature, Section
  from NEWSPAPER;
```

Listing the column names in the header of the **create view** command removes the column aliases from the query—and thus prevents you from seeing them via USER_VIEWS. The only way to see the view's column names would be by querying USER_TAB_COLUMNS. If the column names are in the query, then you only need to query one data dictionary view (USER_VIEWS) for both the query and the column names.

For example, given the NEWSPAPER_VIEW view created in the last example, if you were to query USER_VIEWS, you would see:

```
select Text
   from USER_VIEWS
 where View_Name ='NEWSPAPER_VIEW';

TEXT
----------------------------------------
select Feature, Section from NEWSPAPER
```

This query does *not* show you the new column names you assigned, since you did not make those column names part of the view's query. To make those column names show up in USER_VIEWS, add them as column aliases in the view's query:

```
create view NEWSPAPER_VIEW
    as select Feature SomeFeature, Section SomeSection
  from NEWSPAPER;
```

Now when you query USER_VIEWS, the column aliases will be displayed as part of the view's query text:

```
select Text
  from USER_VIEWS
 where View_Name ='NEWSPAPER_VIEW';


TEXT
----------------------------------------
select Feature SomeFeature, Section SomeSection
  from NEWSPAPER
```

The ALL_VIEWS view lists all of the views owned by the user as well as any to which the user has been granted access. Since ALL_VIEWS can contain entries for multiple users, it contains an Owner column in addition to the columns listed earlier in this section. DBA_VIEWS, which lists all views in the database, has the same column definitions as ALL_VIEWS.

Synonyms: USER_SYNONYMS (SYN)

USER_SYNONYMS lists all of the synonyms that a user owns. The columns are:

Synonym_Name	The name of the synonym.
Table_Owner	The owner of the table that the synonym refers to.
Table_Name	The name of the table that the synonym refers to.
DB_Link	The name of the database link used in the synonym.

USER_SYNONYMS is useful when debugging programs or resolving problems with users' access to objects within applications. USER_SYNONYMS is also known by the public synonym SYN.

The DB_Link column will be NULL if the synonym does not use a database link. Therefore, if you want to see a list of the database links currently in use by the synonyms owned by your account, execute the query

```
select distinct DB_Link
  from USER_SYNONYMS
 where DB_Link is not null;
```

This same sort of query can be performed by DBAs at the database level, using the DBA_SYNONYMS view instead.

The ALL_SYNONYMS view lists all of the synonyms owned by the user, PUBLIC synonyms, and all synonyms to which the user has been granted access. Since ALL_SYNONYMS can contain entries for multiple users, it contains an Owner column in addition to the columns listed earlier in this section. DBA_SYNONYMS, which lists all synonyms in the database, has the same column definitions as ALL_SYNONYMS.

Sequences: USER_SEQUENCES (SEQ)

To display the attributes of sequences, you can query the USER_SEQUENCES data dictionary view. This view can also be queried using the public synonym SEQ. The columns of USER_SEQUENCES are listed in Table 24-4.

The Last_Number column is not updated during normal database operation; it is used during database restart/recovery operations.

ALL_SEQUENCES lists all of the sequences owned by the user or to which the user has been granted access. Since ALL_SEQUENCES can contain entries for multiple users, it contains an Owner column in addition to the columns listed in Table 24-4. DBA_SEQUENCES, which lists all sequences in the database, has the same column definitions as ALL_SEQUENCES.

COLUMN NAME	DESCRIPTION
Sequence_Name	Name of the sequence.
Min_Value	Minimum value of the sequence.
Max_Value	Maximum value of the sequence.
Increment_By	Increment between sequence values.
Cycle_Flag	A flag to indicate whether the values should cycle back to the Min_Value once the Max_Value is reached.
Order_Flag	A flag to indicate whether sequence numbers are generated in order.
Cache_Size	The number of sequence entries cached in memory.
Last_Number	The last sequence number written to disk or cached.

TABLE 24-4. *Columns in USER_SEQUENCES*

Constraints and Comments

Constraints and comments help you to understand how tables and columns relate to each other. Comments are strictly informational; they do not enforce any conditions on the data stored in the objects they describe. Constraints, on the other hand, define the conditions under which that data is valid. Typical constraints include NOT NULL, UNIQUE, PRIMARY KEY, and FOREIGN KEY. In the next sections you will see how to retrieve data about constraints and comments from the data dictionary.

Constraints: USER_CONSTRAINTS

Constraint information is accessible via the USER_CONSTRAINTS view. This information is very useful when trying to alter data constraints or resolve problems with an application's data. The columns of this view are listed in Table 24-5.

Note that although this is a "USER" view, it contains an Owner column; in this view, Owner refers to the owner of the *constraint*, not the owner of the table (which is the user).

Valid values for the Constraint_Type column are shown in Table 24-5. Understanding the constraint types is crucial when you are trying to get useful information about your constraints.

FOREIGN KEY constraints will always have values for the R_Owner and R_Constraint_Name columns in USER_CONSTRAINTS. These two columns will tell you which constraint the FOREIGN KEY references. Note that the FOREIGN KEY references another *constraint*, not another column.

USER_CONSTRAINTS lists all of the constraints on a table. NOT NULL constraints on columns are stored as CHECK constraints, so they have a Constraint_Type of 'C'. Querying USER_CONSTRAINTS will give you the names of all the constraints on a table, which is important when trying to interpret error messages that only provide the name of the constraint that was violated.

Once you know the name and type of a constraint, you can then check the columns associated with it via the USER_CONS_COLUMNS view, described in the next section.

For example, you may want to know which columns comprise the PRIMARY KEY of a certain table. To do this, you will first need to identify the name of the PRIMARY KEY constraint on that table. This query will return that information:

```
select Owner, Constraint_Name
  from USER_CONSTRAINTS
 where Table_Name = 'BIRTHDAY'
   and Constraint_Type = 'P';
```

```
OWNER       CONSTRAINT_NAME
----------  -------------------
TALBOT      SYS_C0008791
```

The Constraint_Name shown here is system-generated; you may also give constraints names at the time you create them. See "Integrity Constraint" in the Alphabetical Reference for further details.

ALL_CONSTRAINTS lists the constraints on all of the tables that the user can access. DBA_CONSTRAINTS lists all of the constraints in the database. Each of these views has the same set of columns as USER_CONSTRAINTS (since they all include the Owner column).

COLUMN NAME	DESCRIPTION
Owner	The owner of the constraint.
Constraint_Name	The name of the constraint.

Constraint_Type	The type of constraint:
	  C: CHECK constraint; includes NOT NULLs.
	  P: PRIMARY KEY constraint.
	  R: FOREIGN KEY (reference) constraint.
	  U: UNIQUE constraint.
	  V: WITH CHECK OPTION constraint (for views).

Table_Name	The name of the table associated with the constraint.
Search_Condition	The search condition used (for CHECK constraints).
R_Owner	The owner of the table referenced by a FOREIGN KEY constraint.
R_Constraint_Name	The name of the constraint referenced by a FOREIGN KEY constraint.
Delete_Rule	The action to take on the foreign key tables when a PRIMARY KEY record is deleted ('CASCADE' or 'NO ACTION').
Status	The status of the constraint ('ENABLED' or 'DISABLED').

TABLE 24-5. *Columns in USER_CONSTRAINTS*

Constraint Columns: USER_CONS_COLUMNS

You can view the columns associated with constraints via the USER_CONS_COLUMNS data dictionary view. If you have already queried USER_CONSTRAINTS to obtain the types and names of the constraints involved, then you can use USER_CONS_COLUMNS to determine which columns are involved in the constraint. The columns in this view are listed in Table 24-6.

There are only two columns in this view that are not in USER_CONSTRAINTS: Column_Name and Position. A sample query of this table, using the Constraint_Name from the USER_CONSTRAINTS example, is shown in the following listing.

```
select Column_Name, Position
  from USER_CONS_COLUMNS
 where Owner = 'TALBOT'
   and Constraint_Name = 'SYS_C0008791';


COLUMN_NAME   POSITION
-----------   --------
FIRSTNAME            1
LASTNAME             2
```

As shown in the preceding listing, the combination of FirstName and LastName forms the primary key for the BIRTHDAY table.

The Position column is significant. In ORACLE7, when you create a UNIQUE or PRIMARY KEY constraint, the database automatically creates a unique index on the set of columns you specify. The index is created based on the column order you specify. The column order, in turn, affects the performance of the index. An index comprised of multiple columns will not be used by the optimizer unless the leading column of that index (Position = '1') is used in the query's **where** clause. See Chapter 18 for further details on indexes.

The ALL_CONS_COLUMNS and DBA_CONS_COLUMNS views have the same column definitions as USER_CONS_COLUMNS. ALL_CONS_COLUMNS can

COLUMN NAME	DESCRIPTION
Owner	The owner of the constraint.
Constraint_Name	The name of the constraint.
Table_Name	The name of the table associated with the constraint.
Column_Name	The name of the column associated with the constraint.
Position	The position of the column within the constraint definition.

TABLE 24-6. *Columns in USER_CONS_COLUMNS*

be used to display column information about constraints on all tables that the user can access regardless of owner. DBA_CONS_COLUMNS lists the column-level constraint information for the entire database.

Constraint Exceptions: EXCEPTIONS

When enabling constraints on tables that already contain data, you may encounter constraint violations within the data. For example, you may attempt to create a PRIMARY KEY constraint on a column that contains the same value for multiple records. Attempting to create a PRIMARY KEY constraint on such a column would fail.

ORACLE7 allows you to capture information about the rows that cause constraint creations to fail. First, you must create a table called EXCEPTIONS in your account (also called a *schema*); a SQL script that should be used to create this table is named UTLEXCPT.SQL, and is usually located in the /rdbms/admin directory under the ORACLE home directory.

After creating the EXCEPTIONS table, attempt to enable the constraint:

```
alter table NEWSPAPER enable PRIMARY KEY
exceptions into EXCEPTIONS;
```

The EXCEPTIONS table contains four columns: Row_ID (the RowID of each row that violated the constraint), Owner (the owner of the violated constraint), Table_Name (the table on which the violated constraint was created), and Constraint (the constraint violated by the row). You can then compare the Row_ID in the EXCEPTIONS table to the RowID in the table on which the constraint was being placed (in the previous example, the NEWSPAPER table).

For example, if the primary key constraint in the last example generated exceptions, then you could query the EXCEPTIONS table as shown in the following listing.

```
select * from EXCEPTIONS;

ROW_ID                 OWNER       TABLE_NAME CONSTRAINT
-------------------    ----------  ---------- ----------
00008971.000B.0001 TALBOT          NEWSPAPER  SYS_C00516
00008971.000B.0002 TALBOT          NEWSPAPER  SYS_C00516
```

The output from this query shows that two rows violated the constraint named SYS_C00516 (which in this example is the constraint name given to the primary key constraint for the NEWSPAPER table). You can determine which rows of the

NEWSPAPER table correspond to these exceptions by joining the Row_ID column of the EXCEPTIONS table to the RowID pseudo-column of the NEWSPAPER table:

```
select *
  from NEWSPAPER
 where RowID in
       (select Row_ID from EXCEPTIONS);
```

The rows that caused the constraint violations will then be displayed.

Table Comments: USER_TAB_COMMENTS

You can add a comment to a table, view, or column after it has been created. Comments on the data dictionary views are the basis for the records displayed via the DICTIONARY and DICT_COLUMNS views. To display comments about your own tables, use the USER_TAB_COMMENTS view.

USER_TAB_COMMENTS contains three columns:

Table_Name	The name of the table or view.
Table_Type	The object type ('TABLE' or 'VIEW').
Comments	Comments that have been entered for the object.

Query USER_TAB_COMMENTS by specifying the Table_Name you wish to see the Comments for, as shown in the following listing.

```
select Comments
from USER_TAB_COMMENTS
where Table_Name = 'BIRTHDAY';
```

To add a comment to a table, use the **comment** command, as shown in the following listing. To remove a comment from a table, set the comment to two single quotes with no space between them (''), as shown below.

```
comment on table BIRTHDAY is 'Birthday list for Blacksburg employees';
```

To remove that comment:

```
comment on table BIRTHDAY is '';
```

You can view the comments on all of the tables you can access via the ALL_TAB_COMMENTS view. ALL_TAB_COMMENTS has an additional column, Owner, which specifies the owner of the table. DBA_TAB_COMMENTS lists all of the tables in the database, and it has an Owner column as well.

Column Comments: USER_COL_COMMENTS

USER_COL_COMMENTS displays the comments that have been entered for columns within your tables. These comments are added to the database via the **comment** command. USER_COL_COMMENTS contains three columns:

Table_Name	The name of the table or view.
Column_Name	The name of the column.
Comments	Comments that have been entered for the column.

Query USER_COL_COMMENTS by specifying the Table_Name and Column_Name you wish to see the Comments for:

```
select Comments
  from USER_COL_COMMENTS
 where Table_Name = 'BIRTHDAY'
   and Column_Name = 'AGE';
```

To add a comment to a table, use the **comment** command, as shown in the following listing. To remove a comment from a table, set the comment to two single quotes with no space between them (''), as shown below.

```
comment on column BIRTHDAY.AGE is 'Age in years';
```

To remove that comment:

```
comment on column BIRTHDAY.AGE is '';
```

You can view the column comments on all of the tables you can access via the ALL_COL_COMMENTS view. ALL_COL_COMMENTS has an additional column, Owner, which specifies the owner of the table. DBA_COL_COMMENTS lists all of the columns in all of the tables in the database, and it has an Owner column as well.

Indexes and Clusters

Indexes and clusters do not change the data that is stored in tables; however, they do change the way that data is stored and accessed. In the following sections, you will see the usage of the data dictionary views that describe indexes and clusters.

Indexes: USER_INDEXES (IND)

In ORACLE7, indexes are very closely related to constraints. The PRIMARY KEY and UNIQUE constraints always have associated unique indexes. Like constraints, there are two data dictionary views that are used to query information about indexes: USER_INDEXES and USER_IND_COLUMNS. USER_INDEXES is also known by its public synonym, IND.

The columns in USER_INDEXES can be grouped into three categories, as shown in Table 24-7.

The name of the index is shown in the Index_Name column. The owner and name for the table being indexed are displayed in the Table_Owner and Table_Name columns. The Uniqueness column will be set to 'UNIQUE' for unique indexes and to 'NONUNIQUE' for non-unique indexes. Table_Type records whether the index is on a table or a cluster.

The "Space-Related" columns are described in the "Storage" entry in the Alphabetical Reference. The "Statistics-Related" columns are populated when the table is analyzed (see the **analyze** command in the Alphabetical Reference).

IDENTIFICATION	SPACE-RELATED	STATISTICS-RELATED
Index_Name	Tablespace_Name	BLevel
Table_Owner	Ini_Trans	Leaf_Blocks
Table_Name	Max_Trans	Distinct_Keys
Table_Type	Initial_Extent	Avg_Leaf_Blocks_Per_Key
Uniqueness	Next_Extent	Avg_Data_Blocks_Per_Key
Status	Min_Extents	Clustering_Factor
	Max_Extents	
	Pct_Increase	
	Pct_Free	

TABLE 24-7. *Columns in USER_INDEXES*

To see all of the indexes on a table, query USER_INDEXES, using the Table_Owner and Table_Name columns in the **where** clause, as shown in the following listing.

```
select Index_Name, Uniqueness
  from USER_INDEXES
 where Table_Owner = 'TALBOT'
   and Table_Name = 'BIRTHDAY';


INDEX_NAME        UNIQUENESS
----------------  ----------
PK_BIRTHDAY       UNIQUE
```

The result of the query in the preceding example shows that an index named "PK_BIRTHDAY" exists on the BIRTHDAY table. By using the same naming standard for all of your indexes, you can make it very easy to identify the purpose and table for an index just by looking at the Index_Name. In this example, "PK" signifies PRIMARY KEY; the constraint name can be specified during constraint creation to supersede the system-generated constraint name.

The Clustering_Factor column is not directly related to clusters, but rather represents the degree to which the rows in the table are ordered. The more ordered those rows are, the more efficient range queries will be (*range queries* are those in which a range of values is given for a column, such as **where LastName like 'A%'**).

To discover which columns are part of the index, and their order within the index, you will need to query the USER_IND_COLUMNS view. USER_IND_COLUMNS is described in the next section.

ALL_INDEXES shows all of the indexes owned by the user as well as any created on tables to which the user has been granted access. Since ALL_INDEXES can contain entries for multiple users, it contains an Index_Owner column in addition to the columns shown in Table 24-7. DBA_INDEXES, which lists all indexes in the database, has the same column definitions as ALL_INDEXES.

NOTE
The "ALL" and "DBA" versions of USER_INDEXES have an added column to define the owner of the index, but that column is called Index_Owner, not Owner.

Indexed Columns: USER_IND_COLUMNS

You can determine which columns are in an index by querying USER_IND_COLUMNS. The columns available via this view are listed in Table 24-8.

COLUMN NAME	DESCRIPTION
Index_Name	The name of the index.
Table_Name	The name of the indexed table.
Column_Name	The name of a column within the index.
Column_Position	The column's position within the index.
Column_Length	The indexed length of the column.

TABLE 24-8. *Columns for USER_IND_COLUMNS*

There are only three columns in this view that are not in USER_INDEXES: Column_Name, Column_Position, and Column_Length. Column_Length, like the statistics-related columns in USER_INDEXES, is populated when the index's base table is analyzed (see the **analyze** command in the Alphabetical Reference). A sample query of this table, using the Index_Name from the USER_INDEXES example, is shown in the following listing. In this example, the Column_Position column is given the alias "Pos".

```
select Column_Name, Column_Position Pos
  from USER_IND_COLUMNS
 where Index_Name = 'PK_BIRTHDAY';


COLUMN_NAME   POS
-----------   ---
FIRSTNAME       1
LASTNAME        2
```

As can be seen from this query, the PK_BIRTHDAY index is comprised of two columns: FirstName and LastName, in that order. The ordering of the columns will determine whether the index can be used for certain queries. If users frequently use the LastName column in their **where** clauses, and do not use the FirstName column in those queries, then this index may need to be reorganized. An index comprised of multiple columns will not be used by the optimizer unless the leading column of that index (Column_Position = '1') is used in the **where** clause. See Chapter 18 for further details on indexes.

The ALL_IND_COLUMNS and DBA_IND_COLUMNS views have the same column definitions as USER_IND_COLUMNS. ALL_IND_COLUMNS can be used to display column information about indexes on all tables that the user can access regardless of owner. DBA_IND_COLUMNS lists the column-level index information for the entire database.

IDENTIFICATION	SPACE-RELATED	STATISTICS-RELATED
Cluster_Name	Tablespace_Name	Avg_Blocks_Per_Key
Cluster_Type	Pct_Free	Hashkeys
Function	Pct_Used	
	Key_Size	
	Ini_Trans	
	Max_Trans	
	Initial_Extent	
	Next_Extent	
	Min_Extents	
	Max_Extents	
	Pct_Increase	

TABLE 24-9. *Columns in USER_CLUSTERS*

Clusters: USER_CLUSTERS (CLU)

The storage and statistics parameters associated with clusters are accessible via USER_CLUSTERS (also known by the public synonym CLU). The columns in this data dictionary view are shown in Table 24-9, separated by type.

The Cluster_Name column contains the name of the cluster. Cluster_Type refers to whether the cluster uses a standard B-tree index or a hashing function for the cluster.

The usage of the "Space-Related" columns is described in the "Storage" entry in the Alphabetical Reference. The "Statistics-Related" columns are populated when the table is analyzed (see the **analyze** command in the Alphabetical Reference).

There is no "ALL_CLUSTERS" view. DBA_CLUSTERS has an additional column, Owner, since it lists all clusters in the database.

Cluster Columns: USER_CLU_COLUMNS

To see the mapping of table columns to cluster columns, query USER_CLU_COLUMNS, whose columns are:

Cluster_Name	The name of the cluster.
Clu_Column_Name	The name of the key column in the cluster.
Table_Name	The name of a table within the cluster.
Tab_Column_Name	The name of the key column in the table.

Since a single cluster can store data from multiple tables, USER_CLU_COLUMNS is useful for determining which columns of which tables map to the cluster's columns.

There is no "ALL" version of this view. There is only USER_CLU_COLUMNS for the user's cluster columns, and DBA_CLU_COLUMNS, which shows the column mappings for all clusters in the database.

Database Links and Snapshots

Database links and snapshots are used to manage access to remote data. Depending on the type of snapshot you use, you may also be able to use snapshot logs. In the following sections you will see descriptions of the data dictionary views that can be used to display information about database links, snapshots, and snapshot logs. For further information on database links, see Chapter 20. For further information on snapshots, see Chapter 23.

Database Links: USER_DB_LINKS

To see the database links created under your account, query USER_DB_LINKS. This view, whose columns are described in Table 24-10, shows the information about the remote connection that the link will be used to establish. The Username and Password values will be used to log into the remote database defined by the Host value.

The Host column can store SQL*Net V1 connect strings or SQL*Net V2 connect descriptors. This column stores the exact character string you specify during the **create database link** command, and does *not* alter its case. You should therefore be careful with the text case used when creating database links. Otherwise

COLUMN NAME	DESCRIPTION
DB_Link	The name of the database link.
Username	The username to use in the remote database.
Password	The password for the username in the remote database.
Host	The SQL*Net string to use for the connection to the remote database.
Created	The timestamp for the creation of the database link.

TABLE 24-10. *Columns in USER_DB_LINKS*

your queries against USER_DB_LINKS will have to take into account inconsistencies in the case of the Host column. For example, looking for a database link that uses the 'HQ' service descriptor would require you to enter

```
select * from USER_DB_LINKS
 where UPPER(Host) = 'HQ';
```

since it is possible that there are entries with a Host value of 'hq' instead of 'HQ'.

NOTE
If you are using default logins to the remote database, then Password will be NULL.

The ALL_DB_LINKS view lists all of the database links that are owned by the user or are PUBLIC database links. DBA_DB_LINKS lists all database links in the database. ALL_DB_LINKS and DBA_DB_LINKS share the same column definitions as USER_DB_LINKS.

See Chapter 20 for further information on the uses of database links.

Snapshots: USER_SNAPSHOTS

You can query USER_SNAPSHOTS to display information about the snapshots owned by your account. This view, whose columns are listed in Table 24-11, shows the structural information about the snapshot as well as its refresh schedule.

When a snapshot is created, several database objects are created. In the local database, ORACLE7 creates a table that is populated with the remote table's data, plus the RowIDs for that data. ORACLE7 then creates a view of this table, using the snapshot's name for the view's name. See Chapter 23 for further details on snapshots.

When you query the snapshot, you are actually querying the snapshot view. The name of the snapshot view is found in the Name column of USER_SNAPSHOTS. The local base table for that view is the Table_Name column in USER_SNAPSHOTS. The table that the snapshot uses in the remote database is defined by the Master_Owner and Master columns.

To determine which database links are being used by your snapshots, query the Master_Link column, as shown in the following example.

```
select Master_Link
  from USER_SNAPSHOTS;
```

COLUMN NAME	DESCRIPTION
Owner	The account that owns the snapshot.
Name	The name of the snapshot.
Table_Name	The base table (in the local database) for the snapshot.
Master_View	The name of the view used during snapshot refreshes.
Master_Owner	The account that owns the base table (in the remote database) for the snapshot.
Master	The base table (in the remote database) for the snapshot.
Master_Link	The database link used to access the master database.
Can_Use_Log	A flag to indicate if the snapshot can use a snapshot log ('YES' or 'NO').
Last_Refresh	A timestamp to record the last time the snapshot's data was refreshed.
Error	Any error that was encountered during the last refresh attempt.
Type	Type of refresh performed ('COMPLETE', 'FAST', or 'FORCE').
Next	The date function used to determine the next refresh date.
Start_With	The date function used to determine the starting and next refresh dates.
Query	The query used as a basis for the snapshot.

TABLE 24-11. *Columns in USER_SNAPSHOTS*

The names of the database links returned by this query can be used as input for queries against USER_DB_LINKS. This query will display all of the database link information available for database links used in your snapshots:

```
select *
  from USER_DB_LINKS
 where DB_Link in
    (select Master_Link
       from USER_SNAPSHOTS);
```

Additional queries that are useful in the management of snapshots are provided in Chapter 23.

The ALL_SNAPSHOTS and DBA_SNAPSHOTS views have the same column definitions as USER_SNAPSHOTS. ALL_SNAPSHOTS can be used to display information about all snapshots that the user can access regardless of owner. DBA_SNAPSHOTS lists snapshot information for all users in the database.

In ORACLE7.1 and above, two additional snapshot-related views—USER_REFRESH and USER_REFRESH_CHILDREN—display information about refresh groups. See Chapter 23 for information about refresh groups.

Snapshot Logs: USER_SNAPSHOT_LOGS

Snapshots logs can be used by simple snapshots to determine which records in the master table need to be refreshed in remote snapshots of that table. Information about a user's snapshot logs can be queried from the USER_SNAPSHOT_LOGS data dictionary view, described in Table 24-12. Restrictions on the use of snapshot logs are discussed in Chapter 23.

USER_SNAPSHOT_LOGS is usually queried for maintenance purposes, such as to determine the name of the trigger used to create the snapshot log records.

There is no "ALL" version of this view. DBA_SNAPSHOT_LOGS has the same column definitions as USER_SNAPSHOT_LOGS, but shows all snapshot logs in the database.

COLUMN NAME	DESCRIPTION
Log_Owner	Owner of the snapshot log.
Master	The name of the base table for which changes are being logged.
Log_Table	The name of the table that holds the log records (which are comprised of RowIDs and timestamps).
Log_Trigger	The name of the AFTER ROW trigger on the base (Master) table that inserts records into the snapshot log table (Log_Table).
Current_Snapshots	The date the snapshot was last refreshed.

TABLE 24-12. *Columns in USER_SNAPSHOT_LOGS*

Triggers, Procedures, Functions, and Packages

You can use procedures, packages, and triggers—blocks of PL/SQL code stored in the database—to enforce business rules or to perform complicated processing. Triggers are described in Chapter 21. Procedures, functions, and packages are described in Chapter 22. In the following sections you will see how to query the data dictionary for information about triggers, procedures, packages, and functions.

Triggers: USER_TRIGGERS

You can query USER_TRIGGERS to display information about the triggers owned by your account. This view, whose columns are listed in Table 24-13, shows the trigger type and body.

In ORACLE7.0, you can only have one trigger per table for each combination of the Trigger_Type and Triggering_Event columns. The following query will list the name, type, and triggering event for all triggers on the LEDGER table.

COLUMN NAME	DESCRIPTION
Trigger_Name	Name of the trigger.
Trigger_Type	The type of trigger ('BEFORE STATEMENT', 'BEFORE ROW', 'AFTER STATEMENT', or 'AFTER ROW').
Triggering_Event	The command that executes the trigger ('INSERT', 'UPDATE', or 'DELETE').
Table_Owner	The owner of the table that the trigger is defined for.
Table_Name	The name of the table that the trigger is defined for.
Referencing_Names	Names used for referencing OLD and NEW values in the trigger (when set to other than the defaults of OLD and NEW).
When_Clause	The **when** clause used for the trigger.
Status	Whether the trigger is ENABLED or DISABLED.
Description	The description for the trigger.
Trigger_Body	The trigger text.

TABLE 24-13. *Columns in USER_TRIGGERS*

```
select Trigger_Name, Trigger_Type, Triggering_Event
  from USER_TRIGGERS
 where Table_Owner = 'TALBOT'
   and Table_Name = 'LEDGER';
```

The ALL_TRIGGERS data dictionary view lists the triggers for all tables to which you have access. DBA_TRIGGERS lists all of the triggers in the database. Both of these views contain an additional column, Owner, that records the owner of the trigger.

A second trigger-related data dictionary view, USER_TRIGGER_COLS, shows how columns are used by a trigger. It lists the name of each column affected by a trigger, as well as how the trigger is used. Like USER_TRIGGERS, "ALL" and "DBA" versions of this data dictionary view are available.

Procedures, Functions, and Packages: USER_SOURCE

The source code for existing procedures, functions, packages, and package bodies can be queried from the USER_SOURCE data dictionary view. The Type column in USER_SOURCE identifies the procedural object as a 'PROCEDURE', a 'FUNCTION', a 'PACKAGE', or a 'PACKAGE BODY'. Each line of code is stored in a separate record in USER_SOURCE.

Select information from the USER_SOURCE view via a query similar to the one shown in the following listing. In this example, the Text column is selected, ordered by the Line number. The Name of the object and the object Type are used to define which object's source code is to be displayed. The following example uses the NEW_WORKER procedure shown in Chapter 22.

```
select Text
  from USER_SOURCE
 where Name = 'NEW_WORKER'
   and Type = 'PROCEDURE'
 order by Line;

TEXT
----------------------------------------------------
procedure NEW_WORKER
  (Person_Name IN varchar2)
AS
  BEGIN
     insert into WORKER
       (Name, Age, Lodging)
```

```
    values
       (Person_Name, null, null);
    END;
```

As shown in the preceding example, the USER_SOURCE view contains one record for each line of the NEW_WORKER procedure. The sequence of the lines is maintained by the Line column; therefore, the Line column should be used in the **order by** clause, as shown.

The ALL_SOURCE and DBA_SOURCE views have all of the columns found in USER_SOURCE, plus an additional Owner column (the owner of the object). ALL_SOURCE can be used to display the source code for all procedural objects that the user can access regardless of owner. DBA_SOURCE lists the source code for all users in the database.

Code Errors: USER_ERRORS

The **show errors** command in SQLPLUS and SQLDBA checks the USER_ERRORS data dictionary view for the errors associated with the most recent compilation attempt for a procedural object. **show errors** will display the line and column number for each error, as well as the text of the error message.

To view errors associated with previously created procedural objects, you may query USER_ERRORS directly. You may need to do this when viewing errors associated with package bodies, since a package compilation that results in an error may not display the package body's error when you execute the **show error** command. You may also need to query USER_ERRORS when you encounter compilation errors with multiple procedural objects.

The columns available in USER_ERRORS are listed in Table 24-14.

COLUMN NAME	DESCRIPTION
Name	The name of the procedural object.
Type	The object type ('PROCEDURE', 'FUNCTION', 'PACKAGE', or 'PACKAGE BODY').
Sequence	The line sequence number, for use in the query's **order by** clause.
Line	The line number within the source code at which the error occurs.
Position	The position within the Line at which the error occurs.
Text	The text of the error message.

TABLE 24-14.   *Columns in USER_ERRORS*

A sample query against USER_ERRORS in shown in the following listing. Queries against this view should always include the Sequence column in the **order by** clause. "ALL and "DBA" versions of this view are also available; they feature an additional column, Owner, which records the owner of the object.

```
select Line, Position, Text
  from USER_ERRORS
 where Name = 'NEW_WORKER'
   and Type = 'PROCEDURE'
 order by Sequence;
```

Code Size: USER_OBJECT_SIZE

The amount of space used in the SYSTEM tablespace for a procedural object can be queried from the USER_OBJECT_SIZE data dictionary view. As shown in the following listing, the four separate size areas can be added together to determine the total space used in the SYSTEM data dictionary tables to store the object. The four "Size" columns, along with the Name and Type columns, comprise all of the columns available in this view. The Type column can have values of 'PROCEDURE', 'PACKAGE', or 'PACKAGE BODY'.

```
select Source_Size+Code_Size+Parsed_Size+Error_Size Total
  from USER_OBJECT_SIZE
 where Name = 'NEW_WORKER'
   and Type = 'PROCEDURE';
```

There are also "ALL" and "DBA" versions of this view available. ALL_OBJECT_SIZE lists the sizes for all objects to which you have been granted access; DBA_OBJECT_SIZE lists the sizes for all objects in the database.

Space Allocation and Usage

You can query the data dictionary to determine the space that is available and allocated for your database objects. In the following sections, you will see how to determine the default storage parameters for objects, your space usage quota, available free space, and the way in which your objects are physically stored. For information on ORACLE7's methods of storing data, see Chapter 18.

Tablespaces: USER_TABLESPACES

You can query the USER_TABLESPACES data dictionary view to determine which tablespaces you have been granted access to, and the default storage parameters in each. A tablespace's default storage parameters will be used for each object stored within that tablespace unless the **create** or **alter** command for that object specifies its own storage parameters. The storage-related columns in USER_TABLESPACES, listed in Table 24-15, are very similar to the storage-related columns in USER_TABLES. See the "Storage" entry of the Alphabetical Reference for further details.

NOTE
In ORACLE7.1 and above, the Status column can also contain the value 'READ ONLY'. See the **alter tablespace** command in the Alphabetical Reference for further details on read-only tablespaces.

There is no "ALL" version of this view. DBA_TABLESPACES shows the storage parameters for all tablespaces.

COLUMN NAME	DESCRIPTION
Tablespace_Name	The name of the tablespace.
Initial_Extent	The default INITIAL parameter for objects in the tablespace.
Next_Extent	The default NEXT parameter for objects in the tablespace.
Min_Extents	The default MINEXTENTS parameter for objects in the tablespace.
Max_Extents	The default MAXEXTENTS parameter for objects in the tablespace.
Pct_Increase	The default PCTINCREASE parameter for objects in the tablespace.
Status	A flag to indicate whether the tablespace is 'ONLINE', 'OFFLINE', or 'INVALID'. An "invalid" tablespace is one that has been dropped; its record is still visible in this view. See also related note.

TABLE 24-15. *Columns in USER_TABLESPACES*

Space Quotas: USER_TS_QUOTAS

USER_TS_QUOTAS is a very useful view for determining the amount of space you have currently allocated and the maximum amount of space available to you, by tablespace. A sample query of USER_TS_QUOTAS is shown in the following listing.

```
select * from USER_TS_QUOTAS;

TABLESPACE_NAME     BYTES   MAX_BYTES    BLOCKS  MAX_BLOCKS
--------------- ---------- ----------- ---------- ----------
USERS                67584           0        33           0
```

There is one record for each Tablespace_Name. The Bytes column reflects the number of bytes allocated to objects owned by the user. Max_Bytes is the maximum number of bytes the user can own in that tablespace; if there is no quota for that tablespace, then Max_Bytes will display a value of 0, as shown in the previous listing. The Bytes and Max_Bytes columns are translated into ORACLE blocks in the Blocks and Max_Blocks columns, respectively.

There is no "ALL" version of this view. DBA_TS_QUOTAS shows the storage quotas for all users for all tablespaces, and is a very effective way to list space usage across the entire database.

Segments and Extents: USER_SEGMENTS and USER_EXTENTS

As described in Chapter 18, space is allocated to objects (such as tables, clusters, and indexes) in *segments*. Segments are the physical counterparts to the logical objects created in the database. You can query USER_SEGMENTS to see the current storage parameters and space usage in effect for your segments. USER_SEGMENTS is very useful when you are in danger of exceeding one of the storage limits; its columns are listed in Table 24-16.

Segments are comprised of contiguous sections called *extents*. The extents that comprise segments are described in USER_EXTENTS. Here you will see the actual size of each extent within the segment—this is very useful for tracking the impact of your changes to the NEXT and PCTINCREASE settings. In addition to the Segment_Name, Segment_Type, and Tablespace_Name columns, USER_EXTENTS has three new columns: Extent_ID (to identify the extent within the segment), Bytes (the size of the extent, in bytes), and Blocks (the size of the extent, in ORACLE blocks).

Both USER_SEGMENTS and USER_EXTENTS have "DBA" versions, which are useful for listing the space usage of objects across owners. Both DBA_SEGMENTS

COLUMN NAME	DESCRIPTION
Segment_Name	The name of the segment.
Segment_Type	The type of segment ('TABLE', 'CLUSTER', 'INDEX', 'ROLLBACK', 'DEFERRED ROLLBACK', 'TEMPORARY', or 'CACHE').
Tablespace_Name	The name of the tablespace in which the segment is stored.
Bytes	The number of bytes allocated to the segment.
Blocks	The number of ORACLE blocks allocated to the segment.
Extents	The number of extents in the segment.
Initial_Extent	The size of the initial extent in the segment.
Next_Extent	The value of the NEXT parameter for the segment.
Min_Extents	The minimum number of extents in the segment.
Max_Extents	The value of the MAXEXTENTS parameter for the segment.
Pct_Increase	The value of the PCTINCREASE parameter for the segment.
Freelists	The number of *process freelists* (lists of data blocks in the segment that can be used during **insert**s) allocated to the segment. If a segment has multiple freelists, then contention for free blocks during concurrent **insert**s will be lessened.
Freelist_Groups	The number of *freelist groups* (the number of groups of freelists, for use with the Parallel Server option) allocated to the segment.

TABLE 24-16.   *Columns in USER_SEGMENTS*

and DBA_EXTENTS have an additional Owner column. If you want to list all of the owners who own segments in a tablespace, you can query based on the Tablespace_Name column in DBA_SEGMENTS and list all of the Owners of segments in that tablespace.

Free Space: USER_FREE_SPACE

In addition to viewing the space you have used, you can also query the data dictionary to see how much space is currently marked as "free" space. USER_FREE_SPACE lists the free extents in all tablespaces accessible to the user.

It lists, by Tablespace_Name, the File_ID and Block_ID of the starting point of the free extent. The size of the free extent is listed in both Bytes and Blocks. DBA_FREE_SPACE is frequently used by DBAs to monitor the amount of free space available and the degree to which it has become fragmented.

Users and Privileges

Users and their privileges are recorded within the data dictionary. In the following sections you will see how to query the data dictionary for information about user accounts, resource limits, and user privileges.

Users: USER_USERS

You can query USER_USERS to list information about your account. You can select your Username, User_ID (a number assigned by the database), Default_Tablespace, Temporary_Tablespace, and your Created date (when your account was created) from this view.

ALL_USERS contains only the Username, User_ID, and Created columns from USER_USERS, but it lists that information for all accounts in the database. ALL_USERS is useful when you need to know the usernames that are available (for example, during **grant** commands). DBA_USERS contains all of the columns in USER_USERS, plus two additional columns: Password (the encrypted password for the account) and Profile (the user's resource profile). DBA_USERS lists this information for all users in the database.

Resource Limits: USER_RESOURCE_LIMITS

In ORACLE7, *profiles* can be used to place limits on the amount of system and database resources available to a user. If no profiles are created in a database, then the default profile, which specifies unlimited resources for all users, will be used. The resources that can be limited are described in the **create profile** entry of the Alphabetical Reference.

To view the limits that are in place for your current session, you can query USER_RESOURCE_LIMITS. Its columns are

Resource_Name	The name of the resource (e.g, SESSIONS_PER_USER).
Limit	The limit placed upon this resource.

There is no "ALL" or "DBA" version of this view; it is strictly limited to the user's current session.

Table Privileges: USER_TAB_PRIVS

To view grants for which you are the grantee, the grantor, or the object owner, query USER_TAB_PRIVS (user table privileges). In addition to its Grantee, Grantor, and Owner columns, this view contains columns for the Table_Name, Privilege, and a flag (set to 'YES' or 'NO') to indicate whether the privilege was granted **with admin option** (Grantable).

USER_TAB_PRIVS_MADE displays the USER_TAB_PRIVS records for which the user is the owner (it therefore lacks an Owner column). USER_TAB_PRIVS_RECD (user table privileges received) displays the USER_TAB_PRIVS records for which the user is the grantee (it therefore lacks a Grantee column). Since both USER_TAB_PRIVS_MADE and USER_TAB_PRIVS_RECD are simply subsets of USER_TAB_PRIVS, you can duplicate their functionality simply by querying against USER_TAB_PRIVS with an appropriate **where** clause to view the subset you want.

There are "ALL" versions available for USER_TAB_PRIVS, USER_TAB_PRIVS_MADE, and USER_TAB_PRIVS_RECD. The "ALL" versions list those objects for which either the user or PUBLIC is the grantee or grantor. There is a "DBA" version of USER_TAB_PRIVS named DBA_TAB_PRIVS that lists all object privileges granted to all users in the database. DBA_TAB_PRIVS and ALL_TAB_PRIVS have the same column definitions as USER_TAB_PRIVS.

Column Privileges: USER_COL_PRIVS

In addition to granting privileges on tables, you can also grant privileges at the column level. For example, you can grant users the ability to update only certain columns in a table. See Chapter 17 and the **grant** command in the Alphabetical Reference for further details.

The data dictionary views used to display column privileges are identical in design to the table privileges views described in the previous section. The only modification is the addition of a Column_Name column to each of the views. USER_COL_PRIVS is analogous to USER_TAB_PRIVS, USER_COL_PRIVS_MADE is analogous to USER_TAB_PRIVS_MADE, and USER_COL_PRIVS_RECD is analogous to USER_TAB_PRIVS_RECD.

There are "ALL" versions available for all of the column privileges views. DBA_COL_PRIVS lists all column privileges that have been granted to users in the database (just as DBA_TAB_PRIVS lists all table privileges granted to users).

System Privileges: USER_SYS_PRIVS

USER_SYS_PRIVS lists the system privileges that have been granted to the user. Its columns are Username, Privilege, and Admin_Option (a flag set to 'YES' or 'NO' to indicate whether the privilege was granted **with admin option**). As shown in the following listing, all system privileges directly granted to a user are displayed via this view. System privileges granted to a user via a role are not displayed here. In this example, the Talbot user has been granted CREATE SESSION privilege via a role; therefore, that privilege is not displayed in this listing.

```
select * from USER_SYS_PRIVS;

USERNAME          PRIVILEGE                                 ADM
---------------   ---------------------------------------   ---
TALBOT            CREATE PROCEDURE                          NO
TALBOT            CREATE TRIGGER                            NO
```

There is no "ALL" version of this view available. To see the system privileges granted to all users in the database, query DBA_SYS_PRIVS, which has the same column definitions as USER_SYS_PRIVS.

Roles

In addition to privileges granted directly to users, sets of privileges may be grouped into *roles*. Roles may be granted to users or to other roles, and may be comprised of both object and system privileges. For information on the use and management of roles, see Chapter 17.

To see which roles have been granted to you, query the USER_ROLE_PRIVS data dictionary view. Any roles that have been granted to PUBLIC will also be listed here. The available columns for USER_ROLE_PRIVS are listed in Table 24-17.

To list all of the roles available in the database, you need to have DBA authority; you can then query DBA_ROLES to list all roles. DBA_ROLE_PRIVS lists the assignment of those roles to all of the users in the database.

Roles may receive three different types of grants, and each has a different corresponding data dictionary view:

Table/column grants	ROLE_TAB_PRIVS. Similar to USER_TAB_PRIVS and USER_COL_PRIVS, except that it has a Role column instead of a Grantee column.
System privileges	ROLE_SYS_PRIVS. Similar to USER_SYS_PRIVS, except that it has a Role column instead of a Username column.
Role grants	ROLE_ROLE_PRIVS. All roles that have been granted to other roles.

COLUMN NAME	DESCRIPTION
Username	The username (may be 'PUBLIC').
Granted_Role	The name of the role granted to the user.
Admin_Option	A flag to indicate whether the role was granted **with admin option** ('YES' or 'NO').
Default_Role	A flag to indicate if the role is the user's default role ('YES' or 'NO').
OS_Granted	A flag to indicate if the operating system is being used to manage roles ('YES' or 'NO').

TABLE 24-17. *Columns in USER_ROLE_PRIVS*

NOTE
If you are not a DBA, then these data dictionary views list only those roles that have been granted to you.

In addition to these views, there are two views, each with a single column, that list the privileges and roles currently enabled for the current session. They are

| SESSION_PRIVS | The Privilege column lists all system privileges available to the session, whether granted directly or via roles. |
| SESSION_ROLES | The Role column lists all roles that are currently enabled for the session. |

SESSION_PRIVS and SESSION_ROLES are available to all users.

NOTE
See Chapter 17 for information on the enabling and disabling of roles and the setting of default roles.

Auditing

As a non-DBA user within an ORACLE7 database, you cannot enable the database's auditing features. If, however, auditing has been enabled, then there are data dictionary views that anyone can use to view the audit trail.

There are many different audit trail data dictionary views available. Most of the audit trail views are based on a single audit trail table in the database (SYS.AUD$). The most generic of the audit trail views available is named USER_AUDIT_TRAIL. Its columns are described in Table 24-18. Since this view shows the audit records for many different types of actions, many of the columns may be inapplicable for any given row. The "DBA" version of this view, DBA_AUDIT_TRAIL, lists all entries from the audit trail table; USER_AUDIT_TRAIL lists only those that are relevant to the user.

As shown in Table 24-18, there is a vast array of auditing capabilities available (see the **audit** command in the Alphabetical Reference for a complete listing).

COLUMN NAME	DESCRIPTION
OS_Username	The audited user's operating system account.
Username	The ORACLE username of the audited user.
UserHost	A numeric ID for the instance used by the audited user.
Terminal	The user's operating system terminal identifier.
TimeStamp	The date and time the audit record was created.
Owner	The owner of the object affected by an action (for action audits).
Obj_Name	The name of the object affected by an action (for action audits).
Action	The numeric code for the audited action.
Action_Name	The name of the audited action.
New_Owner	The owner of the object named in the New_Name column.

TABLE 24-18.   *Columns in USER_AUDIT_TRAIL*

COLUMN NAME	DESCRIPTION
New_Name	The new name of an object that has been **rename**d.
Obj_Privilege	The object privilege that has been **grant**ed or **revoke**d.
Sys_Privilege	The system privilege that has been **grant**ed or **revoke**d.
Admin_Option	A flag to indicate whether the role or system privilege was **grant**ed **with admin option** ('Y' or 'N').
Grantee	The username specified in a **grant** or **revoke** command.
Audit_Option	The auditing options set via an **audit** command.
Ses_Actions	A string of characters serving as a session summary, recording success and failure for different actions.
Logoff_Time	The date and time the user logged off.
Logoff_LRead	The number of logical reads performed during the session.
Logoff_PRead	The number of physical reads performed during the session.
Logoff_LWrite	The number of logical writes performed during the session.
Logoff_DLock	The number of deadlocks detected during the session.
Comment_Text	A text comment on the audit trail entry.
SessionID	The numeric ID for the session.
EntryID	A numeric ID for the audit trail entry.
StatementID	The numeric ID for each command that was executed.
ReturnCode	The return code for each command that was executed. If the command was successful, then the ReturnCode will be 0.
Priv_Used	The system privilege used to execute the action.
Object_Label	The label associated with the object (for Trusted ORACLE).
Session_Label	The label associated with the session (for Trusted ORACLE).

TABLE 24-18. *Columns in USER_AUDIT_TRAIL (continued)*

Each type of audit can be accessed via its own data dictionary view. The available views are:

USER_AUDIT_OBJECT	For statements concerning objects.
USER_AUDIT_SESSION	For connections and disconnections.
USER_AUDIT_STATEMENT	For **grant**, **revoke**, **audit**, **noaudit**, and **alter system** commands issued by the user.

There are "DBA" versions available for each of the "USER" views in the previous list; the "DBA" versions show all of the audit trail records that fit into the view's category.

You can view the auditing options that are currently in effect for your objects by querying USER_OBJ_AUDIT_OPTS. For each object listed in USER_OBJ_AUDIT_OPTS, the audit options for each command that may be performed on that object (identified by the Object_Name and Object_Type columns) are listed. The column names of USER_OBJ_AUDIT_OPTS correspond to the first three letters of the command (for example, Alt for **alter**, Upd for **update**). Each column will record whether that command is audited for that object when the command is successful ('S'), unsuccessful ('U'), or both. The default auditing options in effect for any new objects in the database can be displayed via the ALL_DEF_AUDIT_OPTS view, which has the same column naming conventions as USER_OBJ_AUDIT_OPTS.

The commands that can be audited are stored in a reference table named AUDIT_ACTIONS. There are two columns in AUDIT_ACTIONS: Action (the numeric code for the action) and Name (the name of the action/command). Action and Name correspond to the Action and Action_Name columns of USER_AUDIT_TRAIL.

DBAs can make use of several additional auditing views that do not have "USER" counterparts, including DBA_AUDIT_EXISTS, DBA_PRIV_AUDIT_OPTS, DBA_STMT_AUDIT_OPTS, and STMT_AUDIT_OPTION_MAP. See the *ORACLE7 Server Administrator's Guide* for details on these DBA-only views.

Monitoring: The V$ Dynamic Performance Tables

The views that form the basis of the SQLDBA Monitor may be made available to all users in a database via the UTLMONTR.SQL script. This script creates a role called MONITORER and then grants privileges on system statistics tables to that role. The MONITORER role can then be granted to users. The system statistics tables—also called the *dynamic performance tables*—are commonly referred to as the *V$* (pronounced "Vee-Dollar") *tables* because they all begin with the letter "V" followed by the dollar sign ($).

The definitions and usage of columns within the monitoring views are subject to change with each version of the database that is released. The usage of the views themselves is fairly static, however; their descriptions are listed in Table 24-19. Correctly interpreting the results of ad hoc queries against views usually requires referring to the *ORACLE7 Server Administrator's Guide*. The V$ tables are normally used only via the SQLDBA Monitor.

VIEW NAME	DESCRIPTION
V$ACCESS	The currently held locks on objects in the database.
V$BGPROCESS	Information about the database's background processes.
V$DATAFILE	Information about the database's datafiles.
V$DBFILE	A pre-ORACLE7 view used to list datafiles. Use V$DATAFILE instead.
V$FILESTAT	File read/write statistics for the datafiles.
V$LATCH	The database internal latches, by latch number.
V$LATCHHOLDER	The processes holding each latch.
V$LATCHNAME	A code table that maps latch numbers to latch names.
V$LOCK	Information about non-DDL locks and resources.
V$LOG	Information about the database's redo logs.
V$LOGFILE	Information about the database's redo log files.
V$PARAMETER	The current values of the database's parameters.
V$PROCESS	The currently active processes.
V$ROLLNAME	A code table that maps rollback segment numbers to rollback segment names.
V$ROLLSTAT	Statistics for all online rollback segments, by rollback segment number.
V$SESSION	The currently active sessions.
V$SESSTAT	The current statistics for the current session.
V$SGA	The size of each component of the SGA.
V$SYSSTAT	The current statistics for the entire database.
V$THREAD	Information on redo log threads.
V$TRANSACTION	Information about transactions.

TABLE 24-19. *The V$ Monitoring Views*

Miscellaneous

In addition to the data dictionary views described earlier in this chapter, there are several miscellaneous views and tables that may be available within your data dictionary. These views and tables include DBA-only views and the table used

when the **explain plan** command is executed. In the following sections, you will
see brief descriptions for each of the miscellaneous view types.

ORACLE V6 Views Required for Other ORACLE Products

Two ORACLE7 data dictionary views are created to support ORACLE products that
rely on the data dictionary names that were used in ORACLE Version 6. These two
views are named TABLE_PRIVILEGES and COLUMN_PRIVILEGES. Although these
two views are available as part of the ORACLE7 data dictionary, they should not be
queried because of their status as ORACLE Version 6 views.

ORACLE V5 Views Required for Other ORACLE Products

Nine ORACLE7 data dictionary views are created to support ORACLE products
that rely on the data dictionary names that were used in ORACLE Version 5. These
nine views are SYSCATALOG, CATALOG, TAB, COL, SYSSEGOBJ, TABQUOTAS,
SYSFILES, SYNONYMS, and PUBLICSYN. Although these ORACLE Version 5 views
are available as part of the ORACLE7 data dictionary, and are similar in name to
ORACLE7 views (such as TABS), they should not be queried because of their
status as ORACLE Version 5 views.

CHAINED_ROWS

When a row no longer fits within the data block its row header is stored in, that
row may store the remainder of its data in a different block or set of blocks. Such a
row is said to be chained, and chained rows may cause poor performance due to
the increased number of blocks that must be read in order to read a single row.

The **analyze** command can be used to generate a listing of the chained
rows within a table. This listing of chained rows can be stored in a table called
CHAINED_ROWS. To create the CHAINED_ROWS table in your schema, run the
UTLCHAIN.SQL script (usually found in the /rdbms/admin subdirectory under the
ORACLE home directory).

To populate the CHAINED_ROWS table, use the **list chained rows into** clause
of the **analyze** command, as shown in the following listing.

```
analyze LEDGER list chained rows into CHAINED_ROWS;
```

The CHAINED_ROWS table lists the Owner_Name, Table_Name, Cluster_Name (if the table is in a cluster), Head_RowID (the RowID for the row), and a TimeStamp column that shows the last time the table or cluster was analyzed. You can query the table based on the Head_RowID values in CHAINED_ROWS, as shown in the following example.

```
select * from LEDGER
 where RowID in
       (select Head_RowID
          from CHAINED_ROWS
         where Table_Name = 'LEDGER');
```

If the chained row is short in length, then it may be possible to eliminate the chaining by deleting and reinserting the row.

PLAN_TABLE

When tuning SQL statements, you may wish to determine the steps that the optimizer will take to execute your query. To view the query path, you must first create a table in your schema named PLAN_TABLE. The script used to create this table is called UTLXPLAN.SQL, and is usually stored in the /rdbms/admin subdirectory of the ORACLE home directory.

After you have created the PLAN_TABLE table in your schema, you can use the **explain plan** command. **explain plan** will generate records in your PLAN_TABLE, tagged with the Statement_ID value you specify for the query you wish to have explained:

```
explain plan
set Statement_ID = 'MYTEST'
for
select * from LEDGER
 where Person like 'S%';
```

The ID and Parent_ID columns in PLAN_TABLE establish the hierarchy of steps (Operations) that the optimizer will follow when executing the query. See the *ORACLE7 Server Concepts Manual* for details on the ORACLE optimizer.

Interdependencies: USER_DEPENDENCIES and IDEPTREE

Objects within ORACLE7 databases can depend upon each other. For example, a stored procedure may depend upon a table, or a package may depend upon a package body. When an object within the database changes, any procedural object that depends upon it will have to be recompiled. This recompilation can either take place automatically at run-time (with a consequential performance penalty), or manually (see Chapter 22 for details on compiling procedural objects).

There are two sets of data dictionary views available to help you track dependencies. The first is USER_DEPENDENCIES, which lists all *direct* dependencies of objects. However, this only goes one level down the dependency tree. To fully evaluate dependencies, you must create the recursive dependency tracking objects in your schema. To create these objects, run the UTLDTREE.SQL script (usually located in the /rdbms/admin subdirectory of the ORACLE home directory). This script creates two objects you can query: DEPTREE and IDEPTREE. They contain identical information, but IDEPTREE is indented based on the pseudo-column Level, and is thus easier to read and interpret.

DBA-only Views

Since this chapter is intended for use by developers and end users, the data dictionary views available only to DBAs will not be covered here. The DBA-only views are used to provide information about distributed transactions, lock contention, rollback segments, and other internal database functions. For information on the use of the DBA-only views, see the *ORACLE7 Server Administrator's Guide*.

Trusted Oracle

Users of Trusted Oracle can view two additional data dictionary views, listed below.

ALL_LABELS	All system labels.
ALL_MOUNTED_DBS	All mounted databases.

For details on the usage of these views, see the *Trusted ORACLE7 Server Administrator's Guide*.

SQL*LOADER Direct Load Views

In order to manage the direct load option within SQL*LOADER, ORACLE7 maintains a number of data dictionary views. These generally are only queried for debugging purposes, upon request from Oracle Customer Support. The SQL*LOADER direct load option is described under the "SQLLOAD" entry in the Alphabetical Reference; its supporting data dictionary views are listed in Table 24-20. No descriptive comments are entered in the data dictionary for these views.

National Language Support (NLS) Views

Three data dictionary views are used to display information about the National Language Support (NLS) parameters currently in effect in the database. Nonstandard values for the NLS parameters (such as NLS_DATE_FORMAT and NLS_SORT) can be set via the database's INIT.ORA file or via the **alter session** command. See the **alter session** command of the Alphabetical Reference for further information on NLS settings. To see the current NLS settings for your session, instance, and database, you should query NLS_SESSION_PARAMETERS, NLS_INSTANCE_PARAMETERS, and NLS_DATABASE_PARAMETERS, respectively.

VIEW NAME

LOADER_TAB_INFO

LOADER_COL_INFO

LOADER_CONSTRAINT_INFO

LOADER_INDCOL_INFO

LOADER_IND_INFO

LOADER_PARAM_INFO

LOADER_TRIGGER_INFO

TABLE 24-20. *Data Dictionary Views for the SQL*LOADER Direct Path Option*

PART 4

Designing for Productivity

CHAPTER 25

Good Design Has a Human Touch

Chapter 2 discussed the need to build applications that are understandable and accommodating to users, and made several specific recommendations on how to approach this task successfully. If it's been some time since you read Chapter 2, review it now before moving on, as many of the concepts introduced there will be built upon here.

This chapter looks at a method of approaching a development project that takes into account the real business tasks your end users have to accomplish. This is to distinguish it from the more common data orientation of many developers and development methodologies. Data normalization and CASE technologies have become so much the center of attention with relational application development, that a focus on the data and the issues of referential integrity, keys, normalization, and table diagrams has become almost an obsession. They are so often confused with design—and even believed to *be* design—that the reminder that they are analysis is often met with surprise.

Normalization is analysis, not design. And it is only a part of the analysis necessary to understand a business, and build a useful application. The goal of application development, after all, is to help the business run more successfully. This is accomplished by improving the speed and efficiency with which business tasks are done, and also by making the environment in which people work as meaningful and supportive as possible. Give people control over their information, and intuitive, straightforward access to it, and they will respond gratefully and productively. Remove the control to a remote group, cloud the information in codes and user-hostile interfaces, and they will be unhappy and unproductive. It doesn't take a genius to figure this out.

The methods outlined in this chapter are not intended to be a rigorous elucidation of the process, and the tools you use and are familiar with for data structures or flows are probably sufficient for the task. The purpose here is more to disclose an approach that is effective in creating responsive, appropriate, and accommodating applications.

Understanding the Application Tasks

One of the often neglected steps in building software is really understanding the end user's job—the tasks that computer automation is intended to support. Occasionally, this is because the application itself is quite specialized; more often it is because the approach to design tends to be data-oriented. Frequently, these are the major questions asked in the analysis:

- What data should be captured?
- How should the data be processed?
- How should the data be reported?

These questions expand into a series of subquestions, and include issues such as input forms, codes, screen layouts, computations, postings, corrections, audit trails, retention, storage volumes, processing cycles, report formatting, distribution, and maintenance. These are all vitally important areas. One difficulty, however, is that they all focus solely on data.

People *use* data, but they *do* tasks. One might argue that while this may be true of professional workers, key entry clerks really only transfer data from an input form to a keyboard; their tasks are very data-oriented. This is a fair portrayal of these jobs today. But is this a consequence of the real job that needs to get done, or is it a symptom of the design of the computer application? Using humans as input devices, particularly for data that is voluminous, consistent in format (as on forms), and in a limited range of variability, is an expensive and antiquated, not to mention dehumanizing, method of capturing data. Like the use of codes to accommodate machine limitations, it's an idea whose time has passed.

This may sound like so much philosophy and idealism, but it has practical import in the way application design is done. People *use* data, but they *do* tasks. And they don't do tasks through to completion one at a time. They do several tasks that are subsets of or in intersection with each other, and they do them all at once, in parallel.

When designers allow this idea to direct the analysis and creation of an application, rather than the data orientation that has been historically dominant, the very nature of the effort changes significantly. Why have windowing environments been so successful? Because they allow a user to jump quickly between small tasks, keeping them all active without having to shut down and exit one in order to begin another. The windowing environment comes closer to mapping the way people really think and work than the old "one thing at a time" approach ever did. This lesson should not be lost. It should be built upon.

Understanding the application tasks means going far beyond identifying the data elements, normalizing them, and creating screens, processing programs, and reports. It means really understanding what the users do for a living and what their tasks are, and designing the application to be responsive to those tasks, not just to capture the data associated with them. In fact, when the orientation is toward the data, the resulting design will inevitably *distort* the user's tasks, rather than support them.

How do you design an application that is responsive to tasks rather than data? The biggest hurdle is simply understanding that it is necessary. This allows you to approach the analysis of the business from a fresh, naïve, and skeptical perspective.

Step One in the analysis process is to understand the tasks. What is it that this group, and the people in it, really do for a living? What is the real service or product produced? This seems like a fundamental and even simplistic first question, but you'll find a surprising number of businesspeople are quite unclear about the answer. An amazing number of businesses, from health care to banking, from shipping to manufacturing, think they're in the data processing business. After all, they input data, process it, and report it, don't they? This delusion is yet another symptom of the data orientation our systems designs have had in the past that has led dozens of companies to attempt to market their imagined "real" product, data processing, with disastrous consequences for most of them.

Hence the importance of naïveté and skepticism in learning about a business application: you will often have to challenge pet notions about what the business is, in order to learn what it *really* is. This is a healthy, if sometimes difficult, process.

And just as it is essential that businesspeople become literate users of SQL, and understand the basics of the relational model, so it is important that application designers really understand the service or product being delivered, and the tasks *necessary* to make that happen. A project team that includes end users who have been introduced to the essentials of SQL and the relational approach, such as by this book, and designers who are sensitive to end user's needs and understand the value of a task-oriented, English-based (or native language) application environment, will together turn out extraordinarily good systems. They check, support, and enhance each other's efforts.

One approach to this process is to develop two converging documents: a task document and a data document. It is in the process of preparing the task document that the deep understanding of the application comes about. The data document will help implement the vision and assure that the details and rules are all accounted for, but the task document defines the vision of what the business is.

Outline of Tasks

The task document is a joint effort of the business users and the application designers. It lists the tasks associated with the business from the top down. It begins with a basic description of the business. This should be a simple declarative sentence of three to ten words, in the active voice, without commas and with a minimum of adjectives:

"We sell insurance."

It should not be:

"Amalgamated Diversified is a leading international supplier of financial resources, training, information processing, transaction capture and distribution, communications, customer support, and industry direction in the field of shared risk funding for health care maintenance, property preservation, and automobile liability."

There is a tremendous temptation to cram every little detail about a business and its dreams about itself into this first descriptive sentence. Don't do it. The effort of trimming the descriptive excesses down to a simple sentence, like facing the gallows tomorrow morning, wonderfully focuses the mind. If you can't get the business down to ten simple words, you haven't understood it yet.

But, as an application designer, creating this sentence isn't your task alone; it is a joint task with the business user, and it initiates the task documentation process. It provides you with the opportunity to begin serious questioning about what the business does and how it does it. This is a valuable process for the business itself, quite independent of the fact that an application is being built. There will be numerous tasks and subtasks, procedures and rules that you will encounter that will prove to be meaningless or of very marginal use. Typically, these are artifacts of either a previous problem, long since solved, or of information or reporting requests from managers long since departed.

Some wags have suggested the way to deal with too many reports being created, whether manually or by computer, is to simply stop producing them, one by one, and see if anyone notices. This is a humorous notion, but the seed of truth it contains needs to be a part of the task documentation process.

The naïveté you bring to the joint effort of documenting tasks allows you to ask skeptical questions and look at (and reevaluate the usefulness of) what may be mere artifacts. Be aware, however, that you need to proceed with the frank acknowledgment that you, as a designer, cannot understand the business as thoroughly as the user does. There is an important line between seizing the opportunity of an application development to rationalize what tasks are done and why, and possibly offending the users by presuming to understand the "real" business better than they do.

Ask the user to describe a task in detail and explain to you the reason for each step. If the reason is a weak one, such as "we've always done it this way," or "I think they use this upstairs for something," red flags should go up. Say that you don't understand, and ask again for an explanation. If the response is still unsatisfactory, put the task and your question on a separate list for resolution. Some of these will be answered simply by someone who knows the subject better, others will require talking to senior management, and many tasks will end up eliminated because they are no longer needed. One of the evidences of a good analysis process is the improvement of existing procedures, independent of, and generally long before, the implementation of a new computer application.

General Format of the Task Document

This is the general format for the task document:

- Summary sentence describing the business (three to ten words)

- Summary sentences describing and numbering the major tasks of the business (short sentences, short words)

- Additional levels of task detail, as needed, within each of the major tasks

By all means follow the summary sentence for every level with a short, descriptive paragraph if you wish, but don't use this as an excuse to avoid the effort of making the summary sentence clear and crisp. Major tasks are typically numbered 1.0, 2.0, 3.0, and so on, and are sometimes referred to as *zero level tasks.* The levels below each of these are numbered using additional dots, as in 3.1.14. Each major task is taken down to the level where it is a collection of *atomic tasks*—tasks for which no subtask is meaningful in itself, and that, once started, is either taken to completion or dropped entirely. Atomic tasks are never left half-finished.

Writing a check is an atomic task; filling in the dollar amount is not. Answering the telephone as a customer service representative is not an atomic task; answering the phone and fulfilling the customer's request is atomic. Atomic tasks must be meaningful and must complete an action.

The level at which a task is atomic will vary by task. The task represented by 3.1.14 may be atomic, yet still have several additional sublevels. The task 3.2 may be atomic, or 3.1.16.4 may be. What is important is not the numbering scheme (which is nothing more than a method for outlining a hierarchy of tasks) but the decomposition to the atomic level. The atomic tasks are the fundamental building blocks of the business. Two tasks can still be atomic if one occasionally depends upon the other, but only if each can and does get completed independently. If two tasks always depend upon each other, they are not atomic. The real atomic task includes them both.

In most businesses you will quickly discover that many tasks do not fit neatly into just one of the major (zero level) tasks, but seem to span two or more, and work in a network or "dotted line" fashion. This is nearly always evidence of improper definition of the major tasks, or incomplete atomization of the lower tasks. The goal is to turn each task into a conceptual "object," with a well-defined idea of what it does (its goal in life) and what resources (data, computation, thinking, paper, pencil, and so on) it uses to accomplish its goal.

Insights Resulting from the Task Document

Several insights come out of the task document. First, because the task document is task-oriented rather than data-oriented, it is likely to substantially change the way user screens are designed. It will affect what data is captured, how it is presented, how help is implemented, and how users switch from one task to another. The task orientation will help assure that the most common kinds of jumping between tasks will not require inordinate effort from the user.

Second, the categorization of major tasks will change as conflicts are discovered; this will affect how both the designer and the business user understand the business.

Third, even the summary sentence itself will probably change. Rationalizing a business into atomic task "objects" forces a clearing out of artifacts, misconceptions, and unneeded dependencies that had long weighed down the business unnecessarily.

This is not a painless process, but the benefits, in terms of the business's self-understanding, the cleanup of procedures, and the automation of the tasks, will usually far exceed the emotional costs and time spent. It helps immensely if there is general understanding going into the project that uncomfortable questions will be asked, incorrect assumptions corrected, and step-by-step adjustments made to the task document until it is completed.

Understanding the Data

In conjunction with the decomposition and description of the tasks, the resources required at each step are described in the task document, especially in terms of the data required. This is done on a task-by-task basis, and the data requirements are then included in the data document. This is a conceptually different approach from the classical view of the data. You will not simply take the forms and screens currently used by each task and record the elements they contain. This is how many data element lists for projects are built. The flaw in this "piece of paper in a cigar box" approach—first described in Chapter 2—lies in our tendency (even though we don't like to admit it) to accept anything printed on paper as necessary or true.

In looking at each task, you should ask "what data is necessary to do this task?" rather than "what are the data elements on the form you use to do this task?" By requiring that the definition of the data needed come from the task, rather than from any existing forms or screens, you force an examination of the true purpose of the task and the real data requirements. If the person doing the task doesn't know the use to which data is put, the element goes on the list for resolution. An amazing amount of garbage is eliminated by this process.

Once the current data elements have been identified, they must be carefully scrutinized. Numeric and letter codes are always suspect. They disguise real information behind anti-intuitive, meaningless symbols. There are times and tasks where codes are handy, easily remembered, or made necessary by sheer volume. But in your final design these cases should be rare and obvious. If they are not, you've lost your way.

In the scrutiny of existing data elements, codes should be set aside for special attention. In each case ask yourself "why should this be a code?" Its continued use as a code should be viewed very suspiciously. There must be good arguments and compelling reasons for perpetuating the disguise. The process for converting them back into English is fairly simple, but is a joint effort. The codes are first listed, by data element, along with their meanings. These are then examined by users and designers, and short English versions of the meanings are proposed, discussed, and tentatively approved.

In this same discussion, designers and end users should decide on names for the data elements. These will become column names in the database, and will be regularly used in English queries, so the names should be descriptive, avoiding abbreviations other than those very common to the business, and singular (more on this in Chapter 27). Because of the intimate relationship between the column name and the data it contains the two should be named simultaneously. A thoughtful choice of a column name will vastly simplify the naming of its new English contents.

Data elements that are not codes also must be rigorously examined. By this point you have good reason to believe all of the data elements you've identified are necessary to the business tasks, but they are not necessarily well organized. What appears to be one data element in the existing task may in fact be several elements mixed together that require separation. Names, addresses, and phone numbers are very common examples of this, but every application has a wealth of others.

First and last names were mixed together, for example, in Talbot's ledger, and in the table built to store his data. Note, however, that the Name column held both names, even though the tables were in Third Normal Form. This would be an extremely burdensome way to actually implement an application, in spite of the fact that the normalization rules were technically met. To make the application practical and prepare it for English query, the Name column needs to be decomposed into at least two new categories, LastName and FirstName. This same categorization process is regularly needed in rationalizing other data elements, and is often quite independent of normalization.

The degree of decomposition depends on how the particular data elements are likely to be used. It is possible to go much too far, and decompose categories that, though made up of separable pieces, provide no additional value in their new state. Decomposition is application dependent on an element-by-element basis. Once done, these new elements, which will become columns, need to be thoughtfully named, and the data they will contain scrutinized. Text data that will fall into a definable number of values should be reviewed for naming. These column and value names, like those of the codes, are tentative.

The Atomic Data Models

Now the process of normalization begins, and with it the drawing of the atomic data models. There are many good texts on the subject and a wide variety of CASE tools that can speed the process, so this book doesn't suggest any particular method since recommending one method may hinder rather than help. The results will look something like Figure 25-1.

A drawing like this should be developed for each atomic transaction, and should be labeled with the task number to which it applies. Included in the drawing are table names, primary and foreign keys, and major columns. Each normalized relationship (the connecting lines) should have a descriptive name, and estimated row counts and transaction rates should appear with each table. Accompanying each drawing is an additional sheet with all of the columns and data types, their ranges of value, and the tentative names for the tables, columns, and named values in the columns.

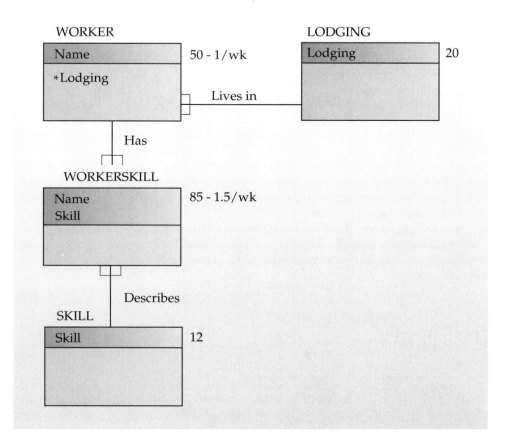

FIGURE 25-1. *A data model for the task of adding a new employee*

The Atomic Business Model

This data document is now combined with the task document. The combined document is a business model. It's reviewed jointly by the application designers and end users for accuracy and completeness.

The Business Model

At this point both the application designers and the end users should possess a clear vision of the business, its tasks, and its data. Once corrected and approved, the process of synthesizing the tasks and data models into an overall business model begins. This part of the process sorts common data elements between tasks, completes final, large-scale normalization, and resolves consistent, definitive names for all of the parts.

This can be quite a large drawing for major applications, with supporting documentation that includes the tasks, the data models (with corrected element names, based on the full model), and a list of each of the full-scale tables and their column names, datatypes, and contents. A final check of the effort is made by tracing the data access paths of each transaction in the full business model to determine that all the data the transaction requires is available for selection or insertion, and that no tasks insert data with elements missing that are essential to the model's referential integrity.

With the exception of the effort spent to properly name the various tables, columns, and common values, virtually everything to this point has been analysis, not design. The aim has been to promote understanding of the business and its components.

Data Entry

Screen design does not proceed from the business model. It is not focused on tables, but on tasks, so screens are created that support the task orientation and the need to jump between subtasks when necessary. In practical terms, this will often map readily to a primary table used by the task, and to other tables that can be queried for values or updated as the primary table is accessed.

But there will also be occasions where there simply is no main table, but instead a variety of related tables, all of which will supply or receive data to support the task. These screens will look and act quite differently from the typical table-oriented screens developed in most applications, but they will significantly amplify the effectiveness of their users and their contribution to the business. And that's the whole purpose of this approach.

The interaction between the user and the machine is critical; the input and query screens should consistently be task oriented and descriptive, in English. The use of icons and graphical interfaces will play an important role as well. Screens must reflect the way work is actually done, and be built to respond in the language in which business is conducted.

Query and Reporting

If anything sets the relational approach, and SQL, apart from more traditional application environments, it is the ability for end users to easily learn and execute *ad hoc queries*. These are those reports and one-time queries that are outside of the basic set usually developed and delivered along with the application code.

With SQLPLUS (and SQL*REPORTWRITER), end users are given unprecedented control over their own data. Both the users and developers benefit from this ability: the users, because they can build reports, analyze information, modify their queries, and re-execute them all in a matter of minutes, and the developers, because they are relieved of the undesirable requirement of creating new reports.

Users are granted the power to look into their data, analyze it, and respond with a speed and thoroughness unimaginable just a few years ago. This leap in productivity is greatly extended if the tables, columns, and data values are carefully crafted in English; it is greatly foreshortened if bad naming conventions and meaningless codes and abbreviations are permitted to infect the design. The time spent in the design process to name the objects consistently and descriptively will pay off quickly for the users, and therefore for the business.

It is supposed, fearfully, by some who have not built major relational applications, that turning query facilities over to end users will cripple the machine on which the facilities are used. The fear is that users will write inefficient queries that will consume overwhelming numbers of CPU cycles, slowing the machine and every other user. Experience shows that this is not generally true. Users quickly learn what kinds of queries run quickly, and which do not. Their concern may not be specifically with CPU cycles, but they are interested in getting their information quickly. This pushes them to learn the skills that make speed and efficiency possible. Those same skills reduce cycle usage. In practice, the demand users make on a machine only occasionally gets out of hand, but the benefit they derive far exceeds the cost of the processing. Remember the machine cost versus labor cost discussion in Chapter 2. Virtually anytime you can move effort from a person to a machine, you save money.

Review

Design includes issues other than naming conventions, data entry, and reporting. Depending upon the size and nature of the application, issues of transaction volume, performance, and ease of query often force a violation of Third Normal Form. This is not an irredeemable sin, but it does require putting certain controls in place to assure the concurrence and integrity of the data. These issues will be addressed in Chapter 26.

Aside from these concerns, the real goal of design is to clarify and satisfy the needs of the business and business users. If there is a bias, it must always be toward making the application easier to understand and use, particularly at the expense of CPU or disk, but less so if the cost is an internal complexity so great that maintenance and change become difficult and slow.

The purpose of this chapter has not been to direct you to a particular set of tools or diagramming techniques, but rather to explain the need to deeply understand the business, the data, and the needs of users when designing and building an effective relational application. Data can be mapped trivially into a relational database. But people do not organize their tasks based on the Third Normal Form of their data. A design that properly supports the way a person works must go beyond a view of the data; it requires significant thought and development to implement successfully in any environment.

CHAPTER 26

Performance and Design

No major application will run in Third Normal Form.

This is probably as heretical a statement as can be made in the face of modern relational theology, but it needs to be said. Perhaps, as CPUs get faster and parallel processing architecture is better exploited, this will no longer be true; more likely, the size of major applications will also increase. Demand for information and analysis will probably continue to outpace the ability of machines to process it in a fully normalized fashion.

Now, before cries for another inquisition begin, this heresy needs to be explained. The issue of normalization has several components. This chapter does not challenge either the relational model, which is both simple and elegant, or the process of normalization, which is an excellent and rational method of analyzing data and its fundamental relationships. It does challenge these fallacies:

- Normalization completely rationalizes data.

- Normalization accurately maps how humans work with data.

- Normalized data is the best representation of data.

- Data stored nonredundantly will be accessed faster than data stored many times.

- Normalized tables are the best way to store data.

- Referential integrity requires fully normalized tables.

The use of theological language here is intentional. Some people present relational techniques as if they were revealed law. Normalization, for instance, is simply a method to analyze elements of data and their relationships, and the relational model is the theoretical superstructure that supports the process. Together, these provide a way of viewing the world of data.

But they are not the only correct or useful ways to view the data. In fact, in a complex set of relationships, even Third Normal Form becomes insufficient rather quickly. Higher forms have been conceived to cope with these more difficult relations, although they are not often used outside of academia. Theorists readily acknowledge that these also fail to completely model reality (according to the number theorist Gödel, any model must remain incomplete).

Nevertheless, both the sufficiency of the relational model, and the necessity of Third Normal Form, have become virtual dogma in some circles. Some vendors (not including Oracle, to their credit) are even beginning to *enforce* Third Normal Form in their data dictionary. You won't be *allowed* to violate it—never mind that your application may not run.

ORACLE is based on a much more practical approach. It acknowledges the genius of the relational model, even to the degree of obeying Codd's rules, but it also provides, unapologetically, tools that permit developers to use their brains and make their own decisions about normalization, referential integrity, procedural language access, non-set-oriented processing, and other heretical techniques. In the real world, with real data, real users, and real demands for performance and ease of use, this flexibility is fundamental to success. Normalization is analysis, not design. Design encompasses issues, particularly related to performance, ease of use, maintenance, and straightforward completion of business tasks, that are unaccounted for in simple normalization.

Denormalization and Data Integrity

When analyzing the data of a business, normalizing the data to at least Third Normal Form assures that each nonkey column in each table is dependent only on the whole primary key of the table. If the data relationships are complex enough, normalizing to a higher form does a fine, if not complete, job of giving you a deep understanding of the data, and of relations between the various elements that must be protected and sustained as the application and database are built.

For a major application, however, or even a simple application where tasks do not readily map to fully normalized tables, once the analysis is complete, the design process may need to denormalize some of the tables in order to build an application that is responsive, maps to the user's tasks, and will actually complete its processing in the time windows available. There are a couple of useful approaches to this task.

However, any recommendations attempting to produce better response will have to differ from application to application. They will also differ over time, as query optimization methods improve, and as more and more CPU power is pushed out to the peripheral devices in the computer system and network. Benchmarking your application on your system is the only way to truly optimize your database.

Meaningful Keys

The tables put into Third Normal Form in Chapter 2 included one of the techniques you'll learn here, although it was not mentioned at the time. Once normalized, the tables and columns looked like this first version:

```
WORKER Table      WORKERSKILL Table    SKILL Table       LODGING Table
-------------     ------------------    -----------       -------------
Name              Name                  Skill             Lodging
Age               Skill                 Description       LongName
Lodging           Ability                                 Manager
                                                          Address
```

In a more typical design, particularly for a large application with many tables, these would have looked more like the following second version:

```
WORKER Table      WORKERSKILL Table    SKILL Table       LODGING Table
-------------     ------------------    -----------       -------------
WorkerID          WorkerID              SkillID           LodgingID
Name              SkillID               Skill             ShortName
Age               Ability               Description       LongName
LodgingID                                                 Manager
                                                          Address
```

The shift to WorkerID instead of Name is probably unavoidable. Too many of us have the same name for Name to be a unique primary key. However, the same is not necessarily true of the other keys. In this kind of design, all of the ID columns are usually sequentially assigned, unique, and meaningless numbers. Their sole function is to link one table to another. LodgingID, a number, is a foreign key in the WORKER table that points to just one row of the LODGING table. SkillID, a number, is a foreign key in the WORKERSKILL table that points to one row in the SKILL table.

To learn anything at all about a worker's skills and lodging, all four of these tables must be combined in a single join. Yet the task analysis shows that many of the most common queries seek the name of a worker's Skill and the name of his or her lodging. The additional detailed description of the Skill and the lodging Address and Manager are called for only infrequently. By using the first version of the table design, where the Skill and Lodging are meaningful keys—where they actually contain information, not just an assigned number—only the first two tables need to be joined for the most frequent queries, as in the following:

The WORKER Table

NAME	AGE	LODGING
Adah Talbot	23	Papa King
Bart Sarjeant	22	Cranmer
Dick Jones	18	Rose Hill
Elbert Talbot	43	Weitbrocht
Helen Brandt	15	
Jed Hopkins	33	Matts
John Pearson	27	Rose Hill
Victoria Lynn	32	Mullers
Wilfred Lowell	67	

The WORKER SKILL Table

NAME	SKILL	ABILITY
Adah Talbot	Work	Good
Dick Jones	Smithy	Excellent
Elbert Talbot	Discus	Slow
Helen Brandt	Combine Driver	Very Fast
John Pearson	Combine Driver	
John Pearson	Woodcutter	Good
John Pearson	Smithy	Average
Victoria Lynn	Smithy	Precise
Wilfred Lowell	Work	Average
Wilfred Lowell	Discus	Average

instead of this:

```
            The WORKER Table

NAME                          AGE LODGINGID
------------------------      ----- ---------
Adah Talbot                    23       4
Bart Sarjeant                  22       1
Dick Jones                     18       5
Elbert Talbot                  43       6
Helen Brandt                   15
Jed Hopkins                    33       2
John Pearson                   27       5
Victoria Lynn                  32       3
Wilfred Lowell                 67
```

```
            The WORKERSKILL Table

NAME                          SKILLID ABILITY
------------------------      ------- ---------
Adah Talbot                      6 Good
Dick Jones                       4 Excellent
Elbert Talbot                    2 Slow
Helen Brandt                     1 Very Fast
John Pearson                     1
John Pearson                     5 Good
John Pearson                     4 Average
Victoria Lynn                    4 Precise
Wilfred Lowell                   6 Average
Wilfred Lowell                   2 Average
```

Several points need to be made here.

First, meaningful primary keys must by definition be unique; they must provide the same relational integrity that a simple number key does.

Second, meaningful primary key names should be chosen with care: they may be more than one word long, and may contain spaces, so long as they are short, descriptive, memorable, in English, and avoid codes (other than those that are widely known and common to the business). This will make using them in queries simpler, and will reduce common entry errors when they are used in data entry.

Third, the choice of which keys to make meaningful comes from the task analysis; the need for it is virtually indiscernible from the data normalization process, since normalization can proceed with meaningless keys (as in the second example) without any awareness of their impact on tasks. Anyone with practical experience in a major application knows that table joins involving three or more tables, even if only two of them are large, consume a substantial number of CPU cycles. Yet many of these multi-table joins can be avoided if a task analysis has resulted in an understanding of what information will be often queried. This may imply that good performance is the criterion by which good design is measured; it is rather only one of several criteria, including simplicity, understandability, maintainability, and testability. The use of meaningful keys will contribute to these other goals as well.

Fourth, although the simplicity of a query can be improved with views, by making the four tables appear as one to the user, this method will not solve the performance problem (if there is one). In fact, it will worsen it by forcing, in this case, a four-way join when information from only one or two of the tables may be needed.

Fifth, the use of meaningful keys is not really denormalization. Referential integrity is still maintained in the same way, and **update** and **delete** anomalies of forms below third are not created by the technique. Some purists object to the use of meaningful keys, but the purity they pursue comes often at an unattainable price. Only when CPUs become infinitely fast can such purity be practical. Further, the real issue is not with meaningful keys, but with "intelligent" composite keys. These are dealt with separately in Chapter 27.

Sixth, if your query is just for the column that is indexed, ORACLE can retrieve the data from the index alone, without ever going to the underlying table, thereby speeding retrieval. With a meaningful key, this data is useful. With a meaningless key it is not.

In building a major relational application, the use of meaningful keys can simplify relationships between tables, and make the application faster and more intuitive. Meaningful keys require additional analysis and design work in creating the application, but quickly pay back the effort expended. However, if the application is small and the computer resources more than sufficient, the same simplicity and intuitiveness can be delivered through the use of views that hide the table joins from the end user.

Real Denormalization

The use of meaningful keys may not be enough. **select**s, **insert**s, **update**s, and **delete**s, and online and batch programs may all still run too slowly on a major application—usually because too many tables have been joined. Again, the task analysis will show the areas where the information requested is forcing access to too many tables at once.

One solution to this is to intentionally violate Third Normal Form in the table design by pushing data redundantly into a table where it is not wholly dependent on the primary key. This should not be done lightly, as the cost of denormalization is increased difficulty in maintaining the code. And the arguments given in Chapter

2 about the cost of equipment still apply. It is often cheaper to buy more memory and CPU power than to pay for the additional programming and maintenance costs. Assuming, however, that it is clear that performance must be attacked in some other way, denormalization is an effective means.

For example, suppose that whenever Talbot needed a profile of a worker, he always also wanted the name of the manager of the worker's lodging. This column is therefore added to the WORKER table itself:

WORKER Table	WORKER SKILL Table	SKILL Table	LODGING Table
Name	Name	Skill	Lodging
Age	Skill	Description	LongName
Lodging	Ability		Manager
Manager			Address

The data in the WORKER table now contains redundancy. The data on every worker living in Cranmer, for instance, now contains this information in addition to Name and Age:

LODGING	MANAGER
Cranmer	Thom Cranmer

If 50 of Talbot's workers live at Cranmer, "Thom Cranmer" appears in the WORKER table 50 times. However, if the application is designed carefully, Third Normal Form is still maintained *logically,* even though it is violated in the *physical* design of the tables. This is accomplished by continuing to maintain a LODGING table, and enforcing two rules:

- Whenever a new worker is added to the WORKER table, the data for the Manager column must come from the LODGING table only. It may not be keyed in independently. If a new worker lives in quarters not yet in the LODGING table, those quarters must be added to the LODGING table first, before the worker can be added to the WORKER table.

- Whenever a change is made to the LODGING table, such as the change of a manager at Cranmer, every row in the WORKER table that contains Cranmer must immediately be updated. To put it in task terminology, the update of the LODGING table, and the related columns and rows in the WORKER table, are together an atomic task. Both must be completed and committed at the same time. This is a trade-off between performance and transaction complexity.

These rules historically have been implemented in the application. You also can design a data dictionary that supports either *assertion,* where an atomic task such as this is stored and executed automatically when a change is made to the LODGING table, or *procedural logic,* which is executed from the dictionary if certain conditions are met. PL/SQL and triggers implement these rules in ORACLE7.

Rows, Columns, and Volume

One might sensibly ask what this will accomplish. Won't queries actually run slower with all that redundant data in the WORKER table? The answer is no. They will almost always run substantially faster. With only one or a few columns of redundant data, odds are excellent that queries, particularly, will run much faster without the table join being required. This is because when a row is fetched from a related table (such as LODGING), all of the columns are brought back to the CPU's memory, and those columns not named in the **select** are then discarded before the join is made. If only a portion of the LODGING table's data is kept in the WORKER table, a substantially smaller volume of data is fetched and processed by the CPU for a **select**. Further, if the same data is sought by multiple queries, ORACLE's buffer caching will make this even faster. Multiple tables and joins are never cached. Updates, however, particularly to the LODGING table, will be slower, because the rows in the WORKER table need to be updated as well.

What about the case when a majority, or even all, of a related table's data is stored in a table—such as putting Lodging, LongName, Manager, and Address all within the WORKER table (still using the LODGING table for data integrity, of course)? What are the competing claims?

A query using a table join, where only the foreign key (to the LODGING table) is kept in the WORKER table, and the LODGING data is kept in the LODGING table, will move less data, overall, to the CPU from the tables stored on disk. The data in the Cranmer LODGING row, for instance, will only be retrieved once, and then joined to each related row of the WORKER table in the CPU's memory. This moves less data over the disk I/O channel than having all of the same Cranmer data retrieved, over and over again, for every worker who lives at Cranmer, if all of the LODGING columns are replicated in the WORKER table.

Substantially less data is being moved from the disk, so will the table join, in this case, be faster? Surprisingly, it may not be.

Memory Binding

Relational database systems are usually *CPU-memory-bound*—that is, the system resource that most limits their performance is usually CPU memory, not disk access speed or disk I/O rate for the initial retrieval. This may seem counterintuitive, and many a designer (including the author) has spent hours carefully organizing tables on disk, avoiding discontinuity, minimizing head movement, and more, only to gain marginal increases in throughput. A highly tuned database system, where all resources have been balanced, tested, and balanced again, may run into binding other than CPU memory. But CPU memory is usually the first place a relational system becomes bound. This binding is memory size, rather than CPU speed.

When memory size is too small, *paging* occurs, and the operation of storing, sorting, and joining tables together suddenly becomes not a memory task, but is dropped back onto the disk I/O, which is millions of times slower than memory. The effect is like slamming the brakes on the CPU. If additional memory can be added to the machine (and taken advantage of by increasing array sizes or the SGA), it is usually worth the expense. Even so, querying a single table with redundant data will often still be faster than a join.

In any event, ORACLE provides monitoring facilities that can be used by a DBA to determine where the real bottlenecks lie, and common queries can be tested readily, perhaps with several alternative physical table designs, using the **set timing on** in SQLPLUS, or other CPU and disk consumption monitoring tools provided with the operating system. Benchmark alternatives when performance becomes an issue. What intuitively seems likely to be faster will often not be.

The Kitchen Junk Drawer

Another practical design technique, one that will often send the same purists mentioned earlier screaming into the woods, is the use of a *common codes table*. This is the design equivalent of that one drawer in every kitchen that collects all of the implements, string, tools, and assorted pieces of junk that don't really fit anywhere else.

Any real application has bits of information and (when unavoidable) codes that occur in extremely small volume, often only a single instance. But there may be dozens of such instances, all unrelated. Theoretically, these do not all belong in the same place. They should each have separate tables all their own. Practically, this would be a pain to manage. The solution is the construction of a relational kitchen junk drawer.

The junk drawer may contain several columns, each of which is a primary key for just one of the rows, and null for all the others. It may contain columns with names so general no one could guess what they meant, and that contained vastly different kinds of data depending upon the row being fetched.

These tables can be useful and effective; however, observe a few warnings: First, these tables should usually not themselves be visible to users. They may be a part of a view, but an end user shouldn't know it. Second, they usually contain information used internally, such as by SQL*FORMS screens, perhaps to manage a process, or to supply a piece of common information (your own company's address, for instance). Third, their integrity must be assured by carefully designed screens and programs, which only a limited, qualified group of systems people can access. If some of the information in them needs to be accessible to users, access should be strictly governed, and should probably be through a view that hides the true form of the table.

Should You Do Any of This?

These techniques, and others like them, are sometimes referred to as "violating normal form," the implication being that you've done something illogical or wrong. You've done neither. In fact, in most of the examples here, normal form was maintained logically, if not in the physical table design. The danger is in violating the integrity of the data, in particular its referential integrity: this is the glue that connects related data together and keeps it consistent. Fail to maintain it and you lose information, nearly always irretrievably. This should be of genuine concern. How you design your tables, on the other hand, is a case-by-case issue: what works best for this user and this application?

The Computation Table

A "table look up"—solving computations that contain well-defined parts by looking up the answer in a table rather than recomputing it each time—is a technique older than data processing. This use is obvious for something like a table of prime numbers, but it can prove valuable in other areas as well.

Many financial computations, for example, use two variables, say x and y, and include fractional exponents and quite extensive multiplication and division; the x variable part of each is involved only in one of the four basic arithmetic functions (such as multiplication).

These equations can be calculated once, with the variable x set to 1, for the whole range of possible values of y. The result for a given x and y is then found by looking up the y (which is indexed), retrieving the computed and stored result, and multiplying it by actual x. As with table denormalization, benchmarking is the best way to determine for which calculations this is most productive.

Review

Probably the most disheartening awareness stemming from all of this discussion of denormalization, referential integrity, memory-binding, benchmarking, and the like, is that the design process extends well beyond the first vision produced by the task and data analysis efforts. Unfortunately, the truth is that it does. Particularly with major applications, the portion of design time spent in rearranging the tables, benchmarking, and rearranging yet again can exceed that of the initial design work by a considerable amount. This is not mere adjustment or afterthought. You need to expect it, budget for it, and plan to do it rigorously. It is as integral to the design process as determining primary keys. The friendliest application in the world will lose its popularity rapidly if it moves too slowly.

To sensibly build an application you must strike a balance among three primary factors: ease of use, performance, and maintainability. In a perfect world these would all be maximized. But in a world where projects have limited development time frames, machines have limited power, and ease of use usually means additional program complexity, not favoring one factor at the expense of others is a challenge. The real message of this chapter is to convey how serious a process development is, and how important it is to be attentive to the competing forces at work.

CHAPTER 27

The Ten Commandments of Humane Design

This chapter reviews some of the issues in database application design a bit more thoroughly, proposes strategies to implement the ideas presented, presents a new idea or two for consideration by the relational community, and ends with "The Ten Commandments of Humane Design," which might more accurately be called the "Ten Suggestions." They are intended to help assure productive and accommodating applications, and avoid the deep chasms some designers (the authors included) have fallen into.

Toward Object Name Normalization

By now you've read quite a lot of comment on naming conventions, first in Chapter 2, and then in Chapters 25 and 26. These ideas have been presented rather informally: the basic approach is to choose meaningful, memorable, and descriptive English (or the country's official tongue, if not English) names, avoiding abbreviations and codes, and using underlines either consistently or not at all. In a large application, table, column, and data names will often be multiword, as in the case of ReversedSuspenseAccount, or Last_GL_Close_Date. The goal of thoughtful naming methods is ease of use: the names must be easily remembered, and must follow rules that are easily explained and applied. In the pages ahead, a somewhat more rigorous approach to naming will be spelled out, with the ultimate goal of developing a formal process of object name normalization.

Level-Name Integrity

In a relational database system, the hierarchy of objects ranges from the database, to the table owners, to the tables, to the columns, to the data values. In very large systems, there may even be multiple databases, and these may be distributed within locations. For the sake of brevity, the higher levels will be ignored for now, but what is said will apply to them as well. See Figure 27-1.

OWNER						
Table1			**Table2**			
Column 1	Column 2		Column 1	Column 2		
Value 1	Value 1		Value 1	Value 1		
Value 2	Value 2		Value 2	Value 2		
Value 3	Value 3		Value 3	Value 3		
			.	.		
			.	.		
			.	.		

FIGURE 27-1. *Database hierarchy*

Each level in this hierarchy is defined within the level above it, and each level should be given names appropriate to its own level, and not incorporate names from outside its own level. For example, consider the objects in Figure 27-2.

The full name of a column shows its heritage: George.WORKER.Name. Each level of the hierarchy is separated from those above or below it by a single dot or period. Names must be unique within their own parents: WORKER cannot have two columns called Name. The owner George cannot have two tables named WORKER. If Name is a primary key, it cannot have two data values of Adah Talbot. This is perfectly sensible and logical.

There is no requirement that each of George's tables have a name that is unique throughout the entire database. Other owners may have WORKER tables as well. Even if George is granted access to them, there is no confusion, because he can identify them uniquely by prefixing their owner's name to the table name, as in Dietrich.WORKER. If George combines a WORKER table of his own with one of Dietrich's, then the Name column in the **select** clause must contain its full identification, that is, Dietrich.WORKER.Name.

It would not be logically consistent to incorporate George's owner name into the name of each of his tables, as in GEOWORKER, GEOWORKERSKILL, and so on. This confuses and complicates the table name by placing part of its parent's name in its own, in effect a violation of *level-name integrity*.

Neither would it be logical or appropriate to tag each data value in a column with a portion of the column's name, as in NamAdah Talbot, NamBart Sarjeant, NamDick Jones. This is also a violation of level-name integrity.

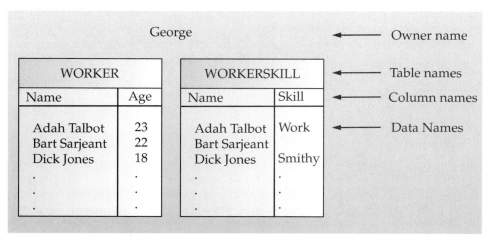

FIGURE 27-2. *Database example*

Nevertheless, many designers of tables have adopted the habit of creating column names that attempt to be unique across all tables, and they do this by inserting a part of the table name into each column name, as in WK_Name, WK_Age, WS_Name, and WS_Skill. In some cases, this is simply a bad habit acquired from experience with DBMS technologies of the 1970s, where all field names in the entire database were required to be unique. In other cases, this is done apparently in an attempt to eliminate the occasional need for table names in **select** and **where** clauses, producing listings like this:

```
select WK_Name, WK_Age, WS_Skill
  from WORKER, WORKERSKILL
 where WK_Name = WS_Name;
```

instead of this:

```
select WORKER.Name, Age, Skill
  from WORKER, WORKERSKILL
 where WORKER.Name = WORKERSKILL.Name;
```

This approach has enormous problems. The first example doesn't accomplish very much. The prefixes require extra keying, they confuse the meaning of the columns, and they don't readily disclose which tables they refer to. Some designers even use just the first letter of a table as a prefix. For them, the problem of abbreviation gets severe almost immediately, and is worse if several tables all start with the same letter or letters. In the previous example, in a less limited technique, WK and WS were taken as abbreviations for the two tables, but the abbreviation method is not defined anywhere, and the portion of the column name that defines what the column means is pushed off to the right.

One alternative sometimes used is to prefix only those column names that appear in more than one table with a table abbreviation:

```
select WK_Name, Age, Skill
  from WORKER, WORKERSKILL
 where WK_Name = WS_Name;
```

The difficulty here is obvious as well. How does a user remember which columns have prefixes and which don't? What happens to a column that is without a prefix if a column by the same name is later added to another table? Does it get renamed? If so, what happens to all the reports and views that rely upon it? If its name is left the same, but the new column gets a prefix, how will users remember which is prefixed and which is not?

The claim is sometimes made that this approach allows more brevity in a SQL statement because table names don't have to be keyed in to the **select** or **where** clauses. Yet the same degree of brevity can be accomplished by simple use of table aliases, as shown in the following:

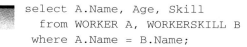

```
select A.Name, Age, Skill
  from WORKER A, WORKERSKILL B
 where A.Name = B.Name;
```

This method has the added benefit of including the abbreviation chosen for each table right in front of your eyes, in the **from** clause.

Brevity should never be favored over clarity. Including pieces of table names in column names is a bad technique because it violates the logical idea of levels, and the level-name integrity that this requires. It also confuses, requiring users to look up column names virtually every time they want to write a query.

Object names must be unique within their parent, but no incorporation of names from outside an object's own level should be permitted.

Foreign Keys

The one area of difficulty with this approach is the occasional appearance of a foreign key in a table where another column has the same name that the foreign key column does in its home table. One possible long-term solution is to allow the use of the full foreign key name, including the table name of its home table, as a column name in the local table, as shown in Figure 27-3.

If just the EMPLOYEE table were being queried, BRANCH.Badge would identify that column. If the two tables were joined, BRANCH.Badge would unambiguously refer to the Badge column of the BRANCH table. To select it from the EMPLOYEE table would require referencing it as EMPLOYEE.BRANCH.Badge. This method for identifying foreign keys should be sufficiently rigorous, but in reality today it is not supported. It's proposed here as an idea to be explored.

The practical need to solve the same-name column problem requires one of the following actions:

■ Invent a name that incorporates the source table of the foreign key in its name without using the dot (using an underline for instance).

■ Invent a name where an abbreviation of the source table of the foreign key is incorporated in its name.

■ Invent a name different from its name in its source table.

■ Change the name of the conflicting column.

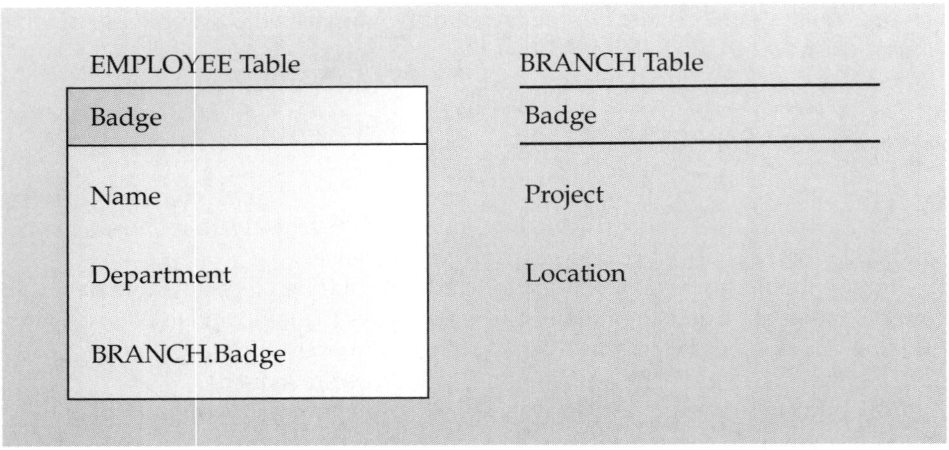

FIGURE 27-3. *Foreign key with complete name*

None of these is particularly attractive, but if you come across the same-name dilemma, you'll need to follow one of these steps.

Singularity

One area of great inconsistency and confusion is the question of whether objects should have singular or plural names. Should it be the WORKER table or the WORKERS table? Should it be the Name column or the Names column?

Some argue that table names should be plural, because they refer to all the rows they contain, hence: WORKERS. And column names should be plural because they refer to all the rows they contain, hence: Names.

Others argue that a table is really a set of rows, and it is a row that the column and table names refer to, hence: WORKER and Name.

One vendor proposes that all table names be plural, and all column names be singular, hence: WORKERS and Name. Another vendor proposes that all table names should be singular and each user should decide for themselves about the columns. Is it any wonder designers are confused, and with them their long-suffering users?

There are two helpful ways to think about this issue. First, consider some columns common to nearly every database: Name, Address, City, State, and Zip.

Other than the first column, does it ever occur to anyone to make these column names plural? It is nearly self-evident when considering these names that they describe the contents of a single row, a record. Even though relational databases are "set-oriented," clearly the fundamental unit of a set is a row, and it is the content of that row that is well-described by singular column names. When designing a data entry screen to capture a person's name and address, should it look like this?

```
Names: _____

Addresses: _____

Cities: _____ States __ Zips _____-____
```

Or will you make these column names singular on the screen, since you're capturing *one* name and address at a time, but tell the users that when they write queries they must all be converted to plural? It is simply more intuitive and straightforward to restrict column names to singular.

The argument for table names is less straightforward. They contain the set of rows. Your "photo" album contains a set of many photos. Your "address" book or your "phone" book contains the set of your regular business and personal contacts. You wouldn't expect an "address" book to contain just one address; obviously it contains a set, each instance of which is characterized as an address. You may have a car club, an investment portfolio, and a best restaurant list.

On the other hand, people sometimes talk about a receivables ledger, a singles group, or a favorite foods list. Groups get named both ways, though the singular form is more common when there is no preposition. You might say "address book," but would always say "book of addresses." It would always be "table of workers," but "worker table" (besides which, "workers table" sounds like something workers own, rather than something that contains worker information).

So, although both sides have merit when tables are concerned, the singular usage is more common in everyday speech about sets and groups.

The second way to think about this is consistency and usefulness. If all objects are named consistently, neither you nor a user has to try to remember the rules for what is plural and what isn't. The benefit of this should be obvious. Suppose we decide that all objects will henceforth be plural. We now have an "s" or an "es" on the end of virtually every object, perhaps even on the end of each word in a long multiword object name. Of what possible benefit is it to key all of these extra letters, all of the time? Is it easier to use? Is it easier to understand? Is it easier to remember? Obviously, it is none of these.

Therefore, the best solution is this: all object names are always singular. The sole exception to this rule is any widely accepted term already commonly used in the business, such as "sales."

Brevity

As mentioned earlier, clarity should never be sacrificed for brevity, but given two equally meaningful, memorable, and descriptive names, always choose the shorter. For example, suppose you are to assign a name to a column that is a part of a description of a company's structure. It includes division, department, project, and employee columns. The company is acquired by a conglomerate, and your database is to become the reporting mechanism for the new parent. This means a higher level of organization, by company, is going to be required. What will you call it? Here are some alternatives:

```
Corporation
Enterprise
Business
Company
Firm
```

Depending upon how the business is organized, any one of these names could be appropriate (all of them have been used in table designs by one designer or another). Firm, however, is about one-third the size of Corporation, and it is meaningful, memorable, and descriptive. Although it is not as commonly used as Company, for instance, it is certainly more common than Enterprise, which has become quite fashionable, and it is learned and remembered after one use.

Another example is in the name chosen for the LODGING table and column. It could have been any of these:

```
Accommodation
Domicile
Dwelling
Lodging
Abode
Home
```

Because Home is less than one-third the size of Accommodation, and just over half the size of Lodging, it would have been a better choice. Brevity saves keying, and makes object names concise and quickly understood, but it is less important than clarity.

During application development, propose alternative names such as these to a group of users and developers and get their input on choosing the clearest name. How do you build lists of alternatives like these examples? Use a thesaurus and a dictionary. On a project team dedicated to developing superior, productive applications, every team member should be given a thesaurus and a dictionary as basic equipment, and then be reminded over and over again of the importance of careful object naming.

Object Name Thesaurus

Ultimately, relational databases should include an Object Name Thesaurus, just as they include a Data Dictionary. This thesaurus would enforce the company's naming standards, and assure consistency of name choice and abbreviation (where used).

An object being named must often have multiple words in its name, such as Firm_Home_City. If a new name were proposed, such as Company_Domicile_City, the thesaurus would analyze the component words and rate them. For each of the words, it would approve the choice, or declare a violation of standards and suggest an approved alternative, or tell you the word or abbreviation was not recognized. The use of an unapproved name in the creation of an object would either require approval from a standards group or person, or produce a report to the DBA specifying the violation.

Such a thesaurus may require the use of underlines in object naming, in order to make the parsing of the name into component parts a straightforward task. This also helps enforce the consistent use of underlines, rather than the scattered, inconsistent usage within an application that they frequently receive now, and keyboard manufacturers might be encouraged to place the underline key within easier reach than it is currently (usually on the top row of the keyboard and requiring the use of the SHIFT key—most people can't type it without looking).

Intelligent Keys and Column Values

Intelligent keys are so named because they contain nontrivial combinations of information. The term is misleading in the extreme, because it implies something positive or worthwhile. A more meaningful term might be "overloaded" keys. General ledger and product codes often fall into this category, and contain all of the difficulties associated with other codes, and more. Further, the difficulties found in intelligent or overloaded keys also apply to nonkey columns that are packed with more than one piece of meaningful data.

Typical of an overloaded key or column value would be this description: "The first character is the region code. The next four characters are the catalog number. The final digit is the cost center code, unless this is an imported part, in which case an 'I' is tagged on to the end of the number, or if it is a high volume item, such as screws, in which case only three digits are used for catalog number, and the region code is HD."

Eliminating overloaded key and column values is essential in good relational design. The dependencies built on pieces of these keys (usually foreign keys into other tables) are all at risk if the structure is maintained. Unfortunately, many application areas have overloaded keys that have been used for years and are deeply embedded in the company's tasks. Some of them were created during earlier efforts at automation, using databases that could not support multiple key columns for composite keys. Others came about through historical accretion, by forcing a short code, usually numeric, to mean more and to cover more cases than it was ever intended to at the beginning. Eliminating the existing overloaded keys may have practical ramifications that make it impossible to do immediately. This makes building a new, relational application more difficult.

The solution to this problem is to create a new set of keys, both primary and foreign, that properly normalizes the data; then make sure that people can access tables only through these proper keys. The overloaded key is then kept as an additional, and unique, table column. Access to it is still possible using historical methods (matching the overloaded key in a query, for instance), but the newly structured keys are promoted as the preferred method of access. Over time, with proper training, users will gravitate to the new keys. Eventually, the overloaded keys (and other overloaded column values) can simply be nulled out.

Failing to eliminate overloaded keys and values makes extracting information from the database, validating the values, assuring data integrity, and modifying the structure all extremely difficult and costly.

The Commandments

All of the major issues in designing for productivity have now been introduced and discussed, primarily in Chapters 2, 25, 26, and this chapter, but also briefly in other chapters as well. It will probably prove worthwhile to sum these up in a single place, thus "The Ten Commandments." As was noted at the beginning of the chapter, these issues might better be characterized as the "Ten Suggestions." They are presented, not assuming that you need to be told what to do, but rather assuming that you are capable of making rational judgments, and can benefit from the experience of others facing the same challenges. The purpose here is not to describe the development cycle, which you probably understand better than you want to, but rather to bias that development with an orientation that will radically change how the application will look, feel, and be used. Careful attention to these ideas can dramatically improve the productivity and happiness of an application's users.

The Ten Commandments of Humane Design

1. Include users. Put them on the project team, and teach them the relational model and SQL.

2. Name tables, columns, keys, and data jointly with the users. Develop an application thesaurus to assure name consistency.

3. Use English words that are meaningful, memorable, descriptive, short, and singular. Use underline consistently or not at all.

4. Don't mix levels in naming.

5. Avoid codes and abbreviations.

6. Use meaningful keys where possible.

7. Decompose overloaded keys.

8. Analyze and design from the tasks, not just the data. Remember that normalization is not design.

9. Move tasks from users to the machine. It is profitable to spend cycles and storage to gain ease of use.

10. Don't be seduced by development speed. Take time and care in analysis, design, testing, and tuning.

PART 5

Alphabetical Reference

CHAPTER 28

Alphabetical Reference

This chapter contains references for most major ORACLE commands, keywords, products, features, and functions, with extensive cross-referencing of topics. Subtopics within a reference can be found in the index. The reference is intended for use by both developers and users of ORACLE, but assumes some familiarity with the products. Reading the first six pages of this reference will help you make the most productive use of the entries.

What This Alphabetical Reference Includes

This alphabetical reference contains entries for virtually every ORACLE command in SQL, PL/SQL, and SQLPLUS, as well as definitions of all relevant terms used in ORACLE and SQL. Each command is listed with its correct format or syntax, an explanation of its purpose and use, the product or products in which it is used, and important details, restrictions, and hints about it, along with examples to illustrate proper usage. Topics are in alphabetical order, and are heavily cross-referenced, both within the alphabetical reference, and to preceding chapters in the book.

What This Alphabetical Reference Does Not Include

This is not a tutorial; it does not explain the screen-oriented development tools in products such as SQL*FORMS and SQL*REPORTWRITER, since these are relatively easy to learn and use. Additionally, there are a few areas where usage is likely to be so specialized or infrequent that inclusion here did not seem of much benefit. In these instances, the text refers you to the ORACLE manual, or another book, where you can find the needed information.

General Format of Entries

Entries in this reference are typically either definitions of terms or descriptions of functions, commands, and keywords. These are usually structured in seven sections: the keyword, its type, the products in which it is used, a "*See also*" cross-reference, the format in which the keyword appears, a description of its components, and an example of its use. A typical entry looks like the following:

RPAD

Type   SQL function

Products   All

See also   CHARACTER FUNCTIONS, **LPAD**, **LTRIM**, **RTRIM**, Chapter 5

Format

```
RPAD(string,length [,'set'])
```

Description   **R**ight **PAD**. RPAD makes a string a certain length by adding a certain set of characters to the right. If *set* is not specified, the default pad character is a space.

Example

```
select RPAD('HELLO ',24,'WORLD') from DUAL;
```

produces this:

```
HELLO WORLDWORLDWORLDWOR
```

The Sections of Each Entry

The **KEYWORD** usually appears on a line by itself. In some cases a brief definition follows. If a keyword has more than one definition, either in different ORACLE tools or in different ORACLE versions, the keyword will be followed by a brief qualifier, such as (Form 1 - Schema Objects), in order to indicate that more than one listing exists for this keyword.

Type is a general indication of what the keyword is used for, such as "SQL function," "SQL*FORMS command," and so on.

Products tells which products use each listed keyword. "All" means any product with the authority to use the command. If specific products are named, then the command or keyword applies only to them. If only certain versions of the product are able to use the keyword, the product versions will be named.

See also suggests other topics that are closely related to the keyword, or gives the chapter or chapters in the book that give detailed descriptions of how the keyword is used in practice. Occasionally you will be referred to the ORACLE manual or other reference book that contains detail beyond the scope of this reference.

Format generally follows the notation of ORACLE manuals, with all SQL and other keywords in uppercase. In actual use, these must be entered exactly as they are shown (except that case is irrelevant). Variables and variable parameters are shown in lowercase *italic*. This indicates that some appropriate value should be substituted. When parentheses are shown, they must be entered where they appear, just as are words shown in uppercase.

Standard Usages for Variables

Some standard usages for variables follow:

THIS VARIABLE	INDICATES
column	The name of a column
database	The name of a database
link	The name of a link in SQL*NET
password	A password
segment	The name of a segment
table	The name of a table
tablespace	The name of a tablespace
user	The name of a user or owner
view	The name of a view

Other Formatting Guidelines

Some other guidelines for formatting follow:

character means the value must be a single character.

string typically represents a character column or an expression or column that can be treated like a CHAR or VARCHAR2 column after automatic data conversion.

value usually represents a NUMBER column or an expression or column that can be treated like a NUMBER column after automatic data conversion.

date usually represents a date column or an expression or column that can be treated like a date column after automatic data conversion.

integer must be a whole number, such as –3, 0, or 12.

expression means any form of a column. This could be a literal, a variable, a mathematical computation, a function, or virtually any combination of functions and columns whose final result is a single value, such as a string, a number, or a date.

Occasionally other notation is used as well, such as **condition** or **query**. This is explained or apparent in context.

Optional items are enclosed in square brackets, as in **[user.]**, meaning that *user* is not necessarily required.

Alternative items in a list are separated by a single broken vertical bar, as in **OFF ¦ ON**, which should be read "OFF or ON." On some systems this vertical bar is displayed as a solid vertical bar.

Required options, where one item of a list of items is required, are surrounded by curly braces, as in **{OFF ¦ ON}**.

The **default** item in a list, if there is one, will be listed first.

Three periods (or ellipses) indicate that the previous expression can be repeated any number of times, as in **column [,column]. . .** which means that **,column** may be any number of additional columns separated by commas.

In rare instances normal notation is either insufficient or inappropriate for what is being shown. In these cases, the **Description** will spell out more fully what is intended in the **Format**.

Other Elements of a Listing

A few commands have a **Return type**, which indicates the data type of the value returned by a function.

Description is a verbal explanation of the command and its parts. **Boldface** words within the description usually direct references to either commands or variables shown in the **Format** section.

Examples will show either the results of a function, or how a keyword is used in a real query or application. The style of the examples is not the same as that of the **Format** section. Instead, it follows the style of the first part of this book (described in Chapter 3), since this is more typical of real coding practice.

The Order of the Listings

This reference is in alphabetical order, with all entries that begin with symbols coming before the first entry beginning with the letter A.

Words that are hyphenated, such as BLOCK-LEVEL, or that have an underscore character in them, such as GO_FIELD, are alphabetized as if the hyphen or underscore were a space.

Symbols

The symbols are listed in order of appearance with a short definition or name. Those symbols with definitions in **boldface** have full entries dedicated to them, or are prefixes to words that are covered in the pages that follow.

_	**underline (also called underscore, underbar)**
¬	not sign, used on some systems for ¬ (not equal)
!	exclamation mark
"	**double quotation mark**
#	**pound sign**
$	**dollar sign**
%	**percent sign**
&	**ampersand**

&&	double ampersand
'	single quotation mark or apostrophe
( )	parentheses
*	asterisk or multiplication
**	exponentiation in PL/SQL
+	plus
–	subtraction or hyphen
- -	double hyphen, SQL comment minus or hyphen
.	period or dot, a name or variable separator
..	to
/	division or slash
/*	slash asterisk, SQL comment divided by or slash
:	colon
:=	is set equal to in PL/SQL
;	semicolon
<< >>	label name delimiter in PL/SQL
<	less than
<=	less than or equal to
< >	not equal
!=	not equal
=	equal
>	greater than
>=	greater than or equal to
@	at sign
@@	double at sign
[ ]	square brackets
^	caret
^=	not equal
{ }	curly braces
¦	broken vertical bar
¦¦	concatenation

_ (Underscore)

The underscore represents a single position with the **LIKE** operator. *See* **LIKE**.

_EDITOR

See **EDIT**.

" (Double Quotation Mark)

Type   SQL delimiter

Products   All

See also   **ALIAS**, **TO_CHAR**, Chapters 5 and 7

Description   " surrounds a table or column alias that contains special characters or a space, or surrounds literal text in a date format clause of **TO_CHAR**.

Example   Here it is used as an alias:

```
select NEXT_DAY(CycleDate,'FRIDAY') "Pay Day!"
  from PAYDAY;
```

and here it is used as a formatting portion of **TO_CHAR**:

```
select FirstName, Birthdate, TO_CHAR(BirthDate,
       '"Baby Girl on" fmMonth ddth, YYYY, "at" HH:MI "in the Morning"')
       "Formatted"
  from BIRTHDAY
 where FirstName = 'VICTORIA';
```

```
FIRSTNAME       BIRTHDATE Formatted
--------------- --------- -------------------------------
VICTORIA        20-MAY-49 Baby Girl on May 20th, 1949,
                          at 3:27 in the Morning
```

(Pound Sign)

Type   SQL*PLUS command

Product   SQL*PLUS

See also   **DOCUMENT**, **REMARK**, /* */, Chapter 4

Description   # completes a block of documentation in a SQLPLUS start file where the block is begun by the word DOCUMENT. SQL*PLUS ignores all lines from the line where it sees the word DOCUMENT until the line after the **#**.

$ (Dollar Sign)

Type   SQL*PLUS command

Product   SQLPLUS

See also   **@, @@, HOST, START**

Format

```
$ host command
```

Description   **$** passes any host command back to the operating system for execution without exiting SQL*PLUS. **$** is shorthand for **HOST**. This doesn't work on all hardware or operating systems.

% (Percent)

% is a wild card used to represent any number of positions and characters with the LIKE operator. *See* **LIKE**.

%FOUND

Type   cursor attribute

Products   PL/SQL

See also   %ISOPEN, %NOTFOUND, %ROWCOUNT, **CURSOR**, **SQL CURSOR**

Format

```
cursor%FOUND
```

or

```
SQL%FOUND
```

Description   **%FOUND** is a success flag for **select**, **insert**, **update**, and **delete**. *cursor* is the name of an explicit cursor **declare**d in a PL/SQL block, or the implicit cursor named **SQL**. **%FOUND** can be attached to a cursor name as a suffix. The two together are a success flag for the execution of **select**, **insert**, **update**, and **delete** statements in PL/SQL blocks.

   PL/SQL temporarily sets aside a section of memory as a scratchpad for the execution of SQL statements, and for storing certain kinds of information (or *attributes*) about the state of that execution. If the SQL statement is a **select**, this area will contain one row of data.

%FOUND is one of those attributes. It is used in PL/SQL logic as part of an IF/THEN test, and always evaluates TRUE, FALSE, or NULL. **%NOTFOUND** is the logical opposite. It is FALSE when **%FOUND** is TRUE, TRUE when **%FOUND** is FALSE, and NULL when **%FOUND** is NULL.

Here are the states of **%FOUND** under various conditions:

CURSOR ACTIVITY	EXPLICIT CURSOR	IMPLICIT (SQL) CURSOR
Explicit cursor not opened yet	(ERROR)	n/a
Cursor OPEN but no FETCH executed yet	NULL	n/a
FETCH returned a row	TRUE	TRUE
FETCH returned no rows	FALSE	FALSE
Before any SQL executed in implicit cursor	n/a	NULL
insert inserted a row	n/a	TRUE
insert failed to insert a row	n/a	FALSE
update affected at least one row	n/a	TRUE
update failed to affect any rows	n/a	FALSE
delete eliminated at least one row	n/a	TRUE
delete failed to eliminate any rows	n/a	FALSE

Testing **%FOUND** for the condition of an explicit cursor before it is **OPEN**ed raises an EXCEPTION (error code ORA-01001, INVALID CURSOR).

You'll notice that many conditions here are "n/a," or "not applicable." This is because only the implicit cursor is used for any **insert**, **update**, or **delete**, and any testing of its value must be done using **SQL%FOUND** after its execution, and before any other SQL is executed in the SQL cursor.

%ISOPEN

Type   cursor attribute

Products   PL/SQL

See also   SQL CURSOR

Format

```
cursor%ISOPEN
```

Description   *cursor* must be either the name of an explicitly declared cursor or the implicit cursor named **SQL**. Evaluates to TRUE if the named cursor is open, FALSE if it is not. **SQL%ISOPEN** will *always* evaluate FALSE, because the SQL cursor is opened and closed automatically when a SQL statement not explicitly declared is executed (*see* SQL CURSOR). **%ISOPEN** is used in PL/SQL logic; it cannot be a part of a SQL statement.

Example

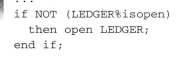

```
...
if NOT (LEDGER%isopen)
  then open LEDGER;
end if;
...
```

%NOTFOUND

See **%FOUND**.

%ROWCOUNT

Type   Cursor attribute

Products   PL/SQL

See also   **CLOSE, DECLARE, DELETE, FETCH, INSERT, OPEN, SELECT, UPDATE**

Format

```
cursor%ROWCOUNT
```

Description   *cursor* must be either the name of an explicitly declared cursor, or the implicit cursor named SQL. **cursor%ROWCOUNT** contains the cumulative total number of rows that have been **FETCH**ed from the active set in this cursor. This can be used to intentionally process only a fixed number of rows, but is more commonly used as an exception handler for **select**s that are intended to return just one row (for example **select. . . into**). In these cases, **%ROWCOUNT** is set to 0 if no rows are returned (**%NOTFOUND** can make this test as well), and to 2 if more than one row is returned, regardless of the actual number.

　　%ROWCOUNT is used in PL/SQL logic; it cannot be a part of a SQL statement. If **SQL%ROWCOUNT** is used, it can only refer to the most recently opened implicit cursor. If no implicit cursor has been opened, **SQL%ROWCOUNT** returns NULL.

%ROWTYPE

Type   variable attribute

Products   PL/SQL

See also   FETCH

Format

```
{[user.]table | cursor}%ROWTYPE
```

Description   **%ROWTYPE** declares a record variable to have the same structure as an entire row in a table (or view), or as a row retrieved by the named cursor. This is used as part of a variable declaration and assures that the variable will contain the appropriate fields and data types to handle all of the columns being fetched. If [*user.*]*table* is used, the table (or view) must exist in the database.

For example, recall the WORKER table:

```
Column          Data type
-------------   ----------------
Name            VARCHAR2(25) not null
Age             NUMBER
Lodging         VARCHAR2(15)
```

To create a variable that will contain corresponding fields, use **declare**, a variable name, and **%ROWTYPE** with the table name, and then select a row into the record. (Note the *****, which gets all columns. This is required for the form that uses a table name as a prefix to **%ROWTYPE**.)

```
DECLARE
 WORKER_RECORD     WORKER%rowtype;

BEGIN
    select * into WORKER_RECORD from WORKER
     where Name = 'BART SARJEANT';

    if WORKER_RECORD.Age > 65
       then ...
    end if;

END;
```

Because the WORKER_RECORD has the same structure as the table WORKER, you can reference the Age field as WORKER_RECORD.Age, using notation similar to table.column used in SQL statements. **select. . .into** and **fetch. . .into** are the only methods for loading an entire record variable. Individual fields within the record can be loaded using **:=**, as shown here:

```
WORKER_RECORD.Age := 44;
```

If a cursor is used as the prefix for **%ROWTYPE**, then it can contain a **select** statement with only as many columns as are needed. However, if a column that is **fetch**ed from a named cursor is an expression, rather than a simple column name, the expression must be given an alias in the **select** statement before it can be referenced using this technique. For instance, suppose the cursor **select** statement was this:

```
DECLARE
cursor employee is select Name, Age + 10 from WORKER;
```

There would be no way to reference the expression Age + 10, so redo it this way:

```
DECLARE
cursor employee is select Name, (Age + 10) New_Age
  from WORKER;
```

The previous example would then look like this:

```
DECLARE
   cursor EMPLOYEE is select Name, (Age + 10) New_Age
 from WORKER
 where Name = 'BART SARJEANT';

   WORKER_RECORD    EMPLOYEE%rowtype;

BEGIN
   open EMPLOYEE;
   fetch EMPLOYEE into WORKER_RECORD;

   if WORKER_RECORD.new_age > 65
      then ...
   end if;
   close EMPLOYEE;

END;
```

New_Age is the alias for Age + 10, and it now can be referenced as a field in WORKER_RECORD.

%ROWTYPE is used in PL/SQL logic; it cannot be a part of a SQL statement.

%TYPE

Type   variable attribute

Products   PL/SQL

See also   **%ROWTYPE**

Format

```
{[user.]table.column ¦ variable}%TYPE
```

Description   **%TYPE** is used to declare a new variable to be of the same type as a previously declared variable, or as a particular column in a table that already exists in the database you're connected to.

Example   In this example a new variable, Employee, is made to be the same type as the Name column in the WORKER table. Since Employee now exists, it can be used to declare yet another new variable, New_Worker:

```
Employee     WORKER.Name%type;
New_Worker   Employee%type;
```

& or && (Ampersand or Double Ampersand)

Type   Prefixes for variables

Product   SQL*PLUS

See also   **:**, **ACCEPT**, **DEFINE**, **START**, Chapters 12 and 19.

Format

```
&integer
&variable
&&variable
```

Description   **&** and **&&** can be used in several ways (**&&** applies only to the second definition below):

- Prefix for parameters in a SQL*PLUS start file. Words are substituted for &1, &2, etc. *See* **START**.

- Prefix for a substitution variable in a SQL command in SQL*PLUS. SQL*PLUS will prompt for a value if an undefined **&** or **&&** variable is found. **&&** will define the variable and thereby preserve its value; **&** will not define or preserve the value, but only substitute what is entered one time. *See* **ACCEPT** and **DEFINE**.

■ A prefix indicating indirection—the use of a variable to contain the name of another variable in SQL*FORMS.

' (Single Quotation Mark)

Type   SQL literal string delimiter

Products   All

See also   " (Double Quotation Mark), Chapter 5

Format

```
'string'
```

Description   ' surrounds a literal, such as a character string or date constant. To use one quotation mark or an apostrophe in a string constant, use two ' marks (*not* a double quotation mark). Avoid the use of apostrophes in data (and elsewhere) whenever possible.

Example

```
select 'William' from DUAL;
```

produces this:

```
William
```

whereas this:

```
select 'William''s brother' from DUAL;
```

produces this:

```
William's brother
```

( ) (Parentheses)

Type   SQL delimiter

Products   All

See also   **PRECEDENCE**, **SUBQUERY**, **UPDATE**, Chapters 3, 10, and 13

Description   ( ) surrounds subqueries or lists of columns, or controls precedence.

* (Multiplication)

Type   SQL operator

Products   All

See also   +, –, /, Chapter 6

Format

```
value1 * value2
```

Description   *value1* * *value2* means *value1* multiplied by *value2*.

* * (Exponentiation)

Type   PL/SQL operator

Products   PL/SQL

See also   **POWER**

Format   *x* ** *y*

Description   The *x* is raised to the power *y*. *x* and *y* may be constants, variables, columns, or expressions. Both must be numeric.

Example

```
4**4 = 256
```

+ (Addition)

Type   SQL operator

Products   All

See also   –, *, /, Chapter 6

Format

```
value1 + value2
```

Description   *value1* + *value2* means *value1* plus *value2*.

– (Subtraction [Form 1])

Type   SQL operator

Products   All

See also   +, *, /, Chapter 6

Format

```
value1 - value2
```

Description   *value1 – value2* means *value1* minus *value2*.

- (Hyphen [Form 2])

Type   SQL*PLUS command

Product   SQL*PLUS

See also   Chapter 12

Format

```
command text -
text -
text
```

Description   SQL*PLUS command continuation. - continues a command on the following line.

Example

```
ttitle left 'Current Portfolio' -
      right 'April 1st, 1995'        skip 1 -
      center 'Industry Listings    '  skip 4;
```

-- (Comment)

Type   SQL single-line embedded comment delimiter

Products   All

See also   /* */, **REMARK**, Chapter 4

Format

```
-- any text
```

Description   -- tells ORACLE a comment has begun. Everything it sees from that point to the end of the line, it regards as a comment. These delimiters are used only within SQL itself or in PL/SQL and must appear before the SQLTERMINATOR.

Example

```
select Feature, Section, Page
-- this is just a comment
   from NEWSPAPER    -- this is another comment
 where Section = 'F'
```

. (Period or Dot [Form 1])

Type   SQL operator

Product   SQL*PLUS

Format

```
&variable.suffix
```

Description   The . is a variable separator, used in SQL*PLUS to separate the variable name from a suffix, so that the suffix is not considered a part of the variable name.

Example   Here the suffix "st" is effectively concatenated to the contents of the variable &Avenue.

```
define Avenue = 21
select '100 &Avenue.st Street' from DUAL;
```

produces this:

```
100 21st Street
```

This same technique might also be used in a **where** clause.

. (Period or Dot [Form 2])

Type   SQL operator

Products   All

See also SYNTAX OPERATORS, Chapters 20 and 27.

Format

```
[user.][table.]column
```

Description The . is a name separator, used to specify the complete name of a column, including (optionally) its table or user.

Example

```
select Talbot.WORKER.Name
  from Talbot.WORKER, Wallbom.WORKER
 where Talbot.WORKER.Name = Wallbom.WORKER.Name;
```

.. (To)

See **LOOP**.

/ (Division [Form 1])

Type SQL operator

Products All

See also +, –, *, Chapter 6

Format

```
value1 / value2
```

Description *value1 / value2* means *value1* divided by *value2*.

/ (Slash [Form 2])

Type SQL*PLUS command

Product SQL*PLUS

See also ;, **BUFFER**, **EDIT**, **GET**, **RUN**, **SET**, SQLTERMINATOR, Chapter 12

Description / executes the SQL in the SQL buffer without displaying it, unlike **RUN**, which displays it first.

/* */ (Comment)

Type   SQL embedded comment delimiters

Products   All

See also   **REMARK**, Chapter 4

Format

```
/* any text */
```

Description   /* tells ORACLE a comment has begun. Everything it sees from that point forward, even for many words and lines, it regards as a comment until it sees the ending */—which tells it the comment is finished. These delimiters are used only within SQL itself or in a PL/SQL program and must appear before the SQLTERMINATOR. Comments cannot be embedded within comments—that is, a /* is terminated by the first following */, even if there is an intervening /*.

Example

```
select Feature, Section, Page
/* this is just a comment */
   from NEWSPAPER    /* this is another comment */
 where Section = 'F'
```

The following is incorrect, because it embeds one comment in another:

```
select Feature, Section, Page
/* this is a comment /* with an embedded comment */ inside it */
   from NEWSPAPER
 where Section = 'F'
```

: (Colon, Host Variable Prefix)

Type   prefix

Products   PL/SQL, precompilers

See also   INDICATOR VARIABLE

Format

```
:name
```

Description   name is the name of a host variable. When PL/SQL is embedded in a host language through an ORACLE precompiler, host variables can be referenced from within the PL/SQL blocks by prefixing their host language names with a colon. In effect, this *is* the host variable. If PL/SQL changes its value through an assignment (:=), the value of the host variable is changed. Currently these variables must be single value (that is, arrays are not supported). They may be used anywhere a PL/SQL variable can be used. The one exception is in assigning the value NULL to a host variable, which is not supported directly, but requires the use of an indicator variable.

Example

```
BEGIN
  select COUNT(*) into :RowCount from LEDGER;
END;
```

:= (Set Equal To)

Type   Assignment operator

Products   PL/SQL

See also   **DECLARE**, **FETCH**, **SELECT INTO**

Format

```
variable := expression
```

Description   The PL/SQL *variable* is set equal to the *expression*, which may be a constant, NULL, or a calculation with other variables, literals, and PL/SQL functions.

Example

```
Extension := Quantity * Price;
Title := 'BARBERS WHO SHAVE THEMSELVES';
Name := NULL
```

; (Semicolon)

Type   SQL and PL/SQL terminator

Products   All

See also   **/** (Slash), **BUFFER**, **EDIT**, **GET**, **RUN**, **SQLTERMINATOR**

Description   **;** executes the SQL or the command that precedes it.

< < > > (PL/SQL Label Name Delimiter)

See **BEGIN**, BLOCK STRUCTURE, **END**, **GOTO**, **LOOP**.

@ ("At" Sign [Form 1])

Type   SQL*PLUS command

Product   SQL*PLUS

See also   **@@**, **START**

Format

```
@file
```

Description   @ starts the SQL*PLUS start file named *file*. @ is similar to **START**, but does not allow command line arguments.

@ ("At" Sign [Form 2])

Type   SQL syntax operator

Products   All

See also   **CONNECT**, **COPY**, **DATABASE LINK**

Format

```
CON[NECT] user[/password] [@database];


COPY [FROM user/password@database]
     [TO user/password@database]
         {APPEND ¦ CREATE ¦ INSERT ¦ REPLACE}
   table [ (column, [column]...) ]
         USING query;


SELECT...   FROM [user.]table[link]  [, [user.]table[@link] ]...
```

Description   @ prefixes a database name in a **CONNECT**, **COPY**, or a link name in a **from** clause.

@@ (Double "At" Sign)

Type   SQL*PLUS command

Product   SQL*PLUS

See also   **@ (Form 1)**, **START**

Format

```
@@file
```

Description   @ starts a nested SQL*PLUS start file named *file*. @@ is similar to @, but differs in that @@, when used in a command file, will search for a start file in the same directory as the command file that called it (rather than in the directory you are in when you execute the command file).

¦ (Broken Vertical Bar)

Type   SQL*PLUS operator

Product   SQL*PLUS

See also   **BTITLE**, **HEADSEP**, **TTITLE**, Chapter 4

Format

```
text¦text
```

Description   When used in SQL*PLUS **column** or **ttitle** or **btitle**, ¦ is the default **headsep** character, and is used to denote the splitting of a line onto a second line. (When used in listings in this Reference, ¦ denotes a break between alternative choices: variable ¦ literal would be read "variable or literal." On some machines this shows as a solid vertical bar.)

Example   Here's how it is used as a **headsep** character.

```
TTITLE 'This is the First Line¦and This is the Second'
```

produces this:

```
This is the First Line
and This is the Second
```

¦¦ (Concatenation)

Type   SQL function

Products   All

See also   . (Period or Dot [Form 1]), **SUBSTR**, Chapter 5

Format

```
expression1 || expression2
```

Description || glues or concatenates two strings together. The | symbol is called a broken vertical bar. On some computers this bar may be solid instead of broken.

Example   Use || to display a column of cities, followed by a comma, a space, and the country:

```
select City||', '||Country from LOCATION
```

ABS (Absolute Value)

Type   SQL, PL/SQL functions

Products   All

See also   NUMBER FUNCTIONS, Chapter 6

Format

```
ABS(value)
```

value must be a number, whether a literal number, the name of a number column, a literal character string containing a valid number, or a character column containing only a valid number.

Description   Absolute value is the measure of the magnitude of something, and is always a positive number.

Examples

```
ABS(146) = 146

ABS(-30) =  30

ABS('-27.88') = 27.88
```

ACCEPT

Type   SQL*PLUS command

Product   SQL*PLUS

See also   **&**, **&&**, **DEFINE**, Chapter 12

Format

```
ACC[EPT] variable [NUM[BER]¦CHAR] [PROMPT text ¦ NOPR[OMPT]] [HIDE]
```

Description   **ACCEPT** takes input from a user's keyboard and puts it in the named variable. If the variable has not been previously DEFINED, it is created. NUMBER or CHAR determines the data type of the variable as it is input. CHAR will accept any numbers or characters. NUMBER will accept only numbers and an optional decimal point and minus sign, otherwise **ACCEPT** will produce an error message. PROMPT displays the text to the user before accepting the input. NOPROMPT skips a line and waits for input without displaying any prompt. Using neither PROMPT nor NOPROMPT causes **ACCEPT** to invent a prompt asking for the value of the variable. HIDE suppresses the user's entry, and is valuable for passwords and the like.

Examples   The following displays the prompt "Nickname:" and puts the user's entry into a character variable named Taunt, suppressing the display of the entry:

```
ACCEPT Taunt CHAR PROMPT 'Nickname: ' HIDE
```

Next, **ACCEPT** prompts the user with "How hot?" and puts the user's entry in a number variable named Temperature:

```
ACCEPT Temperature NUMBER PROMPT 'How hot? '
```

ADD_MONTHS

Type   SQL, PL/SQL function

Products   All

See also   DATE FUNCTIONS, Chapter 7

Format

```
ADD_MONTHS(date,integer)
```

Description   ADD_MONTHS adds a number of months to *date*, and returns the date that is that many months in the future. *date* must be a legitimate ORACLE date. *integer* must be an integer; a non-integer value will be truncated to the next smallest integer. A negative value for *integer* will return a date in the past.

Example   ADD_MONTHS is executed on April 1, 1995 at 11 P.M.

```
select ADD_MONTHS(SysDate,1), ADD_MONTHS(SysDate,.3) from DUAL;

ADD_MONTH ADD_MONTH
--------- ---------
01-MAY-95 01-APR-95
```

ADDRESS (ROW)

See **ROWID**.

ALIAS

Alias is a temporary name assigned to a table or a column within a SQL statement and used to refer to it elsewhere in the same statement (if a table), or in a SQL*PLUS command (if a column). In ORACLE7.1 and above, you can use the AS keyword to separate the column definition from its alias. *See* " (Double Quotation Mark), **AS**, and **SELECT**.

ALL

Type   SQL Logical Operator

Products   All

See also   **ANY**, **BETWEEN**, **EXISTS**, **IN**, LOGICAL OPERATORS, Chapter 10

Format

```
operator ALL list
```

Description   != **ALL** is the equivalent of **NOT IN**. *operator* can be any one of =, >, >=, <, <=, != and *list* can be a series of literal strings (such as 'Talbot', 'Jones', 'Hild'), or a series of literal numbers (such as 2, 43, 76, 32.06, 444), or a column from a subquery, where each row of the subquery becomes a member of the list, such as this:

```
LOCATION.City != ALL (select City from WEATHER)
```

It also can be a series of columns in the **where** clause of the main query, as shown here:

```
Prospect != ALL (Vendor, Client)
```

Restrictions   *list* cannot be a series of columns in a subquery, such as this:

```
Prospect != ALL (select Vendor, Client from . . .)
```

Many people find this operator and the **ANY** operator very difficult to remember, because the logic for some of their cases is not immediately intuitive. As a result, some form of **EXISTS** is usually substituted. The combination of an operator with **ALL** and a list can be illustrated with the following explanations:

Page = ALL (4,2,7)	Page is equal to every item in the list—no number qualifies. A subquery *could* return a list where all the items were identical, and a value of Page could be equal to every one of them, but this would be very rare.
Page > ALL (4,2,7)	Page is greater than the greatest item in the list (4,2,7)—anything larger than 7 qualifies.
Page >= ALL (4,2,7)	Page is greater than or equal to the greatest item in the list (4,2,7)—anything equal to or larger than 7 qualifies.
Page < ALL (4,2,7)	Page is less than the lowest item in the list (4,2,7)—anything below 2 qualifies.
Page <= ALL (4,2,7)	Page is less than or equal to the lowest item in the list (4,2,7)—anything equal to or lower than 2 qualifies.
Page != ALL (4,2,7)	Page is not equal to any item in the list—any number qualifies except 4, 2, and 7.

Examples   Consider this table:

```
select * from NEWSPAPER
 order by Page, Section;


FEATURE          S   PAGE
--------------   -   -----
National News    A      1
Modern Life      B      1
Sports           D      1
Business         E      1
Bridge           B      2
```

```
Weather         C     2
Movies          B     4
Comics          C     4
Obituaries      F     6
Doctor Is In    F     6
Television      B     7
Births          F     7
Classified      F     8
Editorials      A    12
```

The logic of **ALL** when used against the preceding table is shown by the following queries. Keep in mind that the list of values (4,2,7) could just as well be a subquery:

```
select * from NEWSPAPER
  where Page = ALL (4,2,7);
```

```
no rows selected
```

However, note what happens when a subquery produces only rows that have Page = 1:

```
select * from NEWSPAPER
  where Page = ALL (select Page from NEWSPAPER
                    where Section IN ('D','E'));
```

```
FEATURE           S   PAGE
--------------- - -----
National News     A     1
Sports            D     1
Business          E     1
Modern Life       B     1
```

Sections A and B also appear. Here are some other examples:

```
select * from NEWSPAPER
  where Page > ALL (4,2,7);
```

```
FEATURE           S   PAGE
--------------- - -----
Editorials        A    12
Classified        F     8
```

```
select * from NEWSPAPER
  where Page >= ALL (4,2,7);
```

```
FEATURE          S  PAGE
--------------   -  -----
Editorials       A    12
Television       B     7
Births           F     7
Classified       F     8


select * from NEWSPAPER
 where Page < ALL (4,2,7);

FEATURE          S  PAGE
--------------   -  -----
National News    A     1
Sports           D     1
Business         E     1
Modern Life      B     1


select * from NEWSPAPER
 where Page <= ALL (4,2,7);

FEATURE          S  PAGE
--------------   -  -----
National News    A     1
Sports           D     1
Business         E     1
Weather          C     2
Modern Life      B     1
Bridge           B     2


select * from NEWSPAPER
 where Page != ALL (4,2,7);

FEATURE          S  PAGE
--------------   -  -----
National News    A     1
Sports           D     1
Editorials       A    12
Business         E     1
Classified       F     8
```

```
Modern Life     B      1
Obituaries      F      6
Doctor Is In    F      6
```

ALTER CLUSTER

Type   SQL command

Products   All

See also   **CREATE CLUSTER**, **CREATE TABLE**, **STORAGE**, "Clusters" in Chapter 18

Format

```
ALTER CLUSTER [user.]cluster
[INITRANS integer]
[MAXTRANS integer]
[PCTFREE integer]
[PCTUSED integer]
[SIZE integer[{K | M}]]
[STORAGE storage]
[ALLOCATE EXTENT [(([SIZE integer[{K | M}]]
     [DATAFILE 'filename']
     [INSTANCE integer])]
[NOCACHE|CACHE]
[PARALLEL|PARALLEL [DEGREE n][INSTANCES n]]
```

Description   Descriptions of the parameters can be found under **CREATE TABLE**. They have the same purpose and effect, except that here they are used to alter a cluster. Size is described under **CREATE CLUSTER**. In order to alter a cluster, you must either own the cluster or have ALTER ANY CLUSTER system privilege.

All tables in a cluster use the values for **PCTFREE**, **PCTUSED**, **INITRANS**, **MAXTRANS**, **TABLESPACE**, and **STORAGE** set by **CREATE CLUSTER**. **ALTER CLUSTER** changes these values for future cluster blocks, but does not affect those that already exist. **ALTER CLUSTER** does not allow changing the **MINEXTENTS** parameter in **STORAGE**.

Several of the **ALTER CLUSTER** options are only available in ORACLE7.1 and above.

When blocks are read from the database, ORACLE stores them in the SGA. ORACLE maintains a list (the *LRU list*) of the *least recently used* blocks; when extra space is needed in the SGA, the least recently used data blocks are removed from the SGA.

CACHE overrides this behavior by specifying that the blocks for this cluster are to be read to be placed at the "most recently used" end of the LRU list. Therefore, the blocks will stay in the SGA longer. This option is useful if the cluster contains small lookup tables. **NOCACHE** (the default) reverts the cluster back to the normal LRU list behavior.

PARALLEL, along with **DEGREE** and **INSTANCES**, specifies the parallel characteristics of the cluster (for databases using the Parallel Query option). **DEGREE** specifies the number of query servers to use; **INSTANCES** specifies how the cluster is to be split among instances of a Parallel Server for parallel query processing. An integer *n* specifies that the cluster is to be split among the specified number of available instances.

Example

```
alter cluster WORKERandSKILL size 1024 storage (maxextents 30);
```

ALTER DATABASE

Type   SQL command

Products   All

See also   **ALTER ROLLBACK SEGMENT, CREATE DATABASE, RECOVER, START UP, SHUT DOWN**

Format

```
ALTER DATABASE [database]
{ADD LOGFILE
    [THREAD integer] [GROUP integer]
    file_definition [,file_definition]... |
ADD LOGFILE MEMBER
    file [REUSE][, file [REUSE]...]
    TO {GROUP integer |
        (file[,file]...) |
        file}
    [file [REUSE][, file [REUSE]...]
    TO {GROUP integer |
        (file[,file]...) |
        file}]...|
DROP LOGFILE
    {GROUP integer | (file[,file]...) | file}
    [GROUP integer | (file[,file]...) | file]... |
DROP LOGFILE MEMBER file[, file] |
```

```
RENAME FILE file TO file |
NOARCHIVELOG | ARCHIVELOG |
MOUNT [EXCLUSIVE | PARALLEL] |
OPEN [RESETLOGS | NORESETLOGS] |
ENABLE [PUBLIC] THREAD integer |
DISABLE THREAD integer |
BACKUP CONTROLFILE TO file [TRACE] [REUSE] |
DATAFILE file [ONLINE | OFFLINE [DROP]] |
[AUTOEXTEND file [,file][ON | OFF]
     [NEXT integer[K | M]]
   [MAXSIZ [UNLIMITED | integer[K | M]]]]
[RESIZE integer [K | M]]
CREATE DATAFILE file[,file]
   AS file_definition[,file_definition]... |
RENAME GLOBAL_NAME TO database [.domain]|
RECOVER recover_clause [PARALLEL|NOPARALLEL] |
RESET COMPATIBILITY
SET {DBMAC {ON | OFF} | DBHIGH = string | DBLOW = string}
```

To alter a database, you must have the ALTER DATABASE system privilege.
database is the database name, and must be eight or fewer characters long.
DB_NAME in **init.ora** contains the default database name. If database isn't
specified, the name DB_NAME is used by default. ADD LOGFILE adds a redo file
or files to the database. *file_definition* specifies the LOGFILE names and sizes:

```
'file' [SIZE integer [K | M] [REUSE]
```

SIZE is the number of bytes set aside for this file. Suffixing this with **K** multiplies
the value by 1024; using **M** multiplies it by 1048576. **REUSE** (without **SIZE**) means
destroy the contents of any file by this name and give the name to this database.
SIZE with **REUSE** creates the file if it doesn't exist, and checks its size if it does.
SIZE alone will create the file if it doesn't exist, but will return an error if it does.
The log file is assigned to a thread, either explicitly with the **thread** clause or to the
thread assigned to the current instance of ORACLE. A **GROUP** is a collection of log
files. You can add a **GROUP** of log files by listing them, and you can name the
group with an integer.

ADD LOGFILE MEMBER adds new files to an existing log file group, either by
specifying the **GROUP** integer or by listing all the log files in the group.

DROP FILE drops an existing redo log file group. **DROP LOGFILE MEMBER**
drops one or more members of a log file group.

RENAME changes the name of an existing database or log file.

ARCHIVELOG and **NOARCHIVELOG** define the way redo log files are used.
NOARCHIVELOG is the default, and using it means that redo files will be reused
without saving their contents elsewhere. This provides instance recovery except

from a media failure, such as a disk crash. **ARCHIVELOG** forces redo files to be archived (usually to another disk or a tape), so that you can recover from a media failure. This mode also supports instance recovery.

When a database is first created, it is **MOUNT**ed in EXCLUSIVE mode, meaning no one but its creator has access to it. To allow multiple instances (user, processes, and so on) to access the database, use **MOUNT PARALLEL** if you have installed the ORACLE7 Parallel Server option.

After mounting a database, you **OPEN** it. **RESETLOGS** resets the redo log, cleaning out any redo entries. You use this option to restore a database after a media failure. The **NORESETLOGS** option leaves everything the same when you **OPEN** the database.

You can **ENABLE** or **DISABLE** a **THREAD**. **PUBLIC** makes the thread available to any instance not requesting a specific thread.

You can **BACKUP** a CONTROLFILE to the specified file.

You can bring a file **ONLINE** or take it **OFFLINE** with the datafile clause.

In ORACLE7.2, the **AUTOEXTEND** clause can be used to dynamically extend datafiles as needed, in increments of **NEXT** size, to a maximum of **MAXSIZ** (or UNLIMITED). You can use the **RESIZE** clause to increase or decrease the size of an existing datafile.

You can **CREATE** a new **DATAFILE** to replace an old one to re-create a data file lost without backup.

You can **RENAME GLOBAL_NAME** to change the name of the database. If you specify a domain, tell ORACLE where the database is on the network. You must change references to the database from remote databases as well.

You can **RECOVER** the database with a *recover* clause. This command performs media recovery for a lost database. In ORACLE7.1 and above, you can use multiple recovery processes to apply redo entries to datafiles for each instance.

You can use the **RESET COMPATIBILITY** option, in conjunction with the COMPATIBLE parameter in the **init.ora** file, to revert from ORACLE7.1 to ORACLE7.0.

You can **SET DBMAC ON** or **OFF** for Trusted ORACLE, or **SET DBHIGH** or **DBLOW** to an operating system string.

Example

```
alter database add logfile group 1 'biglog.006' size 1m reuse;
```

ALTER FUNCTION

Type   SQL command

Products   All

See also   **CREATE FUNCTION**, **DROP FUNCTION,** Chapter 22.

Format

```
ALTER FUNCTION [user.]function COMPILE
```

Description   **ALTER FUNCTION** recompiles a PL/SQL function. You can avoid runtime overhead and error messages by explicitly compiling a function in advance. To alter a function, you must either own the function or have the ALTER ANY PROCEDURE system privilege.

ALTER INDEX

Type   SQL command

Products   All

See also   **CREATE INDEX**, **DROP INDEX**, **STORAGE**

Format

```
ALTER INDEX [user.]index
[INITRANS integer]
[MAXTRANS integer]
[STORAGE storage]
```

Description   *user* is the user whose index you wish to alter (if you are not that user, you must have DBA privileges). *index* is the name of an existing index. *See* **CREATE TABLE** for a description of **INITRANS** and **MAXTRANS**. The default for **INITRANS** for indexes is 2; **MAXTRANS** is 255. **STORAGE** contains subclauses that are all described under **STORAGE**. In addition to the table INDEX privilege required to alter the index, you must also either own the index or have the ALTER ANY INDEX system privilege.

ALTER PACKAGE

Type   SQL command

Products   All

See also   **CREATE PACKAGE**, **DROP PACKAGE**, Chapter 22.

Format

```
ALTER PACKAGE [user.]package COMPILE [PACKAGE ¦ BODY]
```

Description **ALTER PACKAGE** recompiles a package specification or body. If you recompile the specification using **PACKAGE**, you recompile both the specification and the body. Recompiling the specification will cause referencing procedures to be recompiled. You can recompile the **BODY** without affecting the specification. To alter a package, you must either be the owner of the package or have ALTER ANY PROCEDURE system privilege.

ALTER PROCEDURE

Type   SQL command

Products   All

See also   **CREATE PROCEDURE**, **DROP PROCEDURE**, Chapter 22.

Format

```
ALTER PROCEDURE [user.]package COMPILE
```

Description **ALTER PROCEDURE** recompiles a PL/SQL procedure. You can avoid runtime overhead and error messages by explicitly compiling a procedure in advance. To alter a procedure, you must either own the procedure or have ALTER ANY PROCEDURE system privilege.

ALTER PROFILE

Type   SQL command

Products   All

See also   **CREATE PROFILE**, **DROP PROFILE**

Format

```
ALTER PROFILE profile LIMIT
{{SESSIONS_PER_USER |
CPU_PER_SESSION |
CPU_PER_CALL |
CONNECT_TIME |
IDLE_TIME |
LOGICAL_READS_PER_SESSION |
LOGICAL_READS_PER_CALL |
COMPOSITE_LIMIT} {integer | UNLIMITED | DEFAULT} |
PRIVATE_SGA {integer{K | M} | UNLIMITED | DEFAULT}}
```

Description   **ALTER PROFILE** lets you modify a particular profile setting. *See* **CREATE PROFILE** for details.

ALTER RESOURCE COST

Type   SQL command

Products   All

See also   **CREATE PROFILE**

Format

```
ALTER RESOURCE COST
{CPU_PER_SESSION integer |
CONNECT_TIME integer |
LOGICAL_READS_PER_SESSION integer |
PRIVATE_SGA integer}
```

Description   The resource cost formula calculates the total cost of resources used in an ORACLE7 session. **ALTER RESOURCE COST** lets you assign a weight to several resources. CPU_PER_SESSION is the amount of CPU used in a session in hundredths of a second. CONNECT_TIME is the elapsed time of the session in minutes. LOGICAL_READS_PER_SESSION is the number of data blocks read from both memory and disk during a session. PRIVATE_SGA is the number of bytes in a private System Global Area (SGA), which is only relevant if you are using the multi-threaded server. By assigning weights, you change the formula used to calculate total resource cost.

ALTER ROLE

Type   SQL command

Products   All

See also   **CREATE ROLE**, **DROP ROLE**, Chapter 17.

Format

```
ALTER ROLE role
{NOT IDENTIFIED |
IDENTIFIED {BY password | EXTERNALLY}}
```

Description   **ALTER ROLE** lets you modify a role. *See* **CREATE ROLE** and Chapter 17 for details.

ALTER ROLLBACK SEGMENT

Type   SQL command

Products   All

See also   **CREATE DATABASE, CREATE ROLLBACK SEGMENT, CREATE TABLESPACE, DROP ROLLBACK SEGMENT, STORAGE**

Format

```
ALTER ROLLBACK SEGMENT segment
[STORAGE storage]
[ONLINE | OFFLINE]
[SHRINK[TO SIZE]]
```

Description   *segment* is a name assigned to this rollback segment. **STORAGE** contains subclauses that are all described under **STORAGE**. The **INITIAL** and **MINEXTENTS** options are not applicable. A rollback segment can be taken **ONLINE** or **OFFLINE** while the database is open. In Oracle 7.2, you can **SHRINK** it to a specified size (the default is its **OPTIMAL** size).

ALTER SEQUENCE

Type   SQL command

Products   All

See also   **AUDIT, CREATE SEQUENCE, DROP SEQUENCE, GRANT, NEXTVAL, REVOKE**, and **CURRVAL** under PSEUDO-COLUMNS

Format

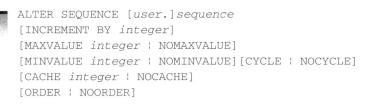

```
ALTER SEQUENCE [user.]sequence
[INCREMENT BY integer]
[MAXVALUE integer | NOMAXVALUE]
[MINVALUE integer | NOMINVALUE][CYCLE | NOCYCLE]
[CACHE integer | NOCACHE]
[ORDER | NOORDER]
```

Description   All of these options affect the future use of an existing sequence. (Note that **start with** is not available. To change the value with which a sequence starts, you must **DROP** and **CREATE** it again.) *sequence* is the name given to the sequence. The default INCREMENT BY is 1. A positive number will cause ascending incrementing of the sequence number in an interval equal to the integer. A negative number will cause descending incrementing (decrementing) in the same way.

MINVALUE is the lowest number the sequence will generate. The default is 1 for ascending sequences. **MAXVALUE** is the highest number the sequence will generate. For descending sequences the default is –1. To allow sequences to progress without limitation, specify only **MINVALUE** for ascending or **MAXVALUE** for descending sequences. To stop creating sequence numbers and force an error when an attempt is made to get a new one, specify a **MAXVALUE** on an ascending sequence, or a **MINVALUE** on a descending sequence, plus **NOCYCLE**. To restart either type of sequence at the number where its **MAXVALUE** or **MINVALUE** made it begin, specify **CYCLE**. A new **MAXVALUE** cannot be specified that is lower than the existing **CURRVAL** on an ascending sequence. A similar rule applies for **MINVALUE** on a descending sequence.

CACHE allows a preallocated set of sequence numbers to be kept in memory. The default is 20. The value set must be less than **MAXVALUE** minus **MINVALUE**. **ORDER** guarantees that sequence numbers will be assigned to instances requesting them in the order the requests are received. This is useful in applications requiring a history of the sequence in which transactions took place.

In order to alter a sequence, you must have ALTER privilege on the sequence or have the ALTER ANY SEQUENCE system privilege.

ALTER SESSION

Type   SQL command

Products   All

See also   *ORACLE7 Server Performance Tuning Guide, Trusted ORACLE Administrator's Guide, ORACLE7 Server Administrator's Guide*

Format

```
ALTER SESSION
    {SET
        [SQL_TRACE {TRUE : FALSE}]
        [GLOBAL_NAMES {TRUE : FALSE}]
        [NLS_LANGUAGE = language]
        [NLS_TERRITORY = territory]
        [NLS_DATE_FORMAT = format]
        [NLS_DATE_LANGUAGE = language]
        [NLS_NUMERIC_CHARACTERS = string]
        [NLS_ISO_CURRENCY = territory]
        [NLS_CURRENCY = string]
        [NLS_SORT = sort]
        [LABEL = {string : DBHIGH : DBLOW : OSLABEL}]
```

```
   [MLS_LABEL_FORMAT = format] |
   [OPTIMIZER_GOAL = {ALL_ROWS|FIRST_ROWS|RULE|CHOOSE}]|
CLOSE DATABASE LINK link |
ADVISE {COMMIT | ROLLBACK | NOTHING} |
{ENABLE | DISABLE} COMMIT IN PROCEDURE}
```

Description   To generate performance statistics for SQL statement processing by ORACLE, set SQL_TRACE to TRUE. To turn them off, set it to FALSE. The INIT.ORA parameter SQL_TRACE sets the initial value for this trace.

GLOBAL_NAMES controls whether or not global names resolution is enforced for your session. The INIT.ORA parameter GLOBAL_NAME sets the initial value for your session.

The various NLS options let you set up the national language support for a specific session if you have the ALTER SESSION system privilege. NLS_LANGUAGE is the language for errors and other messages and controls the language for month and day names and the sorting mechanism. NLS_TERRITORY sets the date format, decimal character, group separator, local and ISO currency symbols, the first week day for the D date format, and the calculation of ISO week numbers in date functions. NLS_DATE_FORMAT sets the default date format; NLS_DATE_LANGUAGE controls the day and month names; NLS_NUMERIC_CHARACTERS gives the decimal character and group separator in the format 'dg', where d is the decimal character and g is the group separator; NLS_ISO_CURRENCY gives a territory for a currency symbol; NLS_CURRENCY gives a specific currency symbol; and NLS_SORT changes the linguistic sort sequence. LABEL and MLS_LABEL_FORMAT are part of Trusted ORACLE.

OPTIMIZER_GOAL tells the database optimizer which goal to use for your session: rule-based (RULE), cost-based for best throughput (ALL_ROWS), cost-based for best response time (FIRST_ROWS), or cost-based if applicable (CHOOSE).

You can **CLOSE** a **DATABASE LINK** to eliminate the session's link to a remote database. You can issue advice for distributed transactions in remote databases with **ADVISE**. You can specify whether procedures can **COMMIT** or not.

ALTER SNAPSHOT

Type   SQL command

Products   All

See also   **CREATE SNAPSHOT**, **DROP SNAPSHOT**, Chapter 23.

Format

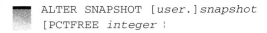
```
ALTER SNAPSHOT [user.]snapshot
[PCTFREE integer |
```

```
PCTUSED integer |
INITRANS integer |
MAXTRANS integer |
STORAGE storage]
[USING INDEX
       [PCTFREE integer]
       [INITRANS integer]
       [MAXTRANS integer]
       [STORAGE storage]]
[REFRESH {FAST | COMPLETE | FORCE}
   [START WITH date] [NEXT date]]
```

Description   **ALTER SNAPSHOT** lets you change the storage characteristics or refresh mode and times of a snapshot. To alter a snapshot, you must own the snapshot or have ALTER ANY SNAPSHOT system privilege. *See* **CREATE SNAPSHOT** and Chapter 23 for details. The **USING INDEX** clause is only available in ORACLE7.2.

ALTER SNAPSHOT LOG

Type   SQL command

Products   All

See also   **CREATE SNAPSHOT, CREATE SNAPSHOT LOG, DROP SNAPSHOT LOG**, Chapter 23.

Format

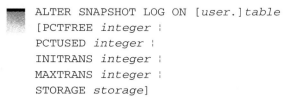

```
ALTER SNAPSHOT LOG ON [user.]table
[PCTFREE integer |
PCTUSED integer |
INITRANS integer |
MAXTRANS integer |
STORAGE storage]
```

Description   **ALTER SNAPSHOT LOG** lets you change the storage characteristics of a snapshot log table. To alter a snapshot log, you must either have ALTER privilege on the snapshot log table, or you must have the ALTER ANY TABLE system privilege. *See* Chapter 23.

ALTER SYSTEM

Type   SQL command

Products   All

See also ALTER SESSION, ARCHIVE_LOG, CREATE PROFILE

Format

```
ALTER SYSTEM
{SET {RESOURCE_LIMIT = {TRUE | FALSE} |
   MTS_SERVERS = integer |
   MTS_DISPATCHERS = 'protocol, integer'} |
 GLOBAL_NAMES={TRUE|FALSE}
 LICENSE_MAX_SESSIONS=integer
 LICENSE_SESSIONS_WARNING=integer
 LICENSE_MAX_USERS=integer
SWITCH LOGFILE |
{CHECKPOINT | CHECK DATAFILES} {GLOBAL | LOCAL} |
{ENABLE | DISABLE}
   {DISTRIBUTED RECOVERY | RESTRICTED SESSION} |
ARCHIVE LOG archive_log |
FLUSH SHARED_POOL |
KILL SESSION 'integer1, integer2'}
```

Description   **ALTER SYSTEM** lets you change your ORACLE instance in one of several ways, listed following:

RESOURCE_LIMIT enables or disables resource limits.

MTS_SERVERS changes the number of shared server processes.

MTS_DISPATCHERS sets a new number of dispatcher processes using the network protocol for the processes.

GLOBAL_NAMES specifies whether global naming should be enforced for the database.

LICENSE_MAX_SESSIONS, **LICENSE_SESSIONS_WARNING**, and **LICENSE_MAX_USERS** allow you to set threshold and maximum limits for the number of sessions and users in your database.

SWITCH LOGFILE changes log file groups.

CHECKPOINT performs a checkpoint for (**GLOBAL**) all instances or (**LOCAL**) your instance of ORACLE. **CHECK DATAFILES** verifies that (**GLOBAL**) every instance or (**LOCAL**) your instance of ORACLE can access all online data files.

ENABLE or **DISABLE RESTRICTED SESSION** turns on or off a restricted session, accessible only to users with that system privilege.

ENABLE or **DISABLE DISTRIBUTED RECOVERY** turns this option on or off, respectively.

ARCHIVE LOG manually archives the redo log files or enables automatic archiving. *See* **ARCHIVE_LOG**.

FLUSH SHARED_POOL clears all data from the SGA shared pool.

KILL SESSION ends a session with either the SID column or the SERIAL# column of the V$SESSION table identifying the session.

ALTER TABLE

Type   SQL command

Products   All

See also   **CREATE TABLE**, **DISABLE**, **DROP**, **ENABLE**, Chapter 18

Format

```
ALTER TABLE [user.] table
{[ADD ( {column_element ¦ table_constraint}
    [, column_element ¦ table_constraint} ]...) ]
[MODIFY ( column_element [, column_element]...)]
[DROP drop]...
[PCTFREE integer]
[PCTUSED integer]
[INITRANS integer]
[MAXTRANS integer]
[STORAGE storage]
ALLOCATE EXTENT
    [([SIZE integer [K ¦ M]]
    [DATAFILE file]
    [INSTANCE integer]}
[ENABLE enable ¦ DISABLE disable]
[NOCACHE¦CACHE]
[PARALLEL¦PARALLEL [DEGREE n][INSTANCES n]]
NO
```

Description   **ADD** allows you to add a new column to the end of an existing table, or add a constraint to the table's definition. These follow the same format used in **CREATE TABLE**.

   MODIFY changes an existing column, with some restrictions:

■ You may change the type of column or decrease its size only if every row for the column is NULL.

■ A NOT NULL column may be added only to a table with no rows.

■ An existing column can be modified to NOT NULL only if it has a non-NULL value in every row.

■ Increasing the length of a NOT NULL column without specifying NULL will leave it NOT NULL.

■ Views that reference a table with **select * from** will not work after a column has been added to the table unless they are dropped and re-created.

ALLOCATE EXTENT lets you allocate a new extent explicitly. **ENABLE** and **DISABLE** enable and disable constraints. All other features of **ALTER TABLE** work as they do in **CREATE TABLE**, except that they apply to an existing table. *See* **CREATE TABLE** for details.

In order to alter a table, you must either have the ALTER privilege for that table or the ALTER ANY TABLE system privilege.

Several of the **ALTER TABLE** options are only available in ORACLE7.1 and above:

When blocks are read from the database, ORACLE stores them in the SGA. ORACLE maintains a list (the *LRU list*) of the *least recently used* blocks; when extra space is needed in the SGA, the least recently used data blocks are removed from the SGA.

CACHE overrides this behavior by specifying that the blocks for this table are to be read to be placed at the "most recently used" end of the LRU list. Therefore, the blocks will stay in the SGA longer. This option is useful if the tables are small and fairly static. **NOCACHE** (the default) reverts the table back to the normal LRU list behavior.

PARALLEL, along with **DEGREE** and **INSTANCES**, specifies the parallel characteristics of the table (for databases using the Parallel Query option). **DEGREE** specifies the number of query servers to use; **INSTANCES** specifies how the table is to be split among instances of a Parallel Server for parallel query processing. An integer *n* specifies that the table is to be split among the specified number of available instances.

ALTER TABLESPACE

Type   SQL command

Products   All

See also   **CREATE TABLESPACE, DROP TABLESPACE, STORAGE**

Format

```
ALTER TABLESPACE tablespace
{ ADD DATAFILE file_definition [,file_definition] |
[AUTOEXTEND file_definition[, file_definition] [ON | OFF]
      [NEXT integer[K | M]]
    [MAXSIZ [UNLIMITED | integer [K | M]]]]
RENAME DATAFILE file [,file]... TO file [,file]... |
DEFAULT STORAGE storage |
[READ WRITE | READ ONLY] |
ONLINE | OFFLINE [NORMAL | IMMEDIATE] |
{BEGIN | END} BACKUP }
```

Description *tablespace* is the name of an existing tablespace. **ADD DATAFILE** adds to the tablespace a file or series of files described according to a *file_definition*, which specifies the database file names and sizes:

```
'file' [SIZE integer [K ¦ M]] [REUSE]
```

The file name format is operating system specific. **SIZE** is the number of bytes set aside for this file. Suffixing this with K multiplies the value by 1024; using M multiplies it by 1048576. **REUSE** (without SIZE) means destroy the contents of any file by this name and give the name to this database. **SIZE** and **REUSE** create the file if it doesn't exist, and check its size if it does. **SIZE** alone will create the file if it doesn't exist, but will return an error if it does.

In ORACLE7.2, you can use the **AUTOEXTEND** clause to dynamically resize your datafiles as needed, in increments of **NEXT** size, to a maximum of **MAXSIZ** (or UNLIMITED).

RENAME changes the name of an existing tablespace file. The tablespace should be offline while the renaming takes place. Note that **RENAME** does not actually rename the files; it only associates their new names with this tablespace. Actually renaming operating system files must be done with the operating system itself. To properly rename files, first **ALTER TABLESPACE OFFLINE**, rename the files in the operating system, **RENAME** them with **ALTER TABLESPACE**, and then **ALTER TABLESPACE ONLINE.**

DEFAULT STORAGE defines the default storage for all future objects created in this tablespace, unless those defaults are overridden, such as by **CREATE TABLE**. **ONLINE** brings the tablespace back online. **OFFLINE** takes it offline, either without waiting for its users to logoff (**IMMEDIATE**), or after they've all stopped using it (**NORMAL**).

READ ONLY tablespaces are never updated by ORACLE7, and can be placed on read-only media. Read-only tablespaces are not backed up. All tablespaces are created read-write. To change a read-only tablespace back to read-write status, use the **READ WRITE** clause.

BEGIN BACKUP can be executed at any time. It assures that all of the database files in this tablespace will be backed up the next time a system backup is done. **END BACKUP** indicates the system backup is finished. If the tablespace is online, any system backup must also back up archive redo logs. If it is offline, this is unnecessary.

ALTER TRIGGER

Type SQL command

Products All

See also **CREATE TRIGGER, DISABLE, DROP TRIGGER, ENABLE, TRIGGER,** Chapter 21

Format

```
ALTER TRIGGER [user.]trigger {ENABLE ¦ DISABLE ¦ COMPILE}
```

Description **ALTER TRIGGER** enables, disables, or recompiles a PL/SQL trigger. *See* TRIGGER and Chapter 21 for a discussion of triggers. To use the ALTER TRIGGER command, you must either own the trigger or have ALTER ANY TRIGGER system privilege.

ALTER USER

Type SQL command

Products All

See also **CREATE TABLESPACE, GRANT,** Chapter 17.

Format

```
ALTER USER user [IDENTIFIED {BY password ¦ EXTERNALLY}]
[DEFAULT TABLESPACE tablespace]
[TEMPORARY TABLESPACE tablespace]
[QUOTA {integer{K ¦ M} ¦ UNLIMITED} ON tablespace]
[,QUOTA {integer{K ¦ M} ¦ UNLIMITED} ON tablespace]...
[PROFILE profile]
[DEFAULT ROLE {role[,role]... ¦
   ALL [EXCEPT role[,role] ¦
   NONE]
```

Description You use **ALTER USER** to change a user's password, or the DEFAULT tablespace (for objects the user owns) or TEMPORARY tablespace (for temporary segments used by the user). Without **ALTER USER**, the defaults for both of these are set by the defaults of the first tablespace (both for objects and temporary segments) to which the user is **GRANT**ed resource. **ALTER USER** can also change the quota, the resource profile, or the default role (*see* **CREATE USER**). **GRANT** can also change the user's password. To alter a user, you must have the ALTER USER system privilege.

ALTER VIEW

Type SQL command

Products All

See also **CREATE VIEW**, **DROP VIEW**

Format

```
ALTER VIEW [user.]view COMPILE
```

Description ALTER VIEW recompiles a view. Use it to find errors before executing the view. This is particularly useful after changing a base table in some way. To alter a view, you must either own the view or have ALTER ANY TABLE system privilege.

ANALYZE

Type SQL command

Products All

Format

```
ANALYZE
{INDEX      [user.]index¦
 TABLE      [user.]table¦
 CLUSTER    [user.]cluster }
   {COMPUTE STATISTICS ¦
     ESTIMATE STATISTICS [SAMPLE integer {ROWS¦PERCENT}]¦
     DELETE STATISTICS} ¦
 VALIDATE STRUCTURE [CASCADE] ¦
 LIST CHAINED ROWS [INTO [user.]table]}
```

Description **ANALYZE** lets you collect statistics about a table, cluster, or index for the optimizer, storing them in the data dictionary; it lets you delete these statistics; it validates the structure of an object; and it identifies migrated and chained rows of a table or cluster with a listing in a local table. Estimating is usually faster and pretty much as accurate as **COMPUTE** for optimizer statistics. You use the VALIDATE STRUCTURE clause to test an object for possible data corruption. To analyze a table, you must either own the table or have the ANALYZE ANY system privilege.

The **LIST CHAINED ROWS** clause records information about row chaining in a table you specify. See Chapter 24 for information on the CHAINED_ROWS table.

ANALYZE can only analyze a single object at a time. To analyze an entire schema, you can use the DBMS_UTILITY.ANALYZE_SCHEMA procedure; that procedure takes two parameters—the schema name and the method to use (COMPUTE or ESTIMATE). See Appendix A of the *ORACLE7 Server Application Developer's Guide*.

AND

See LOGICAL OPERATORS, PRECEDENCE.

ANSI

The American National Standards Institute sets standards for the SQL language and its many elements.

ANY

Type   SQL logical operator

Products   All

See also   **ALL**, **BETWEEN**, **EXISTS**, **IN**, LOGICAL OPERATORS, Chapter 10

Format

```
operator ANY list
```

Description   = **ANY** is the equivalent of **IN**. *operator* can be any one of =, >, >=, <, <=, != and *list* can be a series of literal strings (such as 'Talbot', 'Jones', or 'Hild'), or series of literal numbers (such as 2, 43, 76, 32.06, or 444), or a column from a subquery, where each row of the subquery becomes a member of the list, as shown here:

```
LOCATION.City = ANY (select City from WEATHER)
```

It also can be a series of columns in the **where** clause of the main query, as shown here:

```
Prospect = ANY (Vendor, Client)
```

Restrictions   *list* cannot be a series of columns in a subquery, like this:

```
Prospect = ANY (select Vendor, Client from . . .)
```

Many people find this operator and the **ALL** operator very difficult to remember, because the logic for some of their cases is not immediately intuitive. As a result, some form of **EXISTS** is usually substituted.

The combination of an operator with **ANY** and a list can be illustrated with these explanations:

Page = ANY (4,2,7)	Page is in the list (4,2,7)—2, 4, and 7 all qualify.
Page > ANY (4,2,7)	Page is greater than any single item in the list (4,2,7)—even 3 qualifies, because it is greater than 2.

Page >= ANY (4,2,7)	Page is greater than or equal to any single item in the list (4,2,7)—even 2 qualifies, because it is equal to 2.
Page < ANY (4,2,7)	Page is less than any single item in the list (4,2,7)—even 6 qualifies, because it is less than 7.
Page <= ANY (4,2,7)	Page is less than or equal to any single item in the list (4,2,7)—even 7 qualifies.
Page != ANY (4,2,7)	Page is not equal to any single item in the list (4,2,7)—any number qualifies so long as the list has more than one value. With only one value, != ANY is the equivalent of !=.

Examples   Consider this table:

```
select * from NEWSPAPER
  order by Page, Section;
```

```
FEATURE           S   PAGE
--------------    -   -----
National News     A      1
Modern Life       B      1
Sports            D      1
Business          E      1
Bridge            B      2
Weather           C      2
Movies            B      4
Comics            C      4
Obituaries        F      6
Doctor Is In      F      6
Television        B      7
Births            F      7
Classified        F      8
Editorials        A     12
```

The logic of **ANY** in the preceding is shown by the following queries. Keep in mind that the list of values (4,2,7) could just as well be a subquery. Observe carefully the page numbers that pass the query successfully in each of these cases:

```
select * from NEWSPAPER
  where Page = ANY (4,2,7);
```

```
FEATURE          S  PAGE
---------------  -  -----
Weather          C    2
Television       B    7
Births           F    7
Comics           C    4
Movies           B    4
Bridge           B    2


select * from NEWSPAPER
 where Page > ANY (4,2,7);

FEATURE          S  PAGE
---------------  -  -----
Editorials       A   12
Television       B    7
Births           F    7
Classified       F    8
Comics           C    4
Movies           B    4
Obituaries       F    6
Doctor Is In     F    6


select * from NEWSPAPER
 where Page >= ANY (4,2,7);

FEATURE          S  PAGE
---------------  -  -----
Editorials       A   12
Weather          C    2
Television       B    7
Births           F    7
Classified       F    8
Comics           C    4
Movies           B    4
Bridge           B    2
Obituaries       F    6
Doctor Is In     F    6
```

```
select * from NEWSPAPER
 where Page < ANY (4,2,7);
```

FEATURE	S	PAGE
National News	A	1
Sports	D	1
Business	E	1
Weather	C	2
Modern Life	B	1
Comics	C	4
Movies	B	4
Bridge	B	2
Obituaries	F	6
Doctor Is In	F	6

```
select * from NEWSPAPER
 where Page <= ANY (4,2,7);
```

FEATURE	S	PAGE
National News	A	1
Sports	D	1
Business	E	1
Weather	C	2
Television	B	7
Births	F	7
Modern Life	B	1
Comics	C	4
Movies	B	4
Bridge	B	2
Obituaries	F	6
Doctor Is In	F	6

```
select * from NEWSPAPER
 where Page != ANY (4,2,7);
```

```
FEATURE         S  PAGE
--------------  -  -----
National News   A     1
Sports          D     1
Editorials      A    12
Business        E     1
Weather         C     2
Television      B     7
Births          F     7
Classified      F     8
Modern Life     B     1
Comics          C     4
Movies          B     4
Bridge          B     2
Obituaries      F     6
Doctor Is In    F     6
```

APPEND

Type   SQL*PLUS command

Product   SQL*PLUS

See also   **CHANGE**, **DEL**, **EDIT**, **LIST**, Chapter 4

Format

A[PPEND] *text*

Description   APPEND is a feature of the SQL*PLUS command line editor. **APPEND** places the text at the very end of the current line in the current buffer, with no intervening spaces. If you want a space between the end of the current line and *text*, put two spaces between **APPEND** and *text*. If you want to append a semicolon at the end of a line, put two of them together (one of them will be regarded as a command terminator and discarded).

Example

APPEND ;;

APPLICATION

An application is a set of forms, menus, reports, and other components that satisfies a particular business function. For example, you might build an application to serve as an order entry system.

ARCH PROCESS

One of the background processes used by ORACLE7, ARCH performs automatic archiving of redo log files when the database is used in **ARCHIVELOG** mode. *See* BACKGROUND PROCESS.

ARCHIVE

In a general sense, archiving means to save data for possible later use. In a specific sense, it means to save the data found in the online redo logs, in the event that the logs are needed to restore media.

ARCHIVE_LOG

Type   SQL command

Products   All

Format

```
ARCHIVE_LOG [THREAD integer]
{{SEQ integer |
   CHANGE integer |
   CURRENT |
   GROUP integer |
   LOGFILE file |
   NEXT |
   ALL |
   START} [TO location]} |
STOP}
```

Description   ARCHIVE_LOG is a part of the **ALTER SYSTEM** command. It lets you control the archiving of the redo log file groups in a specific **thread**.

SEQ identifies the group to manually archive in the **thread**. **CHANGE** manually archives a group specified by system change number and performs a log switch if it is the current redo log file group. **CURRENT** manually archives the current group, forcing a log file switch. **GROUP** manually archives a specific group. **LOGFILE** manually archives a group specified by its log file name. **NEXT** manually archives the next file group. **ALL** manually archives all log file groups in the thread that are full but have not been archived.

START enables automatic archiving of log file groups. **STOP** disables automatic archiving.

TO specifies an archive location. This location must be a fully specified file location.

ARGUMENT

An argument is an expression within the parentheses of a function, supplying a value for the function to use.

ARRAY PROCESSING

Array processing is processing performed on batches of data rather than one row at a time. In some ORACLE utilities such as Export/Import and the precompilers, users can set the size of the array; increasing the array size will generally improve performance.

ARRAYSIZE (SQL*PLUS)

See **SET**.

AS

Type   SQL delimiter

Products   All

See also   **ALIAS**, **TO_CHAR**, Chapters 5 and 7

Description   In ORACLE7.1 and above, AS is used to separate column formulas from column aliases.

Example   Here AS separates the column alias PayDay from its column formula:

```
select NEXT_DAY(CycleDate,'FRIDAY') AS PayDay
from PAYDAY;
```

ASCII

Type   SQL function

Products   All

See also   CHARACTER FUNCTIONS, **CHR**

Format

```
ASCII(string)
```

Description   ASCII is an acronym for "American Standard Code for Information Interchange." It is a convention for using digital data to represent printable characters.

The **ASCII** function will return the ASCII value of the first (leftmost) character in the string. The ASCII value of a character is an integer between 0 and 254. Those between 0 and 127 are well defined. Those above 127 ("extended ASCII set") tend to differ by country, application, and computer manufacturer. The letter A, for instance, is equal to the ASCII number 65; B is 66; C is 67, and so on. The decimal point is 46. A minus sign is 45. The number 0 is 48; 1 is 49; 2 is 50, and so on.

Example

```
select Midnight, ASCII(Midnight) from COMFORT;

MIDNIGHT ASCII(MIDNIGHT)
-------- ---------------
    42.3              52
    71.9              55
    61.5              54
    39.8              51
    -1.2              45
    66.7              54
    82.6              56
    -1.2              45


select ASCII('.'), ASCII(.5),
       ASCII('M'), ASCII('MULLER')
from DUAL;

ASCII('.') ASCII(.5) ASCII('M') ASCII('MULLER')
---------- --------- ---------- ---------------
        46        46         77              77
```

ASYNCHRONOUS TERMINAL

An asynchronous terminal is a terminal that transmits and receives data a character at a time (as opposed to a field or screen at a time). *See* **SYNCHRONOUS TERMINAL**.

ATTRIBUTE

An attribute can be one of two things:

- A synonym of "characteristic" or "property." A field, such as in SQL*FORMS, has certain characteristics or attributes.

- Another name for column.

AUDIT (Form 1 - Schema Objects)

Type   SQL command

Products   All

See also   CREATE DATABASE LINK, DATA DICTIONARY, NOAUDIT, PRIVILEGE

Format

```
AUDIT { option, option, ... ¦ ALL }
ON {[user.]object ¦ DEFAULT}
[ BY SESSION ¦ ACCESS} ]
[ WHENEVER [NOT] SUCCESSFUL ]
```

Description   *option* refers to the options described next. *user* is the name of the object owner. *object* can be a table, view, or a synonym. To audit any of these, you must either own them or have AUDIT ANY system privilege. *option* specifies which commands should be audited for an object. Options are **ALTER**, **AUDIT**, **COMMENT**, **DELETE**, **EXECUTE**, **GRANT**, **INDEX**, **INSERT**, **LOCK**, **RENAME**, **SELECT**, and **UPDATE**. **GRANT** audits both **GRANT** and **REVOKE** commands. **ALL** audits all of these.

ON object names the object to be audited, and includes a table, view, synonym of a table or view, sequence, procedure, stored function, package, or snapshot. **ON DEFAULT** means a change to the **DEFAULT** table options, which controls the auditing options assigned to all tables, and requires DBA authority. This default for all tables is set using the word **DEFAULT** instead of a table name:

```
audit grant, insert, update, delete on default;
```

ALTER, **EXECUTE** and **INDEX** cannot be used for views. The default options of a view are created by the union of the options of each of the underlying tables plus the **DEFAULT** options. The auditing of tables and views are independent.

For synonyms, the options are the same as tables.

For sequences, the options are **ALTER**, **AUDIT**, **GRANT**, and **SELECT**.

EXECUTE cannot be used for anything but procedures, functions, or packages, for which you also can audit **AUDIT**, **GRANT**, and **RENAME** options.

You can only audit **SELECT** on snapshots.

BY ACCESS or **BY SESSION** writes a row to an audit table for each command or each user session using the table being audited. If this clause is missing, it is **BY SESSION** by default. **BY ACCESS** also does **BY SESSION**.

NOAUDIT reverses the effect of **AUDIT**.

If remote tables are accessed through a database link, any auditing on the remote system is based on options set there. Auditing information is written to a table named SYS.AUD$; *see* DATA DICTIONARY VIEWS and Chapter 24 for information about views of this table.

Examples   The following audits all attempts to use **update** or **delete** on the WORKER table:

```
audit update, delete on WORKER by access;
```

The following audits all unsuccessful accesses to WORKER:

```
audit all on WORKER whenever not successful;
```

AUDIT (Form 2 - SQL Statements)

Type   SQL command

Products   All

See also   **CREATE DATABASE LINK, DATA DICTIONARY, NOAUDIT, PRIVILEGE**

Format

```
AUDIT {statement option | system privilege}
    [,{statement option | system privilege}]...
[BY user[,user]...]
[BY SESSION | ACCESS]
[WHENEVER [NOT] SUCCESSFUL]
```

Description   The second format of the **AUDIT** command audits use of a system facility, and requires that you have AUDIT SYSTEM system privilege.
The *statement options* are:

OPTION	AUDITS
CLUSTER	create, alter, drop, or truncate cluster
DATABASE LINK	create or drop database link
EXISTS	SQL statements that fail because an object already exists (Trusted Oracle)
INDEX	create, alter, or drop index
NOT EXISTS	SQL statements that fail because an object does not exist
PROCEDURE	create, alter, or drop procedure, function, or package, and create package body
PROFILE	create, alter, or drop profile

OPTION	AUDITS
PUBLIC DATABASE LINK	create or drop public database link
PUBLIC SYNONYM	create or drop public synonym
ROLE	create, alter, drop, or set role
ROLLBACK SEGMENT	create, alter, or drop rollback segment
SEQUENCE	create, alter, or drop sequence
SESSION	logon attempts
SYNONYM	create or drop synonym
SYSTEM AUDIT	audit or noaudit of SQL statements
SYSTEM GRANT	audit or noaudit of system privileges and roles
TABLE	create, alter, drop, or truncate table
TABLESPACE	create, alter, or drop tablespace
TRIGGER	create, alter, or drop trigger, alter table ENABLE¦DISABLE ALL TRIGGERS
USER	create, alter, or drop user
VIEW	create or drop view

You may also audit each individual command covered by the statement option. ORACLE7 also provides the following groups of statement options:

- **CONNECT** audits ORACLE logons and logoffs.

- **DBA** audits commands that require DBA authority, such as **GRANT**, **REVOKE**, **AUDIT**, **NOAUDIT**, **CREATE**, or **ALTER PARTITION**, and **CREATE** or **DROP PUBLIC SYNONYM**.

- **RESOURCE** audits **CREATE** and **DROP** for tables, clusters, views, indexes, space, and synonyms.

- **ALL** audits all of these facilities.

BY user audits only SQL statements issued by particular users. The default is to audit all users.

WHENEVER [NOT] SUCCESSFUL writes a row to an audit table only when an attempted access to an audited table or system facility is (or is **NOT**) successful. Omitting this optional clause causes a row to be written whether an access is successful or not.

NOAUDIT reverses the effect of **AUDIT**.

Both formats commit any pending changes to the database. If remote tables are accessed through a database link, any auditing on the remote system is based on options set there. Auditing information is written to a table named SYS.AUDIT_TRAIL; *see* DATA DICTIONARY VIEWS and Chapter 24 for information about views of this table.

Examples   This audits all successful logons:

```
audit CONNECT whenever successful;
```

AUDIT TRAIL

An audit trail is a database table written to the RDBMS when auditing is enabled (by the **init.ora** parameter) and auditing options have been selected by users or the DBA. One base table owned by SYS contains all audit trail rows.

AUDITING

Auditing is a set of ORACLE installation and data dictionary features that allow the DBA and users to track usage of the database. The DBA can set default auditing activity. The auditing information is stored in the data dictionary, and SQL statements control which information is stored. For example, you can have all attempts to update a table's data be recorded, or only unsuccessful attempts. Alternatively, you can have all logins to ORACLE be recorded, or only unsuccessful attempts to do DBA activities.

AUTHORIZATION

See PRIVILEGE.

AUTOCOMMIT

AUTOCOMMIT is a SQL*PLUS command used to automatically commit changes to the database following any SQL command that **insert**s, **update**s, or **delete**s data in the database. *See* **SET**.

AVG

Type   SQL function

Products   All

See also   **COMPUTE**, GROUP FUNCTIONS, Chapter 6

Format

```
AVG([DISTINCT] value)
```

    AVG is the average of value for a group of rows. **DISTINCT** forces only unique values to be averaged. NULL rows are ignored by this function, which may affect results.

B-TREE

B-TREE is a high performance indexing structure used by ORACLE to create and store indexes.

BACKGROUND PROCESS

A background process is one of the processes used by an instance of multiple-process ORACLE to perform and coordinate tasks on behalf of concurrent users of a database. The base processes are named ARCH (archiver), DBWR (database writer), LGWR (log writer), PMON (process monitor), and SMON (system monitor), and exist as long as an instance does.

BEGIN

Type   PL/SQL statement

Products   PL/SQL

See also   **BLOCK STRUCTURE, DECLARE, END, EXCEPTION, TERMINATOR**

Format

```
[<<block>>] [DECLARE] BEGIN

... block logic ...

END [block];
```

Description   BEGIN is the opening statement of a PL/SQL block's executable section. It can be followed with any legal PL/SQL logic, and an exception handler, and is closed with the END statement. At least one executable statement is required between BEGIN and END. *See* **BLOCK STRUCTURE** for more details.

block is a name given to a PL/SQL block that starts with the word BEGIN and finishes with the word END. The word END is followed by a terminator, usually a semicolon (*see* **TERMINATOR** for exceptions). *block* follows normal naming conventions for objects, and must be bracketed by << and >>. These symbols tell PL/SQL that this is a label. BEGIN may optionally be preceded by a section called DECLARE (which follows the block label) and may optionally contain a section called EXCEPTION.

BETWEEN

See **LOGICAL OPERATORS**.

BIND PHASE

The bind phase is the phase of SQL statement processing during which all variables are made known to the RDBMS so that actual values can be used during execution of the statement.

BIND VARIABLE

A bind variable is a variable in a SQL statement that must be replaced with a valid value or address of a value in order for the statement to successfully execute.

BLOCK

Basic unit of storage (physical and logical) for all ORACLE data. The number of blocks allocated per ORACLE table depends on the tablespace in which the table is created. The ORACLE block size varies by operating system and may differ from the block size of the host operating system. Common block sizes are 512 bytes (characters) and 2048 bytes. For the size of a block on your specific operating system, refer to your *Installation and User's Guide*. Same as a "page" of memory.

BLOCK STRUCTURE

A block structure is a structure of block sections in PL/SQL.

Products   PL/SQL

See also   **BEGIN, DECLARE, END, EXCEPTION, GOTO**

Description   PL/SQL blocks can currently be embedded in SQL*PLUS, SQL*FORMS, and any of several programming languages, through the use of the ORACLE precompilers. PL/SQL blocks are structured like this:

```
[<<block>>]
[DECLARE
.. declarations (CURSOR, VARIABLE and EXCEPTION)...]
```

```
BEGIN

... block logic (executable code)...

[EXCEPTION

... exception handling logic (for fatal errors)...]

END [block];
```

As the brackets show, both the DECLARE and EXCEPTION sections are optional. A block may optionally be labeled by a block name, which must be bracketed by << and >>.

The sections of a block must be in this order, although blocks may nest inside of other blocks in either the block logic or exception handling logic sections. blocks may be used for branching using a **GOTO**, or as a prefix in referencing a variable in another block (*see* **DECLARE** for details on this). If a variable will be referenced in a cursor declaration, it must be declared before the cursor is declared.

Example

```
<<overage>>
DECLARE
    cursor EMPLOYEE is
        select Age from WORKER
            for update of Age;


    WORKER_RECORD    EMPLOYEE%rowtype;
    age_has_junk     exception;
BEGIN
    open EMPLOYEE;
    loop
        fetch EMPLOYEE into WORKER_RECORD;
        exit when EMPLOYEE%notfound;
        if WORKER_RECORD.Age >= 65
            then delete WORKER where current of EMPLOYEE;
        if WORKER_RECORD.Age < 12
```

```
            then raise age_has_junk;
      end loop;
      commit;
      close EMPLOYEE;
EXCEPTION
   when not_logged_on
         then :error := 'Not logged on to ORACLE.';
   when age_has_junk
         then :error := 'WORKER table has bad Age data.';
         rollback;
         exit;
   when others
         then :error := 'Undefined error. Get help.';
         rollback;
         exit;
END overage;
```

BRANCH

Branches are a series of connected nodes of a logical tree. *See* **CONNECT BY**.

BREAK

Type   SQL*PLUS command

Product   SQL*PLUS

See also   **CLEAR**, **COMPUTE**, Chapters 4 and 12

Format

```
BRE[AK] ON { REPORT | expression | ROW | PAG[E] } ...
[ SKI[P] lines | [SKIP] PAGE ]
[ NODUP[LICATES] | DUP[LICATES] ]

BRE[AK]
```

Description   A break occurs when SQL*PLUS detects a specified change, such as the end of a page or a change in the value of an expression. A break will cause SQL*PLUS to perform some action you've specified in the **BREAK** command, such as **SKIP**, and to print some result from a **COMPUTE** command, such as averages or totals for a column. Only one **BREAK** command may be in effect at a time. A new

BREAK command may specify changes, and their associated actions, that are to cause a break.

ON REPORT causes a break at the end of a report or query.

A change in the value of an expression may occur at any time prior to the REPORT or PAGE break, and there may be several **ON** expression clauses in a single **BREAK** statement; however, their order in the **BREAK** command should be the same as in the **order by** of the **select** statement. That is, each expression that appears in the **BREAK** command also should be placed in the **order by** clause of **select**, in identical sequence, or the result will be meaningless. In addition, their order should be from the largest grouping to the smallest (for example, ON Corporation, ON Division, ON Project).

ON ROW causes a break for every row selected.

ON PAGE causes a break at the end of each page, and is independent of breaks caused by expression, ON ROW, or ON REPORT.

SKIP skips a number of *lines*, and PAGE or SKIP PAGE skips to a new page, before printing the result of the associated **COMPUTE** for the break.

NODUPLICATES suppresses the printing of the values in the expression or column in the **BREAK** for every row except the first one after the BREAK occurs.

BREAK by itself will display the current break settings.

CLEAR BREAKS will remove any existing **BREAK**s.

For examples of these in use *see* Chapter 12.

BTITLE (bottom title)

Type SQL*PLUS command

Product SQL*PLUS

See also **ACCEPT**, **DEFINE**, **PARAMETERS**, **SET HEADSEP**, **TTITLE**, Chapter 12

Format

```
BTI[TLE] [option ['text'|variable]... | OFF | ON]

BTI[TLE] text (old form)
```

Description btitle puts *text* (may be multi-line) at the bottom of each page of a report. OFF and ON suppress and restore the display of the *text* without changing its contents. **btitle** by itself displays the current **btitle** options and text or variable. *text* is a bottom title you wish to give this report, and *variable* is a user-defined variable or a system maintained variable, including SQL.LNO, the current line number, SQL.PNO, the current page number, SQL.RELEASE, the current ORACLE release number, SQL.SQLCODE, the current error code, and SQL.USER, the user name.

SQL*PLUS uses **btitle** in the new form if the first word after **btitle** is a valid option:

COL[UMN]*n* skips directly to position *n* (from the left margin) of the current line.

S[KIP]*n* prints *n* blank lines. If no *n* is specified, one blank line is printed. If *n* is 0, no blank lines are printed and the current position for printing becomes position 1 of the current line (leftmost on the page).

TAB*n* skips forward *n* positions (backward if *n* is negative).

LE[FT], **CE[NTER]**, and **R[IGHT]** left-justify, center, and right-justify data respectively on the current line. Any text or variables following these commands are justified as a group, up to the end of the command, or a LEFT, CENTER, RIGHT, or COLUMN. CENTER and RIGHT use the value set by the **SET LINESIZE** command to determine where to place the text or variable.

FORMAT string specifies the format model that will control the format of following text or variables, and follows the same syntax as **FORMAT** in a **COLUMN** command, such as **FORMAT** A12 or **FORMAT** $999,999.99. Each time a **FORMAT** appears, it supercedes the previous one that was in effect. If no **FORMAT** model has been specified, the one set by **SET NUMFORMAT** is used. If **NUMFORMAT** has not been set, the default for SQL*PLUS is used.

Data values are printed according to the default format unless a variable has been loaded with a date reformatted by **TO_CHAR**.

Any number of options, text, and variables may be used in a single **btitle**. Each is printed in the order specified, and each is positioned and formatted as specified by the clauses that precede it.

SQL*PLUS uses **btitle** in the old form if the first word after BTITLE is not a valid option. It simply prints the text at the bottom of each page, preceded by a blank line. The **HEADSEP** character (usually !) may be used in this form of **btitle**.

BUFFER

Generally speaking, a buffer is a scratchpad, usually in the computer's memory, where commands are staged for editing and execution.

In SQL*PLUS, a buffer is an area in memory for editing SQL and SQL*PLUS commands. *See* **EDIT** and **SET**.

BUFFERS (DATABASE)

Buffers are temporary storage places for database blocks that are currently being accessed and changed by database users.

BUFFERS (REDO LOG)

Buffers are temporary storage places for redo log blocks that are currently being accessed and changed by database users.

C LANGUAGE

C is a programming language popular for its portability to many different types of computers. ORACLE is itself written primarily in C.

CACHE MANAGER

The cache manager is the process responsible for making sure all changes made by software are propagated to disk in the right order.

CACHES

Caches are temporary holding places for either database data that is currently being accessed or changed by users or data that ORACLE requires to support users.

CEIL

Type   SQL functions

Products   All

See also   **FLOOR**, NUMBER FUNCTIONS

Format

```
CEIL(value)
```

Description   **CEIL** is the smallest integer higher than or equal to value.

Example

```
CEIL(2)    =   2
CEIL(1.3)  =   2
CEIL(-2)   =  -2
CEIL(-2.3) =  -2
```

CHAINED BLOCK

A chained block is a second or subsequent ORACLE block designated to store table data, when the originally allocated block is out of space, and rows in that block expand due to **update**s. It is most often used for table data, but index data also can be chained. Chained blocks will have an impact on performance, so if they occur, the PCTFREE space definition parameter may be set too low.

CHAINED ROW

A chained row is a row that is stored in more than one database block, and that therefore has several row pieces. Long rows (or LONG data) whose data is greater than the size of a block always have multiple row pieces. In ORACLE7, the **ANALYZE** command can identify chained rows and can also provide statistics on the number of chained rows. *See* **ANALYZE**.

CHANGE

Type   SQL*PLUS command

Product   SQL*PLUS

See also   **APPEND**, **DEL**, **EDIT**, **LIST**, Chapter 4

Format

```
C[HANGE] /old text/new text/
```

Description   **CHANGE** is a feature of the SQL*PLUS command line editor. It changes *old text* to *new text* in the current line of the current buffer (the line marked with an * in the LIST).

CHANGE ignores case in searching for old text. Three dots are a wild card. If *old text* is prefixed with '. . .', everything up to and including the first occurrence of *old text* is replaced by *new text*. If *old text* is suffixed with '. . .', everything including and after the first occurrence of *old text* is replaced by *new text*. If *old text* has . . . embedded in it, everything from the part of *old text* before the dots, through the part of *old text* after the dots, is replaced by *new text*.

The space between the **CHANGE** and the first / may be omitted; the final delimiter is unnecessary if no trailing spaces need to be inserted. A delimiter other than / may be used. Any character following the word CHANGE (other than a space) is assumed to be the delimiter.

Examples   If this is the current line of the current buffer:

```
where Skill in ('Smithy', 'Grave Digger', 'Combine Driver')
```

then this:

```
C /Smithy/Discus
```

would change it to this:

```
where Skill in ('Discus', 'Grave Digger', 'Combine Driver')
```

This:

```
C ?Smithy',...?Discus')
```

(note the ? used as delimiter) would change it to this:

```
where skill in ('Discus')
```

This:

```
C /Grave...Combine/Truck
```

would change it to this:

```
where Skill in ('Smithy', 'Truck Driver')
```

CHAR DATA TYPE

An ORACLE CHAR data type is one that may contain any printable character such as "A", "3", "&", or "blank." It may be any length from zero characters up to the maximum defined for that particular column. The CHAR column may be from 1 to 255 characters long. ORACLE7 pads CHAR values with blanks to the length specified.

See also   DATA TYPES, **VARCHAR**, **VARCHAR2**, and Chapter 16

CHARACTER FUNCTIONS

Type   SQL functions

Products   All

See also   CONVERSION FUNCTIONS, NUMBER FUNCTIONS, OTHER FUNCTIONS, Chapter 5

Description   This is an alphabetical list of all current character functions in ORACLE's SQL. Each of these is listed elsewhere in this reference under its own name, with its proper format and use.

Function Name and Use

‖

‖ glues or concatenates two strings. The ‖ symbol is called a broken vertical bar, although on some computers it may be a solid bar.

ASCII(*string*)

> **ASCII** gives the ASCII value of the first character of a string.

CHR(*integer*)

> **CHR** gives you the character with ASCII value equal to a given positive integer.

CONCAT(*string1*,*string2*)

> **CONCAT** concatenates two strings. It is equivalent to ||.

INITCAP(*string*)

> This stands for **INIT**ial **CAP**ital. It changes the first letter of a word or series of words into uppercase.

INSTR(*string, set* [, *start* [,*occurrence*]])

> **INSTR** finds the location of the beginning of a set of characters **IN** a **STR**ing.

LENGTH(*string*)

> This tells the **LENGTH** of a string.

LOWER(*string*)

> This converts every letter in a string to lowercase.

LPAD(*string*,*length* [,'*set*'])

> **LPAD** stands for **L**eft **PAD**. It makes a string a specific length by adding a specified set of characters to the left.

LTRIM(*string* [,'*set*'])

> **LTRIM** stands for **L**eft **TRIM**. It trims all the occurrences of any one of a set of characters off of the left side of a string.

NLS_INITCAP(*string*[,'NLS_SORT=*sort*'])

> **NLS_INITCAP** stands for **N**ational **L**anguage **S**upport **Init**ial **Cap**ital. This version of **INITCAP** uses the collating sequence sort to do the case conversion.

NLS_LOWER(*string*[,'NLS_SORT=*sort*'])

> **NLS_LOWER** stands for **N**ational **L**anguage **S**upport **Lower** case. This version of **LOWER** uses the collating sequence sort to do the case conversion.

NLS_UPPER(*string*[,'NLS_SORT=*sort*'])

> **NLS_UPPER** stands for **N**ational **L**anguage **S**upport **Upper** case. This version of **UPPER** uses the collating sequence sort to do the case conversion.

NLSSORT(*character*)

ORACLE7 uses **N**ational **L**anguage **S**upport **SORT**. This gives the collating sequence value of the given character based on the National Language Support option chosen for the site.

REPLACE(*string*, *if* [,*then*])

REPLACE returns *string* with every occurrence of *if* replaced with *then* (zero or more characters). If no *then* string is specified, then all occurrences of *if* are removed. *See* **TRANSLATE**.

RPAD(*string*,*length* [,'*set*'])

RPAD stands for **R**ight **PAD**. It makes a string a specific length by adding a specified set of characters to the right.

RTRIM(*string* [,'*set*'])

RTRIM stands for **R**ight **TRIM**. It trims all the occurrences of any one of a set of characters off of the right side of a string.

SOUNDEX(*string*)

SOUNDEX converts a string to a code value. Names with similar sounds tend to have the same code value. You can use **SOUNDEX** to compare names that might have small spelling differences but are still the same.

SUBSTR(*string*, *start* [,*count*])

SUB STRing clips out a piece of a string beginning at *start* position and counting for *count* characters from *start*.

SUBSTRB(*string*, *start* [,*count*])

SUB STRing **B**yte is the same as **SUBSTR** except that it can deal with multiple-byte strings for National Language Support.

TRANSLATE(*string*,*if*,*then*)

This **TRANSLATE**s a string, character by character, based on a positional matching of characters in the *if* string with characters in the *then* string. *See* **REPLACE**.

UPPER(*string*)

UPPER converts every letter in a string into uppercase.

USERENV(*option*)

USERENV returns information about the **USER ENV**ironment, usually for an audit trail. Options are 'ENTRYID', 'SESSIONID', and 'TERMINAL'.

```
VSIZE(string)
```

VSIZE gives storage size of *string* in ORACLE.

CHARTOROWID

Type SQL function

Products All

See also CONVERSION FUNCTIONS, **ROWIDTOCHAR**

Format

```
CHARTOROWID(string)
```

Description This stands for **CHAR**acter **TO ROW ID**entifier. It changes a character string to act like an internal ORACLE row identifier, or **ROWID**. This might be used to make a literal character string equal to a **ROWID**, as in a **where** clause like this for example:

```
where CHARTOROWID('00000320.0001.0002') = ROWID
```

NOTE
ORACLE will do this kind of conversion automatically, so this function isn't really needed. It is apparently a debugging tool that has made its way into general availability.

CHECKPOINT

A checkpoint is a point at which, on a session basis, changed blocks are written to the database. A checkpoint occurs when the number of redo log file blocks written equals LOG_CHECKPOINT_INTERVAL, and also when an online redo log file fills up.

CHILD

In tree-structured data, a child is a node that is the immediate descendent of another node. The node that the child belongs to is called the parent.

CHR

Type SQL function

Products All

See also **ASCII**, CHARACTER FUNCTIONS

Format

```
CHR(integer)
```

Description **CHR** will return the character with the ASCII value of *integer*. (*integer* means an integer between 0 and 254, since the ASCII value of a character is an integer between 0 and 254.) Those between 0 and 127 are well defined. Those above 127 (called the extended ASCII set) tend to differ by country, application, and computer manufacturer. The letter A, for instance, is equal to the ASCII number 65, B is 66, C is 67, and so on. The decimal point is 46. A minus sign is 45. The number 0 is 48, 1 is 49, 2 is 50, and so on.

Examples

```
select CHR(77), CHR(46), CHR(56) from DUAL;

C C C
- - -
M . 8
```

CLAUSE

A clause is a major section of a SQL statement, and is begun by a keyword such as **select**, **insert**, **update**, **delete**, **from**, **where**, **order by**, **group by**, or **having**.

CLEAR

Type SQL*PLUS command

Product SQL*PLUS

See also **BREAK**, **COLUMN**, **COMPUTE**

Format

```
CL[EAR] option
```

Description

> **CLEAR** clears the option:

> ■ **BRE[AKS]** clears breaks set by the **BREAK** command.

> ■ **BUFF[ER]** clears the current buffer.

> ■ **COL[UMNS]** clears options set by the **COLUMN** command.

- **COMP[UTES]** clears options set by the **COMPUTE** command.
- **SCR[EEN]** clears the screen.
- **SQL** clears the SQL buffer.
- **TIMI[NG]** deletes all timing areas created by the **TIMING** command.

Examples   To clear computes, use this:

```
clear computes
```

To clear column definitions, use this:

```
clear columns
```

CLIENT

Client is a general term for a user, software application, or computer that requires the services, data, or processing of another application or computer.

CLOSE

Type   PL/SQL statement

Products   PL/SQL

See also   **DECLARE, FETCH, FOR, OPEN**

Format

```
CLOSE cursor;
```

Description   **CLOSE** closes the named cursor, and releases its resources to ORACLE for use elsewhere. *cursor* must be the name of a currently open cursor.

Even though a cursor has been closed, its definition has not been lost. You can issue **OPEN** *cursor* again, so long as it was explicitly declared. A FOR loop will also implicitly **OPEN** a declared cursor. *See* **OPEN**.

CLOSED DATABASE

A closed database is a database that is associated with an instance (the database is mounted) but not open. Databases must be closed for a few database maintenance functions. This can be accomplished via the SQL statement **ALTER DATABASE**.

CLUSTER

A cluster is a means of storing together data from multiple tables, when the data in those tables contains common information and is likely to be accessed concurrently. *See* **CREATE CLUSTER** and Chapter 18.

CLUSTER COLUMNS

See **CLUSTER KEY**.

CLUSTER INDEX

A cluster index is one manually created after a cluster has been created and before any DML (that is **select**, **insert**, **update**, or **delete**) statements can operate on the cluster. This index is created on the cluster key columns with the SQL statement **CREATE INDEX**. In ORACLE7, you can define a hash cluster to index on the primary key. *See* HASH CLUSTER.

CLUSTER KEY

A cluster key is the column or columns that clustered tables have in common, and which is chosen as the storage/access key. For example, two tables, WORKER and WORKERSKILL, might be clustered on the column Name. A cluster key is the same thing as a CLUSTER COLUMN.

CMDSEP

See **SET**.

COLLATION

Type   Definition

Product   SQL

See also   **GROUP BY**, **INDEX**, **ORDER BY**, "Dates in where Clauses" in Chapter 7

Description   The collation or collating sequence is the order in which characters, numbers, and symbols will be sorted because of an **order by** or **group by** clause. These sequences differ based on the collation sequence of the computer's operating system or the national language. EBCDIC (usually IBM and compatible mainframes) and ASCII (most other computers) sequences differ significantly. The

Spanish "ll" comes at a certain place in the sequence of characters. In spite of these differences, the following rules always apply:

- A number with a larger value is considered "greater" than a smaller one. All negative numbers are smaller than all positive numbers. Thus, −10 is smaller than 10; −100 is smaller than −10.

- A later date is considered greater than an earlier date.

Character strings are compared position by position, starting at the leftmost end of the string, up to the first character that is different. Whichever string has the "greater" character in that position is considered the greater string. One character is considered greater than another if it appears after the other in the computer's collation sequence. Usually this means that a B is greater than an A, but the value of A compared to a, or compared to the number 1, will differ by computer.

The collation comparison varies slightly depending on whether you are using CHAR or VARCHAR2 strings.

If two VARCHAR2 strings are identical up to the end of the shorter one, the longer string is considered greater. If two strings are identical and the same length, they are considered equal.

With CHAR strings, the shorter string is padded with blanks out to the length of the longer string. If the strings are not identical after this padding, the comparison treats the padded blanks as less than any other character, resulting in the same truth value as the VARCHAR comparison. If the strings are identical after, but not before the padding, the CHAR comparison would treat them as equal whereas the VARCHAR2 comparison would not.

In SQL it is important that literal numbers be typed without enclosing single quotes, as '10' would be considered smaller than '6', since the quotes will cause these to be regarded as character strings rather than numbers, and the '6' will be seen as greater than the '1' in the first position of '10'.

COLUMN (Form 1 - Definition)

A column is a subdivision of a table with a column name and a specific data type. For example, in a table of workers, all of the worker's ages would constitute one column. *See* **ROW**.

COLUMN (Form 2 - SQL*PLUS)

Type　　SQL*PLUS command

Product　　SQL*PLUS

See also   ALIAS, Chapters 4 and 12

Format

```
COL[UMN]    {column ¦ expression}
            [ ALI[AS] alias ]
            [ CLE[AR] ¦ DEF[AULT] ]
            [ FOR[MAT] format ]
            [ HEA[DING] text
              [ JUS[TIFY] {L[EFT]¦C[ENTER]¦C[ENTRE]¦R[IGHT]} ] ]
            [ LIKE {expression ¦ label} ]
            [ NEWL[INE] ]
            [ NEW_V[ALUE] variable ]
            [ NUL[L] text ]
            [ NOPRI[NT]¦PRI[NT] ]
            [ ON ¦ OFF ]
            [ OLD_V[ALUE] variable ]
            [ WRA[PPED]¦WOR[D_WRAPPED]¦TRU[NCATED] ]...
```

Description   **COLUMN** controls column and column heading formatting. The options are all cumulative, and may be entered either simultaneously on a single line, or on separate lines at any time; the only requirement is that the word **COLUMN** and the column or expression must appear on each separate line. If one of the options is repeated, the most recent use will be in effect. **COLUMN** by itself displays all the current definitions for all columns. **COLUMN** with only a column or expression will show that column's current definition.

column or *expression* refers to a column or expression used in the **select**. If an expression is used, the expression must be entered exactly the same way that it is in the **select** statement. If the expression in the **select** is **Amount * Rate**, then entering **Rate * Amount** in a **COLUMN** command will not work. If a column or expression is given an alias in the **select** statement, that alias must be used here.

If you **select** columns with the same name from different tables (in sequential selects), a **COLUMN** command for that column name will apply to both. Avoid this by assigning the columns different aliases in the **select** (not with the **COLUMN** command's **alias** clause), and entering a **COLUMN** command for each column's alias.

ALIAS gives this column a new name, which then may be used to reference the column in **BREAK** and **COLUMN** commands.

CLEAR drops the column definition.

DEFAULT leaves the column defined and ON, but drops any other options.

BLACK refers to the background color of the output, and **WHITE** represents its contrast color. On printed output, the background is normally white and the ink is black, so the normal meanings of **BLACK** and **WHITE** are reversed.

FORMAT specifies the display format of the column. The format must be a literal like A25 or 990.99. Without format specified, the column width is the length as defined in the table.

A LONG column's width defaults to the value of the **SET LONG**. Both regular CHAR and LONG fields can have their width set by a format like **FORMAT A*n*,** where *n* is an integer that is the column's new width.

A number column's width defaults to the value of **SET NUMWIDTH**, but is changed by the width in a **format** clause such as FORMAT 999,999.99. These options work with both **set numformat** and the **column format** commands:

9999990	Count of nines or zeros determines maximum digits that can be displayed.
9,999,999.99	Commas and decimals will be placed in the pattern shown. Display will be blank if the value is zero.
999990	Displays a zero if the value is zero.
099999	Displays numbers with leading zeros.
$99999	Dollar sign placed in front of every number.
B99999	Display will be blank if value is zero. This is the default.
99999MI	If number is negative, minus sign follows the number. Default is negative sign on left.
99999PR	Negative numbers bracketed with < and >.
99999EEEE	Display will be in scientific notation. Must be exactly four E's.
999V99	Multiplies number by 10n where *n* is number of digits to right of V. 999V99 turns 1234 into 123400.
DATE	Formats a number column that is a Julian date as MM/DD/YY (version 3.0 of SQL*PLUS).

HEADING relabels a column heading. The default is the column name or the expression. If text has blanks or punctuation characters, it must be in single quotes. The **HEADSEP** character (usually ' ¦ ') in text makes SQL*PLUS begin a new line. The **COLUMN** command will remember the current **HEADSEP** character when the column is defined, and continue to use it for this column unless the column is redefined, even if the **HEADSEP** character is changed.

JUSTIFY aligns the heading over the column. By default this is RIGHT for number columns and LEFT for anything else.

LIKE replicates the column definitions of a previously defined column for the current one, where either the expression or label was used in the other column definition. Only those features of the other column that have not been explicitly defined for the current column are copied.

NEWLINE starts a new line before printing the column value.

NEW_VALUE names a variable to hold the column's value for use in the **ttitle** command. *See* Chapter 12 for usage information.

NOPRINT and **PRINT** turn the column's display off or on.

NULL sets text to be displayed if the column has a NULL value. The default for this is a string of blanks as wide as the column is defined.

OFF or **ON** turns all these options for a column off or on without affecting its contents.

OLD_VALUE names a variable to hold the column's value for use in the **btitle** command. *See* Chapter 12 for usage information.

WRAPPED, **WORD_WRAPPED**, and **TRUNC** control how SQL*PLUS displays a heading or string value too wide to fit the column. **WRAP** folds the value to the next line. **WORD_WRAP** folds similarly, but breaks on words. **TRUNC** truncates the value to the width of the column definition. *See* Chapters 4 and 12 for examples, and **SET RECSEP** for examples of the effect of the record separator character.

COLUMN CONSTRAINT

A column constraint is an integrity constraint placed on a specific column of a table. *See* INTEGRITY CONSTRAINT.

COMMAND

See **STATEMENT**.

COMMAND LINE

A command line is a line on a computer display where you enter a command.

COMMENT

Product   SQL*PLUS

See also   DATA DICTIONARY VIEWS, Chapter 24.

Format

```
COMMENT ON {TABLE table ¦ COLUMN table.column} IS text
```

Description   **COMMENT** inserts the comment text about a table or column into the data dictionary. For information on seeing and setting comments, *see* Chapter 24.

You drop a comment from the database only by setting it to a Null value (set *text* to ' ').

COMMIT

To commit means to make changes to data (**insert**s, **update**s, and **delete**s) permanent. Before changes are stored, both the old and new data exist so that changes can be made, or so that the data can be restored to its prior state ("rolled back"). When a user enters the ORACLE SQL command **COMMIT**, all changes from that transaction are made permanent.

COMMIT (Form 1 - Embedded SQL)

Type   SQL command

Product   Precompilers

See also   **ROLLBACK, SAVEPOINT, SET TRANSACTION**

Format

```
EXEC SQL [AT database] COMMIT [WORK] [RELEASE]
```

Description   You use **COMMIT** to commit work at various stages within a program. Without the explicit use of **COMMIT**, an entire program's work will be considered one transaction, and will not be committed until the program terminates. Any locks obtained will be held until that time, blocking other users from access. **COMMIT** should be used as often as logically feasible.

WORK is optional and has no effect on usage; it is provided for ANSI compatibility. **AT** references a remote database accessed by the **DECLARE DATABASE** command. **RELEASE** disconnects you from the database, whether remote or local.

COMMIT (Form 2 - PL/SQL statement)

Type   PL/SQL statement

Products   PL/SQL

See also   **ROLLBACK, SAVEPOINT**

Format

```
COMMIT [WORK];
```

Description   **COMMIT** commits any changes made to the database since the last **COMMIT** was executed implicitly or explicitly. **WORK** is optional and has no effect on usage.

COMMUNICATIONS PROTOCOL

Communications protocol is any one of a number of standard means of connecting two computers together so that they can share information. Protocols consist of several layers of both software and hardware, and may connect homogeneous or heterogeneous computers.

COMPOSITE KEY

A composite key is a primary or foreign key composed of two or more columns.

COMPRESSED INDEX

A compressed index is an index for which only enough index information is stored to identify unique index entries; information that an index stores with the previous or following key is "compressed" (truncated) and not stored to reduce the storage overhead required by an index. *See also* NONCOMPRESSED INDEX.

COMPUTE

Type   SQL*PLUS command

Product   SQL*PLUS

See also   **BREAK**, GROUP FUNCTIONS

Format

```
COMP[UTE] [AVG¦COU[NT]¦MAX[IMUM]¦MIN[IMUM]¦NUM[BER]¦STD¦SUM¦VAR[IANCE]]...
        OF {expression} [, expression]...
        ON [expression ¦ PAGE ¦ REPORT ¦ ROW]...
```

Description   *expression* is a column or expression. **COMPUTE** performs computations on columns or expressions selected from a table. It works only with the **BREAK** command.

   OF names the column or expression whose value is to be computed. These columns also must be in the **select** clause, or the **COMPUTE** will be ignored.

   ON coordinates the **COMPUTE** with the **BREAK** command. **COMPUTE** prints the computed value and restarts the computation when the ON *expression*'s value changes, or when a specified ROW, PAGE, or REPORT break occurs. *See* **BREAK** for coordination details.

   COMPUTE by itself displays the computes in effect.

AVG, **MAXIMUM**, **MINIMUM**, **STD**, **SUM**, and **VARIANCE** all work on expressions that are numbers. **MAXIMUM** and **MINIMUM** also work on character expressions, but not DATEs. **COUNT** and **NUMBER** work on any expression type. All of these computes except **NUMBER** ignore rows with NULL values:

AVG	Gives average value
COUNT	Gives count of non-NULL values
MAXIMUM	Gives maximum value
MINIMUM	Gives minimum value
NUMBER	Gives count of all rows returned
STD	Gives standard deviation
SUM	Gives sum of non-null values
VARIANCE	Gives variance

Successive computes are simply put in order without commas, such as in this case:

```
compute sum avg max of Amount Rate on report
```

This will compute the sum, average, and maximum of both Amount and Rate for the entire report.

Examples   To calculate for each Item classification and for the entire report, enter this:

```
break on Item skip 2 on report skip 1
compute sum avg max of Amount Rate on Item report

select Item, Rate, Amount
  from Ledger
 order by Item;
```

Note the importance of **order by Item** for this to work properly.

CONCAT

See **SET**, ¦¦.

CONCATENATED INDEX (or KEY)

A concatenated index is one that is created on more than one column of a table. It can be used to guarantee that those columns are unique for every row in the table and to speed access to rows via those columns. *See* COMPOSITE KEY.

CONCATENATION

Concatenation is the joining together of strings, represented by the operator "¦¦" (not to be confused with table joins). For example, concatenation of the strings 'ABC' and 'XYZ' would be denoted 'ABC'¦¦'XYZ', and the resulting value would be 'ABCXYZ'.

CONCURRENCY

Concurrency is a general term meaning the access of the same data by multiple users. In database software, concurrency requires complex software programming to assure that all users see correct data and that all changes are made in the proper order.

CONDITION

A condition is an expression whose value evaluates to either TRUE or FALSE, such as Age > 65.

CONNECT

To connect is to identify yourself to ORACLE by your user name and password, in order to access the database.

CONNECT (Form 1)

Type   SQL*PLUS command

Product   SQL*PLUS

See also   **COMMIT**, **DISCONNECT**, *SQL*Net User's Guide*

Format

```
CON[NECT] user[/password] [@database];
```

Description   You must be in SQL*PLUS to use this command, although you don't need to be logged on to ORACLE (see **DISCONNECT**). **CONNECT** commits any pending changes, logs you off of ORACLE, and logs on as the specified *user*. If the *password* is absent, you are prompted for it. It is not displayed when you type it in response to a prompt.

   @database connects to the named database. It may be on your host, or on another computer connected via SQL*NET.

CONNECT (Form 2 - Embedded SQL)

Type   SQL command

Product   Precompilers

See also   **COMMIT, DECLARE DATABASE**

Format

```
EXEC SQL CONNECT :user_password
        [AT database]
        [USING :connect_string]
EXEC SQL CONNECT :user IDENTIFIED BY :password
        [AT database]
        [USING :connect_string]
```

Description   **CONNECT** connects a host program to a local or remote database. It may be used more than once to connect to multiple databases. :*user_password* is a host variable that contains the ORACLE user name and password separated by a slash (/). Alternatively, :*user* and :*password* can be separated by using the second format.

   AT is used to name a database other than the default for this user. It is a required clause to reach any databases other than the user's default database. This name can be used later in other SQL statements with **AT**. This database must be first identified with **DECLARE DATABASE**. **USING** specifies an optional SQL*NET string (such as a node name) used during the connecting. Without the **USING** string, you will be connected to the user's default database, regardless of the database named in the **AT** line.

CONNECT BY

Type   SQL command operator

Products   All

See also   Chapter 11

Format

```
SELECT expression [,expression]...
  FROM [user.]table
 WHERE condition
CONNECT BY [PRIOR] expression = [PRIOR] expression
 START WITH expression = expression
 ORDER BY expression
```

Description   **CONNECT BY** is an operator used in a **select** statement to create reports on inheritance in tree-structured data, such as company organization, family trees, and so on. **START WITH** tells where in the tree to begin. These are the rules:

- The position of **PRIOR** with respect to the **CONNECT BY** expressions determines which expression identifies the root and which identifies the branches of the tree.

- A **where** clause will eliminate individuals from the tree, but not their descendants (or ancestors, depending on the location of **PRIOR**).

- A qualification in the **CONNECT BY** (particularly a not equal instead of the equal sign) will eliminate both an individual and all of its descendants.

- **CONNECT BY** cannot be used with a table join in the **where** clause.

Example

```
select Cow, Bull, LPAD(' ',6*(Level-1))||Offspring Offspring,
       Sex, Birthdate
  from BREEDING
connect by Offspring = PRIOR Cow
  start with Offspring = 'DELLA'
  order by Birthdate;
```

In this example, the following clause:

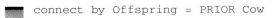

```
connect by Offspring = PRIOR Cow
```

means the offspring is the cow **PRIOR** to this one. *See* Chapter 11 for an extensive discussion of **CONNECT BY**.

CONSISTENCY

Consistency is a general database term and issue requiring that all related data be updated together in the proper order, and that if there is redundant data, all data be consistent.

CONSISTENCY CHECK (SQL*FORMS)

A consistency check tests to make certain that two related pieces of data make sense together. An example would be a check that the worker being inserted in the WORKERSKILL table already exists in the WORKER table. Block-level triggers are often used for such tests.

CONSTRAINT

- (DATABASE) *See* INTEGRITY CONSTRAINT.
- A rule or restriction concerning a piece of data (such as a NOT NULL restriction on a column) that is enforced at the data level, rather than the object or application level.

CONTEXT AREA

A context area is work area in memory where ORACLE stores the current SQL statement, and if the statement is a query, one row of the result. The context area holds the state of a cursor.

CONTROL BLOCK (SQL*FORMS)

A control block is a block not associated with any table or view.

CONTROL FILE

A control file is a small administrative file required by every database, necessary to start and run a database system. A control file is paired with a database, not with an instance. Multiple identical control files are preferred to a single file, for reasons of data security.

CONVERSION FUNCTIONS

Type   SQL functions

Products   All

See also   CHARACTER FUNCTIONS, NUMBER FUNCTIONS

Description   The following is an alphabetical list of all current conversion and transformation functions in ORACLE's SQL. Each of these is listed elsewhere in this reference under its own name, with its proper format and use.

Function Name and Use

CHARTOROWID(*string*)

CHARTOROWID stands for **CHAR**acter **TO ROW ID**entifier. It changes a character string to act like an internal ORACLE row identifier, or **ROWID**.

CONVERT(*string*,[*destination_set*,[*source_set*]])

CONVERTs the characters in string from one standard bit representation to another, such as from US7ASCII to WE8DEC.

DECODE(*value*,*if1*,*then1*,*if2*,*then2*,*if3*,*then3*,. . .,*else*)

DECODEs a character string, a DATE, or a NUMBER into any of several different strings, DATEs, or NUMBERs, based on value. This is a very powerful IF, THEN, ELSE function. Chapter 15 is devoted to it.

HEXTORAW(*hex_string*)

HEXTORAW stands for **HEX**adecimal **TO RAW**. It changes a character string of hex numbers into binary.

RAWTOHEX(*binary_string*)

RAWTOHEX stands for **RAW TO HEX**adecimal. It changes a string of binary numbers to a character string of hex numbers.

REPLACE(*string*, *if* [,*then*])

REPLACE returns *string* with every occurrence of *if* replaced with *then* (zero or more characters). If no *then* string is specified, then all occurrences of *if* are removed. *See* **TRANSLATE**.

ROWIDTOCHAR(*RowId*)

ROWIDTOCHAR stands for **ROW ID**entifier **TO CHAR**acter. It changes an internal ORACLE row identifier, or RowId, to act like a character string.

TO_CHAR(*value*)

TO_CHAR stands for **TO CHAR**acter. It converts a NUMBER so that it acts like a character string.

TO_DATE(*string*, ['*format*'])

TO_DATE converts a NUMBER, CHAR, or VARCHAR2 to act like a DATE (a special ORACLE data type).

TO_LABEL(*string*[,'*format*'])

TO_LABEL converts a character string to a value of RAW MLSLABEL data type. *See* the *Trusted ORACLE Administrator's Guide* for more information.

TO_MULTI_BYTE(*string*)

TO_MULTI_BYTE converts a character string containing single-byte characters to the corresponding multi-byte characters. If a particular character has no equivalent, the character appears as a single-byte character. This function lets you mix single- and multi-byte characters in a given string.

TO_NUMBER(*string*)

TO_NUMBER converts a string to act like a number.

TO_SINGLE_BYTE(*string*)

TO_SINGLE_BYTE converts a character string containing multi-byte characters to the corresponding single-byte characters. If a particular character has no equivalent, the character appears as a multi-byte character. This function lets you mix single- and multi-byte characters in a given string.

TRANSLATE(*string*,*if*,*then*)

TRANSLATEs characters in a string into different characters.

CONVERT

Type   SQL function

Products   All

See also   CONVERSION FUNCTIONS, *ORACLE7 Server Administrator's Guide*

Format

CONVERT(*string*,[*destination_set*,[*source_set*]])

Description   **CONVERT**s the characters in *string* from one standard bit representation to another, such as from US7ASCII (the default if either set isn't entered) to WE8DEC. This is typically done when data entered into a column on one computer contains characters that can't be properly displayed or printed on another computer. **CONVERT** allows a reasonable translation of one to the other in most cases. The most common sets include:

F7DEX	DEC's 7-bit ASCII set for France
US7ASCII	Standard US 7-bit ASCII set
WE8DEC	DEC's 8-bit ASCII set for Western Europe
WE8HP	HP's 8-bit ASCII set for Western Europe
WE8ISO8859P1	ISO 8859-1 Western Europe 8-bit character set

COPY

Type   SQL*PLUS command

Product   SQL*PLUS

See also   **CREATE DATABASE LINK**, *SQL*Net User's Guide*, Chapter 20.

Format

```
COPY [FROM user/password@database]
    [TO user/password@database]
        {APPEND | CREATE | INSERT | REPLACE}
  table[  (column [,column]...)  ]
        USING query;
```

Description   **COPY** copies **FROM** a table **TO** a table in another computer over SQL*NET. **FROM** is the user name, password, and database of the source table, and **TO** is the destination table. Either **FROM** or **TO** may be omitted, in which case the user's default database will be used for the missing clause. The source and destination databases must not be the same, so only one of the **from** and **to** clauses may be absent.

   APPEND adds to the destination table; if the table does not exist, it is created. **CREATE** requires that the destination table be created; if it already exists, a 'table already exists' error occurs. **INSERT** adds to the destination table; if the table does not exist, a 'table does not exist' error occurs. **REPLACE** drops the data in the destination table and replaces it with the data from the source table; if the table does not exist, it is created.

   table is the name of the destination table. *column,* is the name(s) of the column(s) in the destination table. If named, the number of columns must be the same as in the query. If no columns are named, the copied columns will have the same names in the destination table as they had in the source table. *query* identifies the source table and determines which rows and columns will be copied from it.

   SET LONG (*see* **SET**) determines the length of a long field that can be copied. Long columns with data longer than the value of LONG will be truncated. **SET COPYCOMMIT** determines how many sets of rows get copied before a commit. **SET ARRAYSIZE** determines how many rows are in a set.

Example   This example copies totaled records from LEDGER in EDMESTON to the database the local SQL*PLUS user is connected to. The table LEDGER_TOTAL is created by the copy. Only two columns are copied, and one of them is a computed column, a sum. These columns are renamed Item and Amount at the destination. Note the use of the dash (-) at the end of each line. This is required.

```
     copy from GEORGE/TAL@EDMESTON -
  create LEDGER_TOTAL (Item, Amount) -
   using select Item, SUM(Amount) -
          from LEDGER -
          group by Item;
```

COPYCOMMIT

See **SET**.

CORRELATED QUERY

A correlated query is a subquery that is executed repeatedly, once for each value of a candidate row selected by the main query. The outcome of each execution of the subquery depends on the values of one or more fields in the candidate row; that is, the subquery is correlated with the main query. *See* Chapter 10.

COS

Type   SQL command

Products   All

See also   **COSH**, **EXP**, **LN**, **LOG**, **SIN**, **SINH**, **TAN**, **TANH**

Format

```
COS(value)
```

Description   **COS** returns the cosine of a value, an angle expressed in radians. You can convert a degree angle into radians by multiplying it by pi/180.

Example

```
COL COSINE_180 HEADING "Cosine of 180 degrees"

SELECT COS(180*3.14159/80) COSINE_180 FROM DUAL;

Cosine of 180 degrees
--------------------
                  -1
```

COSH

Type   SQL command

Products   All

See also   **COS**, **EXP**, **LN**, **LOG**, **SIN**, **SINH**, **TAN**, **TANH**

Format

COSH(*value*)

Description   **COSH** returns the hyperbolic cosine of a **value**.

Example

```
COL HCOSINE HEADING "Hyperbolic cosine of 0"

SELECT COSH(0) HCOSINE FROM DUAL;

Hyperbolic cosine of 0
----------------------
                     1
```

COUNT

Type   SQL group function

Products   All

See also   GROUP FUNCTIONS, Chapter 6

Format

COUNT([DISTINCT] *expression* ¦ *)

Description   **COUNT** counts the number of rows where *expression* is non-NULL, which are then returned by the query. With **DISTINCT**, **COUNT** counts only the distinct non-NULL rows. With *****, it counts all rows, whether NULL or not.

CREATE CLUSTER

Type   SQL command

Products   All

See also   **CREATE INDEX**, **CREATE TABLE**, "Clusters" in Chapter 18

Format

```
CREATE CLUSTER [user.]cluster
  ( column datatype
    [ ,column datatype ]... )
    [INITRANS integer]
    [MAXTRANS integer]
     [PCTFREE integer]
     [PCTUSED integer]
        [SIZE integer]
      [STORAGE storage]
  [TABLESPACE tablespace]
    [INDEX ¦ [HASH IS column] HASHKEYS integer]
[NOCACHE¦CACHE]
[NOPARALLEL¦PARALLEL [DEGREE n][INSTANCES n]]
```

Description   **CREATE CLUSTER** creates a cluster for two or more tables. Tables are added to the cluster using **CREATE TABLE** with the **cluster** clause. **CREATE CLUSTER** commits pending changes to the database. It requires at least one cluster column from each of the tables. These must have the same data type and size, but are not required to have the same name. For the tables in a cluster, rows with the same cluster column values are kept together on disk in the same area, the same logical block(s). This can improve performance when the cluster columns are the columns by which the tables are usually joined.

Each distinct value in each cluster column is stored only once, regardless of whether it occurs once or many times in the tables and rows. This typically can reduce the amount of disk space needed to store the tables, but each table continues to appear as if it contained all of its own data. The maximum length of all the cluster columns combined (for one **CLUSTER** command) is 239 characters. Tables with LONG columns cannot be clustered.

cluster is the name created for the cluster. *column* and *datatype* follow the method of **CREATE TABLE**, except that NULL and NOT NULL cannot be specified. However, in the actual **CREATE TABLE** statement, at least one cluster column in a cluster must be NOT NULL. **SIZE** sets the size in bytes for a logical block (not a physical block). **SPACE** is the cluster's initial disk allocation, as used in **CREATE TABLE**.

SIZE should be the average amount of space needed to store all the rows from all the clustered tables that are associated with a single cluster key. A small **SIZE** value may increase the time needed to access tables in the cluster, but can reduce disk space usage. **SIZE** should be a proper divisor of the physical block size. If not, ORACLE will use the next larger divisor. If **SIZE** exceeds the physical block size, ORACLE will use the physical block size instead.

By default, the cluster is indexed, and you must create an index on the cluster key before putting any data in the cluster. If you specify the hash cluster form, however, you don't need to (and can't) create an index on the cluster key. Instead, ORACLE7 uses a hash function to store the rows of the table.

You can create your own hash value as a column of the table and use that for hashing with the **hash is** clause to tell ORACLE to use that column as the hash value. Otherwise, ORACLE uses an internal hash function based on the columns of the cluster key. The **hashkeys** clause actually creates the hash cluster and specifies the number of hash values, rounded to the nearest prime number. The minimum value is 2.

Several of the **CREATE CLUSTER** options are only available in ORACLE7.1 and above:

When blocks are read from the database, ORACLE stores them in the SGA. ORACLE maintains a list (the *LRU list*) of the *least recently used* blocks; when extra space is needed in the SGA, the least recently used data blocks are removed from the SGA.

CACHE overrides this behavior by specifying that the blocks for this cluster are to be placed at the "most recently used" end of the LRU list. Therefore, the blocks will stay in the SGA longer. This option is useful if the cluster contains small lookup tables. **NOCACHE** (the default) reverts the cluster back to the normal LRU list behavior.

PARALLEL, along with **DEGREE** and **INSTANCES**, specifies the parallel characteristics of the cluster (for databases using the Parallel Query option). **DEGREE** specifies the number of query servers to use; **INSTANCES** specifies how the cluster is to be split among instances of a Parallel Server for parallel query processing. An integer *n* specifies that the cluster is to be split among the specified number of available instances.

CREATE CONTROLFILE

Type   SQL command

Products   All

See also   ALTER DATABASE, CREATE DATABASE

Format

```
CREATE CONTROLFILE [REUSE] [SET] DATABASE database
LOGFILE            [GROUP integer] file
                     [, [GROUP integer] file] ...
                   {RESETLOGS ¦ NORESETLOGS}
DATAFILE           file [, file]
                   [MAXLOGFILES    integer]
```

```
[MAXLOGMEMBERS integer]
[MAXLOGHISTORY integer]
[MAXDATAFILES  integer]
[MAXINSTANCES  integer]
[ARCHIVELOG ¦ NOARCHIVELOG]
```

Description   The **CREATE CONTROLFILE** command re-creates a control file when you have either lost your current control file to media failure, or you want to change the name of your database, or you want to change one of the options for the log file for a datafile. Fully back up all of your database files before doing this.

The **REUSE** option lets existing control files be reused rather than giving an error if any exist. The **SET** option changes the name of the database, specified by the database clause. The LOGFILE line specifies the redo log file groups, all of which must exist. The **RESETLOGS** versus **NORESETLOGS** option tells ORACLE to reset the current logs or not. The DATAFILE line specifies the data files for the database, all of which must exist.

The **MAXLOGFILES** option specifies the maximum number of redo log file groups that can be created. The **MAXLOGMEMBERS** option specifies the number of copies for a redo log group. The **MAXLOGHISTORY** option specifies the number of archived redo log file groups for the Parallel Server. The **MAXDATAFILES** option specifies the maximum number of data files that can ever be created for the database. The **MAXINSTANCES** option gives the maximum number of ORACLE instances that can mount and open the database. The **ARCHIVELOG** and **NOARCHIVELOG** options turns archiving of the redo log files on and off, respectively.

The **CREATE CONTROLFILE** command needed for an existing database can be generated via the **ALTER DATABASE BACKUP CONTROLFILE TO TRACE** command.

CREATE DATABASE

Type   SQL command

Products   All

See also   **ALTER DATABASE, CREATE CONTROLFILE, CREATE ROLLBACK SEGMENT, CREATE TABLESPACE, SHUT DOWN, START UP**

Format

```
      CREATE  DATABASE [database]
   [CONTROLFILE  REUSE]
      [LOGFILE  [GROUP integer] file_definition
                [,[GROUP integer] file_definition]... ]
   [MAXLOGFILES  integer]
[MAXLOGMEMBERS] integer]
```

```
[MAXLOGHISTORY] integer]
    [DATAFILE  file_definition [,file_definition]... ]
    [AUTOEXTEND file definition[,file_definition] [ON ¦ OFF]
        [NEXT integer [K ¦ M]]
        [MAXSIZ
            [UNLIMITED ¦ integer [K ¦ M]]]]
  [MAXDATAFILES integer]
  [MAXINSTANCES integer]
  [ARCHIVELOG ¦ NOARCHIVELOG]
    [EXCLUSIVE]
 {CHARACTER SET charset]
```

Description   *database* is the database name, and must have eight characters or
fewer. DB_NAME in **init.ora** contains the default database name. **file_definition**
specifies the LOGFILE and DATAFILE names and sizes:

```
'file' [SIZE integer [K ¦ M] [REUSE]
```

SIZE is the number of bytes set aside for this file. Suffixing this with K multiplies
the value by 1024; M multiplies it by 1048576. **REUSE** (without **SIZE**) means destroy
the contents of any file by this name and associate the name with this database.
SIZE with **REUSE** creates the file if it doesn't exist, and checks its size if it does.
CONTROLFILE REUSE overwrites the existing control files defined by
CONTROL_FILES in **init.ora**.

LOGFILE names the files to be used as redo log files. If this parameter is
not used, ORACLE creates two by default. **MAXLOGFILES** overrides the **init.ora**
LOG_FILES parameter, and defines the maximum number of redo log files that can
ever be created for this database. This number cannot be increased later. Minimum
is 2. Maximum is 256. A high number only makes a somewhat larger control file.

DATAFILE names the files to be used for the database itself. These files
will automatically be in the SYSTEM tablespace. Omitting this clause causes
ORACLE to create one file by default. Its name and size differ by operating system.
MAXDATAFILES sets the absolute upper limit for files that can be created for this
database, and overrides the DB_FILES parameter in **init.ora**. Maximum is 255.
Default is 32. A high number only makes a somewhat larger control file.

In ORACLE7.2, the **AUTOEXTEND** option can be used for datafiles. When
turned ON, this option will dynamically extend a datafile as needed in increments
of **NEXT** size, to a maximum of **MAXSIZ** (or UNLIMITED).

MAXINSTANCES overrides the INSTANCES parameter in **init.ora** and sets the
maximum number of simultaneous instances that can mount and open this database.
Maximum is 255.

ARCHIVELOG and **NOARCHIVELOG** define the way redo log files are used
when the database is first created. **NOARCHIVELOG** is the default, and means that
redo files will get reused without saving their contents elsewhere. This provides

instance recovery but will not recover from a media failure, such as a disk crash. **ARCHIVELOG** forces redo files to be archived (usually to another disk or a tape), so that you can recover from a media failure. This mode also supports instance recovery. This parameter can be reset by **ALTER DATABASE**.

The **MAXLOGMEMBERS** option specifies the maximum number of copies of a redo log file group. The **MAXLOGHISTORY** option specifies the maximum number of archived redo log files, useful only for the Parallel Server when you are archiving log files. The **CHARACTER SET** option specifies the character set used to store data, which depends on the operating system.

EXCLUSIVE is completely optional, and is used here as a reminder that all databases are created to allow only one instance that has exclusive access to the database. To allow multiple instances (users, processes, and so on) to access the database, you must use the **ALTER DATABASE DISMOUNT** and **ALTER DATABASE MOUNT PARALLEL** commands.

WARNING
Using **CREATE DATABASE** on an existing database will destroy it.

CREATE DATABASE LINK

Type   SQL command

Products   All

See also   **CREATE SYNONYM**, **SELECT**, *SQL*Net User's Guide*, Chapter 20.

Format

```
CREATE [PUBLIC] DATABASE LINK link
     CONNECT TO user IDENTIFIED BY password
          USING 'connect_string';
```

Description   *link* is the name given to the link. *connect_string* is the definition of the remote database that can be accessed through SQL*NET and defines the link between a local database and a username on a remote database. **PUBLIC** links can only be created by a DBA, but are then available to all users except those who have created a private link with the same name. If **PUBLIC** isn't specified, the link is only available to the user who executed the **CREATE DATABASE LINK** statement. *connect_string* is the SQL*Net connection string or connect descriptor for the remote database.

Remote tables can be accessed just like local tables, except that the table name must be prefixed by *@link* in the **from** clause of the **select** statement. Most systems set the maximum number of simultaneous links to four. The DBA can increase this number with the OPEN_LINKS parameter in **init.ora**.

Tree-structured queries are limited. They may not use the **PRIOR** operator except in the **connect by** clause. **START WITH** cannot contain a subquery. **CONNECT BY** and **START WITH** cannot use the function **USERENV**('ENTRYID'), or RowNum.

To create a database link, you must have CREATE DATABASE LIN privilege and CREATE SESSION privilege in a remote database. To create a public database link, you must have CREATE PUBLIC DATABASE LINK system privilege. *See* Chapter 20 for further details and examples for database links.

Examples   The following defines a link named BOSS to George with password TAL on database D:EDMESTON:

```
create database link BOSS
connect to George identified by TAL
  using 'D:EDMESTON';
```

You now can query George's tables like this:

```
select ActionDate, Item, Amount
  from LEDGER@BOSS;
```

A synonym could also be created to hide the remoteness of George's tables:

```
create synonym TALBOT_LEDGER for LEDGER@BOSS;
```

CREATE FUNCTION

Type   SQL command

Products   PL/SQL

See also   **ALTER FUNCTION**, BLOCK STRUCTURE, **CREATE PACKAGE**, **CREATE PROCEDURE**, DATA TYPES, **DROP FUNCTION**, Chapter 22.

Format

```
CREATE [OR REPLACE] FUNCTION [user.]function
[(argument[IN] datatype[, parameter [IN] datatype]...)]
RETURN datatype {IS | AS} block
```

Description   *function* is the name of the function being defined. A function may have parameters, named arguments of a certain datatype, and every function returns a value of a certain datatype as specified by the return clause. The PL/SQL block defines the behavior of the function as a series of declarations, PL/SQL program statements, and exceptions.

The IN qualifier means that you have to specify a value for the parameter when you call the function, but since you always have to do this for a function, the syntax is optional. In a procedure, you can have other kinds of parameters. The difference between a function and a procedure is that a function returns a value to the calling environment.

In order to create a function, you must have the CREATE PROCEDURE system privilege. To create a function in another user's account, you must have CREATE ANY PROCEDURE system privilege.

In ORACLE7.0, You can only use a function or a procedure in a PL/SQL statement, not as part of a SQL expression. In ORACLE7.1, user-defined functions can be used as part of SQL expressions; *see* Chapter 22. In ORACLE7.2, parameters may also be declared as OUT.

CREATE INDEX

Type   SQL command

Products   All

See also   **ANALYZE, ALTER INDEX, DROP INDEX**, INTEGRITY CONSTRAINT, **STORAGE**

Format

```
CREATE [UNIQUE] INDEX [user.]index
    ON [user.]table (column [ASC | DESC][, column [ASC | DESC]] ...)
        [CLUSTER [user.]cluster]
        [INITRANS integer]
        [MAXTRANS integer]
        [PCTFREE integer]
        [STORAGE storage]
        [TABLESPACE tablespace]
        [NOSORT]
        [NOPARALLEL|PARALLEL [DEGREE n][INSTANCES n]]
        [UNRECOVERABLE | RECOVERABLE]
```

Description   *index* is a name you assign to this index. It's usually a good idea to make it reflect the table and columns being indexed. *table* and *column*(s) are the table and column(s) for which the index is to be created. A **UNIQUE** index guarantees that each indexed row is unique on the values of the index columns. In ORACLE7 you can use the unique constraint on the columns to automatically create unique indexes. Specifying multiple columns will create a composite index. **ASC** and **DESC** mean ascending and descending, and are allowed for DB2 compatibility, but have no effect. (Indexes in ORACLE7 are always ascending.) **CLUSTER** is the name of the cluster key that is indexed for a cluster. Clusters must have their keys indexed for their associated tables to be accessed. (*See* **CREATE TABLE** for a description of **INITRANS** and **MAXTRANS**.) The default for **INITRANS** for indexes is 2; **MAXTRANS** is 255. **PCTFREE** is the percentage of space to leave free in the index for new entries and updates. The minimum is zero. If making a **UNIQUE** index, skip this clause.

TABLESPACE is the name of the tablespace to which this index is assigned. **STORAGE** contains subclauses that are all described under **STORAGE**. **NOSORT** is an option whose primary value is in reducing the time to create an index if, and only if, the values in the column being indexed are already in ascending order. It doesn't harm anything if they later fall out of ascending order, but **NOSORT** will only work if they are in order when **INDEX** is run. If the rows are not in order, **INDEX** will return an error message, will not damage anything, and will allow you to rerun it without the **NOSORT** option.

PARALLEL, along with **DEGREE** and **INSTANCES**, specifies the parallel characteristics of the index (for databases using the ORACLE7.1 Parallel Query option). **DEGREE** specifies the number of query servers to use; **INSTANCES** specifies how the index is to be split among instances of a Parallel Server for parallel query processing. An integer *n* specifies that the index is to be split among the specified number of available instances.

In ORACLE7.2, you can disable logging during the **CREATE INDEX** command by using the **UNRECOVERABLE** keyword. This eliminates the overhead created by the writing of the redo log information that the database would use during recoveries.

In order to create an index, you must either own the indexed table, have INDEX privilege on the table, or have CREATE ANY INDEX system privilege.

CREATE PACKAGE

Type   SQL command

Products   PL/SQL

See also   **ALTER PACKAGE**, **CREATE FUNCTION**, **CREATE PACKAGE BODY**, **CREATE PROCEDURE**, CURSOR, **DROP PACKAGE**, EXCEPTION, RECORD, TABLE, VARIABLE DECLARATION, Chapter 22.

Format

```
CREATE [OR REPLACE] PACKAGE [user.]package {IS | AS}
{variable_declaration |
 cursor_specification |
 exception_declaration |
 record_declaration |
```

```
 plsql_table_declaration ¦
 procedure_specification ¦
 function_specification};
[{variable_declaration ¦
  cursor_specification ¦
  exception_declaration ¦
  record_declaration ¦
  plsql_table_declaration ¦
  procedure_specification ¦
  function_specification};]...
END [package]
```

Description   **CREATE PACKAGE** sets up the specification for a PL/SQL package, a group of public procedures, functions, exceptions, variables, constants, and cursors. Adding OR REPLACE replaces the package specification if it already exists, which invalidates the package and requires recompilation of the package body and any objects that depend on the package specification.

Packaging your procedures and functions lets them share data through variables, constants, and cursors. It gives you the ability to grant the whole collection at once as part of a role. ORACLE accesses all the elements of a package more efficiently than it would if they were separate. If you change the package body, which ORACLE stores separately, you do not have to recompile anything that uses the package.

In order to create a package, you must have the CREATE PROCEDURE system privilege; to create a package in another user's account, you must have the CREATE ANY PROCEDURE system privilege.

CREATE PACKAGE BODY

Type   SQL command

Products   PL/SQL

See also   **ALTER PACKAGE**, **CREATE FUNCTION**, **CREATE PACKAGE**, **CREATE PROCEDURE**, CURSOR, **DROP PACKAGE**, EXCEPTION, RECORD, TABLE, VARIABLE DECLARATION, Chapter 22.

Format

```
CREATE [OR REPLACE] PACKAGE BODY [user.]package {IS ¦ AS}
{variable_declaration ¦
 cursor_body ¦
 exception_declaration ¦
 record_declaration ¦
 table_declaration ¦
```

```
 procedure_body |
 function_body};
[{variable_declaration |
  cursor_body |
  exception_declaration |
  record_declaration |
  table_declaration |
  procedure_body |
  function_body};]...
END [package]
```

Description   **CREATE PACKAGE BODY** builds the body of a previously specified package created with **CREATE PACKAGE**. Adding **OR REPLACE** replaces the package body if it already exists. You must have CREATE PROCEDURE system privilege to create a package body; to create a package body in another user's account, you must have CREATE ANY PROCEDURE system privilege.

CREATE PROCEDURE

Type   SQL command

Products   PL/SQL

See also   **ALTER PROCEDURE**, BLOCK STRUCTURE, **CREATE FUNCTION**, **CREATE PACKAGE**, DATA TYPES, **DROP PROCEDURE**, Chapter 22.

Format

```
CREATE [OR REPLACE] PROCEDURE [user.]procedure
[(argument[IN | OUT | IN OUT] datatype
[, argument [IN | OUT | IN OUT] datatype]...)]
{IS | AS} block
```

Description   **CREATE PROCEDURE** creates the specification and body of a procedure. A procedure may have parameters, named arguments of a certain datatype. The PL/SQL block defines the behavior of the function as a series of declarations, PL/SQL program statements, and exceptions.

The IN qualifier means that you have to specify a value for the argument when you call the procedure. The OUT qualifier means that the procedure passes a value back to the caller through this argument. The IN OUT qualifier combines the meaning of both IN and OUT—you specify a value, and the procedure replaces it with a value. If you don't have any qualifier, the argument defaults to IN. The difference between a function and a procedure is that a function returns a value to the calling environment.

You can only use a function or a procedure in a PL/SQL statement, not as part of a SQL expression. Do not confuse the PL/SQL function with the SQL functions such as **INSTR** or **TO_CHAR**.

CREATE PROFILE

Type   SQL command

Products   ALL

See also   **ALTER PROFILE, ALTER RESOURCE COST, ALTER SYSTEM, ALTER USER, CREATE USER, DROP PROFILE**

Format

```
CREATE PROFILE profile LIMIT
{SESSIONS_PER_USER |
 CPU_PER_SESSION |
 CPU_PER_CALL |
 CONNECT_TIME |
 IDLE_TIME |
 LOGICAL_READS_PER_SESSION |
 LOGICAL_READS_PER_CALL |
 COMPOSITE_LIMIT |
 PRIVATE_SGA} {integer [K|M] | UNLIMITED | DEFAULT}
[{SESSIONS_PER_USER |
  CPU_PER_SESSION |
  CPU_PER_CALL |
  CONNECT_TIME |
  IDLE_TIME |
  LOGICAL_READS_PER_SESSION |
  LOGICAL_READS_PER_CALL |
  COMPOSITE_LIMIT |
  PRIVATE_SGA} {integer [K|M] | UNLIMITED | DEFAULT}]...
```

Description   **CREATE PROFILE** creates a set of limits on the use of database resources. When you associate the profile with a user with **CREATE** or **ALTER USER**, you can control what the user does by those limits. To use **CREATE PROFILE**, you must enable resource limits through the initialization parameter RESOURCE_LIMIT or through the **ALTER SYSTEM** command.

SESSIONS_PER_USER limits the user to integer concurrent SQL sessions. CPU_PER_SESSION limits the CPU time in hundredths of seconds. CPU_PER_CALL limits the CPU time for a parse, execute, or fetch call in hundredths of seconds.

CONNECT_TIME limits elapsed time of a session in minutes. IDLE_TIME disconnects a user after this number of minutes; this does not apply while a query is running. LOGICAL_READS_PER_SESSION limits the number of blocks read per session; LOGICAL_READS_PER_CALL does the same thing for parse, execute, or fetch calls. PRIVATE_SGA limits the amount of space you can allocate in the SGA as private; the K and M options apply only to this limit. COMPOSITE_LIMIT limits the total resource cost for a session in service units based on a weighted sum of CPU, connect time, logical reads, and private sga resources.

UNLIMITED means there is no limit on a particular resource; DEFAULT picks up the limit from the DEFAULT profile, which you can change through the **ALTER PROFILE** command.

If a user exceeds a limit, ORACLE aborts and rolls back the transaction, then ends the session. You must have CREATE PROFILE system privilege in order to create a profile. You associate a profile to a user with the **ALTER USER** command.

CREATE ROLE

Type   SQL command

Products   All

See also   **ALTER ROLE, DROP ROLE, GRANT, REVOKE, SET ROLE**, Chapter 17

Format

```
CREATE ROLE role
[[NOT IDENTIFIED | IDENTIFIED] [BY password | EXTERNALLY]
```

Description   With **CREATE ROLE**, you can create a named role or set of privileges. When you grant the role to a user, you grant him or her all the privileges of that role. You first create the role with **CREATE ROLE**, then grant privileges to the role using the **GRANT** command. When a user wants to access something that the role allows, he or she enables the role with **SET ROLE**.

If you put password protection on the role, the user who wants to use the privileges must supply the password in the **SET ROLE** command to enable the role.

ORACLE automatically creates several roles: CONNECT, RESOURCE, DBA, EXP_FULL_DATABASE, and IMP_FULL_DATABASE. The first three roles provide compatibility with prior versions of ORACLE. The last two roles let you use the import and export utilities. *See* Chapter 17 for examples.

CREATE ROLLBACK SEGMENT

Type SQL command

Products All

See also **ALTER ROLLBACK SEGMENT, CREATE DATABASE, CREATE TABLESPACE, DROP ROLLBACK SEGMENT, STORAGE**

Format

```
CREATE [PUBLIC] ROLLBACK SEGMENT segment
      [TABLESPACE tablespace]
      [STORAGE storage]
```

Description *segment* is a name assigned to this rollback segment. *tablespace* is the name of the tablespace to which this rollback segment is assigned. One TABLESPACE may have multiple ROLLBACK SEGMENTS. You must be online to use this command.

STORAGE contains subclauses that are all described under **STORAGE**. If **PUBLIC** is used, this rollback segment can be used by any instance that requests it; otherwise it is available only to instances that named it in their **init.ora** files.

CREATE SCHEMA

Type SQL command

Products All

See also **CREATE TABLE, CREATE VIEW, GRANT**

Format

```
CREATE SCHEMA AUTHORIZATION schema
{CREATE TABLE command |
 CREATE VIEW command |
 GRANT command}
[{CREATE TABLE command |
 CREATE VIEW command |
 GRANT command}]...
```

Description The **CREATE SCHEMA** command creates a collection of tables, views, and privilege grants as a single transaction. The schema name is the same as your ORACLE user name. The **CREATE TABLE**, **CREATE VIEW**, and **GRANT** commands are the standard commands, and the order in which the commands appear is not important, even if there are internal dependencies.

CREATE SEQUENCE

Type   SQL command

Products   All

See also   **ALTER SEQUENCE, AUDIT, DROP SEQUENCE, GRANT, REVOKE, NEXTVAL** and **CURRVAL** under PSEUDO-COLUMNS

Format

```
CREATE SEQUENCE [user.]sequence
        [INCREMENT BY integer]
        [START WITH integer]
        [MAXVALUE integer | NOMAXVALUE]
        [MINVALUE integer | NOMINVALUE]
        [CYCLE | NOCYCLE]
        [CACHE integer | NOCACHE]
        [ORDER | NOORDER]
```

Description   *sequence* is the name given to the sequence. The default **INCREMENT BY** is 1. A positive number will cause ascending incrementing of the sequence number in an interval equal to the integer. A negative number will cause descent in the same way. **START WITH** is the number with which the sequence will begin. The default **START WITH** is **MAXVALUE** for descending sequences and **MINVALUE** for ascending; use **START WITH** to override this default.

MINVALUE is the lowest number the sequence will generate. The default is 1 for ascending sequences. **MAXVALUE** is the highest number the sequence will generate. For descending sequence the default is –1. To allow sequences to progress without limitation, specify only **MINVALUE** for ascending and **MAXVALUE** for descending sequences. To stop creating sequence numbers and force an error when an attempt is made to get a new one, specify a **MAXVALUE** on an ascending sequence, or a **MINVALUE** on a descending sequence, plus **NOCYCLE**. To restart either type of sequence where its **MAXVALUE** or **MINVALUE** made it begin, specify **CYCLE**.

CACHE allows a preallocated set of sequence numbers to be kept in memory. The default is 20. The value set must be less than **MAXVALUE** minus **MINVALUE**.

ORDER guarantees that sequence numbers will be assigned to instances requesting them in the order the requests are received. This is useful in applications requiring a history of the sequence in which transactions took place.

To create a sequence in your own schema, you must have the CREATE SEQUENCE system privilege; to create a sequence in another user's schema, you must have the CREATE ANY SEQUENCE system privilege.

CREATE SNAPSHOT

Type   SQL command

Products   All

See also   **ALTER SNAPSHOT, CREATE SNAPSHOT LOG, DROP SNAPSHOT, STORAGE**, Chapter 23.

Format

```
CREATE SNAPSHOT [user.]snapshot
   {[  PCTFREE integer :
        PCTUSED integer :
      INITRANS integer :
      MAXTRANS integer :
    TABLESPACE tablespace :
       STORAGE storage] :
    [  CLUSTER cluster (column[,column]...]}
    [USING INDEX
        [PCTFREE integer]
        [INITRANS integer]
        [MAXTRANS integer]
    [TABLESPACE tablespace]
        [STORAGE storage]]
    [  REFRESH [FAST : COMPLETE : FORCE]
        [START WITH date] [NEXT date]]
    AS query
```

Description   **CREATE SNAPSHOT** creates a snapshot, a table that holds the results of a query, usually on one or more tables, called master tables, in a remote database. This lets you maintain a read-only copy of the data locally for improved speed in queries of the data. You can have the data refreshed at intervals using the **refresh** clause. In ORACLE7.0, you cannot modify data in a snapshot; in ORACLE7.1, you can create snapshots whose data can be modified. *See* Chapter 23. Snapshots cannot contain LONG columns.

The first group of options sets up the storage of the local table. You can alternatively set up the snapshot in a cluster using the **CLUSTER** clause. The **USING INDEX** clause, available in ORACLE7.2, allows you to specify the storage parameters for the snapshot's index.

A **FAST** refresh uses the snapshot log associated with the master table to refresh the snapshot. A **COMPLETE** refresh reexecutes the query. A **FORCE** refresh lets ORACLE make the choice between a **FAST** or a **COMPLETE** refresh. ORACLE first refreshes the snapshot on the **START WITH date**. If you give a **NEXT date**, ORACLE refreshes the snapshot at intervals specified by the difference between the **START WITH** and **NEXT** dates.

A **simple** snapshot selects data from a single master table using a simple query. A **complex** snapshot selects data using a **GROUP BY**, **CONNECT BY**, subquery, join, or set operation in the query. ORACLE can do a **FAST** refresh only on simple snapshots that have snapshot logs.

Because of the local objects which snapshots create, the name of a snapshot cannot exceed 23 characters in length. In order to create a snapshot in your schema, you must have the CREATE SNAPSHOT system privilege. To create a snapshot in another user's schema, you must have the CREATE ANY SNAPSHOT system privilege.

CREATE SNAPSHOT LOG

Type   SQL command

Products   All

See also   **ALTER SNAPSHOT LOG, CREATE SNAPSHOT, DROP SNAPSHOT LOG, STORAGE**, Chapter 23.

Format

```
CREATE SNAPSHOT LOG ON [user.]table
   [   PCTFREE integer |
       PCTUSED integer |
      INITRANS integer |
      MAXTRANS integer |
    TABLESPACE tablespace |
       STORAGE storage]
```

Description   **CREATE SNAPSHOT LOG** creates a table associated with the master table of a snapshot that tracks changes to the master table's data. ORACLE uses the snapshot log to **FAST** refresh the snapshots of a master table. The storage options specify the storage of the table. ORACLE logs changes only if there is a simple snapshot based on the master table. You can have only one log for a given master table. Because of the local objects that are created to support the snapshot log, the name of the base table on which the snapshot is based cannot exceed 24 characters in length. In order to create a snapshot log, you must have the CREATE TABLE, CREATE TRIGGER, and CREATE INDEX system privileges.

CREATE SYNONYM

Type   SQL command

Products   All

See also   CREATE DATABASE LINK, **CREATE TABLE**, **CREATE VIEW**, Chapters 17 and 20.

Format

```
CREATE [PUBLIC] SYNONYM [user.]synonym
    FOR [user.]table [@database_link];
```

Description   **CREATE SYNONYM** creates a synonym for a table or view name, including those on a remote database. It commits pending changes to the database.

PUBLIC makes the synonym available to all users, but can only be created by a DBA. Without **PUBLIC**, users must prefix the synonym with your user name. *synonym* is the synonym name. *user.table* is the name of the table, view, or synonym to which the synonym refers. You can have a synonym of a synonym.

@database_link is a database link to a remote database. The synonym refers to a table in the remote database as specified by the database link.

Example

```
create synonym TALBOT_LEDGER for LEDGER@BOSS;
```

CREATE TABLE

Type   SQL command

Products   All

See also   **ALTER TABLE**, **CREATE CLUSTER**, **CREATE INDEX**, **CREATE TABLESPACE**, DATA TYPES, **DROP TABLE**, INTEGRITY CONSTRAINT, **OBJECT NAMES**, **STORAGE**, Chapter 16

Format

```
CREATE TABLE [user.]table
    ({column datatype [DEFAULT expr] [column_constraint] ¦
     table_constraint}
    [,{column datatype [DEFAULT expr] [column_constraint] ¦
     table_constraint}]... )
        [CLUSTER cluster (column [,column]...)]
        [INITRANS integer]
```

```
        [MAXTRANS integer]
         [PCTFREE integer]
         [PCTUSED integer]
         [STORAGE storage]
     [TABLESPACE tablespace]
           [ENABLE enable |
         DISABLE disable]...
  [NOCACHE|CACHE]
  [NOPARALLEL|PARALLEL [DEGREE n][INSTANCES n]]
  [UNRECOVERABLE|RECOVERABLE]
      [AS query]
```

Description   *user* is the table owner. If the table owner is absent, *user* defaults to the user issuing this command. *table* is the table name, and follows ORACLE naming conventions.

column is the name of a column, and *datatype* is CHAR, VARCHAR, VARCHAR2, DATE, LONG, NUMBER, ROWID, MLSLABEL, RAW MLSLABEL, RAW, or LONG RAW (see DATA TYPES). DEFAULT specifies a value to be assigned to the column if a row is inserted without a value for this column. The value can be a simple literal or the result of an expression. The expression, however, cannot include a reference to a column, to Level, or to RowNum.

See INTEGRITY CONSTRAINT for a full description of the column and table constraints.

CLUSTER includes this table in the named cluster. The table columns listed must correspond in order and datatype to the cluster's cluster columns. The names need not be the same as the corresponding cluster's columns, although matching names can help the user to understand what is being done.

INITRANS tells the initial number of transactions that can update a data block concurrently (**select**s are not counted). INITRANS ranges from 1 to 255. 1 is the default. Every transaction takes space (23 bytes in most systems) in the data block itself until the transaction is completed. When more than the **INITRANS** number of transactions are created for the block, space is automatically allocated for them, up to **MAXTRANS**.

MAXTRANS tells the maximum number of transactions that can update a data block concurrently (**select**s are not counted). **MAXTRANS** ranges from 1 to 255. 255 is the default. Every transaction takes space (23 bytes in most systems) in the data block itself until the transaction is completed. Transactions queueing up for execution will occupy more and more free space in the block, although usually there is more free space than is needed for all concurrent transactions.

Whenever ORACLE inserts a row into a table, it first looks to see how much space is available in the current block (the size of a block is operating system dependent—*see* the *ORACLE Installation and User's Guide* for your system). If the size of the row will leave less than PCTFREE percent in the block, it puts the row in a newly allocated block instead. Default is 10; 0 is the minimum.

PCTUSED defaults to 40. This is the percentage minimum of available space in a block that will make it a candidate for insertion of new row's. In ORACLE version 5, a deleted row's space could not be recovered. In ORACLE version 6, this is no longer true. ORACLE tracks how much space in a block has been made available by deletions. If it falls below PCTUSED, ORACLE makes it available for insertions.

STORAGE contains subclauses that are all described under STORAGE. **TABLESPACE** is the name of the tablespace to which this table is assigned.

The **enable** and **disable** clauses enable or disable constraints. *See* **ENABLE** and **DISABLE**.

PARALLEL, along with **DEGREE** and **INSTANCES**, specifies the parallel characteristics of the table (for ORACLE7.1 and above databases using the Parallel Query option). **DEGREE** specifies the number of query servers to use; **INSTANCES** specifies how the table is to be split among instances of a Parallel Server for parallel query processing. An integer *n* specifies that the table is to be split among the specified number of available instances.

The **AS** clause creates the rows of the new table through the returned query rows. The columns and types of the query must match those defined in the **CREATE TABLE**. The query used in the **AS** clause may not contain any LONG datatype columns. In ORACLE7.2, you can turn off logging during the **create table ... as select** operation via the **UNRECOVERABLE** keyword. This option disables the redo log entries that would normally be written during the population of the new table, thus improving performance while impacting your ability to recover that data if an instance failure occurs prior to the next backup.

CREATE TABLESPACE

Type SQL command

Products All

See also **ALTER TABLESPACE, DROP TABLESPACE**

Format

```
CREATE TABLESPACE tablespace
    DATAFILE file_definition [,file_definition]...
[AUTOEXTEND file_definition [file_definition][ON | OFF]
      [NEXT integer [K | M]]
    [MAXSIZ [UNLIMITED| integer [K | M]]]]
    [DEFAULT STORAGE storage]
    [ONLINE | OFFLINE]
```

Description   *tablespace* is the name of the tablespace, and follows ORACLE naming conventions. The DATAFILE is a file or series of files described according to a *file_definition*, which specifies the database file names and sizes:

```
'file' [SIZE integer [K ┆ M] [REUSE]
```

The file format is operating-system specific. **SIZE** is the number of bytes set aside for this file. Suffixing this with K multiplies the value by 1024; M multiplies it by 1048576. **DEFAULT STORAGE** defines the default storage for all objects created in this tablespace, unless those defaults are overridden, such as by **CREATE TABLE**. **ONLINE**, the default, indicates that this tablespace will become available to users as soon as it is created. **OFFLINE** prevents access to it until **ALTER TABLESPACE** changes it to **ONLINE**. DBA_TABLESPACES gives the status of all the tablespaces.

SIZE and **REUSE** together will tell ORACLE to reuse the file if it already exists (anything it contains will be wiped out), or create it if it doesn't already exist. **SIZE** without **REUSE** will create a file that does not exist, but return an error if it does. Without **SIZE**, the file must already exist.

In ORACLE7.2, the **AUTOEXTEND** option can be used for datafiles. When turned ON, this option will dynamically extend a datafile as needed in increments of **NEXT** size, to a maximum of **MAXSIZ** (or UNLIMITED).

CREATE TRIGGER

Type   SQL command

Products   All

See also   **ALTER TABLE**, **ALTER TRIGGER**, BLOCK STRUCTURE, **DROP TRIGGER**, Chapter 21.

Format

```
CREATE [OR REPLACE] TRIGGER [user.]trigger
  {BEFORE ┆ AFTER}
  {DELETE ┆ INSERT ┆ UPDATE [OF column[, column]...}
  [OR {DELETE ┆ INSERT ┆ UPDATE [OF column[, column]...}]...
  ON [user.]table
  [REFERENCING {OLD [AS] old ┆ NEW [AS] new}]
  [FOR EACH ROW]
  [WHEN (condition)]
  block
```

Description   **CREATE TRIGGER** creates and enables a database trigger, a stored procedure block associated with a table, specified in the **on** clause, that ORACLE automatically executes when the specified SQL statement executes against the table. You can use triggers to enforce complex constraints and to propagate changes throughout the database instead of doing this in your applications. That way you implement the triggered code once instead of having to do it in every application.

You must have CREATE TRIGGER or CREATE ANY TRIGGER privilege to create a trigger, and the user must have been directly granted all privileges necessary to execute the stored procedure.

The main clause of the **CREATE TRIGGER** command specifies the SQL operation that triggers the block (**delete**, **insert**, or **update**) and when the trigger fires (**BEFORE** or **AFTER** executing the triggering operation). If you specify an **of** clause on an **update** trigger, the trigger fires only when you update those specific columns.

The **referencing** clause specifies a correlation name for the table for the OLD and NEW versions of the table. This lets you use the name when referring to columns to avoid confusion, particularly when the table name is OLD or NEW. The default names are OLD and NEW.

The **for each row** clause specifies the trigger to be a row trigger, a trigger fired once for each row affected by the triggering operation. The **when** clause restricts the execution of the trigger to happen only when the **condition** is met. This condition is a SQL condition, not a PL/SQL condition.

The PL/SQL block cannot contain any transaction control statements (COMMIT, ROLLBACK, or SAVEPOINT).

You can disable and enable triggers through the **ALTER TRIGGER** and **ALTER TABLE** commands. If a trigger is disabled, ORACLE does not fire the trigger when a potentially triggering operation occurs. The **CREATE TRIGGER** command automatically enables the trigger. To create a trigger on a table you own, you must have the CREATE TRIGGER system privilege. To create a trigger on another user's table, you must have the CREATE ANY TRIGGER system privilege.

See Chapter 21 for examples.

CREATE USER

Type   SQL command

Products   All

See also   **ALTER USER**, **CREATE PROFILE**, **CREATE ROLE**, **CREATE TABLESPACE**, **GRANT**, Chapter 17

Format

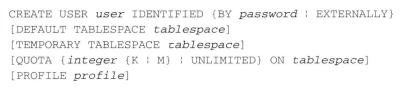

```
CREATE USER user IDENTIFIED {BY password | EXTERNALLY}
[DEFAULT TABLESPACE tablespace]
[TEMPORARY TABLESPACE tablespace]
[QUOTA {integer {K | M} | UNLIMITED} ON tablespace]
[PROFILE profile]
```

Description **CREATE USER** creates a user account that lets you log onto the database with a certain set of privileges and storage settings. If you specify a password, you must supply that password to logon; if you specify the **EXTERNALLY** option, access is verified through the operating system security. External verification uses the OS_AUTHENT_PREFIX initialization parameter to prefix the operating system user id, so the user name you specify in **CREATE USER** should contain that prefix (usually, OPS$).

The DEFAULT TABLESPACE is the tablespace in which the user creates objects. The TEMPORARY TABLESPACE is the tablespace in which temporary objects are created for the user's operations.

You can put a QUOTA on either of these tablespaces that limits the amount of space, in bytes (kilobytes or megabytes for K or M options, respectively), that a user can allocate. The **profile** clause assigns a named profile to the user to limit usage of database resources. ORACLE assigns the DEFAULT profile to the user if you don't specify a profile.

When you first create a user, the user has no privileges. You must use the **GRANT** command to grant roles and privileges to the user. You should usually grant **CREATE SESSION** as a minimal privilege.

CREATE VIEW

Type SQL command

Products All

See also **CREATE SYNONYM**, **CREATE TABLE**, **DROP VIEW**, **RENAME**, INTEGRITY CONSTRAINT, Chapter 16

Format

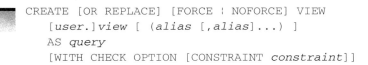

```
CREATE [OR REPLACE] [FORCE ¦ NOFORCE] VIEW
    [user.]view [ (alias [,alias]...) ]
    AS query
    [WITH CHECK OPTION [CONSTRAINT constraint]]
```

Description **CREATE VIEW** defines a view. It commits pending changes to the default database. The **OR REPLACE** option re-creates the view if it already exists. The **FORCE** option creates the view regardless of whether the tables to which the view refers exist or whether the user has privileges on them. The user still can't execute the view, but he or she can create it. The **NOFORCE** option creates the view only if the base tables exist and the user has privileges on them.

user is the name of the user for whom the view is created. *view* is the name assigned to the view.

If an alias is specified, the view uses the alias as the name of the corresponding column in the query. If an alias is not specified, the view inherits the column name from the query; in this case each column in a query must have a unique name, one that follows normal ORACLE naming conventions. It cannot be an expression or a table column. An alias in the query itself also can serve to rename the column.

AS *query* identifies the columns of tables and other views that are to appear in this view. Its **where** clause will determine which rows are to be retrieved.

WITH CHECK OPTION restricts **insert**s and **update**s performed through the view to prevent them from creating rows that the view cannot itself select, based on the **where** clause of the **CREATE VIEW** statement. Thus this:

```
create or replace view WOMEN
   as select Name, Department, Sex
   from EMPLOYEE  where Sex = 'F'
   with check option;
```

prevents you from inserting a row into WOMEN where Sex was either M or NULL, or from changing the value in Sex using an **update**.

WITH CHECK OPTION may be used in a view that is based on another view; however, if the underlying view also has a **WITH CHECK OPTION**, it is ignored.

constraint is a name given to the **CHECK OPTION**. *constraint* is an optional name assigned to this constraint. Without it, ORACLE will assign a name in the form **SYS_C***n,* where *n* is an integer. An ORACLE-assigned name will usually change during an import, while a user-assigned name will not change.

update and **delete** will work on rows in a view if the view is based on a single table and its query does not contain the **group by** clause, the **distinct** clause, group functions, or references to the pseudo-column RowNum. You may **update** views containing other pseudo-columns or expressions, as long as they are not referenced in the **UPDATE**.

You may **INSERT** rows through a view if the view is based on a single table and if its query does not contain the **group by** clause, the **distinct** clause, group functions, references to any pseudo-columns, or any expressions.

In order to create a view, you must have the CREATE VIEW system privilege. To create a view in another user's schema, you must have the CREATE ANY VIEW system privilege.

CREATING A DATABASE

Creating a database is the process of making a database ready for initial use. It includes clearing the database files and loading initial database tables required by the RDBMS. This is accomplished via the SQL statement **CREATE DATABASE**.

CRT

CRT can be used in either of two ways:

- CRT is an ORACLE utility used to define or alter how terminals interact with ORACLE software. It is most often used to define which keys perform which functions.
- (SQL*PLUS) *See* **SET**.

CRT FILE

A CRT file is one containing information about one hardware terminal, its keys, and their mapping to ORACLE programs, and general escape sequences to enable different settings on the terminal.

CURRENT BUFFER

The current buffer is the one that SQL*PLUS editing commands will affect, and that can be saved to a file with the **SAVE** command. *See* **CHANGE**.

CURRENT LINE

The current line is the one in the current buffer that SQL*PLUS command line editor commands will affect. *See* **CURRENT BUFFER** and **CHANGE**.

CURRVAL

See PSEUDO-COLUMNS.

CURSOR

Cursor has two definitions:

- A cursor is a marker such as a blinking square or line, that marks your current position on a CRT screen.
- Cursor is also a synonym for context area—a work area in memory where ORACLE stores the current SQL statement. For a query, the area in memory also includes column headings and one row retrieved by the **select** statement.

CURSOR - PL/SQL

Type SQL command

Products All

See also **CREATE PACKAGE, CREATE PACKAGE BODY**

Format

```
CURSOR cursor [(parameter datatype[,parameter datatype]...]
[IS query]
```

Description You can specify a cursor in a PL/SQL package and you can declare its body. The specification contains only the list of parameters with their corresponding datatypes, not the **IS** clause, while the body contains both. The parameters may appear anywhere in the query that a constant could appear. You can specify the cursor as a part of the public declarations of the package specification, and then the cursor body as part of the hidden package body.

CURSOR COORDINATES

The cursor coordinates are the coordinates of the horizontal and vertical position of a cursor on the screen. Coordinate labels and ranges vary by terminal type.

CURSOR DESCRIPTOR

A cursor descriptor is an area reserved for every cursor (context area) that contains certain cursor information.

CURSOR ID

The cursor ID is the name given to each cursor or context area.

DATA CONTROL LANGUAGE (DCL) STATEMENTS

DCL statements are one category of SQL statements. DCL statements, such as **grant connect**, **grant select**, **grant update**, and **revoke dba**, control access to the data and to the database. The other categories are data definition language (DDL) and data manipulation language (DML) statements.

DATA DEFINITION LANGUAGE (DDL) STATEMENTS

DDL statements are one category of SQL statements. DDL statements define (create) or delete (drop) database objects. Examples are **create view**, **create table**, **create index**, **drop table**, and **rename table**. The other categories are data control language (DCL) and data manipulation language (DML) statements.

DATA DEFINITION LOCKS

Data definition locks are locks placed on the data dictionary during changes to the structures (definitions) of database objects (such as tables, indexes, views, and clusters) so that those changes occur with no negative impact on the database data. There are three kinds: dictionary operation locks, dictionary definition locks, and table definition locks.

DATA DICTIONARY

The data dictionary is a comprehensive set of tables and views owned by the DBA users SYS and SYSTEM, which activates when ORACLE is initially installed, and is a central source of information for the ORACLE RDBMS itself and for all users of ORACLE. The tables are automatically maintained by ORACLE, and hold a set of views and tables containing information about database objects, users, privileges, events, and use. *See* Chapter 24.

DATA DICTIONARY VIEWS

Type   Definitions
Products   All

See also   Chapter 24

Description   The ORACLE7 data dictionary views are described in Chapter 24. Most of the following listing, describing all of the available data dictionary views, was generated by selecting records from the DICTIONARY view in ORACLE7.1, via a non-DBA account. The views are listed here in alphabetical order; Chapter 24 lists them by function, and describes them.

VIEW NAME	COMMENTS
ACCESSIBLE_COLUMNS	Synonym for ALL_TAB_COLUMNS.
ALL_ARGUMENTS	Arguments for accessible procedural objects.
ALL_CATALOG	All tables, views, synonyms, sequences accessible to the user.
ALL_COL_COMMENTS	Comments on columns of accessible tables and views.
ALL_COL_GRANTS	Synonym for COLUMN_PRIVILEGES.
ALL_COL_GRANTS_MADE	Grants on columns for which the user is owner or grantor.
ALL_COL_GRANTS_RECD	Grants on columns for which the user or PUBLIC is the grantee.
ALL_COL_PRIVS	Grants on columns for which the user is the grantor, grantee, owner, or an enabled role or PUBLIC is the grantee.
ALL_COL_PRIVS_MADE	Grants on columns for which the user is owner or grantor.
ALL_COL_PRIVS_RECD	Grants on columns for which the user, PUBLIC or enabled role is the grantee.
ALL_CONSTRAINTS	Constraint definitions on accessible tables.
ALL_CONS_COLUMNS	Information about accessible columns in constraint definitions.
ALL_DB_LINKS	Database links accessible to the user.
ALL_DEF_AUDIT_OPTS	Auditing options for newly created objects.
ALL_DEPENDENCIES	Dependencies to and from objects accessible to the user.
ALL_ERRORS	Current errors on stored objects that user is allowed to create.
ALL_INDEXES	Descriptions of indexes on tables accessible to the user.

VIEW NAME	COMMENTS
ALL_IND_COLUMNS	Columns comprising indexes on accessible tables.
ALL_JOBS	Synonym for USER_JOBS.
ALL_OBJECTS	Objects accessible to the user.
ALL_OBJECT_SIZE	Code sizes for objects accessible to the user.
ALL_REFRESH	All the refresh groups that the user can touch.
ALL_REFRESH_CHILDREN	All the objects in refresh groups, where the user can touch the group.
ALL_SEQUENCES	Description of sequences accessible to the user.
ALL_SNAPSHOTS	Snapshots the user can look at.
ALL_SOURCE	Current source on stored objects that user is allowed to create.
ALL_SYNONYMS	All synonyms accessible to the user.
ALL_TABLES	Description of tables accessible to the user.
ALL_TAB_COLUMNS	Columns of all tables, views, and clusters.
ALL_TAB_COMMENTS	Comments on tables and views accessible to the user.
ALL_TAB_GRANTS	Synonym for TABLE_PRIVILEGES.
ALL_TAB_GRANTS_MADE	User's grants and grants on user's objects.
ALL_TAB_GRANTS_RECD	Grants on objects for which the user or PUBLIC is the grantee.
ALL_TAB_PRIVS	Grants on objects for which the user is the grantor, grantee, owner, or an enabled role or PUBLIC is the grantee.
ALL_TAB_PRIVS_MADE	User's grants and grants on user's objects.
ALL_TAB_PRIVS_RECD	Grants on objects for which the user, PUBLIC or enabled role is the grantee.
ALL_TRIGGERS	Triggers accessible to the current user.
ALL_TRIGGER_COLS	Column usage in user's triggers or in triggers on user's tables.
ALL_USERS	Information about all users of the database.
ALL_VIEWS	Text of views accessible to the user.

VIEW NAME	COMMENTS
AUDIT_ACTIONS	Description table for audit trail action type codes. Maps action type numbers to action type names.
CAT	Synonym for USER_CATALOG.
CLU	Synonym for USER_CLUSTERS.
COLS	Synonym for USER_TAB_COLUMNS.
COLUMN_PRIVILEGES	Grants on columns for which the user is the grantor, grantee, owner, or an enabled role or PUBLIC is the grantee.
DBA_AUDIT_CONNECT	Synonym for USER_AUDIT_CONNECT.
DBA_AUDIT_RESOURCE	Synonym for USER_AUDIT_RESOURCE.
DBA_REFRESH_CHILDREN	Synonym for USER_REFRESH_CHILDREN.
DICT	Synonym for DICTIONARY.
DICTIONARY	Description of data dictionary tables and views.
DICT_COLUMNS	Description of columns in data dictionary tables and views.
DUAL	One-row, one-column table used in logic queries. *See* **DUAL** and Chapter 7.
GLOBAL_NAME	Global database name.
IND	Synonym for USER_INDEXES.
OBJ	Synonym for USER_OBJECTS.
RESOURCE_COST	Cost for each resource.
ROLE_ROLE_PRIVS	Roles which are granted to roles.
ROLE_SYS_PRIVS	System privileges granted to roles.
ROLE_TAB_PRIVS	Table privileges granted to roles.
SEQ	Synonym for USER_SEQUENCES.
SESSION_PRIVS	Privileges which the user currently has set.
SESSION_ROLES	Roles which the user currently has enabled.
SYN	Synonym for USER_SYNONYMS.
TABLE_PRIVILEGES	Grants on objects for which the user is the grantor, grantee, owner, or an enabled role or PUBLIC is the grantee.

VIEW NAME	COMMENTS
TABS	Synonym for USER_TABLES.
USER_AUDIT_CONNECT	Audit trail entries for user logons/logoffs.
USER_AUDIT_OBJECT	Audit trail records for statements concerning objects, specifically: table, cluster, view, index, sequence, [public] database link, [public] synonym, procedure, trigger, rollback segment, tablespace, role, user.
USER_AUDIT_SESSION	Session audit records for the user.
USER_AUDIT_STATEMENT	Audit trail records concerning **grant**, **revoke**, **audit**, **noaudit**, and **alter system**.
USER_AUDIT_TRAIL	Audit trail entries relevant to the user.
USER_CATALOG	Tables, views, synonyms, and sequences owned by the user.
USER_CLUSTERS	Descriptions of user's own clusters.
USER_CLU_COLUMNS	Mapping of table columns to cluster columns.
USER_COL_COMMENTS	Comments on columns of user's tables and views.
USER_COL_GRANTS	Grants on columns for which the user is the owner, grantor, or grantee.
USER_COL_GRANTS_MADE	All grants on columns of objects owned by the user.
USER_COL_GRANTS_RECD	Grants on columns for which the user is the grantee.
USER_COL_PRIVS	Grants on columns for which the user is the owner, grantor, or grantee.
USER_COL_PRIVS_MADE	All grants on columns of objects owned by the user.
USER_COL_PRIVS_RECD	Grants on columns for which the user is the grantee.
USER_CONSTRAINTS	Constraint definitions on user's own tables.
USER_CONS_COLUMNS	Information about accessible columns in constraint definitions.
USER_CROSS_REFS	Cross references for user's views and synonyms.
USER_DB_LINKS	Database links owned by the user.

VIEW NAME	COMMENTS
USER_DEPENDENCIES	Dependencies to and from a users objects.
USER_ERRORS	Current errors on stored objects owned by the user.
USER_EXTENTS	Extents comprising segments owned by the user.
USER_FREE_SPACE	Free extents in tablespaces accessible to the user.
USER_INDEXES	Description of the user's own indexes.
USER_IND_COLUMNS	Columns comprising user's indexes or on user's tables.
USER_JOBS	All jobs owned by this user.
USER_OBJECTS	Objects owned by the user.
USER_OBJECT_SIZE	Sizes, in bytes, of various pl/sql objects.
USER_OBJ_AUDIT_OPTS	Auditing options for user's own tables and views.
USER_REFRESH	All the refresh groups.
USER_REFRESH_CHILDREN	All the objects in refresh groups, where the user owns the refresh group.
USER_RESOURCE_LIMITS	Display resource limit of the user.
USER_ROLE_PRIVS	Roles granted to current user.
USER_SEGMENTS	Storage allocated for all database segments.
USER_SEQUENCES	Description of the user's own sequences.
USER_SNAPSHOTS	Snapshots the user can look at.
USER_SNAPSHOT_LOGS	All snapshot logs owned by the user.
USER_SOURCE	Source of stored objects accessible to the user.
USER_SYNONYMS	The user's private synonyms.
USER_SYS_PRIVS	System privileges granted to current user.
USER_TABLES	Description of the user's own tables.
USER_TABLESPACES	Description of accessible tablespaces.
USER_TAB_AUDIT_OPTS	Auditing options for user's own tables and views.
USER_TAB_COLUMNS	Columns of user's tables, views, and clusters.
USER_TAB_COMMENTS	Comments on the tables and views owned by the user.
USER_TAB_GRANTS	Grants on objects for which the user is the owner, grantor, or grantee.
USER_TAB_GRANTS_MADE	All grants on objects owned by the user.

VIEW NAME	COMMENTS
USER_TAB_GRANTS_RECD	Grants on objects for which the user is the grantee.
USER_TAB_PRIVS	Grants on objects for which the user is the owner, grantor, or grantee.
USER_TAB_PRIVS_MADE	All grants on objects owned by the user.
USER_TAB_PRIVS_RECD	Grants on objects for which the user is the grantee.
USER_TRIGGERS	Triggers owned by the user.
USER_TRIGGER_COLS	Column usage in user's triggers.
USER_TS_QUOTAS	Tablespace quotas for the user.
USER_USERS	Information about the current user.
USER_VIEWS	Text of views owned by the user.
V$ACCESS	Objects that are currently locked, and the sessions that are accessing them.
V$ARCHIVE	Archivelog status for each redo log thread.
V$BACKUP	Backup status of all online datafiles.
V$BGPROCESS	Descriptions of background processes.
V$CIRCUIT	Information about virtual circuits (used by the mult-threaded server).
V$COMPATIBILITY	Version compatibility status.
V$CONTROLFILE	Control file status.
V$DATABASE	Database information, from the control file.
V$DATAFILE	Datafile status.
V$DBFILE	Version 6 view of datafiles, superseded by V$DATAFILE in ORACLE7.
V$DBLINK	Database link status.
V$DB_OBJECT_CACHE	Library cache contents. *See* SHARED SQL POOL.
V$DISPATCHER	Dispatcher process information (for the multi-threaded server).
V$ENABLEDPRIVS	Currently enabled privileges.
V$FILESTAT	File I/O statistics.
V$FIXED_TABLE	Fixed tables, views, and derived objects.

VIEW NAME	COMMENTS
V$LATCH	Latch status.
V$LATCHHOLDER	Processes currently holding latches.
V$LATCHNAME	Names of current latches.
V$LIBRARYCACHE	Library cache usage statistics. *See* SHARED SQL POOL.
V$LICENSE	License limit settings.
V$LOADCSTAT	SQL*LOADER Direct Path load statistics for an entire load.
V$LOADTSTAT	SQL*LOADER Direct path load statistics for the current table.
V$LOCK	Lock status for non-DDL locks.
V$LOG	Redo log status.
V$LOGFILE	Redo log file group descriptions.
V$LOGHIST	Version 6 version of V$LOG_HISTORY.
V$LOG_HISTORY	Redo log history information from the control file.
V$MTS	Multi-threaded server status.
V$NLS_PARAMETERS	Current values of NLS parameters.
V$NLS_VALID_VALUES	Valid values for NLS parameters.
V$OPEN_CURSOR	Cursors opened and parsed by session.
V$PARAMETER	Current parameter values.
V$PROCESS	Status of active processes.
V$QUEUE	Multi-threaded server message queue information.
V$RECOVERY_LOG	Archived redo log files needed to complete media recovery, derived from V$LOG_HISTORY.
V$RECOVER_FILE	Status of files needing recovery.
V$REQDIST	A histogram of request time distribution.
V$RESOURCE	Resource status.
V$ROLLNAME	Names of online rollback segments.
V$ROLLSTAT	I/O and space usage statistics for online rollback segments.
V$ROWCACHE	Data dictionary cache activity statistics.

VIEW NAME	COMMENTS
V$SESSION	Current sessions descriptions.
V$SESSION_WAIT	Resources or events the active sessions are waiting for.
V$SESSTAT	Current session statistics values.
V$SESS_IO	Session I/O statistics.
V$SGA	SGA memory distribution.
V$SGASTAT	Detailed SGA memory distribution.
V$SHARED_SERVER	Information on shared servers (for the multi-threaded server).
V$SQLAREA	Shared SQL area statistics.
V$SQLTEXT	Text of cursors currently in the shared SQL area.
V$STATNAME	Statistics names for the V$SESSTAT view.
V$SYSSTAT	System-wide statistics.
V$THREAD	Thread status of redo logs.
V$TIMER	Current time, in hundredths of seconds.
V$TRANSACTION	Transaction status information.
V$TYPE_SIZE	Component sizes, for use in estimating data block capacity.
V$VERSION	Version numbers of database components.
V$WAITSTAT	Statistics for block contention.

DATA INDEPENDENCE

Data independence is the property of well-defined tables that allows the physical and logical structure of a table to change without affecting applications that access the table.

DATA LOCKS

When a user executes a SQL statement, the data to which the statement refers is locked in one of several lock modes. The user can also lock data explicitly with a LOCK statement. These data locks appear as TX or TM locks on the SQLDBA Monitor Lock display.

DATA MANIPULATION LANGUAGE (DML) STATEMENTS

DML statements are one category of SQL statements. DML statements, such as **select**, **insert**, **delete**, and **update**, query and update the actual data. The other categories are data control language (DCL) and data definition language (DDL) statements.

DATA TYPES

Type   Data definitions

Products   All

See also   CHARACTER FUNCTIONS, CONVERSION FUNCTIONS, DATE FUNCTIONS, LIST FUNCTIONS, NUMBER FUNCTIONS, OTHER FUNCTIONS

Description   When a table is created and the columns in it are defined, they must each have a data type specified. ORACLE's primary data types are VARCHAR2, CHAR, DATE, LONG, LONG RAW, NUMBER, RAW, and ROWID, but for compatibility with other SQL databases, its **create table** statements will accept several versions of these:

DATA TYPE	DEFINITION
CHAR(*size*)	Fixed-length character data, *size* characters long. Maximum size is 255. Default is 1 byte. Padded on right with blanks to full length of *size*.
DATE	Valid dates range from January 1, 4712 B.C. to December 31, 4712 A.D.
DECIMAL	Same as NUMBER. Does not accept size or decimal digits as an argument.
FLOAT	Same as NUMBER.
INTEGER	Same as NUMBER. Does not accept decimal digits as an argument.
INTEGER(*size*)	Integer of specified *size* digits wide.
LONG	Character data of variable size up to 2 Gb in length. Only one LONG column may be defined per table. LONG columns may not be used in subqueries, functions, expressions, **where** clauses, or indexes. A table containing a LONG column may not be clustered.

DATA TYPE	DEFINITION
LONG RAW	Raw binary data; otherwise the same as LONG.
LONG VARCHAR	Same as LONG.
MLSLABEL	4-byte representation of a secure operating system label.
NUMBER	For NUMBER column with space for 40 digits, plus space for a decimal point and sign. Numbers may be expressed in two ways: first, with the numbers 0 to 9, the signs + and –, and a decimal point (.); second, in scientific notation, such as, 1.85E3 for 1850. Valid values are 0, and positive and negative numbers with magnitude 1.0E-130 to 9.99.. E125.
NUMBER(*size*)	For NUMBER column of specified *size*.
NUMBER(*size,d*)	For NUMBER column of specified *size* with *d* digits after decimal point. For example, NUMBER(5,2) could contain nothing larger than 999.99 without an error.
NUMBER(*)	Same as NUMBER.
SMALLINT	Same as NUMBER.
RAW(*size*)	Raw binary data, *size* bytes long. Maximum size is 255 bytes.
RAW MLSLABEL	Binary format for secure operating system label.
ROWID	A value that uniquely identifies a row in an ORACLE database. It is returned by the pseudo-column ROWID. Table columns may not be assigned this type.
VARCHAR2(*size*)	Variable length character string having a maximum of *size* bytes (up to 2000).
VARCHAR(*size*)	Same as VARCHAR2. Use VARCHAR2, since VARCHAR's usage may change in future versions of ORACLE.

DATABASE

Database can be one of two definitions:

- A set of dictionary tables and user tables that are treated as a unit.

- One or more operating system files in which ORACLE stores tables, views, and other objects; also, the set of database objects used by a given application.

DATABASE ADMINISTRATOR (DBA)

A DBA is an ORACLE user authorized to **grant** and **revoke** other users' access to the system, modify ORACLE options that affect all users, and perform other administrative functions.

DATABASE FILE

A database file is simply any file used in a database. A database is made up of one or more tablespaces, which in turn are made up of one or more database files.

DATABASE LINK

A database link is an object stored in the local database that identifies a remote database, a communication path to the remote database, and, optionally, a username and password for it. Once defined, the database link is used to perform queries on tables in the remote database. *See* Chapter 20.

DATABASE NAME

A database name is a unique identifier used to name a database. It is assigned in the **create database** command or in the **init.ora** file.

DATABASE OBJECT

A database object is something created and stored in a database. Tables, views, synonyms, indexes, sequences, clusters, and columns are all types of database objects.

DATABASE SPECIFICATION

Database specification is an alphanumeric code that identifies an ORACLE database, used to specify the database in SQL*NET operations and to define a database link.

DATABASE SYSTEM

A database system is a combination of an instance and a database. If the instance is started and connected to an open database, then the database system is available for access by users.

DATATYPE

See DATA TYPES.

DATE

DATE is a standard ORACLE datatype to store date and time data. Standard date format is 01-APR-95. A DATE column may contain a date and time between January 1, 4712 B.C. and December 31, 4712 A.D.

DATE FORMATS

Type   SQL function parameters

Products   All

See also   DATE FUNCTIONS, Chapter 7

Description   These date formats are used with both **TO_CHAR** and **TO_DATE**:

FORMAT	MEANING
MM	Number of month: 12
RM	Roman numeral month: XII
MON	Three-letter abbreviation of month: AUG
Mon	Same as MON, but with initial capital: Aug
mon	Same as MON, but all lowercase: aug
MONTH	Month fully spelled out: AUGUST
Month	Month with initial capital: August
month	Month all lowercase: august
DDD	Number of the day in the year, since Jan 1: 354
DD	Number of the day in the month: 23
D	Number of the day in the week: 6

FORMAT	MEANING
DY	Three-letter abbreviation of day: FRI
Dy	Same as DY, but with initial capital: Fri
dy	Same as DY, but all lowercase: fri
DAY	Day fully spelled out: FRIDAY
Day	Day with initial capital: Friday
day	Day all lowercase: friday
YYYY	Full four-digit year: 1946
SYYYY	Signed year if B.C. 1000 B.C. = −1000
IYYY	ISO four-digit standard year
YYY	Last three digits of year: 946
IYY	Last three digits of ISO year
YY	Last two digits of year: 46
IY	Last two digits of ISO year
Y	Last digit of year: 6
I	Last digit of ISO year
RR	Last two digits of year, possibly in other century
YEAR	Year spelled out: NINETEEN-FORTY-SIX
Year	Spelled with initial capitals: Nineteen-Forty-Six
year	Year in lowercase: nineteen-forty-six
Q	Number of quarter: 3
WW	Number of week in year: 46
W	Number of week in month: 3
IW	Week of year from ISO standard
J	"Julian" - days since December 31, 4713 B.C.: 2422220
HH	Hour of day, always 1-12: 11
HH12	Same as HH
HH24	Hour of day, 24-hour clock: 17
MI	Minute of hour: 58
SS	Second of minute: 43
SSSSS	Seconds since midnight, always 0-86399: 43000
/,-:.	Punctuation to be incorporated in display for **TO_CHAR** or ignored in format for **TO_DATE**
A.M.	Displays A.M. or P.M., depending on time of day

FORMAT	MEANING
a.m.	Same as A.M. but lowercase
P.M.	Same effect as A.M.
p.m.	Same effect as A.M.
AM	Same as A.M. but without periods
am	Same as A.M. but without periods
PM	Same as P.M. but without periods
pm	Same as P.M. but without periods
CC or SCC	Century; S prefixes BC with "-"
B.C.	Displays B.C. or A.D. depending upon date
A.D.	Same as B.C.
b.c.	Same as B.C., but lowercase
a.d.	Same as B.C.
BC or AD	Same as B.C. but without periods
bc or ad	Same as B.C. but without periods

These date formats work only with **TO_CHAR**. They do not work with **TO_DATE**:

FORMAT	MEANING
"*string*"	string is incorporated in display for **TO_CHAR**.
fm	Prefix to Month or Day: fmMONTH or fmday. Suppresses padding of Month or Day (defined earlier) under format. Without fm, all Months are displayed at same width. The same is true for days. With fm, padding is eliminated. Months and days are only as long as their count of characters.
TH	Suffix to a number: ddTH or DDTH produces 24th or 24TH. Capitalization comes from the case of the number—DD—not from the case of the TH. Works with any number in a date: YYYY, DD, MM, HH, MI, SS, and so on.
SP	Suffix to a number that forces number to be spelled out: DDSP, DdSP, or ddSP produces THREE, Three, or three. Capitalization comes from case of number—DD—not from the case of SP. Works with any number in a date: YYYY, DD, MM, HH, MI, SS, and so on.

FORMAT	MEANING
SPTH	Suffix combination of TH and SP that forces number to be both spelled out and given an ordinal suffix: Mmspth produces Third. Capitalization comes from case of number—DD—not from the case of SP. Works with any number in a date: YYYY, DD, MM, HH, MI, SS, and so on.
THSP	Same as SPTH.

DATE FUNCTIONS

Type   SQL command

Products   All, PL/SQL

See also   DATE FORMATS, Chapter 7

Description   This is an alphabetical list of all current date functions in ORACLE's SQL. Each of these is listed elsewhere in this reference under its own name, with its proper format and use.

FUNCTION	DEFINITION
ADD_MONTHS(*date,count*)	Adds *count* months to *date*.
GREATEST(*date1,date2,date3,. . .*)	Picks latest of list of dates.
LAST_DAY(*date*)	Gives date of last day of month that *date* is in.
MONTHS_BETWEEN(*date2,date1*)	Gives *date2-date1* in months (can be fractional months).
NEXT_DAY(*date,'day'*)	Gives date of next 'day' after *date*.
NEW_TIME('*date*','*this*','*other*')	*date* is the date (and time) in this time zone. *this* is a three-letter abbreviation for the current time zone. *other* is a three-letter abbreviation of the other time zone for which you'd like to know the time and date. Time zones are as follows:
AST/ADT	Atlantic standard/daylight time
BST/BDT	Bering standard/daylight time
CST/CDT	Central standard/daylight time

FUNCTION	DEFINITION
EST/EDT	Eastern standard/daylight time
GMT	Greenwich mean time
HST/HDT	Alaska-Hawaii standard/daylight time
MST/MDT	Mountain standard/daylight time
NST	Newfoundland standard time
PST/PDT	Pacific standard/daylight time
YST/YDT	Yukon standard/daylight time
ROUND(*date*, '*format*')	Rounds a date to 12 A.M. (midnight, the beginning of the day) if time of *date* is before noon, otherwise rounds up to next day, or according to *format*. Look up **ROUND** later in this reference for details of *format*.
TO_CHAR(*date*, '*format*')	Reformats date according to *format* (*see* DATE FORMATS).
TO_DATE(*string*, '*format*')	Converts a string in a given *format* into an ORACLE date. Also accepts a number instead of a string, with certain limits. *format* is restricted.
TRUNC(*date*, '*format*')	Sets a date to 12 A.M. (midnight, the beginning of the day), or according to *format*. Look up **TRUNC** later in this reference for details of *format*.

DATUM

Singular for the word data, datum represents a single unit of data.

DBA

See DATABASE ADMINISTRATOR (DBA).

DBA PRIVILEGE

Database privileges are given via the **grant dba** command, and should be limited to very few users.

DBWR PROCESS

One of the background processes used by ORACLE7. The **D**ata**b**ase **Wr**iter process writes new data to the database.

DCL

See DATA CONTROL LANGUAGE (DCL) STATEMENTS.

DDL

See DATA DEFINITION LANGUAGE (DDL) STATEMENTS.

DDL LOCK

When a user executes a DDL command, ORACLE locks the objects referred to in the command with DDL locks. A DDL lock locks objects in the data dictionary. (Contrast this to parse locks, the other type of dictionary lock.)

DEADLOCK

A deadlock is a rare situation in which two or more user processes of a database cannot complete their transactions. This occurs because each process is holding a resource that the other process requires (such as a row in a table) in order to complete. Although these situations occur rarely, ORACLE detects and resolves deadlocks by rolling back the work of one of the processes.

DECLARATIVE SQL STATEMENT

A declarative SQL statement is one that does not generate a call to the database, and is therefore not an executable SQL statement. Examples are **BEGIN DECLARE**

SECTION or **DECLARE CURSOR**. Declarative statements are used primarily in precompiled and PL/SQL programs. Compare to executable SQL statements.

DECLARE CURSOR (Form 1 - Embedded SQL)

Type   Precompiler declarative SQL command

Product   Precompilers

See also   **CLOSE**, **DECLARE DATABASE**, **DECLARE STATEMENT**, **FETCH**, **OPEN**, **PREPARE**, **SELECT**, **SELECT** (Embedded SQL)

Format

```
EXEC SQL [AT {database | :host_variable}]
DECLARE cursor CURSOR
FOR {SELECT command | statement}
```

Description   The **DECLARE CURSOR** statement must appear before any SQL that references this cursor, and must be compiled in the same source as procedures that reference it. Its name must be unique to the source.

   database is the name of a database already declared in a **DECLARE DATABASE** and used in a SQL CONNECT; *host_variable* is a variable with such a name as its value. *cursor* is the name you assign to this cursor. **SELECT** command is a query with no INTO clause. Alternatively, a SQL statement or a PL/SQL block already declared in a SQL **DECLARE STATEMENT** statement can be used.

   When the FOR UPDATE OF clause is included in the SELECT statement, an UPDATE can reference the cursor with WHERE CURRENT OF CURSOR, although the cursor must still be open, and a row must be present from a **FETCH**.

Example

```
exec sql at TALBOT declare FRED cursor
    for select ActionDate, Person, Item, Amount
         from LEDGER
       where Item = :Item
         and ActionDate = :ActionDate
         for update of Amount
```

DECLARE CURSOR (Form 2 - PL/SQL)

Type   PL/SQL statement

Products   PL/SQL

See also CLOSE, FETCH, OPEN, SELECT. . .INTO

Format

```
DECLARE
CURSOR cursor (parameter datatype [,parameter datatype]...)
IS select_statement
[FOR UPDATE OF column [,column]...];
```

Description A cursor is a work area that ORACLE uses to control the row currently in process. **DECLARE CURSOR** names a cursor and declares that it IS (the result of) a certain select_statement. The *select_statement* is required, and may not contain an INTO clause. The cursor must be declared. It can then be **OPEN**ed, and rows can then be **FETCH**ed into it. Finally, it can be **CLOSE**d.

Variables cannot be used directly in the **where** clause of the *select_statement* unless they've first been identified as parameters, in a list that precedes the select. Note that DECLARE CURSOR does not execute the **select** statement, and the parameters have no values until they are assigned in an **OPEN** statement (an example will follow shortly). Parameters have standard object names, and data types, including VARCHAR2, CHAR, NUMBER, DATE, and BOOLEAN, all without size or scale, however.

FOR UPDATE OF is required if you wish to affect the current row in the cursor using either **update** or **delete** commands with the CURRENT OF clause.

```
DECLARE
    cursor EMPLOYEE (Moniker CHAR, Age NUMBER) is
        select Name, Age, Lodging from WORKER
          where Age > EMPLOYEE.Age or Name = Moniker
            for update of Lodging;
    WORKER_RECORD    EMPLOYEE%rowtype;
    Appellation      CHAR(30);

BEGIN

    Appellation := 'BART SARJEANT';
    open EMPLOYEE(Appellation, 65);
    ...
    fetch EMPLOYEE into WORKER_RECORD;

    update WORKER set Lodging = 'South 40'
     where current of EMPLOYEE;
    ...
    close EMPLOYEE;

END;
```

This is an example of an extremely simple PL/SQL block. The . . . represents missing logic, perhaps including a FOR loop or EXCEPTIONs that are raised. Several of the options of **DECLARE CURSOR** are shown in this example. Consider these three related lines:

```
cursor EMPLOYEE (Moniker CHAR, Age NUMBER) is

       where Age > EMPLOYEE.Age or Name = Moniker

   open EMPLOYEE(Appellation, 65);
```

The first line shows how parameters are defined. They sit in parentheses between the cursor name and the word is. Their character type is declared immediately after their names, but size and precision are never used (it will be implicit from the **OPEN**). Moniker and Age are the parameters; these are invented variable names and are *not* the names of columns in the table. However, they do appear in the **where** clause of the **select** statement, as Moniker and EMPLOYEE.Age. Moniker can stand on its own because there is no column named Moniker in the WORKER table.

However, there is an Age column in the WORKER table, so to avoid ambiguity, the parameter named Age is distinguished by prefixing it with the cursor name, EMPLOYEE.

NOTE
Since it is usually confusing to give parameters the same name as columns, it's better to avoid doing so. It is done here only to show the method of distinguishing parameters and columns with the same name. It is not recommended as a technique.

Now whatever value the parameters Moniker and EMPLOYEE.Age are given by the **OPEN** will be used in the **where** clause of the **select** when it is executed. What are the values? Look at the third related line:

```
   open EMPLOYEE(Appellation, 65);
```

The cursor named in the OPEN, EMPLOYEE, is followed by (Appellation, 65). These are the values that will be plugged into the **where** clause when it executes, and they are in the exact order (and of appropriate data types) as are the parameters shown here:

```
   cursor EMPLOYEE (Moniker CHAR, Age NUMBER) is
```

The result is that the parameter Age, and therefore the **where** clause field EMPLOYEE.Age, is set equal to 65, and Moniker is set equal to the value of Appellation, which is a PL/SQL variable. If you'll look back to just after the word BEGIN, you'll see that Appellation is set equal to BART SARJEANT, and therefore Moniker is also equal to BART SARJEANT. This *indirection* can be used to modify the values in the **where** clause prior to the **OPEN** statement. Although Appellation was simply set equal to the literal string 'BART SARJEANT,' it could also have been set equal to a host variable, or have been the result of a query to a different table.

Finally, consider these related lines:

```
where Age > EMPLOYEE.Age or Name = Moniker
   for update of Lodging;
```

```
update WORKER set Lodging = 'South 40'
 where current of EMPLOYEE;
```

The **for update** is used in the DECLARE CURSOR section so that the **current of employee** can be used in the **update**. **current of EMPLOYEE** refers to that single row that was last **FETCH**ed into the cursor EMPLOYEE; it is this row that the **update** will affect. It is the current row in the cursor, hence "current of" EMPLOYEE.

DECLARE DATABASE (Embedded SQL)

Type Precompiler declarative SQL command

Product Precompilers

See also **COMMIT RELEASE** (Embedded SQL), **CONNECT** (Embedded SQL), *Programmer's Guide to the ORACLE Precompilers*

Format

```
EXEC SQL DECLARE database DATABASE
```

Description **DECLARE DATABASE** declares the name of a remote database for use in later AT clauses of SQL statements, including **COMMIT**, **DECLARE CURSOR**, **DELETE**, **INSERT**, **ROLLBACK**, **SELECT**, and **UPDATE**.

DECLARE EXCEPTION

Type PL/SQL statement

Products PL/SQL

See also BLOCK STRUCTURE, **EXCEPTION**, EXCEPTION_INIT, **RAISE**

Format

```
DECLARE
exception EXCEPTION;
```

Description   *exception* is the label given to a user-defined exception variable (sometimes called an "error flag"), and it follows normal object-naming conventions. The exception is raised (that is, the flag is raised) with the **RAISE** statement. The exception label might be thought of as a BOOLEAN variable (with some restrictions) usually equal to FALSE. To RAISE it means to set it equal to TRUE. This is immediately detected by ORACLE (it sees the raised flag), and control is transferred to the exception handling block (*see* **EXCEPTION**). The exception variables are restricted in that they cannot be passed as arguments to functions or procedures.

   PL/SQL has a considerable number of system-defined exception names. ZERO_DIVIDE is an example. Whenever you program attempts to divide a number by zero (which is mathematically undefined), ZERO_DIVIDE is set to TRUE (the ZERO_DIVIDE flag is raised), and the program jumps to the PL/SQL EXCEPTION section. There you can test each of the exception flags, your own as well as the system's, to see which one is TRUE (up), and then take appropriate action in the program to recover or quit. For example, suppose you decide to make sure the integrity of the relationship between your WORKERSKILL table and your WORKER table is intact. This means any Name in the WORKERSKILL table has to be in the WORKER table. In a section of logic shown next, you've **FETCH**ed a Name from WORKERSKILL, and are now looking it up in WORKER.

> **NOTE**
> Don't model this code. It's an inefficient solution to the stated problem, and included here only to illustrate a point.

```
DECLARE    cursor SKILL is
     select Name from WORKERSKILL;

  cursor EMPLOYEE (Moniker CHAR) is
     select Name from WORKER
       where Name = Moniker;

  worker_name     char(30);
  Appellation     char(30);
```

```
    big_trouble       exception;

BEGIN
    ...
    fetch SKILL into Appellation;
    open EMPLOYEE(Appellation);
    fetch EMPLOYEE into worker_name;
    if EMPLOYEE%NOTFOUND
       then RAISE big_trouble;


    ...
    close EMPLOYEE;

EXCEPTION
    when big_trouble
        then ...

END;
```

When the **%NOTFOUND** is TRUE, it means no rows were returned, which in turn means a Name in the WORKERSKILL table is not also in the WORKER table. This would be big trouble, so you raise the big_trouble exception flag. The program immediately jumps to the EXCEPTION section. There may be several tests there (for other exceptions raised for other reasons), but this time the when big_trouble then. . . logic determines the program's next action, such as adding the Name to a report file.

PL/SQL blocks can be nested, with an entire DECLARE-BEGIN-[EXCEPTION]-END block within the BEGIN section of another block. In this case, use caution when naming exceptions. If an exception in a nested block has the same name as the exception in an enclosing block, the exception handler (the EXCEPTION section) of the enclosing block will be unaware of that exception being raised in the inner block. The inner block could have its own EXCEPTION section, which could handle locally raised exceptions, or, if the inner block lacks an EXCEPTION section, the exception flag will be passed back to the enclosing block and its EXCEPTION section—as long as the inner exception flag does not have the same name as one also declared in the outer block. If it does, control will still be passed to the outer EXCEPTION section, but it won't be able to test the value of the inner exception flag, because it has one of its own by the same name.

This common-name problem can be worked around by prefixing the inner block exception flag with its block's name. If the inner block happened to be named skill_set, for instance, then this is the exception flag's full name:

```
skill_set.big_trouble
```

which the outer EXCEPTION section can distinguish from its own

```
big_trouble
```

exception flag. You can avoid all of this trouble by never giving the same name to exception flags in inner and outer blocks. If they all have different names, then a single EXCEPTION section in the outermost block can handle them all, if necessary—although a preferred design technique is to use exceptions sparingly, and limit exception scope as much as possible, preferably to the block in which the exception occurs.

Exception propagation to outer blocks is there to trap exceptions that have been overlooked in the design and coding, not as a general method of design.

DECLARE STATEMENT (Embedded SQL)

Type   Precompiler declarative SQL command

Product   Precompilers

See also   **CLOSE, FETCH, OPEN, PREPARE**

Format

```
EXEC SQL [AT {database ¦ :host_variable}]
DECLARE STATEMENT {statement ¦ block_name} STATEMENT
```

Description   *statement* is the name of the statement in a **DECLARE CURSOR**, and must be identical to the statement name here. *database* is the name of a database previously declared with **DECLARE DATABASE**; *host_variable* may contain such a name as its value. This command is only needed if **DECLARE CURSOR** will come before a **PREPARE**. When it is used, it should come prior to **DECLARE, DESCRIBE, OPEN,** or **PREPARE,** and must be compiled in the same source as procedures that reference it.

DECLARE TABLE

Type   Precompiler command

Product   Precompilers

See also   **CREATE TABLE**

Format

```
EXEC SQL DECLARE table TABLE
(column datatype [NULL¦NOT NULL],
...);
```

DB2 Compatibility Format

```
EXEC SQL DECLARE table TABLE
(column datatype [NOT NULL [WITH DEFAULT]],
...);
```

Description   *table* is the name of the table being declared. *column* is a column name and *datatype* is its data type. This structure is nearly identical to that of **create table**, including the use of NULL and NOT NULL. There is a second format as well, purely for DB2 compatibility.

You use **DECLARE TABLE** to tell precompilers to ignore actual ORACLE database table definitions when running with SQLCHECK=FULL. The precompilers will regard the table description here as relevant to the program and ignore the table definitions in the database. Use this when table definitions will change, or when a table has not yet been created. If SQLCHECK is not equal to FULL (which means tables and columns will not be checked against the database anyway), this command is ignored by the precompiler and becomes simply documentation.

Example

```
EXEC SQL DECLARE COMFORT TABLE (
City           VARCHAR2(13) NOT NULL,
SampleDate     DATE NOT NULL,
Noon           NUMBER(3,1),
Midnight       NUMBER(3,1),
Precipitation NUMBER
);
```

DECLARE VARIABLE

Type   PL/SQL statement

Products   PL/SQL

See also   **%ROWTYPE**, **%TYPE**

Format

```
DECLARE
variable [CONSTANT]
{datatype ¦ identifier%TYPE ¦ identifier%ROWTYPE}   [NOT NULL]
[:= expression];
```

Description   **DECLARE VARIABLE** allocates space for a variable, defines the variable's type, and assigns a name for reference. *variable* is the name that can be referenced in a PL/SQL block. The optional word CONSTANT means that the value assigned to this variable by the expression cannot be modified. A variable may have its datatype assigned in one of three ways:

- By the use of a standard ORACLE data type assignment, including NUMBER (with optional precision and scale), CHAR(length), and DATE. BOOLEAN is also available, and always evaluates to TRUE, FALSE, or NULL. BOOLEAN can be used only as a PL/SQL variable. It cannot be loaded from a **FETCH** (or **SELECT. . .INTO**), nor can it be inserted in the database.

- By assigning it the same datatype as an already defined variable or column name, using **%TYPE**. *See* **%TYPE** for details.

- By assigning it a record variable type using **%ROWTYPE** to give it the same structure as a table, or a series of named columns in a **DECLARE CURSOR**. *See* %**ROWTYPE** for details.

NOT NULL forces the variable to always have a value. If an attempt is made to make it NULL, the VALUE_ERROR exception is raised. If NOT NULL is used, you must also use := *expression* in order to give it its initial value.

:= *expression* is an optional (except for CONSTANT and NOT NULL, which require it) clause that gives the variable its initial value.

DECLAREd variables are not available just anywhere within PL/SQL, but are confined to the block in which they're declared, or blocks nested within that block. If a nested block also declares a variable with the same name (names are not case sensitive) as an enclosing block's variable, the local definition takes effect, and the enclosing block's variable becomes inaccessible by that name. Any blocks nested within the block which re**DECLARE**d the name, will have access only to the local, redeclared, variable. PL/SQL blocks which follow one another (that is, that are not nested) do not know about each other's variables.

However, if your blocks are *named,* variables within the block can be accessed by other PL/SQL blocks, whether nested or following, simply by prefixing the variable's name with the block name, as shown here:

```
block.variable
```

where *block* is the name of the block, and *variable* is the name of a variable declared within it.

DECODE

Type   SQL command

Products   All

See also   OTHER FUNCTIONS, **TRANSLATE**, Chapter 15

Format

```
DECODE(value,if1,then1[,if2,then2,]... ,else)
```

Description   *value* represents any column in a table, regardless of data type, or any result of a computation, such as one date minus another, a **SUBSTR** of a character column, one number times another, and so on. For each row, *value* is tested. If it equals *if1*, then the result of the **DECODE** is *then1*; if value equals *if2*, then the result of the **DECODE** is *then2*, and so on, for virtually as many if/then pairs as you can construct. If *value* equals none of the *if*s, then the result of the **DECODE** is *else*. Each of the *if*s, *then*s, and the *else* also can be a column or the result of a function or computation. Chapter 15 is devoted entirely to **DECODE**.

Example

```
select DISTINCT City,
DECODE(City, 'SAN FRANCISCO', 'CITY BY THE BAY', City) from
COMFORT;

CITY            DECODE(CITY,'SA
------------- ---------------
KEENE           KEENE
SAN FRANCISCO CITY BY THE BAY
```

DEFAULT

Default is a clause or option value that is used if no alternative is specified.

DEFAULT VALUE

The default value is a value that is used unless a different one is specified or entered. In SQL*FORMS, it is a value automatically assigned to a field, but which the user may change if the field is enterable.

DEFERRED ROLLBACK SEGMENT

A deferred rollback segment is one containing entries that could not be applied to the tablespace, because the given tablespace was offline. As soon as the tablespace comes back online, all the entries are applied.

DEFINE (SQL*PLUS)

See **SET**.

DEFINE PHASE

The define phase is one phase of executing a SQL query, in which the program defines buffers to hold the results of a query to be executed.

DEL

Type   SQL*PLUS command

Product   SQL*PLUS

See also   **APPEND**, **CHANGE**, **EDIT**, **INPUT**, **LIST**, Chapter 4

Format

```
DEL
```

Description   **DEL** deletes the current line of the current buffer.

Example   List the contents of the current buffer with this:

```
list
```

```
  1  select Person, Amount
  2    from LEDGER
  3   where Amount > 10000
  4*     and Rate = 3;
```

The asterisk shows that 4 is the current line. To delete the second line, you'd first enter this:

```
list 2
```

```
  2*    from LEDGER
```

which makes 2 the current line in the current buffer. Then you'd enter this:

```
del
```

and the line would be gone. The old line 3 would now be line 2; line 4 would be line 3, and so on.

DELETE (Form 1 - PL/SQL)

Type   SQL command

Products   PL/SQL

See also   **DECLARE CURSOR**, **UPDATE**

Description   In PL/SQL, **DELETE** follows the normal SQL command rules, with these added features:

- A PL/SQL function and/or variable can be used in the **where** clause just as a literal could be.

- **DELETE. . .WHERE CURRENT OF cursor** can be used in conjunction with a SELECT FOR UPDATE to delete the last row **FETCH**ed. The **FETCH** can either be explicit or implicit from a FOR LOOP.

- Like **update** and **insert**, the **delete** command executes only within the SQL cursor. The SQL cursor's attributes can be checked for the success of the **delete**. SQL%ROWCOUNT will contain the number of rows deleted. If this is 0, none were **delete**d. (Also, SQL%FOUND will be FALSE if none were **delete**d.)

Example   To eliminate all workers who are 65 or over from the worker table (an idea Talbot would have found silly), use this:

```
DECLARE
    cursor EMPLOYEE is
        select Age from WORKER
            for update of Age;

    WORKER_RECORD    EMPLOYEE%rowtype;

BEGIN
    open EMPLOYEE;
    loop
        fetch EMPLOYEE into WORKER_RECORD;
```

```
   exit when EMPLOYEE%notfound;
   if WORKER_RECORD.Age >= 65
      then delete WORKER where current of EMPLOYEE;
end loop;
 close EMPLOYEE;

END;
```

DELETE (Form 2 - SQL command)

Type   SQL command

Products   All

See also   **DROP TABLE**, **FROM**, **INSERT**, **SELECT**, **UPDATE**, **WHERE**, Chapter 13

Format

```
DELETE FROM [user.]table[@link] [alias] [ WHERE condition ];
```

Description   **DELETE** deletes all rows that satisfy condition from table. The
condition may include a correlated query and use the alias for correlation. If the
table is remote, a database link has to be defined. *@link* specifies the link. If *link* is
entered, but *user* is not, the query seeks a table owned by the user on the remote
database.

Example   This example deletes all rows for the city of Keene from the
COMFORT table:

```
delete from COMFORT
 where City = 'KEENE';
```

DEPENDENT PARAMETERS

Dependent parameters are **init.ora** parameters that should not be altered by users
or DBAs because ORACLE automatically calculates their values based on the
values of one or more other **init.ora** parameters.

DESCRIBE

Type   SQL*PLUS command

Product   SQL*PLUS

See also   **CREATE TABLE**

Format

```
DESC[RIBE]  [user.]table
```

Description   **DESCRIBE** displays a specified table's definition. If *user* is omitted, SQL*PLUS displays the table owned by you. The definition includes the table and its columns, with each column's name, NULL or NOT NULL status, data type, and width or precision.

Example

```
describe COMFORT

Name                               Null?     Type
--------------------------------   --------  ----
CITY                               NOT NULL  VARCHAR2(13)
SAMPLEDATE                         NOT NULL  DATE
NOON                                         NUMBER(3,1)
MIDNIGHT                                     NUMBER(3,1)
PRECIPITATION                                NUMBER
```

DESCRIBE PHASE

The describe phase is one phase of executing a SQL query, in which the program gathers information about the results of the query to be executed.

DETACHED PROCESS

See BACKGROUND PROCESS.

DEVICE

A device is a display terminal (CRT) such as an IBM 3270, DEC VT100, or VT220.

DICTIONARY CACHE

A dictionary cache is any one of several caches of data dictionary information contained in the SGA. Caching dictionary information improves performance because the dictionary information is used frequently.

DICTIONARY CACHE LOCKS

Dictionary cache locks are one of three types of internal locks on entries in the dictionary caches.

DICTIONARY LOCKS

A dictionary lock is a shared lock owned by users parsing DML statements, or an exclusive lock owned by users doing DDL commands, to prevent a table from being altered while the dictionaries are queried. There may be many such locks concurrently.

DICTIONARY OPERATION LOCKS

A dictionary operation lock is an exclusive lock in effect while the dictionary is being updated. There is only one, and it is always exclusive.

DISABLE

Type   SQL command clause

Products   All

See also   **ALTER TABLE**, **CREATE TABLE**, **ENABLE**, INTEGRITY CONSTRAINT

Format

```
DISABLE {{UNIQUE(column[,column]...) ¦
        PRIMARY KEY ¦
        CONSTRAINT constraint} [CASCADE]} ¦
      ALL TRIGGERS
```

Description   The **DISABLE** clause disables an integrity constraint or trigger. UNIQUE disables a particular unique constraint. PRIMARY KEY disables the single primary key constraint. CONSTRAINT disables the named integrity constraint. CASCADE disables any integrity constraints that depend on the specified constraints as well. So, for example, if there is a referential integrity constraint defined in another table that refers to a unique or primary key in this one, you must specify CASCADE to disable the unique or primary key constraint.

In an **ALTER TABLE** statement, you can specify **ALL TRIGGERS** to disable all triggers associated with the table. You can't use this clause in **CREATE TABLE**.

You also can disable a constraint in **CREATE TABLE** by specifying the **DISABLE** keyword in the CONSTRAINT clause. *See* INTEGRITY CONSTRAINT.

DISCONNECT

Type   SQL*PLUS command

Product   SQL*PLUS

See also   **CONNECT**, **EXIT**, **QUIT**

Format

```
DISC[ONNECT]
```

Description   **DISCONNECT** commits pending changes to the database and logs you off of ORACLE. Your SQL*PLUS session remains active and the features of SQL*PLUS continue to function, but without any connection to the database. You can edit buffers, use your own editor, spool and stop spooling, or connect to ORACLE again, but until a connection is established, no SQL can be executed.

EXIT or **QUIT** will return you to your host's operating system. If you are still connected when you **EXIT** or **QUIT**, you will be automatically disconnected and logged off of ORACLE.

DISMOUNTED DATABASE

A dismounted database is one that is not mounted by any instance, and thus cannot be opened and is not available for use.

DISTINCT

Distinct means unique. It is used as a part of **select** statements and group functions. *See* GROUP FUNCTIONS, **SELECT**.

DISTRIBUTED DATABASE

A distributed database is a collection of databases that can be operated and managed separately and also share information.

DISTRIBUTED PROCESSING

Distributed processing is performing computation on multiple CPUs to achieve a single result.

DISTRIBUTED QUERY

A distributed query is one that selects data from databases residing at multiple nodes of a network.

DML

See DATA MANIPULATION LANGUAGE (DML) STATEMENTS.

DML LOCK

A DML lock is a synonym for DATA LOCKS.

DOCMENU

Type   Utility

Product   SQL*MENU V5

See also   GENMENU, RUNMENU, SQLMENU

Format

```
DOCMENU [application] [user/password] [-b] [-f] [-o] [-s]
```

Description   DOCMENU is a command line alternative to choosing the Print Doc (in the action menu) option from SQL*MENU Design in version 5 of SQL*MENU. It produces documentation on the application menus.

application is the name of the application menu that you wish to enter.

user and *password* allow you to log on to ORACLE. If these are not entered, you will be prompted for them.

-b means that a brief overview of the application should be produced.

-f produces a full set of documentation on the application.

-o produces references for objects.

-s suppresses the normal display of the logging on program banner information.

-? forces DOCMENU to display all of these options.

DOCUMENT

Type   SQL*PLUS command

Product   SQL*PLUS

See also   #, /* */, REMARK

Format

```
DOC[UMENT]
```

Description   **DOCUMENT** tells SQL*PLUS that a block of documentation is beginning. The pound sign (#) on a line by itself ends the block. DOCUMENT must also be SET to ON for this to work. If **DOCUMENT** is SET to OFF, SQL*PLUS will try to execute the lines in between **DOCUMENT** and #. Thus, this could be used to execute or not execute a sequence of commands based on a prior result (a start file, which would have to issue SET DOCUMENT OFF or ON, using spooling and START techniques described in Chapter 19).

If you are spooling an interactive session to a file, typing the word **DOCUMENT** will change the SQLPROMPT from SQL> to DOC>. Everything you type until you type # will go into the file without SQL*PLUS attempting to execute it.

SQL*PLUS will always display the lines in the DOCUMENT section unless TERMOUT is SET to OFF.

The SQL*PLUS command line editor cannot input a # directly into a buffer (in the first position on the line), so enter another character, followed by the #, and then delete the other character.

DOCUMENT is considered an obsolete command; **REMARK** is recommended for general documentation purposes instead.

Example   The following would be executed if **DOCUMENT** were **SET** to OFF:

```
DOCUMENT
column password print

REM changes the display of the passwords
#
```

DROP CLUSTER

Type   SQL command

Products   All

See also   CREATE CLUSTER, DROP TABLE

Format

```
DROP CLUSTER [user.]cluster
[INCLUDING TABLES [CASCADE CONSTRAINTS]]
```

Description   **DROP CLUSTER** deletes a cluster from the database. You must have DROP ANY CLUSTER privilege if the cluster is not in your own schema. **DROP CLUSTER** commits pending changes to the database. You cannot drop a cluster that contains tables. The tables must be dropped first. The INCLUDING TABLES clause will drop all the clustered tables automatically. The **CASCADE CONSTRAINTS** option drops all referential integrity constraints from tables outside the cluster that refer to keys in the clustered tables.

Individual tables cannot be removed from a cluster. To accomplish the same effect, copy the table under a new name (use **CREATE TABLE** with AS SELECT), drop the old one (this will remove it from the cluster), **RENAME** the copy to the name of the table you dropped, and then issue the appropriate **GRANT**S, and create the needed indexes.

DROP DATABASE LINK

Type   SQL command

Products   All

See also   **CREATE DATABASE LINK**, *SQL*Net Users Guide*

Format

```
DROP [PUBLIC] DATABASE LINK link
```

Description   **DROP DATABASE LINK** drops a database link you own. For a public link, the optional **PUBLIC** keyword must be used, and you must be a DBA to use it. **PUBLIC** cannot be used when dropping a private link. link is the name of the link being dropped. You must have DROP PUBLIC DATABASE LINK system privilege to drop a public database link. You may drop private database links in your account.

Example   The following will drop a database link named ADAH_AT_HOME:

```
drop database link ADAH_AT_HOME;
```

DROP FUNCTION

Type   SQL command

Products   All

See also   **ALTER FUNCTION, CREATE FUNCTION**, Chapter 22.

Format

```
DROP FUNCTION [user.]function
```

Description   **DROP FUNCTION** drops the specified function. It commits pending changes to the database. ORACLE invalidates any objects that depend on or call the function. You must have DROP ANY PROCEDURE system privilege to drop a function that you do not own.

DROP INDEX

Type   SQL command

Products   All

See also   **ALTER INDEX, CREATE INDEX, CREATE TABLE**

Format

```
DROP INDEX [user.]index
```

Description   **DROP INDEX** drops the specified index. You must either own the index or have DROP ANY INDEX system privilege.

DROP PACKAGE

Type   SQL command

Products   All

See also   **ALTER PACKAGE, CREATE PACKAGE**, Chapter 22.

Format

```
DROP PACKAGE [BODY] [user.]package
```

Description   **DROP PACKAGE** drops the specified package. Using the optional **BODY** clause drops only the body without dropping the package specification. It commits pending changes to the database. ORACLE invalidates any objects that depend on the package if you drop the package specification but not if you just drop the body. You must either own the package or have DROP ANY PROCEDURE system privilege.

DROP PROCEDURE

Type   SQL command

Products   All

See also   **ALTER PROCEDURE**, **CREATE PROCEDURE**, Chapter 22.

Format

```
DROP PROCEDURE [user.]procedure
```

Description   **DROP PROCEDURE** drops the specified procedure. It commits pending changes to the database. ORACLE invalidates any objects that depend on or call the procedure. You must either own the procedure or have DROP ANY PROCEDURE system privilege.

DROP PROFILE

Type   SQL command

Products   All

See also   **ALTER PROFILE**, **CREATE PROFILE**

Format

```
DROP PROFILE [user.]profile
```

Description   **DROP PROFILE** drops the specified profile. It commits pending changes to the database. You must have DROP PROFILE system privilege.

DROP ROLE

Type   SQL command

Products   All

See also   **ALTER ROLE**, **CREATE ROLE**, Chapter 17.

Format

```
DROP ROLE [user.]role
```

Description   **DROP ROLE** drops the specified role. It commits pending changes to the database. You must have either been granted the role WITH ADMIN OPTION or you must have DROP ANY ROLE system privilege.

DROP ROLLBACK SEGMENT

Type   SQL command

Products   All

See also   **ALTER ROLLBACK SEGMENT, CREATE ROLLBACK SEGMENT, CREATE TABLESPACE, SHUT DOWN, START UP**

Format

```
DROP [PUBLIC] ROLLBACK SEGMENT segment
```

Description   *segment* is the name of an existing rollback segment to be dropped. The segment must not be in use when this statement is executed. **PUBLIC** is required for dropping public rollback segments.

The Data Dictionary View DBA_ROLLBACK_SEGS can reveal which rollback segments are in use in its STATUS column. If the segment is in use, you can either wait until it no longer is in use, or SHUTDOWN the database using IMMEDIATE, and then bring it up in EXCLUSIVE mode using **STARTUP**. You must have DBA privilege in order to drop a rollback segment.

DROP SEQUENCE

Type   SQL command

Products   All

See also   **ALTER SEQUENCE, CREATE SEQUENCE**, Chapter 18.

Format

```
DROP SEQUENCE [user.]sequence
```

Description   *sequence* is the name of the sequence being dropped. To drop a sequence, you must either own the sequence or have DROP ANY SEQUENCE system privilege.

DROP SNAPSHOT

Type   SQL command

Products   All

See also   **ALTER SNAPSHOT, CREATE SNAPSHOT**, Chapter 23.

Format

```
DROP SNAPSHOT [user.]snapshot
```

Description **DROP SNAPSHOT** drops the indicated snapshot. It commits pending changes to the database. You must either own the snapshot or you must have DROP ANY SNAPSHOT system privilege. *See* Chapter 23 for snapshot implementation details.

DROP SNAPSHOT LOG

Type SQL command

Products All

See also **ALTER SNAPSHOT LOG**, **CREATE SNAPSHOT LOG**, Chapter 23.

Format

```
DROP SNAPSHOT LOG ON [user.]table
```

Description DROP SNAPSHOT LOG drops the indicated log table. It commits pending changes to the database. You must either own the snapshot or you must have DROP ANY SNAPSHOT system privilege. After dropping the log, any snapshots on the master table will get COMPLETE refreshes, not FAST ones.

DROP SYNONYM

Type SQL command

Products All

See also **CREATE SYNONYM**, Chapter 20.

Format

```
DROP [PUBLIC] SYNONYM [user.]synonym
```

Description **DROP SYNONYM** drops the specified synonym and commits pending changes to the database. To drop a public synonym, you must have DROP ANY PUBLIC SYNONYM system privilege. To drop a private synonym, you must own the synonym or have DROP ANY SYNONYM system privilege.

DROP TABLE

Type   SQL command

Products   All

See also   **ALTER TABLE, CREATE INDEX, CREATE TABLE, DROP CLUSTER**

Format

```
DROP TABLE [user.]table [CASCADE CONSTRAINTS]
```

Description   **DROP TABLE** drops the table and commits pending changes to the database. To drop a table, you must either own the table or have DROP ANY TABLE system privilege. Dropping a table also drops indexes and grants associated with it. Objects built on dropped tables are marked invalid and cease to work.

The **CASCADE CONSTRAINTS** option drops all referential integrity constraints referring to keys in the dropped table.

You can drop a cluster and all of its tables by using the INCLUDING TABLES clause on **DROP CLUSTER**.

DROP TABLESPACE

Type   SQL command

Products   All

See also   **ALTER TABLESPACE, CREATE DATABASE, CREATE TABLESPACE**

Format

```
DROP TABLESPACE tablespace
[INCLUDING CONTENTS]
```

Description   *tablespace* is the name of the tablespace being dropped. The **INCLUDING CONTENTS** option allows you to drop a tablespace that contains data. Without **INCLUDING CONTENTS**, only an empty tablespace can be dropped. Tablespaces should be offline (*see* **ALTER TABLESPACE**) before dropping, or the dropping will be prevented by any users accessing data, index, rollback, or temporary segments in the tablespace. You must have DROP TABLESPACE system privilege to use this command.

DROP TRIGGER

Type   SQL command

Products   All

See also   **ALTER TRIGGER**, **CREATE TRIGGER**, Chapter 21.

Format

```
DROP TRIGGER [user.]trigger
```

Description   **DROP TRIGGER** drops the indicated trigger. It commits pending changes to the database. You must either own the trigger or you must have DROP ANY TRIGGER system privilege.

DROP USER

Type   SQL command

Products   All

See also   **ALTER USER, CREATE USER**

Format

```
DROP USER user [CASCADE]
```

Description   **DROP USER** drops the indicated user. It commits pending changes to the database. You must have DROP USER system privilege. The **CASCADE** option drops all the objects in the user's schema before dropping the user, and you *must* specify **CASCADE** if the user has any objects in the schema.

DROP VIEW

Type   SQL command

Products   All

See also   **CREATE SYNONYM, CREATE TABLE, CREATE VIEW**

Format

```
DROP VIEW [user.]view
```

Description   **DROP VIEW** drops the specified view and commits pending changes to the database. Only DBAs can drop views created by other users. Views and synonyms built on dropped views are marked invalid and cease to work. The view must either be in your schema or you must have DROP ANY VIEW system privilege.

DUAL

Type   ORACLE work table

Products   All

See also   **FROM**, **SELECT**, Chapter 7

Description   DUAL is a tiny table with only one row and one column in it. Since ORACLE's many functions work on both columns and literals, it is possible to demonstrate some of its functioning using just literals or pseudo-columns, such as SysDate. When doing this, the **select** statement doesn't care which columns are in the table, and a single row is more than sufficient to demonstrate a point.

Example   The following shows the current User and SysDate:

```
select User, SysDate from DUAL;
```

DUMP

Type   SQL command

Products   All

See also   **RAWTOHEX**

Format

```
DUMP( string [,format [,start [,length] ] ] )
```

Description   **DUMP** displays the value of *string* in internal data format, in ASCII, octal, decimal, hex, or character format. *format* defaults to ASCII or EBCDIC, depending upon your machine; 8 produces octal, 10 decimal, 16 hex, and 17 character (the same as ASCII or EBCDIC). *start* is the beginning position in the string, and *length* is the number of characters to display. *string* can be a literal or an expression.

Example   The following shows how characters 1 through 8 are represented in hex for just the first row of the COMFORT table:

```
select City, dump(City,16,1,8) a from COMFORT where rownum < 2;

CITY           DUMP(CITY,16,1,8)
------------   ------------------------------------
SAN FRANCISCO Typ=1 Len= 13: 53,41,4e,20,46,52,41,4e
```

DUMPREP

Type   Utility report program

Product   SQL*REPORTWRITER

See also   **EBCDIC, GENREP, LOADREP, PRINTDEF, RUNREP,** SQL*REPORTWRITER, **SQLPLUS, SQLREP, TERMDEF**

Format

DUMPREP [REPORTS=]*reportlist* [USERID=*user/password*] [FILE=*file*]

Description   **DUMPREP** creates a flat ASCII file of a report definition to use in transporting the definition to another system. It is then loaded using **LOADREP**. This process works even from an ASCII- to an EBCDIC-based machine.

REPORTS is a required parameter, and is either the name of a report or a list of reports, separated by commas, with the list in parentheses:

REPORTS=(George.ledger, Talbot.worker)

Note that these are not file names, but the database-stored names of report definitions. As shown in the example, reports may be prefixed by the names of their owners. If no owner is specified, the username of the person logged on is assumed. Report names can include wild card characters of % and _. *See* **LIKE** for an explanation of how these functions.

USERID is your ORACLE username and password (followed optionally by an @link location). If these are not entered you will be prompted for them. Entering a slash (/) either on the command line or in response to the prompt will cause ORACLE to attempt to use your OPS$ login id (*see* OPS$LOGINS for details).

FILE gives the name of the file into which the report definition must go. The default is **expdat.rex**.

EBCDIC

EBCDIC is an acronym for **E**xtended **B**inary **C**oded **D**ecimal **I**nterchange **C**ode—the collation sequence used by IBM's mainframe computers and other computers compatible with them.

ECHO (SQL*PLUS)

See **SET**.

EDIT

Type   SQL*PLUS command

Products   SQL*PLUS

See also   **DEFINE**, Chapter 4

Format

```
EDIT [file[.ext]]
```

Description   **EDIT** calls an external standard text editor and passes to it the name of the file. If *.ext* is omitted, the extension SQL is appended. If *file* and *ext* are both omitted, the editor is called and passed the name of a file (invented by SQLPLUS) that contains the contents of the current buffer. The local user variable _EDITOR determines which text editor is used by **EDIT**. _EDITOR can be changed with **DEFINE**, and this is usually best done in the LOGIN.SQL file, which is read whenever SQL*PLUS is invoked.

EDIT will fail if the current buffer is empty and **EDIT** is called without a file name.

EMBEDDED (SQL*PLUS)

See **SET**.

ENABLE

Type   SQL command clause

Products   All

See also   **ALTER TABLE**, **CREATE INDEX**, **CREATE TABLE**, **DISABLE**, INTEGRITY CONSTRAINT, Chapter 24

Format

```
ENABLE {{UNIQUE(column[,column]... |
        PRIMARY KEY |
        CONSTRAINT constraint}
   [USING INDEX    [INITRANS integer]
                   [MAXTRANS integer]
                 [TABLESPACE tablespace]
                   [STORAGE storage]
                   [PCTFREE integer]]
   [EXCEPTIONS INTO [user.]table] |
   ALL TRIGGERS}
```

Description   The **ENABLE** clause enables a disabled integrity constraint or a trigger. When you enable a UNIQUE or PRIMARY KEY constraint, ORACLE builds an index on the columns of the key. The **USING INDEX** clause specifies the parameters for the index. If you enable a referential integrity constraint, the foreign key must also be enabled.

The **EXCEPTIONS INTO** clause specifies the name of an existing exceptions table, which must be stored locally. When ORACLE detects an integrity constraint violation, it stores the information in this table. You create this table with the **UTLEXCPT.SQL** script, or the equivalent on your operating system. *See* "Exceptions" in Chapter 24.

The **ALL TRIGGERS** clause can only appear in an **ALTER TABLE** statement, and it enables all the triggers associated with the table.

END

Type   Block bracketing statement

Products   PL/SQL

See also   **BEGIN**, BLOCK STRUCTURE, **DECLARE EXCEPTION**

Format

```
END [block] ;
```

Description   **END** is unrelated to the END IF and END LOOP statements. *See* IF and LOOP for details on either of them.

END is the closing statement of a PL/SQL block's executable section (and the entire block). If the block is named at the **BEGIN**, the name must also follow the word **END**. At least one executable statement is required between **BEGIN** and **END**. *See* BLOCK STRUCTURE for more details.

ENQUEUE

Enqueue is the lock on a given resource. Those waiting for a given resource have not yet gotten the enqueue. Enqueues exist for many database resources.

ENTITY

An entity is a person, place, or thing represented by a table. In a table, each row represents an occurrence of that entity.

ENTITY-RELATIONSHIP MODEL

An entity-relationship model is a framework used to model systems for a database. It divides all elements of a system into two categories: entities or relationships. Figure 25-1 in Chapter 25 is a simple example.

EQUI-JOIN

An equi-join is a join in which the join comparison operator is an equality, such as where WORKER.Name = WORKERSKILL.Name.

ESCAPE (SQL*PLUS)

See **SET**.

EXCEPTION

Type   Section bracketing statement

Products   PL/SQL

See also   BLOCK STRUCTURE, **DECLARE EXCEPTION**, **RAISE**, Chapter 22

Format

```
EXCEPTION
{WHEN {OTHERS | exception [OR exception]...}
THEN statement; [statement;]...}
[ WHEN {OTHER | exception [OR exception]...}
THEN statement; [statement;]...]...
```

Description   The EXCEPTION section of a PL/SQL block is where program control is transferred whenever an exception flag is raised. Exception flags are either user-defined or system exceptions raised automatically by PL/SQL. *See* **DECLARE EXCEPTION** and **RAISE** for details on user-defined exception flags. The system exception flags are all, in effect, BOOLEAN variables that are either TRUE or FALSE. The **WHEN** clause is used to test these. For example, the NOT_LOGGED_ON flag is raised if you attempt to issue a command to ORACLE without being logged on. You do not need to have **DECLARE**d an exception, or **RAISE**d this flag yourself. PL/SQL will do it for you.

When any exception flag is raised, the program immediately halts whatever it was doing and jumps to the EXCEPTION section of the current block. This section, however, doesn't know automatically which exception flag was raised, nor what to do. Therefore, you must code the EXCEPTION section first to check all of the exception flags that are likely to have occurred, and then give action instructions for each. This is what the **WHEN...THEN** logic does.

Example   Here three exception flags are tested in the EXCEPTION section. The age_has_junk flag is raised if the data in the WORKER table appears to be bad. The NOT_LOGGED_ON is raised automatically if the program isn't properly connected to ORACLE when it executes (for instance if the database has been brought down). The OTHERS is a catch-all flag that tests TRUE if any exception flag is raised. It therefore can be used to handle unanticipated errors, rather than having to code **WHEN...THEN** statements for all possibilities.

```
<<overage>>
DECLARE
    cursor EMPLOYEE is
        select Age from WORKER
            for update of Age;

    WORKER_RECORD    EMPLOYEE%rowtype;
    age_has_junk     exception;
BEGIN
  open EMPLOYEE;
  loop
     fetch EMPLOYEE into WORKER_RECORD;
     exit when EMPLOYEE%notfound;
     if WORKER_RECORD.Age >= 65
        then delete WORKER where current of EMPLOYEE;
     if WORKER_RECORD.Age < 12
        then raise age_has_junk;
  end loop;
  commit;
```

```
      close EMPLOYEE;
EXCEPTION
   when not_logged_on
      then :error := 'Not logged on to ORACLE.';
   when age_has_junk
      then :error := 'WORKER table has bad Age data.';
      rollback;
      exit;
   when others
      then :error := 'Undefined error. Get help.';
      rollback;
      exit;
END overage;
```

The system-raised exception flags follow:

CURSOR_ALREADY_OPEN is raised if an **OPEN** statement tries to open a cursor that is already open. SQLCODE is set to –6511 (error is ORA-06511).

DUP_VAL_ON_INDEX is raised if an **insert** or **update** would have caused a duplicate value in a unique index. SQLCODE is set to –1 (error is ORA-00001).

INVALID_CURSOR is raised if you attempted to **OPEN** an undeclared cursor, or **CLOSE** one that was already closed, or **FETCH** from one that wasn't open, and so on. SQLCODE is set to –1001 (error is ORA-01001).

INVALID_NUMBER is raised on a conversion error from a character string to a number when the character string doesn't contain a legitimate number. SQLCODE is set to –1722 (error is ORA-01722).

LOGIN_DENIED is raised if ORACLE rejects the user/password in the attempt to log on. SQLCODE is set to –1017 (error is ORA-01017).

NO_DATA_FOUND is raised if a **select** statement returns zero rows. (This is not the same as a **FETCH** returning no rows. NO_DATA_FOUND means the **select** returned nothing.) SQLCODE is set to +100 (error code is ORA-01403). The error numbers differ here because the +100 is now the ANSI standard code for no data found. ORACLE's 1403 predates the standard. Note that this error number is positive, which generally indicates a recoverable, nonfatal error. Your EXCEPTION section logic may want to branch and attempt something other than an **EXIT**.

NOT_LOGGED_ON is raised if you attempt any sort of database call without being logged on. SQLCODE is set to –1012 (error is ORA-01012).

PROGRAM_ERROR is raised if PL/SQL itself has a problem executing code. SQLCODE is set to –6501 (error is ORA-06501).

STORAGE_ERROR is raised if PL/SQL needs more memory than is available, or if it detects corruption of memory. SQLCODE is set to –6500 (error is ORA-06500).

TIMEOUT_ON_RESOURCE is raised when a resource ORACLE is waiting for isn't available when it should be. This usually means an instance has had an abnormal termination. SQLCODE is set to –51 (error is ORA-00051).

TOO_MANY_ROWS is raised when a **select** statement that is supposed to return just one row returns more than one (this is also raised by a subquery that is only supposed to return one row). SQLCODE is –1427 (error is ORA-01427).

TRANSACTION_BACKED_OUT is raised when the remote part of a transaction is rolled back. SQLCODE is –61 (error is ORA-00061).

VALUE_ERROR is raised when the value of a column or PS/SQL variable is damaged, such as by truncation. This kind of problem usually occurs during a conversion of one datatype to another, the copying of a value from one data field to another, or a numeric calculation that violates the precision of the variable. This flag is not raised when a string is truncated while being copied into a host variable (such as by a **FETCH**). In this case the host variable indicator (if one is used) is set to the number that is the correct length of the string (before it was truncated). If the copy is successful the indicator variable is 0. *See* INDICATOR VARIABLE. VALUE_ERROR sets SQLCODE to –6502 (error is ORA-01476).

ZERO_DIVIDE is raised when a statement tries to divide a number by zero. SQLCODE is –1476 (error is ORA-01476).

OTHERS is the catch-all for any exception flags you did not check for in your EXCEPTION section. It must always be the last WHEN statement, and must stand alone. It cannot be included with any other exceptions.

Exception handling, particularly as it relates to exceptions you declare, should really be reserved for errors that are fatal—that mean normal processing should stop.

If an exception flag is raised that is not tested for in the current block, the program will branch to the EXCEPTION block in the enclosing block, and so on, until either the exception raised is found, or control falls through to the host program.

EXCEPTION sections can reference variables in the same manner that the execution block can. That is, they can reference local variables directly, or variables from other blocks by prefixing them with the other block's name.

Use caution in testing for certain kinds of exceptions. For instance, if your EXCEPTION section takes the error message and inserts it into a database table, a NOT_LOGGED_ON exception would put the EXCEPTION section into an infinite loop. Design your statements that follow THEN not to duplicate the error that got the program there in the first place. You also may use **RAISE** without an exception name. This will automatically pass control to the next outer exception block, or the main program. *See* **RAISE** for further details.

EXCEPTION_INIT

Type   PL/SQL function

Products   PL/SQL

See also   **DECLARE EXCEPTION**, **EXCEPTION**, **SQLCODE**

Format

```
PRAGMA EXCEPTION_INIT(exception,integer);
```

Description   The standard system exceptions, such as ZERO_DIVIDE, which are referenced by name, are actually no more than the association of a name with the internal ORACLE error number. There are hundreds of these error numbers, and only the most common dozen have been given names. Any that are not named will still raise an exception flag and transfer control to the EXCEPTION block, but they will all be caught by OTHERS, rather than by name.

You can change this by assigning your own names to other ORACLE error numbers. EXCEPTION_INIT allows you to do this. *exception* is the one-word name you assign to the integer error number (*see* ORACLE's *Error Messages and Codes Manual* for a complete list). *integer* should be negative if the error code is negative (true for fatal errors), and *exception* must follow normal object naming rules.

Note that the format of this command requires the word PRAGMA before EXCEPTION_INIT. A pragma is an instruction to the PL/SQL compiler, rather than executable code. The pragma must be in the DECLARE section of a PL/SQL block, and must be preceded by an exception declaration.

Example

```
DECLARE
    some_bad_error          exception;
    pragma                  exception_init(some_bad_error -666);
BEGIN
 ...
EXCEPTION
    when some_bad_error
        then ...
END;
```

EXCLUSIVE LOCK

An exclusive lock is one that permits other users to query data, but not change it. It differs from a SHARE lock because it does not permit another user to place any type of lock on the same data; several users may place SHARE locks on the same data at the same time.

EXCLUSIVE MODE

Exclusive mode is a type of lock on a resource that excludes any other access to that resource; the holder of the lock has exclusive rights to alter that resource.

EXCLUSIVE MODE LOCKING

See EXCLUSIVE MODE.

EXECUTABLE SQL STATEMENT

An executable SQL statement is one that generates a call to the database. It includes almost all queries, DML, DDL, and DCL statements. (Compare to DECLARATIVE SQL STATEMENT.)

EXECUTE

Type   SQL command

Products   All

See also   **CREATE PROCEDURE, CREATE FUNCTION, CREATE PACKAGE, CREATE PACKAGE BODY, GRANT** (Form 2 - Object Privileges), Chapter 17 and 22.

Format

```
execute procedural_object_name [arguments];
```

Description   Executes a procedure, package, or function. To execute a procedure within a package, specify both the package name and the procedure name in the execute command, as shown in the following example. This example executes a procedure named NEW_WORKER, in a package named LEDGER_PACKAGE; the value 'ADAH TALBOT' is passed as input to the procedure.

```
execute LEDGER_PACKAGE.NEW_WORKER('ADAH TALBOT');
```

To execute a procedural object, you must have been granted EXECUTE privilege on that object. *See* **GRANT** (Form 2 - Object Privileges).

EXECUTE (Dynamic Embedded SQL)

Type   Precompiler SQL command

Products   Precompiler

See also   **EXECUTE IMMEDIATE, PREPARE**

Format

```
EXEC SQL [FOR :integer]
EXECUTE {statement_name ¦ block_name}
[USING :variable[:indicator][,:variable[:indicator]...]
```

Description   *database* is the name of a database connection other than the default. *:integer* is a host variable used to limit the number of iterations when the **where** clause uses arrays. *statement_name* is the name of a prepared **insert**, **delete**, or **update** statement to be executed (**select** is not allowed). *block_name* is the name of a prepared PL/SQL block. **USING** introduces a list of substitutions into the host variables of the previously prepared statement.

Example

```
work_string : string(1..200);
worker_name : string(1..25);
get(work_string);
exec sql at TALBOT prepare ADAH from :work_string;
exec sql execute ADAH using :worker_name;
```

EXECUTE IMMEDIATE (Dynamic Embedded SQL)

Type   Precompiler SQL command

Products   Precompiler

See also   **EXECUTE, PREPARE**

Format

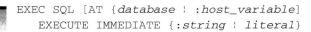

```
EXEC SQL [AT {database ¦ :host_variable]
   EXECUTE IMMEDIATE {:string ¦ literal}
```

Description   *database* is the name of a database connection other than the default; *host_variable* may contain such a name as its value. *:string* is a host variable string containing a SQL statement. *literal* is a character string containing a SQL statement. The **EXECUTE IMMEDIATE** statement cannot contain host variable references other than an executable SQL statement in *:string*. The SQL statement is parsed, put into executable form, executed, and the executable form is destroyed. It is intended only for statements to be executed just once. Statements that require multiple executions should use **PREPARE** and **EXECUTE**, as this eliminates the overhead of parsing for each execution.

Example

```
get(work_string);
exec sql execute immediate :work_string;

exec sql execute immediate
        "delete from SKILL where Skill = 'Grave Digger'";
```

EXECUTE PHASE

The execute phase of SQL statement execution is when all the information necessary for execution is obtained and the statement is executed.

EXISTS

Type   SQL operator

Products   All

See also   ANY, ALL, IN, NOT EXISTS

Format

```
select...
where EXISTS (select...)
```

Description   EXISTS returns *true* in a **where** clause if the subquery that follows it returns at least one row. The **select** clause in the subquery can be a column, a literal, or an asterisk—it doesn't matter. (Convention suggests an asterisk or an 'x'.)

Many people prefer **EXISTS** over **ANY** and **ALL** because it is easier to remember and understand, and most formulations of **ANY** and **ALL** can be reconstructed using **EXISTS**. Note, however, that although ORACLE treats properly constructed **NOT EXISTS** and > **ALL** formulations as equivalent, some SQL databases do not. Refer to *A Guide to the SQL Standard* by C. J. Date (1989, Addison-Wesley, N.Y.) for a discussion of this.

Example   The query shown in the following example uses EXISTS to list from the SKILL table all those records that have matching Skills in the WORKERSKILL table. The result of this query will be the list of all skills that the current workers possess.

```
select SKILL.Skill
  from SKILL
 where EXISTS
       (select 'x' from WORKERSKILL
        where WORKERSKILL.Skill = SKILL.Skill);
```

EXIT (Form 1 - PL/SQL)

Type   PL/SQL function

Products   PL/SQL

See also   END, **LOOP**

Format

```
EXIT [loop] [WHEN condition];
```

Description   Without any of its options, **EXIT** simply takes you out of the current loop, and branches control to the next statement following the loop. If you are in a nested loop, you can exit from any enclosing loop simply by specifying the loop name. If you specify a condition, you will exit when the condition evaluates to TRUE. Any cursor within a loop is automatically closed when you **EXIT**.

Example

```
<<adah>>
for i in 1..100 loop
   ...
   <<george>>
   for k in 1..100 loop
      ...
      exit when...
      delete...
      exit adah when...;
   end loop george;
   ...
end loop adah;
```

EXIT (Form 2 - SQL*PLUS)

Type   SQL*PLUS command

Product   SQL*PLUS

See also   COMMIT, DISCONNECT, QUIT, START

Format

```
{EXIT | QUIT} [SUCCESS|FAILURE|WARNING|integer|variable]
```

Description   **EXIT** ends a SQL*PLUS session and returns user to the operating system, calling program, or menu. **EXIT** commits pending changes to the database.

A return code is also returned. SUCCESS, FAILURE, and WARNING have values that are operating-system specific; FAILURE and WARNING may be the same on some operating systems.

integer is a value you can pass back explicitly as the return code; *variable* allows you to set this value dynamically. This can be a user-defined variable, or a system variable, such as sql.sqlcode, which always contains the sqlcode of the last SQL statement executed, either in SQL*PLUS or an embedded PL/SQL block.

EXP

Type   SQL command

Products   All

See also   **LN,** NUMBER FUNCTIONS, Chapter 6

Format

```
EXP(n)
```

Description   **EXP** returns *e* raised to the *n*th power; e = 2.718281828....

EXPLAIN PLAN

Type   Procedure

Products   SQL*PLUS

Format

```
EXPLAIN PLAN
[SET STATEMENT ID = name] [INTO [user.]table[@dblink]]
FOR sql_statement
```

Description   *name* identifies this plan explanation for this *sql_statement* when it appears in the output table, and follows normal object naming conventions. If *name* is not specified, the STATEMENT_ID column in the table will be NULL. *table* is the name of the output table into which the plan explanation will go. It must be previously created before this procedure can be executed. The start file **UTLXPLAN.SQL** contains the format and can be used directly to create the default table, named PLAN_TABLE. If table is not specified, EXPLAIN PLAN will use PLAN_TABLE. *sql_statement* is the simple text of any **select**, **insert**, **update**, or **delete** statement you wish to have analyzed for ORACLE's execution plan for it.

EXPORT

Export can be either of two definitions:

- Export is the ORACLE utility used to store ORACLE database data in export format files for later retrieval into an ORACLE database via Import.

- To export is to use the Export utility to write selected table data to an export file.

For information on the Export utility, *see* the *Oracle7 Server Utilities User's Guide*.

EXPRESSION

An expression is any form of a column. This could be a literal, a variable, a mathematical computation, a function, or virtually any combination of functions and columns whose final result is a single value, such as a string, a number, or a date.

FEEDBACK (SQL*PLUS)

See **SET**.

FETCH

One phase of query execution is the fetch phase, where actual rows of data meeting all search criteria are retrieved from the database.

FETCH (Form 1 - Embedded SQL)

Type   Embedded SQL command

Product   Precompilers

See also   **CLOSE, DECLARE CURSOR, DESCRIBE**, INDICATOR VARIABLE, **OPEN, PREPARE**

Format

```
EXEC SQL [FOR :integer] FETCH cursor
INTO :variable[[ INDICATOR ]:indicator]
[,:variable[[ INDICATOR ]:indicator] ]...
```

```
EXEC SQL [FOR :integer] FETCH cursor
USING DESCRIPTOR descriptor
```

Description   *integer* is a host variable that sets the maximum number of rows to fetch into the output variables. *cursor* is the name of a cursor previously set up by **DECLARE CURSOR**. :*variable*[:*indicator*] is one or more host variables into which fetched data will be placed. If any of the host variables is an array, then all of them (in the **INTO** list) must be arrays. The **INDICATOR** keyword is optional.

   descriptor is a descriptor from a previous **DESCRIBE** statement.

Example

```
exec sql fetch CURSOR1 into :Name, :Skill;
```

FETCH (Form 2 - PL/SQL)

Type   PL/SQL statement

Products   PL/SQL

See also   **%FOUND**, **%ROWTYPE**, **CLOSE**, **DECLARE CURSOR**, **DECLARE VARIABLE**, **LOOP**, **OPEN**, **SELECT. . .INTO**

Format

```
FETCH cursor INTO {record ¦ variable [,variable]...};
```

Description   **FETCH** gets a row of data. The named cursor's select statement determines which columns are retrieved, and its **where** statement determines which (and how many) rows can be retrieved. This is called the "active set," but it is not available to you for processing until you fetch it, row by row, using the **FETCH** statement. The **FETCH** gets a row from the active set and drops its values into the record (or string of variables), which has been defined in the **DECLARE.**

   If you use the variable list method, then each column in the select list of the cursor must have a corresponding variable, and each of them must have been declared in the **DECLARE** section. The datatypes must be the same or compatible.

   If you use the record method, the record is **DECLARE**d using the **%ROWTYPE** attribute, which declares the structure of the record to be the same (with the same data types) as the column list in the **select**. Each variable within this record can then be accessed individually using the record name as a prefix, and a variable name that is the same as the column name. *See* **DECLARE VARIABLE** for more details.

Example

```
DECLARE
    cursor EMPLOYEE is select Name, Age, Lodging
                        from WORKER
                        where Age < 21;

    WORKER_RECORD   EMPLOYEE%rowtype;

BEGIN

    open EMPLOYEE;
    fetch EMPLOYEE into WORKER_RECORD;

    if WORKER_RECORD.Lodging = 'ROSE HILL'
        then ...
    end if;
    close EMPLOYEE;

END;
```

Or alternatively use this:

```
DECLARE
    cursor EMPLOYEE is select Name, Age, Lodging
                        from WORKER
                        where Age < 21;

    Person              VARCHAR2(25);
    Age                 NUMBER;
    Home                VARCHAR2(25);
BEGIN
    open EMPLOYEE;
    fetch EMPLOYEE into Person, Age, Home;

    if Home = 'ROSE HILL'
        then...
    end if;
    close EMPLOYEE;

END;
```

This second example shows that the variables into which the data will be fetched must be of the proper data type, but may either have the same name, or different names, than the columns from which the data comes.

FIELD

In a table, a field is the information stored at the intersection of a row and a column. Field is generally synonymous with a column, but also can mean an actual column value.

FILE

A file is a storage area used to store all database data. A database must have one physical file (in the SYSTEM tablespace) but may have many files in multiple tablespaces. A file is a part of a tablespace.

FILE MANAGEMENT LOCKS

File management locks are one of three types of internal locks. These locks exist on physical files (control files, redo log files, and database files) to make sure they are read and updated properly.

FILE TYPES

Files usually have a name and an extension, for example **comfort.tab** where **comfort** is the file name, and **tab** is the extension, or file "type." In SQL*PLUS, **start** files that are created using **EDIT** are given the default extension SQL if no extension is specified. In other words, this:

```
edit misty
```

will create or edit a file named **misty.sql**, while this:

```
start misty
```

will attempt to start a file named **misty.sql** because no extension was specified. Similarly, this:

```
spool bellwood
```

will create an output file named **bellwood.lst**, because **lst** is the default extension for spooled files. Of course, if either **edit** or **spool** is followed by both a file name and extension, the given extension will be used, not the default.

FLOOR

Type   SQL command

Products   All

See also   **CEIL**, NUMBER FUNCTIONS, Chapter 6

Format

```
FLOOR(value)
```

Description   **FLOOR** is the largest integer smaller than or equal to *value*.

Example

```
FLOOR(2)     =   2
FLOOR(1.3)   =   1
FLOOR(-2)    =  -2
FLOOR(-2.3)  =  -3
```

FLUSH (SQL*PLUS)

See **SET**.

FOR (Form 1 - Embedded SQL)

Type   Embedded SQL clause

Product   Precompilers

See also   **EXECUTE**, **FETCH**

Format

```
FOR :integer
```

Description   :*integer* is a host variable set as the maximum number of iterations of array processing during **delete**, **execute**, **fetch**, **insert**, **update**, and **select** statements. This is an optional clause. In its absence, the size of the smallest array determines the number of components processed.

Example   The delete will execute 30 times. Note that if the *name_array* had been 15 instead of 50, the delete would have executed 15 times:

```
lid: constant integer := 30
```

```
Name : name_array (1 ... 50)

exec sql for :lid
    delete from WORKER where Name = :Name
```

FOR (Form 2 - PL/SQL)

See **LOOP**.

FOREIGN KEY

A foreign key is one or more columns whose values are based on the primary or candidate key values from another table.

FORMAT

See **BTITLE**, CHAR FORMAT, **COLUMN**, DATE FORMAT, **TO_CHAR**, **TO_DATE**, **TTITLE**.

FORMAT MODEL

A format model is a clause that controls the appearance of numbers, dates, and character strings. Format models for DATE columns are used in date conversion functions such as **TO_CHAR** and **TO_DATE**.

FORMFEED

Formfeed is a control character that signals a printer to skip to the top of the next sheet of paper.

FRAGMENTED DATABASE

A fragmented database is one that has been used for a while so that data belonging to various tables is spread all over the database and free space may be in many small pieces rather than fewer large pieces, due to much database activity or use. Fragmentation makes space usage less efficient and can be remedied by exporting and importing some or all data.

FREE EXTENTS

Free extents are extents of database blocks that have not yet been allocated to any table or index segment. *Free extents* is another term for free space.

FREE SPACE

See FREE EXTENTS.

FROM

Type   SQL clause

Products   All

See also   **DELETE**, **SELECT**, Chapter 3

Format

```
DELETE FROM [user.]table[@link] [alias]
WHERE condition

SELECT... FROM [user.]table[@link] [, [user.]table[@link] ]...
```

Description   *table* is the name of the table used by **delete** or **select**. *link* is the link to a remote database. Both **delete** and **select** commands require a **from** clause to define the tables from which rows will be deleted or selected. If the table is owned by another user, its name must be prefixed by the owner's user name.

   If the table is remote, a database link has to be defined. *@link* specifies the link. If link is entered, but *user* is not, the query seeks a table owned by the user on the remote database. The *condition* may include a correlated query and use the *alias* for correlation.

FULL TABLE SCAN

A full table scan is a method of data retrieval in which ORACLE directly searches in a sequential manner all the database blocks for a table (rather than using an index), when looking for the specified data.

FUNCTION

A function is a predefined operation, such as "convert to uppercase," which may be performed by placing the function's name and arguments in a SQL statement. *See*

CHARACTER FUNCTIONS, CONVERSION FUNCTIONS, DATE FUNCTIONS, GROUP FUNCTIONS, LIST FUNCTIONS, NUMBER FUNCTIONS, and individual functions.

GENMENU

Type   Utility

Products   SQL*MENU V5

See also   DOCUMENT, SQLMENU

Format

```
GENMENU [application] [user/password]
[[-e] ¦ [{-g ¦ -ge ¦ -gd ¦ -ga ¦ -r} user]] [-s]
```

Description   GENMENU is a command line alternative to choosing the Generate or Unload (in the action menu) or Grant Access options (in the admin menu within the action menu) from SQL*MENU Design in version 5 of SQL*MENU. It generates the executable library files for an application, and can also be used to grant or revoke access for users.

application is the name of the application menu that you wish to enter.

user and *password* allow you to log on to ORACLE. If these are not entered, you will be prompted for them.

-e creates a file of the application with the name **application.sql**.

-g user gives the user SELECT access to the SQL*MENU base tables, so that menus can be used.

-ge user is the same as *-g*.

-ga user gives the user UPDATE, INSERT, and DELETE privileges, WITH GRANT OPTION (the ability to pass privileges on).

-gd user gives the user UPDATE, INSERT and DELETE privileges, without the GRANT OPTION.

-r user revokes all privileges from the user.

-s suppresses the normal display of the logging on program banner information.

-? forces GENMENU to display all of these options.

GENREP

Type   Utility report program

Products   SQL*REPORTWRITER

See also   DUMPREP, LOADREP, MOVEREP, PRINTDEF, RUNREP, SQL*REPORTWRITER, SQLPLUS, SQLREP, TERMDEF

Format

```
GENREP {[FILE=file | [REPORT=report [USERID=user/password]]}
       [PATH=path]
```

Description   **GENREP** creates a runfile that can be executed by **RUNREP**. With the first option, **GENREP** reads a flat ASCII file of a report definition created by **DUMPREP** to load the definition into another system. This process works even from an ASCII- to an EBCDIC-based machine. FILE is the name of the file created by **DUMPREP**. If no extension is given, .rex is assumed. This file will then be used to create a "runfile," which is subsequently interpreted by **RUNREP**, directly from the flat ASCII file that **GENREP** produces.

To use **GENREP** with a report definition in the database, do not use FILE, but instead specify REPORT along with the name of the report in the database. Note that it is only in this mode that USERID is needed.

PATH is the path in which to put the runfile that **GENREP** produces.

GET

Type   SQL*PLUS command

Products   SQL*PLUS

See also   EDIT, SAVE

Format

```
GET file [LIST | NOLIST]
```

Description   **GET** loads a host system file named *file* into the current buffer (whether the SQL buffer or a named buffer). If the file type is not included, **GET** assumes a file type of SQL. **LIST** makes SQL*PLUS list the lines being loaded into the buffer. This is the default. **NOLIST** gets the file without listing its contents.

Example   This example gets a file called **work.sql**:

```
get work
```

GLB

Type   SQL function

Products   All

See Also   DATA TYPES, GROUP FUNCTIONS

Format

```
GLB(label)
```

Description   The GLB group function returns the greatest lower bound of a secure operating system label. The label must be either an expression evaluating to an MLSLABEL value or a quoted text literal in the standard MLS label format. This function is available only in Trusted ORACLE; *see* the *Trusted ORACLE 7 Server Administrator's Guide* for more information.

GOTO

Type   PL/SQL statement

Products   PL/SQL

See also   BLOCK STRUCTURE

Format

```
GOTO label;
```

Description   **GOTO** transfers control to a section of code preceded by the named *label*. Such a label can be used to precede any legitimate statement within an execution block, or within an EXCEPTION section. There are certain restrictions:

- A **GOTO** cannot transfer control to a block enclosed in the current block, or inside of a FOR LOOP or an IF statement.

- A **GOTO** cannot transfer to a label outside of its own block unless it is to a block that encloses its block.

Example   Here's an informal loop built from a **GOTO** that, without actually knowing ahead of time what the top number will be, **insert**s a geometric progression from 1 to about 10,000 into a table:

```
DECLARE
  ...
BEGIN
  x := 0;
```

```
   y := 1;
   <<alpha>>
   x := x + 1;
   y := x*y;
   insert ...
   if y > 10000
      then goto beta;
   goto alpha;
<<beta>>
   exit;
```

GRANT (Form 1 - System Privileges and Roles)

Type   SQL command

Products   All

See also   **ALTER USER**, **CREATE USER**, PRIVILEGE, **REVOKE**, ROLE, Chapter 17

Format

```
GRANT {system_privilege : role}
     [, {system_privilege : role}] ...
   TO {user : role : PUBLIC}[, {user : role : PUBLIC}]...
   [WITH ADMIN OPTION]
```

Description   **GRANT** extends one or more system privileges to users and roles. A system privilege is an authorization to perform one of the various data definition or control commands, such as **ALTER SYSTEM**, **CREATE ROLE**, or **GRANT** itself. *See* PRIVILEGE for details of these privileges. A user is created by **CREATE USER** and is then granted system privileges to enable logging into the database and other operations. A user without grants is unable to do anything at all in ORACLE7. A *role* is a collection of privileges created by **CREATE ROLE**. As with a user, a role has no privileges when created, but gets them through one or more **GRANT**s. One can grant one role to another role to create a nested network of roles, which gives the database administrator a great deal of flexibility in managing the security of the system.

The **WITH ADMIN OPTION** option lets the granted user or role (the grantee) grant the system privilege or role to other grantees. The grantee can also alter or drop a role granted **WITH ADMIN OPTION**.

Example   The following grants the role BASIC permission to log into ORACLE, to change session parameters, and to create tables, views, and synonyms. It also lets a user granted the BASIC role grant these permissions to other users or roles.

```
grant CREATE SESSION, ALTER SESSION, CREATE TABLE,
      CREATE VIEW, CREATE SYNONYM
   to BASIC
with admin option;
```

GRANT (Form 2 - Object Privileges)

Type   SQL command

Products   All

See also   **GRANT** (Form 1), PRIVILEGE, ROLE, Chapter 17

Format

```
GRANT object_privilege[,object_privilege]...
      [(column[,column]...)]
   ON [user.]object
   TO {user ¦ role ¦ PUBLIC}[,{user ¦ role ¦ PUBLIC}]... }
[WITH GRANT OPTION]
```

Description   The second form of the **GRANT** command grants object privileges, privileges that affect specific kinds of objects in ORACLE databases, to any user or role. *object* can be a table, view, sequence, procedure, function, package, snapshot, or a synonym for one of these objects. **GRANT**s on a synonym actually become grants on the underlying object that the synonym references. *See* PRIVILEGE for a complete list of object privileges and a discussion of which can be granted for the various objects.

If you are granting INSERT, REFERENCES, or UPDATE privileges on a table or view, **GRANT** can also specify a list of columns of the table or view to which the **GRANT** applies. The **GRANT** applies only to those columns. If **GRANT** has no list of columns, the **GRANT** applies equally to all columns in the table or view.

PUBLIC grants the privileges to all users present and future.

The **WITH GRANT OPTION** passes along the right to grant the granted privileges to another user or role.

GREATEST

Type   SQL function

Products   All

See also   COLLATION, **LEAST**, **MAX**, OTHER FUNCTIONS, Chapters 6 and 7

Format

```
GREATEST(value1, value2, ...)
```

Description   **GREATEST** chooses the greatest of a list of values. These can be columns, literals, or expressions, and CHAR, VARCHAR2, NUMBER, or DATE data types. A number with a larger value is considered greater than a smaller one. All negative numbers are smaller than all positive numbers. Thus, –10 is smaller than 10; –100 is smaller than –10.

A later date is considered greater than an earlier date.

Character strings are compared position by position, starting at the leftmost end of the string, up to the first character that is different. Whichever string has the greater character in that position is considered the greater string. One character is considered greater than another if it appears after the other in the computer's collation sequence. Usually this means that a B is greater than an A, but the value of A compared to a, or compared to the number 1, will differ by computer.

If two strings are identical through to the end of the shorter one, the longer string is considered greater. If two strings are identical and the same length, they are considered equal. In SQL, it is important that literal numbers be typed without enclosing single quotes, as '10' would be considered smaller than '6', since the quotes will cause these to be regarded as character strings rather than numbers, and the '6' will be seen as greater than the 1 in the first position of '10'.

Unlike many other ORACLE functions and logical operators, the **GREATEST** and **LEAST** functions will not evaluate literal strings that are in date format as dates. In order for **LEAST** and **GREATEST** to work properly, the **TO_DATE** function must be applied to the literal strings.

GREATEST_LB

Type   SQL Function

Products   All

See also   **LEAST_UB**, LIST FUNCTIONS

Format

```
GREATEST_LB(label[,label]...)
```

Description   Returns the greatest lower bound of a list of labels in Trusted ORACLE.

GROUP BY

Type   SQL clause

Products   All

See also   **HAVING**, **ORDER BY**, **WHERE**, Chapter 9

Format

```
SELECT expression [,expression]...
GROUP BY expression [,expression]...
HAVING condition
...
```

Description   **GROUP BY** causes a **select** to produce one summary row for all selected rows that have identical values in one or more specified columns or expressions. Each expression in the **select** clause must be one of these things:

- A constant

- A function without parameters (SysDate, User)

- A group function like **SUM**, **AVG**, **MIN**, **MAX**, **COUNT**

- Matched identically to an expression in the **GROUP BY** clause

Columns referenced in the **GROUP BY** clause need not be in the **select** clause, though they must be in the table.

You use **HAVING** to determine which groups the **GROUP BY** is to include. A **where** clause, on the other hand, determines which rows are to be included in groups.

group by and **having** follow **where**, **connect by**, and **start with**. The **order by** clause is executed after the **where**, **group by**, and **having** clauses (which execute in that order). It can employ group functions, or columns from the **group by**, or a combination. If it uses a group function, that function operates on the groups, then the **order by** sorts the *results* of the function in order. If the **order by** uses a column from the **group by**, it sorts the rows that are returned based on that column. Group functions and single columns can be combined in the **order by** (so long as the column is in the **group by**).

In the **order by** clause you can specify a group function and the column it affects even though they have nothing at all to do with the group functions or columns in the **select**, **group by**, or **having** clause. On the other hand, if you specify a column in the **order by** that is not part of a group function, it must be in the **group by** clause.

Example

```
select Person, COUNT(Item), SUM(Amount) Total
  from LEDGER
 where Action = 'PAID'
 group by Person
having COUNT(Item) > 1
 order by AVG(Amount);
```

GROUP FUNCTIONS

Type   SQL functions

Products   All, PL/SQL

See also   **AVG**, **COUNT**, **GLB**, **LUB**, **MAX**, **MIN**, NUMBER FUNCTIONS, **STDDEV**, **SUM**, VARIANCE, Chapter 6

Description   A GROUP FUNCTION computes a single summary value (such as sum or average) from the individual number values in a group of values. This is an alphabetical list of all current group functions in ORACLE's SQL. Each of these is listed elsewhere in this reference under its own name, with its proper format and use. Group functions are useful only in queries and subqueries. **DISTINCT** makes a group function summarize only distinct (unique) values.

Function Name and Use

AVG([DISTINCT ¦ ALL] *value)* gives the average of the values for group of rows.

COUNT([DISTINCT ¦ ALL] *value* ¦*)* gives the count of rows for a column, or for a table (with *).

GLB(*label***)** gives the greatest lower bound of a secure operating system label.

LUB(*label***)** gives the least upper bound of a secure operating system label.

MAX([DISTINCT ¦ ALL] *value)* gives the maximum of all values for a group of rows.

MIN([DISTINCT ¦ ALL] *value)* gives the minimum of all values for a group of rows.

STDDEV([DISTINCT ¦ ALL] *value)* gives the standard deviation of all values for a group of rows.

SUM([DISTINCT ¦ ALL] *value)* gives the sum of all values for a group of rows.

VARIANCE([DISTINCT ¦ ALL] *value)* gives the variance of all values for a group of rows.

HASH CLUSTER

A hash cluster is a cluster stored by a hash key instead of by an index key. A hash key is a value computed from the key values that represents the location on disk. An index key requires ORACLE to look up the location in the index, while a hash key lets ORACLE calculate the location.

HAVING

See **GROUP BY**.

HEADING (SQL*PLUS)

See **SET**.

HEADSEP (SQL*PLUS)

See **SET**.

HELP

Type   SQL*PLUS command

Products   SQL*PLUS

Format

```
HELP {topic ¦ COMMANDS ¦ CLAUSES}

HELP
```

Description   If **HELP** is available on a topic, typing the word **HELP**, followed by the topic name, will cause SQL*PLUS to retrieve the relevant information from the HELP database table and display it. **HELP COMMANDS** shows a list of commands for which help is available. **HELP CLAUSES** shows a list of clauses and other topics. **HELP** alone shows the topics for which help is available. The HELP table may be created and loaded during database creation.

HEXADECIMAL NOTATION

Hexadecimal notation is a numbering system with a base of 16 instead of the decimal base of 10. The numbers 10 through 15 are represented by the letters A through F. This system is often used to display the internal data stored in a computer.

HEXTORAW

Type   SQL command

Products   All

See also   **RAWTOHEX**

Format

HEXTORAW(*hex_string*)

Description   **HEX**adecimal **TO RAW, HEXTORAW** changes a character string of hex numbers into binary.

HOST (SQL*PLUS)

Type   SQL*PLUS

Product   SQL*PLUS

See also   **$, @, @@, START**

Format

HO[ST] *host command*

Description   A host is a computer on which the ORACLE RDBMS is running. The **HOST** command in SQL*PLUS passes any host command back to the operating system for execution without exiting SQL*PLUS. SQL*PLUS permits embedding local or PL/SQL variables in the host command string. This doesn't work on all hardware or operating systems.

IF

Type   PL/SQL statement

Products   PL/SQL

See also   LOOP

Format

```
IF condition
    THEN statement; [statement;]...
 [ELSEIF condition THEN statement; [statement;]...
 [ELSEIF condition THEN statement; [statement;]...]... ]
[ELSE statement; [statement;]...]
END IF;
```

Description   The IF statement will execute one or more *statements* if *condition* evaluates to TRUE, after which the program branches to END IF. If the *condition* is FALSE, then any number of a series of optional ELSEIF conditions are tested. If any one is TRUE, the associated *statements* (following THEN) are executed, and then the program branches to END IF. If none of the ELSEIF conditions are TRUE (and the original IF condition was not TRUE), then the statements following the optional ELSE are executed. Note that the final ELSE does not have a condition.

Example

```
IF Age >= 65
    THEN insert into RETIRED values (Name, Age, Lodging);
ELSEIF Age < 18
    THEN insert into UNDERAGE values (Name, Age, Lodging);
ELSE insert into WORKFORCE values (Name, Age, Lodging);
END IF;
```

IMPORT

Import is the ORACLE utility used to retrieve ORACLE database data found in export format files into an ORACLE database. To import is to use the Import utility to move data from an export file into database table(s). *See* EXPORT. For details on using Import, *see* the *ORACLE7 Server Utilities Users Guide.*

IN

Type   Logical Operator for **where** clause

Products   All

See also   **ALL**, **ANY**, LOGICAL OPERATORS, Chapter 3

Format

```
where expression IN ({'string' [,'string']... ¦ select...})
```

Description   **IN** is equivalent to **=ANY**. In the first option, **IN** means the expression is equal to any member of the following list of literal *strings*. In the second option, it means the expression is equal to any value in any row selected from the subquery. The two are logically equivalent, with the first giving a list made of literal strings, and the second building a list from a query. **IN** works with VARCHAR2, CHAR, DATE, and NUMBER data types, as well as RowID.

INDEX

Index is a general term for an ORACLE/SQL feature used primarily to speed execution and impose uniqueness upon certain data. Indexes provide a faster access method to one table's data than doing a full table scan. There are several types of indexes; *see* CONCATENATED INDEX, COMPRESSED INDEX, and UNIQUE INDEX. An index has an entry for each value found in the table's indexed field(s) (except those with a NULL value) and pointer(s) to the row(s) having that value.

INDEX SEGMENT

The index segment is the storage that is allocated for the indexes on a table, as compared to storage allocated to the data in a table.

INDICATOR VARIABLE

Type   Data field

Products   PL/SQL, ORACLE precompilers (versions 1.3 and up)

See also   : (colon, the host variable prefix)

Format

```
:name[INDICATOR]:indicator
```

Description   An indicator variable—used when both name and indicator are host language variable names—is a data field whose value indicates whether a host variable should be regarded as NULL. (The INDICATOR keyword is for readability and has no effect.)

name may be any legitimate host variable data name used in the host program and included in the precompiler's DECLARE SECTION. *indicator* is defined in the precompiler's DECLARE SECTION as a two-byte integer.

Few procedural languages directly support the idea of a variable with a NULL or unknown value, although ORACLE and SQL do so easily. In order to extend languages for which ORACLE has developed precompilers to support the NULL concept, an indicator variable is associated with the host variable, almost like a flag, to indicate whether it is NULL. The host variable and its indicator variable may be referenced and set separately in the host language code, but are always concatenated in SQL or PL/SQL.

Example

```
BEGIN
    select Name, Skill into :Worker, :JobSkill:JobSkillInd
      from WORKERSKILL
     where Name = :First||' '||:Last;

    IF :JobSkill:JobSkillInd IS NULL
    THEN :JobSkill:JobSkillInd := 'No Skills'
    END IF;
END;
```

Note that the test to see if the variable is NULL, and the assignment of No Skills to it if it is, are both done with the concatenated variable name. PL/SQL knows enough to check the indicator in the first case, and set the variable value in the second case. The two variables together are treated just like a single ORACLE column. These important points must be noted:

- Within any single PL/SQL block, a host variable must either always stand alone, or always be concatenated with its indicator variable.

- An indicator variable cannot be referenced alone within PL/SQL, although it can be in the host program.

When setting host variables within the host program, but outside of PL/SQL, note these points:

- Setting the indicator variable equal to –1 will force the concatenated variable to be regarded within PL/SQL as NULL, both in logic tests and for **insert**s or **update**s.

- Setting the indicator variable greater than or equal to 0 will force the concatenated variable to be regarded as equal to the value in the host variable, and NOT NULL.

- PL/SQL tests the value of all indicator variables on entering a block, and sets them on exiting the block.

When loading concatenated host variables within PL/SQL, via a SQL statement with an INTO clause, the following rules apply when checking the indicator variable within the host program, but outside of PL/SQL:

- The indicator variable will be equal to –1 if the value loaded from the database was NULL. The value of the host variable is uncertain, and should be treated as such.

- The indicator variable will be equal to 0 if the value from the database is loaded completely and correctly into the host variable.

- The indicator variable will be greater than 0 and equal to the actual length of the data in the database column if only a portion of it could fit in the host variable. The host variable will contain a truncated version of what was in the database column.

init.ora

init.ora is a database system parameter file that contains numerous settings and file names used when a system is started using the **CREATE DATABASE**, **START UP**, or **SHUT DOWN** command. *See* the *ORACLE7 Server Administrator's Guide.*

INITCAP

Type   SQL function

Products   All

See also   CHARACTER FUNCTIONS, **LOWER**, **UPPER**, Chapter 5

Format

```
INITCAP(string)
```

Description   **INIT**ial **CAP**ital changes the first letter of a word or series of words into uppercase. Also it notes the presence of symbols, and will **INITCAP** any letter that follows a space or a symbol, such as a comma, period, colon, semicolon, !, @, #, $, and so on.

Example

```
INITCAP('this.is,an-example of!how@initcap#works')
```

produces this:

```
This.Is,An-Example Of!How@Initcap#Works
```

INPUT

Type   SQL*PLUS line editor command

Products   All

See also   **APPEND**, **CHANGE**, **DEL**, **EDIT**, Chapter 4

Format

```
I[NPUT] [text]
```

Description   **INPUT** adds a new line of text after the current line in the current buffer. Using **INPUT** by itself allows multiple lines to be keyed in after the current line, which stops when the system encounters ENTER with nothing else on the line. The space between **INPUT** and *text* will not be added to the line but any additional spaces will be. *See* **DEL** for a discussion of current line.

INSERT (Form 1 - Embedded SQL)

Type   Embedded SQL command

Product   Precompilers

See also   **EXECUTE**, **FOR**

Format

```
EXEC SQL [AT{database¦:host_variable] [FOR :integer]
INSERT INTO [user.]table[@db_link] [ (column [,column]...)]
          { VALUES (expression[,expression]...) ¦ query }
```

Description   *database* is a database other than the user's default, and *host_variable* contains the name of the database. *:integer* is a host value that limits the number of times the **INSERT** will be processed (*see* **FOR**). *table* is any existing table, view, or synonym, and *db_link* is the name of a remote database where the table is stored. (*See* the **INSERT** Form 3 definition for a discussion of the **VALUES** clause, columns, and query.) *expression* here can be an expression or a host variable in the form *:variable[:indicator]*.

INSERT (Form 2 - PL/SQL)

Type   PL/SQL statement

Products   PL/SQL

See also   SQL CURSOR

Format

```
INSERT INTO [user.]table[@db_link] [(column [,column]...)]
     VALUES (expression [,expression]...) : query...);
```

Description   PL/SQL's use of **INSERT** is identical to its general form (Form 3 in the following section), with these exceptions:

- You may use a PL/SQL variable in an expression for the value in the VALUES list.

- Each variable will be treated in the same way that a constant, with the value of the variable, would be treated.

- If you use the *query. . .* version of the **INSERT**, you cannot use the **INTO** clause of the **select**.

INSERT (Form 3 - SQL Command)

Type   SQL command

Products   All

See also   **CREATE TABLE**

Format

```
INSERT INTO [user.]table[@db_link] [ (column [,column]...) ]
            { VALUES (expression[,expression]...) : query }
```

Description   **INSERT** adds one or more new rows to the table or view. The optional *user* must be a user to whose table you have been granted insert authority. *table* is the table into which rows are to be inserted. If a list of columns is given, an expression (SQL expression) must be matched for each of those columns. Any columns not in the list receive the value NULL, and none of them can be defined NOT NULL or the **INSERT** will fail. If a list of columns is not given, values must be given for all columns.

    INSERT with a query adds as many rows as the query returns, with each query column being matched, position for position, with columns in the column list. If no column list is given, the tables must have the same number and type of columns. USER_TAB_COLUMNS data dictionary view shows these, as does DESCRIBE in SQL*PLUS.

Example   The following inserts a row into the COMFORT table:

```
insert into COMFORT values ('KEENE','23-SEP-93',99.8,82.6,NULL);
```

The following inserts City, SampleDate (both NOT NULL columns), and Precipitation into COMFORT:

```
insert into COMFORT (City, SampleDate, Precipitation) values
                   ('KEENE','22-DEC-93',3.9);
```

To copy just the data for the city of KEENE into a new table named NEW_HAMPSHIRE, use this:

```
insert into NEW_HAMPSHIRE select * from COMFORT
                   where City = 'KEENE';
```

INSTANCE

An instance is everything required for ORACLE to run: background processes (programs), memory, and so on. An instance is the means of accessing a database.

INSTANCE IDENTIFIER

An instance identifier is a means of distinguishing one instance from another when multiple instances exist on one CPU.

INSTANCE RECOVERY

Instance recovery is recovery in the event of software or hardware failure. This occurs if the software aborted abnormally due to a severe bug, deadlock, or destructive interaction between programs. *See also* MEDIA RECOVERY.

INSTR

Type   SQL function

Products   All

See also   CHARACTER FUNCTIONS, **SUBSTR**, Chapter 5

Format

```
INSTR(string,set[,start[,occurrence]])
```

Description   **INSTR** finds the location of a *set* of characters in a *string*, starting at position *start* in the string, and looking for the first, second, third, and so on, *occurrence* of the *set*. This function will also work with NUMBER and DATE data types. *start* also can be negative, meaning the search begins with the characters at the end of the string and searches backward.

Example   To find the third occurrence of PI in this string, use this:

```
INSTR('PETER PIPER PICKED A PECK OF PICKLED PEPPERS','PI',1,3)
```

The result of this function is 30, the location of the third occurance of 'PI'.

INSTRB

Type   SQL command

Products   All

See also   CHARACTER FUNCTIONS, **INSTR**, Chapter 5

Format

```
INSTRB(string,set[,start[,occurrence]])
```

Description   **INSTRB** finds the location of a *set* of characters in a *string*, starting at the byte position *start* in the string, and looking for the first, second, third, and so on, *occurrence* of the set. This function also works with NUMBER and DATE data types. *start* also can be negative, which means the search begins with the characters at the end of the string and searches backward.

This function is the same as **INSTR** for single-byte character sets.

INTEGRITY CONSTRAINT

Integrity constraint is a rule that restricts the range of valid values for a column. It is placed on a column when the table is created.

column_constraint

column_constraint defines the restrictions placed on this column and consists of the following:

```
[CONSTRAINT constraint]
  {[NOT] NULL |
  [{UNIQUE | PRIMARY KEY}
    [USING INDEX
      [   PCTFREE integer]
      [  INITRANS integer]
      [  MAXTRANS integer]
      [TABLESPACE tablespace]
      [   STORAGE storage]]]
  [REFERENCES [user.]table[(column)] [ON DELETE CASCADE]
  [CHECK (condition)]
  [EXCEPTIONS INTO [user.]table]
  [DISABLE]
```

constraint is an optional name assigned to this constraint. Without it, ORACLE assigns a name in the form SYS_C*n*, where *n* is an integer. An ORACLE-assigned name will usually change during an import, while a user-assigned name will not change.

NULL permits NULL values. NOT NULL specifies that every row must have a non-NULL value for this column.

UNIQUE forces column values to be unique. There can be only one PRIMARY KEY constraint on a table. If a column is UNIQUE it cannot also be declared the PRIMARY KEY (PRIMARY KEY also enforces uniqueness). An index enforces the unique or primary key, and the USING INDEX clause and its options specify the storage characteristics of that index. *See* **CREATE INDEX** for more information on the options.

REFERENCES identifies this column as a foreign key from [*user.*]*table* [*(column)*]. Omitting *column* implies that the name in the *user.table* is the same as the name in this table. Note that when REFERENCES is used in a *table_constraint* (described shortly) it must be preceded by FOREIGN KEY. This is not used here, as only this column is referenced; *table_constraint* can reference several columns for FOREIGN KEY. ON DELETE CASCADE instructs ORACLE to maintain referential integrity automatically by removing foreign key rows in the dependent tables if you remove the primary key row in this table.

CHECK assures that the value for this column pass a condition such as this:

```
Amount number(12,2) CHECK (Amount >= 0)
```

condition may be any valid expression that tests TRUE or FALSE. It can contain functions, any columns from this table, and literals.

The **EXCEPTIONS INTO** clause specifies a table into which ORACLE puts information about rows that violate an enabled integrity constraint. This table must be local.

The **DISABLE** option lets you disable the integrity constraint when you create it. When the constraint is disabled, ORACLE does not automatically enforce it. You can later enable the constraint with the **ENABLE** clause in **ALTER TABLE**.

table_constraint

table_constraint is identical to *column_constraint* except that it can reference multiple columns with a single constraint—for example in declaring three columns as a primary or foreign key. This is the format for table_constraint:

```
[CONSTRAINT constraint]
  {[NOT] NULL |
  [{UNIQUE | PRIMARY KEY} (column[,column])
    [USING INDEX
      [   PCTFREE integer]
      [  INITRANS integer]
      [  MAXTRANS integer]
      [TABLESPACE tablespace]
      [   STORAGE storage]]]
  [FOREIGN KEY (column[,column])
    REFERENCES [user.]table [ (column[,column])]
    [ON DELETE CASCADE]]
  [CHECK (condition)]
  [EXCEPTIONS INTO [user.]table]
  [DISABLE]
```

INTERSECT

Type   SQL command

Products   All

See also   **MINUS**, QUERY OPERATORS, **UNION**, Chapter 10

Format

```
    select...
INTERSECT
    select...
```

Description   **INTERSECT** combines two queries and returns only those rows from the first **select** statement that are identical to at least one row from the second **select** statement. The number of columns and data types must be identical between

select statements, although the names of the columns do not need to be. The data, however, must be identical in the rows produced for the **INTERSECT**ion to pass them. *See* Chapter 10 for a discussion of the important differences and effects of **INTERSECT**, **UNION**, and **MINUS**.

IS NULL

Type   Logical operator

Products   All

See also   LOGICAL OPERATORS, Chapters 3 and 6

Format

```
WHERE column IS [NOT] NULL
```

Description   **IS NULL** tests column (or an expression) for the absence of any data. A NULL test is distinctly different from a test for equality, because NULL means that the value is unknown or irrelevant, and it therefore cannot be said to be equal to anything, including another NULL. *See* Chapter 6 for a discussion of NULL.

JOIN

Type   Definition

Products   All

See also   **SELECT**, Chapter 3

Format

```
WHERE {table.column = table.column}
```

Description   A join combines columns and data from two or more tables (and in rare cases, of one table with itself). The tables are all listed in the **from** clause of the **select** statement, and the relationship between the two tables is specified in the **where** clause, usually by a simply equality, such as this:

```
where WORKER.Lodging = LODGING.Lodging
```

This is often called an *equi-join* because it uses the equal sign in the **where** clause. You could join tables using other forms of equality, such as >=, <, and so on, but the results are seldom meaningful. There also are cases in which one or both sides of the equal sign contain an expression, perhaps a **SUBSTR** or a combination of columns, which is used for equality with the other side. This is a fairly common usage.

Joining two tables together without a **where** clause produces a Cartesian product, which combines every row in one table with every row in another table. An 80-row table combined with a 100-row table would produce an 8000-row result (which is usually quite meaningless).

An *outer join* is a method for intentionally retrieving selected rows from one table that don't match rows in the other table. A classic example of this is Talbot's workers and their skills. Suppose you combined the WORKER table and the SKILL table with an equi-join, like this:

```
select WORKER.Name, Skill
  from WORKER, WORKERSKILL
 where WORKER.Name = WORKERSKILL.Name
```

Unfortunately, you would get only those workers who have skills, and therefore have rows in the WORKERSKILL table. But what if you want to list *all* workers and skills, including those who have none? An outer join, accomplished with a + sign, will allow you to do it:

```
select WORKER.Name, Skill
  from WORKER, WORKERSKILL
 where WORKER.Name = WORKERSKILL.Name(+);
```

The plus says, effectively, "if a row exists in the WORKER table that doesn't correspond to a row in the WORKERSKILL table, add one to make the match." It's like adding a NULL row, but it allows rows from the WORKER table to be in the result, even if there is no match for them in the WORKERSKILL table. *See* Chapter 10 for a full discussion.

JOIN COLUMN

A join column is a column used to join one table to another. You identify a join column by using it in a **where** clause that specifies the relationship between the join columns in the two tables.

JULIAN DATE

Julian dates are a means of converting date data so that every date can be expressed as a unique integer. Julian dates can be obtained by using the format mask 'J' with functions on date data. *See* DATE FORMATS.

KERNEL

Kernel is the base ORACLE RDBMS program code (a collection of many modules) that can be called by the background processes.

KEY

A key is a column or columns used to identify rows; it is not the same as an index, although indexes are often used with such columns. *See* FOREIGN KEY, PRIMARY KEY, and UNIQUE KEY.

LABEL (PL/SQL)

A label is a word associated with an executable statement, usually for the purpose of being the target of a GOTO statement.

LAST_DAY

Type   SQL function

Products   All

See also   **ADD_MONTHS**, DATE FUNCTIONS, **NEXT_DAY**, Chapter 7

Format

```
LAST_DAY (date)
```

Description   **LAST_DAY** gives the date of the last day of the month that *date* is in.

Example   This:

```
LAST_DAY ('05-NOV-95')
```

produces a result of 30-NOV-95.

LEAF

In a tree-structured table, a leaf is a row that has no child row.

LEAST

Type   SQL function

Products   All

See also   **GREATEST**, LIST FUNCTIONS, Chapter 7

Format

```
LEAST(value1, value2, ...)
```

Description   **LEAST** is the value of a list of columns, expressions, or values. Values may be VARCHAR2, CHAR, DATE, or NUMBER data types, although **LEAST** will not properly evaluate literal dates (such as '20-MAY-49') without the **TO_DATE** function. *See* **GREATEST** for a discussion of evaluating relative values.

LEAST_UB

Type   SQL Function

Products   All

See also   **GREATEST_LB**, LIST FUNCTIONS

Format

```
LEAST_UB(label[,label]...)
```

Description   Returns the least upper bound of a list of labels in Trusted ORACLE. A label is used in Trusted ORACLE to assign a security level to a record. For further information, *see* the *Trusted ORACLE7 Server Administrator's Guide*.

LENGTH

Type   SQL function

Products   All

See also   CHARACTER FUNCTIONS, **VSIZE**, Chapter 5

Format

```
LENGTH(string)
```

Description   **LENGTH** tells the length of a string, a number, date, or expression.

LENGTHB

Type   SQL function

Products   All

See also   CHARACTER FUNCTIONS, **LENGTH**, **VSIZE**, Chapter 5

Format

```
LENGTHB(string)
```

Description   **LENGTHB** tells the length of a string, a number, date, or expression, in bytes (a series of eight bits) rather than in characters. This gives the number of bytes in multi-byte character strings, while **LENGTH** gives you the length in terms of number of characters.

LEVEL

Type   Pseudo-column

Products   All

See also   **CONNECT BY**, PSEUDO-COLUMNS, Chapter 11

Format

```
LEVEL
```

Description   Level is a pseudo-column, used with **CONNECT BY**, that is equal to 1 for a root node, 2 for a child of a root, 3 for a child of a child of a root, and so on. Level tells basically how far down a tree you've traveled. Chapter 11 contains an extended discussion of **CONNECT BY** and level.

LGWR

LGWR (**LoG WR**iter process) writes redo log entries from the System Global Area to the online redo logs. *See* BACKGROUND PROCESS.

LIKE

Type   SQL command

Products   All

See also   LOGICAL OPERATORS, Chapter 3

Format

WHERE *string* LIKE *string*

Description   **LIKE** performs pattern matching. An underline represents exactly one space. A percent sign represents any number of spaces or characters. If **LIKE** uses either the _ or % in the first position of a comparison (as in the second and third examples following), any index on the column is ignored.

Examples

```
Feature LIKE 'MO%'    "Feature begins with the letters MO."
Feature LIKE '__I%'   "Feature has an I in the third position."
Feature LIKE '%0%0%'  "Feature has two 0's in it."
```

LINESIZE (SQL*PLUS)

See **SET**.

LIST

Type   SQL*PLUS line editor command

Products   SQL*PLUS

See also   **APPEND, CHANGE, EDIT, INPUT, RUN**, Chapter 4

Format

L[IST] [{*start*¦*} [*end*¦*]]

Description   **LIST** lists lines of the current buffer starting at *start* and ending at *end*, both of which are integers. The end line becomes the current line of the buffer, and is flagged with an asterisk. **LIST** without *start* or *end* lists all lines. An asterisk in either place will set it to the current line. **LIST** with a single number will display just that line, and **LIST** with just an asterisk will display just the current line. The space between **LIST** and *start* is not necessary but it does help readability.

Example   Use this to list the current SQL buffer:

```
list

    1   select Person, Amount
    2     from LEDGER
    3   where Amount > 10000
    4*     and Rate = 3;
```

The asterisk shows that 4 is the current line. To list just the second line, use this:

```
LIST 2
```

```
2*   from LEDGER
```

This also makes 2 the current line in the current buffer.

LIST FUNCTIONS

Type   List

Products   All

See also   All other function lists, Chapter 7.

Description   The following is an alphabetical list of all current list functions in ORACLE's SQL. Each of these is listed elsewhere in this reference under its own name, with its proper format and use.
This gives the greatest value of a list:

```
GREATEST(value1, value2, ...)
```

This gives the least value of a list:

```
LEAST(value1, value2, ...)
```

LN

Type   SQL function

Products   All

See also   NUMBER FUNCTIONS, Chapter 6

Format

```
LN(number)
```

Description   **LN** is the "natural", or base e, logarithm of a **number**.

LOADREP

Type   Utility report program

Product   SQL*REPORTWRITER

See also **DUMPREP**, **GENREP**, **MOVEREP**, **PRINTDEF**, **RUNREP**, SQL*REPORTWRITER, **SQLPLUS, SQLREP, TERMDEF**

Format

```
LOADREP [[FILE=]file] [[USERID=]user/password]
```

Description **LOADREP** loads a flat ASCII file of a report definition into the ORACLE database. This file is created using **DUMPREP**. The process works even from an ASCII- to an EBCDIC-based machine.

   FILE gives the name of the file from which the report definition is loaded. The default is **expdat.rex**. If the file extension is not specified, **.rex** is assumed.

   USERID is your ORACLE user name and password.

LOCAL DATABASE

The local database is usually a database on your host computer. *See also* REMOTE DATABASE.

LOCK

To lock is to temporarily restrict other users' access to data. The restriction that is placed on such data is called "a lock." The modes are SHARE, SHARE UPDATE, EXCLUSIVE, SHARE EXCLUSIVE, ROW SHARE, and ROW EXCLUSIVE. Not all locks can be acquired in all modes.

LOCK TABLE

Type SQL command

Products All

See also **COMMIT, DELETE, INSERT, ROLLBACK, SAVEPOINT, UPDATE**

Format

```
LOCK TABLE [user.]table[@db_link]
           [,[user.]table[@db_link]]...
      IN mode MODE [NOWAIT];
```

Description **LOCK TABLE** locks a table in one of several specified modes, allowing it to be shared, but without loss of data integrity. Using **LOCK TABLE** allows you to give other users continued but restricted access to the table.

Regardless of which option you choose, the table will remain in that lock mode until you **commit** or **rollback** your transactions.

Lock modes include ROW SHARE, ROW EXCLUSIVE, SHARE UPDATE, SHARE, SHARE ROW EXCLUSIVE, and EXCLUSIVE.

EXCLUSIVE locks permit users to query the locked table but not to do anything else. No other user may lock the table. SHARED locks permit concurrent queries but no updates to the locked table.

With a ROW SHARE or SHARE UPDATE lock, no user can lock the whole table for exclusive access, allowing concurrent access for all users to the table. The two types of lock are synonymous, and SHARE UPDATE exists for compatibility with previous versions of ORACLE.

ROW EXCLUSIVE locks are similar to ROW SHARE but they prohibit shared locking, so only one user may access the table at a time.

If a **LOCK TABLE** command cannot be completed (usually because someone else has executed a prior and competing **LOCK TABLE** of some sort) then your **LOCK TABLE** will wait until it can complete. If you wish to avoid this, and simply have control returned to you, use the **NOWAIT** option.

LOG

Type   SQL function

Products   All

See also   NUMBER FUNCTIONS, Chapter 6

Format

```
LOG(base, number)
```

Description   **LOG** gives the *base*10 logarithm of a number.

Example

```
LOG(base, value)
```

```
LOG(EXP(1),3) = 1.098612   // log(e) of 3
LOG(10,100)   = 2          // log(10) of 100
```

LOG WRITER PROCESS (LGWR)

See **LGWR**.

LOGICAL EXPRESSION

A logical expression is one whose value evaluates to either TRUE or FALSE. It is a synonym for CONDITION.

LOGICAL OPERATORS

Type   SQL command

Products   All

See also   PRECEDENCE

Format   The following lists all current logical operators in ORACLE's SQL. Most of these are listed elsewhere in this reference under their own names with their proper format and use. All of these operators work with columns or literals.

Logical Operators that Test a Single Value

```
=    expression     is equal to expression
>    expression     is greater than expression
>=   expression     is greater than or equal to expression
<    expression     is less than expression
<=   expression     is less than or equal to expression
!=   expression     is not equal to expression
^=   expression     is not equal to expression
<>   expression     is not equal to expression

EXISTS (query)
NOT EXISTS (query)

LIKE expression
NOT LIKE expression

expression IS NULL
expression IS NOT NULL
```

Logical Operators that Test More than a Single Value

```
ANY (expression [,expression]... ¦ query)
ALL (expression [,expression]... ¦ query)
```

ANY and **ALL** require an equality operator as a prefix, such as **>ANY**, **=ALL**, and so on.

```
IN (expression [,expression]... | query)
NOT IN (expression [,expression]... | query)

BETWEEN expression AND expression
NOT BETWEEN expression AND expression
```

Other Logical Operators

()	Overrides normal precedence rules, or encloses a subquery
NOT	Reverses logical expression
AND	Combines logical expressions
OR	Combines logical expressions
UNION	Combines results of queries
INTERSECT	Combines results of queries
MINUS	Combines results of queries

LOGICAL UNIT OF WORK

See TRANSACTION.

LOGIN ACCOUNT

A login account is a username and password that allows people to use the ORACLE RDBMS. This account is usually separate from your operating system account.

LOGON ACCOUNT

Logon account is the same as LOGIN ACCOUNT.

LONG (SQL*PLUS)

See **SET**.

LONG DATATYPE

A LONG datatype is a standard ORACLE datatype that may contain any printable characters such as "A", "3", "&", or "blank". It may be any length from 0 to 2 gigabytes in ORACLE7. Only one LONG column may be defined per table. LONG columns may not be used in functions arguments, expressions, or **where** clauses, and have certain other restrictions.

LONG RAW DATATYPE

A LONG RAW column contains raw binary data, but is otherwise the same as a LONG column. Values entered into LONG RAW columns must be in hex notation.

LOOP

Type   PL/SQL statement

Products   PL/SQL

See also   **%ROWTYPE, CLOSE, DECLARE CURSOR, EXIT, FETCH, OPEN**

Format

```
<<label>> [WHILE condition ¦
     FOR counter IN [REVERSE] computation .. computation ¦
     FOR record  IN
         [cursor [(value [,value]...)] ¦select... ]]
  LOOP statement [,statement] END LOOP [label];
```

Description   label is an optional name for a loop. If it has a label, it must be bracketed by << >> when it appears at the beginning of the loop. If used at the beginning of the loop, it should also be used at the end, following the **END LOOP**, but should not be bracketed. The <<label>> can be referenced from elsewhere in the program by a **GOTO**, and can be used within the **LOOP** with **EXIT** label, which will branch program control to the first statement after the **LOOP**. There are four kinds of loops: unconstrained (also called basic or infinite), **WHILE**, **FOR** counter, and **FOR** record **IN** (also called a cursor loop).

An unconstrained loop has no constraints placed directly on the loop itself. It simply continues to loop until a condition test in one of the statements it contains directs the program to branch elsewhere. The condition test is done with an IF, and the branching with **EXIT**, **GOTO**, or **RAISE**. A system **RAISE**d exception would also break the loop, and would transfer control to the EXCEPTION section.

A WHILE loop specifies a condition that is tested on entering the loop, and with each iteration (looping around), to see if it is TRUE. If it is, the loop's statements are executed again. Of course, one or more of those statements could also be condition tests with **EXIT**, **GOTO**, or **RAISE**. As soon as an iteration of the loop begins where the condition tests FALSE, the loop is immediately exited, and control passes to the next program line after the loop.

Example   For 10 rows, **FETCH** Name and Age from the EMPLOYEE cursor, and **INSERT** them into the table NAME:

```
DECLARE
...
BEGIN
   WHILE EMPLOYEE%ROWCOUNT < 11 LOOP
      FETCH adah into EMPLOYEE;
      insert into NAME values (Name, Age);
   END LOOP;
END;
```

A FOR loop is really a very restricted form of a WHILE loop, where a counter is set up and incremented (or decremented with REVERSE) from a low value to a high value. These values can either be constants, or the result of a computation that is made once and once only just as the loop is entered. The computations must evaluate to an integer (if necessary using **ROUND** or **TRUNC**), and the counter is merely a variable name that is implicitly defined to be a number. You do not need to, and should not, include it in your DECLARE section. PL/SQL will declare its data type automatically on encountering its name following the word FOR. The FOR loop is executed over and over again until the counter is equal to or greater than the final value. If you use the REVERSE option, the counter is decremented starting with the high value (still the right number of the pair), until it is equal to or lower than the low value.

Example   With the following, add one to x as many times as it takes to count from 10 to 20:

```
DECLARE
x      NUMBER;

BEGIN
x := 0;
FOR i IN 10..20 LOOP
   x := x+1;
END LOOP
```

The same routine, in a little more complicated fashion, is shown here:

```
DECLARE
x NUMBER;
s NUMBER;
t NUMBER;

BEGIN;
s := 5;
t := 10;
x := 0;
<<fashion_loop>>
FOR i IN 2*s..2*t LOOP
    x := x+1;
END LOOP fashion_loop
```

If the loop you wish to execute will be fetching and processing every row from a **select**, there is a shorthand way to accomplish what would normally be done with a **DECLARE** cursor, an **OPEN**, and a WHILE loop with **FETCH**es. This method is called a cursor loop. A cursor loop automatically opens a previously **DECLARE**d cursor, **FETCH**es and processes each row until all rows satisfying the **where** clause in the cursor declaration have been retrieved, and then automatically closes the cursor and exits the loop.

Example

```
DECLARE
    cursor TALBOT is select W.Name Name, Skill,
                            W.Lodging Home, Manager
                    from WORKER W, WORKERSKILL WS, LODGING L
                    where W.Lodging = L.Lodging
                        and W.Name = WS.Name;
    know_how    SKILL%ROWTYPE;
BEGIN    for know_how in TALBOT loop
        when SQL%notfound exit;
        if know_how.Skill = 'Discus'
            then insert into HELPER_LIST
                    values (Talbot.Name, Talbot.Skill, Talbot.Home,
                        Talbot.Manager);
        endif;
    end loop;
    commit;
END;
```

Here, four columns are retrieved from two joined tables, WORKERSKILL and LODGING. A cursor loop begins with **for know_how in TALBOT loop**, which loops through the cursor TALBOT, **FETCH**ing columns into the record know_how. The column Skill in the record know_how is tested during each loop cycle to see if this worker knows how to use a discus. If the worker knows how, the lodging and manager's name for the worker are written into a HELPER_LIST table, along with name and skill.

Note the use of two aliases in the **select** statement in the cursor. This is to remove the presence of the dot (.) in a column name, which could conflict with the record.column naming convention used later.

LOWER

Type   SQL function

Products   All

See also   CHARACTER FUNCTIONS, **INITCAP**, **UPPER**, Chapter 5

Format

```
LOWER(string)
```

Description   **LOWER** converts every letter in a string to lowercase.

Example

```
LOWER('PENINSULA') = peninsula
```

LPAD

Type   SQL function

Products   All

See also   CHARACTER FUNCTIONS, **LTRIM**, **RPAD**, **RTRIM**, Chapter 5

Format

```
LPAD(string,length [,'set'])
```

Description   **L**eft **pad** makes a *string* a certain *length* by adding a certain *set* of characters to the left of the string. If *set* is not specified, the default pad character is a space.

Example

```
LPAD('>',11,'- ')
```

produces

```
- - - - - >
```

LTRIM

Type   SQL function

Products   All

See also   CHARACTER FUNCTIONS, **LPAD**, **RPAD**, **RTRIM**, Chapter 5

Format

```
LTRIM(string [,'set'])
```

Description   Left **trim** trims all the occurrences of any one of a *set* of characters off of the left side of a *string*.

Example

```
LTRIM('NANCY','AN')
```

produces this:

```
CY
```

LUB

Type   SQL function

Products   All

See also   **COMPUTE**, **GLB**, GROUP FUNCTIONS, Chapter 6

Format

```
LUB(label)
```

Description   **LUB** gives the least upper bound of a secure operating system label. The label expression must have data type MLSLABEL or be a quoted text literal in the standard label format. The resulting value is datatype RAW MLSLABEL. This function is available only with Trusted ORACLE. *See* the *Trusted ORACLE Administrator's Guide* for more information.

■ MAIN QUERY

A main query is the outermost or top query in a query containing a subquery. It's the query whose columns produce a result.

■ MAINTENANCE RELEASE

The maintenance release is the second number in ORACLE software version numbering. In ORACLE version 7.0.16, the maintenance release is 0.

■ MAX

Type   SQL function

Products   All

See also   **COMPUTE**, GROUP FUNCTIONS, **MIN**, Chapter 6

Format

```
MAX([DISTINCT | ALL] value)
```

Description   **MAX** is the maximum of all *values* for a group of rows. **MAX** ignores NULL values. The **DISTINCT** option is not meaningful, since the maximum of all values is identical to the maximum of the distinct values.

■ MAXDATA (SQL*PLUS)

See **SET**.

■ MEDIA RECOVERY

Media recovery is recovery in the event of hardware failure, which would prevent reading or writing of data and thus operation of the database. *See also* INSTANCE RECOVERY.

MIN

Type   SQL function

Products   All

See also   **COMPUTE**, GROUP FUNCTIONS, **MAX**, Chapter 6

Format

```
MIN([DISTINCT | ALL] value)
```

Description   **MIN** is the minimum of all *values* for a group of rows. **MIN** ignores NULL values. The **DISTINCT** option is not meaningful, since the minimum of all values is identical to the minimum of the distinct values.

MINUS

Type   SQL function

Products   All

See also   **INTERSECT**, QUERY OPERATORS, **UNION**, Chapter 10

Format

```
    select...
MINUS
    select...
```

Description   **MINUS** combines two queries. It returns only those rows from the first **select** statement that are not produced by the second **select** statement (the first **select MINUS** the second **select**). The number of columns and data types must be identical between **select** statements, although the names of the columns do not need to be. The data, however, must be identical in the rows produced for the **MINUS** to reject them. *See* Chapter 10 for a discussion of the important differences and effects of **INTERSECT**, **MINUS**, and **UNION**.

MOD

Type   SQL function

Products   All

See also   NUMBER FUNCTIONS, Chapter 6

NEXT_DAY

See DATE FUNCTIONS.

Format

```
MOD(value, divisor)
```

~~tion~~ MOD divides ~~value by a divisor,~~ and gives the remainder.

NEXTVAL

See PSEUDO-COLUMNS.

NLSSORT

Type   SQL function

Products   All

See also   *ORACLE7 Server Administrator's Guide*

Format

```
NLSSORT(character)
```

Description   **N**ational **L**anguage **S**upport **SORT** gives the collating sequence value (an integer) of the given *character* based on the National Language Support option chosen for the site.

NLS_INITCAP

Type   SQL function

Products   All

See also   CHARACTER FUNCTIONS, **INITCAP**, Chapter 6

Format

```
NLS_INITCAP(number[, nls_parameters])
```

Description   **NLS_INITCAP** is like the **INITCAP** function except with the addition of a parameter string. The *NLS parameters* string, enclosed in single quotation marks, gives a sort sequence for capitalizing special linguistic sequences. You would usually use **INITCAP** with the default sort sequence for the session, but this function lets you specify the exact sort sequence to use.

NLS_LOWER

Type   SQL function

Products   All

See also   CHARACTER FUNCTIONS, **LOWER**, Chapter 6

Format

```
NLS_LOWER(number[, nls_parameters])
```

Description   **NLS_LOWER** is like the **LOWER** function except with the addition of a parameter string. The *NLS parameters* string, enclosed in single quotation marks, gives a sort sequence for lowercasing special linguistic sequences. You would usually use **LOWER** with the default sort sequence for the session, but this function lets you specify the exact sort sequence to use.

NLS_UPPER

Type   SQL function

Products   All

See also   CHARACTER FUNCTIONS, **UPPER**, Chapter 6

Format

```
NLS_UPPER(number[, nls_parameters])
```

Description   **NLS_UPPER** is like the **UPPER** function except with the addition of a parameter string. The *NLS parameters* string, enclosed in single quotation marks, gives a sort sequence for capitalizing special linguistic sequences. You would usually use **UPPER** with the default sort sequence for the session, but this function lets you specify the exact sort sequence to use.

NOAUDIT (Form 1 - Schema Objects)

Type   SQL command

Products   All

See also   **AUDIT**, **CREATE DATABASE LINK**, DATA DICTIONARY VIEWS

Format

```
NOAUDIT { option [,option]... | ALL }
         ON {user.object }
         [ WHENEVER [NOT] SUCCESSFUL ]
```

Description   This form of NOAUDIT stops the audit for an option of the use of a table, view, or synonym. To stop the audit of any table, view, or synonym, you must either own them or have DBA authority. *option* refers to the options described shortly. *user* is the username of the object owner. *object* is a table, view, or synonym. *option* specifies what commands the audit should be stopped for. For a table, options are **ALTER**, **AUDIT**, **COMMENT**, **DELETE**, **GRANT**, **INDEX**, **INSERT**, **LOCK**, **RENAME**, **SELECT**, and **UPDATE**. For procedures, functions, and packages, **EXECUTE** commands can be audited. For snapshots, **SELECT**s can be audited. **GRANT** audits both **GRANT** and **REVOKE** commands. **NOAUDIT GRANT** stops both of them. **ALL** stops the audits of all of these.

ON *object* names the object being audited, and includes a table, view, or a synonym of a table, view or sequence.

For views, **ALTER** and **INDEX** cannot be used. The default options of a view are created by the union of the options of each of the underlying tables plus the DEFAULT options.

For synonyms, the options are the same as tables.

For sequences, the options are **ALTER**, **AUDIT**, **GRANT**, and **SELECT**.

WHENEVER SUCCESSFUL turns off auditing for successful writes to the table. **WHENEVER NOT SUCCESSFUL** turns auditing off for unsuccessful writes to the table. Omitting this optional clause turns off both kinds of auditing.

Both formats commit any pending changes to the database. If remote tables are accessed through a database link, any auditing on the remote system is based on options set there. Auditing information is written to a table named **SYS.AUD$**. *See* Chapter 24 for details on the auditing views.

Examples   The following stops auditing of all attempts at **update** or **delete** on the WORKER table:

```
noaudit update, delete on WORKER;
```

This stops auditing of all unsuccessful access to WORKER:

```
noaudit all on WORKER whenever not successful;
```

NOAUDIT (Form 2 - SQL Statements)

Type   SQL command

Products   All

See also   **AUDIT**, **NOAUDIT** (Form 1), PRIVILEGE

Format

```
NOAUDIT {statement | system_privilege}
        [,{statement | system_privilege}]...
        [BY user[,user]...]
        [ WHENEVER [NOT] SUCCESSFUL ]
```

Description   NOAUDIT stops auditing of SQL statements being audited as a result of the **AUDIT** command (Form 2). It stops auditing either a statement (*see* **AUDIT**) or a statement authorized by a system privilege (*see* PRIVILEGE). If there is a BY clause with a list of users, the command stops the auditing of statements issued by these users. If there is no BY clause, ORACLE stops auditing the statements for all users. The **WHENEVER SUCCESSFUL** option stops auditing only for those statements that successfully complete; **WHENEVER NOT SUCCESSFUL** stops only for those statements that result in an error.

NODE

Node can be either of two definitions:

- In a tree-structured table, a node is one row.
- In a network, a node is the location in the network where a computer is attached.

NONDISPLAYABLE CHARACTERS

Nondisplayable characters are command strings used to achieve certain screen functions (such as Clear Screen or Move Cursor Right) that are not displayed on the screen.

NON-EQUI-JOIN

A non-equi-join is a join condition other than "equals" (=). *See* EQUI-JOIN.

NOT

Type   SQL operator

Products   All

See also   LOGICAL OPERATORS, Chapter 3

Description   **NOT** comes before and reverses the effect of any of these logical operators: **BETWEEN**, **IN**, **LIKE**, and **EXISTS**. **NOT** can also come before NULL, as in **IS NOT NULL**.

NOT EXISTS

Type   SQL operator

Products   All

See also   ANY, ALL, EXISTS, IN, Chapter 10.

Format

```
select ...
where NOT EXISTS (select...);
```

Description   **NOT EXISTS** returns false in a **where** clause if the subquery that follows it returns one or more rows. The **select** clause in the subquery can be a column, a literal, or an asterisk—it doesn't matter. The only part that matters is whether the **where** clause in the subquery will return a row.

Example   **NOT EXISTS** is frequently used to determine which records in one table do not have matching records in another table. The query shown in the following example uses **NOT EXISTS** to exclude from the SKILL table all those records that have matching Skills in the WORKERSKILL table. The result of this query will be the list of all skills that no workers possess.

```
select SKILL.Skill
  from SKILL
 where NOT EXISTS
       (select 'x' from WORKERSKILL
         where WORKERSKILL.Skill = SKILL.Skill);


SKILL
----------------
GRAVE DIGGER
```

NULL (Form 1 - PL/SQL)

Type   PL/SQL statement

Products   PL/SQL

See also   BLOCK STRUCTURE

Format

```
NULL;
```

Description   The NULL statement has nothing to do with NULL values. Its main purpose is to make a section of code more readable by saying, in effect, "do nothing." It also provides a means of having a null block (since PL/SQL requires at least one executable statement between **BEGIN** and **END**). It is usually used as the statement following one (usually the last) of a series of condition tests.

Example

```
IF Age > 65 THEN
   ...
ELSEIF AGE BETWEEN 21 and 65 THEN
   ...
ELSE
   NULL;
ENDIF;
```

NULL (Form 2 - SQL Column Value)

Type   SQL column value

Products   All

See also   **CREATE TABLE**, GROUP FUNCTIONS, INDICATOR VARIABLE, **NVL**, Chapter 3

Description   A NULL value is one that is unknown, irrelevant, or not meaningful. Any ORACLE data type can be NULL. That is, any ORACLE column in a given row can be without a value (unless the table was created with NOT NULL for that column). NULL in a NUMBER data type is not the same as zero.

Few procedural languages directly support the idea of a variable with a NULL or unknown value, although ORACLE and SQL do so easily. In order to extend languages for which ORACLE has developed precompilers to support the NULL concept, an INDICATOR VARIABLE is associated with the host variable, almost like a flag, to indicate whether it is NULL. The host variable and its indicator variable may be referenced and set separately in the host language code, but are always concatenated in SQL or PL/SQL.

You use the **NVL** function to detect the absence of a value for a column, and convert the NULL value into a real value of the data type of the column. For instance, **NVL**(Name,'NOT KNOWN') converts a NULL value in the column Name into the words NOT KNOWN. For a non-NULL value (that is, where a name is present), the **NVL** function simply returns the name. **NVL** works similarly with NUMBERs and DATEs.

Except for **COUNT**(*) and **COMPUTE NUMBER**, group functions ignore null values. Other functions return a null value when a NULL is present in the value or values they are evaluating. Thus, the following example:

```
NULL + 1066 is NULL.
LEAST(NULL,'A','Z') is NULL.
```

Since NULL represents an unknown value, two columns that are each NULL are not equal to each other. Therefore, the equal sign and other logical operators (except for IS NULL and IS NOT NULL) do not work with NULL. For example, this:

```
where Name = NULL
```

is not a valid **where** clause. NULL requires the word IS:

```
where Name IS NULL
```

During **order by** sorts, NULL values always come first when the order is ascending, and last when it is descending.

When NULL values are stored in the database, they are represented with a single byte if they fall between two columns that have real values, and no bytes if they fall at the end of the row (last in the column definition in the **create table**). If some of the columns in a table are likely to often contain NULL values, those columns can be usefully grouped near the end of the **create table** column list; this will save disk space.

NULL values do not appear in indexes, except in the single case where all the values in a cluster key are NULL.

NUMBER DATATYPE

A NUMBER datatype is a standard ORACLE datatype that may contain a number, with or without a decimal point and a sign. Valid values are 0, and positive and negative numbers with magnitude 1.0E-130 to 9.99.. E125.

NUMBER FORMATS

Type   SQL*PLUS command options

Product   SQL*PLUS

See also   **COLUMN**, Chapter 12

Description   These options work with both **set numformat** and the **column format** command.

FORMAT	DEFINITION
9999990	Count of nines or zeroes determines maximum digits that can be displayed.

FORMAT	DEFINITION
999,999,999.99	Commas and decimals will be placed in the pattern shown. Display will be blank if the value is zero.
999990	Displays a zero if the value is zero.
099999	Displays numbers with leading zeros.
$99999	Dollar sign placed in front of every number.
B99999	Display will be blank if value is zero. This is the default.
99999MI	If number is negative, minus sign follows the number. Default is negative sign on left.
99999S	Same as 99999MI.
S99999	If number is negative, minus sign precedes the number; if number is positive, plus sign precedes the number.
99D99	Displays a decimal character in this position.
C99999	Displays the ISO currency character in this position.
L99999	Displays the local currency character in this position.
RN	Displays the number as a roman numeral.
99999PR	Negative numbers displayed surrounded by < and >.
9.999EEEE	Display will be in scientific notation (must be exactly four E's).
999V99	Multiplies number by $10n$ where n is number of digits to right of V. 999V99 turns 1234 into 123400.

NUMBER FUNCTIONS

This is an ordered list of all current number functions in ORACLE's SQL. Each of these is listed elsewhere in this reference under its own name, with its proper format and use. Each can be used as a regular SQL as well as a PL/SQL function, except for **VSIZE**, which is not available in PL/SQL.

FUNCTION	MEANING
value1 + value2	Addition
value1 – value2	Subtraction
*value1 * value2*	Multiplication
value1 / value2	Division
ABS(*value*)	Absolute Value of *value*
CEIL(*value*)	Smallest integer larger than or equal to *value*
COS(*value*)	Cosine of the *value*
COSH(*value*)	Hyperbolic cosine of the *value*
EXP(*value*)	*e* raised to the *value*th power

FUNCTION	MEANING
FLOOR(*value*)	Largest integer smaller than or equal to *value*
LN(*value*)	Natural (base *e*) logarithm of *value*
LOG(*base, value*)	Base *base* logarithm of *value*
MOD(*value,divisor*)	Modulus of *value* divided by *divisor*
NVL(*value,substitute*)	*Substitute* for *value* if *value* is NULL
POWER(*value,exponent*)	*Value* raised to an *exponent*
ROUND(*value,precision*)	Rounding of *value* to *precision*
SIGN(*value*)	1 if *value* is positive, −1 if negative, 0 if zero
SIN(*value*)	Sine of *value*
SINH(*value*)	Hyperbolic sine of *value*
SQRT(*value*)	Square root of *value*
TAN(*value*)	Tangent of *value*
TANH(*value*)	Hyperbolic tangent of *value*
TRUNC(*value,precision*)	*Value* truncated to *precision*
VSIZE(*value*)	Storage size of *value* in ORACLE

NUMWIDTH (SQL*PLUS)

See **SET**.

NVL

Type   SQL function

Products   All, PL/SQL

See also   GROUP FUNCTIONS, NULL, OTHER FUNCTIONS, Chapter 6

Format

```
NVL(value, substitute)
```

Description   If *value* is NULL, this function is equal to *substitute*. If *value* is not NULL, this function is equal to *value*. *value* can be any ORACLE datatype. *Substitute* can be a literal, another column, or an expression, but must be the same data type as *value*.

OBJECT

An object is a named element in the ORACLE database, such as a table, index, synonym, procedure, or trigger.

OBJECT NAMES

These database objects may be given names: tables, views, synonyms, aliases, columns, indexes, users, sequences, tablespaces, and so on. The following rules govern naming objects.

- The name of an object can be from 1 to 30 characters long, except for database names, which are eight characters, and host file names, which are usually eight characters or fewer, plus an extension. Snapshot names may not exceed 23 characters in length, and the name of the base table for a snapshot log may not exceed 24 characters in length.

- A name may not contain a quotation mark.

A name must:

- Begin with a letter
- Contain only the characters A-Z, 0-9, $, #, and _
- Not be an ORACLE reserved word (*see* RESERVED WORDS)
- Not duplicate the name of another database object owned by the same user

Object names are not case sensitive. Object names should follow a sensible naming convention, such as is discussed in Chapter 2 and in more detail in Chapter 27.

OFFLINE REDO LOG

Using the redo log in ARCHIVELOG mode, the offline redo log is a log file that has been archived.

ONLINE BACKUP

Online backup is the ability of ORACLE to archive data while the database is still running. The DBA does not need to shut down the database to archive data. Even data currently being accessed can be archived.

ONLINE REDO LOG

Online redo logs are Redo log files that are not yet archived. They may be available to the instance for recording activity, or have previously been written but are awaiting archiving.

OPEN

Type   PL/SQL statement

Product   PL/SQL

See also   **CLOSE, DECLARE CURSOR, FETCH, LOOP**

Format

```
OPEN cursor [(parameter[,parameter]...]
```

Description   **OPEN** works in conjunction with **DECLARE** cursor and **FETCH**. The **DECLARE** cursor sets up a **SELECT** statement to be executed, and establishes a list of parameters (PL/SQL variables) that are to be used in its **where** clause, but it does not execute the query.

   OPEN cursor, in effect, executes the query in the named cursor and keeps its results in a staging area, where they can be called in, a row at a time, with **FETCH**, and their column values put into local variables with the INTO clause of the **FETCH**. If the cursor **SELECT** statement used parameters, then their actual values are passed to the **SELECT** statement in the parameter list of the **OPEN**. They must match in number and position and have compatible data types.

   There is also an alternative method of associating the values in the **OPEN** with those in the **SELECT** list:

```
DECLARE
    cursor talbot(Moniker, Age) is select ...
BEGIN
    open talbot(new_employee => Moniker, 50 => Age);
```

   Here, new_employee, a PL/SQL variable, loaded perhaps from a data entry screen, is pointed to Moniker, and therefore loads it with whatever is currently in the variable new_employee. Age is loaded with the value 50, and these then become the parameters of the cursor talbot. (*See* **DECLARE CURSOR** for more details on parameters in cursors.)

   You also may combine pointed associations with positional ones, but the positional ones must appear first in the **OPEN**'s list.

   You cannot reopen an open cursor, though you can **CLOSE** it and re**OPEN** it, and you cannot use a cursor for which you have a current **OPEN** statement in a cursor FOR LOOP.

OPEN CURSOR (Embedded SQL)

Type   Embedded SQL command

Products   Precompilers

See also   **CLOSE, DECLARE CURSOR, FETCH, PREPARE**

Format

```
EXEC SQL OPEN cursor
   [USING {:variable[ INDICATOR ]:indicator_variable
          [,:variable[ INDICATOR ]:indicator_variable]...
          DESCRIPTOR descriptor}]
```

Description   *cursor* is the name of a cursor previously named in a **DECLARE CURSOR** statement. The optional USING references either the host variable list of variables that are to be substituted in the statement in the **DECLARE CURSOR**, based on position (the number and type of variables must be the same), or a descriptor name that references the result of a previous DESCRIBE.

OPEN cursor allocates a cursor, defines the active set of rows (the host variables are substituted when the cursor is opened), and positions the cursor just before the first row of the set. No rows are retrieved until a **FETCH** is executed. Host variables do not change once they've been substituted. To change them, you must reopen the cursor (you don't have to **CLOSE** it first).

Example   This example **DECLARE**s a cursor, **OPEN**s it, **FETCH**es rows, and after no more are found, **CLOSE**s the cursor as shown in the following:

```
EXEC SQL at TALBOT declare FRED cursor
     for select ActionDate, Person, Item, Amount
          from LEDGER
          where Item = :Item
            and ActionDate = :ActionDate
            for update of Amount;

EXEC SQL open FRED;

ledger: loop

  EXEC SQL fetch FRED into :Check_Date, :Buyer, :Choice, :Value;

  if sqlca.sqlcode = oracle.error.not_found
    then exit loop ledger;
  end if;
```

```
end loop ledger;

EXEC SQL close FRED;
```

OPEN DATABASE

An open database is a database available for access by users.

OPERATING SYSTEM

An operating system is a computer program that manages the computer's resources and mediates between the computer hardware and programs.

OPERATOR

An operator is a character or reserved word used in an expression to perform an operation, such as addition or comparison, on the elements of the expression. Some examples of operators are * (multiplication), > (greater than comparison), and **ANY** (compares a value to each value returned by a subquery).

OPS$ LOGINS

OPS$ LOGINS are a type of ORACLE username in which OPS$ is prefixed to the user's operating system account ID, to simplify logging in to ORACLE from that ID. *See* the *ORACLE7 Server Administrator's Guide.*

OPTIMIZER

An optimizer is the part of an ORACLE kernel that chooses the best way to use the tables and indexes to complete the request made by a SQL statement.

OR

Type   SQL operator

Products   All

See also   **AND**, Chapter 3

Description   **OR** combines logical expressions so that the result is true if either logical expression is true.

Example   The following will produce data for both KEENE and SAN FRANCISCO:

```
select * from COMFORT
 where City = 'KEENE' OR City = 'SAN FRANCISCO'
```

ORACLE PROGRAM INTERFACE (OPI)

The OPI is the ORACLE half of the Program Interface, which provides security between the user program and the ORACLE program. *See* USER PROGRAM INTERFACE (UPI).

ORDER BY

Type   SQL clause

Products   All

See also   **COLLATION, FROM, GROUP BY, HAVING, SELECT, WHERE**

Format

```
ORDER BY { expression [,expression]... |
           position [,position]... }
           alias [,alias]... }
[ ASC | DESC ]
```

Description   The **ORDER BY** clause causes ORACLE to sort the results of a query before they are displayed. This can be done either by *expression*, which can be a simple column name or a complex set of functions, an *alias* (*see* Note), or a column *position* in the **select** clause (*see* Note). Rows are ordered first by the first expression or position, then by the second, and so on, based on the collating sequence of the host. If **ORDER BY** is not specified, the order in which rows are selected from a table is indeterminate, and may change from one query to the next.

NOTE
In ORACLE7.1 and above, you can use column aliases in the ORDER BY clause.

NOTE
As of ORACLE7.1, the use of column positions in ORDER BY clauses should be discontinued; this feature is no longer part of the SQL standard. ORACLE7.1 still supports the use of column positions in ORDER BY clauses, but that usage is not guaranteed to be supported in future releases. Use column aliases instead.

ASC or DESC specifies ascending or descending order, and may follow each expression, position, or alias in the **ORDER BY**. Null values precede ascending and follow descending rows in ORACLE7.

ORDER BY follows any other clauses except FOR UPDATE OF.

If **ORDER BY** and **DISTINCT** are both specified, the **ORDER BY** clause may only refer to columns or expressions that are in the **SELECT** clause.

When the **UNION**, **INTERSECT**, or **MINUS** operator is used, **ORDER BY** must use column positions, not column names, in spite of the SQL standard changes cited in the Note above.

Only CHAR, VARCHAR2, NUMBER, and DATE data types—and the special data type RowID—can appear in an **ORDER BY**.

Example

```
select Name, Age from WORKER
 order by Age;
```

OTHER FUNCTIONS

This is an alphabetical list of all current functions in ORACLE's SQL that do not readily fall into any other function category. Each of these is listed elsewhere in this reference under its own name, with its proper format and use.

```
DUMP( string [,format [,start [,length] ] ] )
```

DUMP displays the value of *string* in internal data format, in ASCII, octal, decimal, hex, or character format.

```
NVL(value, substitute)
```

If *value* is NULL, the **NVL** function is equal to *substitute*. **NVL** also can be used as a PL/SQL function.

```
VSIZE(expression)
```

VSIZE tells how many bytes ORACLE needs in order to store the *expression* in its database.

OUTER JOIN

See JOIN for a detailed explanation.

PACKAGE

A package is a PL/SQL object that groups PL/SQL types, variables, SQL cursors, exceptions, procedures, and functions. Each package has a specification and a body. The specification shows the objects you can access when you use the package. The body fully defines all the objects and can contain additional objects used only for the internal workings. You can change the body (for example, by adding procedures to the package) without invalidating any object that uses the package.

   See **CREATE PACKAGE** and **CREATE PACKAGE BODY**. *See also* CURSOR, EXCEPTION, FUNCTION, TABLE (PL/SQL), RECORD (PL/SQL), and PROCEDURE.

PAGE

A page is a unit of disk storage. *See* BLOCK.

PAGESIZE (SQL*PLUS)

See **SET**.

PARAMETER

A parameter is a value, a column name, or an expression, usually following a function or module name, specifying additional functions or controls that should be observed by the function or module. *See* PARAMETERS for an example.

PARAMETERS

Type   SQL*PLUS argument

Product   SQL*PLUS

See also   **&, &&, ACCEPT, DEFINE**, Chapter 14

Description   Parameters allow the execution of a start file with values passed on the command line. These are simply spaced apart following the name of the start file. Within the file they are referenced by the order in which they appeared on the command line. &1 is the first, &2 the second, and so on. Aside from this, the rules for use are the same as for variables loaded using **DEFINE** or **ACCEPT**, and may be used in SQL statements in the same way.

There is one limitation, however. There is no way to pass a multiple word argument to a single variable. Each variable can take only one word, date, or number. Attempting to solve this by putting the parameters in quotes on the command line results in the words being concatenated.

Example   Suppose you have a start file named **fred.sql** that contains this SQL:

```
select Name, Age
  from WORKER
 where Age > &1;
```

Starting it with this command line:

```
start fred.sql 21
```

produces a report of all workers who are older than 21 years of age.

PARENT

In tree-structured data, a parent is a node that has another node as a descendent, or child.

PARENT QUERY

The parent query is the outermost query (the one that displays a result) in a main query containing a subquery. *See* MAIN QUERY.

PARENTHESES

See LOGICAL OPERATORS and PL/SQL KEY WORDS AND SYMBOLS.

PARSE

Parsing is the mapping of a SQL statement to a cursor. At parse time, several validation checks are made, such as, do all referenced objects exist, are grants proper, and is statement syntax correct? Also, decisions regarding execution and optimization are made, such as which indexes will be used.

PASSWORD

A password is a set of characters that you must enter when you connect to your host computers operating system or to an ORACLE database. Passwords should be kept confidential.

PAUSE (Form 1 - SQL*PLUS)

See **SET**.

PAUSE (Form 2 - SQL*PLUS)

Type   SQL*PLUS command

Product   SQL*PLUS

See also   **ACCEPT**, **PROMPT**, Chapter 4

Format

```
PAU[SE] [text];
```

Description   **PAUSE** is similar to **PROMPT**, except **PAUSE** first displays an empty line, then a line containing *text*, then waits for the user to press RETURN. If *text* is not entered, **PAUSE** displays two empty lines, then waits for user to press RETURN.

NOTE
PAUSE waits for a RETURN from the terminal even if the source of command input has been redirected to be from a file, which means a start file with SET TERMOUT OFF could hang, waiting for a RETURN, with no message as to why it was waiting (or that it was waiting). Use **PAUSE** with caution.

Example

```
prompt Report Complete.
pause Press RETURN to continue.
```

PCTFREE

PCTFREE is a portion of the data block that is not filled by rows as they are inserted into a table, but is reserved for later updates made to the rows in that block.

PCTUSED

PCTUSED is the percentage of space in a data block, which ORACLE attempts to fill before it allocates another block.

PHYSICAL BLOCK

A physical block is a storage location on a disk, often 512 bytes. A physical block is different from an ORACLE block; *see* BLOCK. Different computers have different size physical blocks.

PL/SQL Key Words and Symbols

These key words and symbols, each separately listed in this Alphabetical Reference, are directly or indirectly related to PL/SQL.

SYMBOLS	DESCRIPTION
( )	Parentheses, used to control precedence.
+ − * / **	Addition, subtraction (or negation), multiplication, division and exponentiation.
- -	Single-line comment. *See* **COMMENT** and - -.
/* */	Multiple-line comment. *See* **COMMENT** and /*.
;	Terminator. *See* SQLTERMINATOR.
%	Prefix for PL/SQL attributes.
,	Comma, to separate a list if items.
.	Period. Separates portions of compound identifiers.
..	Range operator. *See* LOOP.
@	"At sign," used to reference remote databases.
'	Single quote. Delimits a literal character string.
"	Double quote. Delimits a literal character string to be a legal identifier. Not recommended.

SYMBOLS	DESCRIPTION
[]	Used only internally by ORACLE, or to bracket options in showing the format of a command.
:	Colon. Prefixes a host variable.
<> !=~= ^=	All mean not equal in SQL and PL/SQL logic.
< <= > >=	Less than, less than or equal to, greater than, greater than or equal to. Used in SQL and PL/SQL logic.
=>	Association operator.
:=	Assignment. Assigns a value to a PL/SQL or host variable "to." Used in **FOR LOOP**.
¦¦	Concatenation
<< >>	Delimiters for a label in a **LOOP**, **GOTO**, or **BLOCK**.

KEYWORDS

%FOUND	CREATE TRIGGER
%ISOPEN	CURSOR
%NOTFOUND	DECLARE CURSOR
%ROWCOUNT	DECLARE EXCEPTION
%ROWTYPE	DECLARE VARIABLE
%TYPE	DELETE
ALTER FUNCTION	END
ALTER PACKAGE	EXCEPTION
ALTER TRIGGER	EXCEPTION_INIT
BEGIN	EXIT
BLOCK STRUCTURE	FETCH
CLOSE	FOR
COMMIT	GOTO
CREATE FUNCTION	IF
CREATE PACKAGE	INDICATOR VARIABLE
CREATE PACKAGE BODY	INSERT
CREATE PROCEDURE	LABEL

KEYWORDS

LOCK TABLE	SET TRANSACTION
LOOP	SQL CURSOR
NULL	SQLCODE
OPEN	SQLERRM
PACKAGE	SQLTERMINATOR
PRAGMA	TABLE
PROCEDURE	TERMINATOR
RAISE	TRIGGER
RECORD	UPDATE
ROLLBACK	VARIABLE DECLARATION
SAVEPOINT	WHILE
SELECT ... INTO	

In addition, the following functions, which are identical in format to the SQL functions of the same names, may be used directly in a PL/SQL statement, thus avoiding a SQL call to the database. To learn the proper format and operation of each of these, look them up in this alphabetical reference under their own names:

ABS	GREATEST_LB
ADD_MONTHS	HEXTORAW
ASCII	INITCAP
CEIL	INSTR
CHARTOROWID	INSTRB
CHR	LAST_DAY
CONCAT	LEAST
CONVERT	LEAST_UB
COS	LENGTH
COSH	LENGTHB
DECODE	LN
DUMP	LOG
EXP	LOWER
FLOOR	LPAD
GREATEST	LTRIM

MOD	SQRT
MONTHS_BETWEEN	SUBSTR
NEW_TIME	SUBSTRB
NEXT_DAY	SYSDATE
NLS_INITCAP	TAN
NLS_LOWER	TANH
NLS_UPPER	TO_BINARY_INTEGER
NLSSORT	TO_CHAR
NVL	TO_DATE
POWER	TO_LABEL
RAWTOHEX	TO_MULTI_BYTE
REPLACE	TO_NUMBER
ROUND	TO_SINGLE_BYTE
ROWIDTOCHAR	TO_VARCHAR2
RPAD	TRANSLATE
RTRIM	TRUNC
SIGN	UPPER
SIN	USERENV
SINH	VSIZE
SOUNDEX	

▇ PMON PROCESS

The **P**rocess **MON**itor is a background process used for recovery when a process accessing a database fails. *See* BACKGROUND PROCESS.

▇ POWER

Type   SQL command

Products   All, PL/SQL

See also   **SQRT**, Chapter 6

Format

```
POWER(value,exponent)
```

Description   **POWER** is *value* raised to an *exponent*.

Example

```
POWER(2,4) = 16
```

PRAGMA

A pragma statement is a directive to the compiler, rather than a piece of executable code. Even though a pragma statement looks like executable code, and appears in a program (such as a PL/SQL block), it is not actually executable and doesn't appear as a part of the execution code of that block. Rather, it gives instructions to the compiler. *See* **EXCEPTION_INIT**.

PRECEDENCE

Type   Execution order rules

Products   All

See also   LOGICAL OPERATORS, QUERY OPERATORS, Chapter 10

The following operators are listed in descending order of precedence. Operators with equal precedence are on the same line. Operators of equal precedence are evaluated in succession from left to right. All **AND**s are evaluated before any **OR**. Each of these is listed and described separately under its own symbol or name in this alphabetical reference.

OPERATOR	FUNCTION
-	SQL*PLUS command continuation. Continues a command on the following line.
&	Prefix for parameters in a SQL*PLUS start file. Words are substituted for &1, &2, and so on. *See* START.
& &&	Prefix for a substitution in a SQL command in SQL*PLUS. SQL*PLUS will prompt for a value if an undefined & or **&&** variable is found. **&&** also defines the variable and saves the value; '**&**' does not. *See* & and **&&**, **DEFINE**, and **ACCEPT**.
:	Prefix for a host variable in PL/SQL.
.	Variable separator, used in SQL*PLUS to separate the variable name from a suffix, so that the suffix is not considered a part of the variable name.
( )	Surrounds subqueries or lists of columns.

OPERATOR	FUNCTION
'	Surrounds a literal, such as a character string or date constant. To use a ' in a string constant, use two ' marks (not a double quotation mark).
"	Surrounds a table or column alias that contains special characters or a space.
"	Surrounds literal text in a date format clause of TO_CHAR.
@	Precedes a database name in a COPY, or a link name in a **from** clause.
( )	Overrides normal operator precedence.
+ −	Prefix sign (positive or negative) for a number or number expression.
* /	Multiplication and division.
+ −	Addition and subtraction.
¦¦	Char value concatenation.
NOT	Reverses result of an expression.
AND	True if both conditions are true.
OR	True if either condition is true.
UNION	Returns all distinct rows from both of two queries.
INTERSECT	Returns all matching distinct rows from two queries.
MINUS	Returns all distinct rows in first query that are not in the second.

PRECOMPILER

A precompiler program reads specially structured source code, and writes a modified (precompiled) source program file that a normal compiler can read.

PREDICATE

The predicate is the **where** clause and, more explicitly, a selection criteria clause based on one of the operators (=, !=, **IS**, **IS NOT**, >, >=) and containing no **AND**, **OR**, or **NOT**.

PREPARE (Embedded SQL)

Type   SQL command

Product   Precompilers

See also   **CLOSE, DECLARE, CURSOR, FETCH, OPEN**

Format

```
EXEC SQL PREPARE statement_name FROM {:string | text}
```

Description   **PREPARE** parses SQL in the host variable *:string* or the literal *text*. It assigns a *statement_name* as a reference to the SQL. If the *statement_name* has been used previously, this reference replaces it. The SQL is a select statement, and may include a **for update of** clause. *:string* is not the actual name of the host variable used, but a placeholder. **OPEN CURSOR** assigns input host variables in its **using** clause, and **FETCH** assigns output host variables in its **into** clause, based on position. A statement only needs to be **PREPARE**d once. It can then be executed multiple times.

Example

```
query_string : string(1..100)
get(query_string);

EXEC SQL prepare FRED from :query_string;
EXEC SQL execute FRED;
```

PRIMARY KEY

The primary key is the column(s) used to uniquely identify each row of a table.

PRINT

Type   SQL*PLUS command

Product   SQL*PLUS

See also   BIND VARIABLE, **VARIABLE**

Format

```
PRINT variable
```

Description   Displays the current value of the specified variable (which is created via the **VARIABLE** command).

PRINTDEF

Type   Utility report program

Product   SQL*REPORTWRITER

See also   **DUMPREP**, **GENREP**, **LOADREP**, **RUNREP**, SQL*PLUS, SQLREP, SQL*REPORTWRITER, **TERMDEF**

Format

```
PRINTDEF [PRINTER=]printer [OUTFILE=]outfile [[PDFILE=]pdfile]
```

Description   **PRINTDEF** creates a new printer definition in the outfile from a description in the pdfile (which defaults to **printdef.dat**). *See the SQL*ReportWriter Reference Manual for details.*

PRIOR

See **CONNECT BY**.

PRIVILEGE

A privilege is a permission granted to an ORACLE user to execute some action. In ORACLE, no user can execute any action without having the privilege to do so.

There are two kinds of privileges: system privileges and object privileges. System privileges extend permission to execute various data definition and data control commands such as **CREATE TABLE** or **ALTER USER**, or even to log on to the database. Object privileges extend permission to operate on a particular named database object.

System privileges in ORACLE7 include CREATE, ALTER, and DROP privileges for the various **CREATE**, **ALTER**, and **DROP** commands. Privileges with the keyword **ANY** in them mean that the user can exercise the privilege on any schema for which the privilege has been granted, not just his or her own schema. The standard privileges in the list following just give permission to execute the indicated command, and don't require further explanation. Some of the privileges aren't intuitively clear; these are explained here.

PRIVILEGE	PERMISSION TO
ALTER ANY CLUSTER	ALTER CLUSTER
ALTER ANY INDEX	ALTER INDEX
ALTER ANY PROCEDURE	ALTER PROCEDURE, ALTER FUNCTION, ALTER PACKAGE
ALTER ANY ROLE	ALTER ROLE
ALTER ANY SEQUENCE	ALTER SEQUENCE
ALTER ANY SNAPSHOT	ALTER SNAPSHOT
ALTER ANY TABLE	ALTER TABLE
ALTER ANY TRIGGER	ALTER TRIGGER
ALTER DATABASE	ALTER DATABASE
ALTER PROFILE	ALTER PROFILE
ALTER RESOURCE COST	ALTER RESOURCE COST
ALTER ROLLBACK SEGMENT	ALTER ROLLBACK SEGMENT
ALTER SESSION	ALTER SESSION
ALTER SYSTEM	ALTER SYSTEM
ALTER TABLESPACE	ALTER TABLESPACE
ALTER USER	ALTER USER
ANALYZE ANY	ANALYZE
AUDIT ANY	AUDIT (FORM 1)
AUDIT SYSTEM	AUDIT (FORM 2)
BECOME USER	Allow import of objects from any schema
BACKUP ANY TABLE	Allow export of objects from any schema
COMMENT ANY TABLE	COMMENT
CREATE ANY CLUSTER	CREATE CLUSTER
CREATE ANY INDEX	CREATE INDEX
CREATE ANY PROCEDURE	CREATE PROCEDURE
CREATE ANY SEQUENCE	CREATE SEQUENCE
CREATE ANY SNAPSHOT	CREATE SNAPSHOT
CREATE ANY SYNONYM	CREATE SYNONYM
CREATE ANY TABLE	CREATE TABLE
CREATE ANY TRIGGER	CREATE TRIGGER
CREATE ANY VIEW	CREATE VIEW
CREATE CLUSTER	CREATE CLUSTER

PRIVILEGE	PERMISSION TO
CREATE DATABASE LINK	CREATE DATABASE LINK
CREATE PROCEDURE	CREATE PROCEDURE, CREATE FUNCTION, CREATE PACKAGE
CREATE PROFILE	CREATE PROFILE
CREATE PUBLIC DATABASE LINK	CREATE PUBLIC DATABASE LINK
CREATE PUBLIC SYNONYM	CREATE PUBLIC SYNONYM
CREATE ROLE	CREATE ROLE
CREATE ROLLBACK SEGMENT	CREATE ROLLBACK SEGMENT
CREATE SESSION	CREATE SESSION (logon to database)
CREATE SEQUENCE	CREATE SEQUENCE
CREATE SNAPSHOT	CREATE SNAPSHOT
CREATE SYNONYM	CREATE SYNONYM
CREATE TABLE	CREATE TABLE
CREATE TABLESPACE	CREATE TABLESPACE
CREATE TRIGGER	CREATE TRIGGER
CREATE USER	CREATE USER
CREATE VIEW	CREATE VIEW
DELETE ANY TABLE	DELETE (from tables or views)
DROP ANY CLUSTER	DROP CLUSTER
DROP ANY INDEX	DROP INDEX
DROP ANY PROCEDURE	DROP PROCEDURE, DROP FUNCTION, DROP PACKAGE
DROP ANY ROLE	DROP ROLE
DROP ANY SEQUENCE	DROP SEQUENCE
DROP ANY SNAPSHOT	DROP SNAPSHOT
DROP ANY SYNONYM	DROP SYNONYM
DROP ANY TABLE	DROP TABLE
DROP ANY TRIGGER	DROP TRIGGER
DROP ANY VIEW	DROP VIEW
DROP PROFILE	DROP PROFILE
DROP PUBLIC DATABASE LINK	DROP PUBLIC DATABASE LINK
DROP PUBLIC SYNONYM	DROP PUBLIC SYNONYM
DROP ROLLBACK SEGMENT	DROP ROLLBACK SEGMENT

PRIVILEGE	PERMISSION TO
DROP TABLESPACE	DROP TABLESPACE
DROP USER	DROP USER
EXECUTE ANY PROCEDURE	Allow execution of any function or procedure or reference to any public package variable
FORCE ANY TRANSACTION	Allow forcing of commit or rollback of any in-doubt transaction (*see* TWO-PHASE COMMIT)
FORCE TRANSACTION	Allow forcing of commit or rollback of user's own in-doubt transactions
GRANT ANY PRIVILEGE	GRANT system privilege
GRANT ANY ROLE	GRANT a role
INSERT ANY TABLE	INSERT
LOCK ANY TABLE	LOCK TABLE
MANAGE TABLESPACE	Allows taking tablespaces on and off line and tablespace backups
READUP	Allows query of data with a higher access class than the current session possesses (Trusted ORACLE7)
RESTRICTED SESSION	Allows logon after instance startup in restricted access mode by SQL*DBA
SELECT ANY SEQUENCE	SELECT from sequences
SELECT ANY TABLE	SELECT
UNLIMITED TABLESPACE	Allows overriding of assigned quotas
UPDATE ANY TABLE	UPDATE
WRITEDOWN	Allows CREATE, ALTER, DROP, INSERT, UPDATE, or DELETE of objects with access classes lower than the current session's (Trusted ORACLE7)
WRITEUP	Allows CREATE, ALTER, DROP, INSERT, UPDATE, or DELETE of objects with access classes higher than the current session's (Trusted ORACLE7)

Object privileges apply only to certain kinds of objects. The following table shows the relationships. The REFERENCES privilege allows a user to create a constraint that refers to the base table.

PRIVILEGE	TABLES	VIEWS	SEQUENCES	PROCEDURES FUNCTIONS PACKAGES	SNAPSHOTS
ALTER	X		X		X
DELETE	X	X			
EXECUTE				X	
INDEX	X				
INSERT	X	X			
REFERENCES	X				
SELECT	X	X	X		X
UPDATE	X	X			

As shown in this table, you can select from tables, views, sequences, or snapshots (that is, the local view named after the snapshot; *see* Chapter 23).

PRO*ADA

PRO*ADA is an extension to Ada that lets you develop user exits and other programs that access the ORACLE database. A precompiler converts PRO*ADA code into normal Ada code, which can then be compiled.

PRO*C

PRO*C is an extension to C that lets you develop user exits and other programs that access the ORACLE database. A precompiler converts PRO*C code into normal C code, which can then be compiled.

PRO*COBOL

PRO*COBOL is an extension to COBOL that lets you develop user exits and other programs that access the ORACLE database. A precompiler converts PRO*COBOL code into normal COBOL code, which can then be compiled.

PRO*FORTRAN

PRO*FORTRAN is an extension to FORTRAN that lets you develop user exits and other programs that access the ORACLE database. A precompiler converts PRO*FORTRAN code into normal FORTRAN code, which can then be compiled.

PRO*PASCAL

PRO*PASCAL is an extension to Pascal that lets you develop user exits and other programs that access the ORACLE database. A precompiler converts PRO*PASCAL code into normal Pascal code, which can then be compiled.

PRO*PL/I

PRO*PL/I is an extension to PL/I that lets you develop user exits and other programs that access the ORACLE database. A precompiler converts PRO*PL/I code into pure PL/I code.

PROCEDURE

A procedure is a set of instructions (usually combining SQL and PL/SQL commands) saved for calling and repeated execution. *See* **CREATE PROCEDURE**.

PRODUCT_USER_PROFILE

A PRODUCT_USER_PROFILE is a SYSTEM table in ORACLE used to restrict use of individual ORACLE products, by disabling one or more commands available in the product. *See* Appendix E in *SQL*Plus User's Guide and Reference*.

PROFILE

A profile is a collection of settings in ORACLE7 that limit database resources. *See* **CREATE PROFILE**.

PROMPT

Type   SQL*PLUS command

Product   SQL*PLUS

See also   ACCEPT

Format

```
PROMPT [text]
```

Description   Displays the *text* to the user's screen. If no *text* is specified, then a blank line will be displayed. To display a variable, *see* **PRINT**.

PSEUDO-COLUMNS

Type   Definitions

Products   All

Description   A pseudo-column is a "column" that yields a value when selected, but which is not an actual column of the table. An example is RowID or SysDate. Here are the current ORACLE pseudo-columns:

PSEUDO-COLUMN	VALUE RETURNED
Sequence.CurrVal	Current value for this sequence name.
Level	Equal to 1 for a root node, 2 for a child of a root, and so on. Tells basically how far down a tree you've traveled.
sequence.**NextVal**	Next value for this sequence name. Also increments the sequence.
NULL	A null value.
RowID	Returns the row identifier for a row. Use the RowID in the UPDATE ... WHERE and SELECT ... FOR UPDATE. This guarantees that only a certain row is updated, and no others.
RowNum	Returns the sequence number in which a row was returned when selected from a table. The first row RowNum is 1, the second is 2, and so on. An order **by** will affect the sequence of the ROWNUMs. *See* **RowNum** in this Alphabetical Reference and Chapter 15 for a discussion.

PSEUDO-COLUMN	VALUE RETURNED
SysDate	The current date and time.
UID	User ID. A unique number assigned to each user.
User	Name by which current user is known.

PUBLIC

Public can be either of two definitions:

- Something public can be visible or available to all users. Synonyms and database links can be public. In ORACLE7, a user must have CREATE PUBLIC SYNONYM or CREATE PUBLIC DATABASE LINK privilege. Users may GRANT PUBLIC access to their own objects.

- A group to which every database user belongs—the name of that group.

PUBLIC SYNONYM

A public synonym is a synonym for a database object that a user with CREATE PUBLIC SYNONYM privilege has created for use by all ORACLE users.

QUERY

A query is a SQL instruction to retrieve data from one or more tables or views. Queries begin with the SQL keyword **select**.

QUERY OPERATORS

The following is an alphabetical list of all current query operators in ORACLE's SQL. Each of these is listed elsewhere in this reference under its own name, with its proper format and use. *See also* Chapter 10.

OPERATOR	PURPOSE
UNION	Returns all distinct rows from both of two queries.
UNION ALL	Returns all rows from both of two queries.
INTERSECT	Returns all matching distinct rows from two queries.

OPERATOR	PURPOSE
MINUS	Returns all distinct rows in first query that are not in the second.

QUIT

Type   SQL*PLUS command

Product   SQL*PLUS

See also   **COMMIT, DISCONNECT, EXIT, SET AUTOCOMMIT, START**

Format

```
QUIT
```

Description   **QUIT** ends a SQL*PLUS session and returns the user to an operating system, calling program, or menu.

QUOTA

A quota is a resource limit. Quotas can limit the amount of storage used by each user of the database. *See* **CREATE USER** and **ALTER USER**.

RAISE

Type   PL/SQL statement

Products   PL/SQL

See also   **DECLARE EXCEPTION, EXCEPTION, EXCEPTION_INIT**

Format

```
RAISE [exception]
```

Description   **RAISE** names the exception flag you want to raise, based on a condition that is being tested. The exception must either be one you've explicitly **DECLARE**d, or an internal system exception such as DIVIDE_BY_ZERO (*see* EXCEPTION for a complete list).

A **RAISE** statement causes control to be transferred to the EXCEPTION section of the current block, where you must test to see which exception was raised. If no EXCEPTION section is present, control is passed to the nearest EXCEPTION section of an enclosing block (basically backward through the nesting of the blocks). If no logic is found to handle the exception, control is passed from the PL/SQL to the calling program or environment with an unhandled exception error. (The use of OTHERS can avoid this. *See* EXCEPTION.)

RAISE without an explicitly named exception can only be used in one circumstance: within an EXCEPTION section, in order to force the current exception to be handled by an enclosing block's EXCEPTION section, rather than the current one. If, for instance, a NOT_LOGGED_ON error had occurred, and your local EXCEPTION section says this:

```
when not_logged_on
    then raise;
```

it would pass control back to the EXCEPTION section of the next enclosing block that had one, or to the program if none were found. That EXCEPTION block could also test for NOT_LOGGED_ON. The benefit here is that for a certain class of errors, particularly where the recovery, tracing, or error-logging steps you want to take may be extensive, you can set every nested block's EXCEPTION section to simply hand the EXCEPTION backward to a single spot for disposition.

RAW DATATYPE

A RAW column contains binary data in whatever form the host computer stores it. Raw columns are useful for storing binary (non-character) data.

Maximum width for RAW columns is 255 in ORACLE7.

RAWTOHEX

Type   SQL command

Products   All

See also   **HEXTORAW**

Format

```
RAWTOHEX(binary_string)
```

Description   **RAW TO HEX**adecimal changes a string of binary numbers to a character string of hex numbers.

RDBMS

See RELATIONAL DATABASE MANAGEMENT SYSTEM.

READ CONSISTENCY

Read consistency is a state that guarantees that all data encountered by a statement/transaction is a consistent set throughout the duration of the statement/transaction. *See* **SET TRANSACTION**.

RECORD

Record is a synonym for row.

RECORD (PL/SQL)

Type   PL/SQL data type

Products   All

See also   TABLE (PL/SQL), DATA TYPES

Format

```
TYPE new_type IS RECORD
    (field {type ¦ table.column%TYPE}[NOT NULL]
    [,field {type ¦ table.column%TYPE}[NOT NULL]...]);
```

Description   A RECORD declaration declares a new type that can then be used to declare variables of that type. The individual components of the record are fields, and each has its own data type. That data type can either be one of the standard PL/SQL data types (including another RECORD but not a TABLE), or it can be a reference to the type of a particular column in a specific table. Each field also may have a NOT NULL qualifier that specifies that the field must always have a non-null value.

You can refer to the individual fields in a record using dot notation.

Example

```
type SkillRecord is record(name char(25), skill
    WORKERSKILL.Skill%TYPE);
SkillRecord MySkill;
```

```
MySkill.Name = 'DICK JONES';
MySkill.Skill = 'SMITHY';
```

RECORD LOCKING

Record locking protects two users from updating the same row of data at the same time.

RECOVER

Type   SQL command

Products   All

See also   **ALTER DATABASE**, SQL*DBA, *ORACLE7 Server Administrator's Guide*

Format

```
RECOVER [AUTOMATIC] [FROM location]
{{[DATABASE]
     {UNTIL CANCEL :
      UNTIL TIME date :
      UNTIL CHANGE integer :
      USING BACKUP CONTROLFILE]}} :
TABLESPACE tablespace[,tablespace]... :
  DATAFILE filename[,filename]... :
   LOGFILE filename :
  CONTINUE [DEFAULT] :
    CANCEL}
```

Description   The **RECOVER** clause of the **ALTER DATABASE** command recovers a database using various options. **AUTOMATIC** recovery generates the redo log file names automatically during recovery. The **FROM** clause specifies the location of the archived redo log file group and must be a fully qualified filename. The default is set by the initialization parameter LOG_ARCHIVE_DEST.

The **DATABASE** option recovers the entire database and is the default. The **UNTIL CANCEL** alternative recovers the database until you cancel the recovery with the **CANCEL** option. The **UNTIL TIME** alternative recovers up to a specified date. The **UNTIL CHANGE** alternative recovers up to a *system change number* (a unique number assigned to each transaction) specified by an integer. The **USING BACKUP CONTROLFILE** alternative recovers by applying the redo log in a backup controlfile.

The **TABLESPACE** option recovers only the specified tablespaces. The **DATAFILE** option recovers only the specified data files. The **LOGFILE** option applies the specified redo log file. The **CONTINUE** option continues applying the redo log file. **CANCEL** terminates the recovery.

RECSEP (SQL*PLUS)

See **SET**.

RECSEPCHAR (SQL*PLUS)

See **SET**.

RECURSIVE CALLS

A recursive call is a nested invocation of the RDBMS; for example, auditing information is recorded in system tables using a recursive call. That is, during a normal database operation, such as an **update**, another database operation is executed to write log, auditing, or other vital information *about* the normal database operation underway.

REDO LOG

A redo log is a sequential log of actions that are to be reapplied to the database if they did not get written to disk. The log always consists of at least two files; one is optionally being spooled while the other is being written. When the one currently being written fills, the next one is reused.

REDO LOG SEQUENCE NUMBER

The redo log sequence number is a number used to identify a redo log, used when applying the log file for recovery.

REFERENTIAL INTEGRITY

Referential integrity is the property that guarantees that values from one column depend on values from another column. This property is enforced through integrity constraints. *See* INTEGRITY CONSTRAINT.

REFERENTIAL INTEGRITY RULE

A referential integrity rule is an integrity constraint that enforces referential integrity.

RELATION

See TABLE and Chapter 1.

RELATIONAL DATABASE MANAGEMENT SYSTEM

An RDBMS is a computer program for general-purpose data storage and retrieval that organizes data into tables consisting of one or more units of information (rows), each containing the same set of data items (columns). ORACLE is a relational database management system.

RELATIONAL OPERATOR

A relational operator is a symbol used in search criteria to indicate a comparison between two values, such as the equal sign in "where Amount = .10". Only those rows are returned (fetched) for which the comparison results in TRUE.

REMARK

Type   SQL*PLUS command

Product   SQL*PLUS

See also   /* */, - -, DOCUMENT, Chapter 4

Format

```
REM[ARK] text
```

Description **REMARK** begins a single line of remarks, usually documentation, in a start file. It is not interpreted as a command. **REMARK** cannot appear within a SQL statement.

Example

```
REM Reduce the default column width for this data field:
column ActionDate format a6 trunc
```

REMOTE COMPUTER

A remote computer refers to any computer in a network other than one's own host computer.

REMOTE DATABASE

A remote database is one that resides on a remote computer, in particular, one that you use through a database link.

RENAME

Type SQL command

Products All

See also COPY, CREATE SYNONYM, CREATE TABLE, CREATE VIEW

Format

```
RENAME old TO new
```

Description RENAME changes the name of a table, view, or synonym from its old name to a new one. No quotes are used around the names, and the new name must be neither a reserved word nor the name of an existing object for the user.

Example The following changes the WORKER table to the EMPLOYEE table:

```
rename WORKER to EMPLOYEE;
```

REPEATABLE READ

Repeatable read is a feature in which multiple subsequent queries return a consistent set of results, as though changes to the data were suspended until all the queries finished.

REPLACE

Type   SQL function

Products   All, PL/SQL

See also   CHARACTER FUNCTIONS, **TRANSLATE**

Format

```
REPLACE(string,if,then)
```

Description   **REPLACE** replaces a character or characters in a string with 0 or more characters. *if* is a character or characters. Every time it appears in *string*, it is replaced by the contents of *then*.

Example

```
REPLACE('ADAH','A','BLAH') = BLAHDBLAHH
REPLACE('GEORGE','GE',null) = OR
REPLACE('BOB','BO','TA') = TAB
```

RESERVED WORDS

Type   Object naming restriction

Products   Described in this section

See also   OBJECT NAMES

Description   This is an exhaustive list of the reserved words in ORACLE. A reserved word is one that has a special meaning to SQL, and therefore may not be used as the name of an object. Contrast this to keyword, which may be used as an object name, but may become a reserved word in the future. Not every word is reserved in all products, so this list is structured to show which products reserve which words. The following are the keys:

- **V6SQL** means this word is *reserved* in the SQL language as of ORACLE version 6. SQL reserved words usually cannot be used in any ORACLE product, including those not explicitly listed here.

- **V6SQLk** means this word is a *keyword* in ORACLE version 6, but is not yet reserved. You can use it for object names, but this is highly discouraged, as it will probably become a reserved word with a later release. SQL reserved words usually cannot be used in any ORACLE product.

- **V7SQL** means this word is *reserved* in the SQL language as of ORACLE7. If there is no V6SQL entry for this word, then it became reserved as of ORACLE7. SQL reserved words usually cannot be used in any ORACLE product, including those not explicitly listed here.

- **V7SQLk** means this word is a *keyword* in ORACLE7, but is not yet reserved. You can use it for object names, but this is highly discouraged, as it will probably become a reserved word with a later release. SQL reserved words cannot usually be used in any ORACLE product.

- **ANSI** means this word is *reserved* in the ANSI SQL standard.

- **PLSQL** means this word is *reserved* in ORACLE7 PL/SQL, whether it appears in a SQL*FORM, in SQL*PLUS, in a precompiler program, or anywhere else. It's generally not a good idea to use SQL reserved words or keywords as PL/SQL names either.

- **LOAD** means this word is a *reserved* word in SQL*LOADER.

- **V2FRM** means this word is a *reserved* word in SQL*Forms V2.

- **V3FRM** means this word is a *reserved* word in SQL*Forms V3.

ABORT						PLSQL	
ACCEPT						PLSQL	
ACCESS	V7SQL	V6SQL	ANSI	V2FRM	V3FRM	PLSQL	LOAD
ADD	V7SQL	V6SQL	ANSI	V2FRM	V3FRM	PLSQL	LOAD
ADMIN	V7SQLk						
AFTER	V7SQLk						
ALL	V7SQL	V6SQL	ANSI	V2FRM	V3FRM	PLSQL	LOAD
ALLOCATE	V7SQLk						
ALTER	V7SQL	V6SQL	ANSI	V2FRM	V3FRM	PLSQL	LOAD
ANALYZE	V7SQLk						
AND	V7SQL	V6SQL	ANSI	V2FRM	V3FRM	PLSQL	LOAD

	V7SQL	V6SQL	ANSI	V2FRM	V3FRM	PLSQL	LOAD
ANY	V7SQL	V6SQL	ANSI	V2FRM	V3FRM	PLSQL	LOAD
APPEND				V2FRM	V3FRM		
ARCHIVE	V7SQLk						
ARCHIVELOG	V7SQLk	V6SQLk		V2FRM	V3FRM	PLSQL	LOAD
ARRAY					V3FRM	PLSQL	
AS	V7SQL	V6SQL	ANSI	V2FRM	V3FRM	PLSQL	LOAD
ASC	V7SQL	V6SQL	ANSI	V2FRM	V3FRM	PLSQL	LOAD
ASSERT				V2FRM	V3FRM		
ASSIGN				V2FRM	V3FRM	PLSQL	LOAD
AT						PLSQL	
AUDIT	V7SQL	V6SQL			V3FRM	PLSQL	
AUTHORIZATION	V7SQLk	V6SQLk	ANSI			PLSQL	
AVG	V7SQLk	V6SQL				PLSQL	LOAD
BACKUP	V7SQLk	V6SQLk				PLSQL	
BADDN							LOAD
BADFILE							LOAD
BECOME	V7SQLk						
BEFORE	V7SQLk						
BEGIN	V7SQLk	V6SQLk	ANSI		V3FRM	PLSQL	
BEGINDATA							LOAD
BETWEEN	V7SQL	V6SQL	ANSI	V2FRM	V3FRM	PLSQL	LOAD
BINARY_INTEGER						PLSQL	
BLOCK	V7SQLk			V2FRM	V3FRM		
BLOCKSIZE							LOAD
BODY	V7SQLk					PLSQL	
BOOLEAN						PLSQL	
BY	V7SQL	V6SQL	ANSI	V2FRM	V3FRM	PLSQL	LOAD
CACHE	V7SQLk	V6SQLk					
CANCEL	V7SQLk						
CASCADE	V7SQLk						
CASE				V2FRM	V3FRM	PLSQL	LOAD
CHANGE	V7SQLk						
CHAR	V7SQL	V6SQL	ANSI	V2FRM	V3FRM	PLSQL	LOAD

	V7SQL	V6SQL	ANSI	V2FRM	V3FRM	PLSQL	LOAD
CHAR_BASE						PLSQL	
CHARACTER	V7SQLk	V6SQLk	ANSI				
CHECK	V7SQL	V6SQL	ANSI	V2FRM	V3FRM	PLSQL	LOAD
CHECKPOINT	V7SQLk						
CLOSE	V7SQLk	V6SQLk	ANSI		V3FRM	PLSQL	
CLUSTER	V7SQL	V6SQL	ANSI	V2FRM	V3FRM	PLSQL	LOAD
CLUSTERS					V3FRM	PLSQL	
COBOL	V7SQLk	V6SQLk	ANSI				
COLAUTH						PLSQL	LOAD
COLUMN	V7SQL	V6SQL		V2FRM	V3FRM		LOAD
COLUMNS						PLSQL	LOAD
COMMENT	V7SQL	V6SQL		V2FRM	V3FRM		LOAD
COMMIT	V7SQLk	V6SQLk	ANSI		V3FRM	PLSQL	
COMPILE	V7SQLk						
COMPRESS	V7SQL	V6SQL	ANSI	V2FRM	V3FRM	PLSQL	LOAD
CONCATENATE							LOAD
CONNECT	V7SQL	V6SQL	ANSI	V2FRM	V3FRM	PLSQL	LOAD
CONSTANT						PLSQL	LOAD
CONSTRAINT	V7SQLk	V6SQLk	ANSI				
CONSTRAINTS	V7SQLk						
CONTAIN				V2FRM	V3FRM		
CONTAINS				V2FRM	V3FRM		
CONTENTS	V7SQLk	V6SQLk					
CONTINUE	V7SQLk	V6SQLk	ANSI				
CONTINUEIF							LOAD
CONTROLFILE	V7SQLk	V6SQLk					LOAD
COUNT	V7SQLk					PLSQL	LOAD
CRASH		V6SQLk		V2FRM	V3FRM	PLSQL	
CREATE	V7SQL	V6SQL	ANSI	V2FRM	V3FRM	PLSQL	LOAD
CURRENT	V7SQL	V6SQL	ANSI	V2FRM	V3FRM	PLSQL	LOAD
CURRVAL						PLSQL	
CURSOR	V7SQLk	V6SQLk	ANSI		V3FRM	PLSQL	
CYCLE	V7SQLk	V6SQLk					

DATA						LOAD
DATA_BASE					PLSQL	
DATABASE	V7SQLk V6SQLk			V3FRM	PLSQL	
DATAFILE	V7SQLk V6SQLk					
DATAPAGES			V2FRM	V3FRM		
DATE	V7SQL V6SQL		V2FRM	V3FRM	PLSQL	LOAD
DBA	V7SQLk V6SQL		V2FRM	V3FRM	PLSQL	LOAD
DEBUGOFF				V3FRM	PLSQL	
DEBUGON					PLSQL	
DEC	V7SQLk V6SQLk ANSI					
DECIMAL	V7SQL V6SQL ANSI	V2FRM	V3FRM	PLSQL	LOAD
DECLARE	V7SQLk V6SQLk ANSI		V3FRM	PLSQL	
DEFAULT	V7SQL V6SQL ANSI	V2FRM	V3FRM	PLSQL	LOAD
DEFAULTIF						LOAD
DEFINITION			V2FRM	V3FRM	PLSQL	
DELAY				V3FRM	PLSQL	
DELETE	V7SQL V6SQL ANSI	V2FRM	V3FRM	PLSQL	LOAD
DELTA					PLSQL	
DESC	V7SQL V6SQL ANSI	V2FRM	V3FRM	PLSQL	LOAD
DIGITS				V3FRM	PLSQL	
DISABLE	V7SQLk					
DISCARDDN						LOAD
DISCARDFILE						LOAD
DISCARDMAX						LOAD
DISCARDS						LOAD
DISMOUNT	V7SQLk V6SQLk					
DISPOSE				V3FRM	PLSQL	
DISTINCT	V7SQL V6SQL ANSI	V2FRM	V3FRM	PLSQL	LOAD
DO				V3FRM	PLSQL	
DOES			V2FRM	V3FRM		
DOUBLE	V7SQLk V6SQLk ANSI				LOAD
DROP	V7SQL V6SQL		V2FRM	V3FRM	PLSQL	LOAD
DUMP	V7SQL					

EACH	V7SQLk			V2FRM	V3FRM		
ELSE	V7SQL	V6SQL		V2FRM	V3FRM	PLSQL	
ELSIF					V3FRM	PLSQL	
ENABLE	V7SQLk						
ENCLOSED							LOAD
END	V7SQLk	V6SQLk	ANSI		V3FRM	PLSQL	
ENTRY					V3FRM	PLSQL	
ERASE				V2FRM	V3FRM		
ESCAPE	V7SQLk	V6SQLk	ANSI				
EVALUATE				V2FRM	V3FRM		
EVENTS	V7SQLk	V6SQLk					
EXCEPTION					V3FRM	PLSQL	
EXCEPTIONS	V7SQLk						
EXCEPTION_INIT					V3FRM	PLSQL	
EXCLUSIVE	V7SQL	V6SQL		V2FRM	V3FRM		LOAD
EXEC	V7SQLk	V6SQLk	ANSI				
EXECUTE	V7SQLk						
EXISTS	V7SQL	V6SQL	ANSI	V2FRM	V3FRM	PLSQL	LOAD
EXIT					V3FRM	PLSQL	
EXPLAIN	V7SQLk						
EXTENT	V7SQLk						
EXTERNAL							LOAD
EXTERNALLY	V7SQLk						
FALSE					V3FRM	PLSQL	
FETCH	V7SQLk	V6SQLk	ANSI		V3FRM	PLSQL	
FIELD				V2FRM	V3FRM		
FIELDS							LOAD
FILE	V7SQL	V6SQL		V2FRM	V3FRM		LOAD
FIXED							LOAD
FLOAT	V7SQL	V6SQL	ANSI	V2FRM	V3FRM	PLSQL	LOAD
FLUSH	V7SQLk						
FOR	V7SQL	V6SQL	ANSI	V2FRM	V3FRM	PLSQL	LOAD
FORCE	V7SQLk						

	V7SQL	V6SQL	ANSI	V2FRM	V3FRM	PLSQL	LOAD
FOREIGN	V7SQLk	V6SQLk	ANSI				
FORM				V2FRM	V3FRM	PLSQL	
FORMAT				V2FRM	V3FRM		LOAD
FORTRAN	V7SQLk	V6SQLk	ANSI				
FOUND	V7SQLk	V6SQLk	ANSI				
FREELIST	V7SQLk						
FREELISTS	V7SQLk	V6SQLk	ANSI	V2FRM	V3FRM		LOAD
FROM	V7SQL	V6SQL	ANSI	V2FRM	V3FRM	PLSQL	LOAD
FUNCTION	V7SQLk				V3FRM	PLSQL	
GENERIC					V3FRM	PLSQL	
GLOBAL				V2FRM	V3FRM		
GO	V7SQLk	V6SQLk	ANSI				
GOTO	V7SQLk	V6SQLk	ANSI		V3FRM	PLSQL	
GRANT	V7SQL	V6SQL	ANSI	V2FRM	V3FRM	PLSQL	LOAD
GRAPHIC		V6SQL		V2FRM	V3FRM		LOAD
GROUP	V7SQL	V6SQL	ANSI	V2FRM	V3FRM	PLSQL	LOAD
GROUPS	V7SQLk						
HAVING	V7SQL	V6SQL	ANSI	V2FRM	V3FRM	PLSQL	LOAD
IDENTIFIED	V7SQL	V6SQL		V2FRM	V3FRM	PLSQL	LOAD
IF		V6SQL		V2FRM	V3FRM	PLSQL	LOAD
IMAGE				V2FRM	V3FRM		
IMMEDIATE	V7SQL	V6SQL	ANSI	V2FRM	V3FRM	PLSQL	LOAD
IN	V7SQL	V6SQL	ANSI	V2FRM	V3FRM	PLSQL	LOAD
INCLUDING	V7SQLk	V6SQLk					
INCREMENT	V7SQL	V6SQL		V2FRM	V3FRM		LOAD
INDDN							LOAD
INDEX	V7SQL	V6SQL		V2FRM	V3FRM	PLSQL	LOAD
INDEXED				V2FRM	V3FRM		
INDEXES					V3FRM	PLSQL	
INDEXPAGES				V2FRM	V3FRM		
INDICATOR	V7SQLk	V6SQLk	ANSI		V3FRM	PLSQL	
INFILE	V7SQLk	V6SQLk	ANSI		V3FRM	PLSQL	LOAD
INITIAL	V7SQL	V6SQL		V2FRM	V3FRM		LOAD

INITRANS	V7SQLk	V6SQLk					
INSERT	V7SQL						
INSTANCE	V7SQLk	V6SQL	ANSI	V2FRM	V3FRM	PLSQL	LOAD
INT	V7SQLk	V6SQLk	ANSI				
INTEGER	V7SQL	V6SQL	ANSI	V2FRM	V3FRM	PLSQL	LOAD
INTERSECT	V7SQL	V6SQL		V2FRM	V3FRM	PLSQL	LOAD
INTO	V7SQL	V6SQL	ANSI	V2FRM	V3FRM	PLSQL	LOAD
IS	V7SQL	V6SQL	ANSI	V2FRM	V3FRM	PLSQL	LOAD
KEY	V7SQLk	V6SQLk	ANSI				
LANGUAGE	V7SQLk	V6SQLk	ANSI				
LAST							LOAD
LAYER	V7SQLk						
LEVEL	V7SQL	V6SQL		V2FRM	V3FRM	PLSQL	LOAD
LIKE	V7SQL	V6SQL	ANSI	V2FRM	V3FRM	PLSQL	LOAD
LIMITED					V3FRM	PLSQL	
LINK	V7SQLk	V6SQLk			V3FRM	PLSQL	LOAD
LIST				V2FRM	V3FRM		
LISTS	V7SQLk						
LOAD							LOAD
LOCK	V7SQL	V6SQL		V2FRM	V3FRM		LOAD
LOG							LOAD
LOGFILE	V7SQLk	V6SQLk					
LONG	V7SQL	V6SQL		V2FRM	V3FRM		LOAD
LOOP					V3FRM	PLSQL	
MANAGE	V7SQLk						
MANUAL	V7SQLk						
MAX	V7SQLk				V3FRM	PLSQL	LOAD
MAXDATAFILES	V7SQLk	V6SQLk					
MAXEXTENTS	V7SQL	V6SQL		V2FRM	V3FRM	PLSQL	LOAD
MAXINSTANCES	V7SQLk	V6SQLk					
MAXLOGFILES	V7SQLk	V6SQLk					
MAXLOGHISTORY	V7SQLk						
MAXLOGMEMBERS	V7SQLk						

MAXTRANS	V7SQLk V6SQLk					
MAXVALUE	V7SQLk V6SQLk					
MIN	V7SQLk			V3FRM	PLSQL	
MINEXTENTS	V7SQLk V6SQLk					
MINUS	V7SQL V6SQL		V2FRM	V3FRM	PLSQL	LOAD
MINVALUE	V7SQLk V6SQLk					
MLSLABEL					PLSQL	
MOD				V3FRM	PLSQL	
MODE	V7SQL V6SQL		V2FRM	V3FRM		LOAD
MODIFY	V7SQL V6SQL ANSI		V2FRM	V3FRM		LOAD
MODULE	V7SQLk V6SQLk ANSI					
MOUNT	V7SQLk V6SQLk					
MOVE			V2FRM	V3FRM		
NATURAL					PLSQL	
NEW	V7SQLk V6SQL		V2FRM	V3FRM	PLSQL	LOAD
NEXT	V7SQLk V6SQLk ANSI					LOAD
NEXTVAL					PLSQL	
NO						LOAD
NOARCHIVELOG	V7SQLk V6SQLk					
NOAUDIT	V7SQL V6SQL		V2FRM	V3FRM		LOAD
NOCACHE	V7SQLk V6SQLk					
NOCOMPRESS	V7SQL V6SQL		V2FRM	V3FRM	PLSQL	LOAD
NOCYCLE	V7SQLk V6SQLk					
NOLIST			V2FRM	V3FRM		
NOMAXVALUE	V7SQLk V6SQLk					
NOMINVALUE	V7SQLk V6SQLk					
NONE	V7SQLk					
NOORDER	V7SQLk V6SQLk					
NORESETLOGS	V7SQLk					
NORMAL	V7SQLk V6SQLk					
NOSORT	V7SQLk V6SQLk					
NOSYSSORT			V2FRM	V3FRM		
NOT	V7SQL V6SQL		V2FRM	V3FRM	PLSQL	LOAD

	V7SQL	V6SQL	ANSI	V2FRM	V3FRM	PLSQL	LOAD
NOWAIT	V7SQL	V6SQL		V2FRM	V3FRM		LOAD
NULL	V7SQL	V6SQL	ANSI	V2FRM	V3FRM	PLSQL	LOAD
NULLIF							LOAD
NUMBER	V7SQL	V6SQL		V2FRM	V3FRM	PLSQL	LOAD
NUMBER_BASE					V3FRM	PLSQL	
NUMERIC	V7SQLk	V6SQLk	ANSI				
OF	V7SQL	V6SQL	ANSI	V2FRM	V3FRM	PLSQL	LOAD
OFF	V7SQLk						
OFFLINE	V7SQL	V6SQLk		V2FRM	V3FRM		
OLD	V7SQLk			V2FRM	V3FRM		
ON	V7SQL	V6SQL	ANSI	V2FRM	V3FRM	PLSQL	LOAD
ONLINE	V7SQL	V6SQL		V2FRM	V3FRM		LOAD
ONLY	V7SQLk	V6SQLk	ANSI				
OPEN	V7SQLk	V6SQLk	ANSI		V3FRM	PLSQL	
OPTIMIZE				V2FRM	V3FRM		
OPTION	V7SQL	V6SQL	ANSI	V2FRM	V3FRM	PLSQL	LOAD
OPTIONALLY							LOAD
OPTIONS							LOAD
OR	V7SQL	V6SQL	ANSI	V2FRM	V3FRM	PLSQL	LOAD
ORDER	V7SQL	V6SQL	ANSI	V2FRM	V3FRM	PLSQL	LOAD
OTHERS					V3FRM	PLSQL	
OUT					V3FRM	PLSQL	
OWN	V7SQLk						
PACKAGE	V7SQLk				V3FRM	PLSQL	
PARALLEL	V7SQLk						
PART							LOAD
PARTITION				V2FRM	V3FRM	PLSQL	
PASCAL	V7SQLk	V6SQLk	ANSI				
PCTFREE	V7SQL	V6SQL		V2FRM	V3FRM	PLSQL	LOAD
PCTINCREASE	V7SQLk	V6SQLk					
PCTUSED	V7SQLk	V6SQLk					
PLAN	V7SQLk						
PLI	V7SQLk	V6SQLk	ANSI				

POSITION					LOAD
POSITIVE				PLSQL	
PRAGMA			V3FRM	PLSQL	
PRECISION	V7SQLk V6SQLk ANSI				
PRIMARY	V7SQLk V6SQLk ANSI				
PRIOR	V7SQL V6SQL	V2FRM	V3FRM	PLSQL	LOAD
PRIVATE	V7SQLk		V3FRM	PLSQL	
PRIVILEGES	V7SQL V6SQL ANSI	V2FRM	V3FRM		LOAD
PROCEDURE	V7SQLk V6SQLk ANSI		V3FRM	PLSQL	
PROFILE	V7SQLk				
PUBLIC	V7SQL V6SQL ANSI	V2FRM	V3FRM	PLSQL	LOAD
QUOTA	V7SQLk				
RAISE			V3FRM	PLSQL	
RANGE			V3FRM	PLSQL	LOAD
RAW	V7SQL V6SQL	V2FRM	V3FRM		LOAD
RAW MLSLABEL				PLSQL	
RCLEN					LOAD
READ	V7SQLk V6SQLk ANSI				
REAL	V7SQLk V6SQLk ANSI			PLSQL	
RECNUM					LOAD
RECORD		V2FRM	V3FRM	PLSQL	LOAD
RECOVER	V7SQLk				
REFERENCES	V7SQLk V6SQLk ANSI				
REFERENCING	V7SQLk				
RELEASE	V6SQL		V3FRM	PLSQL	LOAD
REM			V3FRM	PLSQL	
RENAME	V7SQL V6SQL	V2FRM	V3FRM	PLSQL	LOAD
REPLACE					LOAD
RESETLOGS	V7SQLk V6SQLk				
RESOURCE	V7SQL V6SQL	V2FRM	V3FRM	PLSQL	LOAD
RESTRICTED	V7SQLk				
RESUME					LOAD
RETURN			V3FRM	PLSQL	

REUSE	V7SQLk	V6SQLk				PLSQL	
REVERSE					V3FRM	PLSQL	
REVOKE	V7SQL	V6SQL	ANSI	V2FRM	V3FRM	PLSQL	LOAD
ROLE	V7SQLk						
ROLES	V7SQLk						
ROLLBACK	V7SQLk	V6SQLk	ANSI		V3FRM	PLSQL	
ROW	V7SQL	V6SQL		V2FRM	V3FRM		LOAD
ROWID	V7SQL	V6SQL		V2FRM	V3FRM	PLSQL	LOAD
ROWLABEL	V7SQL					PLSQL	
ROWNUM	V7SQL	V6SQL		V2FRM	V3FRM	PLSQL	LOAD
ROWS	V7SQL	V6SQL		V2FRM	V3FRM		LOAD
ROWTYPE					V3FRM	PLSQL	
RUN				V2FRM	V3FRM	PLSQL	
SAVEPOINT	V7SQLk	V6SQLk			V3FRM	PLSQL	
SCHEMA	V7SQLk	V6SQLk	ANSI		V3FRM	PLSQL	
SCN	V7SQLk						
SECTION	V7SQLk	V6SQLk	ANSI				
SEGMENT	V7SQLk	V6SQLk					
SELECT	V7SQL	V6SQL	ANSI	V2FRM	V3FRM	PLSQL	LOAD
SEPARATE					V3FRM	PLSQL	
SEQUENCE	V7SQLk	V6SQLk					LOAD
SESSION	V7SQL	V6SQL	ANSI	V2FRM	V3FRM		LOAD
SET	V7SQL	V6SQL	ANSI	V2FRM	V3FRM	PLSQL	LOAD
SHARE	V7SQL	V6SQL		V2FRM	V3FRM		LOAD
SHARED	V7SQLk	V6SQLk					
SIZE	V7SQL	V6SQL		V2FRM	V3FRM	PLSQL	LOAD
SMALLINT	V7SQL	V6SQL	ANSI	V2FRM	V3FRM	PLSQL	LOAD
SNAPSHOT	V7SQLk						
SOME	V7SQLk	V6SQLk	ANSI				
SORT	V7SQLk	V6SQLk					
SORTDEVT							LOAD
SORTNUM							LOAD
SPACE				V2FRM	V3FRM	PLSQL	

SPECIFIED		V6SQLk				
SQL	V7SQLk	V6SQLk	ANSI		V3FRM	PLSQL
SQL/DS							LOAD
SQLCODE	V7SQLk	V6SQLk	ANSI		V3FRM	PLSQL
SQLERRM		V6SQLk	ANSI		V3FRM	PLSQL
SQLERROR	V7SQLk	V6SQLk	ANSI			
START	V7SQL	V6SQL	ANSI	V2FRM	V3FRM	PLSQL	LOAD
STATEMENT		V6SQLk			V3FRM	PLSQL
STATEMENT_ID	V7SQLk					
STATISTICS	V7SQLk					
STDDEV					V3FRM	PLSQL
STOP	V7SQLk					
STORAGE	V7SQLk	V6SQLk				
STREAM							LOAD
SUBTYPE					V3FRM	PLSQL
SUCCESSFUL	V7SQL	V6SQL		V2FRM	V3FRM		LOAD
SUM	V7SQLk				V3FRM	PLSQL
SWITCH	V7SQLk	V6SQLk				
SYNONYM	V7SQL	V6SQL		V2FRM	V3FRM		LOAD
SYSDATE	V7SQL	V6SQL		V2FRM	V3FRM		LOAD
SYSSORT				V2FRM	V3FRM	
SYSTEM	V7SQLk	V6SQLk	ANSI	V2FRM	V3FRM	
TABAUTH					V3FRM	PLSQL
TABLE	V7SQL	V6SQL	ANSI	V2FRM	V3FRM	PLSQL	LOAD
TABLES	V7SQLk	V6SQLk			V3FRM	PLSQL
TABLESPACE	V7SQLk	V6SQLk				
TASK					V3FRM	PLSQL
TEMPORARY	V7SQLk	V6SQLk	ANSI		V3FRM	
TERMINATE						PLSQL	LOAD
THEN	V7SQL	V6SQLk		V2FRM	V3FRM	PLSQL
THIS							LOAD
THREAD	V7SQLk					
TIME	V7SQLk					

TO	V7SQL	V6SQL	ANSI	V2FRM	V3FRM	PLSQL	LOAD
TRACING	V7SQLk						
TRANSACTION	V7SQLk	V6SQL	ANSI				
TRIGGER	V7SQL	V6SQL			V3FRM		
TRIGGERS	V7SQLk						
TRUE					V3FRM	PLSQL	
TRUNCATE	V7SQLk						
TYPE					V3FRM	PLSQL	
UID	V7SQL	V6SQL		V2FRM	V3FRM		LOAD
UNDER	V7SQLk						
UNION	V7SQL	V6SQL	ANSI	V2FRM	V3FRM	PLSQL	LOAD
UNIQUE	V7SQL	V6SQL	ANSI	V2FRM	V3FRM	PLSQL	LOAD
UNLIMITED	V7SQLk						
UNLOAD							LOAD
UNTIL	V7SQLk						
UPDATE	V7SQL	V6SQL	ANSI	V2FRM	V3FRM	PLSQL	LOAD
USE	V7SQLk				V3FRM	PLSQL	
USER	V7SQL	V6SQL	ANSI	V2FRM	V3FRM		LOAD
USING	V7SQLk	V6SQLk	ANSI		V3FRM		
VALIDATE	V7SQL	V6SQL		V2FRM	V3FRM		LOAD
VALUES	V7SQL	V6SQL	ANSI	V2FRM	V3FRM	PLSQL	LOAD
VARCHAR	V7SQL	V6SQL	ANSI	V2FRM	V3FRM	PLSQL	LOAD
VARCHAR2	V7SQL					PLSQL	LOAD
VARGRAPHIC		V6SQL		V2FRM	V3FRM		LOAD
VARIABLE							LOAD
VARIANCE					V3FRM	PLSQL	
VIEW	V7SQL	V6SQL	ANSI	V2FRM	V3FRM	PLSQL	LOAD
VIEWS					V3FRM	PLSQL	
WHEN	V7SQLk				V3FRM	PLSQL	LOAD
WHENEVER	V7SQL	V6SQL	ANSI	V2FRM	V3FRM		LOAD
WHERE	V7SQL	V6SQL	ANSI	V2FRM	V3FRM	PLSQL	LOAD
WHILE					V3FRM	PLSQL	
WHITESPACE							LOAD

WITH	V7SQL	V6SQL	ANSI	V2FRM	V3FRM	PLSQL	LOAD
WORK	V7SQLk	V6SQLk	ANSI		V3FRM	PLSQL	
WORKDDN							LOAD
WRITE	V7SQLk	V6SQLk	ANSI		V3FRM		
XOR					V3FRM	PLSQL	
YES							LOAD

RESOURCE

Resource is a general term for a logical database object or physical structure that may be locked. Resources that users can directly lock are rows and tables; resources that the RDBMS can lock are numerous and include data dictionary tables, caches, and files.

REVOKE (Form 1 - System Privileges and Roles)

Type   SQL command

Products   All

See also   **DISABLE**, **ENABLE**, **GRANT**, **REVOKE** (Form 2), PRIVILEGE, Chapter 17

Format

```
REVOKE {system_privilege : role}
       [,{system_privilege : role}]...
  FROM {user : role : PUBLIC}
       [,{user : role : PUBLIC}]...
```

Description   The **REVOKE** command takes privileges and roles away from users or privileges away from roles. Any system privilege may be revoked; *see* PRIVILEGE.

If you revoke a privilege from a user, the user can no longer execute the operations allowed by the privilege. If you revoke a privilege from a role, no user granted the role can execute the allowed operations, unless they are permitted by another role or directly as a user. If you revoke a privilege from **PUBLIC**, no user granted the privilege through **PUBLIC** can execute the operations allowed by the privilege.

If you revoke a role from a user, the user can no longer enable the role (*see* **ENABLE**) but may continue exercising the privilege in a current session. If you revoke a role from a role, users granted the role can no longer enable the role but may continue using the privilege during the current session. If you revoke a role from **PUBLIC**, users granted the role through **PUBLIC** can no longer enable the role.

REVOKE (Form 2 - Object Privileges)

Type   SQL command

Products   All

See also   **GRANT**, **REVOKE** (Form 1), PRIVILEGE, Chapter 17

Format

```
REVOKE object_privilege[,object_privilege]...
    ON [user.]object
  FROM {user ¦ role ¦ PUBLIC}
       [,{user ¦ role ¦ PUBLIC}]...
       [CASCADE CONSTRAINTS]
```

Description   The **REVOKE** command takes object privileges on a specific object away from a user or role. If a user's privileges are revoked, the user may not execute the operations allowed by the privilege on the object. If a role's privileges are revoked, no user granted the role may execute those operations unless they are granted through another role or directly to the user. If the PUBLIC's privileges are revoked, no user granted the privilege through **PUBLIC** may execute those operations.

The **CASCADE CONSTRAINTS** clause drops any referential integrity constraints defined by the user or by users granted the role. This applies to a REFERENCES privilege.

ROLE

A role is a set of privileges that an ORACLE7 user can grant to another user. ORACLE version 6 privileges DBA, CONNECT, and RESOURCE have become system-supplied roles in ORACLE7, and there are also two new roles for importing and exporting a database. *See* **CREATE ROLE** for details.

ORACLE has five system-supplied roles: CONNECT, RESOURCE, DBA, EXP_FULL_DATABASE, and IMP_FULL_DATABASE. The first three provide compatibility with ORACLE version 6; the last two are for convenience in using the export and import utilities.

These default roles have the following granted roles and privileges (*see* PRIVILEGE):

ROLE	PRIVILEGES
CONNECT	ALTER SESSION, CREATE CLUSTER, CREATE DATABASE LINK, CREATE SEQUENCE, CREATE SESSION, CREATE SYNONYM, CREATE TABLE, CREATE VIEW
RESOURCE	CREATE CLUSTER, CREATE PROCEDURE, CREATE SEQUENCE, CREATE TABLE, CREATE TRIGGER, UNLIMITED TABLESPACE
DBA	All system privileges WITH ADMIN OPTION, EXP_FULL_DATABASE role, IMP_FULL_DATABASE role
EXP_FULL_DATABASE	SELECT ANY TABLE, BACKUP ANY TABLE, INSERT, UPDATE, DELETE ON SYS.INCEXP, SYS.INCVID, SYS.INCFIL
IMP_FULL_DATABASE	BECOME USER

See Chapter 17 for examples of creating and using roles.

ROLL FORWARD

Roll forward is the reapplying of changes to the database. You sometimes need it for media recovery and sometimes for instance recovery. The **REDO LOG** contains the redo entries used for roll forward.

ROLLBACK

A rollback discards part or all of the work you have done in the current transaction, since the last **COMMIT** or **SAVEPOINT**.

ROLLBACK (FORM 1 - SQL)

Type   SQL command

Products   All, PL/SQL

See also   **COMMIT**, **SET AUTOCOMMIT**, Chapter 13

Format

```
ROLLBACK [WORK] {[TO [SAVEPOINT] savepoint] ¦ [FORCE text]}
```

Description   **ROLLBACK** reverses all changes made to tables in the database since changes were last committed or rolled back and releases any locks on the tables. An automatic rollback occurs whenever a transaction is interrupted, such as by an execution error, a power failure, and so on. **ROLLBACK** affects not just the last **insert**, **update**, or **delete** statement but any that have occurred since the last **COMMIT**. This allows you to treat blocks of work as a whole and only **COMMIT** when all of the changes you want are completed.

With **SAVEPOINT**, **ROLLBACK** goes to a specific, named place in the sequence of transactions being processed, the **SAVEPOINT**. It erases any interim **SAVEPOINT**s and releases any table or row locks that occurred after the **SAVEPOINT** was made.

With **FORCE**, **ROLLBACK** manually rolls back an in-doubt transaction identified by the literal text, which is a local or global transaction ID from the data dictionary view DBA_2PC_PENDING.

> **NOTE**
> If **SET AUTOCOMMIT** is ON, however, then every **insert**, **update**, or **delete** will immediately and automatically commit the changes to the database. Typing the word **ROLLBACK** will produce this message:
>
> ```
> ROLLBACK COMPLETE
> ```
>
> but it won't mean anything. The changes will stay, because **ROLLBACK** only rolls back to the last *COMMIT*, and that happened automatically after your last change.

ALTER, AUDIT, CONNECT, CREATE, DISCONNECT, DROP, EXIT, GRANT, NOAUDIT, QUIT, REVOKE, and **SAVE** all cause a **COMMIT**.

ROLLBACK (Form 2 - Embedded SQL)

Type   Embedded SQL command

Products   Precompilers

See also   **COMMIT, SAVEPOINT, SET TRANSACTION**

```
EXEC SQL [AT database ¦ :variable]
        ROLLBACK [WORK]
            {[TO [SAVEPOINT] savepoint] [RELEASE] ¦
            [FORCE text]}
```

Description   **ROLLBACK** ends the current transaction, reverses any changes resulting from the current transaction, and releases any locks being held, but does not affect host variables or program flow. *database* indicates the name of the database where the **ROLLBACK** should take effect. Its absence indicates the default database for the user. **SAVEPOINT** allows a rollback to a named **SAVEPOINT** that has been previously declared. (*See* **SAVEPOINT**.)

FORCE manually rolls back an in-doubt transaction specified by a literal text containing the transaction ID from the DBA_2PC_PENDING data dictionary view. WORK is entirely optional and is for readability only.

Both **ROLLBACK** and **COMMIT** have **RELEASE** options. **RELEASE** should be specified by one of them after the last transaction, otherwise locks put on during the program will block other users. **ROLLBACK** occurs automatically (with a **RELEASE**) if the program abnormally terminates.

ROLLBACK SEGMENT

A rollback segment is a storage space within a tablespace that holds transaction information used to guarantee data integrity during a rollback and used to provide read consistency across multiple transactions.

ROOT

In a table with tree-structured data, the root is the origin of the tree, a row that has no parent, and whose children, grandchildren, and so on, constitute the entire tree. In a tree-structured query, the root is the row specified by the **START WITH** clause.

ROUND (Form 1 - for Dates)

Type   SQL function

Products   All, PL/SQL

See also   DATE FUNCTIONS, **ROUND** (NUMBER), **TRUNC**, Chapter 7

Format

ROUND (*date*, '*format*')

Description   **ROUND** is the rounding of date according to format. Without a format, date is rounded to 12 A.M. of the next date as of 12:00:00 P.M. (exactly noon) today, or to today's date if before noon. The resulting date has its time set to 12 A.M., the very first instant of the day.

Formats Available for Rounding

FORMAT	MEANING
cc,scc	century (rounds up to January 1st of next century, as of midnight exactly on the morning of January 1st of 1950, 2050, and so on).
syear,syyyy,y,yy,yyy,yyyy and year	year (rounds up to January 1st of the next year as of midnight exactly on the morning of July 1st).
q	quarter (rounds up in the 2nd month of the quarter as of midnight exactly on the morning of the 16th, regardless of the number of days in the month).
month,mon,mm	month (rounds up as of midnight exactly on the morning of the 16th regardless of the number of days in the month).
ww	rounds to closest Monday (see text following list).
w	rounds to closest day which is the same day as the first day of the month (see text following list).
ddd,dd,j	rounds up to the next day as of noon exactly. This is the same as ROUND with no format.
day,dy,d	rounds up to next Sunday (first day of the week) as of noon exactly on Wednesday.
hh,hh12,hh24	rounds up to the next whole hour as of 30 minutes and 30 seconds after the hour.
mi	rounds up to the next whole minute as of 30 seconds of this minute.

ww produces the date of the nearest Monday with the time set at 12 A.M. Since a week is seven days long, this means any date and time up to three and one-half days after a Monday (the next Thursday at 11:59:59 A.M.), or three and one-half days before (the previous Thursday at noon exactly), will be rounded to the Monday at 12 A.M. (midnight) in the morning.

w works similarly, except that instead of producing the date of the nearest Monday at 12 A.M., it produces the date of the nearest day that is the same day as the first day of the month. If the first day of a month was Friday, for instance, then, since a week is seven days long, this means any date and time up to three and one-half days after a Friday (the next Monday at 11:59:59 A.M.), or three and one-half days before (the previous Monday at noon exactly), will be rounded to the Friday at 12 A.M. (midnight) in the morning.

When **ww** and **w** round, the time of the date being rounded is compared to a date (either Monday or the day of the first day of the month) which is set to 12 A.M., the very beginning of the day. The result of **ROUND** is a new date, which is also set to 12 A.M.

ROUND (Form 2 - for Numbers)

Type   SQL function

Products   All, PL/SQL

See also   **CEIL**, **FLOOR**, NUMBER FUNCTIONS, **ROUND** (DATE), **TRUNC**, Chapter 6

Format

```
ROUND(value,precision)
```

Description   ROUND rounds *value* to *precision*. *precision* is an integer and may be positive, negative, or zero. A negative integer rounds to the given number of places to the left of the decimal point, a positive integer rounds to the given number of places to the right of the decimal point.

Example

```
ROUND(123.456,2)  = 123.46
ROUND(123.456,0)  = 123
ROUND(123.456,-2) = 100
ROUND(-123.456,2) = -123.46
```

ROW

Row can be either of two definitions:

- One set of fields in a table; for example, the fields representing one worker in the table WORKER.
- One set of fields in the output of a query. RECORD is a synonym.

ROW-HEADER

A row-header is the portion of each row that contains information about the row other than row data, such as the number of row pieces, columns, and so on.

ROW-LEVEL LOCK MANAGER

The row-level lock manager is the portion of the kernel that allows locking on the row level rather than on the table level, thus allowing a high level of concurrency and transaction throughout.

ROW-LEVEL LOCKING

A row-level locking is a type of locking in which **update**s to data occur through locking rows in a table and not the entire page.

ROW PIECE

A row piece is a portion of a row, containing row-header information and row data.

ROW SEQUENCE NUMBER

A row sequence number is a number assigned to a row as it is inserted into a data block for a table. This number is also stored as row overhead and forms a part of the ROWID.

ROWID

Type   Pseudo-column

Products   All

See also   **CHARTOROWID**, PSEUDO-COLUMNS, **ROWIDTOCHAR**, Chapter 8

Format

```
00001F20.000C.0001
```

Description   ROWID is the logical address of a row, and it is unique within the database. The ROWID is broken into three sections: left, middle, and right (corresponding to 00001F20, 000C, and 0001, just shown). The numbering is in hexadecimal notation.

The left section is the block in the file, the middle is the row sequence number within the block (numbering starts with 0, not 1), and the right is the file number within the database. Note that the file numbers are unique within the whole database. The tablespace they are in is not relevant to the ROWID.

ROWID can be **select**ed, or used in a **where** clause, but cannot be changed by an **insert**, **update**, or **delete**. It is not actually a data column, but merely a logical address, made of the three pieces of information just described. ROWID is useful when used in a **where** clause for rapid **update**s or **delete**s of rows. However, it can change if the table it is in is exported and imported.

ROWIDTOCHAR

Type   SQL command

Products   All

See also   **CHARTOROWID**, CONVERSION FUNCTIONS

Format

```
ROWIDTOCHAR(RowId)
```

Description   **Row Id**entifier **TO CHAR**acter changes an internal ORACLE row identifier, or RowId, to act like a character string. This might be used to make a RowId equal to a literal character string, as in a **where** clause, for example:

```
where '00000320.0001.0002' = ROWIDTOCHAR(RowId)
```

However, ORACLE will do this kind of conversion automatically, so this function isn't really needed. It seems to be a debugging tool that has made its way into general availability.

ROWNUM

Type   Pseudo-column

Products   All

See also   PSEUDO-COLUMNS, Chapter 15

Format

```
ROWNUM
```

Description   ROWNUM returns the sequence number in which a row was returned when first selected from a table. The first row has a ROWNUM of 1, the second is 2, and so on. Note, however, that even a simple **order by** in the **select** statement will *disorder* the ROWNUMs, which are assigned to the rows before any ordering takes place. *See* Chapter 15 for a discussion of this.

RPAD

Type   SQL function

Products   All, PL/SQL

See also   CHARACTER FUNCTIONS, **LPAD**, **LTRIM**, **RTRIM**, Chapter 5

Format

```
RPAD(string,length [,'set'])
```

Description   **R**ight **PAD** makes a string a certain length by adding a certain *set* of characters to the right. If *set* is not specified, the default pad character is a space.

Example

```
select RPAD('HELLO ',24,'WORLD') from DUAL;
```

produces this:

```
HELLO WORLDWORLDWORLDWOR
```

and this:

```
select RPAD('CAROLYN',15,'-') from DUAL;
```

produces this:

```
CAROLYN--------
```

RTRIM

Type   SQL function

Products   All, PL/SQL

See also   CHARACTER FUNCTIONS, **LPAD**, **LTRIM**, **RPAD**, Chapter 5

Format

```
RTRIM(string [,'set'])
```

Description   **R**ight **TRIM** trims all the occurrences of any one of a *set* of characters off of the right side of a string.

Example

```
RTRIM('GEORGE','OGRE')
```

produces *nothing*, a NULL, empty string with zero length! On the other hand, this:

```
RTRIM('EDYTHE','HET')
```

produces this:

```
EDY
```

RUN

Type   SQL*PLUS command

Product   SQL*PLUS

See also   **/**, **@**, **@@**, **EDIT**, **START**

Format

```
R[UN]
```

Description   **RUN** displays the SQL command in the SQL buffer, and then executes it. **RUN** is similar to the **/** command, except that the **/** doesn't display the SQL first.

RUNFORM

Type   SQL*PLUS command

Products   SQL*PLUS

Format

```
RUNFORM [options] form_name
```

Description   **RUNFORM** runs a SQL*Forms application from within SQL*PLUS. You cannot specify a new username/password combination when running the form; it will use the account you are currently logged into.

RUNMENU

Type   Utility

Products   SQL*MENU version 5

See also   **DOCMENU**, **GENMENU**, SQL*MENU

Format

```
RUNMENU [application] [user/password] [-c crt] [-m {p ¦ b ¦ f}]
[-q] [-s] [-z] [-r file] [-w file] [-e file] [?]
```

Description   **RUNMENU** is a command line alternative to choosing the Run Menu option from SQL*MENU Design in version 5 of SQL*MENU. It displays menus and executes the programs or commands each menu choice represents.

    application is the name of the application menu that you wish to enter.

    user and *password* allow you to log on to ORACLE. If these are not entered, you will be prompted for them (followed optionally by an @*link* location). Entering only a slash (/) either on the command line or in response to the prompt, will cause ORACLE to attempt to use your OPS$ login ID. (*See* OPS$ LOGINS.)

    -c indicates use of a non-default crt definition, which has a known *crt* name, and an .r file type.

    -m defines the menu style as any one of pull down (p), bar (b), or full screen (f).

    -q makes the terminal quiet by suppressing beeps.

    -s suppresses the normal display of the logging on program banner information.

    -z prevents SQL*MENU from storing the password in the variable &PW; instead, &PW is set to NULL.

    -r takes its input from the file instead of the keyboard. This is useful for testing forms.

    -w puts the display output from SQL*MENU into a file instead of on the screen, so it can be studied later.

    -e echos keystrokes into a file while SQL*MENU is being used. This file later can be used with *-r* to replicate your previous session, such as when testing the menus for compatibility, or with automatic execution of applications.

    -? forces **RUNMENU** to display all of these options.

RUNREP

Type   Utility report program

Products   SQL*REPORTWRITER

See also   **DUMPREP**, **GENREP**, **LOADREP**, **PRINTDEF**, SQLPLUS, SQLREP, SQL*REPORTWRITER, **TERMDEF**

Format

```
RUNREP
[REPORT=]file
[USERID=user/password]
[PARAMFORM={YES¦NO}]
[CMDFILE=file]
[TERM=file]
[ARRAYSIZE=integer]
[DESTYPE={SCREEN¦FILE¦PRINTER¦MAIL}]
[DESNAME=userlist]
[DESFORMAT=format]
[COPIES=integer]
[CURRENCY=symbol]
[THOUSANDS=symbol]
[DECIMAL=symbol]
[READONLY={NO¦YES}]
[LOGFILE=file]
[BUFFERS=integer]
[LANGUAGE=language]
[BATCH={NO¦YES}]
[parameter=value]
```

Description   Although these options are listed on several lines, in actual use they must appear on the same line as **RUNREP**. The keywords and equal signs can be eliminated if the arguments all appear, and in the order shown here (although eliminating keywords can confuse others looking at the code, and should be avoided). If keywords are used, no spaces should appear on either side of the equal signs, and each keyword/parameter pair is separated from the others by spaces. On some operating systems the names chosen for files, terminal definitions, formats, or users may be case sensitive (none of the other keywords or arguments are). File names may include path names as well. On some operating systems, arguments must be entered in either single or double quotation marks. Entering just **RUNREP** followed by a question mark will produce the list of options (it, too, may need quotation marks).

REPORT is the name of the SQL*REPORTWRITER file that contains the report definitions. This is a required argument.

USERID is your ORACLE username and password (followed optionally by an @*link* location). If these are not entered, you will be prompted for them. Entering only a slash (/) either on the command line or in response to the prompt, will cause ORACLE to attempt to use your OPS$ login if (*see* OPS$ LOGINS).

PARAMFORM defaults to YES, which will offer the user the parameter form to enter runtime parameters for reports.

CMDFILE is a file that contains any of the command line arguments for **RUNREP**, including CMDFILE itself (which will point to another file with arguments in it). These may be on one or more lines, separated by spaces on the lines where more than one argument appears. Any arguments on the actual command line will override those in a command file, so command files can be used for your own "default" values, where they differ from **RUNREP**'s.

TERM specifies a file that contains terminal definitions, such as for function keys, for the terminal you are using. The default varies from system to system.

ARRAYSIZE sets aside an area in memory for processing the report. The default is 10 kilobytes. The integer value specifies the number of kilobytes to set aside if you don't choose the default. This value has a profound effect on performance, and some reports may require several megabytes to run effectively.

DESTYPE defines the output destination for the report: SCREEN sends it to the interactive browser; FILE sends it to a file specified by DESNAME; PRINTER sends it to a printer specified in DESNAME; and MAIL sends it via ORACLE*MAIL to another user (or users). SYSOUT will route the report to the standard system output, but only if BATCH=YES is included on the command line. Note that this option is not available with SQLREP.

DESNAME is a single user, or a list of users separated by commas and enclosed in parentheses:

```
DESNAME=(george, victoria, sarjeant, swing, lawson)
```

DESFORMAT specifies the printer format type for the printer named in DESNAME. This will determine control codes included in the output. Typical formats include wide, decwide, hplwide, and so on. Your System Administrator should have a list of those appropriate for your environment.

COPIES controls the number of copies to be printed. It defaults to 1.

CURRENCY determines the symbol with which money fields will be displayed. The default is taken from the database and the National Language Support feature. This can be designated automatically with the LANGUAGE keyword. However, an entry for CURRENCY will override LANGUAGE, and an entry in the runtime PARAMETER FORM will override either of them.

THOUSANDS specifies the symbol used to divide groups of numbers. That is, in some countries the number 63 million would be written 63.000.000 while in others it would be 63,000,000; the character chosen here will be the one used when such numbers are reported. The default is taken from the database and the National Language Support feature. This can be designated automatically with the LANGUAGE keyword. However, an entry for THOUSANDS will override LANGUAGE, and an entry in the runtime PARAMETER FORM will override either of them.

DECIMAL is similar to THOUSANDS. It is the symbol used to designate the presence of decimal digits. In some countries the number nine and thirty-four hundredths would be typed as 9.34 while people in other countries use 9,34 for the same value. The character chosen here will be the one used. The default is taken from the database and the National Language Support feature. This can be designated automatically with the LANGUAGE keyword. However, an entry for DECIMAL will override LANGUAGE, and an entry in the runtime PARAMETER FORM will override either of them.

READONLY is only meaningful in reports that have multiple separate queries, and for which you need to assure consistency of data from the query. This is done by a SET TRANSACTION READ ONLY, which locks just the records that will be queried. In a single query report, the default of NO should be used.

LOGFILE is the file that will get the print requests from the screen, such as to print the screen, the page, or the report. An existing file will have this output appended to the end of the file. If no file name is specified, the output goes to a file named **dfltrep.log** ("default report").

BUFFERS is the integer number of 512 byte buffers available to the executable module, and the default varies from system to system. The more buffers assigned, the more rapidly the program will execute, although significant usage on a shared system could slow other processing. The default has been optimized for reports of up to a few hundred pages.

LANGUAGE defaults to US and automatically designates the correct CURRENCY, THOUSANDS, and DECIMAL characters. It is overridden by any of these three keywords on the command line or in a runtime PARAMETER FORM.

BATCH designates that this report is being run in a batch mode, without human interaction, so all terminal input and output are suppressed. The default is N, which is the usual state for nonbatch reporting. Note that PARAMFORM=Y is nonsensical here, since there is no human user to key values into the PARAMETER FORM.

parameter is a keyword you created when defining the report. The value you enter following its name will be substituted in the report creation wherever that parameter appears.

SAVE

Product　SQL*PLUS

See also　**EDIT**, **GET**, Chapter 4

Format

```
SAV[E] file[.ext] [ CRE[ATE] ¦ REP[LACE] ¦ APP[END] ]
```

Description　**SAVE** saves the contents of the current buffer into a host file with the name *file*. If no file type (extension) is specified, the file type SQL is added to the file name. This default extension can be changed with **SET SUFFIX**. **SAVE** commits pending work to the database.

　　If the file already exists, the **CREATE** option will force **SAVE** to abort and will produce an error message. The **REPLACE** option will replace any existing file, or create a new one if none exists.

　　The **APPEND** option adds this file to the end of any existing file, or creates a new one if none exists.

Example　The following saves the contents of the current buffer into a file named **lowcost.sql**:

```
save lowcost
```

SAVEPOINT

Type　SQL command

Products　All, PL/SQL

See also　**COMMIT, ROLLBACK, SET TRANSACTION**

Format

```
SAVEPOINT savepoint
EXEC SQL SAVEPOINT [AT {database ¦ :variable }] savepoint
```

Description　**SAVEPOINT** is a point within a transaction to which you may rollback. Savepoints allow you to **ROLLBACK** partitions of your current transaction. *See* **ROLLBACK**.

　　The first version here is typical of SQL*PLUS. The second is typical of embedded SQL in a precompiler and includes a way to identify the database on which the SAVEPOINT is created, either by name or by variable containing the name. The purpose of **SAVEPOINT** is to be able to assign a name to the beginning of a group of SQL statements and later, if necessary, **ROLLBACK** to that name, thus undoing the results of *just that group.* These can be nested or sequenced, allowing great control over recovery from errors. The idea here is to collect together a series of SQL statements that make up one logical transaction, and hold the **COMMIT** until all the steps within it have been completed successfully. It may be that an attempted step will fail, but you'll want to be able to try it again without having to undo everything else prior to it. Here is a possible structure, shown logically in pseudo-code:

```
start of logical transaction

    savepoint ALPHA
    SQL statement 1
    function a
    function b

    if (condition) then rollback to savepoint ALPHA

      savepoint BETA
      function c
      SQL statement 2
      SQL statement 3

      if (condition) then rollback to savepoint BETA

    if (condition) then rollback to savepoint ALPHA

        savepoint GAMMA
        SQL statement 4

      if (condition) then rollback to savepoint GAMMA

    if (condition) then rollback to savepoint BETA

  if (condition) then rollback to savepoint ALPHA

if (condition) then either commit or rollback
```

This shows that SQL statements, or groups of them, can be collected together and undone in sets or singly. In a host program, or using PL/SQL in SQL*PLUS or SQL*FORMS, or even interactively in SQL*PLUS, you may want to set up SAVEPOINTs that you can **ROLLBACK** to, based on the results of your most recent SQL statement or condition test. **ROLLBACK** allows you to return to a specific step where you named a SAVEPOINT.

If a function, a section of logic, or an attempted SQL statement fails, you can return the data in the database back to the state it was in before the local step began. You can then try it again.

SAVEPOINT names must be unique to a transaction (defined by where it ends, with either a **COMMIT** or unconditional **ROLLBACK**) but do not have to be unique to all of your database objects. You can give a **SAVEPOINT** the same name as a table, for instance (this might even result in more understandable code if the **SAVEPOINT** had the name of the table being updated). Names for **SAVEPOINT**s follow object-naming conventions.

If you give a new **SAVEPOINT** the same name as a previous one, the new one replaces the earlier one. The earlier one is lost, and you can no longer roll back to it.

The **init.ora** parameter **SAVEPOINT**s determine the maximum number available in a transaction. The default is 5, but you can set it as high as 255.

Once a **COMMIT** or an unconditional **ROLLBACK** (not to a SAVEPOINT) is issued, all previous **SAVEPOINT**s are erased. Recall that all DDL statements (such as **DISCONNECT**, **CREATE TABLE**, **CREATE INDEX**, and so on) automatically issue an implicit **COMMIT**, and any severe failure (if the program terminates abnormally or the computer goes down), will result in an automatic **ROLLBACK**.

SCAN (SQL*PLUS)

See **SET**.

SEGMENT

A segment is another way to classify the space allocated to a table, index, or cluster. A table has one segment that consists of all of its extents. Every index has one segment similarly defined. A cluster has at least two segments, one for its data and one for its cluster key index.

SEGMENT HEADER BLOCK

The segment header block is the first block in the first extent of a segment, which contains, among other things, a list of extents for that segment.

SELECT (Form 1 - SQL)

Type   SQL command

Products   All

See also   COLLATION, **CONNECT BY, DELETE, DUAL, FROM, GROUP BY,
HAVING, INSERT, JOIN**, LOGICAL OPERATORS, **ORDER BY**, QUERY
OPERATORS, SUBQUERY, SYNTAX OPERATORS, **UPDATE, WHERE**

Format

```
SELECT [ ALL ¦ DISTINCT
        { * ¦
         [user.]table.* ¦
         expression [AS alias] [ ,expression [AS alias] ]... }
  FROM [user.]table[@dblink] [alias]
        [ ,[user.]table[@dblink] [alias]...
[ WHERE condition ]
[ CONNECT BY condition [START WITH condition] ]
[ GROUP BY expression [,expression]... ] [HAVING condition]
[ { UNION [ALL] ¦ INTERSECT ¦ MINUS } SELECT ... ]
[ ORDER BY {expression ¦ position} [ASC¦DESC] ...
            [ ,expression ¦ position} [ASC¦DESC] ]...
[ FOR UPDATE [OF [[user.]{table ¦ view}.]column
  [,[[user.]{table ¦ view}.]]...]
  [NOWAIT] ]
```

Description   **select** retrieves rows from one or more tables (or views or
snapshots), either as a command, or as a subquery in another SQL command
(within limitations), including **select**, **insert**, **update**, and **delete**. **ALL** means that
all rows satisfying the conditions will be returned (this is the default). **DISTINCT**
means that only rows that are unique will be returned; any duplicates will be
weeded out first.

An * (asterisk) by itself results in all columns from all tables in the **from** clause
being displayed. *table*.* means that all columns from this table will be displayed.
An asterisk by itself cannot be combined with any other columns, but a *table*.*
can be followed by column names and expressions, including ROWID.

expression means any form of a column. This could be a column name, a
literal, a mathematical computation, a function, or several functions combined.
The most common version is a simple column name, or a column name prefixed
by a table name or table alias. *alias* is a renaming of the column or expression. In
ORACLE7.1 and above, the column alias can be preceded by the word AS. The
column alias will become the column heading in the display, and may be
referenced by the **column**, **ttitle**, and **btitle** commands in SQL*PLUS. In

ORACLE7.0, the column alias cannot be referenced elsewhere within the **select** statement itself, but in ORACLE7.1 and above, it may be used in the **order by** clause. If it is more than one word, or will contain characters that are neither numbers nor letters, it must be enclosed in double quotation marks.

user, *table*, and *dblink* denote the table or view from which the rows will be drawn. *user* and *dblink* are optional, and their absence makes ORACLE default to the current user. However, specifying the user in a query may reduce ORACLE's overhead and make the query run more quickly.

An *alias* here will rename the table for this query. This alias, unlike the expression alias, can be referenced elsewhere within the **select** statement itself, for instance as a prefix to any column name coming from that table. In fact, if a table has an alias, the alias *must* be used whenever a column from that table has a table name prefix. Tables are typically aliased when two tables with long names are joined in a query, and many of their columns have the same name, requiring them to be unambiguously named in the **select** clause. Aliases are also commonly used in correlated subqueries, and when a table is being joined to itself.

condition may be any valid expression that tests true or false. It can contain functions, columns (from these tables), and literals. *position* allows the **order by** to identify the expressions based on their relative position in the **select** clause, rather than on their names. This is valuable for complicated expressions, and essential with **UNION**, **INTERSECT**, and **MINUS** operators. However, users of ORACLE7.1 and above should discontinue the use of ordinal positions in **order by** clauses (except with **UNION**, **INTERSECT**, and **MINUS**); column aliases may be used in their place. The current SQL standard does not include support for ordinal positions in **order by** clauses, and ORACLE may not support them in the future. **ASC** and **DESC** specify whether it is an ascending or descending sequence for each expression in the **order by**. *See* COLLATION for a discussion of what these sequences are.

column is a column in a table listed in the **from** clause. This cannot be an expression, but must be a real column name. **NOWAIT** means that a **select for update** attempt that encounters a locked row will terminate and return immediately to the user, rather than wait and attempt to update the row again in a few moments.

The **for update of** clause puts locks on the rows that have been selected. **select . . . for update of** should be followed immediately by an **update. . .where** command, or, if you decide not to update anything, by a **COMMIT** or **ROLLBACK**. The **for update of** also includes the actions of **insert** and **delete**. Once you have locked a row, other users cannot update it until you free it with a **COMMIT** command (or **AUTOCOMMIT**) or **ROLLBACK**. **select . . . for update of** cannot include **DISTINCT**, **GROUP BY**, **UNION**, **INTERSECT**, **MINUS**, or any group function, such **MIN**, **MAX**, **AVG**, or **COUNT**. The columns named have no effect and are present for compatibility with other dialects of SQL. ORACLE will lock only the tables that appear in the **for update** clause. If you don't have an **of** clause listing any tables, ORACLE will lock all the tables in the **from** clause for update. All the tables must be on the same database, and if there are references to a LONG column or a sequence in the **select**, the tables must be on the same database as the LONG or the sequence.

The other individual clauses in the **select** statement are all described under their own names elsewhere in this reference.

Other Notes

Clauses must be placed in the order shown, except for these:

- **connect by**, **start with**, **group by**, and **having**, which may be in any order in relation to each other.

- **order by** and **for update of**, which may be in any order in relation to each other.

SELECT (Form 2 - Embedded SQL)

Type   Embedded SQL command

Product   Precompilers

See also   **CONNECT, DECLARE CURSOR, DECLARE DATABASE, EXECUTE, FETCH, FOR, PREPARE, UPDATE** (Form 2), **WHENEVER**

Format

```
EXEC SQL [AT {database|:variable}]

SELECT select_list
  INTO :variable [,:variable]...
  FROM table_list
[ WHERE condition ]
[ CONNECT BY condition [START WITH condition] ]
[ GROUP BY expression [,expression]... ] [HAVING condition]
[ { UNION [ALL] | INTERSECT | MINUS } SELECT ... ]
[ ORDER BY {expression | position} [ASC|DESC] ...
            [ ,expression | position} [ASC|DESC] ]...
[ FOR UPDATE [OF column_list] [NOWAIT] ]
```

Description   *See* the description of the various clauses in **SELECT** (Form 1). The following are the elements unique to embedded SQL:

- **AT *database***, which optionally names a database from a previous **CONNECT** statement, for a database name from a previous **DECLARE DATABASE** statement.

- **INTO :*variable* [,:*variable*]** is the list of host variables into which the results of the **select** statement will be loaded. If any variable in this list is an array, all of the variables in the list must be arrays, though they need not all be the same size arrays.

- The **where** clause may reference non-array host variables.

- The **select** clause may reference host variables anywhere a constant would have been used.

You can use the embedded **SQL SELECT** with variable arrays to return multiple rows with a single **FETCH**. You also can use it to either **DECLARE CURSOR** or **PREPARE** statements for use with a later **FETCH**, and may include the **for update of** clause. The later **update** statement can then reference the columns named in the **for update of** using its own **current of** clause. *See* **DECLARE CURSOR** and **UPDATE** (Form 2).

If the embedded **select** returns no rows, SQLCODE is set to +100, and the host variables are left unchanged. In that case, **WHENEVER** lets you change the program flow.

All rows that meet the **select** criteria are locked at the **OPEN**. **COMMIT** releases the locks, and no further **FETCH**ing is permitted. This means you must **FETCH** and process all of the rows you wish to update before you issue a **COMMIT**.

Example

```
exec sql select Name, Age, Lodging, Age - :Retirement
           into :Employee, :Age, :Domicile, :Over_Limit
           from WORKER
           where Age >= :Retirement;
```

SELECT. . .INTO

Type PL/SQL version of SQL statement

Products PL/SQL

See also **%ROWTYPE, %TYPE, DECLARE VARIABLE, FETCH**

Format

```
SELECT expression [,expression]...
  INTO {variable [,variable]... | record}
```

```
FROM [user.]table [,[user.]table]...
[where...][group by... [having...]] [order by...];
```

Description   This is not the form of the **select** statement used in **DECLARE CURSOR**. This form utilizes the implicit cursor named SQL, executes within an execution section of a block (between **BEGIN** and **END**), and copies the values from a single row being returned into either a string of named variables, or a record whose structure is declared by **%ROWTYPE** to be just like the columns being selected. If the form that uses variables is used, they must each be **DECLARE**d and have compatible data types with those being retrieved. The order in which they appear in the **into** clause must correspond to the order of the associated columns in the **select** clause.

This **select** may be used in a loop with PL/SQL variables appearing in the **where** clause (or even acting like constants in the **select** clause), but each time the **select** executes it must return only one row. If it produces more than one row, the TOO_MANY_ROWS exception will be **RAISE**d, and SQL%ROWCOUNT will be set to 2 (*see* EXCEPTION for details). SQL%FOUND will be TRUE.

If it produces no rows, the NO_DATA_FOUND exception is **RAISE**d, and SQL%ROWCOUNT will be set to 0. SQL%FOUND will be FALSE.

Example

```
DECLARE
    EMPLOYEE            WORKER%rowtype;
    ...
BEGIN
    select Name, Age, Lodging into EMPLOYEE
      from WORKER
     where Worker = 'BART SARJEANT';
```

or alternatively,

```
DECLARE
    Who        CHAR(25);
    How_Old    NUMBER;
    Home       CHAR(25);
    ...
BEGIN
    select Name, Age, Lodging into Who, How_Old, Home
      from WORKER
     where Worker = 'BART SARJEANT';
```

SEQUENCE

A sequence is a database object used to generate unique integers for use as primary keys. *See* **CREATE SEQUENCE**.

SERVER PROCESS

Server processes work on behalf of user processes. *See* BACKGROUND PROCESS.

SERVER SYSTEM

Server system is the configuration of ORACLE when a remote user accesses ORACLE via SQL*NET.

SESSION

The session is the series of events that happens between the time a user connects to SQL and the time he or she disconnects.

SET

Type   SQL*PLUS command

Product   SQL*PLUS

See also   **SET TRANSACTION**, **SHOW**, Chapter 4

Format

```
SET feature value
```

where feature and value are from the following list. The default value is listed first.

```
ARRAY[SIZE] {20|integer}
AUTO[COMMIT] {OFF|ON|IMM[EDIATE]}
BLOCKTERMINATOR {.|symbol} (Version 3 SQL*PLUS)
BUF[FER] buffer
CMDS[EP] {OFF|ON|;|symbol}
CONCAT {.|symbol}
CONCAT {ON|OFF}
COPYCOMMIT {0|integer}
```

```
CRT crt (Version 3 SQL*PLUS)
DCL[SEP] {!¦symbol}
DEF[INE] {&¦symbol¦OFF¦ON}
DOC[UMENT] {OFF¦ON}
ECHO {OFF¦ON}
EMBEDDED {OFF¦ON}
ESCAPE {\¦symbol¦OFF¦ON}
FEED[BACK] {6¦integer¦OFF¦ON}
FLUSH {OFF¦ON}
HEA[DING] {OFF¦ON}
HEADS[EP] {¦¦symbol¦OFF¦ON}
LIN[ESIZE] {80¦integer}
LONG {80¦integer}
MAXD[ATA] integer
NEWP[AGE] {1¦integer}
NULL text NUMF[ORMAT] format
NUM[WIDTH] {10¦integer}
PAGES[IZE] {14¦integer}
PAU[SE] {OFF¦ON¦text}
RECSEP {WR[APPED]¦EA[CH]¦OFF}
RECSEPCHAR {_¦symbol}
SCAN {ON¦OFF}
SHOW[MODE] {OFF¦ON}
SPA[CE] {1¦integer}
SQLC[ASE] {MIX[ED]¦LO[WER]¦UP[PER]}
SQLC[ONTINUE] { '>' ¦ text }
SQLN[UMBER] {ON¦OFF}
SQLPRE[FIX] {#¦symbol}
SQLP[ROMPT] { SQL>¦text}
SQLT[ERMINATOR] {;¦symbol¦OFF¦ON}
SUFFIX {SQL¦text}
TAB {OFF¦ON}
TERM[OUT] {ON¦OFF}
TI[ME] {OFF¦ON}
TIMI[NG] {OFF¦ON}
TRIM[OUT] {ON¦OFF}
TRU[NCATE] {OFF¦ON}
UND[ERLINE] {-¦character}
UND[ERLINE] {ON¦OFF}
VER[IFY] {ON¦OFF}
WRAP {ON¦OFF}
```

Description   **SET** turns a SQL*PLUS feature ON or OFF or to a certain value. All of these features are changed with the **SET** command and displayed with the **SHOW** command. **SHOW** will display a particular command if its name follows the word **SHOW**, or all commands if **SHOW** is entered by itself. As there are a large number of options here, it makes sense to **spool** to a file, type **SHOW**, and then **spool off**. This will put all the options and their current state in a file that you can then browse through with your editor.

In the features below, the default value is always the first in the list.

ARRAY[SIZE] {20¦n} will set the size of the batch of rows that SQL*PLUS will fetch at one time. The range is 1 to 5000. Larger values improve the efficiency of queries and subqueries where many rows will be fetched, but use more memory. Values above 100 generally do not produce much improvement. ARRAYSIZE has no other effect on the workings of SQL*PLUS.

AUTO[COMMIT] {OFF¦ON¦IMM} ON or IMM makes SQL immediately commit any pending changes to the database upon the completion of every SQL command. **OFF** stops this automatic committing, and you must instead commit any changes intentionally with the **COMMIT** command. However, many commands, such as **QUIT**, **EXIT**, **CONNECT**, **CREATE**, and so on, will themselves cause a **COMMIT** of any pending changes.

BLOCKTERMINATOR {.¦symbol} sets the symbol to be used to denote the end of a PL/SQL block. This cannot be a letter or a number. To execute the block, use **RUN** or **/** (slash).

In BUF[FER] {buffer} buffer becomes the current buffer. The SQL buffer is always the current buffer when SQL*PLUS first begins.

In CMDS[EP] {OFF¦ON¦;¦symbol} symbol sets the character used to separate multiple SQL*PLUS commands entered on a line. ON or OFF controls whether multiple commands may be entered on a line.

CONCAT {.¦symbol} sets a symbol that may be used to terminate or delimit a user variable that is followed by a symbol, character, or word that would otherwise be interpreted as a part of the user variable name.

CONCAT {ON¦OFF} Setting CONCAT ON resets its value to ' . '.

COPYCOMMIT {0¦n} The **COPY** command will commit rows to the destination database on a cycle of n batches of rows (the number of rows in a batch is **SET** by ARRAYSIZE). Valid values are 0 to 5000. If value is 0, a **COMMIT** will occur only at the end of a copy operation.

CRT crt changes the default crt that will be used whenever the **RUNFORM** command is used (this allows SQL*FORMS to be called directly from within SQL*PLUS). The crt file has **.r** file type.

DCL[SEP] {!¦symbol} sets the symbol used to separate multiple operating system commands entered in SQL*PLUS. When used with HOST or $, it has the effect of a carriage return and line feed (like hitting the ENTER key) after each command. Thus, if the following displays "Hello, World" on your terminal:

```
host echo Hello, World
```

then this:

```
host echo Hello, World!echo Hello, World!echo Hello, World
```

will display this:

```
Hello, World
Hello, World
Hello, World
```

The default DCL separator is !, and it is in effect only in combination with the HOST or $ command. DCL, by the way, is the Digital Equipment VMS operating system command language.

DEF[INE] {&¦symbol} Here, *symbol* defines the character used to prefix and denote a substitution variable.

DEF[INE] {ON¦OFF} determines whether SQL*PLUS will look for and substitute commands for substitution variables and load them with their DEFINEd values.

DOC[UMENT] {OFF¦ON} ON allows the **DOCUMENT** command to work. OFF causes SQL*PLUS to ignore it, even when present, which will cause any lines following **DOCUMENT** to be treated as SQL*PLUS or SQL commands. *See* **DOCUMENT** for further details.

ECHO {OFF¦ON} ON makes SQL*PLUS echo (display) commands to the screen as they execute from a start file. OFF makes SQL*PLUS execute them without displaying them. The results of the commands, on the other hand, are controlled by **TERMOUT**.

EMBEDDED {OFF¦ON} ON allows a new report in a series of reports to begin anywhere on a page, just after the previous one ended. OFF forces the new report to start at the top of a new page.

ESCAPE {\¦symbol} *symbol* defines an ESCAPE character that can be used to prefix the DEFINE symbol so that it can be displayed, rather than interpreted as the beginning of a variable.

ESCAPE {OFF¦ON} OFF disables the ESCAPE character so that it no longer has any effect. ON always defines the ESCAPE character to be \ (backslash). For example, if the ESCAPE character were defined as \, then this:

```
ACCEPT Report prompt 'Please Enter P\&L Report Name:'
```

would display this:

```
Please Enter P&L Report Name:
```

and &L would not be treated as a variable.

FEED[BACK] {6⌐*n*⌐OFF⌐ON} makes SQL*PLUS show "records selected" after a query if at least *n* records are selected. ON or OFF turns this display on or off. **SET FEEDBACK** to 0 is the same as OFF.

FLUSH {ON⌐OFF} OFF is used when a start file can be run without needing any display or interaction until it has completed. The OFF lets the operating system avoid sending output to the display. ON restores output to the user's display. OFF may improve performance.

HEA[DING] {ON⌐OFF} OFF suppresses the headings, both text and underlines, that normally appear above columns. ON allows them to be displayed.

In HEADS[EP] {⌐ ⌐ *symbol*} *symbol* is the heading separator character. The default is the broken vertical bar (a solid vertical bar on some computers). Wherever it appears, SQL*PLUS will break the title or heading down on to a new line. This works both in the **column** command, and in the old method of using **btitle** and **ttitle**.

HEADS[EP] {ON⌐OFF} ON or OFF turns it on or off. If it is off, the heading separator symbol is printed like any other character.

LIN[ESIZE] {80⌐*n*} sets the line width, the total number of characters on a line that can be displayed before wrapping down to the next line. This number is also used when SQL*PLUS calculates the proper position for centered or right-aligned titles. The maximum value of *n* is 999.

LONG {80⌐*n*} is the maximum width for displaying or copying (spooling) LONG values. *n* may range from 1 to 32767, but must be less than the value of **MAXDATA**. *See* Chapter 24.

MAXD[ATA] *n* sets the maximum total row width (including a row folded onto many lines) that SQL*PLUS is able to handle. The default and maximum values for **MAXDATA** are different for different host operating systems. *See* the *ORACLE Installation and User's Guide* for further details.

NEWP[AGE] {1⌐*n*} sets the number of blank lines to be printed between the bottom of one page and the top title of the next. A 0 (zero) sends a form feed at the top of each page. If the output is being displayed, this will usually clear the screen.

NULL text sets the text that will be substituted when SQL*PLUS discovers null value. NULL without text displays blanks.

NUMF[ORMAT] format sets the default number format for displaying number data items. *See* NUMBER FORMATS for details.

NUM[WIDTH] {10⌐*n*} sets the default width for number displays.

PAGES[IZE] {14⌐*n*} sets the number of lines per page. *See* Chapter 4 for use of **pagesize** and **newpage**.

PAU[SE] {OFF⌐ON⌐*text}* ON makes SQL*PLUS wait for you to press RETURN after it displays each page of output. OFF means no pause between pages of display. *text* is the message SQL*PLUS will display at the bottom of the screen as it waits for you to hit the RETURN key. Pause will wait before the very first page is displayed; you'll have to hit RETURN to see it.

RECSEP {WR[APPED]¦EA[CH]¦OFF} Each row SQL*PLUS brings back can be separated from other rows by a character, defined by RECSEPCHAR (*see also* **SET**). By default, the character is a space, and this only happens for records (and therefore columns) that wrap. For example, here the eight rows of the City column are queried, but the format is too narrow for one of the cities, so it wraps just for that city:

```
column City format a9

select City from COMFORT;

CITY
---------
SAN FRANC
ISCO

SAN FRANC
ISCO

SAN FRANC
ISCO

SAN FRANC
ISCO

KEENE
KEENE
KEENE
KEENE
```

However, when RECSEP is OFF, the effect is this:

```
set recsep off

select City from COMFORT;
CITY
---------
SAN FRANC
ISCO
SAN FRANC
ISCO
SAN FRANC
ISCO
SAN FRANC
```

```
ISCO
KEENE
KEENE
KEENE
KEENE
```

RECSEPCHAR { ¦ *symbol*} works with RECSEP. The default is a space, but you can set it to another symbol if you wish.

SCAN {ON¦OFF} Variable substitution normally occurs because SQL*PLUS scans SQL statements for the substitution symbol. If SCAN is set OFF, it won't scan and the substitution of variables will be suppressed.

SHOW[MODE] {OFF¦ON} ON makes SQL*PLUS display the old and new settings of a SET feature and its value when it is changed. OFF stops the display of both of these.

SPA[CE] {1¦*n*} sets the number of spaces between columns in a row in the output. The maximum value is 10.

SQLC[ASE] {MIX[ED] ¦ LO[WER] ¦ UP[PER]} converts all the text, including literals and identifiers, in either SQL or PL/SQL blocks, before it is executed by ORACLE. **MIXED** leaves case just as it is typed. **LOWER** converts everything to lowercase; **UPPER** converts it all to uppercase.

SQLC[ONTINUE] { '> ' ¦ text } sets the character sequence to be displayed as a prompt for a long line that must continue on the next line. When you enter a - (hyphen) at the end of a SQL*PLUS command line, the SQLCONTINUE symbols or text will prompt you from the left of the next screen line.

SQLN[UMBER] {ON¦OFF} If this is ON, then lines of SQL beyond the first one you enter will have line numbers as prompts. If this is OFF, the SQLPROMPT will appear only on additional lines.

SQLPRE[FIX] {#¦*symbol*} sets the SQL prefix character, which can be used to cause immediate execution of a SQL*PLUS command (such as **COLUMN**), even when entering SQL or PL/SQL commands. The SQL*PLUS command will go into effect immediately. Using this with a SQL statement will cause any preceding SQL keyed in thus far to be replaced completely by the text following the #.

SQLP[ROMPT] { SQL>¦*text*} sets the SQL prompt that is displayed if SQLNUMBER is OFF.

SQLT[ERMINATOR] {;¦*symbol*} sets the symbol used to end SQL commands, and start immediate execution of the SQL. OFF means that no SQL symbol will be recognized as a terminator, and the user must instead terminate the command by entering an empty line after the last line of SQL.

SQLT[ERMINATOR] {ON¦OFF} ON always resets the terminator to the default (';'), regardless of what else has been set.

SUFFIX {SQL¦*text*} sets the default file name extension (also called the file type) that SQL*PLUS appends to files you **SAVE**. *See* **SAVE**.

TAB {OFF¦ON} OFF makes SQL use spaces in formatting columns and text on reports. The default value for TAB is system-dependent. **SHOW TAB** will display it. ON sets SQL*PLUS to use tabs instead of spaces.

TERM[OUT] {ON¦OFF} ON displays regular SQL*PLUS output from a start file. OFF suppresses the display, and is valuable when the output is being spooled to a file, but you don't want to see it displayed on the screen as well. OFF will also improve performance.

TI[ME] {OFF¦ON} When TIME is ON, SQL*PLUS displays the current time (from the system clock) before each command prompt. OFF suppresses the display of the current time.

TIMI[NG] {OFF¦ON} ON has SQL*PLUS show timing statistics for each SQL command that is executed. OFF suppresses the display of the timing of each command. (*See* **TIMING** for another command by the same name that operates completely differently.)

TRIM[OUT] {ON¦OFF} SET TAB ON must be in effect for this to operate. When ON, it trims blanks at the end of each displayed line rather than displaying them, which often results in significant performance gains, especially over dial-up lines. OFF allows trailing blanks to be displayed. TRIMOUT ON does not change spooled output.

TRU[NCATE] {OFF¦ON} Use **SET WRAP OFF** instead of **TRUNCATE**, which is an old command. **TRUNCATE** clips the excess off of a column so it will fit in the width allowed it by the **COLUMN FORMAT** command. **SET WRAP OFF** gives the same results as **SET TRUNCATE ON**, but is preferable, because the **SHOW** command can reference it, but cannot reference **TRUNCATE**.

UND[ERLINE] {-¦*character*} sets the character used as the underline for column headings. The default is - (hyphen).

UND[ERLINE] {ON¦OFF} turns underlining on or off without changing the character.

VER[IFY] {ON¦OFF} ON makes SQL*PLUS show the old and new values of variables before executing the SQL in which they are embedded. OFF suppresses the display.

WRAP {ON¦OFF} ON wraps a row to the next line if it exceeds the width set in **COLUMN**. OFF truncates (clips) the right-hand side of a column display if it is too long to fit the current line width. Use the **COLUMN** command's **wrapped** clauses to override WRAP for specific columns.

SET CONDITION

Set condition is a logical expression containing a query, for example "Name IN (select. . .)". The name derives from the idea that the query condition will produce a set of records.

SET OPERATOR

The set operator is always either **UNION**, **INTERSECT**, or **MINUS**. *See also* QUERY OPERATORS.

SET ROLE

Type   SQL command

Products   All, PL/SQL

See also   **ALTER USER**, **CREATE ROLE,** Chapter 17

Format

```
SET ROLE { role [IDENTIFIED BY password]
           [,role [IDENTIFIED BY password]]... ¦
         ALL [EXCEPT role[, role]...] ¦
         NONE }
```

Description   **SET ROLE** enables or disables roles granted to a user for the current SQL session. The first option lets the user enable specific roles, optionally giving a password if the role has one (*see* **CREATE ROLE**). The second option lets the user enable **ALL** roles **EXCEPT** for specific ones; these roles must be directly granted to the user, not roles granted through other roles. The **ALL** option does not enable roles with passwords. The third option, **NONE**, disables all roles for the current session.

SET TRANSACTION

Type   SQL command

Products   All, PL/SQL

See also   **COMMIT**, **ROLLBACK**, **SAVEPOINT**, **TRANSACTION**

Format

```
SET TRANSACTION {READ ONLY ¦ USE ROLLBACK SEGMENT segment}
```

Description   **SET TRANSACTION** starts a transaction. The standard SQL transaction guarantees statement level read consistency, making sure that the data from a query is consistent while the statement is executing. But some transactions need a stronger guarantee that a series of **select** statements, accessing one or more tables, will see a consistent snapshot of all of the data in one instant in time. **SET**

TRANSACTION READ ONLY specifies this stronger read consistency. No changes to the queried data by other users will affect the transaction's view of the data. In a read-only transaction, you can use only the **select**, **lock table**, **set role**, **alter session**, and **alter system** commands.

For transactions that include **insert**, **update**, or **delete** commands, ORACLE assigns a rollback segment to the transaction. **SET TRANSACTION USE ROLLBACK SEGMENT** specifies that the current transaction will use a specific rollback segment.

```
select Name, Manager
  from WORKER, LODGING
 where WORKER.Lodging = LODGING.Lodging;
```

Changes that occur to a Manager after the query is executed, but before all the rows have been fetched, will not appear in the result. However, if the two tables were queried sequentially, as follows:

```
select Name, Lodging from WORKER;

select Manager, Lodging from LODGING;
```

the Manager in LODGING could well change while the first **select** was still executing, and the Lodging in WORKER could change while the second **select** was executing. Attempting to then join the results of these two separate **select**s using program logic (rather than the table join in the first example) would produce inconsistent results. This gives the solution:

```
commit;
set transaction read only;
select Name, Lodging from WORKER;

select Manager, Lodging from LODGING;
commit;
```

This freezes the data (for this user) in both tables before either **select** retrieves any rows. It will be as consistent as the data in the first example with the table join. The data is held constant until a **COMMIT** or **ROLLBACK** is issued.

The use of the two **commit**s (one before and one after) is important. **SET TRANSACTION** must be the first SQL statement in a transaction. The **COMMIT** just before it assures that this is true. The **COMMIT** at the end releases the snapshot of the data. This is important because ORACLE needs to recapture the resources it has set aside to hold the data constant.

If the data you are freezing is from tables with high update volume, or your transaction is lengthy and will take a good deal of time, the DBA may need to **CREATE** additional **ROLLBACK SEGMENT**s to provide the storage space for the frozen data.

SGA

See System Global Area.

SHARE LOCK

A share lock is one that permits other users to query data, but not to change it.

SHARE-MODE LOCKING

Share-mode locking is synonymous with row-level locking, a type of locking in which **update**s to data occur through locking rows in a table, and affect the rows locked, not the entire table.

SHARE-UPDATE LOCK

A share-update lock is one that permits other users to both query and lock data.

SHARED PARTITION SYSTEM

A shared partition system is an ORACLE configuration in which ORACLE systems on multiple network nodes share the same database files. Each node is called an instance.

SHARED SQL POOL

An area in the ORACLE7 SGA that contains both the dictionary cache and a shared area for the parsed versions of all SQL commands within the database. The Shared SQL Pool is also referred to as the Shared SQL Area; its size is determined by the SHARED_POOL_SIZE parameter in the database's **init.ora** file.

SHOW

Type   SQL*PLUS command

Product   SQL*PLUS

See also   SET

Format

```
SHO[W] { feature | ALL | BTI[TLE] | LNO | PNO | REL[EASE]|
SPOO[L] | TTI[TLE] | USER | WRAP }
```

Description **SHOW** displays the value of a feature of SET, or **ALL** features of SET, or of the other SQL*PLUS items. More than one of these (including more than one SET feature) can follow the word SHOW, and each will be displayed on a separate line.

BTI[TLE] displays the current **btitle** definition.

LNO shows the current line number (the line in the current page being displayed).

PNO displays the page number.

REL[EASE] gives the release number of this version of ORACLE.

SPOO[L] tells whether output is being spooled (ON or OFF). *See* **SPOOL**.

SQLCODE shows the error message number of the most recent ORACLE error.

TTI[TLE] displays the current **ttitle** definition.

USER shows the user's ID.

WRAP shows the WRAP setting (**TRUNCATE** does not work with **SHOW**).

SHOWMODE (SQL*PLUS)

See **SET**.

SHUT DOWN

To shut down is to disconnect an instance from the database and terminate the instance. *See* (and contrast with) START UP.

SIGN

Type SQL function

Products All, PL/SQL

See also +, **PRECEDENCE**, Chapter 6

Format

```
SIGN(value)
```

Description It equals 1 if *value* is positive, –1 if negative, 0 if zero.

Example

```
SIGN(33)  =   1
SIGN(-.6) = -1
SIGN(0)   =   0
```

SIN

Type   SQL function

Products   All

See also   **COS**, NUMBER FUNCTIONS, **SINH**, **TAN**, Chapter 6

Format

```
SIN(value)
```

Description   **SIN** returns the sine of an angle *value* expressed in radians.

Example

```
select SIN(30*3.141593/180) Sine -- sine of 30 degrees in radians
   from DUAL;

SINE
----------
       .5
```

SINH

Type   SQL function

Products   All

See also   **COS**, NUMBER FUNCTIONS, **SIN**, **TAN**, Chapter 6

Format

```
SINH(value)
```

Description   **SINH** returns the hyperbolic sine of an angle *value*.

SINGLE PROCESS

Single process is a mode of database operation that allows only one user to access a database.

SMON

The **S**ystem **Mon**itor Process is one of the ORACLE7 background processes used to perform recovery and clean up unused temporary segments. *See* BACKGROUND PROCESS.

SNAPSHOT

A snapshot is a means of creating a local copy of remote data. A snapshot can be used to replicate all or part of a single table, or to replicate the result of a query against multiple tables. The refreshes of the replicated data can be done automatically by the database (at time intervals you specify) or manually. *See* Chapter 23, **CREATE SNAPSHOT, CREATE SNAPSHOT LOG**.

SNAPSHOT REFRESH GROUP

A snapshot refresh group is a set of local snapshots that are all refreshed as a group. Snapshot refresh groups, available as of ORACLE7.1, allow data consistency to be enforced between snapshots. *See* Chapter 23.

SOUNDEX

Type   SQL function

Products   All, PL/SQL

See also   **LIKE**, Chapter 5

Format

SOUNDEX(*string*)

Description   **SOUNDEX** finds words that **SOUND** like an **EX**ample *string*. **SOUNDEX** makes certain assumptions about how letters and combinations of letters are usually pronounced. The two words being compared must begin with the same letter.

Example

```
select LastName
  from ADDRESS
 where SOUNDEX(LastName) = SOUNDEX('SEPP');
```

```
LASTNAME                        FIRSTNAME                    PHONE
----------------------------    ------------------------     ------------
SZEP                            FELICIA                      214-522-8383
SEP                             FELICIA                      214-522-8383
```

SPACE (SQL*PLUS)

See **SET**.

SPOOL

Type   SQL*PLUS command

Product   SQL*PLUS

See also   **SET**, Chapters 4 and 19

Format

```
SPO[OL] [file:OFF:OUT];
```

Description   **SPOOL** starts or stops spooling (copying) of SQL*PLUS output to a host system file or the system printer. **SPOOL** *file* makes SQL*PLUS spool all output to the named file. If the file type is not specified, **SPOOL** adds a default, similarly to what **SAVE** does, usually .LST, but with some variation by host. OFF stops spooling. OUT stops spooling and sends the file to the printer. To spool output to a file without displaying it, **SET TERMOUT OFF** in the start file prior to the SQL statement, but before the **SPOOL** command. **SPOOL** by itself shows the name of the current (or most recent) spool file.

SQL

SQL is the ANSI industry-standard language, used to manipulate information in a relational database and used in ORACLE and IBM DB2 relational database management systems. SQL is formally pronounced "sequel," although common usage also pronounces it "S.Q.L."

The ANSI X3.135-1989 standard defines standard SQL, including the "Integrity Enhancement Option," which includes all the integrity constraints in **CREATE TABLE** (*see* INTEGRITY CONSTRAINT). The ANSI X3-168-1989 standard defines standard embedded SQL. ANSI standard ANSI X3.135-1992, also known as SQL2, defines the next-generation standard for SQL and includes many new and interesting features. It combines the standard and embedded SQL standards. The SQL3 standard, which is slated for approval later in the decade, includes a version of PL/SQL, stored procedures and triggers, and abstract data types.

ORACLE7.0 has been certified as compliant with Level 2 of the SQL89 standard. ORACLE7.1 has been certified as compliant with the SQL92 standard.

SQL CURSOR

Type   PL/SQL implicit cursor

Products   PL/SQL

See also   **%FOUND**, **%ISOPEN**, **%NOTFOUND**, **%ROWCOUNT**

Description   *SQL* is the name of the cursor opened implicitly any time the SQL statement being processed is not part of an explicitly named and opened cursor (*see* **DECLARE**). There is only one of these at any time. The cursor attributes **%FOUND** and **%NOTFOUND** can be tested by checking SQL%FOUND and SQL%NOTFOUND before or after an **insert**, **update**, or **delete** (which are never associated with an explicit cursor) or a single-row **select** that happened to be executed without an explicit cursor.

See **%FOUND** for details on these tests. *See* **%ROWCOUNT** for details on the values this attribute has under different conditions. SQL%ISOPEN always evaluates FALSE because ORACLE closes the SQL cursor automatically after executing the SQL statement.

SQL*DBA

SQL*DBA is an ORACLE utility used by DBAs while performing database maintenance and monitoring.

SQL*LOADER

SQL*LOADER is a utility for loading data into an ORACLE database. *See* **SQLLOAD**.

SQL*MENU

See **SQLMENU**.

SQL*NET

SQL*NET is an optional product that works with the ORACLE RDBMS to enable two or more computers running ORACLE to exchange database data through a network. *See* the *SQL*NET User's Guide* and Chapter 20.

SQL*PLUS

See **SQLPLUS**.

SQL*REPORTWRITER

SQL*REPORTWRITER is ORACLE's report writing, formatting, and distribution environment. It consists of several major programs:

- **SQLREP** supports the creation and running of reports, using fill-in-the-blank screens, prompts, and database storage for the report definitions.

- **RUNREP** executes reports that have been defined in SQLREP. The reports can be run using command-line parameters or screen prompts, and may be browsed or printed after creation.

- **DUMPREP** creates a flat ASCII file that can be used to transfer report definitions to other computers. Similar to the way Export works with the database, this file can move freely between ASCII and EBCDIC machines, and will be properly converted when necessary.

- **LOADREP** moves the file created by **DUMPREP** into the local ORACLE database, thereby allowing reports created elsewhere to be run locally (provided the tables and data exist, of course).

- **GENREP** takes the report definition in the database and uses it to produce a *runfile*, a tokenized or compressed version of the file, which **RUNREP** interprets in producing a report. **GENREP** also can create a runfile from the ASCII or EBCDIC files, as well as from definitions in working storage while in **SQLREP**, by choosing the Execute or Generate options.

- **PRINTDEF** allows you to create definitions for your printers to control boldface, underlining, top of form control, and so on.

- **TERMDEF** allows you to assign key definitions, highlight control codes, line drawing codes, and so on, for your particular terminal.

- For more information about these programs, see the entries under each of their names.

SQLCASE (SQL*PLUS)

See **SET**.

SQLCODE

Type   PL/SQL error function

Products   PL/SQL

See also   EXCEPTION, SQLERRM

Format

```
variable := SQLCODE
```

Description   This is an error function that returns the latest error number, but outside of an exception handler (*see* EXCEPTION WHEN) always returns 0. This is because the occurrence of an exception (that is, when SQLCODE would be nonzero) is expected to immediately transfer control to the EXCEPTION part of the PL/SQL block. Once there, SQLCODE can be tested for its value, or be used to assign a value to a variable.

SQLCODE cannot be used as a part of a SQL statement (such as to insert the value of the error code into a error table). However, you can set a variable equal to SQLCODE, and then use the variable in a SQL statement:

```
sql_error := sqlcode;
insert into PROBLEMLOG values (sql_error);
```

SQLCONTINUE (SQL*PLUS)

See **SET**.

SQLERRM

Type   PL/SQL statement

Products   PL/SQL

See also   EXCEPTION, EXCEPTION_INIT, PRAGMA, SQLCODE

Format

```
SQLERRM[(integer)]
```

Description   Without an *integer* supplied, SQLERRM returns the error message related to the current SQLCODE. With an integer supplied, it returns the error message related to that integer value. Like SQLCODE, this function cannot be used directly in a SQL statement, but can be used in an assignment:

```
error_message := sqlerrm;
```

or, to retrieve the error message associated with the error code 1403:

```
error_message := sqlerrm(1403);
```

Outside of an exception handler (*see* SQLCODE), this function without an integer argument will always return "normal, successful completion." Once in an exception handler, you will get one of these messages:

- The message associated with an ORACLE error.

- The words "User-defined exception" for an explicitly raised user-exception where you did not assign a message text.

- A user-defined message text, loaded using the PRAGMA EXCEPTION_INIT.

SQLLOAD

Type   SQL*LOADER command

Product   SQL*LOADER

See also   *Oracle7 Server Utilities User's Guide, Installation and User's Guide*

Format

```
SQLLOAD [USERID=user/password] CONTROL=file [LOG=file]
[BAD=file]
DATA=file [DISCARD=file] [DISCARDMAX=integer] [SKIP=integer]
[LOAD=integer] [ERRORS=integer] [ROWS=integer]
```

```
[BINDSIZE=integer]
[SILENT=(ALL ¦ [HEADER ¦ FEEDBACK ¦ ERROR ¦ DISCARDS] )]
[DIRECT=TRUE]
```

Description   SQLLOAD loads data from external files into tables in the ORACLE database. SQL*LOADER requires two primary files: the data file, which contains the information to be loaded into ORACLE, and the control file, which contains information on the format of the data, the records and fields within the file, the order in which they are to be loaded, and even, when needed, the names of the multiple files that will be used for data. You also can combine the control file information into the data file itself.

SQLLOAD will automatically create a log and bad file, and a discard file if DISCARDMAX is used. These will have the extensions **.log**, **.bad**, and **.dsc**.

If you wish you can separate the arguments to SQLLOAD with commas. Enter them either with the keywords (such as USERID or LOG), followed by their parameters, or in the order shown in the command, without the associated keywords. The latter technique, however, may confuse others reading the command, and will probably confuse you once you haven't looked at it for a while. Enter them with keywords for clarity's sake.

Keywords are always followed by an equal sign (=) and the appropriate argument.

If USERID is omitted, you will be asked for it. If a slash is given after the equal sign, OPS$ login default ID and password will be used. You also can use a SQL*NET database specification string to log on to a remote database and load the data to it.

CONTROL names the file that has data format and loading instructions. If omitted, you will be asked for it. If you don't give the file extension, **.ctl** will be used.

LOG names the file that will contain a log of the work SQL*LOADER does: names of files used, number of records, and so on. If you don't specify a name, SQLLOAD creates one with the same name as the control file and the extension **.log**.

BAD names the file that will contain a log of the records SQL*LOADER couldn't load. If you don't specify a name, SQLLOAD creates one with the same name as the control file and the extension **.bad**.

DATA names the file that will contain the records SQL*LOADER will load. If you don't specify a name, SQLLOAD assumes one with the same name as the control file and the extension **.dat**. Data also can be included in the control file itself.

DISCARD names the file that will contain the records SQL*LOADER neither rejected nor inserted into the database because they either did not meet the criteria of a **when** clause in the control file, or they contained all blank fields. This file is created if you name it (but will be empty if nothing is discarded) or is created automatically if you specify DISCARDMAX (or any DISCARD control word in the CONTROL file). In the latter case, if you don't specify a name, SQLLOAD assumes one with the same name as the control file and the extension **.dsc**. Its records have the same format as the data file, so they can be easily loaded later if necessary.

DISCARDMAX specifies how many discard records to allow before stopping the load. With DISCARDMAX=0, it will allow no records to be discarded. By eliminating the keyword altogether, as many as all of the records can be discarded.

SKIP tells SQLLOAD how many records at the beginning of the file to skip before it starts loading. Without the keyword, it skips none.

LOAD tells the maximum number of records to load. This doesn't include those that are skipped. Without the keyword, all records are loaded.

ERRORS specifies how many insert errors to permit before stopping the load. To stop immediately on the first error, set ERRORS=0. Without the keyword, the default is 50. To allow unlimited errors, specify a number higher than the number of records to be loaded.

ROWS specifies the number of rows to buffer together for an **insert** and **commit**. The default value is 64 if ROWS is not specified.

BINDSIZE sets the maximum number of bytes to allow for buffering rows for the insert and commit discussed in ROWS. BINDSIZE overrides the default number of bytes (called the Bind Array) on your computer (it differs by machine). If it is smaller than the total bytes required by ROWS, it will reduce the number of rows that can be buffered.

SILENT tells SQLLOAD to suppress certain informative displays:

- HEADER suppresses the SQL*LOADER header.

- FEEDBACK suppresses the feedback at each commit point.

- ERRORS suppresses the logging (in the log file) of each record that caused an ORACLE error, although the count is still logged.

- DISCARDS suppresses the logging (in the log file) of each record that was discarded, although the count is still logged.

- ALL suppresses all of the above.

If more than one of these is entered, separate each with commas and enclose the list in parentheses.

DIRECT invokes the Direct Path load option (see below).

OPTIONS

The last six of these options can also be specified in the control file itself, as an alternative to the command line. They are entered at the top of that file with the keyword OPTIONS, as shown here:

```
OPTIONS ({[SKIP=integer] [LOAD=integer] [ERRORS=integer]
[ROWS=integer]
[BINDSIZE=integer] [SILENT=(ALL ¦ [FEEDBACK ¦ ERROR ¦
DISCARDS] })
```

Note that the HEADER option for SILENT cannot be used in the control file, because by the time SQLLOAD reads it, it has already displayed the header. To silence the header display, you must do it on the command line.

The Control File

The control file contains several kinds of information essential for loading data. If the keyword INFILE is present, it tells the name of the file containing the data. If BEGINDATA is present, it means that the data is in the control file itself, and follows this word immediately (it must be the last keyword in the control file). If neither INFILE nor BEGINDATA is present, the data is assumed to be in the control file named on the command line, or in a file with the same name as the control file but with the extension **.dat**.

The control file also can specify (though with slightly altered syntax) the details of the BAD and DISCARD files, the names of the tables that are to be loaded, the format of the records that will be loaded into the tables, and the correspondence between the fields in the records and the columns in the tables. It also can exercise logic as to which records qualify for loading (using **when**), and whether records are to be **append**ed to the table, **replace** everything already in the table, or **insert** rows into an empty table.

The control file allows control statements to span several lines of the file. You can use SQLLOAD key words as column or table names, but only if you enclose them (the table or column names) in double quotation marks. Although SQLLOAD is not case sensitive, the use of double quotation marks makes anything inside of them case sensitive, so type quoted column or table names in uppercase.

Comments in a SQLLOAD control file are denoted by -- (two dashes). SQLLOAD ignores anything from the -- to the end of the line, so you can use them anywhere except in the data file, or in the data following BEGINDATA.

Commands in the control file override any in the calling command line.

Control File Format

```
OPTIONS ({[SKIP=integer] [LOAD=integer]
[ERRORS=integer][ROWS=integer]
[BINDSIZE=integer] [SILENT=(ALL ¦ [FEEDBACK ¦ ERROR ¦
DISCARDS] })
```

```
LOAD [DATA]
[ { INFILE ¦ INDDN} { file ¦ * }
  [ STREAM ¦ RECORD ¦ FIXED length [BLOCKSIZE size] ¦
VARIABLE[length] ]
[ { BADFILE ¦ BADDN } file ]
[ { DISCARDS ¦ DISCARDMAX } integer ]

[ { INDDN ¦ INFILE } ...]

[ APPEND ¦ REPLACE ¦ INSERT ]
[ RECLEN integer ]

[ { CONCATENATE integer ¦
    CONTINUEIF { [THIS ¦ NEXT ] (start[  :end]) ¦ LAST}
      operator {'string' ¦ X'hex'} } ]

INTO TABLE [user.]table
    [APPEND ¦ REPLACE ¦ INSERT ]
    [WHEN condition [ AND condition ]...]
    [FIELDS  [delimiter] ]
  (
  column         {
     RECNUM   ¦
     CONSTANT value ¦
     SEQUENCE ( { integer ¦ MAX ¦ COUNT } [ ,increment ]) ¦
     [ POSITION ( { start [ end} ¦ * [+integer] } ) ]
datatype
        [TERMINATED [BY] {WHITESPACE ¦ [X]'character'}]
        [[OPTIONALLY] ENCLOSED [BY] [X]'character']
          [ NULLIF condition ]
          [ DEFAULTIF condition ]
    }
   [ ,... ]
  )
  [ INTO TABLE ... ]

  [ BEGINDATA ]
```

Specifying the Data Files

INFILE and INDDN are synonyms; each signifies that a data file name is to follow that contains the data to be loaded. If an * is used instead of a file name, the data is in the control file itself, following the word BEGINDATA (BEGINDATA requires the default record reading method RECORD, specified shortly). You may list multiple files to be read simply by typing the keyword **INFILE** or **INDNN** followed by file names. Each file listed can have several variables specified:

STREAM means the data is to be read a byte at a time. New lines represent new physical records (logical records may be built from several physical records—*see* CONCATENATE, in the upcoming "Building Logical Records" section).

RECORD uses the host operating system's file and record management system. If the data is in the control file, this is the method used.

FIXED *length* means the records to be read are *length* bytes long, regardless of how they are broken into separate lines in the file. That is, if length is 300, SQLLOAD will read 300 bytes of data, whether they appear as one 300-byte record, three hundred one-byte records, or anything in between. BLOCKSIZE specifies the size of the blocks if this is being read from a tape.

VARIABLE means the records will be read with the first two bytes of each record assumed to contain the record's length (these bytes are not used as data). The optional length gives the maximum size any record is likely to be. If this is not specified, ORACLE assumes it to be 8K bytes. This might exceed memory constraints on your machine. If you are certain the value will be a number lower than 8K, specifying it will improve performance.

Some of the following options are not available on some systems:

BADFILE and BADDN are synonyms; each signifies that a data file name is to follow that will receive rejected data (ORACLE was unable to load it into the database). Naming rules are the same as for the command line option.

DISCARDFILE and DISCARDDN are synonyms; each signifies that a data file name is to follow that will receive records that failed the **when** clause. Naming rules are the same as for the command line option.

DISCARDS and DISCARDMAX are synonyms; the integer specifies the number of records in this file that may be discarded before SQLLOAD will terminate its efforts to load this file, and move on to the next one (or quit, if there are no more). Naming rules are the same as for the command line option. The value of integer remains in effect for subsequent files, unless one of them specifies a different integer, at which time that value controls subsequent files.

Specifying the Default Table Load Method

If the following options precede the **into table** clause, they set up the table load method for all tables that do not specify it themselves. The user must have INSERT privilege on the tables.

APPEND merely adds the rows to the table.

INSERT adds rows only to an empty table, otherwise it aborts.

REPLACE empties the table and then adds rows. The user must have DELETE privilege on the table to use this option.

These three options are equivalent to DB2's **resume yes**, **resume no**, and **resume no replace** clauses. For details on DB2 compatibility *see* the *Oracle7 Server Utilities User's Guide*.

Maximum Record Length

RECLEN is used primarily in two cases: where SQLLOAD cannot compute the record length automatically, or if you wish to see an entire bad record in the bad file. In the latter case, ORACLE will, on long records, normally only write the portion of the record up to the error point. If you want to see all of it, specifying length allows records up to that length to be written in full.

SQLLOAD computes the default length for variable length records, and assumes 80 (unless you tell it otherwise) for fixed length files.

Building Logical Records

If several physical records are needed to complete one logical record (for example, Name on line one, address on line two, city, state and zip on line three), with CONCATENATE you can specify the integer that is the number of physical records to be assembled into one logical record. (An alternative concatenation technique combines physical records if they pass certain criteria. These are specified following the CONTINUEIF.)

THIS tests a condition for the current record. If it is TRUE, the next record is concatenated to it.

NEXT tests a condition for the next record. If it is TRUE, this next record is concatenated to the current record.

start: end or start-end specifies the columns to check for the existence of a continuation string in either THIS or the NEXT string, to determine if concatenation should be done. The test is done using an operator that can be either "equal" or "not equal." *Equal* is always =, but *not equal* may be any one of !=, ~= or <>.

For example, to specify that positions 1 through 3 of the NEXT string must contain 'WAG' for it to be concatenated to the current string, use this:

```
continueif next (1-3) = 'WAG'
```

An alternative to the string of characters is the test for the existence of certain hexadecimal characters. Many of these can't be used directly in a control file, so they are called out by their number, being prefixed by one X. For example, this:

```
continueif next (1-3) = X'0D031F'
```

tests for the presence of the hex values 0D, 03, and 1F in positions 1 to 3.

Characters found using THIS and NEXT positions are assumed not to be a part of the logical record. If the field that denotes that concatenation should be done is to be a part of the assembled logical record (such as a comma), then the word **last** is used:

```
continueif last = ','
```

The Tables to be Loaded

INTO TABLE is followed by the name of the table to be loaded, and optionally prefixed with the user name if you do not own it. You must have INSERT privilege on the table. If the table has the same name as a SQLLOAD keyword, enclose it in double quotation marks and type the name in uppercase:

```
into table Talbot."LEDGER"
```

To load multiple tables, create an INTO TABLE section for each table to be loaded, and put them in the same order (and same number) as the files that contain the data. To load the same table from two files, specify the INTO TABLE twice. To load two tables from the same file, specify the file twice.

WHEN is the rough equivalent of the **where** clause in a **select** statement. It will test conditions about the records to determine if they qualify to be loaded into the table.

WHEN can test either the field to be loaded, based on its positions in the logical record, or the value to be loaded into the column, by specifying the column name. No rows will be loaded that fail either test.

The condition that is tested is similar to the one used with CONTINUEIF (and also NULLIF and DEFAULTIF, discussed shortly). The format for condition is as follows:

```
start[ :end]) ¦ column} operator {'string' ¦ X'hex'}
```

That is, either the positions (in the *logical* record, not the physical record) can be tested against a character or hex string, or a column in the table being loaded can have the value that will be loaded into it tested, just before the row is added to the table. *operator* is restricted to equal and not equal (*see* CONTINUEIF, discussed just previously), and several conditions can be joined together with **AND** (**OR** is not available). For example, this:

```
when (3-5) = 'SSM' and (22)   '*'
```

or this:

```
when Section = 'A'
```

Terminating and Enclosing Fields in the Record

FIELDS is used to specify the delimiters (if any) that separate the fields in the record. This is the format for FIELDS:

```
FIELDS [TERMINATED [BY] {WHITESPACE ¦ [X]'character'}]
       [[OPTIONALLY] ENCLOSED [BY] [X]'character']
```

TERMINATED reads fields, starting just after the end of the previous field, until the termination character is found. The character itself is not considered data. WHITESPACE means the terminator is any sort of white space, which includes spaces, tabs, linefeed, formfeed, and carriage return characters. Alternatively, a single character can be specified in quotes, or, prefixed by an X, as a hexadecimal number, such as X'1B'.

OPTIONALLY ENCLOSED indicates data might be enclosed by the specified character, but would also be enclosed by the TERMINATED character (a record where each field is separated by commas, and some are also in quotation marks, would be an example). The use of OPTIONALLY requires the use of TERMINATED. All of the options for fields (without the word FIELDS) can also be used on a column-by-column basis after any column name. If OPTIONALLY is used there, TERMINATED must either also be used there, or be in the FIELDS statement.

ENCLOSED means the data is found between two delimiters. If both ENCLOSED and TERMINATED are used, their order determines the order of evaluation.

BY is purely optional and is only used to improve readability.

Defining the Columns

column is the name of a column in the table. The specification of each column is separated by commas, and the full list of columns is surrounded by parentheses. Each column may get its value in one of four ways:

RECNUM means this column will be assigned an integer value equal to the logical record number (the count) as read from the data file. The first record gets 1, the second 2, and so on.

CONSTANT means this column will be assigned the constant value following the keyword CONSTANT. For CHAR columns this must be enclosed in quotes.

SEQUENCE differs from RECNUM in that the sequence can start at an arbitrarily chosen number and incremented in an amount greater than one. It has this format:

```
SEQUENCE ( {integer ¦ MAX ¦ COUNT } [,increment]
```

The sequence can begin in one of three ways: *integer* gives the number with which the sequence is to begin. **MAX** means start with the maximum value currently in this column in the table plus the amount of the *increment* (which is at least 1). **COUNT** means start with the count of the number of rows already in the table plus the amount of the increment. *increment* defaults to 1, but can be set to any integer value equal to or larger than 1.

Sequence numbers are incremented for every row added, or attempted to be added (rejected). This will leave missing values for rejected records; the missing values must be inserted later and their sequence values manually assigned, but using this technique preserves their original sequential position from the source file.

POSITION specifies the location in the logical record of this column's data. This position can be given in absolute terms, or can be relative to the previous column. This is the format for POSITION:

```
POSITION ( {start[ end] ¦ * [+integer] } )
```

The *start* is the location of the beginning of this column in the logical record, and the optional end gives its final position. Either : or - is acceptable between *start* and *end*. If *end* is not given, SQLLOAD assumes a default length for the column from the datatype specified for it, although a CHAR column without an end will default to 1.

An * means that this field begins immediately after the end of the previous field. Without start or end, SQLLOAD assumes a default length for the column from the datatype specified for it.

The +*integer* tells the number of positions to the right to skip over from the end of the previous field to find the beginning of this one.

If **POSITION** is not used, the default method used is **POSITION(*)**. If more than one method for determining the location of a field's data is involved (for example, delimiters and positions), certain precedence rules are followed. This list shows the order in which they are checked. Those at the beginning of the list override those below:

- Length from a specified datatype
- Length from a start *and* end position
- Length from delimiters
- Length from a start position only

Defining the Data Type

There are 14 possible data types that can be loaded using SQLLOAD. They are listed here:

```
CHAR
DATE
DECIMAL EXTERNAL
DECIMAL
DOUBLE
FLOAT
FLOAT EXTERNAL
GRAPHIC
GRAPHIC EXTERNAL
INTEGER
INTEGER EXTERNAL
SMALLINT
VARCHAR
VARGRAPHIC
```

The formatting options for each of these follows.

For a Character Data Type

CHAR [(*length*)] [*delimiter*]

If *length* is not specified, the POSITION values are used. If neither is used, the length is assumed to be 1. If the database column is a LONG, length must be specified either here or in POSITION. *See* "Terminating and Enclosing Fields in the Record," earlier in this section, for details on the *delimiter* use.

For a Date Data Type

DATE [(*length*)] ['*date format*'] [*delimiter*]

If *length* is not specified, the **POSITION** values are used. The date format may be any valid ORACLE data mask used with **TO_DATE** (*see* DATE FORMATS). If no format is specified, the default ORACLE format DD-MON-YY is assumed. *See* "Terminating and Enclosing Fields in the Record," earlier in this section, for details on the *delimiter* use.

For a Decimal Number in Character Format

DECIMAL EXTERNAL [(*length*)] [*delimiter*]

This format is used for decimal numbers that are in normal character format in the file, rather than packed into a binary format (usually one digit per four bits, rather than the eight bits that characters use). These are numbers you would be able to read if you looked at them in a file.

Binary formatted numbers would display strange symbols. These numbers are therefore treated like character data coming in, and follow the same format as

CHAR. However, when using DEFAULTIF (a discussion of which follows shortly), if you want to set the default value to NULL, use CHAR. If you want it to be 0, use DECIMAL EXTERNAL. If length is not specified, the **POSITION** values are used. *See* "Terminating and Enclosing Fields in the Record," earlier in this section for details on the *delimiter* use.

For a Decimal Number in Packed Decimal Format

```
DECIMAL (digits [,precision])
```

Decimal data is in packed decimal format, with each digit getting four bits, and the whole number followed by a sign, also four bits. The *digits* tell how many digits are in the number (333.33 has 5, not 6). The precision tells how many of these digits fall to the right side of the decimal point (which is implied—it is not there in the data). *Precision* can be greater than the digits (implying a number smaller than one with leading zeros to the right of the decimal). Both digits and precision must be positive integers. If precision is not specified, 0 is assumed, meaning the number is an integer.

The number of character positions a decimal number takes in a file is equal to (digits+2)/2, truncated to a whole number.

For a Double Precision Floating Point Binary Number

```
DOUBLE
```

For this data type, only the start in the **position** clause is used, and length is defined based on the size of a double precision floating point binary number on your system. This corresponds to the DOUBLE and LONG FLOAT data types in C.

For a Normal Floating Point Binary Number

```
FLOAT
```

For this data type, only the start in the **position** clause is used, and length is defined based on the size of a single precision floating point binary number on your system. This corresponds to the FLOAT data type in C.

For a Floating Point Number in Character Format

```
FLOAT EXTERNAL [(length)] [delimiter]
```

This format is used for floating points (either single or double precision) that are in normal character format in the file, rather than packed into a binary format (usually one digit per four bits, rather than the eight bits that characters use). These are numbers you would be able to read if you looked at them in a file.

Binary formatted numbers would display strange symbols. These numbers are therefore treated like character data coming in, and follow the same format as CHAR. However, when using DEFAULTIF (a discussion of which follows shortly), if you want to set the default value to NULL, use CHAR. If you want it to be 0, use DECIMAL EXTERNAL. If length is not specified, the **POSITION** values are used. *See* "Terminating and Enclosing Fields in the Record," earlier in this section, for details on the *delimiter* use.

For Data That Is a Double Byte Character String (DBCS)

GRAPHIC [(*length*)]

While ORACLE doesn't directly support double byte character strings, it can read in the data as a string of single bytes and store it in a column. *Length* is defined in one of two very different ways. Specifying a length is defined as the length in double bytes. This is one-half the value of the actual number of single bytes in the string. That is, a string with 12 8-bit bytes would have a length of 6.

If, on the other hand, the length is indirectly specified with start and end after the **POSITION** keyword, these will simply be the actual beginning and final positions in the file—these are always measured in single bytes.

For Data That Is a Double Byte Character String (DBCS)

GRAPHIC EXTERNAL [(*length*)]

This is identical to GRAPHIC without EXTERNAL, except that here it is assumed that the field is enclosed in shift-in and shift-out characters. The *length*, if specified explicitly, does not include the shift-in and shift-out byte. However, if start and end are specified, start is the location of the shift-in byte, and end is the location of the shift-out byte.

For a Normal Fullword Binary Integer

INTEGER

For this data type, only the start in the **position** clause is used, and length is defined based on the size of a fullword integer on your system. This corresponds to the LONG INT data type in C.

For a Normal Halfword Binary Integer

SMALLINT

For this data type, only the start in the **position** clause is used, and length is defined based on the size of a halfword integer on your system. This corresponds to the SHORT INT data type in C.

For an Integer in Character Format

INTEGER EXTERNAL [(*length*)] [*delimiter*]

This format is used for integers that are in normal character format in the file, rather than packed into a binary format (usually one digit per four bits, rather than the eight bits that characters use). These are numbers you would be able to read if you looked at them in a file.

Binary formatted numbers would display strange symbols. These numbers are therefore treated like character data coming in, and follow the same format as CHAR. However, when using DEFAULTIF (a discussion of which follows shortly), if you want to set the default value to NULL, use CHAR. If you want it to be 0, use DECIMAL EXTERNAL. If length is not specified, the position values are used. *See* "Terminating and Enclosing Fields in the Record," earlier in this section, for details on the *delimiter* use.

For a Normal Halfword Binary Integer

SMALLINT

For this data type, only the start in the **position** clause is used, and length is defined based on the size of a halfword integer on your system. This corresponds to the SHORT INT data type in C.

For a Variable Length Character String

VARCHAR [(*length*)]

For this data type, only the start in the **position** clause is used, and *length* is defined by the first two bytes of the string. The length here is the maximum expected for the field, and does not include the two bytes at the head of each string, which specify its length. Its purpose is to aid in optimizing buffer size.

For Data That Is a Variable Double Byte Character String (DBCS)

VARGRAPHIC [(*length*)]

While ORACLE doesn't directly support double byte character strings, it can read in the data as a string of single bytes and store it in a column. Actual length is stored as the first two bytes of the string; the location of the first of these two bytes is specified with start after the POSITION keyword. This length is in double bytes. This is one-half the value of the actual number of single bytes in the string. That is, a string with 12 8-bit bytes would have a length of 6; 06 would be stored in the first two bytes (these two bytes are not included in the length).

If *length* is specified after VARGRAPHIC, it means maximum length, and is only used for optimization of buffers.

Conditionally or Completely Setting a Column to NULL

A column can be conditionally set to NULL by testing it for a condition using the NULLIF keyword:

```
NULLIF {(start[:end]) ¦ column} operator {'string' ¦ X'hex'}
```

That is, either the positions (in the *logical* record, not the physical record) can be tested against a character or hex string, or a column in the table being loaded can have the value that will be loaded into it tested, just before the row is added to the table. *operator* can be either "equal" or "not equal." *Equal* is always =, but *not equal* may be any one of !=, ~= or < >. Several conditions can be joined together with **AND** (**OR** is not available). For example, this:

```
NULLIF (37-39) = 'DOG' and (22-25} = 'FRED'
```

or this:

```
NULLIF Age = '65'
```

If you want a column's value set to NULL for every row inserted, do not include the column name or any specifications for it in the control file.

Conditionally Setting a Number Column to Zero

The keyword DEFAULTIF can be used in a similar fashion to NULLIF:

```
DEFAULTIF {(start[:end]) ¦ column} operator {'string' ¦
X'hex'}
```

The two keywords are identical in operation for character columns, but for a number column DEFAULTIF sets the column value to zero if the conditions are met, while NULLIF sets the number column's value to NULL if its conditions are met. Usually one or the other of these is sufficient, but both could be used if under some circumstances NULL was desired, and under others zero was desired. DEFAULTIF treats DECIMAL EXTERNAL, FLOAT EXTERNAL, and INTEGER EXTERNAL as numbers: it sets the column value to zero if conditions are met.

Using the Direct Path Load Option

SQL*LOADER, when inserting records, generates a large number of **insert** statements. To avoid the overhead associated with using large number of **insert**s, you may use the *direct path* option in SQL*LOADER. The direct path option creates pre-formatted data blocks and inserts those blocks into the table. As a result, the performance of your load can dramatically improve. In order to use the direct path option, you must not be performing any functions on the values being read from the input file.

Any indexes on the table being loaded will be placed into a temporary DIRECT LOAD state. Once the load has completed, the old index values will be merged with the new values to create the new index. When the index is once again valid, its status will change to VALID. To minimize the amount of space necessary for the temporary index, pre-sort the data according by the indexed columns. The name of the index for which the data is presorted should be specified via a SORTED INDEXES clause in the control file.

To use the direct path option, specify

```
DIRECT=TRUE
```

as a keyword on the SQLLOAD command line.

SQLMENU

Type   Utility

Products   SQL*MENU version 5

See also   **DOCMENU**, **GENMENU**, **RUNMENU**

Format

```
SQLMENU [application] [user/password] [-c crt] [-l language]
        [-q] [-r file] [-w file ] [-e file] [?]
```

Description   SQL*MENU is a product very much like SQL*FORMS, except that its primary function is to produce menus, and menu-trees, that allow users to navigate easily through ORACLE and other applications. For training in the use and development of SQL*MENU screens, see the *SQL*Menu User's Guide and Reference*; this reference entry is for command line syntax and parameters. *See* **RUNMENU**, **GENMENU**, and **DOCMENU**. These are command-line versions of options within SQL*MENU Design.

Typically, you enter SQL*MENU by typing **SQLMENU** without parameters. You are prompted for your username and password, and then put into your first option screen. The command line here is an alternative to that process, and offers a number of useful options.

application is the name of the application menu that you wish to enter.

Your user name and password allow you to log on to ORACLE. If these are not entered, you will be prompted for them (followed optionally by an *@link* location).

Entering a slash (/) either on the command line or in response to the prompt, causes ORACLE to attempt to use your OPS$ login ID. (*See* OPS$ LOGINS.)

-*c* indicates use of a nondefault crt definition, which has a known crt name.

-*q* makes the terminal quiet by suppressing beeps.

-*r* takes its input from the file instead of the keyboard. This is useful for testing forms.

-*w* puts the display output from SQL*MENU into a file instead of on the screen, so it can be studied later.

-*e* echoes keystrokes into a file while SQL*MENU is being used. You later can use this file with **-r** to replicate your previous session, such as when testing the menus for compatibility, or with automatic execution of applications.

-*?* forces SQLMENU to display all of these options.

Packaged Procedures

The following are SQL*MENU's packaged procedures, which are used in PL/SQL or on a menu item command line. Not all of these packaged procedures can run in all of SQL*MENU's six states, AFORM, AMENU, IFORM, LOGIN, MENU, and MFORM.

AFORM occurs when the dialog box for an application's parameters is being displayed.

AMENU occurs when in an application menu.

IFORM occurs when a dialog box for item parameters is being displayed.

LOGIN is the state when SQL*MENU is attempting to log in to ORACLE.

MENU occurs when in an application itself.

MFORM occurs when a dialog box for menu parameters is being displayed for a full-screen menu.

The procedures are:

APPLICATION_MENU takes the user from a SQL*MENU application to the application menu. This works in AFORM, IFORM, MENU, and MFORM states.

APPLICATION_PARAMETER displays the application's current parameter's in a dialog box. This works in MENU and MFORM states.

BACKGROUND_MENU*integer* executes item *integer* from the background menu. *integer* can range from 1 to 10. This works in AFORM, MENU, and MFORM states.

DEBUG_MODE turns the debug mode on or off. If debug mode is off, it turns it on. If it is on, it turns it off. This works only in MENU state.

EXIT_MENU[(***text***)] leaves the menu and displays the optional text on the screen. This works in any state.

MAIN_MENU takes the user to the main menu of the application. This can be used in AFORM, IFORM, MENU, and MFORM states.

MENU_CLEAR_FIELD clears the current field, starting at the current location of the cursor, all the way to the end (right) of the field. If the cursor already is to the right of all displayed (nonblank) characters, then the whole field is cleared and set equal to NULL. This works in any state.

MENU_HELP displays any hint message for the current item. This works in all states.

MENU_NEXT_FIELD moves the user to the next field, whether in a menu or dialog box. This works in any state.

MENU_PARAMETER displays the menu's current parameters in a dialog box. This works in MENU and MFORM (full screen only) states.

MENU_PREVIOUS_FIELD moves the user to the previous field, whether in a menu or dialog box. This works in AFORM, IFORM, LOGIN, or MFORM states.

MENU_SHOW_KEYS displays the keys and their functions. (It is equivalent to the user hitting the [Show Keys] key.) This works in all states.

NEW_APPLICATION(*application*) changes to the menu of the **application**. This works in AFORM, AMENU, IFORM, MENU, and MFORM.

NEW_USER(*user/password*) logs off the current user and logs in the new user with the password. This procedure cannot be used if the menu has been called from SQL*FORMS. This works with AFORM, AMENU, IFORM, MENU, and MFORM states.

NEXT_MENU_ITEM takes the user to the next item in the menu. This works only with AMENU and MENU.

OS_COMMAND(' [(**type**=*integer*)] *command*') executes an operating system command of type 2 (return immediately) or 3 (return after pause for user to hit a key). If type is not specified, it is assumed to be 2. For a full discussion of command types 1 through 7, *see* the *SQL*Menu User's Guide and Reference*. This works in AFORM, IFORM, MENU, and MFORM states.

OS_COMMAND1(' [(**type**=*integer*)] *command*') works the same as OS_COMMAND.

PREVIOUS_MENU takes the user to the previous menu. This works in AFORM, IFORM, MENU, and MFORM states.

PREVIOUS_MENU_ITEM takes the user to the previous item in the menu. This works in AMENU and MENU only.

QUERY_PARAMETER(&*parameter* [&*parameter*]. . .) loads the values of the current substitution parameters into the parameter fields in the list. Each must be preceded by an ampersand (&). These can then be used in PL/SQL, although they are preceded there by a colon (:) instead of an ampersand. This works in AFORM, IFORM, MENU, and MFORM states.

SHOW_BACKGROUND_MENU moves the background menu to the front. This works in AFORM, IFORM, MENU, and MFORM states.

TERMINATE is the same as the user hitting the [Accept] key. It accepts the choice in a dialog box, or the input in a form, and terminates input. This works in all states.

WHERE_DISPLAY toggles (turns on or off) the display of where you are in the menu hierarchy. This works only in AMENU and MENU.

Error-Related Packaged Procedures

You may use the following packaged procedures to check the success or failure of, or provide information about, any packaged procedure during its execution. The first six will evaluate to a boolean TRUE or FALSE after a procedure, but may be affected by a user striking a key, so the testing should follow the procedure immediately.

MENU_FAILURE
MENU_FATAL
MENU_SUCCESS
FORM_FAILURE
FORM_FATAL
FORM_SUCCESS

The last three contain information about the success or failure just tested:

ERROR_CODE
ERROR_TEXT
ERROR_TYPE

ERROR_TEXT should be avoided if you have multi-language support in your application, as it can be implemented in only one language.

Macros

The following macros are available in SQL*MENU:

ASSIGN *parameter=value* assigns value to a two-letter parameter. The only predefined parameter that can have a value assigned is SO, the current menu item. If this is done, the assign should be followed by TRMNATE.

CHRMODE changes the input mode (toggles) between **insert** and **replace**.

DELCHR deletes one character to the left of the current cursor position, and moves the cursor one character left.

DISP allows the screen to display macro-produced **update**s as they occur. DISP works only in character mode displays.

LEFT moves the cursor to the left one space within a field.

NODISP stops the display macro-produced **update**s as they occur. NODISP works only in character mode displays.

RIGHT moves the cursor to the right one space within a field.

SUSPEND stops macro execution until the user hits the [Accept] key.

SQLNUMBER (SQL*PLUS)

See **SET**.

SQLPLUS

Type   ORACLE product

Product   SQL*PLUS

See also   Chapters 4,12, and 19.

Format

```
SQLPLUS [user[/password][@database] [@file] ] [-SILENT] :
        [/NOLOG] [-SILENT] : [-?]
```

Description   SQLPLUS starts up SQL*PLUS. Entering both username and password will log you on to your default database. Entering just your username will cause SQL*PLUS to prompt you for your password, which will not be displayed as you enter it. Entering @*database* will connect you to the named database instead of your default. The @*database* can be anywhere, so long as the computer you are logging onto is connected to it through SQL*NET. There must be no space between *password* and @*database*. For more information about SQL*NET, see the *SQL*Net User's Guide.*@*file* will run the start file immediately after SQL*PLUS is loaded. There must be a space before @*file*. If the username and password are not entered on the command line with SQLPLUS, they must be the first line in the file. If they are in the file, and you enter them on the command line, you'll get an error message but the start file will run correctly anyway. To put user and password at the top of the file, separate them with a slash (/):

```
GEORGE/MISTY
```

/NOLOG makes SQL*PLUS start, but does not log you onto the ORACLE database. You must then use **CONNECT** to attach to ORACLE. (*See* **CONNECT**).

-SILENT suppresses all of SQL*PLUS's screen displays, including the command prompts and even the SQL*PLUS logon and copyright information. It makes the use of SQL*PLUS by another program invisible to the program's user.

-? displays the current version and level number for SQL*PLUS without actually starting it up.

Example   Normal startup of SQL*PLUS follows:

```
sqlplus george/misty
```

To start up on the database EDMESTON, use this:

```
sqlplus george/misty@EDMESTON
```

To start the report file REPORT6, which includes the name and password as its first line, use this:

```
sqlplus @report6
```

To start the report file REPORT6, which includes the name and password as its first line, on the database EDMESTON, use this:

```
sqlplus george/misty@EDMESTON @report6
```

SQLPREFIX (SQL*PLUS)

See **SET**.

SQLPROMPT (SQL*PLUS)

See **SET**.

SQLREP

Type   Utility program

Product   SQL*REPORTWRITER

See also   **DUMPREP**, **GENREP**, **LOADREP**, **PRINTDEF**, **RUNREP**, SQL*REPORTWRITER, SQLPLUS, **TERMDEF**

Format

```
SQLREP
[USERID=user/password]
[PARAMFORM={YES|NO}]
[CMDFILE=file]
[TERM=file]
```

```
[ARRAYSIZE=integer]
[DESTYPE={SCREEN|FILE|PRINTER|MAIL}]
[DESNAME=userlist]
[DESFORMAT=format]
[COPIES=integer]
[CURRENCY=symbol]
[THOUSANDS=symbol]
[DECIMAL=symbol]
[LOGFILE=file]
[BUFFERS=integer]
[LANGUAGE=language]
[parameter=value]
```

Description   Although these options are listed on several lines, in actual use they must appear on the same line as SQLREP. The keywords and equal signs can be eliminated if the arguments all appear in the order shown here (although this is usually not well understood by others looking at the code, and should be avoided). If keywords are used, no spaces should appear on either side of the equal signs, and each keyword/parameter pair should be separated from the others by spaces. On some operating systems the names chosen for files, terminal definitions, formats, or users may be case sensitive. None of the other keywords or arguments are. File names may include path names as well. On some operating systems, arguments must be entered in either single or double quotation marks. Entering just **SQLREP** followed by a question mark will produce the list of options (it, too, may need quotation marks).

USERID is your ORACLE user name and password (followed optionally by an @*link* location). If these are not entered, you will be prompted for them. Entering a slash (/), either on the command line or in response to the prompt, will cause ORACLE to attempt to use your OPS$ login ID (see OPS$ LOGINS).

PARAMFORM defaults to YES, which offers the user the parameter form to enter runtime parameters for reports.

CMDFILE is a file that contains any of the command line arguments for SQLREP, including CMDFILE itself (which will point to another file with arguments in it). These may be on one or more lines, separated by spaces on the lines where more than one argument appears. Any arguments on the actual command line will override those in a command file, so command files can be used for your own "default" values, where they differ from SQLREP's.

TERM specifies a file that contains terminal definitions, such as for function keys, for the terminal you are using. The default varies from system to system.

ARRAYSIZE sets aside an area in memory for processing the report. The default is 10 kilobytes. The integer value specifies the number of kilobytes to set aside if you don't choose the default. This value has a profound effect on performance, and some reports may require several megabytes to run effectively.

DESTYPE defines the output destination for the report: SCREEN sends it to the interactive browser; FILE sends it to a file specified by DESNAME; PRINTER sends it to a printer specified in DESNAME; and MAIL sends it via ORACLE*MAIL to another user (or users).

DESNAME is a single user, or a list of users separated by commas and enclosed in parentheses:

```
DESNAME=(george, victoria, sarjeant, swing, lawson)
```

DESFORMAT specifies the printer format type for the printer named in DESNAME. This determines control codes included in the output. Typical formats include wide, decwide, hplwide, and so on. Your System Administrator should have a list of those appropriate for your environment.

COPIES controls the integer number of copies to be printed. It defaults to 1.

CURRENCY determines the symbol with which money fields will be displayed. The default is taken from the database and the National Language Support feature. This can be designated automatically using the LANGUAGE keyword. However, an entry for CURRENCY will override LANGUAGE, and an entry in the runtime PARAMETER FORM will override either of them.

THOUSANDS specifies the symbol used to divide groups of numbers. That is, in some countries the number 63 million would be written 63.000.000, while in others it would be 63,000,000; the character chosen here will be the one used when such numbers are reported. The default is taken from the database and the National Language Support feature. This can be designated automatically using the THOUSANDS keyword. However, an entry for CURRENCY will override THOUSANDS, and a entry in the runtime PARAMETER FORM will override either of them.

DECIMAL is similar to THOUSANDS. It is the symbol used to designate the presence of decimal digits. People of some countries would type the number nine and thirty-four hundredths as 9.34, while people of other countries might use 9,34 for the same value. The character chosen here will be the one used. The default is taken from the database and the National Language Support feature. This can be designated automatically using the DECIMAL keyword. However, an entry for CURRENCY will override DECIMAL, and a entry in the runtime PARAMETER FORM will override either of them.

LOGFILE is the file that will get the print requests from the screen, such as to print the screen, the page, or the report. An existing file will have this output appended to the end of the file. If no file name is specified, the output goes to a file named **dfltrep.log**.

BUFFERS is the integer number of 512 byte buffers available to the executable module, and the default varies from system to system. The more buffers assigned, the more rapidly the program will execute, although significant usage on shared systems could slow other processing. The default has been optimized for reports of up to a few hundred pages.

LANGUAGE defaults to US, which automatically designates the correct CURRENCY, THOUSANDS, and DECIMAL characters. It is overridden by any of these three keywords on the command line or in a runtime PARAMETER FORM.

parameter is a keyword you created when defining the report. The value you enter following its name will be substituted in the report creation wherever that parameter appears.

SQLTERMINATOR (SQL*PLUS)

See **SET**.

SQRT

Type   SQL command

Products   ALL, PL/SQL

See also   **POWER**

Format

```
SQRT(value)
```

Description   **SQRT** finds the square root of value.

Examples

```
SQRT(64) = 8
SQRT(d2) = 1.414...
SQRT(-1) = NULL
```

The square root of negative numbers is not available in ORACLE (mathematically, it's an imaginary number, which isn't supported).

START

Type   SQL*PLUS command

Product   SQL*PLUS

See also   **@, @@, ACCEPT, DEFINE, SPOOL**

Format

```
STA[RT] file [parameter] [parameter]...
```

Description   **START** executes the contents of the specified start file (so called because it is started by this command). The file may contain any SQL*PLUS commands. If no file type is specified, START assumes it is **.sql**. Any parameters following the file name are substituted into variables in the start file; the variables must be named &1, &2, &3, and so on, and will receive the parameters in order, from left to right. Every occurrence in the start file of &1 will get the first parameter. Parameters are limited to a single word or number each.

Example

```
start skill HELEN
```

where the file **skill.sql** contains the following:

```
select * from WORKERSKILL
 where Name LIKE '&1%';
```

This will produce the following:

```
NAME                         SKILL                        ABILITY
------------------------     ------------------------     -------------
HELEN BRANDT                 COMBINE DRIVER               VERY FAST
```

START UP

Starting up is the process of starting an instance, presumably with the intent of mounting and opening a database in order to make a database system available for use.

STATEMENT

A statement is a SQL instruction to ORACLE comprised of clauses.

STDDEV

Type   SQL group function

Product   SQL*PLUS

See also   GROUP FUNCTIONS, VARIANCE, Chapter 6

Format

```
STDDEV(value)
```

Description   **STDDEV** gives the standard deviation from the norm of values in a group of rows. It ignores NULL values in its calculation.

STORAGE

Type   SQL command clause

Products   All

See also   **BLOCK, CREATE CLUSTER, CREATE INDEX, CREATE ROLLBACK SEGMENT, CREATE SNAPSHOT, CREATE SNAPSHOT LOG, CREATE TABLE, CREATE TABLESPACE**, as well as the **ALTER** statement for each of these.

Format

```
STORAGE ([INITIAL integer [K¦M]]
         [NEXT integer [K¦M]]
         [PCTINCREASE integer]
         [MINEXTENTS integer]
         [MAXEXTENTS integer]
         [OPTIMAL {integer [K¦M] ¦ NULL}]
         [FREELISTS integer]
         [FREELIST GROUPS integer] )
```

Description   The **storage** clause is optional in any of the **CREATE** and **ALTER** statements listed under the "See also" section. It is not a SQL statement, and cannot stand alone. In the following paragraphs, a block is a database block (*see* **BLOCK**) with a size depending on the operating system.

INITIAL allocates the first extent of space to the object. If INITIAL is not specified, it defaults to five data blocks. The smallest initial extent you can allocate is two data blocks, and the largest depends on your operating system. You can express these numbers either as a simple integer or as an integer followed by K or M to indicate kilobytes or megabytes, respectively.

NEXT is the size of the extent allocated after the initial extent has been filled. If not specified, it defaults to five data blocks. The smallest next extent you can allocate is one data block, and the largest depends on the operating system. You can use K and M for kilobytes and megabytes.

PCTINCREASE controls the rate of growth of extents beyond the second. If set to 0, every additional extent will be the same size as the second extent, specified by NEXT. If PCTINCREASE is a positive integer, each succeeding extent will be that percentage larger than the previous one. For example, if PCTINCREASE was 50 (the default, if it is not specified), each additional extent would be 50 percent larger than the previous one. PCTINCREASE cannot be negative. The minimum PCTINCREASE is 0, and the maximum depends on the operating system. ORACLE rounds the extent size up to the next multiple of the operating system block size.

MINEXTENTS defaults to 1 (or 2 for a rollback segment) if it is not specified, meaning that when the object is created, only the initial extent is allocated. A number larger than 1 will create that many total extents (which don't need to be contiguous on disk, as each extent itself does), and the size of each of them will be determined by the values set with INITIAL, NEXT, and PCTINCREASE. All of these will be allocated when the object is created.

MAXEXTENTS sets the limit on the total number of extents that can be allocated. The minimum limit is 1, with the default and maximum depending on the operating system.

OPTIMAL sets an optimal size in bytes for a rollback segment. You can use K and M for kilobytes and megabytes. ORACLE7 will dynamically deallocate extents in the rollback segment to maintain the optimal size. NULL means that ORACLE7 never deallocates the rollback segment extents, and this is the default behavior. You must supply a size greater than or equal to the initial space allocated for the rollback segment by the MINEXTENTS, INITIAL, NEXT, and PCTINCREASE parameters.

FREELIST GROUPS gives the number of groups of free lists, with a default value of 1. This setting applies to the Parallel Server option of ORACLE7 for tables, clusters, or indexes.

FREELISTS sets the number of free lists for each free list group.

In ORACLE7.2, storage parameters for datafile extensions are available. *See* **CREATE TABLESPACE**, **CREATE DATABASE**, **ALTER TABLESPACE**, and **ALTER DATABASE**.

STRUCTURED QUERY LANGUAGE

See SQL.

SUBQUERY

Type   SQL language feature

Product   All, SQL*PLUS

See also   **COPY**, **CREATE TABLE**, **DELETE**, **INSERT**, **SELECT**, **UPDATE**, Chapter 10

Format

```
COPY [FROM user/password@database]
     [TO user/password@database]
```

```
     {APPEND | CREATE | INSERT | REPLACE}
table [ (column [,column]...) ]
     USING query;

CREATE TABLE table ...
     AS query;

DELETE FROM table [alias]
     [ WHERE ... (subquery)];

INSERT INTO table [ (column [,column]...) ]
     query;

SELECT [* | (expression [,expression]...) ]
     FROM table
     [ WHERE ... (subquery)];

UPDATE table [alias]
     SET (column [,column]... ) = (subquery)
     [ WHERE condition ];
```

Description   A query (that is, a **select** statement) may be used as a part of
another SQL statement (called the parent, or outer statement), including **CREATE
TABLE**, **delete**, **insert**, **select**, and **update**, or in the SQL*PLUS **COPY** command, in
order to define the rows or columns that the parent will use in its execution. The
results of the child query (also called a subquery) are not themselves displayed, but
are passed to the parent SQL statement for its use. The following rules apply:

- In an **update** or **CREATE TABLE** command, the subquery must return one
  value for each column to be inserted or updated. The value or values are
  then used by the parent SQL statement to **insert** or **update** the rows.

- A subquery cannot contain **order by** and **for update of** clauses.

- A "correlated" subquery is used in the **where** clause of a **select** statement,
  and references an alias for the table used by the parent select command. It
  is tested once for each row evaluated for selection by the parent select
  statement (a standard subquery evaluated just once for the parent query).
  See Chapter 10 for further details.

Other than these restrictions, normal rules for a **select** statement apply.

SUBSTITUTION

See **&, &&, ACCEPT, DEFINE**

SUBSTR

Type   SQL function

Products   All

See also   ¦¦, CHARACTER FUNCTIONS, **INSTR**, Chapter 5

Format

```
SUBSTR(string, start [,count])
```

Description   **SUBSTR**ing clips out a piece of a string beginning at *start* and going for *count* characters. If *count* is not specified, the string is clipped from *start* and goes to the end of the string.

Example

```
SUBSTR('NEWSPAPER',5)
```

produces this:

```
PAPER
```

SUBSTRB

Type   SQL function

Products   All

See also   ¦¦, CHARACTER FUNCTIONS, **INSTRB**, **SUBSTR**, Chapter 5

Format

```
SUBSTRB(string, start [,count])
```

Description   **SUB STR**ing **B**yte clips out a piece of a string beginning at a *start* byte and going for *count* bytes. If *count* is not specified, the string is clipped from *start* and goes to the end of the string. This function lets you clip multi-byte character strings byte by byte instead of character by character, as **SUBSTR** does.

SUFFIX (SQL*PLUS)

See **SET**.

SUM

Type SQL group function

Products All

See also **COMPUTE**, GROUP FUNCTIONS, Chapter 6

Format

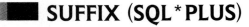

```
SUM([DISTINCT] value)
```

Description **SUM** is the sum of all *values* for a group of rows. **DISTINCT** makes **SUM** add each unique value to the total only once; this is usually not very meaningful.

SYNCHRONOUS TERMINAL

A synchronous terminal is one that transmits and receives data one field or one screen at a time (as opposed to a character at a time). It's also called a BLOCK MODE TERMINAL. *See also* ASYNCHRONOUS TERMINAL.

SYNONYM

A synonym is a name assigned to a table or view that may thereafter be used to refer to it. If you have access to another user's table, you may create a synonym for it and refer to it by the synonym alone, without entering the user's name as a qualifier. *See* Chapter 20 and Chapter 24.

SYNTAX

Syntax is a set of rules that determine how to construct a valid statement in a computer language such as SQL.

SYNTAX OPERATORS

Type SQL operators

Products   All

See also   LOGICAL OPERATORS, PRECEDENCE

Description   Syntax operators have the highest precedence of all operators, and may appear anywhere in a SQL statement. Here they are listed in descending order of precedence. Operators of equal precedence are evaluated from left to right. Most of these are listed and described separately under their own symbols.

OPERATOR	FUNCTION
-	SQL*PLUS command continuation. Continues a command on the following line.
&	Prefix for parameters in a SQL*PLUS start file. Words are substituted for &1, &2, and so on. *See* **START**.
& &&	Prefix for a substitution variable in a SQL command in SQL*PLUS. SQL*PLUS will prompt for a value if an undefined & or && variable is found. && also defines the variable and saves the value; ' & ' does not. *See* **&** and **&&**, **DEFINE**, and **ACCEPT**.
:	Prefix for a variable in SQL*FORMS and for a host variable in PL/SQL.
.	Variable separator, used in SQL*PLUS to separate the variable name from a suffix, so that the suffix is not considered a part of the variable name, and in SQL between user, table, and column names.
( )	Surrounds subqueries, lists of columns, or controls precedence.
'	Surrounds a literal, such as a character string or date constant. To use a ' in a string constant, use two ' marks (not a double quotation mark).
"	Surrounds a table or column alias that contains special character or a space.
"	Surrounds literal text in a **date format** clause of **TO_CHAR**.
@	Precedes a database name in a **COPY**, or a link name in a **from** clause.

SYS (ORACLE USER)

SYS is one of the DBA users that is created when a database system is installed and initialized (the other is SYSTEM). SYS owns most of the data dictionary tables, while SYSTEM owns the views created on those base tables.

SYSDATE

Type   SQL pseudo-column

Product   SQL

See also   PSEUDO-COLUMNS

Format

```
SYSDATE
```

Description   SYSDATE contains the current date and time. SYSDATE acts like a DATE data type.

SYSTEM (ORACLE TABLESPACE)

SYSTEM is the name given to the original tablespace.

SYSTEM (ORACLE USER)

SYSTEM is one of the DBA users that is created when database system is installed and initialized (the other is SYS). While SYS owns most of the data dictionary tables, SYSTEM owns the views created on those base tables.

SYSTEM GLOBAL AREA (SGA)

SGA is a shared storage area in main or virtual memory (depending on your operating system) that is the center of ORACLE activity while the database is running. The size of the SGA (and performance of the system) depends on the values of the variable **init.ora** parameters. The SGA provides communication between the user and the background processes.

SYSTEM PRIVILEGED SQL*DBA COMMANDS

The system privileged SQL*DBA commands are a subset of the SQL*DBA commands that require not only access to the SQL*DBA utility, but a special operating system account. These commands require the highest level of security.

TABLE

A table is the basic data storage structure in a relational database management system. A table consists of one or more units of information (rows), each of which contains the same kinds of values (columns). *See* **CREATE TABLE**.

TABLE - PL/SQL

Type   PL/SQL data type

Products   All

See also   DATA TYPES, **RECORD** (PL/SQL)

Format

```
TYPE new_type IS TABLE OF
   {type ¦ table.column%TYPE}[NOT NULL]
   INDEX BY BINARY_INTEGER;
```

Description   A TABLE declaration declares a new type that can then be used to declare variables of that type. A PL/SQL table has one column and an integer key and can have any number of rows. The data type of the column can either be one of the standard PL/SQL data types (including another RECORD but not a TABLE), or it can be a reference to the type of a particular column in a specific database table. Each field may also have a NOT NULL qualifier that specifies that the field must always have a non-null value.

The **index by binary integer** clause is required and reminds you that the index is an integer. You can refer to any row of the table with the index in parentheses.

If you refer to an index to which you have not assigned any data, PL/SQL raises the NO_DATA_FOUND exception.

Example

```
type SkillTable is table(skill WORKERSKILL.Skill%TYPE);
SkillRecord MySkill;
MySkill(1) := 'GRAVEDIGGER';
MySkill(5) := 'SMITHY';
```

TABLE ALIAS

A table alias is a temporary substitute for a table name, defined in the **from** clause of a **select** statement. *See* **AS** and Chapter 9.

TABLE COLUMN

A table column is one that appears in a table. *See* **COLUMN**.

TABLE CONSTRAINT

A table constraint is an integrity constraint that applies to multiple columns of the same table. *See* INTEGRITY CONSTRAINT.

TABLESPACE

Tablespace is a file or set of files that is used to store ORACLE data. An ORACLE database is composed of the SYSTEM tablespace and possibly other tablespaces.

TABLESPACE LOCKS

See DICTIONARY LOCKS.

TAN

Type   SQL function

Products   All

See also   **COS**, NUMBER FUNCTIONS, **SIN**, **TANH**, Chapter 6

Format

```
TAN(value)
```

Description   **TAN** returns the tangent of an angle *value* expressed in radians.

Example

```
select TAN(135*3.141593/180) Tan -- tangent of 135 degrees in radians
  from DUAL;

TAN
----------
        -1
```

TANH

Type SQL function

Products All

See also **COS**, NUMBER FUNCTIONS, **SIN**, **TAN**, Chapter 6

Format

TANH(*value*)

Description **TANH** returns the hyperbolic tangent of an angle *value*.

TEMPORARY SEGMENT

A temporary segment is a storage space within a tablespace used to hold intermediate results of a SQL statement. For example, temporary segments are used when sorting large tables.

TERMINAL DEFINITION

A terminal definition is a terminal that has a corresponding **.crt** file. The **.crt** file contains information needed by ORACLE to establish the correct functions for terminal keys.

TERMINAL NODE

In a tree-structured table, a terminal node is a row that has no child row. It's the same as LEAF.

TERMINATOR

PL/SQL can be embedded in a host language using an ORACLE precompiler. When it is, the entire section of PL/SQL blocks is treated as a single SQL statement. Thus, it is framed by the precompiler commands EXEC SQL EXECUTE and ENDEXEC. The character that follows ENDEXEC tells the precompiler that this is the end of the PL/SQL code. In Ada, C, Pascal, and PL/I, this character is the semicolon (;). In COBOL it is a period (.), and in FORTRAN an end-of-line character.

TERMDEF

Type   Utility report program

Product   SQL*REPORTWRITER

See also   **DUMPREP**, **GENREP**, **LOADREP**, **MOVEREP**, **PRINTDEF**, **RUNREP**, SQLPLUS, SQLREP, SQL*REPORTWRITER

Format

```
TERMDEF  [TERMINAL=]terminal [OUTFILE=]outfile
[KDFILE=]kdfile
[[USERID=]user/password] [[tdfile=]tdfile]
```

Description   **TERMDEF** creates a new terminal definition named *terminal* in the *outfile* from a description in the *tdfile* (which defaults to **termdef.dat**). This terminal name must be the second name in the tdfile. *kdfile* is the definition file for the keys. *outfile* may include a path. *USERID* is your ORACLE user name and password. If these are not entered, you will be prompted for them (followed optionally by an @*link* location). Entering a slash (/), either on the command line or in response to the prompt, will cause ORACLE to attempt to use your OPS$ login ID (*see* OPS$ LOGINS). *See* the *SQL*ReportWriter Reference Manual* for details.

TERMOUT (SQL*PLUS)

See **SET**.

TIME (SQL*PLUS)

See **SET**.

TIMING (Form 1 - SQL*PLUS)

See **SET**.

TIMING (Form 2 - SQL*PLUS)

Type   SQL*PLUS command

Product   SQL*PLUS

See also   CLEAR, SET

Format

```
TIMI[NG] [ START area ¦ STOP ¦ SHOW ];
```

Description   **TIMING** keeps track of elapsed time from START to STOP by area name. **START** opens a timing area and makes *area* its title. *area* must be a single word. Several areas may exist at once. The most recently created one is the current timing area until it is deleted, when the previously created one becomes current. Timing areas are, in effect, nested. The most recently created will always show the least amount of time, because the elapsed time of those before it will be, by definition, longer. Total time for any timing area is its own net time plus those of all the timing areas that followed it.

SHOW gives the current timing area's name and elapsed time.

STOP gives the current timing area's name and elapsed time, deletes the area, and makes the one previous to it (if there was one) the current timing area. *See* the *SQL*Plus User's Guide and Reference* for your host operating system for details on the precise meaning of time on your machine.

Example   To create a timing area named 1, you enter this:

```
timing start 1
```

To see the current area name and time, but allow it to continue running, enter the following:

```
timing show
```

To see the current timing area's name and accumulated time, stop it, and make the previous one current, use this:

```
timing stop
```

TO_BINARY_INTEGER

Type   PL/SQL function

Products   PL/SQL

See also   TABLE - PL/SQL

Format

```
TO_BINARY_INTEGER(string)
TO_BINARY_INTEGER(number)
```

Description   **TO_BINARY_INTEGER** converts a CHAR or VARCHAR2 string or a NUMBER number into a binary integer. You can use this as an index into a PL/SQL table. The *string* must be a valid number.

TO_CHAR (Form 1 - Date and Number Conversion)

Type   SQL function

Products   All, PL/SQL

See also   DATE FORMATS, DATE FUNCTIONS, NUMBER FORMATS, **TO_DATE**, Chapter 7

Format

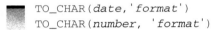

```
TO_CHAR(date,'format')
TO_CHAR(number, 'format')
```

Description   **TO_CHAR** reformats number or date according to *format. date* must be a column defined as a DATE data type in ORACLE. It cannot be a string even if it is in the default date format of DD-MON-YY. The only way to use a string in which *date* appears in the **TO_CHAR** function is to enclose it within a **TO_DATE** function. The formats possible for this function are numerous. They are listed under NUMBER FORMATS and DATE FORMATS.

Example   Note the format in the following example. This is necessary in SQL*PLUS to avoid the current default date width produced by **TO_CHAR**, which is about 100 characters wide:

```
column Formatted format a30 word_wrapped heading 'Formatted'

select BirthDate, TO_CHAR(BirthDate,MM/DD/YY) Formatted
  from BIRTHDAY
 where FirstName = 'VICTORIA';


BIRTHDATE Formatted
--------- ------------------------------
20-MAY-49 05/20/49
```

TO_CHAR (Form 2 - Label Conversion)

Type SQL function

Products All, PL/SQL

See also **TO_CHAR (Form 1), TO_LABEL**

Format

```
TO_CHAR(label,'format')
```

Description For users of Trusted ORACLE7, the **TO_CHAR** function can be used to convert *labels* of the MLSLABEL datatype to VARCHAR2 datatypes, using an optional *format*. If the format is omitted, then the label is converted to a VARCHAR2 value in the default label format. *See* the *Trusted ORACLE7 Server Administrator's Guide.*

TO_DATE

Type SQL function

Products All, PL/SQL

See also DATE FORMATS, DATE FUNCTIONS, **TO_CHAR**, Chapter 7

Format

```
TO_DATE(string,'format')
```

Description **TO_DATE** converts a *string* in a given *format* into an ORACLE date. It also will accept a number instead of a string, with certain limits. *string* is a literal string, a literal number, or a database column containing a string or a number. In every case but one, their format must correspond to that which is described by the *format*. Only if a string is in the format 'DD-MON-YY' can the format be left out. Note that *format* is restricted. *See* DATE FORMATS for a list of acceptable formats for **TO_DATE**.

Example

```
select TO_DATE('02/22/90','MM/DD/YY') from DUAL;

TO_DATE('
---------
22-FEB-90
```

TO_LABEL

Type   PL/SQL function

Products   PL/SQL

See also   DATA TYPES, **TO_CHAR (Form 2)**

Format

```
TO_LABEL(string, format)
```

Description   **TO_LABEL** converts a CHAR or VARCHAR2 *string* into a secure operating system label of type RAW MLSLABEL using a label *format*.

TO_MULTI_BYTE

Type   SQL function

Products   All, PL/SQL

See also   CONVERSION FUNCTIONS, Chapter 8

Format

```
TO_MULTI_BYTE(string)
```

Description   **TO_MULTI_BYTE** converts the single-byte characters in a character *string* to their multi-byte equivalents. If a character has no multi-byte equivalent, the function returns the character unconverted.

TO_NUMBER

Type   SQL function

Products   All, PL/SQL

See also   CONVERSION FUNCTIONS, Chapter 8

Format

```
TO_NUMBER(string)
```

Description   **TO_NUMBER** converts a character *string* to a number data type. It requires that the characters in the string be a properly formatted number with only the characters 0-9, –, +, and . included. This function is largely unnecessary due to automatic data conversion done by ORACLE, except when used for a character column containing numbers in an **order by** or a comparison.

Example

```
TO_NUMBER('333.46')
```

TO_SINGLE_BYTE

Type   SQL function

Products   All, PL/SQL

See also   CONVERSION FUNCTIONS, Chapter 8

Format

```
TO_SINGLE_BYTE(string)
```

Description   **TO_SINGLE_BYTE** converts the multi-byte characters in a character *string* to their single-byte equivalents. If a multi-byte character has no single-byte equivalent, the function returns the character unconverted.

TO_VARCHAR2

Type   PL/SQL function

Products   PL/SQL

See also   DATA TYPES

Format

```
TO_VARCHAR2(string)
TO_VARCHAR2(date)
TO_VARCHAR2(number)
TO_VARCHAR2(index)
```

Description   **TO_VARCHAR2** converts a CHAR *string*, DATE *date*, NUMBER *number*, or BINARY_INTEGER *index* into a VARCHAR2 string.

TRANSACTION

A transaction is a sequence of SQL statements that ORACLE treats as a single unit. The set of changes is made permanent with the **COMMIT** statement. Part or all of a transaction can be undone with the **ROLLBACK** statement.

ORACLE manages transactions both with locking (*see* LOCK) and a *multiversion consistency model,* which essentially behaves as though each transaction had its own copy of the database—that is, that there are multiple, overlapping versions of the database in existence at any given time. A transaction starts with the execution of the first SQL statement in the transaction and ends with either the **COMMIT** or **ROLLBACK** statement. By default, ORACLE guarantees that a transaction has *statement-level read consistency,* which means that when you execute a query, the data stays the same while ORACLE is gathering and returning it. But if a transaction has multiple queries, each query is consistent but not with each other. If you want to be able to maintain a consistent view of the data throughout such a transaction, the transaction needs to have *transaction-level read consistency,* which guarantees that the transaction will not see the effects of the committing of other transactions. This read-only transaction, started with **SET TRANSACTION READ ONLY**, can only execute queries and certain control commands (*see* **SET TRANSACTION**).

TRANSACTION LOCK

A transaction lock is one appearing in the SQLDBA Monitor Lock display indicating that a transaction is holding row locks.

TRANSACTION PROCESSING

Transaction processing is a form of processing oriented toward logical units of work, rather than separate and individual changes, in order to keep the database consistent.

TRANSLATE

Type   SQL function

Products   All, PL/SQL

See also   **REPLACE**, Chapter 8

Format

TRANSLATE(*string*,*if*,*then*)

Description   **TRANSLATE** looks at each character in *string*, and then checks if
to see if that character is there. If it is, **TRANSLATE** notes the position in *if* where it
found the character, and then looks at the same position in *then*. Whatever character it
finds there, it substitutes for the character in *string*.

Example

```
select TRANSLATE('I LOVE MY OLD THESAURUS','AEIOUY','123456')
  from DUAL;

TRANSLATE('ILOVEMYOLDTH
----------------------
3 L4V2 M6 4LD TH2S15R5S
```

TREE-STRUCTURED QUERY

A tree-structured query is one whose result shows hierarchical relationships among
rows in a table. *See* **CONNECT BY**.

TRIGGER

A database trigger is a stored procedure associated with a table that ORACLE7
automatically executes on one or more specified events (**BEFORE** or **AFTER** an **insert**,
update, or **delete**) affecting the table. Triggers can execute for the table as a whole
or for each affected row in the table. *See* Chapter 21 for a full discussion of triggers
and examples, and **CREATE TRIGGER** in this Alphabetical Reference for syntax.

TRIMOUT (SQL*PLUS)

See **SET**.

TRUNC (Form 1 - for Dates)

Type   SQL function

Products   All, PL/SQL

See also   **COLUMN**, DATE FUNCTIONS, **TRUNC** (Form 2 - for Numbers),
Chapter 7

Format

TRUNC(*date*,'*format*')

Description   **TRUNC** is the truncating of *date* according to *format*. Without a *format*, *date* is truncated to 12 A.M. (midnight) in the morning, with the first moment of the new day, today's date, for any time up to and including 11:59:59 P.M. (just before midnight). These are the formats available for truncating:

FORMAT	MEANING
cc, scc	century (truncates up to January 1st of this century, for any date and time up to December 31st, 1999 at 11:59:59 P.M.
syear,syyy,y,yy,yyy,yyyy and year	year (truncates up to January 1st of this year for any date up to December 31st at 11:59:59 P.M.).
q	quarter (truncates to the first day of the current quarter for any date in this quarter, up to 11:59:59 P.M. of the last day of the quarter).
month,mon,mm	month (truncates to the first date of the current month for any date up to 11:59:59 P.M. on the last day of the month)
ww	truncates to Monday of current week for any date up to 11:59:59 P.M. on Sunday.
w	truncates to the last day that is the same day of the week as the first day of the month (*see* text following list).
ddd,dd,j	truncates to 12 A.M. of current day, up to 11:59:59 P.M.. This is the same as **TRUNC** with no format.
day,dy,d	truncates back to Sunday (first day of week) for any date up to 11:59:59 P.M. on Saturday.
hh,hh12,hh24	truncates to the last whole hour, up to 59 minutes and 59 seconds after the hour.
mi	truncates to the last whole minute as of 59 seconds of the current minute.

ww produces the date of the current week's Monday with the time set at 12 A.M., for any day in the week up to Sunday night at 11:59:59 P.M. Any time on Monday is truncated to the same Monday at 12 A.M.

w works similarly, except that instead of producing the date of the current week's Monday at 12 A.M., it produces the date of the current week's day that is the same day of the week as the first day of the month. If the first day of a month was Friday, for instance, since a week is seven days long, this means any date and time up to seven days after a Friday (the next Thursday at 11:59:59 P.M.), will be truncated to the last Friday at 12 A.M. (midnight) in the morning (the first moment of the day on Friday). Any time on Friday is truncated to the same Friday at 12 A.M.

The result of **TRUNC** is always a date with its time set to 12 A.M., the first moment of the day.

TRUNC (Form 2 - for Numbers)

Type SQL function

Products All

See also **COLUMN**, NUMBER FUNCTIONS, **TRUNC** (Form 1 - for Dates), Chapter 6

Format

```
TRUNC(value,precision)
```

Description **TRUNC** is *value* truncated to *precision*.

Examples

```
TRUNC(123.45,1) = 123.4t
TRUNC(123.45,0) = 123
TRUNC(123.45,-1) = 120
TRUNC(123.45,-2) = 100
```

TRUNCATE

Type SQL command

Product All

See also **CREATE CLUSTER, DELETE, DROP TABLE**, TRIGGER

Format

```
TRUNCATE {TABLE [user.]table ¦ CLUSTER [user.]cluster}
         [{DROP ¦ REUSE} STORAGE]
```

Description **TRUNCATE** removes all the rows from a table or cluster. You can only truncate an indexed cluster, not a hash cluster (*see* **CREATE CLUSTER**). If you add the **DROP STORAGE** option, **TRUNCATE** will deallocate the space from the deleted rows; if you add the **REUSE STORAGE** option, **TRUNCATE** will leave the space allocated for new rows in the table. **DROP STORAGE** is the default.

The **TRUNCATE** command is faster than a **DELETE** command because it generates no rollback information, does not fire any **DELETE** triggers (and therefore must be used with caution), and does not record any information in a snapshot log. In addition, using **TRUNCATE** does not invalidate the objects depending on the deleted rows or the privileges on the table.

You cannot roll back a **TRUNCATE** statement.

TTITLE

Type   SQL*PLUS command

Product   SQL*PLUS

See also   **ACCEPT**, **BTITLE**, **DEFINE**, PARAMETERS, Chapter 12

Format

```
TTI[TLE] [option [text|variable]... | OFF | ON]


TTI[TLE] text          (old form)
```

Description   ttitle (top **title**) puts a title (may be multi-line) at the top of each page of a report. OFF and ON suppress and restore the display of the text without changing its contents. **ttitle** by itself displays the current **ttitle** options and *text* or *variable.*

text is a title you wish to give this report, and *variable* is a user-defined variable or a system-maintained variable, including SQL.LNO, the current line number; SQL.PNO, the current page number; SQL.RELEASE, the current ORACLE release number; SQL.SQLCODE, the current error code; and SQL.USER, the username.

SQL*PLUS uses **ttitle** in the new form if the first word after **ttitle** is a valid option. The valid options are:

COL[UMN] *n* skips directly to position *n* from the left margin of the current line.

S[KIP] *n* prints *n* blank lines. If no *n* is specified, one blank line is printed. If *n* is 0, no blank lines are printed and the current position for printing becomes position 1 of the current line (leftmost on the page).

TAB *n* skips forward *n* positions (backward if *n* is negative).

LE[FT], **CE[NTER]**, and **R[IGHT]** left-justify, center, and right-justify data on the current line. Any text or variables following these commands are justified as a group, up to the end of the command, or a LEFT, CENTER, RIGHT, or COLUMN. CENTER and RIGHT use the value set by the **SET LINESIZE** command to determine where to place the text or variable.

FORMAT string specifies the format model that will control the format of subsequent text or variables, and follows the same syntax as FORMAT in a

COLUMN command, such as FORMAT A12 or FORMAT $999,990.99. Each time a FORMAT appears, it supersedes the previous one that was in effect. If no FORMAT model has been specified, the one set by **SET NUMFORMAT** is used. If NUMFORMAT has not been set, the default for SQL*PLUS is used.

Date values are printed according to the default format unless a variable has been loaded with a date reformatted by **TO_CHAR**.

Any number of options, pieces of text, and variables may be used in a single **ttitle**. Each is printed in the order specified, and each is positioned and formatted as specified by the clauses that precede it.

SQL*PLUS uses **ttitle** in the old form if the first word after **ttitle** is not a valid option. It simply prints the text at the top of each page. The HEADSEP character (usually |) may be used in this form of **ttitle**.

TUPLE

TUPLE is a synonym for row. It rhymes with "couple."

TWO-PHASE COMMIT

ORACLE7 manages distributed transactions with a special feature called *two-phase commit*. Two-phase commit guarantees that a transaction is valid at all sites by the time it commits or rolls back. All sites either commit or roll back together, no matter what errors occur in the network or on the machines tied together by the network. You don't need to do anything special to have your applications use a two-phase commit.

UID

Type   SQL pseudo-column

Product   SQL

See also   PSEUDO-COLUMNS

Format

```
UID
```

Description   The User **ID** is a number assigned by ORACLE to each user, and is unique on the current database. It may be used in a **select** statement, but is not a real column and cannot be updated by the user.

UNDEFINE

Type   SQL*PLUS command

Product   SQL*PLUS

See also   **ACCEPT**, **DEFINE**, PARAMETERS, Chapters 12 and 14

Format

```
UNDEF[INE] variable
```

Description   **UNDEFINE** deletes the definition of a user variable that has been defined by **ACCEPT**, **DEFINE**, or as a parameter to the **START** command.

Example   To undefine a variable named Total, use this:

```
undefine Total
```

UNDERLINE (SQL*PLUS)

See **SET**.

UNION

Type   SQL function

Products   All

See also   **INTERSECT**, **MINUS**, QUERY OPERATORS, Chapter 10

Format

```
   select...
UNION [ALL]
   select...
```

Description   **UNION** combines two queries. It returns all distinct rows for both **select** statements, or, when **ALL** is specified, all rows regardless of duplication. The number of columns and data types must be identical between **select** statements, although the names of the columns do not need to be. *See* Chapter 10 for a discussion of the important differences and effects of **INTERSECT**, **UNION**, and **MINUS**, and the role that precedence plays in the results.

UNIQUE INDEX

A unique index is an index that imposes uniqueness on each value it indexes. The index may be one single column or concatenated (multiple columns). *See* UNIQUENESS and INTEGRITY CONSTRAINT.

UNIQUE KEY

A unique key is one or more columns that must be unique for each row of the table. *See* KEY, PRIMARY KEY, and INTEGRITY CONSTRAINT.

UNIT OF WORK

In ORACLE, a transaction is equivalent to a logical unit of work, which includes all SQL statements since you either logged on, last committed, or last rolled back your work. Thus, a transaction can encompass numerous SQL statements, or only one.

UPDATE (Form 1 - Embedded SQL)

Type   Embedded SQL command

Product   Precompilers

See also   **EXECUTE IMMEDIATE, FOR, PREPARE, SELECT** (Form 2)

Format

```
EXEC SQL [AT database ¦ :variable] [FOR :integer]
UPDATE [user.]table[@dblink] [alias]
   SET { column = expression [,column = expression]... ¦
        (column [,column]... ) = (subquery) }
 [ WHERE condition ¦ CURRENT OF cursor];
```

Description   *See* the description of the various clauses in **UPDATE** (Form 3). The elements unique to Embedded SQL follow:

- **AT database**, which optionally names a database from a previous **CONNECT** statement for a database name from a previous **DECLARE DATABASE** statement.

- **FOR** *:integer*, which sets the maximum number of rows that can be fetched. *integer* is a named host variable.

- *expression* may include a host :*variable*[:*indicator*]

- The **where** clause may include host variables or arrays.

- **CURRENT OF** updates the last row fetched for the named **cursor**. However, the cursor must be open and positioned on the row. If it isn't, the **CURRENT OF**, which is a part of the **where** clause, causes the **where** to find no rows, and none will be updated. The cursor must have previously been named in a **DECLARE CURSOR** statement with a **select. . .for update of**.

If any host variable in either the **set** or **where** is an array, then all host variables in both must be arrays, though they do not all need to be the same size arrays. If they are arrays, **update** is executed once for each set of components in the array, and may update zero or more rows. The maximum number depends on either the size of the smallest array, or the integer value in the **for** clause, if one is specified. *See* **FOR** for additional details.

UPDATE (Form 2 - PL/SQL)

Type   SQL statement, PL/SQL version

Products   PL/SQL

See also   **DECLARE CURSOR**, SUBQUERY

Format

```
UPDATE [user.]table[@dblink]
SET { column = expression ¦ column = (select expression...)
    [ [,column = expression]... ¦
      [,column = (select
expression...)]... ] ¦
    (column [,column]...) = (subquery)}
[WHERE {condition ¦ CURRENT OF cursor}];
```

Description   **UPDATE** in PL/SQL works identically to the normal SQL UPDATE statement, with the exception of the alternative **where** clause **WHERE CURRENT OF** cursor. In this instance, the **update** statement affects just the single row currently in the cursor as a result of the last **FETCH**. The cursor **select** statement must have included the words FOR UPDATE.

Like **insert**, **delete**, and **select. . .into**, the **update** statement always uses the implicit cursor named SQL. This is never declared (although the **select. . .for update** statement must be **DECLARE**d in a cursor for **WHERE CURRENT OF cursor** to be used). Its attributes are set as follows:

- SQL%ISOPEN is irrelevant.

- SQL%FOUND is TRUE if one or more rows is updated, FALSE if no rows are updated. SQL%NOTFOUND is the opposite of SQL%FOUND.

- SQL%ROWCOUNT is the number of rows updated.

Example

```
<<overage>>
DECLARE
    cursor EMPLOYEE is
        select Age from WORKER
            for update of Lodging;

    WORKER_RECORD    EMPLOYEE%rowtype;
BEGIN
    open EMPLOYEE;
    loop
        fetch EMPLOYEE into WORKER_RECORD;
        exit when EMPLOYEE%notfound;
        if WORKER_RECORD.Age >= 65
            then update WORKER
                    set Lodging = 'YOUTH HOSTEL'
                where current of EMPLOYEE;
    end loop;
    commit;
    close EMPLOYEE;
END overage;
```

UPDATE (Form 3 - SQL Command)

Type   SQL command

Products   All

See also   **DELETE**, **INSERT**, **SELECT**, SUBQUERY, **WHERE**, Chapter 13

Format

```
UPDATE [user.]table[@dblink] [alias]
   SET { column = expression [,column = expression]... |
         (column [,column]... ) = (subquery) }
  [ WHERE condition ];
```

Description   **update** updates (changes) the values in the listed columns in the specified table. The **where** clause may contain a correlated subquery. A subquery may select from the table that is being updated, although it must return just one row. Without a **where** clause, all rows will be updated. With a **where** clause, only those rows it selects will be updated. The expressions are evaluated as the command is executed, and their results replace the current values for the columns in the row(s).

   A subquery must select the same number of columns (with compatible data types) as are in parentheses on the left side of the **set** clause. Columns set to equal expression may precede columns in parentheses set equal to a subquery, all within a single **update** statement.

Example   To set NULL ages for all workers over the age of 65, use this:

```
update WORKER set Age = NULL where Age > 65;
```

   The following will update the city of Walpole in the COMFORT table, setting the precipitation for all Walpole rows to NULL, the noon temperature equal to that in Manchester, and the midnight temperature equal to the noon temperature minus 10 degrees.

```
update COMFORT set Precipitation = NULL,
             (Noon, Midnight) =
      (select Temperature, Temperature - 10
         from WEATHER
        where City = 'MANCHESTER')
 where City = 'WALPOLE';
```

UPPER

Type   SQL function

Products   All

See also   **LOWER**, Chapter 5

Format

```
UPPER(string)
```

Description   **UPPER** converts every letter in a *string* into uppercase.

Example

```
upper('Look what you''ve done, Lauren!')
```

produces this:

```
LOOK WHAT YOU'VE DONE, LAUREN!
```

USED EXTENTS

Used extents are those that either have been allocated to a data (table) segment—and thus have data in them—or have been reserved for data.

USER

Type   SQL pseudo-column

Products   All

See also   PSEUDO-COLUMNS, UID

Format

USER

Description   *User* is the name by which the current user is known to ORACLE. *User* is a pseudo-column, and as such can be queried in any **select** statement, but because it is not a real column, it cannot be updated.

USER PROGRAM INTERFACE (UPI)

UPI is the user half of the Program Interface, which is responsible for keeping separate the user program and the ORACLE program, for data security.

USER VARIABLES

See **ACCEPT**, **DEFINE**, PARAMETERS

USERENV

Type   SQL function

Products   All

See also   CHARACTER FUNCTIONS

Format

```
USERENV(option)
```

Description   *UserEnv* returns information about the user environment, usually for an audit trail. Options are 'ENTRYID', 'SESSIONID', and 'TERMINAL'.

USERNAME

Username is a word that identifies you as an authorized user of your host computer's operating system or of ORACLE. Associated with each username is a password.

VAR (Embedded SQL)

Type   PL/SQL function

Product   PL/SQL

See also   *See* **SELECT (Form 2)**, VARIABLE DECLARATION.

Format

```
EXEC SQL VAR host_variable IS datatype
```

Description   PL/SQL lets you override the default datatype assignment of a variable via the **VAR** command. Once a variable has been declared, its uses the datatype assigned to it in the **declare** command. **VAR** allows you to change the datatype of a declared variable within a PL/SQL block.

VARCHAR

See DATA TYPES.

VARCHAR2

See DATA TYPES.

VARIABLE

Type   PL/SQL function

Products   PL/SQL, SQL*PLUS

See also   PRINT

Format

```
VAR[IABLE] [variable_name {NUMBER|CHAR|CHAR (n)}]
```

Description   **VARIABLE** declares a bind variable which can be referenced in PL/SQL. Each variable is assigned a *variable_name* and a type (NUMBER or CHAR). For CHAR variables, a maximum length (*n*) can be specified.

Examples   In the following example, a variable named *bal* is created and is set equal to the result of a function.

```
variable bal NUMBER
begin
   :bal := BALANCE_CHECK('ADAH TALBOT');
end;
```

VARIABLE DECLARATION (PL/SQL)

Type   PL/SQL statement

Product   PL/SQL

Format

```
variable [CONSTANT]
   {type | identifier%TYPE | [user.]table%ROWTYPE}
   [NOT NULL]
   [{DEFAULT | :=} expression];
```

PL/SQL lets you declare variables in a PL/SQL block. If you declare the variable to be CONSTANT, you must initialize the variable with a value in the declaration and you cannot assign a new value to the variable.

The type of the variable can be a PL/SQL type (*see* DATA TYPES), the type of another PL/SQL variable or database column given by an identifier, or a ROWTYPE (*see* **%ROWTYPE**) that lets you refer to a record corresponding to a database table.

If you add NOT NULL to the declaration, you cannot assign a NULL to the variable and you must initialize the variable. The initialization (following a DEFAULT or assignment :=) expression is any valid PL/SQL expression that results in a value of the type declared.

VARIABLE PARAMETERS

Variable parameters are certain parameters that may be set in the **init.ora** parameter file that will impact the size of the System Global Area (SGA). If these parameters are increased, the size required by the SGA also increases.

VARIABLES

See **ACCEPT**, **DEFINE**, PARAMETERS.

VARIANCE

Type   SQL group function

Products   All

See also   **COMPUTE**, GROUP FUNCTIONS, **STDDEV**, Chapter 6

Format

```
VARIANCE([DISTINCT] value)
```

Description   **VARIANCE** gives the variance of all *values* for a group of rows. Like other group functions, **VARIANCE** ignores NULL values.

VERIFY (SQL*PLUS)

See **SET**.

VERSION NUMBER

The version number is the primary identifying number of ORACLE software. In V7.1.3.6, 7 is the version number.

VIEW

A view is a database object that is a logical representation of a table. It is derived from a table but has no storage of its own and often may be used in the same manner as a table. See **CREATE VIEW**.

VIRTUAL COLUMN

A virtual column is a column in a query result whose value is calculated from the value(s) of other column(s).

VSIZE

Type   SQL function

Products   All

See also   CHARACTER FUNCTIONS, **LENGTH**, NUMBER FUNCTIONS, Chapter 6

Format

```
VSIZE(value)
```

Description   **VSIZE** is the storage size of value in ORACLE. For character columns, **VSIZE** is the same as LENGTH. For numbers it is usually smaller than the apparent length, because less space is required to store numbers in the database.

Examples

```
VSIZE('VICTORIA') = 8

VSIZE(12.345) = 4
```

WALKING A TREE

Walking a tree is the process of visiting each node of a tree in turn. *See* **CONNECT BY**.

WHENEVER (Form 1 - Embedded SQL)

Type   Embedded SQL command

Product   Precompilers

See also   **EXECUTE, FETCH**

Format

```
EXEC SQL WHENEVER {NOT FOUND : SQLERROR : SQL WARNING}
                  {CONTINUE :
```

```
GOTO label :
STOP :
DO routine}
```

Description   **WHENEVER** is not an executable SQL statement, but rather an instruction to the ORACLE language processor to embed an "IF *condition* THEN GOTO *label*" statement after every SQL statement to follow. As each SQL statement executes, its results are tested to see if they meet the *condition*. If they do, the program branches to the *label*.

WHENEVER may be used with **CONTINUE** or a different label for each of the three possible conditions. Each of these will be in effect for all subsequent SQL statements. A new **WHENEVER** with one of these conditions will completely replace its predecessor for all subsequent SQL statements.

NOT FOUND condition is raised any time SQLCODE is 100, meaning, for instance, that a **FETCH** failed to return any rows (this includes subqueries in **insert** statements).

SQLERROR occurs whenever SQLCODE is less than 0. These are typically fatal errors and require serious error handling.

SQLWARNING occurs when a nonfatal "error" occurs. These include truncation of character strings being loaded into host variables, a select list of columns that doesn't match the INTO list of host variables, and **delete** or **update** statements without **where** clauses.

Usually initial branching, continuation, stopping, or routine execution is set up at the very beginning of a program, before any executable SQL statements, something like this:

```
exec sql whenever not found  goto close_down;
exec sql whenever sqlwarning continue;
exec sql whenever sqlerror   goto fatal_error;
```

However, within particular blocks of logic in the body of the program, any or all of these could be replaced depending upon local needs. Note that **WHENEVER** knows nothing about the host languages scoping rules, calls, or branching. From the moment a **WHENEVER** is asserted, its rules remain in effect until another **WHENEVER** (with the same condition) replaces it. On the other hand, your program must obey language scoping rules with regard to the **GOTO** and label.

The **STOP** option stops program execution; the **DO** option calls a host language routine of some kind, the syntax of which depends on your host language.

Lastly, in an error-handling routine, particularly one that may contain SQL statements, WHENEVER SQLERROR should probably contain **CONTINUE** or **STOP** or should call an exit routine in order to avoid an infinite loop back into the same error-handling routine.

WHENEVER SQLERROR (Form 2 - SQL*PLUS)

Type   SQL command, a modified version of **WHENEVER**

Product   SQL*PLUS

See also   **EXIT**, **WHENEVER** (Form 1)

Format

```
WHENEVER SQLERROR {EXIT
[SUCCESS|FAILURE|WARNING|integer|variable] |
                 CONTINUE}
```

Description   With **EXIT**, WHENEVER SQLERROR ends a SQL*PLUS session and returns user to the operating system or calling program or menu if a fatal error is detected (sqlcode < 0). This does not include warning sqlcodes, such as "no rows selected" or "update without a where clause." It does include "table or view does not exist." It commits pending changes to the database. A return code is also returned. SUCCESS, FAILURE, and WARNING have values that are operating system specific; FAILURE and WARNING may be the same on some operating systems.

With **CONTINUE** (instead of **EXIT**), SQL errors are ignored and succeeding statements continue to be executed. This might be used with a series of start files, where some reports, for instance, were not dependent on the success of earlier SQL statements, and you wanted to avoid leaving SQL*PLUS until they were all completed.

You may place WHENEVER SQLERROR in a start file in front of as many SQL statements as you wish. Each WHENEVER SQLERROR will supersede the one before, and will remain in effect until it is itself superseded.

integer is a value you can pass back explicitly as the return code; *variable* allows you to set this value dynamically. This can be a user-defined variable, or a system variable, such as **sql.sqlcode**, which always contains the sqlcode of the last SQL statement executed, either in SQL*PLUS or an embedded PL/SQL block.

Example   When the **create table** in the following example fails because the literal KEENE is not enclosed in single quotation marks, the subsequent **update** and **select** will never even execute. The WHENEVER SQLERROR will exit SQL*PLUS immediately, and pass the **sql.sqlcode** back to the host:

```
whenever sqlerror exit sql.sqlcode;

create table KEENE as
select * from COMFORT
 where City = KEENE;

update KEENE set Noon = 75;
```

```
select * from KEENE;
```

WHERE

Type   SQL clause

Products   All

See also   **DELETE**, LOGICAL OPERATORS, PRECEDENCE, **SELECT**, SYNTAX OPERATORS, **UPDATE**

Format

```
DELETE FROM [user.]table ...
    [ WHERE condition ]

SELECT ...
    [ WHERE condition ]
       ...

UPDATE [user.]table [alias] ...
    [WHERE condition ]
```

Description   **WHERE** defines those logical conditions that will control which rows a **select** statement will return, a **delete** statement will delete, or an **update** statement will update.

A condition may be defined in one of several ways:

- A comparison between expressions (=, >, !=, and so on).

- A comparison between an expression and a query.

- A comparison between a list of expressions and a list of expressions from a query.

- A comparison between an expression and **ANY** or **ALL** members of a list or between an expression and the values brought back from a query.

- A test to see if an expression is **IN** or **NOT IN** a list, or the results of a query.

- A test for being **BETWEEN** or **NOT BETWEEN** one value and another.

- A test to see if an expression **IS NULL** or **IS NOT NULL**.
- A test to see there **EXISTS** (or **NOT EXISTS**) any results for a query.
- A combination of any of the above, using the conjunctions **AND** and **OR**.

Examples

```
where Amount >= Rate * Quantity;

where Item = 'MEDISON';

where ('GEORGE','VICTORIA') = (select Husband, Wife from COUPLES);

where Section >ANY ('A','C','D');

where City !=ALL (select City from LOCATION);

where Section IN ('A','C','D');

where City NOT IN (select City from LOCATION);

where Page BETWEEN 4 and 7;

where Skill IS NULL;

where EXISTS (select * from WORKER where Age > 90);

where Section = 'A' or Section = 'B' and Page = 1;
```

WHILE in PL/SQL

See **LOOP**.

WRAP (SQL*PLUS)

See **SET**.

WRAPPING

Wrapping is moving the end of a heading or title, or the contents of a column, down to a new line when it is too long to fit on one line. (Contrast with **TRUNCATE**.) *See* **COLUMN**.

PART 6

Appendixes

APPENDIX A

Tables Used in This Book

This appendix contains the complete listings of all the tables used in the examples throughout this book. They can be keyed into a start file "as is" to load into a database using SQL*PLUS. If these tables are a part of your ORACLE database, you can easily work your way through the examples in this book and experiment with the many techniques that are illustrated.

For ease of use, set up a user named **practice**, with a password of **practice**. Give this user CONNECT and RESOURCE authority so that new users can access it to learn ORACLE. If you are a new user on an existing ORACLE installation, check with your DBA to see if this has already been done. If not, you might request it, or at least request that the tables and start files be available to you through public synonyms. Whatever "damage" is done on the **practice** id can always be repaired simply by reloading the tables from their start files.

Ordering a Disk of the Tables in This Book

If you'd rather not type the contents of this appendix, you can order a 3.5" disk (IBM format) with a complete copy of all the tables used in this book. To do so, send $40 to:

> George Koch Disk Offer
> 0 North 512 Herrick Drive
> Wheaton, IL 60187-3069

   Payment must accompany order. No purchase orders. Non-U.S. price is $44 (U.S. dollars only).
   Please allow three to six weeks for shipment. Osborne/McGraw-Hill assumes NO responsibility for this offer. This is solely an offer of the authors, and not of Osborne/McGraw-Hill.
   The first two start files are referenced in early chapters in the book: **activity.sql** is used in Chapter 4 and **math.sql** is used in Chapter 6.

The activity.sql Start File

```
rem          Name: activity.sql   Type: start file report
rem    Written by: G. Koch        Date: 2/1/90
rem
rem   Description: Report on G. B. Talbot sales by product
rem                during second half of 1901.
set headsep !


ttitle 'Sales by Product During 1901!Second Six Months (Jul-Dec)'

btitle 'from G. B. Talbot"s Ledger'

column Item heading 'What Was!Sold'
column Item format a18
column Item truncated
```

```
column Person heading 'To Whom Sold' format a18 word_wrapped
column Rate format 90.99
column ActionDate heading 'Date'
column QuantityType heading 'Type' format a8 truncated
column Quantity heading 'Quan' format 9990
column Ext format 990.99


break on Item skip 2
compute sum of Ext on Item


set linesize 79
set pagesize 50 set
newpage 0

spool activity.lst

select ActionDate, Person, Item, Quantity, QuantityType,
       Rate, Quantity * Rate "Ext"
  from Ledger
 where Action = 'SOLD'                /* last 6 months only */
       and ActionDate BETWEEN '01-JUL-01' AND '31-DEC-01'
 order by Item, ActionDate;

spool off
```

The math.sql Start File

```
rem          Name: math.sql      Type: start file report
rem     Written by: G. Koch      Date: 2/4/90
rem
rem  Description: Illustrates ORACLE math functions. Produces
rem               an output file named MATH.LST
set echo off
set pagesize 32000
set linesize 132
column Plus format 99.999
column Minus format 999.999
column Times format 9999.999999
column Divided format .999999
```

```
column VSIZE(Above) heading 'VSIZE¦(Above)'
column VSIZE(Below) heading 'VSIZE¦(Below)'
column VSIZE(Empty) heading 'VSIZE¦(Empty)'
column NVL(Above,11) heading 'NVL¦(Above,11)'
column NVL(Below,11) heading 'NVL¦(Below,11)'
column NVL(Empty,11) heading 'NVL¦(Empty,11)'
column ROUND(Above,2) heading 'ROUND¦(Above,2)'
column ROUND(Below,2) heading 'ROUND¦(Below,2)'
column TRUNC(Above,2) heading 'TRUNC¦(Above,2)'
column TRUNC(Below,2) heading 'TRUNC¦(Below,2)'
column ROUND(Above,0) heading 'ROUND¦(Above,0)'
column ROUND(Below,0) heading 'ROUND¦(Below,0)'
column TRUNC(Above,0) heading 'TRUNC¦(Above,0)'
column TRUNC(Below,0) heading 'TRUNC¦(Below,0)'
column ROUND(Above,-1) heading 'ROUND¦(Above,-1)'
column ROUND(Below,-1) heading 'ROUND¦(Below,-1)'
column TRUNC(Above,-1) heading 'TRUNC¦(Above,-1)'
column TRUNC(Below,-1) heading 'TRUNC¦(Below,-1)'
set echo on
set numwidth 7
set numformat ""
spool math.lst
select Name, Above, Below, Empty from MATH;

select Name, Above, Below, Empty,
       Above + Below "Plus",
       Above - Below "Minus",
       Above * Below "Times",
       Above / Below "Divided"
  from MATH where Name = 'HIGH DECIMAL';

select Name, Above, Below, Empty,
       Above + Empty "Plus",
       Above - Empty "Minus",
       Above * Empty "Times",
       Above / Empty "Divided"
  from MATH where Name = 'HIGH DECIMAL';

select Name, Above, Below, Empty,
       ABS(Above),
       ABS(Below),
       ABS(Empty)
```

```
     from MATH where Name = 'HIGH DECIMAL';

select Name, Above, Below, Empty,
       VSIZE(Above),
       VSIZE(Below),
       VSIZE(Empty)
  from MATH;

select Name, Above, Below, Empty,
       NVL(Above,11),
       NVL(Below,11),
       NVL(Empty,11)
  from MATH where Name = 'HIGH DECIMAL';

select Name, Above, Below,
       CEIL(Above),
       CEIL(Below)
  from MATH;

select Name, Above, Below,
       FLOOR(Above),
       FLOOR(Below)
  from MATH;

select Name, Above, Below,
       MOD(Above,11),
       MOD(Below,11)
  from MATH where Name = 'HIGH DECIMAL';

set numformat 9999.999999
select Name, Above, Below,
       POWER(Above,2),
       POWER(Below,2)
  from MATH where Name = 'HIGH DECIMAL';

select Name, Above, Below,
       POWER(Above,2.9),
       POWER(Below,2.9)
  from MATH;

set numformat ""
select Name, Above, Below,
```

```
         SQRT(Above),
         SQRT(Below)
   from MATH where Name = 'HIGH DECIMAL';

select Name, Above, Below,
       ROUND(Above,2),
       ROUND(Below,2),
       TRUNC(Above,2),
       TRUNC(Below,2)
   from MATH;

select Name, Above, Below,
       ROUND(Above,0),
       ROUND(Below,0),
       TRUNC(Above,0),
       TRUNC(Below,0)
   from MATH;

select Name, Above, Below,
       ROUND(Above,-1),
       ROUND(Below,-1),
       TRUNC(Above,-1),
       TRUNC(Below,-1)
   from MATH;

select Name, Above, Below,
       SIGN(Above),
       SIGN(Below)
   from MATH where Name = 'HIGH DECIMAL';

spool off
```

The ADDRESS Table

```
drop table ADDRESS;
create table ADDRESS (
LastName    varchar2(25),
FirstName   varchar2(25),
Street      varchar2(50),
City        varchar2(25),
State       char(2),
Zip         number,
```

```
Phone        varchar2(12),
Ext          varchar2(5));
insert into ADDRESS values (
'BAILEY',       'WILLIAM',      null,null,null,null,'213-293-0223',null);
insert into ADDRESS values (
'ADAMS',        'JACK',         null,null,null,null,'415-453-7530',null);
insert into ADDRESS values (
'SEP',          'FELICIA',      null,null,null,null,'214-522-8383',null);
insert into ADDRESS values (
'DE MEDICI',    'LEFTY',        null,null,null,null,'312-736-1166',null);
insert into ADDRESS values (
'DEMIURGE',     'FRANK',        null,null,null,null,'707-767-8900',null);
insert into ADDRESS values (
'CASEY',        'WILLIS',       null,null,null,null,'312-684-1414',null);
insert into ADDRESS values (
'ZACK',         'JACK',         null,null,null,null,'415-620-6842',null);
insert into ADDRESS values (
'YARROW',       'MARY',         null,null,null,949414302,'415-787-2178',null);
insert into ADDRESS values (
'WERSCHKY',     'ARNY',         null,null,null,null,'415-235-7387',null);
insert into ADDRESS values (
'BRANT',        'GLEN',         null,null,null,null,'415-526-7512',null);
insert into ADDRESS values (
'EDGAR',        'THEODORE',     null,null,null,null,'415-525-6252',null);
insert into ADDRESS values (
'HARDIN',       'HUGGY',        null,null,null,null,'617-566-0125',null);
insert into ADDRESS values (
'HILD',         'PHIL',         null,null,null,null,'603-934-2242',null);
insert into ADDRESS values (
'LOEBEL',       'FRANK',        null,null,null,null,'202-456-1414',null);
insert into ADDRESS values (
'MOORE',        'MARY',         null,null,null,601262460,'718-857-1638',null);
insert into ADDRESS values (
'SZEP',         'FELICIA',      null,null,null,null,'214-522-8383',null);
insert into ADDRESS values (
'ZIMMERMAN',    'FRED',         null,null,null,null,'503-234-7491',null);
```

The ASOF Table

```
drop table ASOF;
create table ASOF (
AsOf            date
);

insert into ASOF values ('15-DEC-01');
```

The BIRTHDAY Table

```
drop table BIRTHDAY;
create table BIRTHDAY (
FirstName       varchar2(15),
LastName        varchar2(15),
BirthDate       date,
Age             number
);

insert into BIRTHDAY values ('GEORGE','SAND','12-MAY-46',42);
insert into BIRTHDAY values ('ROBERT','JAMES','23-AUG-37',52);
insert into BIRTHDAY values ('NANCY','LEE','02-FEB-47',42);
insert into BIRTHDAY values ('VICTORIA','LYNN',TO_DATE('20-MAY-49 3:27',
'DD-MON-YY HH24:MI'),45);
insert into BIRTHDAY values ('FRANK','PILOT','11-NOV-42',42);
```

The BREEDING Table

```
drop table BREEDING;
create table BREEDING (
Offspring       varchar2(10),
Sex             char(1),
Cow             varchar2(10),
Bull            varchar2(10),
Birthdate       date
);

insert into BREEDING values ('EVE','F',null,null,null);
insert into BREEDING values ('ADAM','M',null,null,null);
insert into BREEDING values ('BANDIT','M',null,null,null);
insert into BREEDING values ('BETSY','F','EVE','ADAM','02-JAN-00');
insert into BREEDING values ('POCO','M','EVE','ADAM','15-JUL-00');
insert into BREEDING values ('GRETA','F','EVE','BANDIT','12-MAR-01');
insert into BREEDING values ('MANDY','F','EVE','POCO','22-AUG-02');
insert into BREEDING values ('NOVI','F','BETSY','ADAM','30-MAR-03');
insert into BREEDING values ('GINNY','F','BETSY','BANDIT','04-DEC-03');
insert into BREEDING values ('CINDY','F','EVE','POCO','09-FEB-03');
insert into BREEDING values ('DUKE','M','MANDY','BANDIT','24-JUL-04');
insert into BREEDING values ('TEDDI','F','BETSY','BANDIT','12-AUG-05');
insert into BREEDING values ('SUZY','F','GINNY','DUKE','03-APR-06');
insert into BREEDING values ('RUTH','F','GINNY','DUKE','25-DEC-06');
insert into BREEDING values ('PAULA','F','MANDY','POCO','21-DEC-06');
insert into BREEDING values ('DELLA','F','SUZY','BANDIT','11-OCT-08');
```

The CD Table

```
drop table CD;
create table CD (
Account        number not null,
Amount         number not null,
MaturityDate   date not null
);

insert into CD values (573334, 10000, '15-JAN-09');
insert into CD values (677654, 25000, '15-JAN-01');
insert into CD values (976032, 10000, '15-JAN-95');
insert into CD values (275031, 10000, '15-JAN-97');
insert into CD values (274598, 20000, '15-JAN-99');
insert into CD values (538365, 45000, '15-JAN-01');
insert into CD values (267432, 16500, '15-JAN-04');
```

The COMFORT Table

```
drop table COMFORT;
create table COMFORT (
City           varchar2(13) NOT NULL,
SampleDate     date NOT NULL,
Noon           number(3,1),
Midnight       number(3,1),
Precipitation  number
);

insert into COMFORT values ('SAN FRANCISCO','21-MAR-93',62.5,42.3,.5);
insert into COMFORT values ('SAN FRANCISCO','22-JUN-93',51.1,71.9,.1);
insert into COMFORT values ('SAN FRANCISCO','23-SEP-93',NULL,61.5,.1);
insert into COMFORT values ('SAN FRANCISCO','22-DEC-93',52.6,39.8,2.3);
insert into COMFORT values ('KEENE','21-MAR-93',39.9,-1.2,4.4);
insert into COMFORT values ('KEENE','22-JUN-93',85.1,66.7,1.3);
insert into COMFORT values ('KEENE','23-SEP-93',99.8,82.6,NULL);
insert into COMFORT values ('KEENE','22-DEC-93',-7.2,-1.2,3.9);
```

The COMMA Table

```
drop table COMMA;
create table COMMA (
Amount          number,
AmountChar      varchar2(20)
);
insert into COMMA values (0,'0');
insert into COMMA values (0.25,'0.25');
insert into COMMA values (1.25,'1.25');
insert into COMMA values (12.25,'12.25');
insert into COMMA values (123.25,'123.25');
insert into COMMA values (1234.25,'1,234.25');
insert into COMMA values (12345.25,'12,345.25');
insert into COMMA values (123456.25,'123,456.25');
insert into COMMA values (1234567.25,'1,234,567.25');
insert into COMMA values (12345678.25,'12,345,678.25');
insert into COMMA values (123456789.25,'123,456,789.25');
REM insert into COMMA values (1234567890.25,'1,234,567,890.25');
REM insert into COMMA values (12345678901.25,'12,345,678,901.25');
```

The EMPTY Table

```
drop table EMPTY;
create table EMPTY (
Nothing         varchar2(25),
Less            number
);

REMARK No inserts. This table is empty.
```

The HOCKEY Table

```
drop table HOCKEY;
create table HOCKEY (
Team        varchar2(20),
Won         number,
Lost        number,
Tied        number
```

```
);

insert into HOCKEY values ('Quebec'       ,  6,    23,    4);
insert into HOCKEY values ('Detroit'      , 10,    18,    5);
insert into HOCKEY values ('Vancouver'    , 11,    16,    6);
insert into HOCKEY values ('NY Islanders' , 11,    20,    4);
insert into HOCKEY values ('Washington'   , 13,    15,    4);
insert into HOCKEY values ('Pittsburgh'   , 13,    16,    3);
insert into HOCKEY values ('Calgary'      , 14,    11,    9);
insert into HOCKEY values ('St Louis'     , 14,    12,    6);
insert into HOCKEY values ('Winnipeg'     , 14,    13,    5);
insert into HOCKEY values ('NY Rangers'   , 15,    14,    5);
insert into HOCKEY values ('New Jersey'   , 15,    15,    3);
insert into HOCKEY values ('Edmonton'     , 16,    11,    7);
insert into HOCKEY values ('Philadelphia' , 16,    14,    4);
insert into HOCKEY values ('Los Angeles'  , 16,    14,    3);
insert into HOCKEY values ('Hartford'     , 16,    17,    1);
insert into HOCKEY values ('Toronto'      , 16,    18,    0);
insert into HOCKEY values ('Boston'       , 17,    13,    3);
insert into HOCKEY values ('Minnesota'    , 17,    15,    2);
insert into HOCKEY values ('Chicago'      , 19,    13,    2);
insert into HOCKEY values ('Montreal'     , 20,    13,    4);
insert into HOCKEY values ('Buffalo'      , 21,     9,    4);
```

The HOLIDAY Table

```
drop table HOLIDAY;
create table HOLIDAY (
Holiday        varchar2(25),
ActualDate     date,
CelebratedDate date
);
insert into HOLIDAY values ('NEW YEAR DAY','01-JAN-95','01-JAN-95');
insert into HOLIDAY values ('MARTIN LUTHER KING, JR.','15-JAN-95','16-JAN-95');
insert into HOLIDAY values ('LINCOLNS BIRTHDAY','12-FEB-95','20-FEB-95');
REM insert into HOLIDAY values ('VALENTINES DAY','14-FEB-95','14-FEB-95');
insert into HOLIDAY values ('WASHINGTONS BIRTHDAY','22-FEB-95','20-FEB-95');
insert into HOLIDAY values ('FAST DAY, NEW HAMPSHIRE','22-FEB-95','22-FEB-95');
REM insert into HOLIDAY values ('VICTORIA DAY,CANADA','21-MAY-95','21-MAY-95');
insert into HOLIDAY values ('MEMORIAL DAY','30-MAY-95','29-MAY-95');
REM insert into HOLIDAY values ('FLAG DAY','14-JUN-95','14-JUN-95');
REM insert into HOLIDAY values ('FATHERS DAY','18-JUN-95','18-JUN-95');
insert into HOLIDAY values ('INDEPENDENCE DAY','04-JUL-95','04-JUL-95');
insert into HOLIDAY values ('LABOR DAY','04-SEP-95','04-SEP-95');
insert into HOLIDAY values ('COLUMBUS DAY','08-OCT-95','09-OCT-95');
REM insert into HOLIDAY values ('HALLOWEEN','31-OCT-95','31-OCT-95');
```

```
REM insert into HOLIDAY values ('VETERANS DAY','11-NOV-95','11-NOV-95');
insert into HOLIDAY values ('THANKSGIVING','23-NOV-95','23-NOV-95');
REM insert into HOLIDAY values ('CHANUKAH','18-DEC-95','18-DEC-95');
REM insert into HOLIDAY values ('CHRISTMAS','25-DEC-95','25-DEC-95');
```

The LEDGER Table

```
drop table LEDGER;
create table LEDGER (
ActionDate      date,          /* when */
Action          varchar2(8),      /* bought, sold, paid, received */
Item            varchar2(30),     /* what */
Quantity        number,        /* how many */
QuantityType    varchar2(10),     /* type of quantity: lbs, bushels, etc */
Rate            number,        /* how much per Quantity Type  */
Amount          number(9,2),   /* Total amount (extension) Rate * Quantity */
Person          varchar2(25)      /* To or from whom? */
);

insert into ledger values (
'01-APR-01','PAID','PLOWING',1,'DAY',3,3,'RICHARD KOCH AND BROTHERS');
insert into ledger values (
'02-MAY-01','PAID','WORK',1,'DAY',1,1,'DICK JONES');
insert into ledger values (
'03-JUN-01','PAID','WORK',1,'DAY',1,1,'ELBERT TALBOT');
insert into ledger values (
'04-JAN-01','PAID','WORK',1,'DAY',1,1,'GERHARDT KENTGEN');
insert into ledger values (
'04-FEB-01','PAID','WORK',.5,'DAY',1,.5,'ELBERT TALBOT');
insert into ledger values (
'05-APR-01','PAID','WORK',1,'DAY',1,1,'DICK JONES');
insert into ledger values (
'06-AUG-01','PAID','PLOWING',1,'DAY',1.8,1.8,'VICTORIA LYNN');
insert into ledger values (
'07-OCT-01','PAID','PLOWING',.5,'DAY',3,1.5,'RICHARD KOCH AND BROTHERS');
prompt Going into silent mode.
set termout off
insert into ledger values (
'09-SEP-01','PAID','WORK',1,'DAY',1,1,'ADAH TALBOT');
insert into ledger values (
'09-OCT-01','PAID','WORK',.5,'DAY',1.25,.63,'DONALD ROLLO');
insert into ledger values (
'10-NOV-01','PAID','WORK',1,'DAY',1.25,.63,'JOHN PEARSON');
insert into ledger values (
'10-AUG-01','PAID','WORK',1,'DAY',1,1,'HELEN BRANDT');
insert into ledger values (
'11-AUG-01','PAID','WORK',1,'DAY',2,2,'HELEN BRANDT');
insert into ledger values (
'11-SEP-01','PAID','WORK',1,'DAY',.75,.75,'ROLAND BRANDT');
insert into ledger values (
'12-DEC-01','PAID','WORK',1,'DAY',1,1,'BART SARJEANT');
insert into ledger values (
'12-JAN-01','PAID','WORK',1,'DAY',1,1,'GEORGE OSCAR');
insert into ledger values (
```

```
'13-JUN-01','PAID','WORK',1,'DAY',1,1,'PETER LAWSON');
insert into ledger values (
'14-JUL-01','PAID','WORK',1,'DAY',1.2,1.2,'WILFRED LOWELL');
insert into ledger values (
'15-JUL-01','PAID','WORK',1,'DAY',2.25,2.25,'KAY AND PALMER WALLBOM');
insert into ledger values (
'03-OCT-01','SOLD','BOOT BETWEEN HORSES',1,'EACH',12.5,12.5,'GARY KENTGEN');
insert into ledger values (
'01-NOV-01','BOUGHT','CALF',2,'EACH',2,4,'GARY KENTGEN');
insert into ledger values (
'02-NOV-01','BOUGHT','MARE',1,'EACH',5,5,'JAMES COLE');
insert into ledger values (
'03-NOV-01','BOUGHT','PIG',1,'EACH',2,2,'ANDREW DYE');
insert into ledger values (
'04-NOV-01','BOUGHT','HAY',1,'WAGON',5,5,'ANDREW DYE');
insert into ledger values (
'05-NOV-01','BOUGHT','HAY',4,'WAGON',5,20,'ANDREW DYE');
insert into ledger values (
'05-NOV-01','BOUGHT','LINE',1,'SET',.75,.75,'ANDREW DYE');
insert into ledger values (
'06-NOV-01','BOUGHT','COLT',2,'COLT',4.5,9,'ANDREW DYE');
insert into ledger values (
'06-AUG-01','PAID','PLOWING',2,'DAY',2,4,'ANDREW DYE');
insert into ledger values (
'07-NOV-01','PAID','SAWED WOOD',1,'DAY',.5,.5,'ANDREW DYE');
insert into ledger values (
'09-NOV-01','BOUGHT','COLT',1,'EACH',10,10,'ANDREW DYE');
insert into ledger values (
'10-NOV-01','SOLD','HEFER',1,'EACH',28,28,'PAT LAVAY');
insert into ledger values (
'11-NOV-01','SOLD','BOOT BETWEEN HORSES',1,'EACH',6,6,'PAT LAVAY');
insert into ledger values (
'11-NOV-01','SOLD','BUTTER',1,'LB',.15,.15,'PAT LAVAY');
insert into ledger values (
'12-NOV-01','PAID','WORK',2,'DAY',.75,1.5,'PAT LAVAY');
insert into ledger values (
'13-NOV-01','PAID','CUT LOGS',.5,'DAY',.5,.25,'PAT LAVAY');
insert into ledger values (
'13-NOV-01','PAID','DRAWED LOGS',1.5,'DAY',.5,.75,'PAT LAVAY');
insert into ledger values (
'13-DEC-01','PAID','SAWED WOOD',1,'DAY',.5,.5,'PAT LAVAY');
insert into ledger values (
'14-NOV-01','SOLD','HEFER',1,'EACH',35,35,'MORRIS ARNOLD');
insert into ledger values (
'15-NOV-01','SOLD','BEEF',37,'LB',.04,1.48,'FRED FULLER');
insert into ledger values (
'16-NOV-01','SOLD','BUTTER',5,'LB',.16,.8,'VICTORIA LYNN');
insert into ledger values (
'18-NOV-01','SOLD','BUTTER',6,'LB',.16,.96,'JOHN PEARSON');
insert into ledger values (
'20-NOV-01','SOLD','HEFER',1,'EACH',30,30,'PALMER WALLBOM');
insert into ledger values (
'21-NOV-01','SOLD','BEEF',116,'LB',.06,6.96,'ROLAND BRANDT');
insert into ledger values (
'22-NOV-01','SOLD','BEEF',118,'LB',.06,7.08,'GERHARDT KENTGEN');
insert into ledger values (
'01-DEC-01','BOUGHT','BEEF',138,'LB',.05,6.9,'VICTORIA LYNN');
```

```
insert into ledger values (
'01-DEC-01','BOUGHT','BEEF',130,'LB',.06,7.8,'GEORGE B. MCCORMICK');
insert into ledger values (
'03-DEC-01','BOUGHT','BEEF',130,'LB',.05,6.5,'PETER LAWSON');
insert into ledger values (
'03-DEC-01','BOUGHT','BEEF',125,'LB',.06,7.5,'HELEN BRANDT');
insert into ledger values (
'05-DEC-01','BOUGHT','BEEF',140,'LB',.05,7,'ROBERT JAMES');
insert into ledger values (
'05-DEC-01','BOUGHT','BEEF',145,'LB',.05,7.25,'ISAIAH JAMES');
insert into ledger values (
'07-DEC-01','BOUGHT','HORSE',1,'EACH',30,30,'GEORGE AUGUST');
insert into ledger values (
'07-DEC-01','BOUGHT','REAPER/BINDER',1,'EACH',47.5,47.5,'JANICE TALBOT');
insert into ledger values (
'03-JAN-01','BOUGHT','HOMINY',1,'BUSHEL',1.25,1.25,'GENERAL STORE');
insert into ledger values (
'09-JAN-01','BOUGHT','LICE KILLER',1,'BOX',.5,.5,'GENERAL STORE');
insert into ledger values (
'11-JAN-01','BOUGHT','MENDING BRACE',1,'EACH',.15,.15,'GENERAL STORE');
insert into ledger values (
'11-JAN-01','BOUGHT','STOVE BLACKING',1,'BOX',.05,.05,'GENERAL STORE');
insert into ledger values (
'13-JAN-01','BOUGHT','GRINDING BAT',10,'EACH',.03,.3,'GENERAL STORE');
insert into ledger values (
'14-JAN-01','SOLD','BEEF HIDE',1,'EACH',5.46,5.46,'GENERAL STORE');
insert into ledger values (
'14-JAN-01','SOLD','CHEESE FLAT',13,'EACH',3.15,40.95,'GENERAL STORE');
insert into ledger values (
'14-JAN-01','BOUGHT','LANTERN GLOBE',1,'EACH',.1,.1,'GENERAL STORE');
insert into ledger values (
'15-JAN-01','BOUGHT','STAMP FOR LETTER',1,'EACH',.02,.02,'POST OFFICE');
insert into ledger values (
'15-JAN-01','BOUGHT','STOCKING',2,'PAIR',.15,.3,'GENERAL STORE');
insert into ledger values (
'16-JAN-01','BOUGHT','OIL',4,'GALLON',.1,.4,'GENERAL STORE');
insert into ledger values (
'16-JAN-01','BOUGHT','SUGAR',25,'LB',.07,1.75,'GENERAL STORE');
insert into ledger values (
'16-JAN-01','BOUGHT','MOLASSES',1,'GALLON',.6,.6,'GENERAL STORE');
insert into ledger values (
'16-JAN-01','BOUGHT','CARD OF THANKS',1,'EACH',.3,.3,'GENERAL STORE');
insert into ledger values (
'17-JAN-01','BOUGHT','HORSE SHODDING',1,'EACH',.85,.85,'LIVERY');
insert into ledger values (
'17-JAN-01','BOUGHT','CORN',230,'LB',.01,2.3,'FEED STORE');
insert into ledger values (
'18-JAN-01','BOUGHT','CORN MEAL',213,'LB',.01,2.13,'FEED STORE');
insert into ledger values (
'18-JAN-01','BOUGHT','PAPER',50,'SHEETS',.01,.5,'GENERAL STORE');
insert into ledger values (
'18-JAN-01','BOUGHT','COFFEE',1,'LB',.3,.3,'GENERAL STORE');
insert into ledger values (
'18-JAN-01','BOUGHT','SEEDED RAISINS',1,'LB',.12,.12,'GENERAL STORE');
insert into ledger values (
'18-JAN-01','BOUGHT','COTTON STOCKING',3,'PAIR',.08,.24,'GENERAL STORE');
insert into ledger values (
```

```
'19-JAN-01','BOUGHT','COTTON STOCKING',3,'PAIR',.08,.24,'GENERAL STORE');
insert into ledger values (
'19-JAN-01','BOUGHT','GRINDING BAT',24,'EACH',.03,.72,'GENERAL STORE');
insert into ledger values (
'19-JAN-01','BOUGHT','TELEPHONE CALL',1,'EACH',.15,.15,'PHONE COMPANY');
insert into ledger values (
'19-JAN-01','BOUGHT','TEA',.5,'LB',.5,.25,'GENERAL STORE');
insert into ledger values (
'19-JAN-01','BOUGHT','HAT',1,'EACH',.1,.1,'GENERAL STORE');
insert into ledger values (
'19-JAN-01','BOUGHT','SALT PETER',1,'TABLET',.08,.08,'GENERAL STORE');
insert into ledger values (
'19-JAN-01','BOUGHT','ENVELOPES',6,'EACH',.02,.12,'GENERAL STORE');
insert into ledger values (
'19-JAN-01','BOUGHT','CREOAL',2,'QUART',.37,.74,'GENERAL STORE');
insert into ledger values (
'23-JAN-01','SOLD','WOOD',1,'CORD',2,2,'METHODIST CHURCH');
insert into ledger values (
'24-JAN-01','BOUGHT','SCHOOLING',1,'TERM',1,1,'SCHOOL');
insert into ledger values (
'24-JAN-01','BOUGHT','HOMINY',186,'TERM',.01,1.86,'GENERAL STORE');
insert into ledger values (
'28-JAN-01','BOUGHT','GRINDING',1,'EACH',.9,.9,'MILL');
insert into ledger values (
'28-JAN-01','BOUGHT','POPCORN',5,'LB',.04,.2,'GENERAL STORE');
insert into ledger values (
'02-FEB-01','BOUGHT','SULPHER',5,'LB',.25,1.25,'GENERAL STORE');
insert into ledger values (
'03-FEB-01','BOUGHT','OIL',4,'GALLON',.13,.52,'GENERAL STORE');
insert into ledger values (
'03-FEB-01','BOUGHT','SWAMP ROOT',1,'BOTTLE',.75,.75,'GENERAL STORE');
insert into ledger values (
'04-FEB-01','BOUGHT','SHOEING NED',1,'EACH',.5,.5,'BLACKSMITH');
insert into ledger values (
'04-FEB-01','BOUGHT','GRINDING',1,'EACH',.47,.47,'MILL');
insert into ledger values (
'05-FEB-01','BOUGHT','PILLS',1,'BOX',.25,.25,'GENERAL STORE');
insert into ledger values (
'07-FEB-01','BOUGHT','THREAD',2,'SPOOLS',.05,.1,'GENERAL STORE');
insert into ledger values (
'08-FEB-01','BOUGHT','SHIRTS',2,'EACH',.5,1,'GENERAL STORE');
insert into ledger values (
'10-FEB-01','SOLD','BUTTER',9,'LB',.25,2.25,'GENERAL STORE');
insert into ledger values (
'18-FEB-01','BOUGHT','HORSE MEDISON',1,'ENVELOPE',.13,.13,'GENERAL STORE');
insert into ledger values (
'18-FEB-01','BOUGHT','ELBO STOVE PIPE',1,'EACH',.15,.15,'GENERAL STORE');
insert into ledger values (
'18-FEB-01','SOLD','CALF',1,'EACH',4,4,'LILY CARLSTROM');
insert into ledger values (
'25-FEB-01','SOLD','BUTTER',21,'LB',.25,5.25,'GENERAL STORE');
insert into ledger values (
'28-FEB-01','BOUGHT','SWAMP ROOT',1,'BOTTLE',.75,.75,'GENERAL STORE');
insert into ledger values (
'28-FEB-01','BOUGHT','LIVER PILLS',1,'BOX',.2,.2,'GENERAL STORE');
insert into ledger values (
'28-FEB-01','SOLD','BUTTER',3,'LB',.25,.75,'HELEN BRANDT');
```

```
insert into ledger values (
'01-APR-01','BOUGHT','GRINDING',1,'EACH','.45,.45,'MILL');
insert into ledger values (
'06-MAR-01','BOUGHT','MEDISON FOR INDIGESTION',1,'BOTTLE',.4,.4,
'DR. CARLSTROM');
insert into ledger values (
'06-JUN-01','BOUGHT','BREADING POWDER',1,'BOX',.9,.9,'MILL');
insert into ledger values (
'06-MAR-01','BOUGHT','PANTS',1,'PAIR',.75,.75,'GENERAL STORE');
insert into ledger values (
'07-APR-01','BOUGHT','HOMINY',200,'LB',.01,2,'MILL');
insert into ledger values (
'08-MAR-01','BOUGHT','TOBACCO FOR LICE',1,'BOX',.25,.25,'MILL');
insert into ledger values (
'07-MAR-01','BOUGHT','SHOEING',1,'EACH',.35,.35,'BLACKSMITH');
insert into ledger values (
'07-APR-01','BOUGHT','PINS',1,'BOX',.05,.05,'GENERAL STORE');
insert into ledger values (
'07-MAR-01','BOUGHT','MAIL BOX',1,'EACH',1,1,'POST OFFICE');
insert into ledger values (
'10-MAR-1','BOUGHT','STOVE PIPE THIMBLES',2,'EACH',.5,1,'VERNA HARDWARE');
insert into ledger values (
'13-MAR-01','BOUGHT','THERMOMETER',1,'EACH',.15,.15,'GENERAL STORE');
insert into ledger values (
'14-MAR-01','BOUGHT','LOT IN CEMETERY NO. 80',1,'EACH',25,25,'METHODIST CHURCH');
insert into ledger values (
'14-MAR-01','PAID','DIGGING OF GRAVE',1,'EACH',3,3,'JED HOPKINS');
insert into ledger values (
'16-APR-01','BOUGHT','GRINDING',1,'EACH',.16,.16,'MILL');
insert into ledger values (
'16-MAR-01','BOUGHT','GRINDING',1,'EACH',.16,.16,'MILL');
insert into ledger values (
'23-MAR-01','BOUGHT','CLOTH FOR DRESS LINING',2,'YARD',.27,.54,'GENERAL STORE');
insert into ledger values (
'18-AUG-01','BOUGHT','SYRUP THERMOMETER',1,'EACH',1,1,'GENERAL STORE');
insert into ledger values (
'25-MAR-01','BOUGHT','BOOTS FOR SHIRLEY',1,'PAIR',2.5,2.5,'GENERAL STORE');
insert into ledger values (
'27-APR-01','BOUGHT','SYRUP CANS',2,'DOZEN',1.07,2.14,'VERNA HARDWARE');
insert into ledger values (
'22-MAR-01','BOUGHT','MILK CANS',2,'EACH',2.5,5,'VERNA HARDWARE');
insert into ledger values (
'23-APR-01','BOUGHT','DUBBLE STRAINER',1,'EACH',.95,.95,'VERNA HARDWARE');
insert into ledger values (
'25-JUN-01','BOUGHT','MILK STIRRER',1,'EACH',.25,.25,'VERNA HARDWARE');
insert into ledger values (
'27-MAR-01','BOUGHT','HOMINY',77,'LB',.01,.77,'MILL');
insert into ledger values (
'28-APR-01','BOUGHT','CORN',104,'LB',.01,1.04,'MILL');
insert into ledger values (
'06-APR-01','BOUGHT','FUNERAL',1,'EACH',3.19,3.19,'UNDERWOOD BROS');
insert into ledger values (
'30-APR-01','BOUGHT','BRUSH',1,'EACH',.05,.05,'GENERAL STORE');
insert into ledger values (
'30-APR-01','BOUGHT','SAND',5,'BUSHEL',.03,.15,'QUARRY');
insert into ledger values (
```

```
'31-MAR-01','SOLD','MOLASSES',3,'GALLON',1,3,'HAROLD SCHOLE');
insert into ledger values (
'28-MAR-01','SOLD','MOLASSES',1,'GALLON',1,1,'GERHARDT KENTGEN');
insert into ledger values (
'30-MAR-01','BOUGHT','FIXING SHIRLEYS WATCH',1,'EACH',.25,.25,'MANNER JEWELERS');
insert into ledger values (
'04-APR-01','SOLD','BUTTER',9,'LB',.23,2.07,'HAROLD SCHOLE');
insert into ledger values (
'05-APR-01','BOUGHT','SODA',1,'BOTTLE',.05,.05,'GENERAL STORE');
insert into ledger values (
'05-MAR-01','BOUGHT','TELEPHONE CALL',1,'EACH',.2,.2,'PHONE COMPANY');
insert into ledger values (
'06-APR-01','BOUGHT','GLOVES',1,'PAIR',.25,.25,'GENERAL STORE');
insert into ledger values (
'06-APR-01','BOUGHT','SHOES FOR SHIRLEY',1,'PAIR',2,2,'GENERAL STORE');
insert into ledger values (
'09-APR-01','BOUGHT','PEANUTS',1,'BAG',.05,.05,'GENERAL STORE');
insert into ledger values (
'11-APR-01','BOUGHT','BRAN',300,'LB',.01,3,'GENERAL STORE');
insert into ledger values (
'15-APR-01','BOUGHT','SHOEING',2,'EACH',.3,.6,'BLACKSMITH');
insert into ledger values (
'17-APR-01','BOUGHT','HOMINY',173,'LB',.01,1.73,'GENERAL STORE');
insert into ledger values (
'17-APR-01','BOUGHT','BRAN',450,'LB',.01,4.5,'GENERAL STORE');
insert into ledger values (
'17-APR-01','BOUGHT','CALF MEAL',110,'LB',.01,1.1,'GENERAL STORE');
insert into ledger values (
'22-APR-01','BOUGHT','HOMINY',454,'LB',.01,4.54,'GENERAL STORE');
insert into ledger values (
'22-APR-01','BOUGHT','BRAN',300,'LB',.01,3,'GENERAL STORE');
insert into ledger values (
'22-APR-01','SOLD','CALF',1,'EACH',1,1,'PAT LAVAY');
insert into ledger values (
'25-APR-01','BOUGHT','CALF MEAL',100,'EACH',.01,1,'GENERAL STORE');
insert into ledger values (
'27-APR-01','BOUGHT','SHOEING NED',1,'EACH',.5,.5,'BLACKSMITH');
insert into ledger values (
'07-JUN-01','RECEIVED','BREAKING COLT',1,'EACH',5,5,'SAM DYE');
insert into ledger values (
'07-JUN-01','RECEIVED','KEEPING COLT',1,'EACH',4,4,'SAM DYE');
insert into ledger values (
'17-JUN-01','BOUGHT','SCHOOL TAX',1,'EACH',6.56,6.56,'SCHOOL');
insert into ledger values (
'17-JUN-01','RECEIVED','THRESHING',2,'DAY',1,2,'HENRY CHASE');
insert into ledger values (
'18-JUN-01','PAID','THRESHING',.5,'DAY',1,.5,'WILLIAM SWING');
insert into ledger values (
'18-JUN-01','BOUGHT','SHEEP',22,'EACH',.87,19.14,'BOOLE AND JONES');
insert into ledger values (
'15-MAR-01','SOLD','POTATOES',5,'BUSHEL',.25,1.25,'GENERAL STORE');
insert into ledger values (
'15-MAR-01','SOLD','COW',2,'EACH',33,66,'SAM DYE');
insert into ledger values (
'15-MAR-1','RECEIVED','BOOT BETWEEN HORSES',1,'EACH',10,10,'ADAH TALBOT');
insert into ledger values (
```

```
'18-MAR-01','SOLD','WAGON',1,'EACH',5,5,'ADAH TALBOT');
insert into ledger values (
'04-APR-01','SOLD','HARNES',1,'EACH',2,2,'ADAH TALBOT');
insert into ledger values (
'16-APR-01','SOLD','COW',3,'EACH',30,90,'GEORGE B. MCCORMICK');
insert into ledger values (
'09-JUN-1','BOUGHT','USE OF PASTURE',1,'EACH',10,10,'GEORGE B. MCCORMICK');
insert into ledger values (
'28-JUN-01','BOUGHT','SHEEP AND BULL',1,'LOT',97.88,97.88,'EDWARD JOHNSON');
insert into ledger values (
'03-JUL-01','SOLD','HEIFER',1,'EACH',35,35,'SAM DYE');
insert into ledger values (
'18-MAY-01','BOUGHT','MIDDLINGS',180,'LB',.01,1.8,'DEAN FOREMAN');
insert into ledger values (
'20-MAY-01','BOUGHT','MIDDLINGS',450,'LB',.01,4.5,'GEORGE OSCAR');
insert into ledger values (
'22-MAY-01','BOUGHT','MIDDLINGS',640,'LB',.01,6.4,'EDYTHE GAMMIERE');
insert into ledger values (
'23-MAY-01','BOUGHT','MIDDLINGS',110,'LB',.01,1.1,'JOHN AUSTIN');
insert into ledger values (
'28-MAY-01','BOUGHT','COMB',1,'EACH',.07,.07,'GENERAL STORE');
insert into ledger values (
'29-MAY-01','BOUGHT','BUTTONS',1,'BOX',.1,.1,'GENERAL STORE');
insert into ledger values (
'05-JUL-01','BOUGHT','BEANS',6,'LB',.03,.18,'GENERAL STORE');
insert into ledger values (
'29-MAY-01','BOUGHT','RAISONS',3,'LB',.08,.24,'GENERAL STORE');
insert into ledger values (
'29-MAY-01','BOUGHT','CHEESE',3,'LB',.09,.27,'GENERAL STORE');
insert into ledger values (
'04-JUN-01','BOUGHT','BEER',1,'BOTTLE',.2,.2,'GENERAL STORE');
insert into ledger values (
'04-JUN-01','BOUGHT','COUGH SYRUP',1,'BOTTLE',.25,.25,'GENERAL STORE');
insert into ledger values (
'26-JUN-01','BOUGHT','SHOE STRING',2,'PAIR',.04,.08,'GENERAL STORE');
insert into ledger values (
'26-JUN-01','BOUGHT','CLOSE PINS',1,'BOX',.05,.05,'GENERAL STORE');
insert into ledger values (
'26-JUN-01','BOUGHT','CLOSE BRUSH',1,'BOX',.1,.1,'GENERAL STORE');
insert into ledger values (
'06-MAR-01','SOLD','EGGS',14,'DOZEN',.12,1.68,'GENERAL STORE');
insert into ledger values (
'06-MAR-01','SOLD','HENS',12,'EACH',.5,6,'GENERAL STORE');
insert into ledger values (
'15-APR-01','SOLD','EGGS',13,'DOZEN',.1,1.3,'GENERAL STORE');
insert into ledger values (
'27-APR-01','PAID','PLOWING',1,'DAY',3,3,'RICHARD KOCH AND BROTHERS');
insert into ledger values (
'16-APR-01','PAID','PLOWING',1,'DAY',3,3,'RICHARD KOCH AND BROTHERS');
insert into ledger values (
'17-DEC-01','PAID','SAWING',1,'DAY',.75,.75,'DICK JONES');
insert into ledger values (
'28-JUL-01','PAID','SAWING',1,'DAY',.75,.75,'DICK JONES');
insert into ledger values (
'18-AUG-01','PAID','WEEDING',1,'DAY',.9,.9,'ELBERT TALBOT');
insert into ledger values (
'29-SEP-01','PAID','WORK',1,'DAY',1,1,'GERHARDT KENTGEN');
```

```
insert into ledger values (
'19-JAN-01','PAID','WORK',1,'DAY',1,1,'GERHARDT KENTGEN');
insert into ledger values (
'30-JAN-01','PAID','WORK',.5,'DAY',1,.5,'ELBERT TALBOT');
insert into ledger values (
'28-FEB-01','PAID','WORK',1,'DAY',1,1,'ELBERT TALBOT');
insert into ledger values (
'20-MAR-01','PAID','WORK',1,'DAY',1,1,'DICK JONES');
insert into ledger values (
'21-JUL-01','PAID','WORK',1,'DAY',1,1,'VICTORIA LYNN');
insert into ledger values (
'22-OCT-01','PAID','PLOWING',1,'DAY',1.8,1.8,'DICK JONES');
insert into ledger values (
'23-SEP-01','PAID','DISCUS',.5,'DAY',3,1.5,'RICHARD KOCH AND BROTHERS');
insert into ledger values (
'22-AUG-01','PAID','SAWING',1,'DAY',1,1,'PETER LAWSON');
insert into ledger values (
'23-AUG-01','PAID','SAWING',1,'DAY',1,1,'PETER LAWSON');
insert into ledger values (
'24-MAY-01','PAID','WORK',1,'DAY',1.2,1.2,'WILFRED LOWELL');
insert into ledger values (
'11-MAY-01','PAID','WORK',1,'DAY',1.2,1.2,'WILFRED LOWELL');
insert into ledger values (
'26-JUN-01','PAID','PAINTING',1,'DAY',1.75,1.75,'KAY AND PALMER WALLBOM');
insert into ledger values (
'02-JUL-01','BOUGHT','MIDDLINGS',220,'LB',.01,2.2,'EDYTHE GAMMIERE');
insert into ledger values (
'03-JUL-01','BOUGHT','PIG',1,'EACH',3,3,'JOHN AUSTIN');
insert into ledger values (
'08-JUL-01','BOUGHT','CHEESE',1,'LB',.09,.09,'GENERAL STORE');
insert into ledger values (
'09-JUL-01','BOUGHT','BEER',1,'BOTTLE',.2,.2,'GENERAL STORE');
insert into ledger values (
'02-AUG-01','BOUGHT','MILK CANS',3,'EACH',2.5,7.5,'GENERAL STORE');
insert into ledger values (
'05-AUG-01','BOUGHT','HOMINY',120,'LB',.01,1.2,'GENERAL STORE');
insert into ledger values (
'08-AUG-01','BOUGHT','BRUSH',1,'EACH',.06,.06,'GENERAL STORE');
insert into ledger values (
'12-AUG-01','BOUGHT','CORN',90,'LB',.01,.9,'GENERAL STORE');
insert into ledger values (
'25-MAR-01','SOLD','MOLASSES',5,'GALLON',1,5,'SAM DYE');
insert into ledger values (
'29-AUG-01','SOLD','BUTTER',5,'LB',.23,1.15,'GERHARDT KENTGEN');
insert into ledger values (
'06-SEP-01','BOUGHT','TELEPHONE CALL',1,'EACH',.2,.2,'PHONE COMPANY');
insert into ledger values (
'09-SEP-01','BOUGHT','PEANUTS',1,'BAG',.05,.05,'GENERAL STORE');
insert into ledger values (
'12-SEP-01','BOUGHT','BRAN',170,'LB',.01,1.7,'GENERAL STORE');
insert into ledger values (
'13-SEP-01','BOUGHT','SHOEING',4,'EACH',.3,1.2,'BLACKSMITH');
insert into ledger values (
'15-SEP-01','BOUGHT','HOMINY',144,'LB',.01,1.44,'GENERAL STORE');
insert into ledger values (
'20-APR-01','BOUGHT','BRAN',370,'LB',.01,3.7,'GENERAL STORE');
insert into ledger values (
```

```
'17-JUL-01','BOUGHT','CALF MEAL',90,'LB',.01,.9,'GENERAL STORE');
insert into ledger values (
'20-JUL-01','BOUGHT','HOMINY',300,'LB',.01,3,'GENERAL STORE');
insert into ledger values (
'25-JUL-01','SOLD','CALF',1,'EACH',1,1,'SAM DYE');
insert into ledger values (
'19-SEP-01','BOUGHT','BRAN',100,'LB',.01,1,'GENERAL STORE');
insert into ledger values (
'23-SEP-01','BOUGHT','CALF MEAL',110,'LB',.01,1.1,'GENERAL STORE');
insert into ledger values (
'25-SEP-01','BOUGHT','HOMINY',80,'LB',.01,.8,'GENERAL STORE');
insert into ledger values (
'07-OCT-01','PAID','WORK',1,'DAY',1,1,'JED HOPKINS');
set termout on prompt Waking up again.
insert into ledger values (
'12-OCT-01','BOUGHT','SHEEP',12,'EACH',.9,10.8,'BOOLE AND JONES');
insert into ledger values (
'15-OCT-01','SOLD','BEEF',935,'LB',.03,28.05,'GENERAL STORE');
insert into ledger values (
'18-OCT-1','RECEIVED','BOOT BETWEEN HORSES',1,'EACH',10,10,'ADAH TALBOT');
insert into ledger values (
'12-OCT-01','SOLD','HEFER',1,'EACH',35,35,'GEORGE B. MCCORMICK');
```

The LOCATION Table

```
drop table LOCATION;
create table LOCATION (
City        varchar2(25),
Country     varchar2(25),
Continent   varchar2(25),
Latitude    number,
NorthSouth  char(1),
Longitude   number,
EastWest    char(1));

insert into LOCATION values (
'ATHENS','GREECE','EUROPE',37.58,'N',23.43,'E');
insert into LOCATION values (
'CHICAGO','UNITED STATES','NORTH AMERICA',41.53,'N',87.38,'W');
insert into LOCATION values (
'CONAKRY','GUINEA','AFRICA',9.31,'N',13.43,'W');
insert into LOCATION values (
'LIMA','PERU','SOUTH AMERICA',12.03,'S',77.03,'W');
insert into LOCATION values (
'MADRAS','INDIA','INDIA',13.05,'N',80.17,'E');
```

```
insert into LOCATION values (
'MANCHESTER','ENGLAND','EUROPE',53.30,'N',2.15,'W');
insert into LOCATION values (
'MOSCOW','RUSSIA','EUROPE',55.45,'N',37.35,'E');
insert into LOCATION values (
'PARIS','FRANCE','EUROPE',48.52,'N',2.20,'E');
insert into LOCATION values (
'SHENYANG','CHINA','CHINA',41.48,'N',123.27,'E');
insert into LOCATION values (
'ROME','ITALY','EUROPE',41.54,'N',12.29,'E');
insert into LOCATION values (
'TOKYO','JAPAN','EUROPE',35.42,'N',139.46,'E');
insert into LOCATION values (
'SYDNEY','AUSTRALIA','AUSTRALIA',33.52,'S',151.13,'E');
insert into LOCATION values (
'SPARTA','GREECE','EUROPE',37.05,'N',22.27,'E');
insert into LOCATION values (
'MADRID','SPAIN','EUROPE',40.24,'N',3.41,'W');
```

The LODGING Table

```
drop table LODGING;
create table LODGING (
Lodging        varchar2(15) not null,
LongName       varchar2(40),
Manager        varchar2(25),
Address        varchar2(30)
);

insert into LODGING values (
'CRANMER','CRANMER RETREAT HOUSE','THOM CRANMER','HILL ST, BERKELEY');
insert into LODGING values (
'MATTS','MATTS LONG BUNK HOUSE','ROLAND BRANDT','3 MILE RD, KEENE');
insert into LODGING values (
'MULLERS','MULLERS COED LODGING','KEN MULLER','120 MAIN, EDMESTON');
insert into LODGING values (
'PAPA KING','PAPA KING ROOMING','WILLIAM KING','127 MAIN, EDMESTON');
insert into LODGING values (
'ROSE HILL','ROSE HILL FOR MEN','JOHN PELETIER','RFD 3, N. EDMESTON');
insert into LODGING values (
'WEITBROCHT','WEITBROCHT ROOMING','EUNICE BENSON','320 GENEVA, KEENE');
```

The LONGTIME Table

```
drop table LONGTIME;
create table LONGTIME(
Name            varchar2(25) not null,
Lodging         varchar2(15),
Age             number
);

insert into LONGTIME values ('ADAH TALBOT', 'PAPA KING', 23);
insert into LONGTIME values ('DICK JONES', 'ROSE HILL', 18);
insert into LONGTIME values ('DONALD ROLLO', 'MATTS', 16);
insert into LONGTIME values ('ELBERT TALBOT', 'WEITBROCHT', 43);
insert into LONGTIME values ('GEORGE OSCAR', 'ROSE HILL', 41);
insert into LONGTIME values ('PAT LAVAY', 'ROSE HILL', 21);
insert into LONGTIME values ('PETER LAWSON', 'CRANMER', 25);
insert into LONGTIME values ('WILFRED LOWELL', null, 67);
```

The MAGAZINE Table

```
drop table magazine;
create table magazine (
Name        varchar2(16),
Title       varchar2(37),
Author      varchar2(25),
IssueDate   date,
Page        number);

insert into MAGAZINE values (
'BERTRAND MONTHLY','THE BARBERS WHO SHAVE THEMSELVES.',
'BONHOEFFER, DIETRICH','23-MAY-88',70);
insert into MAGAZINE values (
'LIVE FREE OR DIE','"HUNTING THOREAU IN NEW HAMPSHIRE"',
'CHESTERTON, G.K.','26-AUG-81',320);
insert into MAGAZINE values (
'PSYCHOLOGICA','THE ETHNIC NEIGHBORHOOD',
'RUTH, GEORGE HERMAN','18-SEP-19',246);
insert into MAGAZINE values (
'FADED ISSUES','RELATIONAL DESIGN AND ENTHALPY',
'WHITEHEAD, ALFRED','20-JUN-26',279);
insert into MAGAZINE values (
```

```
'ENTROPY WIT','"INTERCONTINENTAL RELATIONS."',
'CROOKES, WILLIAM','20-SEP-50',20);
```

The MATH Table

```
drop table MATH;
create table MATH (
Name            varchar2(12),
Above           number,
Below           number,
Empty           number
);

insert into MATH values ('WHOLE NUMBER',11,-22,null);
insert into MATH values ('LOW DECIMAL',33.33,-44.44,null);
insert into MATH values ('MID DECIMAL',55.5,-55.5,null);
insert into MATH values ('HIGH DECIMAL',66.666,-77.777,null);
```

The NAME Table

```
drop table NAME;
create table NAME (
Name            varchar2(25)
);
insert into NAME values ('HORATIO NELSON');
insert into NAME values ('VALDO');
insert into NAME values ('MARIE DE MEDICIS');
insert into NAME values ('FLAVIUS JOSEPHUS');
insert into NAME values ('EDYTHE P. M. GAMMIERE');
```

The NEWSPAPER Table

```
drop table NEWSPAPER;

create table NEWSPAPER (
Feature         varchar2(15) not null,
Section         char(1),
Page            number
```

```
);

insert into NEWSPAPER values ('National News',  'A'  ,   1);
insert into NEWSPAPER values ('Sports'       ,  'D'  ,   1);
insert into NEWSPAPER values ('Editorials'   ,  'A'  ,  12);
insert into NEWSPAPER values ('Business'     ,  'E'  ,   1);
insert into NEWSPAPER values ('Weather'      ,  'C'  ,   2);
insert into NEWSPAPER values ('Television'   ,  'B'  ,   7);
insert into NEWSPAPER values ('Births'       ,  'F'  ,   7);
insert into NEWSPAPER values ('Classified'   ,  'F'  ,   8);
insert into NEWSPAPER values ('Modern Life'  ,  'B'  ,   1);
insert into NEWSPAPER values ('Comics'       ,  'C'  ,   4);
insert into NEWSPAPER values ('Movies'       ,  'B'  ,   4);
insert into NEWSPAPER values ('Bridge'       ,  'B'  ,   2);
insert into NEWSPAPER values ('Obituaries'   ,  'F'  ,   6);
insert into NEWSPAPER values ('Doctor Is In' ,  'F'  ,   6);
```

The NUMBERTEST Table

```
drop table NUMBERTEST;
create table NUMBERTEST (
Value1      number,
Value2      number,
Value3      number(10,2)
);
insert into NUMBERTEST values (0,0,0);
insert into NUMBERTEST values (.0001,.0001,.0001);
insert into NUMBERTEST values (1234,1234,1234);
insert into NUMBERTEST values (1234.5,1234.5,1234.5);
insert into NUMBERTEST values (null,null,null);
insert into NUMBERTEST values (1234.56,1234.56,1234.56);
insert into NUMBERTEST values (1234.567,1234.567,1234.567);
insert into NUMBERTEST values (98761234.567,98761234.567,98761234.567);
```

The PAY Table

```
drop table PAY;
create table PAY (
Name        varchar2(25) not null,
DailyRate   number
```

```
);

insert into PAY values ('ADAH TALBOT',1);
insert into PAY values ('ANDREW DYE',.75);
insert into PAY values ('BART SARJEANT',.75);
insert into PAY values ('DICK JONES',1);
insert into PAY values ('GEORGE OSCAR',1.25);
insert into PAY values ('PAT LAVAY',1.25);
```

The PAYDAY Table

```
drop table PAYDAY;
create table PAYDAY (
CycleDate       date
);

insert into PAYDAY values ('15-JAN-95');
insert into PAYDAY values ('15-FEB-95');
insert into PAYDAY values ('15-MAR-95');
insert into PAYDAY values ('15-APR-95');
insert into PAYDAY values ('15-MAY-95');
insert into PAYDAY values ('15-JUN-95');
insert into PAYDAY values ('15-JUL-95');
insert into PAYDAY values ('15-AUG-95');
insert into PAYDAY values ('15-SEP-95');
insert into PAYDAY values ('15-OCT-95');
insert into PAYDAY values ('15-NOV-95');
insert into PAYDAY values ('15-DEC-95');
```

The PROSPECT Table

```
drop table PROSPECT;
create table PROSPECT (
Name         varchar2(25) not null,
Address      varchar2(35)
);

insert into PROSPECT values ('ADAH TALBOT','23 ZWING, EDMESTON');
insert into PROSPECT values ('DORY KENSON','GEN. DEL., BAYBAC');
insert into PROSPECT values ('ELBERT TALBOT','3 MILE ROAD, WALPOLE');
insert into PROSPECT values ('GEORGE PHEPPS','206 POLE, KINGSLEY');
```

```
insert into PROSPECT values ('PAT LAVAY','1 EASY ST, JACKSON');
insert into PROSPECT values ('TED BUTCHER','RFD 1, BRIGHTON');
insert into PROSPECT values ('JED HOPKINS','GEN. DEL., TURBOW');
insert into PROSPECT values ('WILFRED LOWELL',NULL);
```

The ROSE Table

```
drop table ROSE;
create table ROSE (
Lodging        varchar2(12)
);

insert into ROSE values ('ROSELYN');
insert into ROSE values ('ROSE HILL');
insert into ROSE values ('ROSE GARDEN');
insert into ROSE values ('ROSE');
```

The SHIPPING Table

```
drop table SHIPPING;
create table SHIPPING (
Client         varchar2(13),
Weight         number
);

insert into SHIPPING values ('JOHNSON TOOL',59);
insert into SHIPPING values ('DAGG SOFTWARE',27);
insert into SHIPPING values ('TULLY ANDOVER',NULL);
```

The SKILL Table

```
drop table SKILL;
create table SKILL (
Skill          varchar2(25) not null,
Description    varchar2(80)
);

insert into SKILL values (
'WOODCUTTER','MARK AND FELL TREES, SPLIT, STACK, HAUL');
```

```
insert into SKILL values (
'COMBINE DRIVER','HARNESS, DRIVE, GROOM HORSES, ADJUST BLADES');
insert into SKILL values (
'SMITHY','STACK FOR FIRE, RUN BELLOWS, CUT, SHOE HORSES');
insert into SKILL values (
'GRAVE DIGGER','MARK AND CUT SOD, DIG, SHORE, FILL, RESOD');
insert into SKILL values (
'DISCUS','HARNESS, DRIVE, GROOM HORSES, BLADE DEPTH');
insert into SKILL values (
'WORK','GENERAL UNSKILLED LABOR');
```

The STOCK Table

```
drop table STOCK;
create table STOCK (
Company         varchar2(20),
Symbol          varchar2(6),
Industry        varchar2(15),
CloseYesterday  number(6,2),
CloseToday      number(6,2),
Volume          number
);
insert into STOCK values (
'AD SPECIALTY'         ,'ADSP','ADVERTISING',    31.75,    31.75, 18333876);
insert into STOCK values (
'APPLE CANNERY'        ,'APCN','AGRICULTURE',    33.75,    36.50, 25787229);
insert into STOCK values (
'AT SPACE'             ,'ATR ','MEDICAL',        46.75,    48.00, 11398323);
insert into STOCK values (
'AUGUST ENTERPRISES'   ,'AGE','MEDICAL',         15.00,    15.00, 12221711);
insert into STOCK values (
'BRANDON ELLIPSIS'     ,'BELP','SPACE',          32.75,    33.50, 25789769);
insert into STOCK values (
'GENERAL ENTROPY'      ,'GENT','SPACE',          64.25,    66.00,  7598562);
insert into STOCK values (
'GENEVA ROCKETRY'      ,'GENR','SPACE',          22.75,    27.25, 22533944);
insert into STOCK values (
'HAYWARD ANTISEPTIC'   ,'HAYW','MEDICAL',       104.25,   106.00,  3358561);
insert into STOCK values (
'IDK'                  ,'IDK','ELECTRONICS',     95.00,    95.25,  9443523);
insert into STOCK values (
'INDIA COSMETICS'      ,'INDI','COSMETICS',      30.75,    30.75,  8134878);
insert into STOCK values (
'ISAIAH JAMES STORAGE','IJS','TRANSPORTATION', 13.25,    13.75, 22112171);
insert into STOCK values (
'KDK AIRLINES'         ,'KDK','TRANSPORTATION', 85.00,    85.25,  7481566);
insert into STOCK values (
'KENTGEN BIOPHYSICS'   ,'KENT','MEDICAL',        18.25,    19.50,  6636863);
insert into STOCK values (
'LAVAY COSMETICS'      ,'LAVA','COSMETICS',      21.50,    22.00,  3341542);
```

```
insert into STOCK values (
'LOCAL DEVELOPMENT'    ,'LOCD','AGRICULTURE',    26.75,     27.25,  2596934);
insert into STOCK values (
'MAXTIDE'              ,'MAXT','TRANSPORTATION',  8.25,      8.00,  2836893);
insert into STOCK values (
'MBK COMMUNICATIONS'   ,'MBK','ADVERTISING',     43.25,     41.00, 10022980);
insert into STOCK values (
'MEMORY GRAPHICS'      ,'MEMG','ELECTRONICS',    15.50,     14.25,  4557992);
insert into STOCK values (
'MICRO TOKEN'          ,'MICT','ELECTRONICS',    77.00,     76.50, 25205667);
insert into STOCK values (
'NANCY LEE FEATURES'   ,'NLF','ADVERTISING',     13.50,     14.25, 14222692);
insert into STOCK values (
'NORTHERN BOREAL'      ,'NBOR','SPACE',          26.75,     28.00,  1348323);
insert into STOCK values (
'OCKHAM SYSTEMS'       ,'OCKS','SPACE',          21.50,     22.00,  7052990);
insert into STOCK values (
'OSCAR COAL DRAYAGE'   ,'OCD','TRANSPORTATION',  87.00,     88.50, 25798992);
insert into STOCK values (
'ROBERT JAMES APPAREL','RJAP','GARMENT',         23.25,     24.00, 19032481);
insert into STOCK values (
'SOUP SENSATIONS'      ,'SOUP','AGRICULTURE',    16.25,     16.75, 22574879);
insert into STOCK values (
'WONDER LABS'          ,'WOND','SPACE',           5.00,      5.00,  2553712);
```

The TROUBLE Table

```
drop table TROUBLE;
create table TROUBLE (
City          VARCHAR2(13) NOT NULL,
SampleDate    DATE NOT NULL,
Noon          NUMBER(4,1),
Midnight      NUMBER(4,1),
Precipitation NUMBER
);

insert into TROUBLE values ('PLEASANT LAKE', '21-MAR-93', 39.99, -1.31, 3.6);
insert into TROUBLE values ('PLEASANT LAKE', '22-JUN-93', 101.44, 86.2, 1.63);
insert into TROUBLE values ('PLEASANT LAKE', '23-SEP-93', 92.85, 79.6, 1.00003);
insert into TROUBLE values ('PLEASANT LAKE', '22-DEC-93', -17.445, -10.4, 2.4);
```

The TWONAME Table

```
drop table TWONAME;
create table TWONAME (
FirstName    varchar2(25),
LastName     varchar2(25)
);
```

The WEATHER Table

```
drop table WEATHER;
create table WEATHER (
City        varchar2(11),
Temperature number,
Humidity    number,
Condition   varchar2(9)
);

insert into WEATHER values ('LIMA',45,79,'RAIN');
insert into WEATHER values ('PARIS',81,62,'CLOUDY');
insert into WEATHER values ('MANCHESTER',66,98,'FOG');
insert into WEATHER values ('ATHENS',97,89,'SUNNY');
insert into WEATHER values ('CHICAGO',66,88,'RAIN');
insert into WEATHER values ('SYDNEY',29,12,'SNOW');
insert into WEATHER values ('SPARTA',74,63,'CLOUDY');
```

The WORKER Table

```
drop table WORKER;
create table WORKER (
Name        varchar2(25) not null,
Age         number,
Lodging     varchar2(15)
)
cluster WORKERandSKILL (Name)
;

insert into WORKER values ('BART SARJEANT',22,'CRANMER');
insert into WORKER values ('ELBERT TALBOT',43,'WEITBROCHT');
insert into WORKER values ('DONALD ROLLO',16,'MATTS');
insert into WORKER values ('JED HOPKINS',33,'MATTS');
insert into WORKER values ('WILLIAM SWING',15,'CRANMER');
insert into WORKER values ('JOHN PEARSON',27,'ROSE HILL');
insert into WORKER values ('GEORGE OSCAR',41,'ROSE HILL');
insert into WORKER values ('KAY AND PALMER WALLBOM',null,'ROSE HILL');
insert into WORKER values ('PAT LAVAY',21,'ROSE HILL');
insert into WORKER values ('RICHARD KOCH AND BROTHERS',null,'WEITBROCHT');
insert into WORKER values ('DICK JONES',18,'ROSE HILL');
insert into WORKER values ('ADAH TALBOT',23,'PAPA KING');
insert into WORKER values ('ROLAND BRANDT',35,'MATTS');
insert into WORKER values ('PETER LAWSON',25,'CRANMER');
```

```
insert into WORKER values ('VICTORIA LYNN',32,'MULLERS');
insert into WORKER values ('WILFRED LOWELL',67,null);
insert into WORKER values ('HELEN BRANDT',15,null);
insert into WORKER values ('GERHARDT KENTGEN',55,'PAPA KING');
insert into WORKER values ('ANDREW DYE',29,'ROSE HILL');
```

The WORKERSKILL Table

```
drop table WORKERSKILL;
create table WORKERSKILL (
Name          varchar2(25) not null,
Skill         varchar2(25) not null,
Ability       varchar2(15)
)
cluster WORKERandSKILL (Name)
;

insert into WORKERSKILL values ('DICK JONES','SMITHY','EXCELLENT');
insert into WORKERSKILL values ('JOHN PEARSON','COMBINE DRIVER',null);
insert into WORKERSKILL values ('JOHN PEARSON','SMITHY','AVERAGE');
insert into WORKERSKILL values ('HELEN BRANDT','COMBINE DRIVER','VERY FAST');
insert into WORKERSKILL values ('JOHN PEARSON','WOODCUTTER','GOOD');
insert into WORKERSKILL values ('VICTORIA LYNN','SMITHY','PRECISE');
insert into WORKERSKILL values ('ADAH TALBOT','WORK','GOOD');
insert into WORKERSKILL values ('WILFRED LOWELL','WORK','AVERAGE');
insert into WORKERSKILL values ('ELBERT TALBOT','DISCUS','SLOW');
insert into WORKERSKILL values ('WILFRED LOWELL','DISCUS','AVERAGE');
```

APPENDIX B

Oracle Glue

There's much talk these days about open systems. So many vendors have rushed to take advantage of the idea that it seems that every system on a computer must be able to talk with every other one.

Unfortunately, at this stage of the game, this is still a dream. Most people who believe in the idea of open systems have had the frustrating experience of using them only to discover that the systems' openness is similar to what Dorothy sees when she first meets the Wizard of Oz—a lot of power and show, but little reality to back it up.

Oracle Corporation is trying to do something about this with the release of Oracle Glue™. Glue, despite the cute name, is a truly useful addition to the software market. It sticks together everything from relational and flat-file databases (such as Paradox and dBase) to mail and file servers and electronic organizers such as the Sharp Wizard.

The main issue in using data from different sources is the ability to get to it. Database technology should do that, but because each DBMS stores data in its own format, mixing data from several sources is difficult. Other technologies, such as word processors or spreadsheets, have no way to get at the DBMS and thus no way to get data from databases. Vendors have built many specific tools for getting data from one application to another, but in the end, as with all custom solutions, the result is of only limited usefulness.

Oracle Glue gets around these problems by providing a simple interface, or API, to client applications. Once you load the API, the application can connect to all kinds of databases, mail and file servers, and electronic organizers—anything with the ability to communicate using standard protocols (DDE for Windows, SQL*Net, SQL*Connect, or MAPI or VIM for mail servers, for example) or with the ability to call functions through dynamic linking (DLLs in Windows). You use the programming capabilities of the application, such as Excel or WordBasic macros, to get data and put it wherever you want in the format you want it.

There are four functions in the Oracle Glue API:

- EXECMAIL for mail system access
- EXECFILE for file system access
- EXECLINK for electronic organizer access
- EXECSQL for database access

The EXECMAIL function lets you send data from your application to a mail server and get mail back. The EXECFILE function lets you get data from and write data to files. The EXECLINK function lets you get data from and write data to palmtop computers linked to your application.

The most interesting function for connectivity, however, is EXECSQL, which lets you execute any SQL statement against a connected database.

Say, for example, that Talbot has an Excel spreadsheet to report on and must summarize the ledger entries for any given month. The ledger spreadsheet contains the date, quantity, and rate information for each ledger entry between two dates. Up to this point, Talbot has been running SQLPLUS scripts to extract the data from the ORACLE7 database into a flat file. He then reads the data into the Excel spreadsheet using the Excel file loading commands.

With Oracle Glue, Talbot could write a simple Excel macro to extract the data and put it into the spreadsheet.

First, to enable Oracle Glue within Excel, Talbot loads two files that Oracle supplies with Glue, XLGLUE.XLA (the Glue DLL) and XLMGLUE.XLA (the Glue menu on the Excel menu bar), by using the File Open menu choice.

Then, to access ORACLE7, Talbot uses the Glue Connect menu choice to connect to ORACLE7 with his username and password.

Talbot opens an Excel macro spreadsheet for entering the macro, then enters the **select** statement on several rows in column A (for readability):

```
for 100
select ActionDate, Quantity, Rate
  into {LEDGER.XLS!A3:A103}, {LEDGER.XLS!B3:B103},
       {LEDGER.XLS!C3:C103}
  from Talbot.LEDGER
 where ActionDate BETWEEN {LEDGER.XLS!B1} and {LEDGER.XLS!D1}
```

Then Talbot enters the following macro in cells B1 and B2:

```
=EXECSQL("{A1:A6}")
=RETURN()
```

The **select** is in rows A1-A6 of the macro sheet, and the EXECSQL command reads it from there as instructed by the range in its argument when you execute the macro.

Talbot then names the macro using the Define Name command. Voilà! He can now get the data from an ORACLE7 database directly into his spreadsheet by running the macro.

The special syntax in the **select** statement lets you refer to data in the spreadsheet and to specify where to put the data coming back from a database. In this case, the syntax is that of Excel ranges. The BETWEEN operator refers to cells B1 and D1 in the spreadsheet. Talbot can enter the two dates in these cells, and the **select** picks up the dates, converts them to SQL format, and embeds the values in the **select**. The **into** clause specifies, for each item in the **select** list, the cell range into which to put the values. The special **for** clause that prefixes the **select** tells Glue to retrieve no more than 100 rows, since the ranges can't handle more than that; Talbot must assume fewer than 100 rows in any given month for the spreadsheet to work.

The cell references all use the complete form that specifies the spreadsheet name. This means that the macro only affects that spreadsheet rather than the active spreadsheet, which may not be set up for the query.

This example works for Excel on Windows; it will also work for Excel for the Macintosh. Talbot could just as easily have gotten the data from a DB2 database or from his Sharp Wizard.

Version 1.0 of Oracle Glue works only with Windows applications. You can access data from the following applications:

■ Any application that can use DDE

■ Any application that can use a generic DDL (such as Lotus Ami Pro)

- Visual Basic
- Excel

You can access data from several servers:

- ORACLE version 5 or 6 or ORACLE7
- DB2 and SQL/DS or NonStop SQL via SQL*Connect
- ORACLE*Mail™
- Sharp Wizard data

Oracle Glue will also support:

- Sybase SQLServer
- Lotus cc:Mail
- Microsoft Mail
- MAPI mail API
- VIM mail API
- PIA standard API
- IDAPI-conforming databases
- ODBC-conforming databases
- DAL-conforming databases

These last three items are database interface standards that let you write a standard SQL query that can access any database that conforms to the standard interface. IDAPI is the Borland standard, ODBC is the Microsoft standard, and DAL is the Apple standard.

Index

A

B

F

G

P

U

V

W